Top Three Reasons that You Need this Book

Learn to Listen

Music is all around you. Through *Take Note*'s progressive listening approach, you'll learn how music really works; discover and get to know some music that may be new to you; and build active listening skills that will prepare you for a lifetime of musical enjoyment.

Discover the Complete Story

In a three-chapter overview and in various features throughout the text, you'll learn the fascinating stories of the people, places, and world events that shaped Western music from the medieval period to the present.

Get the Tools to Succeed in Music Appreciation

Dashboard for *Take Note* provides you with everything that you will need to succeed in your Music Appreciation course, from streaming audio and interactive listening guides to chapter quizzes, study tools, instrument videos, and more! Plus, new copies of the text include a free 12-month subscription to *Oxford Music Online* to help you write papers and for additional study.

Turn the page to learn more ...

Learn to *Really* Listen

Take Note explores the elements of music through a select group of musical works that reflect a variety of styles (piano, winds, brass, and percussion) and genres (jazz, lieder, world, and choral music). By revisiting these core works throughout the term in different contexts, you will develop a complete understanding of all musical elements.

Full chapters devoted to each of the basic elements of the musical experience—form, timbre, rhythm, meter, melody, harmony, and texture—show how all of these elements come together to make music work.

Chapter Objectives

● Define texture and harmony, and learn how their relationship has evolved through various musical periods.

● Distinguish between monophonic and polyphonic textures, as well as dissonance and consonance.

● Understand counterpoint as a significant musical development of the Middle Ages and Renaissance.

● Recognize and distinguish between major and minor chords, and identify the way functional harmony serves as a building block for musical form.

● Hear how harmonic elements have evolved from the Romantic period to the present.

Chapter Objectives open each chapter, providing a quick guide to the contents to be covered and the key ideas that you should learn.

Learning to Listen Guides throughout the text give moment-by-moment explanations of each recorded work to help you identify basic elements in music.

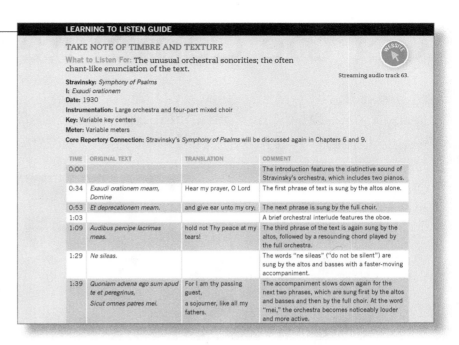

LEARNING TO LISTEN GUIDE

TAKE NOTE OF TIMBRE AND TEXTURE

What to Listen For: The unusual orchestral sonorities; the often chant-like enunciation of the text.

Streaming audio track 63.

Stravinsky: *Symphony of Psalms*
I: *Exaudi orationem*
Date: 1930
Instrumentation: Large orchestra and four-part mixed choir
Key: Variable key centers
Meter: Variable meters
Core Repertory Connection: Stravinsky's *Symphony of Psalms* will be discussed again in Chapters 6 and 9.

TIME	ORIGINAL TEXT	TRANSLATION	COMMENT
0:00			The introduction features the distinctive sound of Stravinsky's orchestra, which includes two pianos.
0:34	*Exaudi orationem meam, Domine*	Hear my prayer, O Lord	The first phrase of text is sung by the altos alone.
0:53	*Et deprecationem meam;*	and give ear unto my cry;	The next phrase is sung by the full choir.
1:03			A brief orchestral interlude features the oboe.
1:09	*Audibus percipe lacrimas meas.*	hold not Thy peace at my tears!	The third phrase of the text is again sung by the altos, followed by a resounding chord played by the full orchestra.
1:29	*Ne sileas.*		The words "ne sileas" ("do not be silent") are sung by the altos and basses with a faster-moving accompaniment.
1:39	*Quoniam advena ego sum apud te et peregrinus,* *Sicut omnes patres mei.*	For I am thy passing guest, a sojourner, like all my fathers.	The accompaniment slows down again for the next two phrases, which are sung first by the altos and basses and then by the full choir. At the word "mei," the orchestra becomes noticeably louder and more active.

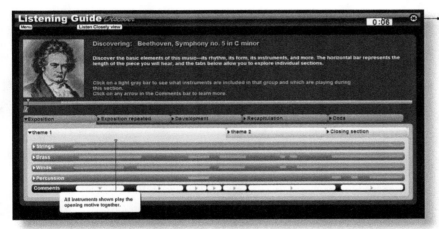

Online interactive listening guides available on the book's Dashboard website combine a visual representation of key works with running commentary to help you follow along in real time while you listen to the music.

If You Liked This Music boxes encourage you to expand your playlists and listening skills beyond the core repertory by offering additional listening suggestions throughout the text.

If You Liked This Music . . .

A Quick Listen to Wagner

Wagner's operas are long and daunting, but for a quick glimpse at his dramatic genius, the following are recommended:

- Wotan's Farewell from *Die Walküre*—The scene in which the king of the gods leaves his daughter Brünnhilde defenseless except for the ring of magic fire with which he surrounds her is deeply affecting, especially if you listen to the duet that precedes it (approximately the last 40 minutes of Act III).
- The song contest from *Die Meistersinger von Nürnberg*. The conclusion of Act III of Wagner's only mature comic opera contrasts Walther von Stolzing's stunning prize song

with a very funny misreading of it by his rival Beckmesser.

- The *Liebestod* from *Tristan und Isolde*—Isolde's "love death," with which the opera concludes, is frequently paired with the prelude in performance.
- After listening to these examples, you might also consider watching the *Star Wars* movies and paying particular attention to John Williams's music. Williams deliberately imitated many of Wagner's techniques, particularly the use of pregnant motives to represent characters and ideas in the plot.

Get the Complete Story

In order to fully appreciate a piece of music, it helps to know where it came from. *Take Note* contains numerous chapters and features that explore the development of Western music over time.

Chapters 2, 3, and 4 provide an overview of Western music from the Medieval period to the present.

Chapter 3
Classical and Romantic Music
TAKE NOTE

Giovanni Pierluigi da Palestrina (ca. 1525–1594)

Chapter 2
Medieval, Renaissance, and Baroque Music
TAKE NOTE

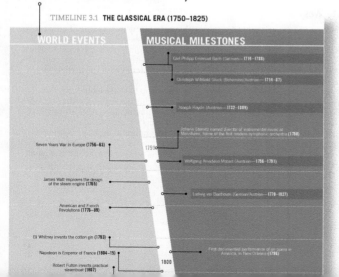

Igor Stravinsky (1882–1971)

Chapter 4
The Twentieth Century and Beyond: Modernism and Jazz
TAKE NOTE

Timelines and Chronologies of Works place selections and key developments in music history in the context of world history.

TIMELINE 3.1 **THE CLASSICAL ERA (1750–1825)**

WORLD EVENTS	MUSICAL MILESTONES
	Carl Philipp Emanuel Bach (German—1714–1788)
	Christoph Willibald Gluck (Bohemian/Austrian—1714–87)
	Joseph Haydn (Austrian—1732–1809)
	Johann Stamitz named director of instrumental music at Mannheim, home of the first modern symphonic orchestra (1750)
Seven Years War in Europe (1756–63)	1750
	Wolfgang Amadeus Mozart (Austrian—1756–1791)
James Watt improves the design of the steam engine (1765)	
American and French Revolutions (1776–89)	Ludwig van Beethoven (German/Austrian—1770–1827)
Eli Whitney invents the cotton gin (1793)	
Napoleon is Emperor of France (1804–15)	First documented performance of an opera in America, in New Orleans (1796)
Robert Fulton invents practical steamboat (1807)	1800

Chronology of Music Discussed in this Chapter

Mid-14th century
Guillaume de Machaut p. 271
Lasse! comment oublieray/Se j'aim mon loyal/Pour quoy me bat mes maris?, motet

1828
Franz Schubert p. 266, 280
Winterreise: Der Lindenbaum; Die Post; Der Leiermann

1840
Robert Schumann
Dichterliebe: Ich grolle nicht, p. 278; *Die alten, bösen Lieder* p. 282

1938–1941
Luigi Dallapiccola p. 284
Canti di prigionia (3 movements).

● Clear and vivid maps help you connect each musical piece and artist with places around the world.

● Focus On boxes draw from Oxford's own distinguished *Grove Music Online* reference site to offer concise background information on composers and other music-related topics. If you purchase a new copy of *Take Note*, you will have access to the entire contents of *Grove Music Online* within *Oxford Music Online*.

Focus On
Claude Debussy (1862–1918)

French composer. One of the most important musicians of his time, his harmonic innovations had a profound influence on generations of composers. He made a decisive move away from Wagnerism in his only complete opera, *Pelléas et Mélisande*, and in his works for piano and for orchestra he created new genres and revealed a range of timbre and color that indicated a highly original musical aesthetic. (François Lesure and Roy Howat, *Grove Music Online*.)

Claude Debussy (1862–1918). Debussy composed many volumes of colorful and evocative music for piano, as well as ensemble and vocal music. (© adoc-photos/Lebrecht Music & Arts)

In 1948, 30 years after the death of Claude Debussy, American composer Virgil Thomson wrote, "Modern music, the full flower of it, the achievement rather than the hope, stems from Debussy. Everybody who wrote before him is just an ancestor and belongs to another time. Debussy belongs to ours." Thomson's essential insight still applies today. All great composers have broken rules, but Debussy was one of the few who have been able to reinvent the language of music. Like the Impressionist painters to whom he is often compared, he worked with colors, both instrumental and harmonic, in ways that defied traditional expectations. While his music has become "classical," it has not lost its edge; it still surprises and delights us.

● Across the Arts boxes examine parallels between music and the other arts, allowing you to discover what music has in common with poetry, storytelling, painting, architecture, and drama.

In History
Schubert's *Winterreise*

Winterreise (*Winter's Journey*), written only months before Schubert's death in 1828, was the second of his two genuine song cycles. Both it and the earlier *Die Schöne Müllerin* (*The Beautiful Maid of the Mill*) deal with unrequited love, one of the favorite subjects of the Romantics. They both consist of settings of a series of poems told from the point of view of a rejected lover and implicitly ending with his death. *Winterreise*, however, is particularly severe. The lover has already been rejected when the cycle begins, and his love is described only in retrospect. The images in the poetry are unrelentingly somber, and Schubert's music follows suit.

It is something of a cliché to say that this subject is an expression of the alienation and loneliness so frequently expressed in modern art of all kinds. In fact, similar images of isolation from a beloved occur in the troubadour poetry of the late Middle Ages. These songs can be linked in many ways, however, to their historical moment.

One is their abundance of nature images, including the linden tree with its rustling leaves and the fierce winter wind. In his poems, Müller treats nature as a place to escape the pressures of modern urban life. Readers of English literature often find this theme in the writing of the early Romantics, such as the poetry of William Wordsworth.

Rest as a metaphor for death and release was also a favorite theme of the Romantics. In *Ode to a Nightingale*, for example, John Keats yearns "to cease upon the midnight with no pain," much as Schubert's singer-hero longs to lie down beneath the tree and its sheltering branches.

The idea of the rootless wanderer as a heroic figure is also typical of Schubert's time; his own

Wanderer Above the Sea of Fog, by Caspar David [...] (1774–1840). Restlessness, longing, and the pow[...] were primary components of the Romantic spir[...] Art Resource, NY)

song *The Wanderer* served as the bas[...] of his most famous piano works, the [...] *Fantasy*. German artists such as Cas[...] Friedrich (1774–1840) often depicted [...] as well.

So if there is such a thing as the Z[...] or "spirit of the times," these songs [...] in a particularly poignant and powe[...] Schubert's music, which does so mu[...] amplify Müller's texts, is a uniquely [...] vehicle for the outlook of the Roman[...]

Across the Arts
The Medieval Worldview

The rhythm of *Lasse! comment oublieray/Se j'aim mon loyal/Pour quoy me bat mes maris?* is difficult for us to understand, but it made perfect sense to medieval listeners. In the medieval worldview, the universe itself was built in interlocking layers, thought to operate according to musical proportions. If you have trouble perceiving Machaut's rhythms, consider that the proportions of the universe cannot be seen or heard either, at least in ordinary terms. Yet in the medieval cosmology they dictate the terms on which life is lived in the visible world.

In this photo, Music is personified in the panels on the left, while the panels on the right illustrate the three levels of the musical universe. On top is *musica mundana*, better known as the "music of the spheres," showing that the universe is constructed according to musical proportions. In the middle is *musica humana*, the "music of human life." *Musica instrumentalis*, sounding music, appears only in the bottom panel, and the female figure of Music points at it reprovingly, as though to remind it that it is only a pale imitation of the higher levels.

This view of music was most notably expressed by Boethius (ca. 480–524), the late Roman philosopher who also provided the text for the second movement of Dallapiccola's *Canti di prigionia*. Though it was based on ideas from the ancient world, Boethius's musical worldview helped to define the way the universe was understood for centuries after his death.

This famous illustration shows the medieval view of the world as consisting of three different kinds of music. (© Lebrecht Music and Arts)

● In History boxes discuss the greater cultural and social contexts of key works in history, providing a compelling narrative of music history.

Get the Tools to Succeed in Music Appreciation

www.oup.com/us/wallace serves as the gateway to everything that you will need for your Music Appreciation course.

Dashboard for *Take Note*

Streaming audio, interactive listening guides, musical instrument videos, and a wealth of additional resources for *Take Note* are available in Dashboard by Oxford University Press. Dashboard delivers quality content, tools, and assessments to track student progress in an intuitive, web-based learning environment.

Interactive Listening Guides and **Streaming Audio** put you in full control of the listening experience. **Interactive listening guides** combine a visual representation of key works with running commentary to help you follow along in real time while you listen to the music. Additionally, all of the **audio examples** discussed in the text are available in streaming audio format.

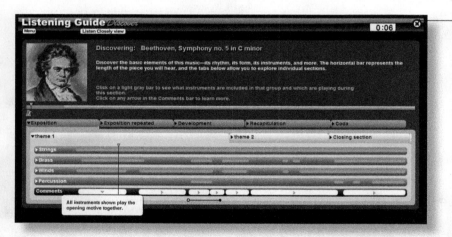

Discover View offers an overview of the piece, including the basic structure of each section.

Listen Closely View displays all the information about the piece, including the melodic "shape" for each instrument so that you can follow the music as it unfolds.

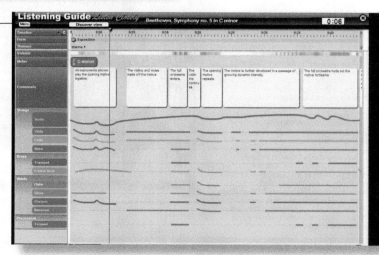

Instrument videos bring individual pieces of the orchestra to life, giving you a closer look at the instruments and actions behind what you hear.

Activities and Additional Study Resources

Dashboard offers brief quizzes on the content of every chapter in *Take Note* so that you can test your knowledge and understanding before taking an in-class exam. Listening exams, featuring excerpts from the book's recordings, allow you to hone your active listening skills. Chapter outlines are handy to use when reviewing key concepts and for quick study before taking tests.

A streamlined interface simplifies the learning experience by putting your progress first.

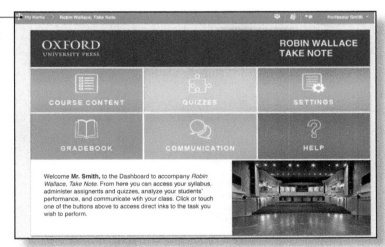

Access to Dashboard requires an access code that can be purchased directly at www.oup.com/us/wallace.

Get the Tools
to Succeed in
Music Appreciation

Oxford Music Online

A free 12-month subscription to *Oxford Music Online* is included for students with all new copies of the text. Within *Oxford Music Online,* you will have access to *Grove Music Online,* the leading online resource for music research. Throughout *Take Note,* you'll find reference to specific articles in *Grove* that offer more in-depth information on the topics covered in the text. With thousands of additional articles on all aspects of music, *Grove Music Online* is an invaluable resource for papers, projects, and additional study.

An **ebook** is available through *CourseSmart©* (www.coursesmart.com)

Visit **www.oup.com/us/wallace** for links to and additional information on all of these resources for *Take Note.*

Take Note

An Introduction to Music Through Active Listening

Robin Wallace
Baylor University

New York Oxford
Oxford University Press

Oxford University Press is a department of the University of Oxford.
It furthers the University's objective of excellence in research,
scholarship, and education by publishing worldwide.

Oxford New York
Auckland Cape Town Dar es Salaam Hong Kong Karachi
Kuala Lumpur Madrid Melbourne Mexico City Nairobi
New Delhi Shanghai Taipei Toronto

With offices in
Argentina Austria Brazil Chile Czech Republic France Greece
Guatemala Hungary Italy Japan Poland Portugal Singapore
South Korea Switzerland Thailand Turkey Ukraine Vietnam

For titles covered by Section 112 of the US Higher Education
Opportunity Act, please visit www.oup.com/us/he for the latest information about pricing and alternate formats.

Published by Oxford University Press
198 Madison Avenue, New York, New York 10016
http://www.oup.com

Library of Congress Cataloging-in-Publication Data

Wallace, Robin.
Take note : an introduction to music through active listening / Robin Wallace.
pages ; cm
ISBN 978-0-19-531433-5.
Music appreciation—Textbooks. I. Title.
MT6.W1666 2014
780—dc23
2013014195

Printing number: 9 8 7 6 5 4 3 2

Printed in the United States of America
on acid-free paper

Dedication

In loving memory of Barbara Elaine Wallace (1956–2011),
who worked harder at listening than anybody I have ever known.

Contents in Brief

Contents

**PART 1
LISTENING
THROUGH
HISTORY**

PART 2
LISTENING
THROUGH
MUSICAL
ELEMENTS

PART 3
BRINGING
IT ALL
TOGETHER

GUIDE TO THE CORE REPERTORY OF MUSICAL WORKS

The following table summarizes the appearances of the recurring repertory of core musical works at the heart of *Take Note*. This diverse collection of works is drawn upon throughout the book to illustrate key historical and thematic elements of music.**

Core Repertory Work	Date	Key discussions and Listening Guides are located in the following chapters:
Gregorian Chant: *Dies Irae*	1250 (circa)	8, 9
Machaut: *Lasse! Comment oublieray!*	1350 (circa)	2, 7, 9, 10
Machaut: *Foy porter*, virelai	1350 (circa)	5, 7, 9
Josquin: *Missa L'homme armé super voces musicales*	1480's (circa)	2, 6, 9, 12
Palestrina: *Sicut cervus*	1584	2, 10
Monteverdi: *Io son pur vezzosetta*	1619	2, 9
Bach: *Mass in B minor, Gloria*	1723–1733	2, 6, 9
Bach: Concerto in D Minor for Harpsichord and Orchestra, BWV 1052	1732–1733	1, 6, 7, 8
Mozart: *Serenade in B-flat Major, K. 361 "Gran Partita"*, K. 361	1781	3, 5, 6, 7, 8, 12
Mozart: *Le Nozze di Figaro, K. 492*	1786	3, 6, 11
Mozart: Symphony No. 40 in G Minor, K. 550	1788	1, 5, 6, 8, 9,12
Haydn: String Quartet in B-flat Major, Op. 64, no. 3	1790	3, 5, 6, 7, 12
Beethoven: Symphony No. 5	1804–1808	3, 8, 12
Schubert: *Winterreise*	1828	5, 10
Chopin, Ballade No. 1 in G Minor, Op. 23	1835–1836	3, 7, 12
Chopin: Nocturne in A-flat Major, Op. 32, No. 2	1836–1837	8, 9, 12
Berlioz, *Roméo et Juliette*	1839	3, 6, 8
Schumann: *Dichterliebe*	1840	10
Wagner: *Tristan und Isolde*	1859	9
Smetana: *Šárka*, from *Má Vlast* (My Homeland)	1872	3, 6, 12
Dvořák: Slavonic Dance in E Minor, Op. 72, No. 10	1886	1, 7, 8, 12
Verdi: *Otello*	1887	6, 11
Sousa: *The Stars and Stripes Forever*	1897	6, 7
Ives: Violin Sonata no. 4 ("Children's Day at the Camp Meeting")	1906–1916	5, 7, 8, 12
Debussy: Sonata for Flute, Viola, and Harp	1915	4, 6, 7, 8, 9
Stravinsky, *Symphony of Psalms*	1930	4, 6, 9, 12
Dallapiccola: *Canti di Prigionia*	1938–1941	6, 8, 10
William "Count" Basie: *Lester Leaps In*	1939	4, 6, 8, 7, 9
Gould: *American Salute*	1947	6
Crumb: *Black Angels*	1970	1, 6, 8, 9
Vandervelde: *Genesis II*	1983	6, 7, 8, 9, 12
Gender Wayang, Sukawati	Traditional	6
Jumping Dance Drums	Traditional	7
Khan: *Raga Bhankar*	Traditional	5, 8

Letter from the Author

Dear Reader:

What does it mean to truly *listen* to music? Most people today experience music many times a day: At work, in the store, on the Internet, at the movies, at the doctor's office, we are bombarded by more kinds of music in a week than most of our ancestors had the opportunity to experience in a lifetime.

Music also serves many purposes. It tells us to relax, to buy, to stay awake, to sit on the edge of our seat. It may evoke a wide range of reactions, causing us to sing along, to tap our feet, or to turn away in indifference. It is hard to get away from music and its role in our lives.

Yet it is rare for us to give music our full attention. This book invites you to become an **active listener** to broaden your enjoyment of music of all kinds.

Central to the successful formula of this book is the use of a recurring or **core repertory of musical examples** that are revisited throughout the chapters. To help you understand these works, the book focuses on fundamental **musical elements** that make up all music: form, timbre, rhythm, meter, melody, harmony, and texture. Each of these elements is used to explore these core works, inviting you to become familiar with great music of many genres and the components that make it tick.

Here's wishing you greater enjoyment of the music already in your playlist as well as a lifetime of musical revelations to come.

Sincerely,

Robin Wallace

ABOUT THE AUTHOR

Dr. Robin Wallace is Professor of Musicology at Baylor University, where he has taught since 2003. He received his Bachelor of Arts degree from Oberlin College, where he studied piano with Thomas Simons and Leon Bates. He holds a master of philosophy and a doctor of philosophy in music history from Yale University. He has also held teaching appointments at Yale, California State University at Long Beach, Scripps College, Concordia University, and Converse College. He is an accomplished pianist, harpsichordist, and recorder player, as well as a composer.

He has written numerous books and essays on music, including *Beethoven's Critics* and *The Critical Reception of Beethoven's Compositions by his German Contemporaries* (series co-editor and translator), and articles and reviews in *Music and Letters*, *The Journal of Musicology*, *The Journal of Musicological Research*, *Music Library Association Notes*, *Beethoven Forum*, *Nineteenth-Century Music Review*, and *The Journal of Music History Pedagogy*. *Take Note* embodies his dedication to teaching the course in music appreciation and applies techniques he has developed for communicating a love of music to his students.

Preface

ENJOY MUSIC THROUGH ACTIVE LISTENING

Take Note is based on the idea that giving music our full attention will deeply enrich our lives, often in ways we may not have anticipated. It is designed both to teach you about music and to teach you how to listen. But it also does more: It allows you to meet the same works of music repeatedly, in different contexts.

MEET THE CORE REPERTORY

A recurring repertory of core musical works is at the heart of *Take Note*. Each of the pieces studied in this book has been carefully selected. They represent a wide range of music, from intimate art songs to grand and exciting orchestral works; from jazz to opera to the music of India and the Caribbean. By the end of the semester, you will have not just heard those works; you will have gotten to know them. They will have become a part of your life. You will also be prepared to get to know new pieces of music that you may encounter, and this will prepare you for a lifetime of musical enjoyment.

LISTEN FOR THE ELEMENTS THAT MAKE MUSIC WORK

Take Note begins with an exploration of musical elements as the key to unlocking the enjoyment of music. There is a chapter devoted to each of the basic elements of the musical experience—form, timbre, rhythm, meter, melody, harmony, and texture—as well as the rich relationship between music, words, drama, and meaning. Every piece in the core repertory of works is examined from multiple angles to illustrate these elements.

GUIDING YOU THROUGH THE LISTENING EXPERIENCE

Take Note's core repertory of listening examples is reinforced by two key features of the text:

1. Each chapter contains a group of **Learning to Listen Guides** that give moment-by-moment explanations of each recorded work through a running commentary. The musical selections are available to you as streaming audio for online listening in Dashboard, an intuitive, web-based learning system from Oxford University Press.

Learning to Listen Guide.

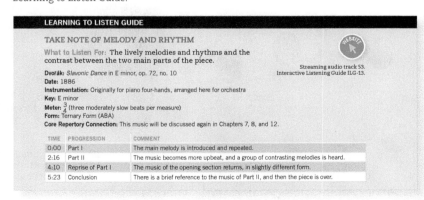

2. Along with streaming audio, Dashboard for *Take Note* also offers online, interactive listening guides, available for key selections. Icons throughout the text will direct you to these unique interactive guides. Each guide presents a visual representation of a work and its component parts and instruments. You follow it in real time as you listen to the music. Whether or not you have ever learned to read music, these interactive guides will give you all the advantages that are available to an orchestral conductor reading a full score. You will be able to see which instruments are playing, who has the melody, and what the other instruments are doing as well. You will be able to see the structure of short sections and entire pieces with ease.

You can read a running commentary explaining what you are hearing and seeing. You can start and stop the music at any point. As a supplement to the book, these interactive listening guides put you in full control of the listening experience.

Online Interactive Listening Guide

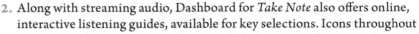

Each chapter includes a diagram showing the Chronology of Works discussed in that chapter.

Music history is placed within the context of world history using timelines in chapters 2, 3, 4.

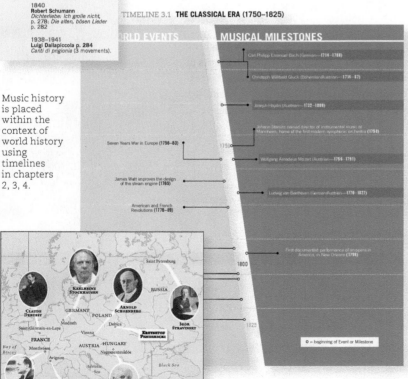

CONNECTING WITH MUSIC HISTORY

Take Note also recognizes the richness of music tradition by building your active listening skills within the context of music history. Chapters 2, 3, and 4 are devoted to an overview of Western music from the Medieval period to the present. The core repertory works—discussed and heard throughout the book—are drawn from the whole of music history. Timelines and chronologies of works discussed are used throughout to reinforce the time and place associated with each musical example. Maps are provided to help the student associate the historical development of music with places around the world.

Maps enable the reader to connect musical history with places around the world. Along with streaming audio, Dashboard for *Take Note* also offers online, interactive listening guides, available for key selections.

Special box features found in all chapters further underscore the historical foundations of music by exploring individual composers, instruments, and developments in related arts such as dance, poetry, and painting.

Focus On boxes provide a profile of key composers and other music topics. These boxes often begin with a background sketch drawn from Oxford's own distinguished *Grove Music Online* reference service. For more in-depth coverage, each new copy of *Take Note* comes with a free one-year subscription to *Grove Music Online*.

In History boxes discuss the greater cultural and social context of key works in history.

Across the Arts boxes emphasize that works of music are not created in isolation from the other arts. Each box examines parallels between music and the other arts, allowing you to discover what music has in common with poetry, story-telling, painting, architecture, and drama.

If You Liked This Music . . . boxes identify other related works from music history that you might enjoy hearing.

Grove Music Online.

Focus On
The Piano

A keyboard instrument distinguished by the fact that its strings are struck by rebounding hammers rather than plucked (as in the harpsichord) or struck by tangents that remain in contact with the strings (as in the clavichord). (Edwin M. Ripin/ Stewart Pollens, *Grove Music Online*.)

Early piano. A fortepiano by Conrad Graf, a Viennese manufacturer of Schubert's time. (© The Metropolitan Museum of Art. Image source: Art Resource, NY)

The modern piano was invented by the Italian instrument maker Bartolomeo Cristofori around 1700, and three of his instruments dating from the 1720s survive to this day. The Cristofori piano was a huge technological innovation—the first instrument to allow hammers to strike the strings and bounce off, leaving them free to vibrate—but was quiet in comparison to today's instruments. Bach was shown an early piano but disliked it. Viennese pianos made during Mozart's time in the late 1700s were quite different from the more dynamic English pianos, which were also widely played. All of these instruments were still much smaller than today's pianos, with fewer keys and a less penetrating sound. By the 1820s, when Schubert wrote the songs discussed in this chapter, the piano was going through a period of rapid changes.

In History
Dvořák's *Slavonic Dance* in E minor, op. 72, no. 10

In the 19th century, if you wanted to hear your favorite music at home, you had to play it yourself. In most middle-class European and American homes, this meant going to the piano. Although our recorded example of this *Slavonic Dance* is arranged for an orchestra, Dvořák first wrote it for piano four-hands, or two people playing the same piano. A great deal of music using this format was written in the 19th century, and even more music intended for other instruments was transcribed so it could be played this way. If you lacked confidence, it helped to have a second player to help out; this made both parts easier to play. Playing and listening to the piano at home was

time to play it. In 1869 composer Johannes Brahms (1833–1897) published his first set of *Hungarian Dances* for piano four-hands. These works, with their perky rhythms and catchy tunes, sold in huge numbers and helped to make Brahms and his publisher wealthy. This was a turning point in the development of a large market for popular music—a market that came of age in the early 20th century.

By 1878, when the first of Dvořák's *Slavonic Dances* were written, Dvořák was motivated to match Brahms's success. So popular were the *Slavonic Dances* that the composer almost immediately arranged them for orchestra. Thus, Dvořák was able to appeal both to the

Across the Arts
Painters Against Fascism

In his painting *The Eternal City* (1934–37), American Peter Blume challenged fascism with specific imagery. Mussolini and others are caricatured against the backdrop of the Roman forum, which they are seen as desecrating. Blume spent the year 1932 in Italy on a Guggenheim grant and, after returning to the United States, was able to produce his painting safely ensconced in his home country. It would have been considerably less safe for the Italian Dallapiccola to compose an overtly antifascist work, which perhaps partly explains why he gravitated to texts about imprisonment in order to express the general atmosphere of oppression. Musical meaning can be much less direct than meaning in figurative art. At the very least, precise meaning in music is much more difficult for authorities to identify, even if that meaning resonates on an intuitive level with its listeners.

The Angel of Hearth and Home. 1937. By Max Ernst

in *The Angel of Hearth and Home* (1937). Whatever was left unclear by the monstrous image itself,

If You Liked This Music. . .
The Diverse World of Romantic Music

Romantic music is incredibly diverse. One composer who does not fit many of the characteristics discussed above is **Johannes Brahms** (1833–1897). Brahms's music is more classical and restrained than that of Berlioz or Smetana. Brahms used smaller orchestras and, unlike many other Romantic composers, wrote a great deal of chamber music. His music is never programmatic, at least in the blatant sense epitomized by Smetana's *Šárka*. Nevertheless, it is rich in expression and written with great care and craftsmanship. Some works by Brahms that you might enjoy include the following:

- *A German Requiem (Ein Deutsches Requiem)*, his best-known choral work, is based on texts from the German Bible rather than the Roman Catholic Requiem Mass.
- **The four symphonies**, written at the height of his maturity, show an alternative view of instrumental music and its aims, eschewing the showiness of Smetana but revealing many inner beauties.
- The **Intermezzos** for piano, published in a number of collections under the opus numbers 76, 116, 117, 118, and 119, show the Romantic character piece at its most intimate.

Bonus Chapter 13, *Actively Listening to Additional Works*, at the companion website.

BONUS ONLINE CHAPTER: SUPPLEMENTARY LISTENING ACTIVITIES

A bonus, online chapter is available in Dashboard for *Take Note* for those students and instructors who would like to practice active listening skills on additional works. Online Chapter 13, *Actively Listening to Additional Works*, introduces four major works spanning Medieval to Modern music. Each example applies listening skills and aspects of musical elements reviewed in chapters 1–12 and presents thoughtful review questions for each.

ENSURING STUDENT SUCCESS

Oxford University Press offers students and instructors a comprehensive ancillary package for *Take Note*.

For Students

- **Dashboard for *Take Note*** at www.oup.com/us/wallace

Streaming audio, interactive listening guides, musical instrument videos, and a wealth of additional resources for *Take Note* are available in Dashboard by Oxford University Press. Dashboard delivers quality content, tools and assessments to track student progress in an intuitive, web-based learning environment. Full access to Dashboard can be packaged with new copies of the text for a discounted price or purchased separately through your college bookstore or at www.oup.com/us/wallace.

- **Online Streaming Audio in Dashboard**

All of the audio examples discussed in the text are available in streaming audio format in Dashbaord for *Take Note*. In addition, interactive listening guides are provided for key works that guide students through the listening experience (see above). Students who purchase Dashboard packaged with the text or separately in their bookstore or online will have full access to the streaming audio and interactive listening guides.

- ***Oxford Music Online***

New copies of *Take Note* come with a free code that will give you one year's access to *Oxford Music Online*, including *Grove Music Online*, the leading online resource for music research. You may freely browse through thousands of articles on all topics in music. Additionally, in the text and on this website, you will find links to specific articles in Grove that offer deeper information on the topics covered in this text for both further review and for assistance in writing term papers.

- **CourseSmart eText**

This textbook is available through CourseSmart (http://www.coursesmart.com/) in eText format for those students who prefer to purchase and read the text online or on a portable digital reader. Students who elect to purchase the text through CourseSmart will be able to purchase separately access to Dashboard including the streaming audio and interactive listening guides.

For Instructors

- **Student Assessments, Online Grade Book, and Course Management in Dashboard**

In addition to streaming audio and interactive listening guides, Dashboard provides instructors with a wealth of assignable assessment materials and a fully integrated grade book that allows them to quickly and easily monitor student progress through the course. Simple and intuitive, Dashboard can be used in place of or alongside any major course management system.

- **Instructor's Manual and PowerPoint™ Slides**

Instructors who adopt *Take Note* will be given access to online instructor's manual for the text, which features chapter summaries, teaching strategies, sample test and essay questions, sample in-class and assignable activities, and links to websites featuring related materials. In addition, a downloadable set of PowerPoint™ slides is offered to accompany in-class lectures or for posting on class websites for student review. Visit www.oup.com/us/wallace for additional information and to register for access to instructor materials.

- **Test bank**

A computerized test bank is available to adopters that can be used to create custom exams. Questions can be edited or rewritten, and additional questions can be added to the bank. Visit www.oup.com/us/wallace for additional information and to register for access to instructor materials.

Packaging Options

Save your students money on their course material by packaging *Take Note* with access to Dashboard, which contains the streaming audio, interactive listening guides, and additional study and assessment material that they'll need for success in Music Appreciation. Use ISBN 9780199385881 to order the complete package and your students will save 20% off the cost of the text and Dashboard access alone.

Additionally, adopters can package *Take Note* with ANY Oxford University Press text for a 20% savings off the total package price. Contact your Oxford Representative for package recommendations, prices, and ISBNs.

ACKNOWLEDGMENTS

The seeds of this book were planted when I was a graduate student at Yale in the early 1980s. At that time the nonmajor curriculum in music contained both a two-semester music history course and a one-semester music appreciation course. I had the privilege of teaching the second semester of the history course two years in a row. The appreciation course was taught by Jane Stevens, and it was completely different. Mrs. Stevens (as Ivy League etiquette demanded that she be called) did not teach the students history or how to read music. She taught them how to listen, using a quirky, out-of-print book by Richard Crocker and Ann Basart called *Listening to Music*. All the other books, she said, dealt with terms about music; this was the only one that dealt with music.

I have not sought, in this book, to recreate Crocker and Basart's pedagogy. Rather, I have drawn on my own experiences teaching introductory, nonmajor music courses at several different schools over the past thirty years. Since I was once Jane Stevens's teaching assistant, it is likely that some of her insights have found their way into what I have written here, particularly in the chapter on opera. I also recall discussing the music appreciation course with Richard Crocker in his office in Berkeley in 1988 after reading a paper at a conference across the bay at Stanford. More recently, I have participated in free-ranging discussions of this topic on ams-l, the email listserv of the American Musicological Society. To all of those—too many to name—who have pitched in there, I owe a collective word of thanks. I must single out Jonathan Bellman, however, for his ongoing advocacy and his unwavering belief in what I was doing. Maureen Buja also went beyond the call of duty to offer advice and assistance.

I am deeply indebted to Jan Beatty, who signed this project on for Oxford and saw it through the early stages of writing and revision. Her successor, Richard Carlin, has ably overseen the later stages, and John Haber and Thom Holmes both did huge amounts of valuable editing at many points along the way. Others who made important contributions to the book include development editors Terese Nemeth and Mary Ann McHugh, editorial assistant Sheena Kowalski, development interns Sam Power, Kateri Woody, and Garon Scott, copy editor Elizabeth Nelson Bortka, and director of design Michele Laseau.

Teaching at a school of music, I was able to draw on the expertise of colleagues in all fields of music when needed. I am particularly indebted to Deborah Williamson for reviewing the section on singing in Chapter 6, Joyce Jones for that on organ, Todd Meehan for percussion, Jeffrey Powers for horn and other brass instruments, Christopher Buddo for strings, and Michael Jacobson for winds. Alex Parker reviewed the section on Basie's *Lester Leaps In* in Chapter 4 and provided valuable feedback from his experience as a jazz musician. Julie Kisacky in the Modern Foreign Languages Department at Baylor and Julia Hejduk in Classics helped with the translations. Baylor generously granted me a summer sabbatical in 2007 and several teaching load reductions to speed my progress on the book.

I also had assistance from a long series of students, including Kyle Babb, Sharon McCarthy, Joanie Brittingham, Courtney Zajac, Ariana Phillips, Anthony Berkley, Michael Groff and Anne-Marie Houy. Michael Berg, Daniel Farris, and Aaron Hufty taught the Introduction to Music class at Baylor from the manuscript and provided valuable feedback.

I owe an unrepayable debt of gratitude to my late wife, Barbara Elaine Wallace. A few years before I began writing this book, Barbara lost her hearing due to the long-term effects of radiation treatment 24 years earlier for a brain tumor. With the benefits of cochlear implants, first in her left ear and then in the right as well, she was able to regain some hearing, but her ability to hear and understand music was extremely limited. She nevertheless doggedly accompanied me to concerts and experimented with listening in a wide variety of formats, struggling to recover whatever enjoyment of music this still nascent technology would allow. Her persistence and stamina were an inspiration to me and to many others. Her death from a cerebral hemorrhage occurred just as I was preparing to make the final round of revisions on this book, which I had always planned to dedicate to her. May the posthumous dedication be a lasting tribute to her unforgettable courage and determination.

MANUSCRIPT REVIEWERS

The first edition of *Take Note* is the result of an extensive period of development both of the concept and content. I am grateful to all who have evaluated the manuscript and provided important feedback on the book's features, including:

Alabama
Todd Campbell, Troy University
Shelly Meggison, University of Alabama
Jenny Mann, University of Alabama

Alaska
Eileen Watabe, University of Alaska–Fairbanks

Arizona
Wayne Bailey, University of Arizona
Trish Jordahl, Eastern Arizona College

Arkansas
Louis Young, University of Central Arkansas

California
Gordon Haramki, San Jose State
Matthew Tresler, Irvine Valley College

Colorado
Jonathan Bellman, University of Northern Colorado
Janice Dickensheets, University of Northern Colorado

Florida
Mary Macklem, University of Central Florida
Kenneth Keaton, Florida Atlantic University
Dr. Sarah Satterfield, Central Florida Community College

Georgia
Marva Griffin Carter, Georgia State University
Craig Resta, Schwob School of Music

Illinois
Lois Veenhoven Guderian, Northwestern University
Michael Barta, Southern Illinois University
Rebecca Bennett, Northwestern University

Indiana
Dwight Monical, Purdue University
Constance Cook Glen, Indiana University

Kentucky
Michael Sprowles, University of Kentucky

Louisiana
David Smyth, Louisiana State University

Massachusetts
Benjamin Korstvedt, Clark University
Robert Eisenstein, Mt. Holyoke College
Rebecca Bennett, Northeastern University

Michigan
Melissa Derechailo, Wayne State University

Mississippi
Darcie Bishop, Jackson State

Nevada
Anthony Barone, University of Nevada–Las Vegas

New Jersey
Anthony Scelba, Kean College
Carol Shansky, Bergen Community College

New York
Lisa Lee Sawyer, Concordia College
Michael E. Ruhling, Rochester Institute of Technology
George Hill, Baruch College
Catherine Coppola, Hunter College

North Carolina
Gregory Carroll, University of North Carolina–Greensboro
Jay Grymes, University of North Carolina–Charlotte

North Dakota
Dorothy Keyser, University of North Dakota

Oregon
Dr. Faun Tiedge, Linfield College

Pennsylvania
John Packard, Pennsylvania State University
Matthew R. Baumer, Indiana University of
    Pennsylvania
Dr. Steven Kreinberg, Boyer College
Anna Nisnevich, University of Pittsburgh

Tennessee
Mary Dave Blackman, East Tennessee State University
Jeff Christmas, Pellissippi State Community College
Andrew Daniel, Northeast Texas Community College
David Bubsey, East Tennessee State University

Texas
Bruce Keeling, South Plains College
Laurine Elkins-Marlow, Texas A&M University
Antonio Briseño, The University of Texas at
    Brownsville—Texas Southmost College
G. Yvonne Kendall, University of Houston–Downtown
Dr. Jana Elam Rader, San Jacinto College South

Utah
Elliott Cheney, University of Utah School of Music

Vermont
Larry Hamberlin, Middlebury College

Washington
Bertil van Boer, Western Washington University

West Virginia
Vicki Stroeher, Marshall University

Wisconsin
Richard Mark Heidel, University of Wisconsin–Eau
    Claire

Wyoming
Dr. Katrina Zook, University of Wyoming

Take Note

Antonín Dvořák (1841–1904)

Learning to Listen Actively

TAKE NOTE

Active listening is a framework for listening awareness that makes the experience of music richer, deeper, and more rewarding. Using a recurring repertory of core musical works as examples is a good way to reinforce one's ability to listen for key elements found in all music.

Music is a rich and varied art form that seems capable of expressing the inexpressible. It cannot, however, speak for itself. That's where the craft of listening comes in. An informed listener soon discovers that music is a powerful form

Chapter Objectives

⬤ Discover active listening as a framework for enhancing the enjoyment of music.

⬤ Learn about the core repertory of music examples that recur throughout the book and are central to the author's approach to music appreciation.

⬤ Understand the key elements of music and how they work together.

⬤ Apply active listening skills to several different works of music.

Chronology of Music Discussed in this Chapter

1734–1738
Johann Sebastian Bach p. 13
Concerto in D minor for harpsichord and strings, BWV 1052, 1st movement

1788
Wolfgang Amadeus Mozart p. 9
Symphony no. 40 in G minor, K. 550, 1st movement

1886
Antonín Dvrořák p. 8
Slavonic Dance in E minor, op. 72, no. 10, orchestral version (originally for piano four hands)

1970
George Crumb p. 14
Black Angels: 13 Images from the Dark Land for electric string quartet, Part I: Departure

of communication on many levels from the emotional to the intellectual. The full enjoyment of music depends on an appreciation of the shared elements that make all music possible.

Learning to recognize, analyze, and interpret these elements is the basis for **active listening**, a framework for improving your listening experience. It enables you to pay attention to music at multiple levels of complexity, making it richer and more rewarding.

Active listening can unlock the secrets of any piece of music, from a short rock song to a jazz suite, a symphony, or even an opera lasting several hours. This is because all music originates from a combination of the same basic elements. These include melody, harmony, texture, rhythm, meter, timbre, and form. Music communicates most effectively if we have some deeper understanding of the way in which this communication takes place. Knowing how to listen for these elements and understanding their function as a tool of musical expression is the key to active listening.

By the time you finish this chapter, you will recognize how an active listener approaches the basic elements of music and see how they function in a diverse selection of musical works.

Active Listening

Music engages both the heart and the mind. It is no surprise that we associate music with some of life's most deeply felt moments. The emotional content of a piece of music is often the first thing to which we respond. Music can communicate emotional content more directly, more immediately, than any other form of artistic expression.

An emotional response to music is an important part of the listening experience, but it is far from the whole picture. The ability to recognize, analyze, and interpret what you hear beyond the emotional response adds to your appreciation of music. That is what it means to be an active listener: You use your intellect as well as your emotions. Active listening does not preclude **emotional listening**, but incorporates it. Knowing more about the fundamental elements that make up a work, and learning how to listen for these elements, can add immeasurably to your musical IQ. A listener with an educated ear can gain an even stronger appreciation of music at the emotional level.

The Listening Situation

We hear music every day. One cannot escape it. It is part of the soundtrack to our lives. Yet we rarely make a special effort to listen to music with undivided attention. When we are given such an opportunity—e.g., going to a concert, attending a wedding, downloading a new recording from a favorite artist, happening upon a gifted street musician—it is often difficult to focus our thoughts solely on the musical content. One reason for this is that we are not accustomed to listening actively and overlook opportunities to do so. Once you know *how* to listen and *what* to listen for, active listening becomes easier.

We can become better listeners by using a few simple techniques:

1. **Tune out distractions.** Create a special time for the musical experience that allows you to listen intently. Do not try to listen closely to music while driving, walking, talking, or doing something else.

2. **Give your undivided attention**. No matter how short or long the piece of music, sustain your attention to the fullest. If you are using a listening guide from this book, follow along closely as you listen.

3. **Concentrate on the beginning**. You may want to listen to the first 15 or 20 seconds repeatedly because they frequently contain the key to the music that follows.

4. **Listen more than once**. Be prepared to listen to the entire piece several times; you will rarely, if ever, hear everything the first time.

5. **Move from emotional to active listening**. On first hearing, it's OK to focus on the overall emotional impression created by the music: the mood, the atmosphere, the associations it evokes. Upon repeated listening, shift your attention to the fundamental musical elements at work in the piece.

Active Listening: A way of paying attention to music at multiple levels of complexity for a richer, more rewarding experience. The active listener builds a framework for listening by learning to recognize, analyze, and interpret the fundamental elements all works of music share.

Emotional Listening: Listening to music primarily for the emotional responses it evokes. Such a listener will be most comfortable with short, uncomplicated pieces that do not stretch the limits of the human attention span.

A Core Repertory of Works

Central to this book's approach is the use of a recurring or *core repertory* of music examples that are revisited throughout the chapters. These are the same works included on the book's online music site. These core works were selected because they serve as excellent examples of the development of music over the centuries as well as the individual elements of music and genres discussed in the book.

The value of the core repertory is that it helps those new to the study of music to isolate, identify, and appreciate the various aspects that constitute an individual composition. Each piece in this repertory merits, even requires, repeated listening. The core repertory of the book allows a work to become more than a passing acquaintance. Listeners can explore new dimensions of an increasingly familiar piece as they develop an awareness of its complexity and the relationships among the different elements that contribute to their enjoyment of it. Each work of the core repertory is accompanied by one or more *Learning to Listen* guides in the chapters. These guides provide a running examination of each work. In addition, many of these works are supported by interactive electronic listening guides on the book's companion website. Each *Learning to Listen* guide in the text includes a "core repertory connection" indicating other places in the book where another element of the same piece is discussed, giving the listener a guide to examining many aspects of the same work.

The core repertory is at the heart of the book. By the end of this text, you should know these works intimately.

Key Elements of Music

Knowing something about the inner workings of music improves active listening skills. All music is created using a combination of common elements for making and organizing sound materials. Understanding the fundamental elements of music provides a framework and a vocabulary for analyzing, comparing, and contrasting different works, regardless of who composed the music and when or how it is performed.

The fundamental elements of music—**form, timbre, rhythm, meter, melody, harmony**, and **texture**—connect all types of musical expression. Music may also combine with text or with drama to create an even richer experience.

These elements are the keys to unlocking the meaning and expressive content of music through active listening.

Form

Form: The way musical material is organized. It is the way in which other musical elements such as melody, harmony, timbre, and texture are combined through the passage of time to create a complete work of music.

Form is the way musical material is organized. It defines a work of music the way a blueprint defines a building or a map defines a city, state, or country. While the sounds themselves are made up of the other elements mentioned above, none of these elements alone normally constitutes a complete work of music. It is the arrangement of these elements that gives music its form. Form and structure define the way that a piece of music begins, continues, develops, and ends. Arranging musical materials is generally accomplished using principles of repetition (AA), contrast (AB, ABA, AABB, etc.), and variation (AA'A", AA'BB', etc.). You should listen for audible markers that signal important junctions in the form, such as changes in instrumentation, tempo, and beat structure.

Active listening exercise: Select a favorite recording. Are there patterns you can recognize? Does the music repeat itself? Is there much contrast? Do the answers to these questions change as the music progresses?

Timbre

Timbre: The distinctive sound of a particular instrument or voice.

Pitch: The highness or lowness of a sound. It is measured relative to other pitches and also to absolute standards like 440 megahertz (the standard orchestral A).

Timbre (pronounced TAM-burr) is the distinctive sound of a given instrument or voice. Also known as musical color or tone color, timbre is the quality that distinguishes the sound of one instrument from another. If we set aside the **pitch** (the highness or lowness) and volume of a sound, timbre is what is left. To put it another way, the melody may change and become louder, but we can still recognize the difference between the sound quality of a saxophone, a guitar, or a singer's individual voice. All of this makes timbre one of the most interesting and flexible aspects of musical expression.

Active listening exercise: Select a recording you enjoy listening to. Use whatever words you want to describe what the music sounds like; recognizing the voices or instruments is less important than verbalizing what they sound like to you.

Rhythm and Meter

Rhythm: The organization of music through time. The term may refer in a general way to the element of time in music, but more specifically to the patterns of long notes, short notes, and rests. Rhythm results from the interrelationship of note duration with beat, meter, accent, and tempo.

Beat: The regular pulse of the music.

Meter: The repeated pattern of stronger and weaker beats.

Common Time: A duple meter consisting of four beats per measure.

Measure: One unit of the regular metrical pattern repeated throughout a piece of music (three beats, four beats, or six beats, as the case may be).

Rhythm is the organization of music in time. It groups longer and shorter notes and silences into patterns based on the **beat**, the regular pulse of the music. This pulse generally comprises a repeated pattern of stronger and weaker beats, called **meter**. The meter of a waltz, for example, is ONE-two-three/ONE-two-three (see Figure 1.1). The meter of a march is ONE-two-THREE-four/ONE-two-THREE-four, which is known as **common time**. In musical notation, each instance of this repeated pattern of strong and weak beats is called a **measure**.

Active listening exercise: Try tapping your foot, clapping your hands, snapping your fingers, or even dancing to the beat as you listen to a piece of music you like. This will allow you to embody the metrical patterns, even if you can't count or recognize them at first.

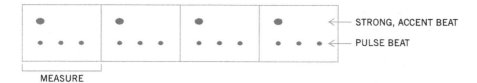

FIGURE 1.1 **Beats, Measures, and Meter.** The strong and weak beats in music divide into measures, creating a regular pulse. In this diagram, the regular pulse of the music, or *beat*, is represented by the smaller dots; the larger dots represent stronger beats forming a repeated pattern, or *meter*. All of these beats are organized into smaller sections called *measures*. Here, the first beat is emphasized to create a pattern of ONE-two-three, ONE-two three (waltz time).

Melody

Melody is a succession of musical notes and rhythms arranged as a recognizable unit. Also called a tune, a melody conveys a sense of forward motion and has a shape in that it uses a succession of high and low notes to form a memorable pattern.

Active listening exercise: Select a favorite song or composition. Listen for the tune, and see if it's one you think you can recognize when you hear it again. What about the melody makes it easy or difficult to remember?

Harmony

Harmony is a way of understanding notes that are played or sung together. To harmonize a melody is to play supporting notes that complement the melody. Harmony may transform the perception of a melody by adding depth that cannot be achieved with a single note at a time. Two or more notes played simultaneously are called **chords**. All notes and chords are heard in relationship to the **key** a piece of music is in. The key centers on a particular note (named by letter) and a **major** or **minor** sound depending on the series of eight notes—known as the **scale**—on which the work is based.

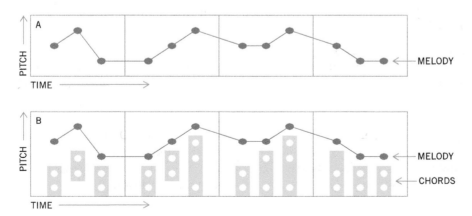

FIGURE 1.2 **Melody and Chords.** Chords are blocks of notes that support the melody and add to the complexity of the sound. In this diagram, the notes of a melody are shown as a series of individual pitches over time, or monophony (A); chords are produced when other supporting notes are played at the same time as the melody, also known as homophony (B).

Melody: A succession of musical notes and rhythms arranged as a recognizable unit.

Harmony: The combination of notes to produce chords, and a way of understanding the progression of chords throughout a piece.

Chords: Two or more notes sounding simultaneously; the foundation of harmony.

Key: The note (named by letter) and mode (major or minor) on which a piece of music is based.

Major: The sound of a melody based on the eight sung syllables "do-re-mi-fa-sol-la-ti-do," or the notes sounded by playing only white keys on the piano between one C and the next. It is typically thought of as having a brighter, happier sound than **minor**.

Minor: The sound of a melody based on the eight sung syllables "la-ti-do-re-mi-fa-sol-la," or the notes sounded by playing only white keys on the piano from one A to the next. It is typically thought of as having a darker, sadder sound than **major**.

Scale: The series of pitches, arranged from low to high or high to low, on which a melody is based. Major and minor, the most common scales, have eight.

Active listening exercise: Select a favorite musical piece. Listen for the notes that play at the same time as the melody. Do they form blocks of accompanying sound that have a pattern of their own (e.g., chords)? Or do they form additional melodic lines that parallel the melody?

Texture

Texture is the relationship between melodic and harmonic elements in a piece of music, especially how many layers of notes are happening at the same time. The texture may be sparse or dense, depending on the plan of the composer, and it may change repeatedly over the course of a piece or section. Conventional approaches to texture include single melodies (monophony), chords that accompany a single melody (homophony), and two or more simultaneous melodies (polyphony).

Texture: The relationship between melodic and harmonic elements in a piece of music, especially how many layers of notes occur at the same time.

Active listening exercise: Choose a piece that you enjoy. Listen for the melody or melodies. Can you identify how many things are going on at once?

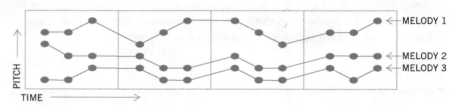

FIGURE 1.3 **Polyphonic Texture.** In a polyphonic texture, different melodies, each with its own distinct shape, are heard at the same time. This diagram shows polyphony, the simultaneous playing of two or more melodies.

Music in Context

In some musical **genres**, or categories, music stands alone. In other genres, it is combined with words or elements of drama.

Genre: A musical category, such as concerto, art song, or character piece.

Music and Text

Music can combine with words in a wide variety of ways. In music with text, it is fascinating to observe how the music and the words mutually support the communication of feelings and ideas.

Active listening exercise: After listening for the first time to an unfamiliar piece of music with text, read the lyrics separately without the music. Then listen to the music while following the text. In each case, how does your response to the music differ? How does your response to the text change when you hear it together with the music?

Music and Drama

A dramatic work may be accompanied by music, either in whole or in part. A dramatic story may be staged with live performers (e.g., opera and musical theater) or may be presented in an electronic medium with recorded music (e.g., motion pictures, television, video games). Music may be integrated in many ways into the telling of a story to provide atmosphere, express moods, influence tension, and communicate plot.

Active listening exercise: Watch a recorded scene from a TV show or movie with the sound turned off. Now watch the same scene again with the sound turned off but play some music at the same time. Do this several times with different musical selections. How does your reaction to the scene differ in each case?

Listening Practice

An excellent way to understand the musical elements is to explore how they work in selected pieces of music. Some elements, such as texture, are more difficult to identify than others. But even the simplest musical elements are sometimes difficult to hear because of the imaginative techniques composers use to organize their musical materials. Active listening involves concentrating on the many layers of a piece of music until we can follow its individual elements. The remainder of this chapter provides several examples to sharpen your skills as an active listener.

An Emotional Response to Music

Your first reaction to new music is typically emotional. Short and engaging, Dvořák's *Slavonic Dances* are a good place to start exploring an emotional response. Listen now to the *Slavonic Dance* in E minor by Antonín Dvořák (1841–1904), op. 72, no. 10.

This piece has a haunting, unforgettable melody that bears frequent repetition, the kind of tune that you are likely to hum or whistle after hearing it.

About two minutes into the piece, the opening tune is followed by a group of more sprightly melodies. The first melody then returns. The piece concludes with a final reference to the more sprightly tunes and a "slow fade." The contrasting melodies, and their repetition, suggest that the music tells a story. Perhaps it involves two or three characters and some simple action. This implied narrative helps hold our interest while we listen.

Another compelling element of this music is its strong dance-like rhythms. We can readily picture traditional Eastern European dancers moving to this music. It is interesting to note that, although it has a regular beat based on the styles and rhythms of Czech folk dances, the *Slavonic Dances* were not intended for dancing.

Finally, the brevity of this work contributes to the ease with which we make an emotional connection to it. It clocks in at about five and a half minutes, only a little longer than today's most popular songs. While a short work may contain many details not evident on first hearing, a piece of music lasting five minutes or less may be understood quite clearly on an emotional level. With longer compositions, our minds may wander and we may lose our initial interest in the music. This is more rare with a short, easy-to-digest piece like this one.

LEARNING TO LISTEN GUIDE

TAKE NOTE OF MELODY AND RHYTHM

What to Listen For: The lively melodies and rhythms and the contrast between the two main parts of the piece.

Streaming audio track 53.
Interactive Listening Guide ILG-13.

Dvořák: *Slavonic Dance* in E minor, op. 72, no. 10
Date: 1886
Instrumentation: Originally for piano four-hands, arranged here for orchestra
Key: E minor
Meter: $\frac{3}{4}$ (three moderately slow beats per measure)
Form: Ternary Form (ABA)
Core Repertory Connection: This music will be discussed again in Chapters 7, 8, and 12.

TIME	PROGRESSION	COMMENT
0:00	Part I	The main melody is introduced and repeated.
2:16	Part II	The music becomes more upbeat, and a group of contrasting melodies is heard.
4:10	Reprise of Part I	The music of the opening section returns, in slightly different form.
5:23	Conclusion	There is a brief reference to the music of Part II, and then the piece is over.

Focus On

Antonín Dvořák (1841–1904)

Czech composer. With Bedřich Smetana (1824–1884), Zdeněk Fibich (1850–1900), and Leoš Janáček (1854–1928) he is regarded as one of the great nationalist Czech composers of the 19th century. Long neglected and dismissed by the German-speaking musical world as a naive Czech musician, he is now considered by both Czech and international musicologists Smetana's true heir. He earned worldwide admiration and prestige for 19th-century Czech music with his symphonies, chamber music, oratorios, songs, and, to a lesser extent, his operas. (Klaus Döge, *Grove Music Online*)

Antonín Dvořák (1841–1904). This Czech nationalist composer was also director of the National Conservatory of Music in New York City from 1892 to 1895.
(© Pictorial Press Ltd/Alamy)

Much of Dvořák's music, like the *Slavonic Dance* in E minor, uses melodies, rhythms, and harmonies characteristic of his native country. From 1892 to 1895 he was director of the National Conservatory of Music in America in New York City. American composers were interested in learning how to write music with a distinctively American flavor. Dvořák obliged them with works like his Symphony no. 9 in E minor ("From the New World"), which remains one of the most popular symphonies ever written.

In History

Dvořák's *Slavonic Dance* in E minor, op. 72, no. 10

In the 19th century, if you wanted to hear your favorite music at home, you had to play it yourself. In most middle-class European and American homes, this meant going to the piano. Although our recorded example of this *Slavonic Dance* is arranged for an orchestra, Dvořák first wrote it for piano four-hands, or two people playing the same piano. A great deal of music using this format was written in the 19th century, and even more music intended for other instruments was transcribed so it could be played this way. If you lacked confidence, it helped to have a second player to help out; this made both parts easier to play. Playing and listening to the piano at home was also a popular social activity, and playing four-hand music created a special kind of intimacy between the two players.

Publishing sheet music for the home was a growing commercial enterprise in the late 19th century. A musically literate middle-class family could afford to own a piano and had free time to play it. In 1869 composer Johannes Brahms (1833–1897) published his first set of *Hungarian Dances* for piano four-hands. These works, with their perky rhythms and catchy tunes, sold in huge numbers and helped to make Brahms and his publisher wealthy. This was a turning point in the development of a large market for popular music—a market that came of age in the early 20th century.

By 1878, when the first of Dvořák's *Slavonic Dances* were written, Dvořák was motivated to match Brahms's success. So popular were the *Slavonic Dances* that the composer almost immediately arranged them for orchestra. Thus, Dvořák was able to appeal both to the amateur home musician and to the growing audience for symphonic music. This music filled a role that today is often associated with jazz, pop, and musical theater rather than with classical music; it was popular in tone, was broadly performed in public, and could easily be played and enjoyed at home as well.

From Emotional to Active Listening

While an emotional response is important to the listening experience, many other aspects of a work can also be explored. The longer a piece of music is, the more important it is to listen actively. Some musical works are so long that they are divided into **movements**, or self-contained parts. The term "movement" literally refers to the **tempo** (speed) and meter of a piece of music: the way it moves. Originally, a piece that contained sections in which the tempo and meter changed was said to have more than one movement. The term later came to be applied to longer pieces grouped together to form an even larger work.

Mozart, Symphony no. 40 in G minor: Listen for form:
Listen now to the first movement of the Symphony no. 40 in G minor, K. 550, by Wolfgang Amadeus Mozart.

Like the arrangement we heard of the Dvořák *Slavonic Dance*, Mozart's symphony is written for **orchestra**, still the most familiar instrumental performing ensemble in classical music. There is no completely standard configuration for an orchestra, and the one Mozart used was much smaller than those used by Dvořák and many later composers. Whereas an orchestra consisting of 35 to 40 musicians is adequate to perform a Mozart symphony, an orchestra containing more than a hundred people is needed to perform a symphony by the late 19th–early 20th-century composer Gustav Mahler (1860–1911).

Movement: A self-contained section of a longer piece. The most common number of movements is four, although there may be only two, and in some cases as many seven, or even more, movements in a single work.

Tempo: The speed of a piece of music.

Orchestra: The most common instrumental performing ensemble in Western classical music. There is no completely standard orchestra, although all orchestras have things in common—a preponderance of string instruments, for example—that distinguish them from other large instrumental ensembles like the band.

This music may already be familiar to you through various popular arrangements of the work's memorable melodies; the opening melody used to be a standard ringtone on many cell phones. The beginning of this work appeals to the emotional listener. From the first note, the orchestra throbs with a sense of urgency, and the melody that emerges is rhythmic and impassioned. The full orchestra enters with loud, fast-moving chords. The piece is off to an engaging start.

However, things start to get more complicated after this initial burst of energy. As in the Dvořák, there is a transition to a second, contrasting melody. But in this piece, several other transitions follow. Then the first two minutes of the work are repeated, and you get the feeling that Mozart is having fun with you but also helping you gain your footing again. Past the four-minute mark, the music becomes more dramatic yet unstable, adding to the sense of confusion. You may also begin to realize by now that you have heard the opening three notes of the piece more than a hundred times! The music then settles down, but a lot of what you heard in the first two minutes is repeated yet again. Why does the composer repeat himself so often?

One possible explanation for this work's unusual organization is that Mozart is using the music to tell a story. Both the contrast and the repetition that we have noticed are essential elements of good storytelling: contrast to keep you interested and repetition to keep you from getting lost. Every good story has characters whose adventures and interactions with other characters may be described at great length. It is reasonable to assume that in this piece, Mozart was attempting to do something similar in musical terms.

There are some obvious problems, though, with comparing a piece of music to a story. When we hear a story, we are accustomed to identifying human characters and character types—Prince Charming, a villain, a damsel in distress, and so forth—and to paying attention to what happens to them. We do this because these characters interest us, and we may even identify with them and come to care about them. Their adventures speak to things that we may have experienced ourselves, or that we may wish to experience. However, most people are not accustomed to caring about what happens to a musical idea. A musical theme is not a character. Or is it?

Actually, much classical music can easily be heard as though the musical themes were participants in a story or drama. A melody is introduced and then repeated in a variety of ways, suggesting that it is changing and growing. Called thematic development, this process resembles the development of an idea in an essay or of a character in a story. It is an important part of what this course will train you to hear. One reason the Mozart symphony movement is so long, yet so repetitive, is that the first three notes undergo considerable development.

Why should we care about what happens to these three notes? It might help to think of this **motive**, or short collection of thematic notes, as a character who grows, ages, and accumulates a variety of life experiences. Everyone experiences tragedy and loss at some point, so this music, with its deeply serious tone, resonates with something in our inner being. At the same time, we are not forced to identify those notes with anything more specific—things such as age, sex, or profession—that might limit our ability to empathize. Because these notes are presented as *music*, rather than as a *person* with human characteristics, we are free to interpret them in very personal terms. Music gains access to our very souls in ways that other art forms often cannot reach.

Motive: A memorable melodic fragment significant to the structure of a piece of music.

After reading the preceding paragraphs, you may wish to listen to the Mozart example again. In fact, a complex piece such as this needs to be listened to several times before it can be fully grasped. This process is similar to that of reading or watching a performance of a Shakespeare play. You know that this is great drama, but many of the words—and the way Shakespeare used them—are unfamiliar. On the first pass, you may understand only some of what you have read or heard. By the second time through, you begin to notice things that went over your head before. You may have to read or watch the play three or four times, though, before it becomes completely clear. Then you can finally understand and enjoy what you are hearing fully.

One of the goals of this book is to make you more fluent in the multilayered way that music communicates, so that listening to *any* music becomes easier.

LEARNING TO LISTEN GUIDE

TAKE NOTE OF MUSICAL FORM

What to Listen For: The careful construction that makes it possible to imagine that this music is telling a story.

Streaming audio track 35.

Mozart: Symphony no. 40 in G minor, K. 550
I: Molto Allegro
Date: 1788
Instrumentation: Small orchestra
Key: G minor
Meter: $\frac{4}{4}$, also known as common time (four rapid beats per measure)
Core Repertory Connection: This music will be discussed again in Chapters 5 and 9.

TIME	PROGRESSION	COMMENT
0:00	Beginning	We "meet" the first character.
0:52	Contrast	A new character is introduced.
1:27	Arrival	An important point in the story seems to have been reached. The first character is reintroduced.
2:02	Repeat	Everything you have heard so far is played again, helping you remember the characters and the differences among them.
4:05	Continuation	The plot thickens as the music you have heard so far is stretched in new directions.
4:21	Dramatic high point	The action seems to have reached some kind of crisis.
4:49	Lessening of tension	The music becomes quieter, as though the crisis is past.
5:06	Sudden outburst	Things become more agitated again.
5:21	Resolution	The music of the opening returns, suggesting that the conflicts of the previous section have been worked out.
6:36	Contrast	The other major character reappears as well.
7:12	Arrival	Now it really sounds like the story is almost over.
8:00	Final flourish	This music underscores the finality of the ending.

Focus On
Wolfgang Amadeus Mozart (1756–1791)

Wolfgang Amadeus Mozart (1756–1791). Mozart, depicted here in Classical fashion, possessed a bawdy sense of humor and a keen understanding of human nature. (© Q-Images/Alamy)

Austrian composer, son of Leopold Mozart (1719–1787). His style essentially represents a synthesis of many different elements, which coalesced in his Viennese years, from 1781 on, into an idiom now regarded as a peak of Viennese Classicism. The mature music, distinguished by its melodic beauty, its formal elegance, and its richness of harmony and texture, is deeply colored by Italian opera though also rooted in Austrian and south German instrumental traditions. Unlike Joseph Haydn (1732–1809), his senior by 24 years, and Ludwig van Beethoven (1770–1827), his junior by 15, he excelled in every medium current in his time. He may thus be regarded as the most universal composer in the history of Western music. (Cliff Eisen and Stanley Sadie, *Grove Music Online*)

Like all great cultural figures, Mozart has been portrayed in ways he could hardly have expected. The sublimely gifted genius, the eternal child, the epitome of classical poise and balance—these are just a few of the popular images of this famous musician. Mozart is still best known to many listeners through his fictional portrayal in the film *Amadeus*. When the movie appeared in 1984, yet another image was added—an obscene, immature prankster with an abrasive laugh who composed using a kind of divinely guided remote control.

Although this film stimulated interest in the composer and his music, it is important to understand that it did not attempt to portray Mozart realistically. Instead, it focused on a largely imaginary conflict between the divinely gifted genius and a self-confessed patron saint of mediocrity, his contemporary Antonio Salieri (1750–1825). In the film, Mozart can be seen tuning in to a kind of celestial radio, which tells him what to write. The clear implication is that Mozart's life and his music occupied different worlds, with little connection to each other.

The reality is much more complex. Mozart, we know, worked hard on his music. Furthermore, despite the music's often placid surface, it shows an amazingly deep understanding of human psychology and character. Mozart's feeling for shifting musical sonorities was uniquely his own; listen to the way he plays with the sounds of his relatively small orchestra in the Symphony no. 40.

If You Liked This Music...
Other Music of Interest

If you enjoyed these first two examples, here is some music that you may also want to hear.

- **Dvořák** wrote 16 *Slavonic Dances* in all, published as op. 46 and op. 72. Both sets were originally written for piano four-hands, but they are more widely available in the orchestral versions, also by the composer.

- **Johannes Brahms** wrote *Hungarian Dances*—21 in all—which are often heard in orchestral arrangements. Brahms and Dvořák were friends, and the popular success of these works by Brahms inspired Dvořák to write his own. All of these pieces feature catchy melodies and lively rhythms, and most are only a few minutes long.

- **Mozart's** Symphony no. 40 is one of three symphonies that Mozart wrote in 1788, three years before his death. All three have been widely recorded. Symphony no. 39, in E-flat major, is lyrical, playful and dramatic by turns: an ideal classical symphony. Symphony no. 41 in C major, the so-called "Jupiter" symphony, ends with one of the most stunning final movements ever written, in which five different motives are combined in various ways and, at the end, played simultaneously. The last 12 symphonies of Joseph Haydn (1732–1809), known as the "London" symphonies, since they were written for public performance in that city, also epitomize the style of the late 18th-century symphony at its best.

Bach, Concerto in D minor: Listen for timbre: Listen now to the first movement of the Concerto in D minor, BWV 1052, for harpsichord and strings, by Johann Sebastian Bach (1685–1750). Though slightly shorter than the Mozart, this piece poses even greater challenges for a novice listener.

These begin with the choice of instrument. Bach wrote this piece for a harpsichord, widely used in his time but much less familiar today. Although it resembles a small piano, the harpsichord is actually a completely different kind of instrument. In a piano, the strings are struck by hammers and the amount of force applied to the keys determines how loud or soft the sound will be. A harpsichord plays a note by plucking a string when a key is depressed. The strings are plucked by a little wedge, or *plectrum*, made of quill or leather in older instruments. The sounds produced are not as loud as those of the piano and fade more quickly. Moreover, the force of the plucking action does not vary much, no matter how hard a key is pressed. The volume of the harpsichord is, therefore, relatively even. Thus, in writing for harpsichord, composers focus on other aspects of the harpsichord's sound.

Bach's Concerto in D minor is performed by a harpsichord and an ensemble of historical string instruments. Like most, but not all, pieces titled **concerto**, it is built on the contrast between a solo instrument (in this case, the harpsichord) and an orchestra (in this case, only strings). Sometimes only the orchestra is heard, sometimes only the harpsichord. Most often, though, they are heard together and play off of each other. Indeed, the opposition between the rich sound of the strings and the clear, brittle sound of the harpsichord is a large part of what makes this music interesting.

Concerto: A genre built on the contrast between a solo instrument or group of instruments and a larger ensemble.

Compared to the Mozart, this piece presents little melodic variety; only one real melody is heard. The beat is extremely steady. The sounds of the instruments, though, are masterfully exploited by the composer. The entire range of the harpsichord is used, from its sonorous low notes to its relatively tinny upper **register** (this word refers to a specific range of low, medium, or high pitches on an instrument or in a voice). The harpsichordist's part is also quite virtuosic: a flurry of rapid-fire notes grabs our attention, even when the harpsichord is nearly drowned out by the full orchestra. At times, the orchestra comes in briefly to punctuate a harpsichord solo, adding an extra rhythmic punch. The orchestra also serves repeatedly to reintroduce the theme with which the movement began; these restatements are an important features of the music's form. Meanwhile, the harpsichord frequently takes off in its own direction.

Register: A specific range of low, medium, or high pitches on an instrument or in a voice.

Despite the limited means the composer has allowed himself, this is a rich and complex piece. Because musical contrast is so minimal, you are forced to concentrate and become hyper-aware of the contrasts that are present. Thus, listening to this music is a rewarding and challenging experience. For most listeners, the strong emotional impact of the beginning of this piece fades in less than a minute. After that, you are virtually forced to become an active listener.

Thus, when you first listen to this selection, you should plan to minimize any and all distractions. Listening to this music will consume your full attention, and you still may have to listen several times before you are fully aware of all that is going on. So be patient, and spread the listening out over several days if necessary. It will be worth it.

Crumb, *Black Angels*: Listen for harmony and texture: The pieces we have examined so far all come from times and places quite distant from our

---

LEARNING TO LISTEN GUIDE

TAKE NOTE OF TIMBRE

What to Listen For: The wide variety of sounds that Bach produces with just a harpsichord and a small orchestra.

Streaming audio track 8.

Bach: Concerto in D minor for harpsichord and strings, BWV 1052
I: Allegro
Date: Early 18th century
Instrumentation: Harpsichord and string orchestra
Key: D minor
Meter: $\frac{4}{4}$, also known as common time (four rapid beats per measure)
Core Repertory Connection: This music will be discussed again in Chapter 7.

TIME	PROGRESSION	COMMENT
0:00	Opening	The orchestra begins the piece; the harpsichord is heard in the background.
0:16	Harpsichord solo	The harpsichord now comes to the fore. This is not a solo in the literal sense, but the harpsichord gets the lion's share of the attention.
0:31	Orchestral passage	The orchestra returns to prominence.
0:55	Second harpsichord solo	Here the harpsichord interacts with the orchestra, playing continual fast notes as the orchestra repeats portions of the opening theme.
2:23	Orchestral passage	The orchestra once again emerges in its own right.
2:39	Third harpsichord solo	We now hear a greater range of sounds from the harpsichord. The orchestral accompaniment is reduced at times to long, sustained notes, only to break forth again with portions of the main theme.
4:26	Orchestral passage	The orchestra powerfully repeats the music heard at the beginning.
4:42	Fourth harpsichord solo	This time the orchestra briefly goes silent.
5:01	Dialogue	The harpsichord and orchestra then carry on a lengthy and varied exchange.
7:58	Orchestral passage	The orchestra concludes the piece in the same way that it began.

Focus On
Original Instruments

Bach's harpsichord music is often played on the piano. In recent years, however, there has been an increasing tendency among classical performers to play older music on the actual instruments for which it was written, or at least on modern copies of such instruments. Performances and recordings made this way are often designated as being on "original," "historical," or "period" instruments. If you compare these performances to ones made on more traditional instruments, you are likely to be able to hear the difference. The sound of the instruments is generally lighter and less sustained. Performers often minimize the dynamic contrasts. These performances are rewarding, but they also pose challenges to listeners unaccustomed to their sounds. They may also help experienced listeners hear familiar music in new ways. Hearing the distinct sounds of the different instruments, called timbre, or *tone color*, is another important part of active listening, and we will study it more fully in Chapter 6.

Inside a harpsichord. The sound is produced by quills plucking the strings. *(© Edwin Remsberg/Alamy)*

own—19th-century Bohemia (now the Czech Republic) and 18th-century Austria and Germany. The final example in this chapter originated much closer to home.

American composer George Crumb was born in West Virginia in 1929. Like many Americans during the 1960s, he had strong feelings about America's involvement in the war in Vietnam. His string quartet *Black Angels*, subtitled *13 Images from the Dark Land*, is a musical commentary on that controversial war. But it is also much more. It deals with the subjects of the fall and redemption of mankind, life and death, God and the devil. These images are conveyed on the surface of the music: The beginning, for example, is meant to sound terrifying. The images are also conveyed symbolically in terms of numerical relationships pertaining to the numbers 13 and 7 that are embedded in the music but nearly impossible to hear. As we will see in Chapters 2 and 12, Crumb is not the only composer to have included this kind of symbolic meaning in his music.

Black Angels challenges the listener in some extraordinary ways. It is written for string quartet—an ensemble of two violins, viola, and cello—a standard small

Chamber Music: Music written for a small ensemble. In modern usage, it usually refers only to instrumental music. Historically, it indicated music meant to be performed in chambers: i.e., in private homes.

Glissando: A series of very rapid notes sliding up or down. On a keyboard, it is produced by sliding the thumb or forefinger along the keys, and on a string instrument, it is produced by sliding the finger up or down the string on the fret board or fingerboard. Glissandos may also be played on the harp by sweeping across the strings.

Dissonant/Dissonance: The result of a combination of notes with strongly clashing overtones, as when two adjacent notes on a keyboard are played simultaneously. (Contrast **Consonant/consonance**.)

group used by classical composers since the 1700s. A string quartet is an example of **chamber music**, written for a small ensemble and intended for performance in a small, private space. When Crumb wrote this piece, there was a very large repertory of works for string quartet. People who came to hear a performance by a string quartet had certain definite expectations about how the music would sound. However, *Black Angels* was dramatically different from what they had learned to expect.

The difference is most evident in the timbres of this work, the most unusual and varied you have heard so far. For one thing, Crumb called for electronic amplification. While most contemporary audiences are accustomed to hearing amplified instruments, classical music performers do not usually employ amplification and often pride themselves on not requiring it. In this case, though, the explicit purpose of the amplification is to make the instruments sound strange, frightening, and unfamiliar.

This strangeness is augmented by a variety of unusual playing techniques. The players are often asked to play *sul ponticello* (close to the bridge, which holds the strings apart from the body of the instrument) and **glissando** (sliding their fingers up and down the strings). They may play their instruments using thimbles, paper clips, and glass rods. They are also asked to play maracas (a kind of rattle) and tam-tams (a kind of gong). They even click their tongues and whisper and shout numbers in Hungarian, Japanese, Russian, German, and Swahili. All players but the cellist are also asked to play on crystal glasses tuned to various pitches by being partially filled with water. Many of the sounds may strike you as abrasive and unpleasant. The harmony, unlike that in the previous pieces we listened to, is often highly **dissonant**, with notes that clash in a way you will easily hear. The texture is complicated by the wide variety of unusual sound effects.

The first section of the piece, titled "Departure," describes mankind's fall from grace. It consists of five short sections, titled "Threnody I: Night of the Electric Insects," "Sounds of Bones and Flutes," "Lost Bells," "Devil-Music," and "*Danse Macabre*." The first of these was inspired by soldiers' stories of swarms of insects they had encountered in the jungles and swamps of Vietnam. "Devil-Music" refers to the *Devil's Trill*, an influential violin sonata by Giuseppe Tartini (1692–1770), while the title of "*Danse Macabre*" recalls a familiar piece by Camille Saint-Saëns (1835–1921). "Devil-Music" and "*Danse Macabre*" also quote the *Dies irae*, a medieval chant from the Requiem, or Mass for the Dead. Taken together, these references suggest that the work is about death and the human confrontation with evil, in Vietnam and perhaps in many other times and places as well.

In short, this piece is both deeply challenging and rich in meaningful associations. On an emotional level, it suggests feelings that are often extreme and may be disagreeable. *Black Angels* is also challenging because of the wide range of impressions it communicates, from the vividness of the insects at the beginning to the obscurity of the numbers and the foreign languages heard at the end. It goes without saying that a single hearing will not suffice for full comprehension of this music.

LEARNING TO LISTEN GUIDE

TAKE NOTE OF HARMONY, TEXTURE, AND TIMBRE

What to Listen For: The unusual sounds and harsh combinations produced by electronic amplification and unorthodox playing techniques.

Streaming audio track 69.

Crumb: *Black Angels*
Date: 1970
Instrumentation: Electronically amplified string quartet
Key: Largely undefined
Meter: Irregular
Core Repertory Connection: This music will be discussed again in Chapters 6 and 9.

TIME	PROGRESSION	COMMENT
	I: Departure	
0:00	1. "Threnody I: Night of the Electric Insects"	Amplified sounds from all the instruments evoke the image of buzzing insects in the swamps of Vietnam. Unusual timbral effects intensify the dissonant harmonies resulting from highly unusual combinations of notes.
1:33	2. "Sounds of Bones and Flutes"	Clucking sounds are introduced, produced both by the performers' mouths and by plucking their instruments. Unusual playing techniques also produce the flute-like sounds heard in this section. The texture increases in complexity compared to the previous section; there is a great deal going on at once.
2:23	3. "Lost Bells"	The eerie, bell-like sounds here are also produced by unusual playing techniques. The harmonies are simpler and reinforce the impression of bells sounding in the distance.
3:51	4. "Devil-Music"	This section is an abrupt contrast that features percussion instruments as well as the strings. Some of the sounds here are quite uncomfortable to listen to.
5:44	5. *"Danse Macabre"*	The conclusion of the Departure section is much more audibly rhythmic than anything heard so far—indeed, a macabre take on the dance. Spoken syllables are included.

Focus On

George Crumb (b. 1929)

American composer. Born to accomplished musical parents, he participated in domestic music-making from an early age, an experience that instilled in him a lifelong empathy with the Classical and Romantic repertory. He studied at Mason College (1947–50), the University of Illinois, Urbana-Champaign (MM 1953), the Berlin Hochschule für Musik (Fulbright Fellow, 1955–6), where he was a student of Boris Blacher, and the

George Crumb, composer of *Black Angels*.
© Lebrecht Music & Arts

(continued)

Focus On (continued)

University of Michigan, Ann Arbor (DMA 1959), where his teachers included Ross Lee Finney. In 1959 he accepted a teaching position at the University of Colorado, Boulder. After receiving a Rockefeller grant in 1964, he became composer-in-residence at the Buffalo Center for the Creative and Performing Arts. His first mature works, composed during these years, include Five Pieces for Piano (1962), *Night Music I* (1963), and Four Nocturnes (1964), in which delicate timbral effects combine with a Webernesque pointillism and echoes of a Virginian folk heritage to create the atmospheric chiaroscuro that became a trademark of his style. (Richard Steinitz, *Grove Music Online*)

Though his is hardly a household name, Crumb has attracted almost a cult following among devotees of contemporary American art music. His fame is based largely on his imaginative use of novel sound effects, often derived from traditional instruments. Crumb's piano works, for example, frequently call for the performer to pluck or strum the strings, and even to sing into the instrument. *Black Angels* is probably his best-known work.

Active Listening

We will return to this piece and to the other examples discussed in this chapter at various points in this book, each time looking at them from a different perspective.

Being an active listener means being as aware as possible of what is going on in the music on different levels. How is the music put together? What kinds of sound are used? How does a work draw upon the basic elements of music discussed in this chapter: form, timbre, rhythm, meter, melody, harmony, texture, and the combination of music with text or drama?

Being an active listener also means paying attention to the meaning or meanings that may be embodied in the music: how it plays on your emotions, how it elicits certain kinds of responses, how it provides unique perspectives on poems, dramas, and even pictures. Being aware of these things will deepen and enrich your experience of music in surprising ways, often allowing you to respond to it in very personal terms. Whatever your reaction to *Black Angels*, for example, you are probably not indifferent to it, even after a single hearing.

SUMMARY

- Active listening is a framework for improving your awareness of the listening experience.
- Active listening enables you to pay attention to music at multiple levels of complexity by examining the common elements that music comprises: form, timbre, rhythm, meter, melody, harmony, texture, and the combination of music with text or drama.

- Active listening does not preclude emotional listening. An emotional response to music is an important part of the listening experience, but it is far from the whole picture.
- The ability to recognize, analyze, and interpret what you hear adds further dimensions to your appreciation of music.

- The first step in learning to listen actively is to provide a situation in which to listen intently by tuning out distractions, giving the music your undivided attention, listening carefully to the beginning of a work, and listening repeatedly to the entire work.

- An excellent way to understand the musical elements described above is to explore how they work in selected pieces of music.

KEY TERMS

Active listening	p. 2	Glissando	p. 16	Orchestra	p. 9
Beat	p. 4	Harmony	p. 5	Pitch	p. 4
Chamber music	p. 16	Key	p. 5	Register	p. 13
Chords	p. 5	Major	p. 5	Rhythm	p. 4
Common time	p. 4	Measure	p. 4	Scale	p. 5
Concerto	p. 13	Melody	p. 5	Tempo	p. 9
Dissonant	p. 16	Meter	p. 4	Texture	p. 6
Emotional listening	p. 2	Minor	p. 5	Timbre	p. 4
Form	p. 4	Motive	p. 10		
Genre	p. 6	Movement	p. 9		

REVIEW QUESTIONS

1. What is the difference between emotional listening and active listening? Do you listen differently at different times?
2. Why is the Dvořák *Slavonic Dance* easy to listen to? What are its most memorable features?
3. Why are the Mozart symphony and the Bach harpsichord concerto more challenging to listen to than the previous two examples?
4. Why is Crumb's *Black Angels* the most challenging example in this chapter?

REVIEW CONCEPTS

1. In what way(s) could the main thematic motive of Mozart's Symphony no. 40 be said to resemble a character in a story? How does a musical theme differ from a human character?
2. What features of Bach's concerto for harpsichord help to maintain your interest, compensating for the small amount of thematic material?
3. What are some of the ways in which George Crumb challenges his listener's expectations about what music for a string quartet should sound like?

LISTENING EXERCISES

1. Listen to some of the other Dvořák *Slavonic Dances* or to the Brahms *Hungarian Dances*, either in the original piano four-hand version or in the later orchestral version. Do these pieces also lend themselves to emotional listening? Why or why not?
2. Listen to Mozart's Symphony no. 40 in its entirety. Is it clear why Mozart joined these four movements together as a single composition? Why or why not?
3. Listen to one or more of the Brandenburg Concertos by Bach, which are among the most popular works in the classical repertory. Does this music appeal to emotional or active listening skills, or both? Give some reasons for your answer.
4. Listen to the first movement of Haydn's String Quartet in B-flat major, op. 64, no. 3, from your listening list. How does the sound of the string quartet in Crumb's *Black Angels* differ from the more traditional sonorities used by Haydn? What means does Crumb use to produce these unusual sounds?

Guide to the Instruments of the Orchestra

The major vehicle for the performance of classical music is the modern symphony orchestra. This guide introduces you to the major instruments of the orchestra and others that you'll be hearing throughout this book.

TABLE 1.1: **Instruments of the Orchestra**

Stringed Instruments	**Bowed Stringed Instruments**	Keyboards	Organ
	Violin		Harpsichord
	Viola		Piano
	Cello		Celesta
	Double-bass		Synthesizer
	Plucked Stringed Instruments	Percussion	**Non-pitched**
	Harp		Snare drum
	Guitar		Bass drum
Woodwinds	Flute		Tom-tom
	Single-reed		Cymbals
	Clarinet		Triangle
	Saxophone		Gong (tam-tam)
	Double-reed		**Pitched**
	Oboe		Timpani
	Bassoon		Xylophone
Brass	Cornet		Marimba
	Trumpet		Vibraphone
	Piccolo trumpet		Glockenspiel
	Horn		Chimes
	Tuba		
	Trombone		

Stringed Instruments

Instruments that create their sound through the vibration of a string (such as a metal wire or a stretched piece of gut) are classified as *stringed instruments*. The very simplest such instrument is called a *monochord*; it consists literally of a stretched piece of twine, animal material, or metal that is attached at either end to a stick. If you pluck a full length of a string, you will hear one tone; if you cut that string exactly in half, the pitch produced will be an octave higher.

THE VIOLIN (© Laurie Lewis/Lebrecht Music & Arts)

THE VIOLA (© T. Martinot/Lebrecht Music & Arts)

The Violin and Other Bowed Stringed Instruments

The *violin* is one of the key melody instruments in the Western classical orchestra. It is part of a family of related instruments, from violin (soprano) to *viola* (alto), *cello* (tenor), and *double bass* (bass). Note that the division of these instruments mirrors the division of vocal ranges commonly found in choirs. One of the most popular of all classical music forms, the string quartet, is performed by a group of two violins, a viola, and a cello.

CORE LISTENING: Haydn's Quartet in B-flat, Op. 64, no. 3, is a great example of a classical string quartet. Listen to how the violins, viola, and cello interact in this piece. You'll hear how the melody is divided between the violins, with the viola and cello providing harmonic support. Contrast this with George Crumb's *Black Angels,* a modern string quartet. Here the division of melody and accompaniment is less clear as Crumb is not tied to the classical division of instrumental roles that Haydn and others had perfected. (**Streaming audio tracks 18–21.**)

Violins developed from earlier stringed instruments that were played with a bow, such as the Renaissance *viol*. The modern violin is a favorite solo instrument, whether played alone, in a string

THE CELLO (bikeriderlondon)

THE DOUBLE-BASS (© Stock MR/Lebrecht)

quartet, or as part of a full orchestra. In the 19th century, great performers such as Nicolò Paganini (1782–1840) were the rock stars of their day; they toured Europe drawing standing-room only crowds who were in awe of their instrumental skills. In the 1990s, violinists like Nigel Kennedy (b. 1956) revived the crowd-pleasing performance style of pop performers, dressing more like a punk rocker than a concert hall star.

See string section streaming video clips V1–V16.

CORE LISTENING: Charles Ives's (1874–1954) Violin Sonata no. 4, 2nd movement, is just one example of how the violin is used as an expressive melodic instrument in classical music. Mozart's Symphony no. 40, 1st movement, and Beethoven's Symphony no. 5 give examples of how the great classical composers employed a full string section in the orchestra to create complex musical textures. (Streaming audio track 59.)

The Harp and Other Plucked Stringed Instruments

Like the violin, the concert harp (or "double-action" harp) is the latest development in a long line of instruments that feature strings stretched across a wooden or metal frame. Folk harps are known all around the world and form the basis for the modern instrument. These harps have a C-shaped body, with the strings anchored to the top and bottom branches, which are separated by a hollow, resonating chamber. The modern harp features a strong metal frame to support its range of strings, and also adds pedals that can be used to change the pitch of individual strings. Traditionally, harpists played either with their fingers or more typically with their finger-nails, plucking individual or groups of notes to play melodies and harmonies. Composers of orchestral music sometimes call for as many as six harps for special effects. The harp also has a large solo repertory.

THE HARP (© Stock MR/Lebrecht)

CORE LISTENING: The sound of the harp can be heard clearly in Claude Debussy's (1862–1918) Sonata for flute, viola, and harp. This piece offers us the opportunity to distinguish between a bowed string (the viola) and a plucked one (the harp), and contrast both with a woodwind (the flute; see below). (Streaming audio tracks 60–62.)

The *guitar* is familiar to listeners of classical and popular music. The traditional acoustic guitar has a hollow wooden body, fretted fingerboard, and six nylon or metal strings. Electric guitars replace the hollow body with a solid one and magnetic pickups for amplifying the sound of the resonating strings. The guitar, in its acoustic (non-electric) form, has a distinguished history, but has only come to be regarded as a medium for classical performers during the past hundred years, largely due to the influence of the guitar virtuoso Andrés Segovia (1893–1987). Classical guitarists often play transcriptions of music originally written for other instruments.

THE GUITAR (© Gerry Walden/Lebrecht Music & Arts)

THE SITAR (© CREATISTA/ShutterStock)

See woodwinds streaming video clips V17–V32.

THE FLUTE (© Chris Stock/Lebrecht Music & Arts)

THE CLARINET (© T. Martinot/Lebrecht Music & Arts)

The *sitar* is an Indian long-necked plucked stringed instrument that has become familiar to listeners outside of India since the 1950s. The sitar is related to an ancient three-stringed instrument found in India and Persia. The modern sitar took shape in the 18th century and typically includes 18 to 20 strings, six or seven of which are plucked for melody. The remaining strings, called *sympathetic* strings, resonate to produce the droning effect that is characteristic of the instrument. The neck of the sitar has 18 moveable frets and its resonating body is made of a gourd. It is played with a plectrum or with the fingernails. The sitar is used primarily in Indian classical music, although it has sometimes been adapted by Western musicians playing classical and popular music.

CORE LISTENING: The sound of the sitar is featured in the work *Raga Bhankar*, played by virtuoso Ustad Vilayat Khan (1928–2004). Notice the way in which the pitches of the melody are dramatically bent and sustained to produce a mesmerizing flow to the music. (**Streaming audio track 74.**)

Woodwinds

Woodwinds are instruments that produce their distinctive sound through the vibration of a column of air. In the simplest woodwind instrument—such as a whistle—the player blows through the end of a hollow tube, setting the air into motion, which produces a sound. By shortening the overall length of the tube—through adding holes that can be "stopped" (covered up) by the player's fingers but also uncovered selectively—the pitch can be raised. Through the addition of specialized mouthpieces and/or reeds, woodwinds have evolved into a variety of expressive instruments.

The *wind*, or *woodwind*, section of the orchestra includes at least three different types of instruments: *flutes; single-reed;* and *double-reed* instruments. The flute features an oval mouthpiece that has a sharp edge; when the player blows across it, the column of air is broken into jagged bursts, creating the unique breathy flute sound. On reed instruments, the mouthpiece is covered by a thin piece of cane that is set into motion by the player's breath. These reeds are attached to the top of the instrument either singly, as on the clarinet, or doubled over, as on the oboe and bassoon.

The basic design of the *flute* is so simple that versions of it are found in cultures from around the world. Western flutes are blown from a mouthpiece on the side of one end of the instrument. Blowing the flute requires finding exactly the right angle from which to blow, the right intensity, and also the right spacing between your lips. Wind players call this finding an *embouchure* (OM-boo-shur). The flute player can also raise the pitch by *overblowing*—blowing harder in order to produce a higher pitch.

CORE LISTENING: As mentioned above, the Debussy sonata for flute, viola, and harp prominently features a flute, heard in contrast with the two stringed instruments. The opening of the second movement of Igor Stravinsky's (1882–1971) *Symphony of Psalms* prominently features both the flute and the oboe. (🔊 **Streaming audio track 64.**)

The *clarinet* is the most common single-reed instrument in modern orchestras, and also the one with the shortest history; it originated in the 18th century, and its only real predecessor appeared less than a century earlier. There is a family of clarinets just like the family of violins, although the standard soprano is most often heard. The bass clarinet is occasionally used in the orchestra for special effects.

The orchestral woodwind section is completed by the *oboe* and the *bassoon*, which are double-reed instruments in the soprano and bass ranges, respectively. They are both blown from the end. Instead of the clarinet mouthpiece, these instruments feature a double reed that is attached to a tube leading into the body of the instrument.

THE OBOE (© *Chris Stock/Lebrecht Music & Arts*)

Unlike the clarinet, the oboe descends from an ancient design that is present in many cultures throughout the world. In Medieval/Renaissance Europe, this instrument was known as a *shawm*. Most shawms, though, are very loud instruments intended for outdoor performance. 17th-century French musicians redesigned the instrument to make it more supple and expressive, and the result was the direct ancestor of the modern oboe. The oboe is regarded as particularly eloquent and lyrical, and this has influenced the ways that composers have written for it.

The *bassoon* has a somewhat different ancestry than the oboe. This instrument is distinguished from the oboe family by its double-bore construction; it consists not of a single tube in which an air column vibrates, but of two separate tubes connected at the bottom. This gives the instrument a richer but less penetrating sound than that of the oboe. The *contrabassoon*, or *double bassoon*, is a larger version of the instrument that extends to an even lower range. Like the bass clarinet, it is used primarily in this low register.

THE BASSOON (© *Chris Stock/Lebrecht Music & Arts*)

CORE LISTENING: Mozart's *Gran Partita*, K. 361 gives us the opportunity to hear a number of these woodwind instruments in action. The piece is scored for two oboes, two clarinets, two basset horns (a single-reed instrument that is similar to the clarinet but instead of having a long, straight body is bent at the mouthpiece), four horns, two bassoons, and bass. The primary melody instrument are the clarinets and oboes, which frequently trade off melodic statements to produce contrasts of timbre. (🔊 **Streaming audio tracks 22–28.**)

The *saxophone*, well known to band musicians and to fans of jazz, is also classified as a woodwind. Its body is made of metal and it has a single-reed mouthpiece and holes covered by keys.

THE TENOR SAXOPHONE (© *JazzSign/Lebrecht Music & Arts*)

It was invented by Antoine-Joseph (Adolphe) Sax (1814–1894) in the early 1840s. As with the clarinet, Sax introduced various instruments in different ranges, with the tenor and alto being the most often played today.

CORE LISTENING: The saxophone can be heard in orchestral settings, but is most commonly heard in jazz. We'll be studying a classic jazz composition, "Lester Leaps In," named for one of the greatest saxophonists of the 20th century, Lester Young (1909–1959). (Streaming audio track 72.)

Brass Instruments

THE TRUMPET (© iStockphoto.com/lisegagne)

Brass instruments are played by blowing air through a cup-shaped mouthpiece connected to a length of metal tubing with a bell-like flare at the end. The action of the lips is important for vibrating the air inside the instrument and also for modulating its tone. In a simple horn, the player blows through a mouthpiece at one end of the instrument; the basic pitch is determined by the horn's length. A modern bugle is played in this way.

A major change in horn design came in the late 18th-early 19th century with the invention of valves that allowed brass instruments to play all notes in the musical scale. Valves played by the fingers can either open or close additional lengths of tubing built into the instrument, enabling the player to access a wider range of notes.

The modern *trumpet* has three valves, which, used either separately or in combination, can yield a surprisingly large variety of pitches. The *piccolo trumpet* is a small, high-pitched trumpet often used to play Baroque music, although it is actually a recent invention. The tone of the trumpet may be modified by placing an object called a *mute* in its bell. A variant of the trumpet played in the 19th and early 20th centuries in bands was the *cornet*, featuring a slightly mellower tone due to differences in the shape and construction of its body. Louis Armstrong and other early jazz musicians began their careers playing the cornet before switching to the louder trumpet.

THE HORN (FRENCH HORN) (© Blend Images/ Alamy)

CORE LISTENING: Instruments from the trumpet family of brass instruments can be heard in several of our core listening selections. The trumpet can be heard in a lively jazz setting both as an accompanying and solo instrument in *Lester Leaps In* by Count Basie (1904–1984). The cornet can be heard prominently in Morton Gould's (1913–1996) *An American Salute*. Gould selected the instrument because of its widespread use in American town bands at the turn of the twentieth century. The piccolo trumpet can be heard in Igor Stravinsky's *Symphony of Psalms*. (Streaming audio track 68.)

The *horn* (often called the *French horn*) is descended from outdoor instruments used in hunting; the resonant tone of the natural horn could be heard up to five miles away. The French horn has three rotary valves to change notes. It is played with the right hand in the bell, and can be muted with the hand to change the tone of the sound.

CORE LISTENING: The French horn is a popular instrument used in the orchestra to add color and a unique melodic voice. Mozart prominently featured it about 18 seconds into his Symphony No. 40, when he abruptly switched from a very soft overall sound (*piano*) to a loud one (*forte*). Berlioz also used French horns prominently in his score for *Romeo et Juliet* in the opening measures of the *Scène d'amour*. (**Streaming audio tracks 35 and 48.**)

The *trombone* uses a slide instead of valves to change notes, allowing the player more flexibility of pitch. Trombones used in today's orchestras are most commonly in the tenor range, although the bass and alto trombone are occasionally heard as well. Thus, the trombone essentially occupies the high end of what is often called the "low brass" section of the orchestra.

The very lowest brass instrument is the *tuba*. In its most common form, it provides the bass component of the brass section. There is also a tenor version of the tuba commonly called the *euphonium*. The tuba is a relatively recent instrument; its earliest predecessors are less than two hundred years old. One familiar variation of the tuba is the *sousaphone*, a curled version of the instrument frequently used in marching bands and developed by famed band leader John Philip Sousa. The tuba is played using valves.

See brass instrument streaming video clips V33–V48.

THE TROMBONE (© Stock MR/Lebrecht)

THE TUBA (© Chris Stock/Lebrecht Music & Arts)

HARPSICHORD. *(© Fred Toulet/Leemage/Lebrecht)*

GRAND PIANO. *(© INTERFOTO/Alamy)*

PIPE ORGAN. *(© R Booth/Lebrecht Music & Arts)*

CORE LISTENING: The trombone and tuba can be clearly heard at the ending of Smetana's Sarka, from Má Vlast, beginning at about 8:58. Their deep voices are used to portray the desperate efforts of the men as they struggle to ward off their attackers. (**Streaming audio track 52.**)

Keyboard Instruments

Keyboard instruments fulfill many functions in music, from playing melodies and solos to providing rhythm or chords to accompany other players. Keyboards are played by both hands using a set of mechanical keys covering several octaves of pitches of a fixed scale. The most common keyboard instruments are the organ, harpsichord, piano and celesta. Electronic keyboards and synthesizers are also widely used to imitate traditional keyboard sounds, to imitate the sounds of other instruments, or to play unique electronic sounds.

Historically, the earliest keyboard is the organ, often called a pipe organ because it features a group of pipes or tubes, each tuned to a single note, that are controlled by a keyboard, also called a *manual*. Organs give players a great range of sounds and can be combined in inventive ways. Pressing a key triggers a mechanism that blows air through the selected pipes. Pipes are often identified by their length, such as 2', 4', and 8', the shorter pipes being for higher pitch ranges. Modern organs have from two to seven manuals, plus pedals that are operated by the player's feet. Organs also come in modern, fully electronic versions, some emulating the sounds of the pipe organ, even using pipe length designations to identify preset pitch ranges.

Various instrument makers experimented over the centuries with ways to create a versatile keyboard-controlled stringed instrument. The *clavichord* was an early design popular in the 17th-18th centuries that featured metal picks or *tangents* that plucked the strings. Unfortunately, it was a very quiet instrument, making it most suitable for being played on its own rather than with other instruments.

More successful was the *harpsichord*, on which a lever connected to a *jack* plucks the string with a quill (recent harpsichords generally use plastic) when a key is depressed. Many harpsichords have two manuals, allowing performers to execute complex hand crossings or to change registrations quickly.

CORE LISTENING: The harpsichord player often served as the informal conductor of larger ensembles in the Baroque era, setting the beat and indicating when the instruments were to play. A great example from this period is Bach's Harpsichord Concerto in D minor. (**Streaming audio track 8.**)

Unlike the harpsichord, the piano (originally named the *pianoforte*) can play both softly (*piano*) and loudly (*forte*). The *piano* is technically a percussion instrument, since its notes are produced by hammers striking a set of tuned strings. When the player releases a key, a felt damper descends on the string, stopping the vibration. Modern pianos have 88 keys, giving them a wide range.

CORE LISTENING: The piano can be heard in many of our core listening examples as an accompanying instrument for vocal music. Dallapiccola (1904–1975) uses two pianos in inventive ways in his *Canti di Prigonia.* Janika Vandervelde's (b. 1955) Genesis II also features the piano played in an unusual manner; towards the end of the piece, the pianist is instructed to percussively play blocks of notes by using his or her forearm to press down on several keys at once. (**Streaming audio tracks 66–67, 73.**)

The *celesta* is a specialty keyboard instrument that has a sound reminiscent of a toy piano. It looks like a small upright piano. The sound of the *celesta* is made by pressing a key that in turn hammers a metal plate suspended over a wooden resonator. Its distinct, bell-like sounds are familiar to many listeners from its use in the *Dance of the Sugarplum Fairy* from Pyotr Il'yich Tchaikovsky's (1840–1893) ballet *The Nutcracker.*

A key development in the evolution of modern instruments was the invention of the electronic music *synthesizer.* Its versatility lies in the ability to use many preset instrumental sounds, to program patterns of sounds, and even create new sounds that will be unique to a given composition or performance. A synthesizer may also be programmed for different scales, other than the standard chromatic scale built into pianos and organs.

See percussion instrument streaming video clips V49–V56.

SNARE (SIDE) DRUM (© *Chris Stock/Lebrecht Music & Arts*)

Percussion Instruments

The *percussion* section includes instruments from all around the world. Every percussion instrument contains something that is struck or hit, either by the player's hand or by sticks or mallets. Some percussion instruments produce a sound that is not perceived as having a specific pitch. Others can produce a wide range of pitches, and are thus capable of performing melodic as well as rhythmic music. Some are made of metal, some of wood, and some use sheets of animal hide, plastic, or other materials as the main resonating surface. Percussion players are versatile musicians because they must know how to play not just one but several instruments, often moving between them in the course of a performance.

BASS DRUM (© *Allan Munsie/Alamy*)

Indefinitely-Pitched Percussion Instruments

Percussion instruments with indefinite pitch are used to add rhythm, a variety of textures, and effects ranging from the explosive roar of artificial thunder to the knocking of a wood block. Most members of the drum family are classified as indefinitely-pitched

TOM TOM (© *discpicture/ShutterStock*)

CYMBALS (© Lelli & Masotti/Alinari/Lebrecht)

THE TRIANGLE (© Richard Haughton/Lebrecht Music & Arts)

THE GONG (© iStockphoto.com/SilviaJansen)

TIMPANI (© SuperStock/Alamy)

THE XYLOPHONE (© ImageDJ/Alamy)

percussion. They are joined by several metallic instruments that are also played by striking them.

Common types of percussion instruments in this category include:

- *Snare drum* (or *side drum*): A drum with two heads, or resonating surfaces. The top head is played with two drumsticks or brushes. The bottom surface is fitted with taut metal snares (wires) that vibrate and rattle slightly to add to the complexity of the sound.

- *Bass drum*: A large, two-sided drum with a deep, bellowing sound. This is also the kind of drum that players in a marching band wear across their stomachs.

- *Tom-toms*: Two-sided drums that are not fitted with snares, available in many sizes and played with sticks, mallets and brushes.

- *Cymbals*: Two metal discs that are clapped together to make a variety of crashing sounds.

- *Triangle*: A metal rod bent into the shape of a triangle, which rings brightly when struck with a metal beater.

- *Gong* (or *tam-tam*): A large metal disc suspended from its rim and struck with a heavy wool- or felt-padded mallet.

Pitched Percussion Instruments

There are several varieties of percussion instruments that play a definite pitch, each with its own role in a musical ensemble.

The *timpani*, or *kettledrums*, are a kind of drum that can play identifiable pitches. There are always at least two timpani, and often three, four, or more, each tuned to a definite pitch. Timpani are tuned by pedals and played with soft or hard mallets. Timpani parts can be quite challenging, because the players are frequently required to retune their instruments while the rest of the orchestra is playing.

Some tuned percussion instruments are designed to play melodies and chords. The most familiar are the *xylophone* and the *marimba*. Antecedents of these mallet instruments are known from Asia, Africa, and South America. The xylophone and marimba each use tuned wooden bars arranged roughly in the format of the black and white keys on a piano. The marimba, in addition to having tuned wooden bars, includes hollow metal tubes suspended beneath the bars to amplify the tone. Both instruments may be played with up to four mallets, two in each hand.

The *vibraphone* uses tuned aluminum bars and is built in the same configuration as the xylophone and marimba. The instrument has pedals for adding vibrato to the tone or sustaining its notes, features that are enhanced by motors and electronic amplification, adding remarkable nuances to the tonalities of the instrument.

CORE LISTENING: The vibraphone, or "vibes," is a popular instrument in jazz ensembles. Our selection from Count Basie's *Lester Leaps In* features an extended vibraphone solo. (**Streaming audio track 72.**)

The *glockenspiel* might be likened to a laptop version of the xylophone. It has two rows of metal tone bars. Its bell-like sounds are produced by striking it with hard mallets.

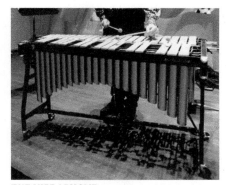

THE VIBRAPHONE (© Wladimir Polak/Lebrecht)

CORE LISTENING: The xylophone and marimba have prominent roles in *Canti di Prigonia* by Luigi Dallapiccola. A variety of other indefinitely-pitched and pitched percussive instruments—including bells, tam-tams, triangle, snare drum, bass drum, and timpani—can be heard used in creative ways throughout the piece. (**Streaming audio tracks 66–67.**)

Chimes consists of a set of tuned, metal tubes suspended in a frame and played with mallets. They produce a strikingly bell-like tone and are often used to create the effect of church bells.

Indonesia is known for its small chamber ensemble of the type collectively known as *gamelan*. The gamelan ensemble uses a variety of instruments such as tuned gongs, drums, flutes, and single- and multi-octave *metallophones* (metal-keyed vibraphones). The latter are mallet-struck instruments tuned to specific pitches, in principle like the vibraphone, but using non-Western scales. Metallophones are often paired with one instrument being tuned slightly higher than the other to produce the distinctive reverberating sound of this music.

THE GLOCKENSPIEL (© Chris Stock/Lebrecht Music & Arts)

CORE LISTENING: *Sukawati*, performed by a *gender wayang* ensemble, is a classic example of a gamelan performance. Listen to how the various percussive instruments blend to form an overall sonic atmosphere. (**Streaming audio track 76.**)

The Orchestra

Just as musical instruments developed over time, the modern orchestra grew out of many earlier experiments in forming larger musical ensembles. In Bach's time, for example, a group would be formed based on whatever musicians were available, either through employment by a member of the aristocracy or by the church. In the 18th century, as newer instruments became available—such as the clarinet in Mozart's time—composers began experimenting with adding them to their larger works. The modern orchestra grew out of the 19th-century interest in composing symphonic works to be performed by increasingly large ensembles. Beethoven's Ninth Symphony, featuring a large orchestra and choir, became a model for many that followed, with composers like Mahler famous for composing for ensembles larger than army brigades!

CHIMES (© Lelli & Masotti/Alinari/Lebrecht)

GAMELAN ENSEMBLE (© Odile Noel/Lebrecht Music & Arts)

Figure 1.4 illustrates the standard layout of the modern orchestra and its instrumental groupings. The placement of instrumental groups is functional in that it arranges the quieter instruments in the front and the loudest instruments on the perimeter. The arrangement also emphasizes the instruments of priority in Western music, notably with the string section front and center. The first violin player is called the *concertmaster*, and usually receives a separate round of applause before the concert begins.

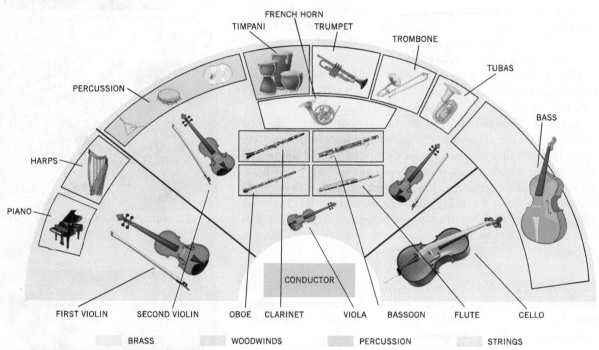

FIGURE 1.4 **Arrangement of the Orchestra**.

Giovanni Pierluigi da Palestrina (ca. 1525–1594)

Medieval, Renaissance, and Baroque Music

TAKE NOTE

History is a silent but supportive partner in the *active listening* process. Compositions from the Medieval, Renaissance, and Baroque periods lay the background for what has come to be the standard repertory of classical music.

Although the performance of music always takes place in the present, music also represents the time in which it was created. This makes history another enormously important topic in the understanding of music. Knowing the factors that influence the creation of music—whether cultural, economic, technological, religious, or political—provides another dimension to one's exploration of music. History is a silent but supportive partner in the active listening process.

33

Chapter Objectives

- Distinguish the major styles and periods of classical music.

- Examine works from the Medieval and Renaissance periods and learn about their position in history.

- Examine two pieces of music from the Baroque period and understand what they have in common.

With this chapter and the next two, we continue our exploration of active listening skills while investigating the history of Western classical music. In the introduction, we discussed the fundamental elements of music that connect all types of musical expression. In these chapters, we will see how the life and times of composers can affect the ways in which they implement these same musical elements.

The Periods of Music History

The styles associated with any period of Western classical music are defined by the ways in which composers worked with the common musical elements introduced in the previous chapter. The composer's choices are affected by many factors, including the purpose of the music and the nature of the audience for which it was written. The way we hear a musical work can also be shaped by such extramusical factors as the reputation of the composer, the social and political arena in which we hear the music performed, and the state of the art in instrument and/or recording technology.

Western classical music is usually divided into six major historical periods (see Table 2.1). In this chapter and the next two, we will explore what gives each period its distinctive style—and often a distinctive kind of performance as well.

TABLE 2.1 Stylistic Periods of Western Classical Music

Medieval: before 1400
Renaissance: 1400–1600
Baroque: 1600–1750
Classical: 1750–1825
Romantic: 1825–1900
Modern: 1900 to the present

Establishing the Periods of Classical Music

The idea of a classical repertory—music that continues to be heard from one generation to the next—began to take shape by the late 18th century. Prior to that, few composers expected their music to be listened to for long after their deaths. It might surprise you that Johann Sebastian Bach, one of the most prolific composers of his time, would have never considered himself to be a composer of classical music.

This attitude toward music began to change after the year 1800, when a permanent repertory started to take shape, with the music of Haydn, Mozart, and—especially—Beethoven at its center. The period in which these composers lived and worked—roughly 1750 to 1825—is now known as the Classical period, with a capital "C." The term **classical music** with a small "c," on the other hand, can be applied to a wide variety of styles ranging from the Middle Ages to the present. The narrower terms now in common use, including Medieval, Renaissance, Baroque, Classical, Romantic, and Modern music, were mostly imposed after the fact. Furthermore, these periods may not always correspond to the periods used in other kinds of history that have similar names. Historians of art and music speak of the Renaissance,

Baroque, and Romantic periods—but they might not agree on when these begin and end. In fact, history rarely offers tidy beginnings and endings. Further complicating the categorization of classical music is the fact that each period encompasses broad stylistic endeavors in many *different* types of music. Baroque music, for example, includes operas, church music, sonatas for ensembles and solo instruments, concertos, organ music, and much more. Even each of these *genres* includes music in different styles. Some scholars would not consider all of the music of Vivaldi or Handel to be "Baroque." There are different styles of jazz, too. Count Basie, whose music we will examine in detail in Chapter 4, is known for the style called *swing*, but you may have heard of Dixieland, bebop, free jazz, and more.

Why, then, do we use these labels at all? We talk about musical styles because they are meaningful to listeners and because knowing the history behind the music makes us more active listeners. Nor are the labels arbitrary; each historical period of classical music embodies meaningful stylistic features of its own.

Chapters 2, 3, and 4 focus on these standard stylistic periods. Each period exhibits a wide variety of musical approaches and genres, and we will not attempt to cover them in their entirety. Instead, representative examples from each period will be examined so that you can begin to develop your active listening skills by hearing this music in historical context. Proceeding chronologically, we will first look at the music of the Medieval, Renaissance, and Baroque periods. In the next chapter we will explore the music of the Classical and Romantic periods, and in Chapter 4 we will examine the diverse music of the 20th century, including a close look at a jazz work.

Medieval Music

There is no single musical style associated with the vast historical period we call the Middle Ages. When we speak of Medieval music, we are describing an array of styles and practices that unfolded over hundreds of years of constant historical change.

The most important collection of written music for most of the Middle Ages is the repertory of church music commonly known as **Gregorian chant**. This music is sung in Latin, without accompaniment or harmonization, and sets the texts used in nearly all services of the Catholic Church. The use of chant was not limited to the Middle Ages; it continued to be used regularly until quite recently, and there are still echoes of chant in some of today's services, both Catholic and Protestant. Chant was also not a coherent body of music in a single style or by a single composer. *Dies irae*, our primary example of chant, is a late composition; its music is anonymous, but its text is attributed to Thomas of Celano, who died around 1250. Most chant originated much earlier, and its authors are unknown. Since it lacks accompaniment, chant is one of the purest examples of melody to be found in Western music, which is why *Dies irae* will be discussed further in Chapter 8, where we will examine its text as well.

To modern ears, the most striking feature of this music is the fact that it is **monophonic**: it consists of a single melody with no accompaniment. Try to remember the last time you heard somebody sing without an accompaniment in public. With the exception of the national anthem at sporting events, an *American Idol* audition, and the occasional rendition of *Amazing Grace*, it simply is not expected these days. Hearing a group of people singing the same melody with no harmony might seem even more unusual today than hearing an instrumental soloist playing

Classical Music: A general category for music that continues to be heard from one generation to the next, commonly broken down into chronological periods known as Medieval, Renaissance, Baroque, Classical, Romantic, and Modern.

Gregorian Chant: A body of monophonic church music standardized in the early Middle Ages. It was long attributed to Pope Gregory I (r. 590–604), but it was likely neither written nor standardized by him, nor even by Pope Gregory II (r. 715–731).

Monophonic: Consisting of a single melodic line with no accompaniment.

36

TIMELINE 2.1   THE MIDDLE AGES (900–1400)

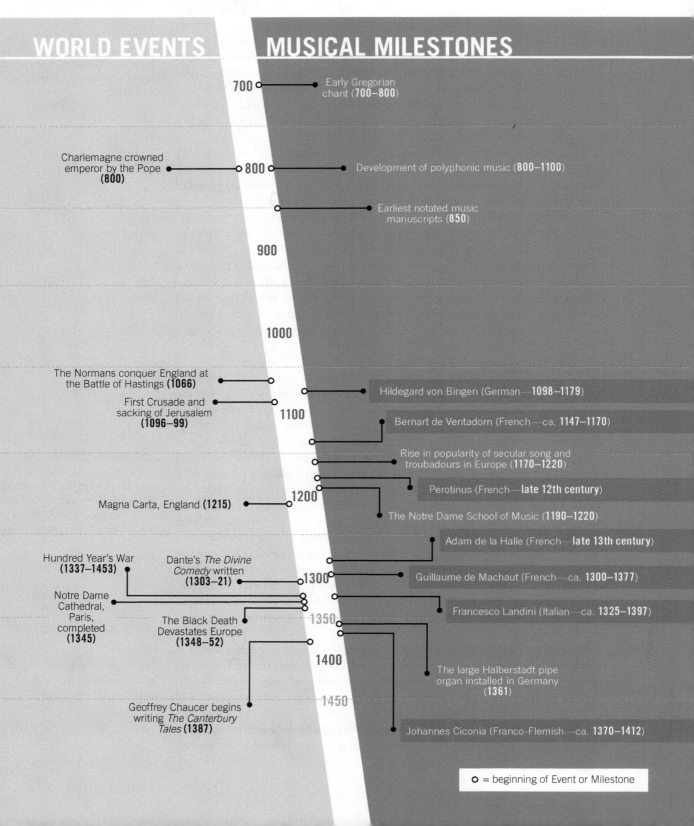

WORLD EVENTS

Charlemagne crowned emperor by the Pope **(800)**

The Normans conquer England at the Battle of Hastings **(1066)**

First Crusade and sacking of Jerusalem **(1096–99)**

Magna Carta, England **(1215)**

Hundred Year's War **(1337–1453)**

Dante's *The Divine Comedy* written **(1303–21)**

Notre Dame Cathedral, Paris, completed **(1345)**

The Black Death Devastates Europe **(1348–52)**

Geoffrey Chaucer begins writing *The Canterbury Tales* **(1387)**

MUSICAL MILESTONES

Early Gregorian chant **(700–800)**

Development of polyphonic music **(800–1100)**

Earliest notated music manuscripts **(850)**

Hildegard von Bingen (German—**1098–1179**)

Bernart de Ventadorn (French—ca. **1147–1170**)

Rise in popularity of secular song and troubadours in Europe **(1170–1220)**

Perotinus (French—**late 12th century**)

The Notre Dame School of Music **(1190–1220)**

Adam de la Halle (French—**late 13th century**)

Guillaume de Machaut (French—ca. **1300–1377**)

Francesco Landini (Italian—ca. **1325–1397**)

The large Halberstadt pipe organ installed in Germany **(1361)**

Johannes Ciconia (Franco-Flemish—ca. **1370–1412**)

700 · 800 · 900 · 1000 · 1100 · 1200 · 1300 · 1350 · 1400 · 1450

o = beginning of Event or Milestone

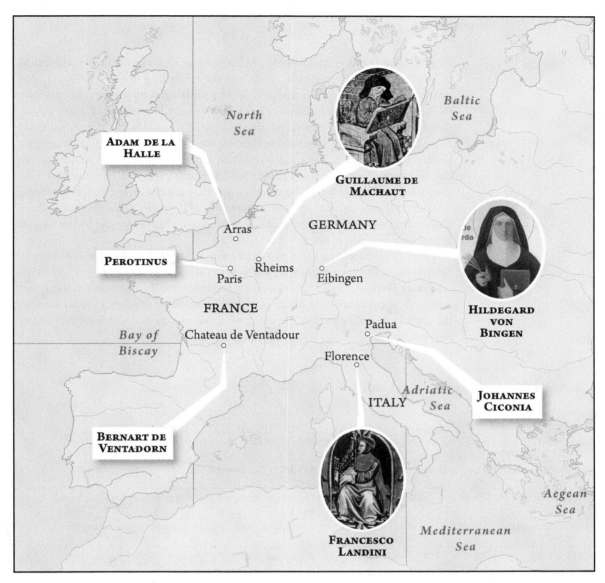

MAP 2.1 **Composers of the Middle Ages.**

that way. However, this is exactly what many medieval listeners were accustomed to hearing. *Dies irae*, with its distinctive, haunting melody, is one of the most familiar monophonic pieces ever written. It has been quoted repeatedly by later composers, including Luigi Dallapiccola (1904–1975) in *Canti di prigionia* (see Chapters 6 and 10) and George Crumb in *Black Angels* (see Chapters 4, 6, and 9).

If you are tempted to think that Medieval music is simple and straightforward, listen next to *Lasse! comment oublieray/Se j'aim mon loyal/Pour quoy me bat mes maris?*, a **motet** (a vocal genre that originated in elaborations on early Christian chant) by the 14th-century composer Guillaume de Machaut (ca. 1300–1377). Unlike *Dies irae*, this piece is **polyphonic**: It features more than one note sounding at a time. If you listen carefully, you will hear that there are three voices singing throughout the piece, each with its own melodic line. A major part of Machaut's artistry lies in making these three melodies blend together while you can still quite clearly hear each separate part.

Motet: One of the most significant genres of the Middle Ages and Renaissance.

Polyphonic: Consisting of multiple parts or voices, allowing more than one note to sound at a time.

37

But there is more. Machaut wrote his texts as well as music. We will examine the words he wrote for this piece and their meaning in Chapter 10, but for now you can practice your active listening skills by simply listening carefully to the words being sung. Although the lyrics are in late medieval French, you should be able to hear one distinctive quality of this piece, the composer's use of multiple texts sung at the same time. Most later vocal music with a text, no matter how complex, has only one set of words. Machaut has written three *different* texts, just as he has written three different melodies. You will not hear the same words sung by all the voices, since they are all singing different things. This contributes to making *Lasse! comment oublieray/Se j'aim mon loyal/Pour quoy me bat mes maris?* sound more dense and complex than most later music in which only one text is sung.

Dies irae is a sacred piece written to be sung in church. *Lasse! comment oublieray/Se j'aim mon loyal/Pour quoy me bat mes maris?* is a secular (i.e., worldly, non-religious) piece written to be enjoyed by connoisseurs. Taken together, these two selections show something of the range and diversity of Medieval music. Both of them are quite unlike most of the music we listen to today—though for very different reasons.

TABLE 2.2 **Major Composers of Medieval Music**

Hildegard von Bingen (German—1098–1179): Prolific composer and religious figure whose music was said to be inspired by her visions; one of the few female composers of the era
Bernart de Ventadorn (French—ca. 1147–1170): A representative of the *troubadours*, the poet-composers who flourished in southern France in the 12th and 13th centuries
Perotinus (French—late 12th century): A central figure in the Notre-Dame School, which played a crucial role in the early development of polyphonic music
Adam de la Halle (French—late 13th century): The most famous of the *trouvères*, the northern French poet-composers who succeeded the *troubadours*
Guillaume de Machaut (French—ca. 1300–1377): Recognized as both the most important French poet and the most important composer of the 14th century
Francesco Landini (Italian—ca. 1325–1397): The most celebrated composer of the Italian *trecento*, or 1300s, when the Renaissance was beginning to take hold there
Johannes Ciconia (Franco-Flemish—ca. 1370–1412): An early representative of the widely traveled northern European composers who helped to create an international style over the next two centuries

---

Renaissance Music

The music of the Renaissance is also diverse, and it is hard to explain exactly what connects it with the art and literature of the same period. There is a reason for this. "Renaissance" means "rebirth," and the period that followed the Middle Ages saw a rebirth of the visual and literary art of ancient Greece and Rome. But although the art, literature, and architecture of ancient Greece and Rome were well understood, little was known about the music of the ancient world. Ancient writers had a great deal to say about the *effects* of music, but they made only tentative attempts to write music down, and very few examples have survived. Thus, Renaissance musicians seeking to revive ancient music had very little to go on.

Nevertheless, musicians in the 15th and 16th centuries changed the language of music in fundamental ways, making it meaningful to say that this period saw the birth of a new style, if not exactly the rebirth of an old one. Perhaps the most famous composer of this period was Josquin des Prez, commonly known as Josquin (ca. 1450–1521). Josquin's music was admired by his contemporaries, who saw in him the musical counterpart to the great Renaissance painters, sculptors, and architects. Modern historians agree, and with the revival of **early music** that took place during the 20th century, his music has once again become widely available to listeners in live performances and recordings.

Compared to the music of the Middle Ages, Josquin's music can sound quite modern, or at least closer to what we are now accustomed to hearing. Like the Machaut motet we just listened to, Josquin's *Missa "L'homme armé" super voces musicales* is polyphonic. Unlike the Machaut piece, this one has only one text, which is that of the **Ordinary** of the Latin Mass (those sections of the Mass that can be sung on any **liturgical** occasion).

Listen to the Kyrie section of Josquin's setting. The text (which, unlike the other sections of the Mass, is in Greek) is quite simple.

Kyrie eleison.	Lord have mercy.
Christe eleison.	Christ have mercy.
Kyrie eleison.	Lord have mercy.

When the Mass is sung in Gregorian chant—which was still the most frequently performed music in the Catholic Church throughout the Renaissance and beyond—each of the three pleas for mercy is sung three times. Josquin's music is divided into three larger sections: an initial setting of *Kyrie eleison*, a setting of *Christe eleison*, and another of *Kyrie eleison*. Each phrase of the text is sung many more than three times, as the four vocal parts repeatedly overlap with one another. In this sense, Josquin's setting of his text resembles that of later composers like Bach and Monteverdi, whom we will examine later in this chapter.

Josquin's music also resembles that of later composers in the way the different parts fit together. If you listen carefully, you will hear that the parts share more than the text; they also share some of the same music. It is possible to imagine the three voice parts of Machaut's *Lasse! comment oublieray/Se j'aim mon loyal/Pour quoy me bat mes maris?* being conceived one at a time and then added together; this is probably how Machaut actually did compose them. The parts in Josquin's music, though, seem to have been written together as a single piece. Listen carefully to both the Machaut and the Josquin until you can hear the difference in the way the parts fit together.

At the same time, Josquin's music, like much music from the Renaissance, communicates meaning in ways that are unfamiliar to modern listeners. The entire Mass is based on a **cantus firmus**, a pre-existing melody that is used by Josquin as a kind of scaffolding around which each section of the music is constructed. This melody would have been familiar to Josquin's contemporaries and thus would have given the piece meaning to them that modern audiences can't share. Josquin teases his listeners by covering up this familiar melody with the other polyphonic voices. He also moves it to successively higher pitches as the music progresses from one section to the next. The tactic of using upwardly moving melodic notes has been interpreted as a musical metaphor symbolizing the rising of the soul toward heaven.

Early Music: A term widely used for music from the 17th century or earlier. Its meaning has shifted over the years, and it refers as much to a style of performance as to a style of music. Even music from the 19th century can be "early music" when played on original instruments by performers who pay close attention to historical performance practice.

Ordinary: The parts of the Mass that are the same for every service and do not change week to week.

Liturgical: Written for a specific function in a church service.

Cantus Firmus: A tune, or melody, from Gregorian chant or another composition used as the structural basis for a new composition. This was a very important practice in the Middle Ages and Renaissance.

TIMELINE 2.2 **THE RENAISSANCE (1400–1600)**

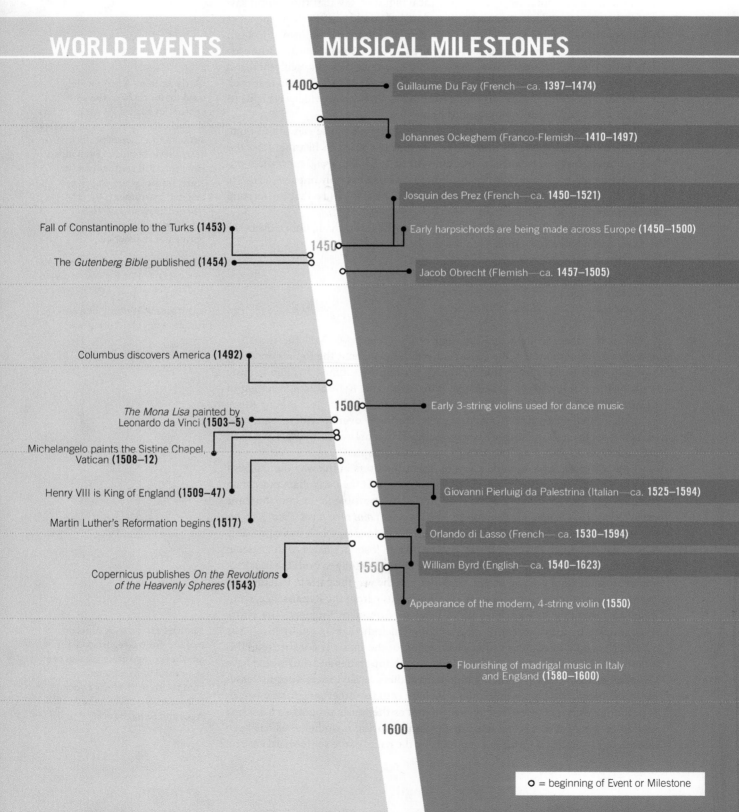

WORLD EVENTS

MUSICAL MILESTONES

1400 — Guillaume Du Fay (French—ca. **1397–1474**)

Johannes Ockeghem (Franco-Flemish—**1410–1497**)

Josquin des Prez (French—ca. **1450–1521**)

Fall of Constantinople to the Turks **(1453)** — Early harpsichords are being made across Europe **(1450–1500)**

The *Gutenberg Bible* published **(1454)** — 1450

Jacob Obrecht (Flemish—ca. **1457–1505**)

Columbus discovers America **(1492)**

1500 — Early 3-string violins used for dance music

The Mona Lisa painted by
Leonardo da Vinci **(1503–5)**

Michelangelo paints the Sistine Chapel,
Vatican **(1508–12)**

Giovanni Pierluigi da Palestrina (Italian—ca. **1525–1594**)

Henry VIII is King of England **(1509–47)**

Martin Luther's Reformation begins **(1517)** — Orlando di Lasso (French— ca. **1530–1594**)

1550 — William Byrd (English—ca. **1540–1623**)

Copernicus publishes *On the Revolutions
of the Heavenly Spheres* **(1543)**

Appearance of the modern, 4-string violin **(1550)**

Flourishing of madrigal music in Italy
and England **(1580–1600)**

1600

○ = beginning of Event or Milestone

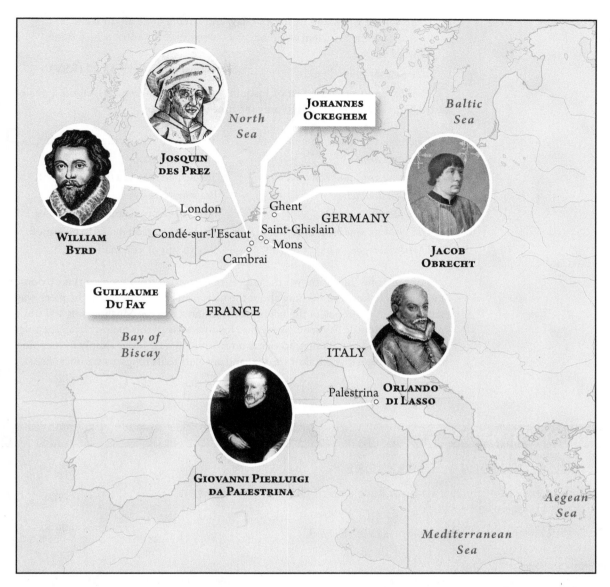

MAP 2.2 **Composers of the Renaissance.**

The song, as Josquin's contemporaries were well aware, is about an armed man, and extols his ability to strike fear into the hearts of one and all. That such a song should have been used as the basis for a Mass—the highest liturgical ceremony of the Roman Catholic Church—may seem incomprehensible to modern listeners. The key to this seeming contradiction lies in a familiar text from the New Testament:

> Put on the whole armor of God, that you may be able to stand against the wiles of the devil. For we are not contending against flesh and blood, but against the principalities, against the powers, against the world rulers of this present darkness, against the spiritual hosts of wickedness in the heavenly places. Therefore take the whole armor of God, that you may

be able to withstand in the evil day, and having done all, to stand. . . .
And take the helmet of salvation, and the sword of the Spirit, which is the
word of God.

Ephesians 6:11–13, 17 (RSV)

Compare this with the text of Josquin's cantus firmus (which is never actually
heard in his setting of the Mass; only the tune is used):

L'homme, l'homme, l'homme armé,	The man, the man, the armed man,
L'homme armé	The armed man,
L'homme armé doibt on doubter,	The armed man is a fearsome sight,
Doibt on doubter.	Is a fearsome sight.
On a fait partout crier	It has been proclaimed everywhere
Que chascun se viengne armer	That each person needs to be armed
D'un haubregon de fer.	With a suit of iron mail.

For someone "in the know," the reference to the text from Ephesians is obvious.
It also helps to know something about the historical context in which the piece was
written, when the shock of the fall of Constantinople to the Muslims was still fresh
on European minds. Suffice it to say that Josquin's use of this melody has very deep
significance, and that its significance is impossible to hear today simply by listening
to the piece, even if you follow the text and are alert to its religious significance.

LEARNING TO LISTEN GUIDE

TAKE NOTE OF MELODY AND TEXTURE

What to Listen For: See if you can hear sections of the *L'homme armé*
tune within this complex music.

Streaming audio track 4.
Interactive Listening Guide ILG-2.

Josquin: *Missa "L'homme armé" super voces musicales,* Kyrie
Date: ca. 1480s
Instrumentation: Four-part choir
Key: There is no key in the modern sense, as the concept of key had not yet developed when this music was written.
Meter: Triple meter (Kyrie eleison I), Duple meter (Christe eleison), Triple meter (Kyrie eleison II)
Core Repertory Connection: Josquin's *Missa "L'homme armé" super voces musicales* will be discussed again in
Chapters 9 and 12.

TIME	SECTION	ORIGINAL TEXT	TRANSLATION	COMMENT
0:00	Kyrie eleison I	Kyrie eleison	Lord have mercy	The tune is most audible at the beginning.
1:22	Christe eleison	Christe eleison	Christ have mercy	This section is based on the middle part of the tune, beginning with "On a fait partout crier."
3:36	Kyrie eleison II	Kyrie eleison	Lord have mercy	The first part of the tune returns, but Josquin disguises it even more thoroughly than before.

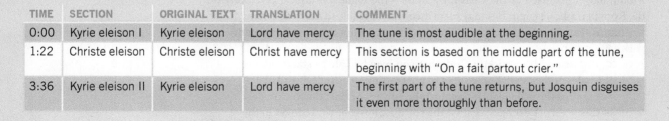

Josquin's music represents a culmination of centuries of development, while at the same time it set patterns that were followed by many later composers. He thus stands at a pivotal point in the entire musical Renaissance.

The most famous composer of the later Renaissance is Giovanni Pierluigi da Palestrina (ca. 1525–1594). Unlike that of Josquin, Palestrina's music did not have to be rediscovered in our own time; it has served as a direct model for composers in most later periods who wanted to learn to write in the musical style of the Renaissance. Later generations have also tended to idealize Palestrina's role in history; it was long believed, for example, that Palestrina had saved polyphonic music from being banned completely from the Catholic Church in the late 16th century.

Listen now to Palestrina's motet *Sicut cervus*. Like the previous examples, this piece is sung a cappella—in this case, by a mixed choir of men and women. The absence of instruments in these examples should not be taken to mean that instruments were not common in these periods. We know from written descriptions,

A Cappella: A performance style in which a singer or, usually, a choir sings without instrumental accompaniment.

Focus On

Giovanni Pierluigi da Palestrina (ca. 1525–1594)

Italian composer. He ranks with Lassus and Byrd as one of the towering figures in the music of the late 16th century. He was primarily a prolific composer of Masses and motets but was also an important madrigalist. Among the native Italian musicians of the 16th century who sought to assimilate the richly developed polyphonic techniques of their French and Flemish predecessors, none mastered these techniques more completely or subordinated them more effectively to the requirements of musical cogency.

Giovanni Pierluigi da Palestrina (ca. 1525–1594). In the spirit of the Counter-Reformation, Palestrina composed so that the words could be understood. (© *Pictorial Press Ltd/Alamy*)

His success in reconciling the functional and aesthetic aims of Catholic church music in the post-Tridentine period earned him an enduring reputation as the ideal Catholic composer, as well as giving his style (or, more precisely, later generations' selective view of it) an iconic stature as a model of perfect achievement. (Lewis Lockwood, Noel O'Regan, and Jessie Ann Owens, *Grove Music Online*.)

Palestrina lived in Rome his entire life. There he worked in a number of positions closely associated with the Counter-Reformation, the Roman Catholic Church's response to the rise of Protestantism in the 16th century. His music served as a model for later generations of composers, who imitated his pure but complex style and his careful text-setting. Performances of his music today tend to make it sound austere and spiritual. That effect is heightened by performance for voices alone, a style known as a cappella.

pictures, and surviving examples that many instruments were widely used. We don't know as much about their use, though, as we do for instruments from later periods, because instrumental music was much less likely to be written down—which is the only way that music from this time could survive to the present day.

LEARNING TO LISTEN GUIDE

TAKE NOTE OF TIMBRE AND TEXTURE

What to Listen For: The lack of strong contrasts; the simple choral sound that makes the words highly audible; the lack of a clear expressive link between the words and the music.

Streaming audio track 6.

Palestrina: *Sicut cervus*
Date: 1584
Motet for four-part a cappella choir
Meter: Duple meter

TIME	ORIGINAL TEXT	TRANSLATION	COMMENT
0:00	*Sicut cervus desiderat ad fontes aquarum;*	Just as the deer longs for water;	Although there is little overall contrast, note that each text phrase is set to different music. The semicolon marks the division between them.
1:33	*ita desiderat anima mea ad te Deus.*	so my soul longs for Thee oh God.	

TABLE 2.3 Major Composers of Renaissance Music

Guillaume Du Fay (French—ca. 1397–1474): The leading musician of the early 15th century, known for both sacred and secular works

Johannes Ockeghem (Franco-Flemish—1410–1497): An exemplar of the rich, complex style of the mid-Renaissance

Josquin des Prez (French—ca. 1450–1521): Perhaps the most famous Renaissance composer, widely respected both in his own time and in our own

Jacob Obrecht (Flemish—ca. 1457–1505): A contemporary of Josquin whose music also helped to establish the styles of the later Renaissance

Roland de Lassus, aka Orlando di Lasso (French—ca. 1530–1594): A versatile, international composer known for both sacred and secular works

Giovanni Pierluigi da Palestrina (Italian—ca. 1525–1594): regarded by many as the outstanding composer of church music in the late Renaissance

William Byrd (English—ca. 1540–1623): A Catholic composer in Protestant England who wrote for services for both faiths and much secular music as well

Baroque Music

When art historians speak of the Baroque period, they are usually referring to a movement that began with the Counter-Reformation of the late 16th century—the Roman Catholic Church's reaction to the Protestant Reformation—and extended through the absolute monarchy and religious wars of the 17th century. This was a turbulent period in European history, when political power became concentrated as never before. Wealthy monarchs commissioned highly decorated buildings such as the Palace of Versailles in France, built by the "Sun King" Louis XIV (1638–1715), to reflect their own power. The opulent decoration and careful design of these architectural monuments may seem to be reflected in the music of such late Baroque composers as Bach and Handel. However, the Baroque period also includes the highly personal, intimate paintings of Rembrandt and the sensual, dramatic sculptures of Bernini. These qualities are also reflected in the music of Baroque composers.

The Hall of Mirrors at Versailles, France. King Louis XIV's palace is one of the great monuments of Baroque architecture. (© *Jose Ignacio Soto/ShutterStock*)

The Baroque Audience

The powerful music of the Baroque period was first heard under very different circumstances than those in which we usually encounter it today. Concerts that were open to the general public were not common until the 18th century, when the period was coming to an end. Originally, most of Bach's vocal music would have been heard in church during actual religious services, and the congregation may even have sung along with parts of it. Operas—the signature form of the Baroque period—were first performed for aristocratic audiences, but by the late 17th century they were being written for the public, making opera a form of entertainment with broad popular appeal. Music for instrumental ensembles was often designated as *da chiesa*—for church—or *da camera*—for chambers, suggesting performance in religious settings or in private homes. Much solo instrumental music may have been intended primarily for the enjoyment of the player. In short, there were many different audiences and venues for music during the Baroque period, as befits a time of growing knowledge and cultural expansion.

Instruments of the Baroque Repertory

While many instruments heard in Baroque music are still familiar—the trumpet, violin, and organ, for example—others, like the harpsichord, the viola da gamba,

The Ecstasy of St. Teresa, by Gian Lorenzo Bernini (1598–1680). This kind of personal intensity was very new in religious art. Baroque artists of all kinds placed strong emphasis on the direct communication of emotion. (*Scala/Art Resource*, NY)

TIMELINE 2.3 **THE BAROQUE ERA (1600–1750)**

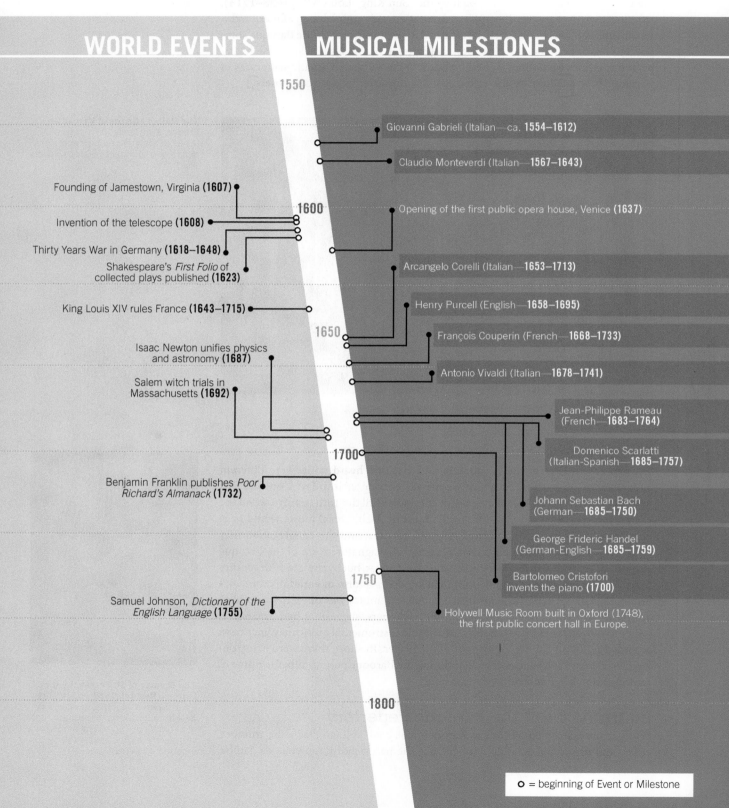

WORLD EVENTS

MUSICAL MILESTONES

1550

Giovanni Gabrieli (Italian—ca. **1554–1612**)

Claudio Monteverdi (Italian—**1567–1643**)

Founding of Jamestown, Virginia **(1607)**

1600

Opening of the first public opera house, Venice **(1637)**

Invention of the telescope **(1608)**

Thirty Years War in Germany **(1618–1648)**

Shakespeare's *First Folio* of collected plays published **(1623)**

Arcangelo Corelli (Italian—**1653–1713**)

Henry Purcell (English—**1658–1695**)

King Louis XIV rules France **(1643–1715)**

1650

François Couperin (French—**1668–1733**)

Isaac Newton unifies physics and astronomy **(1687)**

Antonio Vivaldi (Italian—**1678–1741**)

Salem witch trials in Massachusetts **(1692)**

Jean-Philippe Rameau (French—**1683–1764**)

1700

Domenico Scarlatti (Italian-Spanish—**1685–1757**)

Benjamin Franklin publishes *Poor Richard's Almanack* **(1732)**

Johann Sebastian Bach (German—**1685–1750**)

George Frideric Handel (German-English—**1685–1759**)

1750

Bartolomeo Cristofori invents the piano **(1700)**

Samuel Johnson, *Dictionary of the English Language* **(1755)**

Holywell Music Room built in Oxford (1748), the first public concert hall in Europe.

1800

○ = beginning of Event or Milestone

MAP 2.3 **Composers of the Baroque Era.**

and the wind instrument known descriptively as the serpent, are now heard only in performances and recordings by specialists, so you may not have heard of them, let alone heard them played. Even the more familiar instruments have changed dramatically; a baroque trumpet is both larger and more limited in range than a modern trumpet.

Instrumental ensembles have also changed significantly. Although Baroque composers wrote a great deal of large ensemble music, there was no standard orchestra: even the biggest ensembles were smaller than those of today, and might contain only string instruments or feature other unique combinations. On the other hand, the design of the organ advanced exponentially, as organ builders competed to build larger and more complex instruments with vast ranks of pipes and contrasting registers.

Baroque composers experimented with a wide variety of small ensembles, in which they often combined string and wind instruments in novel ways. Composers like Bach also pushed existing instruments to their limits; his sonatas and suites for unaccompanied violin and cello are rich, complex, and sonically stunning.

The Baroque Style

The term "baroque" originally meant "excessive," even "distorted." Therefore, it is easy to assume that all Baroque music and art is elaborate and highly ornamented. Much Baroque music, however, is not overly fussy, at least as written. The perception of excess stems, rather, from the realization that Baroque composers would go to great stylistic lengths to make an expressive point. The examples we will look at in this chapter are "baroque" in this sense.

Baroque forms often feature strong contrasts. For example, the music may shift from very soft to very loud to express a change in mood. Composers may also alternate different instruments, voices, or groups in a work. The concerto, one of the most popular Baroque genres, alternates a repeated section of music in which the entire ensemble plays—known as the **ritornello**—with sections in which a single instrument or small group plays. These formal contrasts are often emphasized by contrasts in timbre; different instrumental and/or vocal sonorities may be deliberately combined or heard in quick succession.

Baroque melodies are often long and elaborate, and may be highly *ornamented*—featuring quickly-played notes that decorate the basic melodic line—especially in slower tempos. In later Baroque music, extensive use of **counterpoint**—the simultaneous statement of different melodic lines—can make the music dense and challenging but uniquely rewarding as well. Baroque music usually has a regular beat, and the rhythmic patterns established at the beginning of a piece will often continue to its conclusion. These rhythms are frequently lively and dance-like, showing the influence of dances that contemporary listeners would have known well.

Texture is one of the most interesting features of Baroque music. Entire works are often built on the alternation of a fuller texture and a sparer, more limited one.

Baroque harmony can be rich and varied. It is frequently supported by the **basso continuo**, a technical feature that is considered a defining feature of Baroque style. (See box, Focus on the Basso Continuo.)

Monteverdi's *Io son pur vezzosetta*

In performance, the sound of the basso continuo is easy to recognize, and it is the simplest way to identify Baroque music. Listen to *Io son pur vezzosetta*, a *continuo madrigal* by the early Baroque composer Claudio Monteverdi (1567–1643).

Continuo madrigal is a term commonly used to describe compositions from the early 17th century that employ basso continuo with various combinations of voices and, sometimes, instruments. Monteverdi wrote this way beginning with his fifth book of madrigals, published in 1605. His continuo madrigals include several, like this one, written for two sopranos and basso continuo. However, they also include works for solo voice and for vocal ensembles, both with and without instruments.

Ritornello: A section of music to which the entire ensemble returns after sections played by a smaller ensemble.

Counterpoint: The art of combining melodies to produce a polyphonic texture.

Basso Continuo: A form of accompaniment that is often the most recognizable feature of music in Baroque style. It usually makes use of both a melodic bass instrument (e.g., cello or viola da gamba) to play the bass line and a harmonic instrument (e.g., harpsichord or organ) to play chords. Both are traditionally written on a single line of music, with numerical symbols used to indicate the chords. (Hence, this part is often called a *figured bass* line).

Focus On
The Basso Continuo

Continuo playing in varying ensembles was an art practiced by players of chordal instruments throughout Europe for roughly two centuries after about 1600. The instruments used included keyboard (organ, harpsichord), plucked string (chitarrone/theorbo, lute, guitar, harp) and bowed string (*lirone*, bass viol, violoncello). The continuo was fundamental to music in the 17th and 18th centuries.

A basso continuo is an instrumental bass line which runs throughout a piece, over which the player improvises ("realizes") a chordal accompaniment. (Peter Williams, David Ledbetter for *Grove Music Online*).

A cellist and a harpsichordist accompany a soprano in a piece in Baroque style. The cello and harpsichord together constitute the continuo part. *(Photo by Hiroyuki Ito/Getty Images)*

The basso continuo is a form of accompaniment that began to be used around the turn of the 17th century—forms of it may well have been used earlier—and remained in use almost until the end of the 18th.

The continuo is usually performed by a melodic bass instrument—most often a cello, an older, similar instrument known as a bass viol or viola da gamba, or a bassoon—and a harmonic instrument, often a harpsichord,

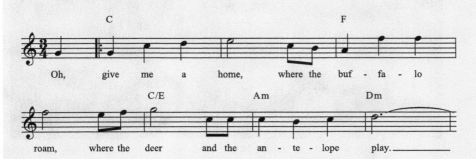

FIGURE 2.1 **Modern chord symbols in the classic folk song, "Home on the Range."**

FIGURE 2.2 **A Baroque piece by Corelli with basso continuo accompaniment.**

(continued)

Focus On (continued)

although it can also be an organ, a lute, a harp, or a guitar. The harmonic instrumentalist plays chords based on numbers written in the score underneath the part for the bass instrument. This type of notation is similar to the chord symbols that are often printed above the melodies of today's popular songs. The continuo part is thus a kind of musical shorthand, from which an accompaniment can be created. The exact nature of that accompaniment is up to the performer, within limits set by the conventions of the style.

A madrigal as sung in the late Renaissance. Madrigal singing was a popular pastime at home and at social gatherings. The natural setting presents an idealized view, since madrigal texts often contain images from nature. *(Erich Lessing/Art Resource, NY)*

While it is not a madrigal in the sense in which many now understand the term— a work for a small a cappella vocal ensemble—*Io son pur vezzosetta* does demonstrate something that later Baroque composers found attractive; it is written in *trio* texture, with two vocal parts supported by a basso continuo. Although the continuo is often performed by two or more instruments, it is technically one part: hence the "trio" designation. Later Baroque composers frequently wrote *trio sonatas*, in which two melodic instruments were accompanied by the continuo. They liked this way of writing because it was not as dense as traditional ensembles with four or more parts, but it still allowed the two upper parts to interact extensively with each other and with the bass.

Another way to describe this piece would be as *vocal chamber music.* The term *chamber music* now typically refers to music written for small instrumental ensembles, but during the Baroque it also encompassed vocal music intended for performance in smaller, more private venues.

Focus On

Claudio Monteverdi (1567–1643)

Claudio Monteverdi (1567–1643). Monteverdi bridged the Renaissance and Baroque and contributed to the development of opera. *(Hulton Fine Art Collection, Getty Images)*

Italian composer. The most important composer in late 16th- and early 17th-century Italy, he excelled in nearly all the major genres of the period. His nine books of madrigals consolidated the achievement of the late Renaissance masters and cultivated new aesthetic and stylistic paradigms for the musical Baroque. In his operas for Mantua and Venice he took the experiments of the Florentines and developed powerful ways of expressing and structuring musical drama. His three major collections of liturgical and devotional music transcend the merely functional, exploiting a rich panoply of text-expressive and contrapuntal-structural techniques. Although he composed little or no independent instrumental music, his writing for instruments was genuinely innovative. (Tim Carter and Geoffrey Chew, *Grove Music Online*.)

Music historian Leo Schrade called Claudio Monteverdi the "creator of modern music," because his music, poised between the Renaissance and the mature Baroque of Bach and Handel, helped to usher in many of the qualities that we take for granted in the music of today. Indeed, Monteverdi was one of the most versatile and significant composers of all time. Works like the *Vespers* of 1610 and his three surviving operas, *L'Orfeo*, *Il ritorno d'Ulisse in patria*, and *L'incoronazione di Poppea* (among the earliest examples of this genre), are just as powerful and moving today as they were 400 years ago. Continuo madrigals like the one heard here helped to expand the expressive range of music in novel directions. This was truly music on the cutting edge of history.

Like all composers, however, Monteverdi reflects the ideas and interests of his time. Florentine scholars of the late 16th century had done extensive research into the theories behind Greek drama and the rhetoric of speech. Their conclusion that the tragedies of Sophocles and Aeschylus had originally been sung throughout provided a theoretical foundation for opera. Their interest in rhetoric—the effective use of speech to influence listeners—helps to explain the extremes to which Monteverdi goes to call attention to the details of his texts. Thus, a work like *Io son pur vezzosetta* would have struck its first audiences as both modern and historically savvy at the same time.

Monteverdi's text is a sonnet, a traditional poetic form. Sonnets always have 14 lines; in this case, each line consists of 11 syllables. Note that some of the syllables have to be run together for the metrical scheme to work. This is not as unnatural as it sounds; it often corresponds to the patterns of spoken language. For example, you and I may say "can't" instead of "cannot," or "gonna" instead of "going to." Similarly, an Italian speaker would pronounce the second line of the poem "*kay lay gwahn-chyo dee roe-zay jell-so-mean-y.*" The "*ce*" of "*guance*" and "*ho*" are joined together, as are the second syllable of "*rose*" and "*e*," rather than being pronounced separately.

Although the text is written as a monologue that is not how Monteverdi presents it. As you listen to the music, you will realize that the interaction between the voices is what makes this piece so interesting. "*Son pur vezzosetta*" ("I am most beautiful"), for example, is heard no fewer than 11 times. First each singer states it in succession.

LEARNING TO LISTEN GUIDE

TAKE NOTE OF TEXTURE AND MUSIC WITH TEXT

What to Listen For: Follow the text carefully and observe how Monteverdi mirrors it in the musical setting.

Monteverdi: *Io son pur vezzosetta*, from Madrigals, Book 7

Streaming audio track 7.

Date: 1619
Instrumentation: Two sopranos and basso continuo
Key: G major
Meter: $\frac{4}{4}$

TIME	SECTION	ORIGINAL TEXT	TRANSLATION	COMMENT
0:00	1st two lines of text	*Io son pur vezzosetta pastorella / che le guance ho di rose e gelsomini*	I am a most beautiful shepherdess / with cheeks of roses and of jasmine,	Listen to the competing voices on "*sun pur vezzosetta*." Each singer is claiming to be more beautiful than the other.
0:29	2nd two lines of text	*e questa fronte e questi aurati crini / mi fann'altrui parer Driada novella.*	and this forehead and these golden curls / make me appear to others to be a new Dryad.	Notice how the progress of the music slows as the speaker(s) begins to admire her/their own features.
1:01	Beginning of the second quatrain (four-line stanza)	*Di Flora non vi è qui nobil donzella / o schiera di pomposi citadini / che quand'in lor m'incontro faccio inchini / il titol non mi dian de la più bella.*	There is none among Flora's noble ladies / and no group of proud townspeople / who, when I meet them and bow to them, / do not name me the most beautiful.	The movement picks up again as the speaker(s) imagine the admiration of the townspeople.
1:31	Beginning of the first terzet (three-line stanza)	*E s'el giorno di festa io vado al ballo, / mi porta ogni Pastor perch'io l'inviti / specchi, fior, frutti o vezzi di corallo*	If, on a holiday, I go to the dance, / every shepherd, in order to make me dance with him, brings me / mirrors, flowers, fruit, and ornaments of coral.	The animated pace continues.
2:08	Volta	*e non saranno a te punto graditi, / caro Lidio, i miei sguardi e sempr'in fallo / ti pregherò, crudel, che tu m'aiuti.*	But to you, dear Lidio, my glances / will not be at all pleasing, and, always deprived, / I will beg you, cruel one, to help me.	The final terzet is marked by a complete change in the tone of the text. This is mirrored in the slow pace and languishing sound of the music.

They then present it several times in quick alternation, making it sound as if each singer is trying to "one-up" the other. Finally, they proclaim the entire first two lines of text simultaneously. The effect is to transform a simple poetic monologue into a passionate declaration. Monteverdi uses an ornate and seemingly overly complicated form to express a simple text in a highly original way, making this music typically Baroque.

In one sense, however, this poem does have two voices. The last three lines constitute a *volta*, or turn-around, in which the mood of the text suddenly changes to something close to its exact opposite. In Monteverdi's text, the turn is from joyful emotions to unhappy ones: the shepherdess admits that, despite all her boasting, the one she truly loves does not care for her, and the poem concludes with a pathetic entreaty. Monteverdi reflects this sudden change of mood in his music.

Across the Arts
Sonnet XXX by William Shakespeare

The convention of a sudden change in mood can also be found in Shakespeare's sonnets. In the example cited here, the change of mood goes in the opposite direction from the Monteverdi text: from serious to happy.

Sonnet XXX by William Shakespeare

First quatrain:
When to the sessions of sweet silent thought
I summon up remembrance of things past,
I sigh the lack of many a thing I sought,
And with old woes new wail my dear time's waste:

Second quatrain:
Then can I drown an eye, unused to flow,
For precious friends hid in death's dateless night,
And weep afresh love's long since cancelled woe,
And moan the expense of many a vanished sight:

Third quatrain:
Then can I grieve at grievances foregone,
And heavily from woe to woe tell o'er
The sad account of fore-bemoanèd moan,
Which I new pay as if not paid before.

Volta:
But if the while I think on thee, dear friend,
All losses are restored and sorrows end.

Note that, unlike the Italian sonnet that Monteverdi set, which has 11-syllable lines, this one is written in iambic pentameter—a common poetic meter in English. The lines all have 10 syllables, alternating unstressed and stressed syllables. How might this difference affect the way a composer would set these texts to music?

Monteverdi loved to write music for texts like this, because they invited him to use the full arsenal of expressive contrasts available to Baroque composers. When the volta begins, the playful interaction between the voices stops, and they proclaim lines 12 and 13 together. The bass line, which "walked" through most of the rest of the piece in steady, fast notes, slows way down, so the accompaniment consists only of sustained chords. The vocal lines also slow down, an effect that most performers instinctively exaggerate. The harmony becomes richer. This music contrasts with the rest of the piece as completely as do the final lines of the poem with the earlier ones. If our ears are searching for unity, one of the age-old criteria of aesthetic beauty, they will not find it here, because the composer's first priority is to express the text.

Bach's Mass in B minor

Bach's Mass in B minor was published more than a hundred years after the Monteverdi piece, during the late Baroque period; Bach assembled the work gradually over the last three decades of his life. Unlike the Monteverdi continuo madrigals, this work is widely performed. This is true at least in part because it can be sung by a skilled choir and, with some changes in instrumentation, played by a symphony orchestra. It is also a setting of one of the most familiar of all texts—the Ordinary of the Roman Catholic Mass, those texts that are said, or sung, on any occasion the Mass is celebrated—by one of the most famous of composers. These are the same texts that Josquin set in his *Missa "L'homme armé" super voces musicales.* The excerpts here are all from the Gloria, an extended hymn of praise that usually forms the second "movement" of a Mass setting.

LEARNING TO LISTEN GUIDE

TAKE NOTE OF TEXTURE, RHYTHM, AND MUSIC WITH TEXT

What to Listen For: Pay attention to how Bach has taken care to reflect the different moods suggested by each of the nine text sections enumerated below.

Streaming audio track 9.

Bach: Mass in B minor, Gloria
Date: 1723–1733
Instrumentation: Five-part mixed choir, vocal soloists, and orchestra
Key and Meter: Varies
Core Repertory Connection: This music will be discussed again in Chapters 6 and 9.
Here is the text of the entire Gloria as Bach set it:

Gloria in excelsis Deo, et in terra pax hominibus bonae voluntatis.
Laudamus te, benedicimus te, adoramus te, glorificamus te. Gratias
agimus tibi propter magnam gloriam tuam. Domine Deus, Rex coelestis,
Deus Pater omnipotens. Domine Fili unigenite, Jesu Christe altissime.
Domine Deus, Agnus Dei, Filius Patris. Qui tollis peccata mundi,
miserere nobis. Qui tollis peccata mundi, suscipe deprecationem nostram.
Qui sedes ad dexteram Patris, miserere nobis. Quoniam tu solus sanctus,
to solus Dominus, tu solus altissimus, Jesu Christe, cum Sancto Spiritu, in
Gloria Dei Patris. Amen.

Glory to God in the highest, and on earth peace to people of good will. We praise thee, we bless thee, we adore thee, we glorify thee. We give thee thanks for thy great glory. Lord God, King of heaven, God the almighty Father. The only begotten Son of God, Jesus Christ most high. Lord God, Lamb of God, Son of the Father. Thou who takest away the sins of the world, have mercy on us. Thou who takest away the sins of the world, hear our prayer. Thou who sittest at the right hand of the Father, have mercy on us. For thou alone art holy, thou alone art the Lord, thou alone art most high, Jesus Christ, with the Holy Spirit, in the glory of God the Father. Amen.

The nine sections, which last up to five minutes each, divide the text as follows:

SECTION	ORIGINAL TEXT	TRANSLATION	COMMENT
1	*Gloria in excelsis Deo,*	Glory to God in the highest,	The choir and orchestra reflect the jubilation of the text in fast, perky music.
2	*et in terra pax hominibus bonae voluntatis.*	and on earth peace to people of good will.	With the second phrase of the text, the music slows down and becomes more peaceful.
3	*Laudamus te, benedicimus te, adoramus te, glorificamus te.*	We praise thee, we bless thee, we adore thee, we glorify thee.	This section features the interaction of a solo violin with the soprano who sings the text.
4	*Gratias agimus tibi propter magnam gloriam tuam.*	We give thee thanks for thy great glory. Lord God, King of heaven, God the almighty Father.	The solemn, measured music to which this text is set features the full choir and an increasingly large number of instruments.
5	*Domine Deus, rex coelestis, Deus Pater omnipotens. Domine Fili unigenite, Jesu Christe altissime. Domine Deus, Agnus Dei, Filius Patris.*	The only begotten Son of God, Jesus Christ most high. Lord God, Lamb of God, Son of the Father.	A flute solo introduces this charming duet for a soprano and a tenor.
6	*Qui tollis peccata mundi, miserere nobis. Qui tollis peccata mundi, suscipe deprecationem nostrum.*	Thou who takest away the sins of the world, have mercy on us. Thou who takest away the sins of the world, hear our prayer.	The choir returns (minus some of the sopranos), but the music slows down and becomes somber for this section of the text.
7	*Qui sedes ad dexteram Patris, miserere nobis.*	Thou who sittest at the right hand of the Father, have mercy on us.	This line of text is set for a solo alto and oboe d'amore, a rarely used member of the oboe family.
8	*Quoniam tu solus sanctus, to solus Dominus, tu solus altissimus, Jesu Christe,*	For thou alone art holy, thou alone art the Lord, thou alone art most high, Jesus Christ,	The distinctive sound of this section results from the combination of the bass voice with a horn and two bassoons.
9	*cum Sancto Spiritu, in Gloria Dei Patris. Amen.*	with the Holy Spirit, in the glory of God the Father. Amen.	The full choir and orchestra return for the rousing final chorus.

Focus On

Johann Sebastian Bach (1685–1750)

Composer and organist. His genius combined outstanding performing musicianship with supreme creative powers in which forceful and original inventiveness, technical mastery, and intellectual control are perfectly balanced. While it was in the former capacity, as a keyboard virtuoso, that in his lifetime he acquired an almost legendary fame, it is the latter virtues and accomplishments, as a composer, that by the end of the 18th century earned him a unique

Johann Sebastian Bach (1685–1750). One of the best-known pictures of Bach shows him holding a page from his remarkable "Canon Triplex," in which three notated voices create a musical puzzle to be solved by combining the voices in different ways.
(© Lebrecht Music and Arts Photo Library/Alamy)

historical position. His musical language was distinctive and extraordinarily varied, drawing together and surmounting the techniques, the styles, and the general achievements of his own and earlier generations and leading on to new perspectives which later ages have received and understood in a great variety of ways. (Walter Emery and Christoph Wolff, *Grove Music Online*.)

Johann Sebastian Bach spent the last few decades of his life working as a musician in the Lutheran Church. As cantor, he was responsible for the music at the four main churches in Leipzig. Thus, he was required to provide substantial service music (not just a short anthem, as in many modern churches) on a regular basis. Most of this music consisted of cantatas, multimovement vocal works featuring (usually) choir, soloists, and orchestra and written for specific occasions in the liturgical year.

The Mass in B minor, on the other hand, was written over an extended period of time and contains a wide variety of musical styles, highlighting the sonic diversity of the Baroque. Bach probably began it in the hopes of obtaining an appointment at the Electoral Court in Dresden, which would have been a significant step up in musical society. He may have completed it in the final years of his life for his own personal satisfaction. Like the other large-scale works of his final years—*The Art of the Fugue* and *A Musical Offering*—it seems to present a self-conscious summary of its composer's abilities.

What Bach set to music was really only a small part of the Mass. An actual Mass celebration includes both the Proper, which pertains to the specific occasion (Christmas, Easter, etc.), and the Ordinary, which, with minor exceptions, is always included. Both Proper and Ordinary contain musical and spoken parts. Like most people who set the Mass to music, Bach set only the musical portions of the Ordinary: Kyrie, Gloria, Credo, Sanctus, and Agnus Dei.

As can be seen, the texts of numbers 1, 2, 8, and 9, which last an average of three or four minutes in performance, are each made up of sentence fragments. It is these particular settings that we will examine here.

Bach's arrangement of the opening phrase, "Gloria in excelsis Deo," begins with a lengthy orchestral introduction that sets the mood. The music is fast and dance-like, letting the listener know that this will be a jubilant piece even before the voices come in. Once the choir enters, the effect can be confusing. The large number of notes and the profusion of voices can easily give the impression that a great deal of text is being sung. Actually, Bach outdoes Monteverdi here; "*son pur vezzosetta*" was repeated only 11 times at the opening of the madrigal we just examined, while the opening word "*Gloria*" is heard 25 times in quick succession! Sometimes it is separated from the rest of the text, so that only the one word is heard; at other times, only "*in excelsis Deo*" is heard repeatedly. For those familiar with the Gospel of Luke—most members of Bach's audience—this is a vivid evocation of the text that inspired the Gloria: "And suddenly there was with the angel a multitude of the heavenly host praising God and saying, 'Glory to God in the highest, and on earth peace among men with whom he is pleased!'" (Luke 2:13–14, RSV) The voices singing the text are indeed a multitude, and the abundant repetitions make their message sound as powerful and persuasive as the Gospel text suggests.

Flinck, Govaert (ca.1615–1660), Annunciation to the Shepherds. 1639 A representation of the scene from Luke. *(RMN-Grand Palais/Art Resource, NY)*

The second part of the phrase, which speaks of peace, evokes a different image. The pace of the music changes and the orchestration thins out; if you listen carefully, you can clearly hear the basso continuo at this point. The previous dance-like music is replaced by smoothly flowing, even notes. Just like Monteverdi at the end of *Io son pur vezzosetta*, Bach has changed gears. As the music progresses, however, it is embellished with additional, faster-moving notes, and the members of the orchestra gradually join back in. As a result, the many restatements of the text give the impression of a mounting and nearly inexorable force. This music is not so much peaceful as it is overwhelming. All sense of balance and proportion is willingly relinquished as Bach repeats these few words of text over and over again. The phrase "*in terra pax*" is actually repeated 48 times—but who's counting?

The two sections that set the final sentence of the text, along with the concluding Amen, are even more sharply contrasting. The first section—featuring the text "*Quoniam tu solus sanctus, tu solus Dominus, tu solus altissimus, Jesu Christe*"—is sung by a bass soloist with a pared down accompaniment (for more on the bass voice and its repertory, see Chapter 6). Here the combination of the horn and the two bassoons produces a highly distinctive sound. Furthermore, since the bassoons play in the same range as the bass soloist, the horn, which has the highest part, is thrown into particular prominence. This is an intriguing and sensuously appealing piece, with the unusual sonorities compensating for the dogmatic nature of the text.

With the final phrase, however—"*cum Sancto Spiritu, in Gloria Dei Patris. Amen*"—intense jubilation breaks out again, surpassing even what was heard at the beginning of the Gloria. This music conveys exactly the kind of ecstatic abandonment that modern Pentecostals associate with the influence of the Holy Spirit. It is wild, even Bacchanalian. If properly performed, the conclusion, with the three trumpets blowing up a storm over the throbbing strings and choir, should leave the audience breathless. This is Baroque expressiveness at its most exalted.

In History

Bach's Mass in B Minor

Bach's Mass in B minor is rightly regarded as a masterwork of human creativity. The conditions that produced it, however, were unique to the time and circumstances in which Bach lived.

The Mass as a compositional form goes back to the late Middle Ages. By the Renaissance, composers like Josquin des Prez gloried in the creation of unified Mass cycles, with a common musical thread. Josquin's *Missa "L'homme armé" super voces musicales*, based entirely on a popular 15th-century tune, is an outstanding example.

In the 18th century, many composers were still writing Mass settings for use in church services; Mozart and Haydn both did so often. Bach's Mass in B minor, though, does not resemble those by either Josquin or Mozart. It is far too long for an actual celebration of the Mass; if it were used this way, it might leave the congregation with the impression of having attended a musical performance rather than a religious service. Bach's Mass in B minor is one of the first in a long line of sacred works that seem more at home in the concert hall than in church. Later works of this kind include Beethoven's *Missa Solemnis* (1819–1823) and Giuseppe Verdi's (1813-1901) *Messa da Requiem* (1874), both of which also follow the traditional liturgy, or order of service, as well as Brahms's *A German Requiem* (1865–1868) and Stravinsky's *Symphony of Psalms* (1930), which do not.

Unlike the other composers just mentioned, Bach was a working church musician for most of his adult life. Although Bach was a Protestant, the Kyrie and Gloria of the Mass were written in the early 1730s for the Catholic Elector of Saxony. (Church composers have often been required to write music to support their patrons' faiths.) In 1748–1749, a few years before the end of his life, Bach then assembled the complete Mass, adding music that he had composed as various earlier stages of his career. In this monumental and unique work, he was summing up his past accomplishments—and the musical ideas of the Baroque itself.

Streaming audio tracks 9–17.

If You Liked This Music. . .

Other Works of Baroque Music

There are many well-known works by Baroque composers that deserve to be a part of any well-stocked library of classical recordings. One of these—*Messiah*, by **George Frideric Handel** (1685–1759)—is discussed in Chapter 13, the chapter which is available online. Here are a few others:

- **Johann Sebastian Bach's** six Brandenburg Concertos, written for different combinations of instruments, are among the most delightful examples of this standard Baroque form.
- **Handel's** *Water Music* consists of three suites of dance-like music meant to be performed from a barge on the Thames river.
- **Antonio Vivaldi's** *The Four Seasons* consists of four concertos for violin, each one representing a different season of the year.

TABLE 2.4 Major Composers of the Baroque Period

Giovanni Gabrieli (Italian—ca. 1554–1612): Worked at St. Mark's Basilica in Venice, whose unusual architecture prompted him to write works for multiple choirs of voices and instruments.

Claudio Monteverdi (Italian—1567–1643): The most important composer of the early Baroque, although his early works are in a late-Renaissance style

Heinrich Schütz (German—1585–1672): The first great German composer and one of the most important figures in Lutheran church music

Henry Purcell (English—ca. 1658–1695): The most outstanding English musician of his time and the composer of one of the best-known English operas, *Dido and Aeneas*

François Couperin (French—1668–1733): The most important French composer of the Baroque and a renowned master of the harpsichord

Arcangelo Corelli (Italian—1653–1713): A violinist and the first composer to write music for instruments exclusively

Antonio Vivaldi (Italian—1678–1741): An important composer of opera, although he is remembered today for hundreds of concertos written for a wide variety of instruments

Johann Sebastian Bach (German—1685–1750): The most famous German composer of the late Baroque, and a master of nearly all Baroque forms except opera

George Frideric Handel (German/English—1685–1759): A musician of international renown, best known today for his English-language oratorios

Jean-Philippe Rameau (French—1683–1764): An important music theorist and composer, and one of the central figures in French opera

Domenico Scarlatti (Italian/Spanish—1685–1757): Known almost exclusively for his short but brilliant sonatas for harpsichord, which are often more pre-Classical than Baroque in style.

SUMMARY

- The history of music, like that of the other arts, is often divided into several broad historical periods. It is important to be familiar with them, because they are central to the way in which classical music is discussed and understood.

- The Medieval period included a wide range of musical styles and genres. Perhaps the most important of these was Gregorian chant, which is sung without harmonic accompaniment, but medieval composers also wrote music with multiple parts and even multiple texts.

- The Renaissance was marked by a rebirth of art and literature from the ancient world. Since we know very little about the music of antiquity, some have questioned whether it is meaningful to associate the music of this time with the Renaissance. Nevertheless, the 15th and 16th centuries produced music of great quality that is often quite accessible to modern listeners.

- The Baroque period extended from about 1600 to about 1750 (the year Bach died). "Baroque" literally means distorted or extravagant, and Baroque music is distinguished by the extraordinary attention that composers gave to expressing feelings through music.

KEY TERMS

A Cappella	p. 43	Early Music	p. 39	Ordinary	p. 39
Basso Continuo	p. 48	Gregorian Chant	p. 35	Polyphonic	p. 37
Cantus Firmus	p. 39	Liturgical	p. 39	Ritornello	p. 48
Classical Music	p. 34	Monophonic	p. 35		
Counterpoint	p. 48	Motet	p. 37		

REVIEW QUESTIONS

1. What are the major periods of music history, as commonly understood?
2. Why is the division of music into historical periods problematic? Why are these periods still important to know and understand?
3. What historical circumstance makes Medieval music particularly difficult to define as a musical style?
4. Why is it problematic to apply the term "Renaissance" to the history of music?
5. What is the definition of "baroque?" How does it apply to the music of Monteverdi and Bach?

REVIEW CONCEPTS

1. In what ways do the two examples of Medieval music, *Dies irae* and *Lasse! comment oublieray/Se j'aim mon loyal/ Pour quoy me bat mes maris?*, differ from each other?
2. What are some features of the pieces by Josquin and Palestrina discussed in this chapter that can make them more accessible to modern listeners than Medieval music?
3. How do the pieces by Monteverdi and Bach discussed in this chapter represent the attitude of Baroque composers toward their texts?

LISTENING EXERCISES

1. Listen to some other examples of Gregorian chant, which is widely available in recordings, or to other monophonic music from the Middle Ages (e.g. Machaut's *Foy porter*, which will be discussed in Chapter 8). What advantages does music without accompaniment offer over other styles? Why do you think this kind of music is so rarely heard?

2. Listen to some different examples of Renaissance music—e.g., English madrigals from the later 16th century, which are widely available in recordings. Do you notice any common features that distinguish this music? How would you describe them?

3. Listen to some other continuo madrigals by Monteverdi to get a better idea of the often extravagant ways in which he integrates text and music. Other fascinating examples from Book VII include (though they are not limited to) *O come sei gentile* (also in trio texture), *Eccomi pronta ai baci* (for three male voices and continuo) and *Con che soavità* (for solo voice and a double string ensemble). Book VIII, known as the "Madrigals of Love and War," contains many striking pieces, including *Hor che'l ciel e la terra* (for vocalists, strings, and continuo), *Non havea Febo ancora* (the *lamento della ninfa* which forms the focal point of this work combines a solo soprano voice with two tenors and a bass who comment on what she says) and the famous dramatic setting *Il combattimento di Tancredi e Clorinda*.

4. Listen to the other sections of the Gloria from Bach's Mass in B minor, and try to find ways in which Bach makes the music express the text. Since the text is in Latin, you will have to follow it carefully, with the translation in front of you (see pages 54–55).

3

Classical and Romantic Music

TAKE NOTE

Compositions from the Classical and Romantic periods illustrate the major tendencies of classical music to create aesthetically pleasing and expressive music. Although the historical period known as Romanticism ended long ago, it continues to influence the culture and style of our time.

In this chapter we will examine the historical periods in music commonly called Classical and Romantic, which roughly correspond to the late 18th and 19th centuries. Works from these periods still form the heart of the repertory performed by most classical musicians. There is also no clear dividing line between them, which is why Beethoven is often considered a part of both periods.

Classical Music

The Classical period in music was considered *classical* by later musicians primarily because it provided a model for later generations. Musicians who composed between the years 1750 and 1825 did not consider themselves classical, any more than Bach considered himself Baroque. Music of this period has provided models that composers have followed ever since. The Classical period saw the emergence of the modern orchestra, the appearance of comic opera as an important genre of "serious" music, and the birth of modern concert-going as a popular social activity.

The Classical Audience

During the Classical period, entrepreneurs and the growing middle class began to make the public concert into the major musical institution that it still is today. Mozart gave very successful subscription concerts in Vienna, and Haydn traveled to London to take advantage of the larger audiences in that growing commercial city.

At the same time, though, much music of the Classical period was still written for music's traditional patrons: the aristocracy and the church. (Franz) Joseph Haydn (like many people of his time—e.g. Johann Chrysostom Wolfgang Amadeus Mozart—he had multiple given names and did not use the first one) worked for most of life for the princes of the Esterházy family, and his music was first presented to highly select audiences. Even Beethoven, who is known for having appealed to a wider and more diverse public than his predecessors—an idea that has become overly romanticized, no doubt—still depended heavily on aristocratic support.

Opera remained the most popular form of musical entertainment, and any composer who wanted to achieve an international reputation had to write in this genre. Other music, though—including the sonatas of Haydn and Mozart, which are now widely performed and recorded—was written mainly for private consumption at home. As printed music grew less expensive and more widely available, the growing number of amateur musicians became an important and influential part of the "audience" at which composers aimed their work.

Instruments of the Classical Repertory

Over the course of the Classical period, the piano gradually replaced the harpsichord and the clavichord—a small and very quiet instrument with great expressive flexibility—as the most common keyboard instrument. Late 18th- and early 19th-century pianos, though, were very different from those in use today, with a lighter but more complex and varied sound.

Classical composers also introduced the clarinet as a major orchestral instrument and virtually stopped writing for older instruments like the viola da gamba ("leg viola") and oboe da caccia ("hunting oboe") that were still widely used by Baroque composers such as Bach. Thus, while the instruments it contains have continued to grow and develop, the orchestra for which Haydn, Mozart, and Beethoven wrote is essentially the same orchestra used today. Later composers continued to add instruments and expand its size, but they have not stopped writing for any of the orchestral instruments that Classical composers used.

Chapter Objectives

- Recognize Classicism and Romanticism as distinct styles and periods of classical music.
- Examine three pieces of music from the Classical period and understand what they have in common.
- Explore the ways in which Beethoven's music forms a bridge into the Romantic period.
- Understand why the musical culture we live in is a form of Romanticism.
- Examine three pieces of music from the Romantic period and understand what they have in common.

Chronology of Music Discussed in this Chapter

1781
Wolfgang Amadeus Mozart p. 66
Serenade no. 10, *Gran Partita*, K. 361, 3rd movement

1786
Wolfgang Amadeus Mozart p. 67
"Dove sono" from *Le nozze di Figaro* (*The Marriage of Figaro*), K. 492

1790
Joseph Haydn p. 69
String Quartet in B-flat major, op. 64, no. 3, 4th movement

1804–8
Ludwig van Beethoven p. 72
Symphony no. 5 in C minor, op. 67, 1st movement

1835–36
Frédéric Chopin p. 81
Ballade no. 1 in G minor, op. 23, for piano solo

1839
Hector Berlioz p. 81
Ohé Capulets! from *Roméo et Juliette*

1872
Bedřich Smetana p. 86
Šárka, from *Má vlast* (*My Homeland*)

64

TIMELINE 3.1 **THE CLASSICAL ERA (1750–1825)**

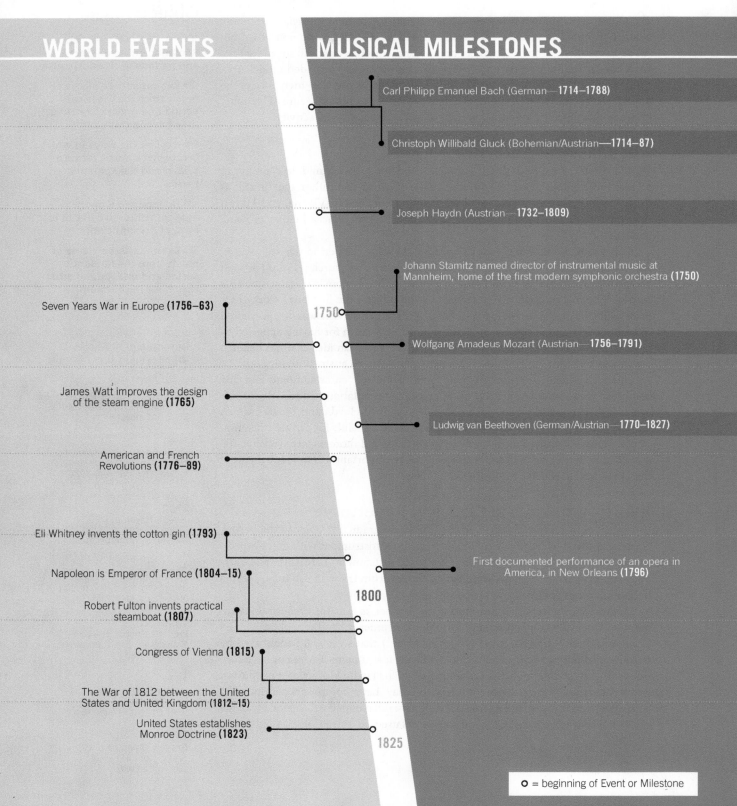

WORLD EVENTS

Seven Years War in Europe **(1756–63)**

James Watt improves the design of the steam engine **(1765)**

American and French Revolutions **(1776–89)**

Eli Whitney invents the cotton gin **(1793)**

Napoleon is Emperor of France **(1804–15)**

Robert Fulton invents practical steamboat **(1807)**

Congress of Vienna **(1815)**

The War of 1812 between the United States and United Kingdom **(1812–15)**

United States establishes Monroe Doctrine **(1823)**

MUSICAL MILESTONES

Carl Philipp Emanuel Bach (German—**1714–1788**)

Christoph Willibald Gluck (Bohemian/Austrian—**1714–87**)

Joseph Haydn (Austrian—**1732–1809**)

Johann Stamitz named director of instrumental music at Mannheim, home of the first modern symphonic orchestra **(1750)**

1750

Wolfgang Amadeus Mozart (Austrian—**1756–1791**)

Ludwig van Beethoven (German/Austrian—**1770–1827**)

First documented performance of an opera in America, in New Orleans **(1796)**

1800

1825

O = beginning of Event or Milestone

North
Sea

Baltic
Sea

**CARL PHILIPP
EMANUEL BACH**

GERMANY   ○ Weimar

Erasbach ○

**LUDWIG VAN
BEETHOVEN**

Vienna
○
Salzburg ○   ○ Rohrau

**CHRISTOPH
WILLIBALD
GLUCK**

Bay of
Biscay

AUSTRIA

Adriatic
Sea

**WOLFGANG
AMADEUS
MOZART**

**FRANZ
JOSEPH
HAYDN**

Aegean
Sea

MAP 3.1 **Composers of the
Classical Era.**

Musical Elements of the Classical Repertory

While Baroque music is often known for its ornamental complexity, Classical music
can be disarmingly straightforward, at least on the surface. On closer hearing, all
is not always as it seems. Classical forms may be clear and easily followed, but
Classical composers delight in surprising the listener. You can expect to hear lots
of short-term contrast and change in this music, especially when compared to that
of the Baroque. You may hear "flashes" of instrumental color; changes in timbre,
or tone color, are one of the ways in which Classical composers like to add interest
and complexity to their music. As a piece progresses, a richer timbre may signal
an expressive high point. So may a more complex texture or unexpected harmonic
changes.

You may also hear sudden rhythmic shifts in Classical music. While the underlying meter is usually clear and easy to detect, you will sometimes encounter notes of different lengths that may fall in unexpected places. This contrasts sharply with the steady "chugging" beat of Baroque music. Classical music also mostly lacks the basso continuo that is almost universally heard in the music of the Baroque.

Phrase: A section of a melody, corresponding to the phrases used in speech.

Classical melodies often consist of distinct sections, or **phrases**, of approximately equal length. They also tend to be built of very short, memorable units known as motives. Those motives, in turn, are often repeated and developed as the music progresses. Listening to this music becomes a learning process; we hear the melodies differently after we have heard what the composer can do with them.

Mozart's Serenade no. 10, *Gran Partita*

Mozart's Serenade no. 10, usually called by the title *Gran partita,* is a rich, varied work that forms one of the pillars of the repertory for wind ensemble. The composer's inventive use of instrumental color is on abundant display here, as is the combination of expressive depth and surface simplicity that mark the Classical style at its best.

LEARNING TO LISTEN GUIDE

TAKE NOTE OF MELODY

What to Listen For: This passage features the oboe-clarinet dialogue described by Salieri in *Amadeus.*

Streaming audio track 24.

Mozart: Serenade no. 10, *Gran Partita*, K. 361
III: Adagio, beginning
Date: 1781
Instrumentation: Two oboes, two clarinets, two bassoons, two horns, and string bass
Key: E-flat major
Meter: $\frac{4}{4}$, also known as common time; in this slow tempo, it may sound like there are eight beats per measure instead of four.
Core Repertory Connection: Mozart's *Gran Partita* will be discussed again in Chapters 5, 6, and 8.

TIME	PROGRESSION	COMMENT
0:00	Introduction	For the first measure, horns, bassoons, and bass play slow notes outlining the harmony.
0:09	Expansion	The scoring now expands to include one basset horn, one clarinet and one oboe, but still only a harmonic accompaniment is heard.
0:25	Entrance of the oboe	The first oboe begins playing on a sustained high note, then reaches downward to encompass a melodic phrase.
0:38	Entrance of the clarinet	As the oboe phrase concludes, the first clarinet begins an "answering" phrase. Notice how the two instruments overlap.
0:56	Entrance of the basset horn	After the clarinet phrase is complete, the first basset horn enters with a phrase that features both ends of its range in quick succession. Because the basset horn is a kind of clarinet, its two registers sound different, and Mozart exploits that fact here.

TIME	PROGRESSION	COMMENT
1:13	Clarinet/basset horn "dialogue"	The clarinet and basset horn seem to converse with each other, with the extreme ranges of both instruments prominently featured.
1:22	The oboe joins in	The first oboe joins the conversation, while the other instruments continue to play the accompaniment that has been heard since the start of the movement.
2:27	End of part I	The first half of the movement ends with a concluding harmonic stop.

In a famous scene from the film *Amadeus*, Mozart's rival Antonio Salieri describes the revelation he received on first hearing the third movement of the *Gran Partita* performed. On the page, he thought, it looked simple-minded and insignificant, and at first it sounded that way as well. As the oboe and clarinet begin their dialogue, however, Salieri is deeply moved, and he concludes by saying that Mozart's music struck him like the voice of God, profound in its simplicity and suggesting far more than it says outright.

Amadeus is a work of fiction, and there is no reason to think that Salieri actually said or even thought anything like this. The fictional Salieri, though, provides an apt description of the musical ideal of the Classical period. Beauty disguised as simplicity, expression that is all the more moving for being understated, even hidden, are the defining characteristics of classicism in the arts, and they are certainly present in this music.

Mozart's *Le nozze di Figaro*

Listen now to the Countess's solo **aria** (song) *"Dove sono,"* from Act III of Mozart's opera *Le nozze di Figaro* (in English, *The Marriage of Figaro*). This selection is preceded by a simple, speech-like **recitative**, a style of opera singing intended to move key plot points along more quickly. As in many operas, the music is divided into recitative and longer, more developed musical numbers such as arias and duets. These elements of opera singing will be discussed in detail in Chapter 11.

The Countess is an aristocratic character, who is not expected to show strong emotion, even though the Count, her philandering husband, freely expresses his rage when things don't go his way. In this scene, she is waiting anxiously to hear from Susanna, one of her servants, with whom she has been conspiring to bring a dose of reality into her husband's privileged life. When Susanna does not appear, the Countess has a perfect opportunity to express her conflicting feelings.

Mozart sets the central text, beginning with the words *"Dove sono i bei momenti,"* in such a way that he appears to ignore the passion and desperation inherent in the words—a passion at which he has hinted in the dramatic orchestral chords that accompany the Countess's introductory speech. The music is slow, relaxed, and bright-sounding, with balanced phrases and an elegant melody. It is the nobility of the Countess's character—not her inner emotional life—that Mozart is holding up for the audience to admire. In the concluding fast section of her aria—beginning with the words *"Ah! se almen la mia costanza"*—she then expresses a resolve that is only hinted at in the text, leaving no doubt that she is a strong character who

Aria: An extended solo in an opera, oratorio, or cantata, intended to show musically how a character reacts to a situation. It is analogous to a song in a Broadway musical or to a monologue in a play.

Recitative: A style of singing usually associated with opera or oratorio. Typically sparsely accompanied, sometimes with only continuo, it is intended to move along the plot of the story by quickly presenting key text or dialogue. (The term is derived from the Italian for "reciting style.")

LEARNING TO LISTEN GUIDE

TAKE NOTE OF MUSIC AND TEXT

What to Listen For: The relative simplicity with which Mozart sets these strongly felt words, mirroring the Countess's nobility of character.

Streaming audio track 33.

Mozart: *Le nozze di Figaro, (The Marriage of Figaro)* K. 492, "*Dove sono*"
Date: 1786
Instrumentation: Soprano and orchestra
Key: C major
Meter: $\frac{4}{4}$ (four beats per measure at variable speeds)—$\frac{2}{4}$ (two moderately slow beats per measure)—$\frac{4}{4}$ (four rapid beats per measure)
Core Repertory Connection: Mozart's *Le nozze di Figaro* will be discussed again in Chapter 11

TIME	ORIGINAL TEXT	TRANSLATION	COMMENT
0:00	*E Susanna non vien! Sono ansiosa* *di saper come il Conte* *accolse la proposta: alquanto ardito* *il progetto mi par, e ad uno sposo* *si vivace geloso . . .* *Ma che mal c'è?* *Cangiando I miei vestiti* *con quelli di Susanna, e I suoi co'miei,* *al favor della notte . . . oh cielo! a quale* *umil stato fatale io son ridotta* *Da un consorte crudel, che dopo avermi* *con un misto inaudito* *d'infedeltà, di gelosie, di sdegni,* *prima amata, indi offesa, e alfin tradita,* *fammi or cercar da una mia serva aita!*	Susanna does not come! I am anxious To know how the Count Received the proposal; so rash Does the project seem to me, and with a husband So spirited and jealous. . . But what's the harm? Changing my clothes For those of Susanna, and hers with mine, Under cover of darkness . . . oh heavens! to what A state of humility am I reduced By a cruel consort, who after having With an unheard of mixture Of infidelity, of jealousy, of scorn, First loved me, then hurt me, and finally betrayed me, Now forces me to seek help from one of my servants!	This long section of text is declaimed quickly with orchestral accompaniment. The music here is full of contrasts, reflecting the conflicting feelings conveyed by the Countess's words.
1:38	*Dove sono i bei momenti* *di dolcezza e di piacer?* *Dove andaro I giuramenti* *di quell labbro menzogner?* *Perché mai, se in pianti e in pene* *per me tutto si cangiò,* *la memoria di quell bene* *dal mio sen non trapassò?*	Where are the beautiful moments Of sweetness and of pleasure? Where have the promises Of that lying mouth gone? Why ever, if everything has changed for me To tears and pain, Has the memory of that happiness Not gone from my heart?	Here begins the countess's aria. The pace of the text slows down and the music becomes more melodic.

TIME	ORIGINAL TEXT	TRANSLATION	COMMENT
4:20	*Ah! Se almen la mia costanza* *nel languire amando ognor,* *mi portasse una speranza* *di cangiar l'ingrato cor.*	Oh! if at least my faithfulness In yearning lovingly for him at all times Could bring some hope Of changing his ungrateful heart!	The final section is faster, expressing a new sense of resolution on the Countess's part.

The Marriage of Figaro. This shot captures the distinct personality and set of emotions Mozart gives each of his all-too-human characters.

(BRENT WOJAHN/*The Oregonian*/Landov)

will ultimately prevail. This section also satisfies our need to hear a musically dynamic conclusion to an extended piece. The music thus blends form and function—another hallmark of classical art in any field.

Mozart was known as a composer who challenged his audience in unprecedented ways. His music reveals unsuspected depths below its seemingly tranquil surface. The same can be said of the Classical style as a whole; it encompasses a little bit of everything, including, not infrequently, a considerable amount of humor. Let us examine this last point further, since humor is not something we normally expect from so-called serious music.

Haydn's String Quartet in B-flat major

Joseph Haydn (1732–1809), Mozart's older, and arguably funnier, contemporary, wrote a huge number of works—108 symphonies, 68 string quartets, 47 piano sonatas, and so forth—that often exemplify the Classical style at its best. Listen carefully to the last movement of his String Quartet in B-flat major, op. 64, no. 3, which the composer indicated should be played in a manner that is "Allegro con spirito" (lively, with spirit). Haydn expected the audience to be amused by this piece. Can you tell why?

Focus On
Joseph Haydn (1732–1809)

Joseph Haydn (1732–1809).
Haydn found many
opportunities for humor
within the graceful
Classical style.
(© GL Archive/Alamy)

Austrian composer, brother of Michael Haydn. . . .
He began his career in the traditional patronage
system of the late Austrian Baroque, and ended as
a "free" artist within the burgeoning Romanticism
of the early 19th century. Famous as early as the
mid-1760s, by the 1780s he had become the
most celebrated composer of his time, and from
the 1790s until his death was a cultural hero
throughout Europe. Since the early 19th century
he has been venerated as the first of the three
"Viennese Classics" (Haydn, Mozart, Beethoven).
He excelled in every musical genre; during the first half of his career his
vocal works were as famous as his instrumental ones, although after his
death the reception of his music focused on the latter (except for *The
Creation*). He is familiarly known as the "father of the symphony" and
could with greater justice be thus regarded for the string quartet; no other
composer approaches his combination of productivity, quality, and
historical importance in these genres. (James Webster and Georg Feder,
Grove Music Online.)

Joseph Haydn is a composer who is widely respected by
musicians but not as well known to the public as Mozart and
Beethoven, with whom he is often linked historically. He was a
friend of Mozart and a teacher to Beethoven. Mozart dedicated a
series of six string quartets to the older composer, leading Haydn
to tell Mozart's father, "Your son is the greatest composer that
I know in person or by name."

Haydn's music provides a perfect example of the rewards of
active listening. Most of his pieces are relatively short, yet they
offer little to the emotional listener who wants to be impressed
immediately. In part, this is because they often reflect the
Enlightenment ideal of rational conversation, in which participants
could cover a wide variety of topics but were expected to keep
their emotions in check.

This quartet is only one of six that Haydn published together as
op. 64. If you listen to all the quartets in the series several times,
you will become aware of Haydn's endless inventiveness. He
seems determined never to do anything the same way twice. He
also had an engaging sense of humor, which grows on you as you
spend more time with his music. Haydn lived a long life, and he
remained productive into his last years.

Like the proverbial knock-knock joke, humor in music often depends on using a conventional pattern to produce unexpected results. This is what Haydn does from the beginning of the piece you just heard. The opening three notes (ba-ba-BUM) could easily be the final three notes, so the rest of the piece is, in a strict sense, unnecessary. The fact that these three notes are repeated three more times, each time more emphatically, only increases the sense of "beginning with an ending." Having started this way, though, Haydn proceeds to write several passages that sound like they will *never* end. The first of these begins at 0:33 and lasts for over 10 seconds—an eternity in a piece this fast. It sounds as though the music has gotten stuck, preparing and preparing for a change, a new idea, *something* different.

When that something finally does come, at 0:45, it is so unexpected as to be disorienting. After the repeated preparatory chords, the pace becomes much slower. The harmony is a complete surprise, seeming to cause the music to lose its moorings. Listen again to this passage and see if you can hear the droll humor that lies beneath Haydn's manipulation of musical language.

Similar passages occur at 1:51, 2:46, and 3:56. Lest the unexpected become the expected, though, the harmonies that enter at these last two points are even more bizarre and surprising each time. What is more, they are always followed by a group of fast notes that move up and down in quick succession, sounding oddly like a sly laugh. Haydn definitely had a sense of humor.

LEARNING TO LISTEN GUIDE

TAKE NOTE OF FORM

What to Listen For: The many, often surprising, humorous effects that Haydn introduces through his manipulation of expectations regarding form.

Streaming audio track 21.

Haydn: String Quartet in B-flat major, op. 64, no. 3
IV: Allegro con spirito
Date: 1790
Instrumentation: Two violins, viola, and cello
Key: B-flat major
Meter: $\frac{2}{4}$ (two rapid beats per measure)
Core Repertory Connection: Haydn's String Quartet in B-flat major will be discussed again in Chapters 5, 6, and 7

TIME	PROGRESSION	COMMENT
0:00	Beginning with an ending	The repeat of the opening three notes makes it sound like the piece is ending over and over again before it even gets underway!
0:09	New idea	A more stable melody begins.
0:33	Never-ending passage	The music hovers and seems "stuck."
0:45	Dramatic change	This shift is so unexpected that the composer undoubtedly expected you to laugh.
0:51	Musical chuckle	Haydn seems to be laughing at his own joke.
0:57	Closing idea	A new musical theme brings this section of the movement to an end.
1:17	Repeat	Everything heard so far is repeated note for note, including the "joke."

TIME	PROGRESSION	COMMENT
2:35	New section	The repeat is concluded, and the music heads in a different direction.
2:46	Never-ending passage	Once again, the music seems to get "stuck."
2:58	Dramatic change	The "joke" is repeated.
3:34	Return	The beginning/ending is heard again, marking the start of a new section.
3:56	Never-ending passage	
4:08	Dramatic change	This time it sounds even more unexpected.
4:17	Musical chuckle	Haydn is still amused with himself.
5:00	Conclusion	The beginning with an ending is made into an actual ending, in an emphatic way.

There are many more humorous touches in this movement, but the above discussion will serve to show, in broad outlines, how music can be funny. The unexpected twists in the Monteverdi and Bach pieces, on the other hand, can be compared to telling a "knock, knock" joke to people who have never heard one before. The surprises really are surprises, and we experience them as such, not as attempts at humor.

Beethoven's Symphony no. 5

Haydn's string quartet also demonstrates another important reason the late 18th century has come to be regarded as "classical" by later musicians. Many, though by no means all, compositions from this period follow established patterns that continued, and sometimes still continue, to be observed by later composers. This was the period in which most of the multimovement forms that we will examine at the end of Chapter 5 were born.

With Ludwig van Beethoven's Symphony no. 5 in C minor, op. 67, however, we encounter something new. In this innovative work, musical material is repeated in all four movements, forging connections *between* the movements and giving them a reason for belonging together. The work is so turbulent and powerful that it has long invited listeners to interpret it in narrative terms. The idea of this symphony as the record of a triumphant struggle goes back so far in history that it has become a part of the work. Without it, many would have had trouble knowing how to listen to a piece of music this long and full of dramatic contrasts.

The Symphony as Musical Story-Telling

Did Beethoven mean to tell a story with this music? His own oft-quoted comment on the beginning of the piece is *"So klopft das Schicksaal an die Pforte"*: "Thus fate pounds at the gate." We can look for additional clues to the work's meaning in what musicians, audiences, and critics have found in it over the years. And they have found some colorful stories. For example, the rhythm of the opening notes is Morse code for the letter "V," which is also the Roman numeral for 5, the symphony's number. With World War II, the association of this music with "V for victory" took hold. This is an acquired meaning that was not associated with the original work.

There was good reason, however, to interpret the Symphony no. 5 and other works of Beethoven as musical records of a victorious struggle. Beethoven had already pointed in that direction with his Symphony no. 3, known as the "Eroica," or "heroic," symphony, and originally written to celebrate the life of Napoleon

Bonaparte. Beethoven himself led a tumultuous life, and he had to reconcile himself to the gradual loss of his hearing. At the time he wrote the Symphony no. 5, he was well on his way to being completely deaf.

Nobody knows for sure why Beethoven went deaf. He began to lose his hearing in his late 20s, and it gradually deteriorated over the next two decades until his deafness became virtually total. When Beethoven wrote the Symphony no. 5, the loss of his hearing was at about the half-way point. Several years earlier, he had written a powerful letter to his two brothers, known by Beethoven scholars as the "Heiligenstadt Testament," in which he spoke of his mental torment. He confessed to having suicidal thoughts, only to be held back by the thought of all the music he had yet to create.

Deafness was not only a creative handicap for Beethoven the musician; it was also a profound force of social isolation for Beethoven the man.

Winston Churchill, prime minister of the UK during WWII, gives the "V for Victory" sign. Both sides in the conflict used Beethoven for moral support. *(© David Cole/Alamy)*

In his later years, all his conversations had to be conducted in writing. Beethoven has come to be known in popular legend as a man who shunned human company and retreated into a world of isolation. Living in the days before sign language, he had little choice but to communicate with others by scribbles, notes, and letters. He was able to continue composing because, as a skilled and highly trained musician, he was able to "hear" the sounds he wrote in his mind's ear, even if he could not hear them in the real world.

The Symphony no. 5, written while Beethoven was struggling to come to terms with this tragic development, seems to express both his struggle and resolve by means of a narrative contour that stretches through all four movements. **Narrative contour** is a dynamic formal trajectory in music that can suggest a story to the listener. It may be contained within a single piece or movement, or it may, as in this case, embrace all the movements of a multimovement work, linking them together into a single expressive unit. If ever there was a piece that shows this process in action, it is this symphony. From the first, commentators recognized that it has an extraordinary emotional impact. One vivid early description comes from German writer and composer E.T.A. Hoffmann, a contemporary of Beethoven. Writing in 1810, before many had heard the symphony, Hoffmann described the effect of the music this way:

> Beethoven's instrumental music . . . opens up to us the kingdom of the gigantic and the immeasurable. Glowing beams shoot through this kingdom's deep night, and we become aware of shadows that surge up and down, enclosing us more and more narrowly and annihilating everything within us, leaving only the pain of that interminable longing, in which every pleasure that had quickly arisen with sounds of rejoicing sinks away and founders, and we live on . . . only in this pain, which, consuming love, hope, and joy within itself, seeks to burst our breast asunder with a full-voiced consonance of all the passions.

Narrative Contour: A formal trajectory in music that can suggest a story. It may be contained within a single piece or movement, or it may embrace all the movements of a multimovement piece.

While Hoffmann refers to Beethoven's instrumental music in general, his words perfectly describe the Symphony no. 5, which was the subject of his review. Listen to the first movement, in particular, and you will hear violent contrasts and enormous intensity of expression. Indeed, its first listeners were probably struck by the immensity and aggressiveness of the music in a manner not unlike those who go to heavy metal concerts today. This experience was overwhelming for Hoffmann. It didn't matter that the emotions he experienced were ones that many people find uncomfortable: pain, longing, even annihilation. Through the arrangement of its four movements, the symphony connects the opposing worlds of tragedy and triumph, providing a simple but tangible narrative contour that has also been described as *per aspera ad astra*: through bitterness to the stars.

Focus On

Ludwig van Beethoven (1770–1827)

Ludwig van Beethoven (1770–1827). The victorious struggle heard in much of his music was an extension of the struggle in his own life. © *Lebrecht Music and Arts Photo Library/ Alamy*

German composer. His early achievements, as composer and performer, show him to be extending the Viennese Classical tradition that he had inherited from Mozart and Haydn. As personal affliction—deafness, and the inability to enter into happy personal relationships—loomed larger, he began to compose in an increasingly individual musical style, and at the end of his life he wrote his most sublime and profound works. From his success at combining tradition and exploration and personal expression, he came to be regarded as the dominant musical figure of the 19th century, and scarcely any significant composer since his time has escaped his influence or failed to acknowledge it. For the respect his works have commanded of musicians, and the popularity they have enjoyed among wider audiences, he is probably the most admired composer in the history of Western music. (Joseph Kerman, Alan Tyson, Scott G. Burnham, Douglas Johnson, and William Drabkin, *Grove Music Online.*)

Grove Music Online.

Ludwig van Beethoven is larger than life— probably more so than any other figure in the history of music. And yes, that includes the Beatles and Michael Jackson! No musician has more irreversibly changed the way music is seen and understood—a change that has profoundly affected the ways people have written and performed music ever since. It is no exaggeration to say that Beethoven invented our musical world. The idea that music is an expression of one's personal identity—and what's on *your* iPod?—was simply not on the radar screen until Beethoven put it there.

Actually, Beethoven never claimed to be expressing his personality in his music. That interpretation was arrived at gradually by those who have performed his music, listened to it, and struggled to come to terms with its meaning. Among the major ideas they have come to agree upon: Much of Beethoven's music can be understood as an autobiographical statement; among other things, it chronicles his coming to terms with his growing deafness—the greatest deprivation that a musician can face. In doing so, it records a powerful testimony to the resilience of the human spirit.

Chuck Berry may have sung "Roll Over Beethoven," but Berry and other influential pop music figures would have been inconceivable without Beethoven's larger-than-life persona guiding the way. *(Library of Congress Prints and Photographs Division Washington, D.C. 20540 USA)*

LEARNING TO LISTEN GUIDE

TAKE NOTE OF MELODY AND FORM

What to Listen For: The way in which the familiar four-note theme is used to anchor the work and introduce dramatic musical contrasts.

Streaming audio track 36.

Beethoven: Symphony no. 5 in C minor, op. 67
I: Allegro con brio
Date: 1807–8
Key: C minor
Meter: $\frac{2}{4}$ (two rapid beats per measure)
Core Repertory Connection: We will return to other sections of the 5th symphony in chapters 8 and 12

TIME	PROGRESSION	COMMENT
0:00	Powerful opening statement	The famous four-note theme is stated twice by the full orchestra, then continues in a passage of mounting intensity.
0:44	Contrast	After a dramatic pause, the music briefly becomes more relaxed, but then begins to build again.

TIME	PROGRESSION	COMMENT
1:07	High point	The full orchestra loudly concludes the first section of the piece.
1:28	Repeat	Everything heard so far is literally repeated. Try to pick out the alternating buildup and relaxation of the music that E.T.A. Hoffmann found so striking.
2:55	Continuation	The four-note theme is repeated, then extended in new ways.
3:17	Build-up and retreat	The music becomes more intense than ever, then seems to back down.
4:12	Return of the orchestra	The full orchestra powerfully reenters and repeats the opening theme and the passages that follow. Do you hear any differences this time?
5:59	Extension	Instead of ending where expected, the music continues to build in intensity, leading to a powerful and emphatic conclusion.

The universality of Beethoven's appeal hinges on his ability to express fundamental conflicts of the human condition. His work has largely defined our understanding of music ever since his time. A work like his Symphony no. 5 in C minor still carries an enormous sense of conviction and an overwhelming, visceral punch that makes it impossible to ignore.

Composers of the century that followed Beethoven, while retaining much of the musical language of the Classical period, often embraced much more ambitious expressive goals. Their music has come to define what we think of as the Romantic period in music.

TABLE 3.1 Major Composers of the Classical Period

(Franz) Joseph Haydn (Austrian—1732–1809): The "father" of the symphony and the string quartet

Christoph Willibald Gluck (Bohemian/Austrian—1714–1787): A major figure in the history of opera

Carl Philipp Emanuel Bach (German—1714–1788): The most famous of J.S. Bach's composer sons

Wolfgang Amadeus Mozart (Austrian—1756–1791): A famous child prodigy who contributed to nearly every musical form practiced during his lifetime

Ludwig van Beethoven (German/Austrian: of Flemish descent—1770–1827): Perhaps the most influential classical composer in history, whose style bridged the Classical and Romantic periods

---

Romantic Music

Why do people like the music they do? Are there any aspects of music about which most people can agree? Answer "true" or "false" to each of the following statements before reading further.

1. Music is a form of personal expression.

2. Music is a universal language.

3. Music can tell a story.

4. The best musicians are major cultural figures and deserve to be treated as celebrities.

If you answered "true" to three or more of these statements—or if you didn't notice that the first two contradict each other—then you are a musical Romantic. You are also a typical citizen of the early 21st century. Some of the most visible cultural figures today are musicians—Lady Gaga and Kanye West, for example—and people often take what they have to say *very* seriously. A musician's actions might be calculated to create publicity, but they may also cause controversy and public outcry.

Historically, Romanticism had its roots in the late 18th century. Many people would date it back to the French Revolution, which began in 1789, or to the writings of Jean-Jacques Rousseau (1712–1778), the philosopher whose theories of an unspoiled human nature shook the foundations of 18th-century thinking. In some ways, Romanticism was a continuation of the Enlightenment, a term given to an 18th-century intellectual movement that applied science and reasoning to all aspects of human affairs—social, political, economic, and artistic. The Enlightenment celebrated a belief in human potential. But Romanticism also appealed to those who thought that the Enlightenment had gone too far, that there was more to life than reason and scientific understanding.

The Romantics firmly believed that music conveyed ideas more directly than any other art, and hence provided broader access to important truths. For them, what mattered most was *personal* expression. As we saw in the last chapter, Baroque composers like Bach and Monteverdi sought to convey the emotional content of their texts. Romantic musicians also expected to express themselves through their music, and Romantic listeners learned to hear music in very individual terms, much as we still do today.

The Romantic Audience

During the Romantic era, the audience for public music-making continued to grow, and the concert became the large, public institution that it remains to this day. Cities in both Europe and America founded civic orchestras with regular concert seasons; many of these, like the Berlin and Vienna Philharmonic Orchestras and the Boston Symphony Orchestra, remain active today.

The concerts given by such groups were attended by the growing middle class, who displaced the church and the nobility as the primary consumers of music. There was a domestic side to this phenomenon as well. As the number of pianos in middle-class homes grew, composers and arrangers produced huge amounts of sheet music for their owners to play. If you have read English novels from this time, you know that being able to play the piano and sing, often at the same time, was an expected mark of social accomplishment for young ladies. Widespread music-making in the home was a defining feature of the Romantic period, when many more people had free time and disposable income than at any previous point in history.

Instruments of the Romantic Repertory

Romantic composers wrote longer pieces for bigger ensembles than ever before: for example, Symphony no. 8 by Gustav Mahler (1860–1911), which lasts nearly two hours and is known as the "Symphony of a Thousand" because of the huge number of performers it requires. Others (e.g., Chopin, see below) specialized in small-scale, intimate pieces for solo piano. The piano, in fact, underwent constant

TIMELINE 3.2   THE ROMANTIC ERA (1825–1900)

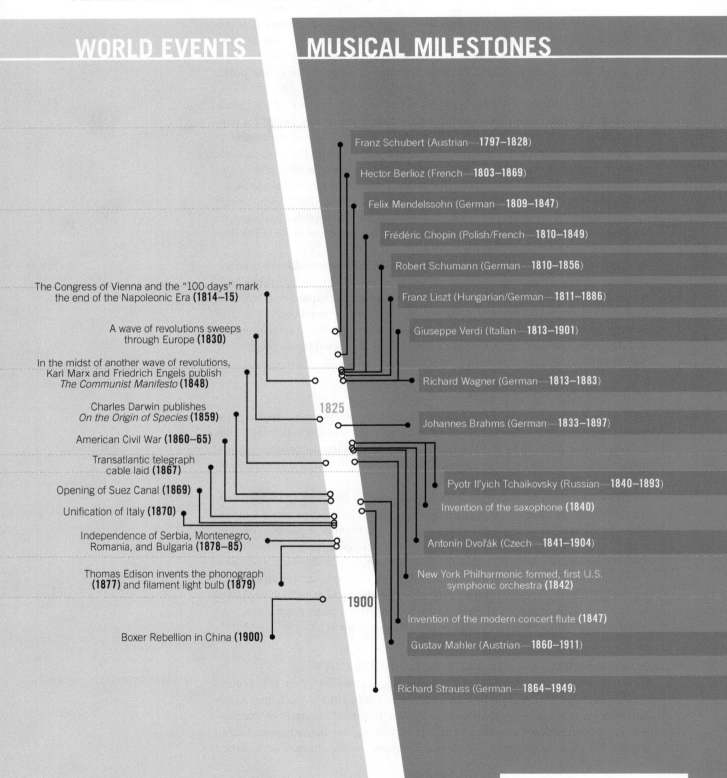

WORLD EVENTS

MUSICAL MILESTONES

Franz Schubert (Austrian—**1797–1828**)

Hector Berlioz (French—**1803–1869**)

Felix Mendelssohn (German—**1809–1847**)

Frédéric Chopin (Polish/French—**1810–1849**)

Robert Schumann (German—**1810–1856**)

The Congress of Vienna and the "100 days" mark
the end of the Napoleonic Era **(1814–15)**

Franz Liszt (Hungarian/German—**1811–1886**)

A wave of revolutions sweeps
through Europe **(1830)**

Giuseppe Verdi (Italian—**1813–1901**)

In the midst of another wave of revolutions,
Karl Marx and Friedrich Engels publish
The Communist Manifesto **(1848)**

Richard Wagner (German—**1813–1883**)

1825

Charles Darwin publishes
On the Origin of Species **(1859)**

Johannes Brahms (German—**1833–1897**)

American Civil War **(1860–65)**

Transatlantic telegraph
cable laid **(1867)**

Opening of Suez Canal **(1869)**

Pyotr Il'yich Tchaikovsky (Russian—**1840–1893**)

Unification of Italy **(1870)**

Invention of the saxophone **(1840)**

Independence of Serbia, Montenegro,
Romania, and Bulgaria **(1878–85)**

Antonín Dvořák (Czech—**1841–1904**)

New York Philharmonic formed, first U.S.
symphonic orchestra **(1842)**

Thomas Edison invents the phonograph
(1877) and filament light bulb **(1879)**

1900

Invention of the modern concert flute **(1847)**

Boxer Rebellion in China **(1900)**

Gustav Mahler (Austrian—**1860–1911**)

Richard Strauss (German—**1864–1949**)

○ = beginning of Event or Milestone

MAP 3.2 **Composers of the Romantic Era.**

development during the Romantic period, growing from the relatively small and quiet instruments of Mozart's time to the nine-foot grands familiar to today's concert audiences.

Other instruments followed suit. String instruments, whose design had been standardized in the Baroque period, underwent transformations that made them louder and more assertive. Woodwind instruments acquired keys that expanded their range, and larger bores (the internal space in which the air can vibrate) that increased their volume. Brass instruments benefited from technological innovations that made it possible to change pitch through the use of valves. The instruments in an orchestra of Beethoven's time would look and sound a bit strange to those

Across the Arts
William Blake's Union of Poetry and Painting

Another Romantic who sought to bridge the gap between the arts was English printmaker, painter, and poet William Blake (1757–1827). In his *Songs of Innocence and Experience* (1794), Blake wove images and decorations around the text for each poem, applying the entire design to one copper plate that could then produce prints to be water colored by hand. To read a text for one of these poems in isolation is to miss the interaction of poetry and painting Blake intended.

Blake exemplified the Romantic spirit in his deep convictions about the necessity of originality, the role of the artist as visionary, the wisdom of nature versus the limitations of reason, and the superiority of unfettered imagination over convention. His fertile imagination and vivid sense of color find direct parallels in Berlioz's richly descriptive music and evocative orchestral timbres.

Songs of Innocence and Experience, by William Blake (Title Page)
© The Trustees of the British Museum / Art Resource, NY

who are accustomed to their modern counterparts. By the time of Mahler, they had largely acquired their modern forms and sonorities.

Musical Elements of the Romantic Repertory

Romantic composers drew on the styles and forms of the Classical period but also changed them. Composers for piano experimented with small pieces that could be constructed in a variety of ways, only one of which was the **ABA** of classical ternary form. Many longer pieces followed forms based on songs or on stories and images specified by the composer. The term **fantasy** was used widely to suggest the freedom of an improvisation.

The orchestra grew ever larger during this time, with composers from Berlioz to Mahler drawing on orchestral tone color in novel and often brilliant ways. Meanwhile, virtuosos like Liszt and Paganini pushed the technical capabilities of their instruments to their limits and, seemingly, beyond. Romantic extravagance can also be heard in the way the music is performed, with rhythmic freedom and frequent changes in tempo making it sound more expressive. Of course, such freedom can be applied to any music in any style, but its use is considered particularly appropriate to Romantic music, with its broad emotional range. That range is also reflected in the often innovative harmony of this music, with surprising chords

ABA: A way of identifying the sections of ternary (three-part) form. After an opening section (A), a contrasting section (B) follows, and then the opening section (A) returns.

Fantasy: A musical genre meant to sound like improvisation.

and key changes occurring more and more frequently with each new generation of composers.

Many of the best-known melodies in the world come from the Romantic era. The instrumental melodies of composers like Chopin, Tchaikovsky, and Rachmaninoff have been set to words countless times, and memorable tunes abound in songs and operas from this time. Romantic composers may use simple textures to highlight the melody, but they often employed more complex textures that may be overwhelming to the ear. They also expanded the classical technique of using short *motives* as the basis for extended works.

In short, it is hard to generalize about this music. For every rule, there are countless exceptions, which is one thing that makes the Romantic period so fascinating to study.

Chopin's Ballade in G minor

Listen to the Ballade in G minor, op. 23, by Frédéric Chopin, written in 1835 by one of the most popular Romantic composers.

This is among the most widely performed Romantic pieces, and it exemplifies the period in several different ways. It is written for the piano. Advances in technology made the piano larger and louder than ever before, and advances in mass production made it possible for members of the growing middle class to have one in their homes. Music publishers, in a way that began to anticipate today's vast music "industry," turned out large amounts of sheet music for amateur home performers.

Like many popular Romantic piano works, however, the Ballade in G minor was written for a virtuoso: a master of the instrument. Chopin himself rarely performed in public, but among his contemporaries were people such as Franz Liszt (1811–1886), a larger-than-life figure who electrified audiences with his showmanship and mastery of his instrument. Liszt is sometimes described, not without justification, as the first rock star. He was musician, technical wizard with the piano, and cultural icon, all rolled into one.

The Ballade in G minor is a vibrant work, but the music is also poetic and intimate. A ballad is a narrative poem with a repeated stanza pattern and, often, a repeated **refrain**. Chopin wrote a total of four pieces with the title **Ballade** (this was the first), and there has been considerable speculation about its meaning—Chopin himself was not very helpful in this regard. As you listen to this piece, you will notice that the music focuses on a few fundamental melodic ideas that are repeated like the stanza pattern of a ballad. They are not simply repeated, though; they seem to grow and develop as the music progresses, much like a narrative story line. Recalling our four statements about Romantic music at the start of the chapter, it is only natural to assume that this music tells some kind of a story, that it does so as a form of personal expression, that it enables one to interpret the language of the music in a concrete way, and that any musician who can make this challenging work speak deserves our rapt attention.

Berlioz's *Roméo et Juliette*

For another perspective on Romantic music, listen to the *Scène d'amour* (Love scene) from *Roméo et Juliette*, a "symphony" by the French composer Hector Berlioz (1803–1869). The word symphony is in quotation marks, since, like many

Franz Liszt (1811–1886). His dashing good looks contributed to his enormous popular success.
(*© Mary Evans Picture Library/Alamy*)

Refrain: A section of music that recurs at predictable intervals. Another word for it is *chorus*.

Ballade: A character piece that gives the impression of telling a story.

LEARNING TO LISTEN GUIDE

TAKE NOTE OF FORM AND MELODY

What to Listen For: The alternating stanza and refrain sections and the mounting tension, which give the music a storytelling structure.

Streaming audio track 43.

Chopin: Ballade No. 1 in G minor, Op. 23
Date: 1831–1835
Instrumentation: Piano
Key: G minor
Meter: $\frac{4}{4}$, also known as common time (4 slow beats per measure)—$\frac{6}{4}$ (a compound meter with two groups of three beats per measure—$\frac{2}{2}$, also known as cut time (2 rapid beats per measure)
Core Repertory Connection: This music will be discussed again in Chapter 7.

TIME	PROGRESSION	COMMENT
0:00	Introduction	A slow beginning functions as a call to attention.
0:33	Refrain	A low note in the bass marks the beginning of the $\frac{6}{4}$ section, and introduces the musical idea that serves as the regular refrain throughout what follows.
2:00	Transition	A more unstable, dramatic section follows. Listen to the contrasts in tempo (speed) and dynamics (loud vs. soft).
3:10	Stanza	Following the above analogy, this theme, which will recur throughout the piece with very different expressive profiles, is like the first stanza of the ballad.
4:22	Refrain	The refrain returns. This time it is shorter and quickly grows louder.
4:54	Stanza	Like the second stanza of the ballad, the earlier theme returns at a fortissimo (very loud) dynamic level.
5:29	Transition	Another unstable passage full of contrasts follows, like the unfolding of the story.
5:44	Dance-like theme	It includes this new theme, which has a light, playful character.
6:13	Preparation	The return of the ballad stanza theme is carefully prepared.
6:22	Stanza	In its final appearance, the theme sounds emphatic and conclusive.
6:53	Refrain	The refrain returns, but here it sounds like a continuation of the music that precedes it.
7:30	Final refrain	The refrain appears for a final time as it was heard at the beginning of the piece.
8:12	Conclusion	A wild, virtuosic passage in duple time brings the piece, and the story, to a climax.
9:01	Reminiscence	Just before the end, there are two brief recollections of the opening refrain.

Romantic works, this one defiantly refuses to behave the way a work of its genre is supposed to behave. The Classical symphonic form consisted of four movements, arranged fast-slow-moderate-fast, played by an orchestra and without a text or story. If you look hard enough, traces of this structure can still be found in Berlioz's work. This seems beside the point, however, because what is most striking about

Focus On
Frédéric Chopin (1810–1849)

Polish composer and pianist. He combined a gift for melody, an adventurous harmonic sense, an intuitive and inventive understanding of formal design, and a brilliant piano technique in composing a major corpus of piano music. One of the leading 19th-century composers who began a career as a pianist, he abandoned concert life early; but his music represents the quintessence of the Romantic piano tradition and embodies more fully than any other composer's the expressive and technical characteristics of the instrument. (Kornel Michałowski and Jim Samson, *Grove Music Online*.)

Frédéric Chopin (1810–1849). This photograph was taken during the last year of his life. (© *Pictorial Press Ltd/Alamy*)

Grove Music Online.

Chopin is unusual among major composers in that he wrote almost exclusively for the piano. Most of his music consists of **character pieces,** short vignettes that may evoke a mood, scene, or idea. Examples of the character piece include the **nocturne** (a "night piece," usually with elegant melodic lines and harmonies blurred by the pedal); the **mazurka** (an evocation of a Polish folk dance); and the **prelude** (which may be in virtually any form and evoke virtually any mood, but generally has an improvisatory quality, as though it were being made up on the spot by the performer). Chopin's ballades are among his larger works. They were apparently inspired by the poetry of fellow Pole Adam Mickiewicz (1798–1855), although the exact nature of the connection has never been established. The first ballade, though, has been convincingly linked to Mickiewicz's poem *Konrad Wallenrod*. It is possible that the two main themes represent Wallenrod, a Lithuanian folk hero who also inspired many in Poland, and Aldona, the object of his ill-starred love. According to this reading, advanced by musicologist and Chopin specialist Jonathan Bellman, the sections of the ballade can be coordinated with particularly important episodes in the development of these two characters, and the concluding section represents the rage-filled suicide of Wallenrod, accompanied by a final scream from Aldona.

Character Piece: A short, Romantic work for piano solo that reflects a scene, idea, or personality, or is simply written in a characteristic genre like the nocturne or mazurka.

Nocturne: "Night piece." A genre of character piece featuring elegant melodic lines.

Mazurka: A character piece evoking the Polish dance of the same name.

Prelude: (1) A short piece that introduces another composition, such as a fugue. (2) A character piece in an improvisatory style.

this work—and deliberately so—is the extent to which it does *not* conform to the classical model.

- There is a story: the familiar one from Shakespeare's play, though with some changes.
- There is a text, in French and freely adapted from Shakespeare.
- There are a chorus and solo singers to help declaim that text.
- The work is divided into seven large sections, some of which can be subdivided further.

Oratorio: A dramatic composition often based on a religious subject and featuring extensive choral writing. It has similar musical content (arias, recitative, etc.) to an opera but lacks staging, costumes, and scenery.

What makes this a symphony, then, rather than an opera or an **oratorio** (an opera-like work without staging: think of Handel's *Messiah*)? The most satisfactory, Romantic answer is that Berlioz called it one. A much less compelling answer is to point to the skeleton of symphonic structure present in the work. A compromise position would be to say that this is a symphony because most of the story is told by the instruments, rather than by the singers. In fact, Berlioz's music for the famous love scene—"O Romeo, Romeo, wherefore art thou Romeo?"—contains only a snippet of text, showing the revelers from the Capulets' ball returning home. Less than four minutes into this 20-minute scene, though, the singers disappear, leaving the orchestra to tell the rest of the familiar story.

LEARNING TO LISTEN GUIDE

TAKE NOTE OF MUSIC AND TEXT

What to Listen For: The minimal preparation provided by the words gives way to a love scene depicted entirely by the instruments.

WEBSITE

Streaming audio track 47.

Berlioz: *Roméo et Juliette, Ohé, Capulets!*
Date: 1839
Instrumentation: Large orchestra and chorus
Key: A major
Meter: $\frac{6}{8}$ (a compound meter with two slowly moving groups of three beats per measure)
Core Repertory Connection: Berlioz's *Roméo et Juliette* will be discussed again in Chapter 6, which also contains a listening guide for the *Scène d'amour.*

TIME	ORIGINAL TEXT	TRANSLATION	COMMENT
0:00	*Ohé, Capulets! Bonsoir, bonsoir!* *Ohé, bonsoir, cavaliers, au revoir!* *Ah, quelle nuit! Quel festin!* *Bal divin! Quel festin!* *Que de folles paroles!* *Belles Véronaises,* *Sous les grands mélèzes* *Allez rêver de bal et d'amour,* *Allez, rêver d'amour* *Jusqu'au jour.* *Tra la la la le ra la. . .* *Allez, rêver d'amour. . .*	Hey, Capulets! Good evening, good evening! Hey, good evening, gentlemen, goodbye! Ah, what a night! What a feast! Divine ball! What a feast! What foolish words! Beautiful Veronese Under the great larch trees Go dream of dancing and of love, Go dream of love Until day. Tra la la la le ra la. . . Go dream of love. . .	A mysterious orchestral introduction sets the scene, and the voices of the revelers are heard quietly, as though from a distance.

Clearly, these words do not even begin to tell the story. Indeed, even with the ambiguities inherent in Romantic music, it seems fairly clear that Berlioz meant to suggest that the music takes over where the words leave off.

Focus On
Hector Berlioz (1803–1869)

Hector Berlioz (1803–1869). This contemporary cartoonist was apparently less than fond of his use of a large and varied orchestra. *(The Pierpont Morgan Library/Art Resource, NY)*

French composer. He stands as the leading musician of his age in a country—France—whose principal artistic endeavour was then literary, and in an art—music—whose principal pioneers were then German. His life presents the archetypal tragic struggle of new ideas for acceptance, to which he gave his full exertions as composer, critic, and conductor. And though there were many who perceived greatness in his music from the beginning, his genius only came to full recognition in the 20th century. (Hugh Macdonald, *Grove Music Online.*)

The musical world has a somewhat limited picture of Hector Berlioz, since he is mostly known to concertgoers through his early work *Symphonie fantastique*. This sumptuous piece

Grove Music Online.

of program music was composed when he was 26 years old and struggling with an infatuation for the Irish actress Harriet Smithson. Berlioz, though, lived almost 40 years longer and continued to produce music of startling originality. In this sense, he epitomizes the refusal of many Romantic artists to play by the rules, even when doing so would make them more popular.

Roméo et Juliette, written almost 10 years after the *Symphonie fantastique*, is at the same time a more mature work and a more revolutionary one. Berlioz based it on the highly adapted version of Shakespeare's play that he had seen in Paris. His work, too, takes considerable liberties with the original. This hardly matters, though, since the distortions are what make it interesting. The story is presented as a series of musical episodes, with just enough text to let the listener know what is going on. When things heat up, as in the *Scène d'amour*, the music always takes over.

Olivia Hussey and Leonard Whiting in the balcony scene from Franco Zeffirelli's 1968 film version of *Romeo and Juliet*. Fascination with this story has continued since Shakespeare's time. *(© Moviestore collection Ltd/Alamy)*

Smetana's Šárka

Program Music: A musical composition based on or alluding to a nonmusical program, usually a pictorial or literary idea, specified by the composer.

Symphonic Poem: A program music genre common in the late 19th century, consisting of a single, often lengthy, movement written for a large orchestra.

Many other Romantic composers wrote **program music**, music associated with a story, image, or other nonmusical subject. Listen to *Šárka* by the Czech composer Bedřich Smetana (1824–1884). This work is a **symphonic poem**, a term used by late-Romantic composers for extended works of program music in a single movement. Unlike the Berlioz work, this is a purely instrumental piece. It does, however, tell a specific story: one that you are not likely to imagine on your own.

Listen to this music, and make some notes about what kind of story it suggests to you. If this were a movie score, what do you think would be going on? What kind of characters or plot developments do you imagine? Fill in the details a bit, and then—only then—read the following.

> A young woman, having been rejected by her lover, swears revenge on all men. She and her band of female warriors contrive a plot. Šárka is tied to a tree, and left to be discovered and "rescued" by the warrior Citrad and his men. Citrad falls in love with her. She summons the other members of her band, and there is general rejoicing. Unknown to the men, though, they have been given a sleeping potion. As soon as they are asleep, the women descend on them and massacre them all.

How did you do? You may have imagined a different scene or story while listening to this music. Chances are, though, you didn't imagine anything like the one just described, in all its gruesome detail. Who would? Smetana probably picked this story precisely because of its unusual qualities, which allowed him to write music that "narrates" while avoiding obvious clichés. Listen again, and try to follow the highlights of the story as described in the Learning to Listen Guide.

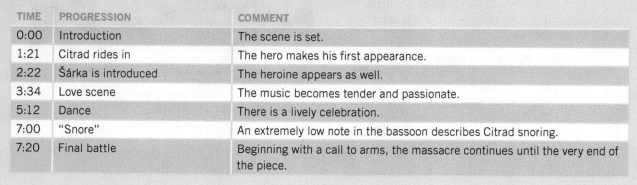

LEARNING TO LISTEN GUIDE

TAKE NOTE OF FORM AND TIMBRE

What to Listen For: The outlines of the story as depicted by the music.

Smetana: *Šárka*, from *Má vlast* (*My Homeland*)
Date: 1875
Instrumentation: Large orchestra
Key: A minor
Meter: $\frac{4}{4}$, also known as common time (four rapid beats per measure)
Core Repertory Connection: This music will be discussed again in Chapter 12.

Streaming audio track 52.

TIME	PROGRESSION	COMMENT
0:00	Introduction	The scene is set.
1:21	Citrad rides in	The hero makes his first appearance.
2:22	Šárka is introduced	The heroine appears as well.
3:34	Love scene	The music becomes tender and passionate.
5:12	Dance	There is a lively celebration.
7:00	"Snore"	An extremely low note in the bassoon describes Citrad snoring.
7:20	Final battle	Beginning with a call to arms, the massacre continues until the very end of the piece.

Romanticism in music lived a long and productive life. Composers like Chopin, Berlioz, and Smetana continue to touch us today, and the music of Romantic composers continues to dominate the concert repertoire, because it delivers many things that listeners still want and expect: a wide range of emotion, powerful and contrasting sounds and the excitement of virtuosic performance. Clearly, Romantic music still resonates with today's society.

Focus On

Bedřich Smetana (1824–1884)

Bedřich Smetana (1824–1884). Like many composers of his time, he was concerned with establishing a national identity through his music. *(Library of Congress Prints and Photographs Division Washington, DC 20540 USA)*

Czech composer, conductor, and critic. The first Czech nationalist composer and the most important of the new generation of Czech opera composers writing from the 1860s. His eight operas established a national canon and have remained in the Czech repertory ever since. Such was the force of his musical personality that his musical style became synonymous with Czech nationalist style, his name a rallying point for the polemics that were to continue in Czech musical life into the next century.

(Marta Ottlová, John Tyrrell, and Milan Pospíšil, *Grove Music Online*)

At the time Smetana was born, the musical mainstream had for years centered on Western Europe, and particularly on the music of Italy, France, and the German-speaking countries. Like many musicians of his time, Smetana was concerned with establishing a musical identity closer to his cultural roots.

Grove Music Online.

These composers, broadly known as nationalists, came mostly from Eastern Europe or Scandinavia, although German composers including Wagner and Brahms, and Italian composers such as Verdi, were also nationalistic.

What distinguishes composers like Smetana, whose deep roots in Slavic culture placed him outside of the Western mainstream, was their conscious attempt to forge different musical styles and to use their music to tell stories that resonated with their compatriots. One of the best-known examples of this is Smetana's *Má vlast* (*My Homeland*), a cycle of six symphonic poems on Czech subjects.

Of these, the most familiar to non-Czech audiences is the second, *The Moldau*, a musical description of a journey down the majestic river that travels through the Czech countryside. It has remained popular in part because the musical imagery that Smetana uses is easy to understand, and because it is based on a tune that sounds like a minor-key version of *Twinkle, Twinkle, Little Star*. The musical selection *Šárka* was chosen here precisely because it is *not* easy to understand and thus challenges you to stretch your musical imagination. It is the third piece from *Má vlast* and is based on a Czech folk legend.

In History
Smetana's *Šárka*

When Smetana wrote *Má vlast* (*My Homeland*), that homeland was not yet an independent country. In fact, it is no exaggeration to say that this music helped that country come into existence. This cycle of six symphonic poems on Czech subjects contributed to a growing sense of pride and national identity.

Smetana completed this monumental work in 1879, when the Czech people were still a part of the Austro-Hungarian Empire. For years, Prague had been a provincial capital of the Hapsburg royalty that ruled Austria. The city had gained many artistic advantages, including its gorgeous baroque architecture and an active musical life. Mozart's opera *Don Giovanni* had its 1787 premiere there. Yet native Czech culture was largely eclipsed during the Hapsburg years. Many educated people spoke German rather than Czech, a language that was not understood by the broader European world.

Interest in Czech culture began to rise in the 19th century, in tandem with nationalistic movements in other areas of Europe. Smetana was one of the first composers to write operas in Czech. The most famous is known in English as *The Bartered Bride*. He also directed the new Provisional Theater—the first native Czech opera house—for ten years until he suddenly lost his hearing in 1874.

Smetana's deafness, which was much more sudden than Beethoven's earlier in the century, ended his conducting career, but it in no way interfered with his work as a composer. *Má vlast* is only the most famous of the many works he composed in the decade before his death in 1884. It is also among the best-known works of musical nationalism, since it presents Czech subject matter in a way that appeals to an international audience.

Parts of the work, though, have never been well known outside of what is now the Czech Republic. The last two movements, *Tábor* and *Blaník*, deal with nationalist legends that originated in the Hussite conflicts of the 15th century, one of the defining moments in Czech national history. Smetana's music incorporates ancient Hussite hymn tunes.

Šárka, too, is based on a legend that is largely unknown to non-Czechs. Its music, though, is in the international style of its day, full of lush melodies and sensuous orchestral colors. Thus, it retains its Czech appeal while catering simultaneously to Czech and broader European tastes—much like its composer himself.

If You Liked This Music. . .
The Diverse World of Romantic Music

Romantic music is incredibly diverse. One composer who does not fit many of the characteristics discussed above is **Johannes Brahms** (1833–1897). Brahms's music is more classical and restrained than that of Berlioz or Smetana. Brahms used smaller orchestras and, unlike many other Romantic composers, wrote a great deal of chamber music. His music is never programmatic, at least in the blatant sense epitomized by Smetana's *Šárka*. Nevertheless, it is rich in expression and written with great care and craftsmanship. Some works by Brahms that you might enjoy include the following:

- *A German Requiem* (*Ein Deutsches Requiem*), his best-known choral work, is based on texts from the German Bible rather than the Roman Catholic Requiem Mass.
- **The four symphonies**, written at the height of his maturity, show an alternative view of instrumental music and its aims, eschewing the showiness of Smetana but revealing many inner beauties.
- The **Intermezzos** for piano, published in a number of collections under the opus numbers 76, 116, 117, 118, and 119, show the Romantic character piece at its most intimate.

TABLE 3.2 **Major Composers of the Romantic Period**

Franz Schubert (Austrian—1797–1828): The greatest master of the *Lied*, or song for voice and piano; also wrote in most instrumental forms

Frédéric Chopin (Polish/French—1810–1849): "The poet of the piano," for which he wrote a huge number of short pieces (nocturnes, mazurkas, preludes, etc.)

Robert Schumann (German—1810–1856): Known for his interest in literature, which is reflected in many of his instrumental works as well as his songs

Felix Mendelssohn (German—1809–1847): A classically-minded composer whose music reflects deep knowledge of 18th-century styles and forms

Hector Berlioz (French—1803–1869): A radical Romantic who wrote large, daring works in forms that are hard to classify

Franz Liszt (Hungarian/German—1811–1886): Perhaps the greatest piano virtuoso of all time, and also a brilliant composer for the instrument

Giuseppe Verdi (Italian—1813–1901): The greatest master of Italian opera in the 19th century

Richard Wagner (German—1813–1883): German opera composer and rival to both Verdi and Brahms

Johannes Brahms (German—1833–1897): A master of traditional instrumental and vocal forms

Antonín Dvořák (Czech—1841–1904): One of the earliest Czech nationalists; also lived and worked briefly in the United States

Gustav Mahler (Austrian—1860–1911): Wrote long, challenging symphonies scored for very large orchestras

Richard Strauss (German—1864–1949): Known for his tone poems, or programmatic orchestral works, and, particularly after the turn of the 20th century, for his operas

Pyotr Il'yich Tchaikovsky (Russian—1840–1893): The most prominent Russian composer of his time, known particularly for his ballets

SUMMARY

- Much of the music played in classical concerts was written during what are called the Classical and Romantic periods, which encompass the late 18th and 19th centuries.
- The Classical period, which centers on the late 18th century, produced music that is more elegant and carefully structured, and often, as in the case of much of Haydn's music, funny. Because of the diversity of details in works from the Classical period, this music is particularly rewarding to the active listener.
- The musical beliefs of the Romantic period are still widely shared, and affect the cultural value that we place on music today, including popular music.
- Those beliefs included the perception that music is both a universal language and a vehicle for personal expression. Composers of the 19th century often used extravagant means to achieve these ends.

KEY TERMS

ABA	p. 80	Mazurka	p. 83	Prelude	p. 83
Aria	p. 67	Narrative Contour	p. 73	Program Music	p. 86
Ballade	p. 81	Nocturne	p. 83	Recitative	p. 67
Character Piece	p. 83	Oratorio	p. 84	Refrain	p. 81
Fantasy	p. 80	Phrase	p. 66	Symphonic Poem	p. 86

REVIEW QUESTIONS

1. What are the two most common definitions of the word "classical?" Which of them best applies to the Classical period in music, and why?
2. Why is Beethoven's music often seen as belonging to both the Classical and Romantic periods?
3. What are the musical goals of the Romantic era, and how are they exemplified in the music by Chopin, Berlioz, and Smetana discussed in this chapter?
4. What is program music, and how does Smetana's *Šárka* represent this approach to composition?

REVIEW CONCEPTS

1. In what ways does "*Dove sono*," from Mozart's *Le nozze di Figaro* (*The Marriage of Figaro*), exemplify the goals of the Classical period in music? How are those goals different from those of the Baroque?

2. How does Haydn use humor as an important element of his music? What makes this appropriate to the Classical period?

3. In what ways does musical Romanticism still survive in today's world?

LISTENING EXERCISES

1. Listen to the other scenes from *Le nozze di Figaro* on your listening list. If you follow the text and translation carefully (see Chapter 11), you will see that the music and the words often fit together perfectly, but without the kind of extravagant text-expression that we observed in the Baroque examples. Thus, Mozart's setting of the text is more restrained and "classical." What are some of the ways in which Mozart achieves this? Make some notes and save them for Chapter 11, where we will look into this question in more detail.

2. Listen to the other movements of Haydn's String Quartet in B-flat, op. 64, no. 3, and listen for examples of musical humor. Does one of the movements seem funnier than the others? Why? (We will return to this question in Chapter 6.)

3. Listen to the other three ballades by Chopin. The recordings by Arthur Rubinstein, available from iTunes, are highly recommended. Does each one seem to have a distinctive character? Do they all contain repetitions of contrasting musical strains, like the stanzas and refrains of a ballad?

4. Listen to some other examples of Romantic program music. Familiar examples include Berlioz's *Symphonie fantastique*, the tone poems of Richard Strauss (e.g., *Also sprach Zarathustra, Don Juan, Till Eulenspiegel*), and the other pieces from Smetana's *Má vlast* (especially *The Moldau*). What are some of the ways in which these composers "tell the story" musically? Would you be able to guess what these pieces were about if you did not know in advance? How can you tell?

Igor Stravinsky (1882–1971)

The Twentieth Century and Beyond: Modernism and Jazz

TAKE NOTE

In the Modern period, the musical mainstream moved away from Western Europe to encompass composers from Eastern Europe and America. American popular music rose to assert itself as a major counterforce to the European classical tradition. Works of jazz provide an excellent listening example for exploring the basic elements of music.

Chapter Objectives

● Understand the characteristics of music of the Modern period and its development during the early 20th century.

● Explore two pieces of music from the early 20th century and understand what they have in common.

● Recognize key aspects of Contemporary classical music.

● Understand the concept of the canon and how it has shaped our musical tastes.

● Develop a basic knowledge of jazz and its elements.

● Apply active listening skills to a single extended work of music and recognize how they enhance the enjoyment of all music.

Chronology of Music Discussed in this Chapter

1915
Claude Debussy p. 100
Sonata for flute, viola, and harp, 1st movement

1911–16
Charles Ives p. 100
Violin Sonata no. 4, 2nd movement

1930
Igor Stravinsky p. 96
Symphony of Psalms, 1st movement

1975
William "Count" Basie p. 104
Lester Leaps In (1939), recorded at the 1975 Montreux Jazz Festival

During the early 20th century, music changed dramatically, although it also retained strong links with the past. The music of this time has enough common features that it can be treated as a single style period like those discussed in the previous chapters. The later 20th through the early 21st century is much harder to classify. This time has produced music in a wide variety of styles, along with popular music that reached an audience of unprecedented size through recordings, broadcasting, and the Internet. In this chapter we will look at a few examples that hint at the diversity of Modern music, and will spend some time with an extended listening exercise that bridges the realms of popular and art music.

Modern Music

By the end of World War I in 1918, Romantic faith in the progress of humankind was shattered by the enormous horrors that the war had revealed. The political and social realities that underlay the destruction were further underscored by the emerging study of modern psychology, exposing the dark underside of the human soul. To many artists and intellectuals, Romanticism seemed to have been a colossal mistake, and the only viable option was to turn back to the past and reinvent the forms and styles of pre-Romantic art and music, as though the 19th century had never happened.

This reaction against Romanticism and its perceived excess is often described as Modernism, with a capital M. While we are still living in modern times, the capitalized term is still used to describe the artistic and intellectual climate of the early 20th century. At least at its beginning, Modernism was driven by the famous imperative expressed by the poet Ezra Pound: "Make it new." Newness was expressed in all kinds of different ways, but innovation and reinvention of traditional forms and styles was the order of the day.

In the Modern period, the musical mainstream moved away from Western Europe, and particularly from Germany and Austria, where it had been centered for most of the previous two centuries, to encompass composers from Eastern Europe (Stravinsky, Bartók) and America (Ives, Copland). For the first time, American popular music began to assert itself as a major counterforce to the European classical tradition.

The Modern Audience

In the 20th century, broadcasting and recording became the primary ways in which people listened to music. Increasingly, nearly everybody could acquire the means to hear music at home without actually being able to perform it. By taking advantage of this growing market, composers and star performers were able to share and distribute their work as never before. The same can be said about the consumption of music to this very day.

The growing accessibility of music in the 20th century also inspired a greater diversity of musical styles and taste. Genres such as jazz, popular song, rhythm and blues, rock and roll, and related styles eclipsed the popularity of Western classical music. As these styles gained larger audiences, they also attracted new groups of people who would never have attended a classical concert. It is no exaggeration to say that by the late 20th century, the audience for music was everyone.

TIMELINE 4.1 THE TWENTIETH CENTURY AND BEYOND (1900 TO THE PRESENT)

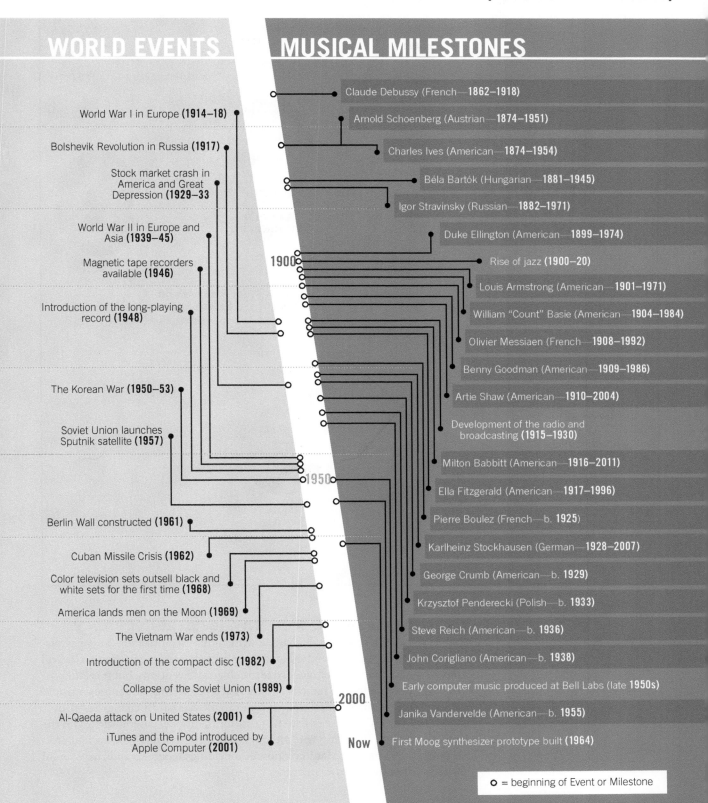

WORLD EVENTS

World War I in Europe (1914–18)

Bolshevik Revolution in Russia (1917)

Stock market crash in America and Great Depression (1929–33)

World War II in Europe and Asia (1939–45)

Magnetic tape recorders available (1946)

Introduction of the long-playing record (1948)

The Korean War (1950–53)

Soviet Union launches Sputnik satellite (1957)

Berlin Wall constructed (1961)

Cuban Missile Crisis (1962)

Color television sets outsell black and white sets for the first time (1968)

America lands men on the Moon (1969)

The Vietnam War ends (1973)

Introduction of the compact disc (1982)

Collapse of the Soviet Union (1989)

Al-Qaeda attack on United States (2001)

iTunes and the iPod introduced by Apple Computer (2001)

MUSICAL MILESTONES

Claude Debussy (French—1862–1918)

Arnold Schoenberg (Austrian—1874–1951)

Charles Ives (American—1874–1954)

Béla Bartók (Hungarian—1881–1945)

Igor Stravinsky (Russian—1882–1971)

Duke Ellington (American—1899–1974)

Rise of jazz (1900–20)

Louis Armstrong (American—1901–1971)

William "Count" Basie (American—1904–1984)

Olivier Messiaen (French—1908–1992)

Benny Goodman (American—1909–1986)

Artie Shaw (American—1910–2004)

Development of the radio and broadcasting (1915–1930)

Milton Babbitt (American—1916–2011)

Ella Fitzgerald (American—1917–1996)

Pierre Boulez (French—b. 1925)

Karlheinz Stockhausen (German—1928–2007)

George Crumb (American—b. 1929)

Krzysztof Penderecki (Polish—b. 1933)

Steve Reich (American—b. 1936)

John Corigliano (American—b. 1938)

Early computer music produced at Bell Labs (late 1950s)

Janika Vandervelde (American—b. 1955)

First Moog synthesizer prototype built (1964)

1900

1950

2000

Now

O = beginning of Event or Milestone

MAP 4.1 **Musicians of the Twentieth Century—Europe.**

Instruments of the Modern Classical Repertory

Ironically, the 20th century, which is known as a time of innovation, has seen relatively little change in the standard instruments of classical music. Some classical composers have made use of modern technological inventions, but it is still possible today to write for the same orchestra that a late Romantic composer would have used. The technology of the piano, for example, has hardly changed at all over the past 100 years. Composers also still write for traditional ensembles such as the string quartet and the piano trio, although they experiment with new and radical combinations as well. Many composers, including George Crumb, have found new ways to use the old instruments.

MAP 4.2 **Musicians of the Twentieth Century—United States.**

Electricity also played a key role in the development of Modern music. Whether used to amplify or modify the sounds of acoustic instruments like the guitar or as the architecture for daring new instruments such as the synthesizer, electricity opened doors to new sounds and new experiences in the performance of music.

Musical Elements of the Modern Repertory

The paradoxical desire to forge links with the past while simultaneously breaking from it characterizes Modern music as a whole. Modern composers treat form with great flexibility. However, if you listen carefully, you can still hear clear formal outlines, just as in the music of the past, showing that Modern composers want you to hear them too. Likewise, while instruments may have changed little in the past century, Modern composers have enjoyed using and combining them in novel ways. Even more importantly, they have often given timbre a lot of attention, using original timbres, and sometimes shifts between them, as a very audible surface feature of their music.

The rhythms and meters of Modern music can be quite hard to follow. In place of the regular, predictable meters that had prevailed since the Baroque, Modern composers enjoyed shifting meters that changed from one measure to the next. This can make it very hard to count to the music of Stravinsky or Debussy. Even in Modern music with a seemingly regular beat, you should be prepared for surprises. The same is true of harmony. Provocative, dissonant harmony, marked by unusual clashes and combinations of notes, has long been considered one of the defining features of Modern music. However, as in other areas, Modern composers also draw freely on the harmonic styles of the past.

Modern composers could also write great melodies; they just didn't always choose to do so. They may also distract attention from melody by drawing more attention to timbre, rhythm and meter, as outlined above. In many cases, you will also hear simple, folk-like melodies in Modern music; some composers, like Copland, use actual folk music extensively. Not surprisingly, the textures of Modern music can also be quite diverse. Here again, composers draw freely on the heritage of the past, creating either dense polyphony or transparent melody and accompaniment textures at will, and sometimes in quick succession. As with other features of Modern music, its complex harmonies and textures make careful, active listening both essential and rewarding.

Stravinsky's *Symphony of Psalms*

Igor Stravinsky, one of the best known early 20th-century composers, wrote his *Symphony of Psalms* in 1930 to celebrate the 50th anniversary of the founding of the Boston Symphony Orchestra. It is an indication of how much had changed in 50 years that the founders of the BSO, an important orchestra born in the Romantic era, would never have imagined a work like this. Stravinsky omitted the upper strings—the heart of the Romantic orchestra—and added two pianos and several other instruments that gave the work an immediately recognizable "Modern" sound. Listen to the first movement, which is a setting of a Latin text from Psalm 39.

The novel scoring of this work results in a sound that is percussive and unusually bright. Many notes are marked **staccato**, meaning that they are to be played in a short, detached manner, with each note clearly distinguishable and not blending with adjacent notes.

A reader examining the text before listening to the music would probably not expect it to sound this way. The psalms often contain very personal statements and entreaties, and these verses are no exception. There is nothing remotely personal, though, about Stravinsky's setting, even if at the end it does acquire an impressively massive sonic punch. This is music in the spirit of the traditional liturgy, in which the repetition of psalm texts was a means of achieving transcendence. The music occasionally evokes Gregorian chant, in which psalms were recited on long passages of repeated notes. However, there is no chance of mistaking this for

Staccato: An articulation mark directing the player to perform the affected notes in a light and detached manner. (Contrast **legato**.)

LEARNING TO LISTEN GUIDE

TAKE NOTE OF TIMBRE AND TEXTURE

What to Listen For: The unusual orchestral sonorities; the often chant-like enunciation of the text.

WEBSITE

Streaming audio track 63.

Stravinsky: *Symphony of Psalms*
I: *Exaudi orationem*
Date: 1930
Instrumentation: Large orchestra and four-part mixed choir
Key: Variable key centers
Meter: Variable meters
Core Repertory Connection: Stravinsky's *Symphony of Psalms* will be discussed again in Chapters 6 and 9.

TIME	ORIGINAL TEXT	TRANSLATION	COMMENT
0:00			The introduction features the distinctive sound of Stravinsky's orchestra, which includes two pianos.
0:34	*Exaudi orationem meam, Domine*	Hear my prayer, O Lord	The first phrase of text is sung by the altos alone.
0:53	*Et deprecationem meam.*	and give ear unto my cry;	The next phrase is sung by the full choir.
1:03			A brief orchestral interlude features the oboe.
1:09	*Audibus percipe lacrimas meas.*	hold not Thy peace at my tears!	The third phrase of the text is again sung by the altos, followed by a resounding chord played by the full orchestra.
1:29	*Ne sileas.*		The words "ne sileas" ("do not be silent") are sung by the altos and basses with a faster-moving accompaniment.
1:39	*Quoniam advena ego sum apud te et peregrinus,* *Sicut omnes patres mei.*	For I am thy passing guest, a sojourner, like all my fathers.	The accompaniment slows down again for the next two phrases, which are sung first by the altos and basses and then by the full choir. At the word "mei," the orchestra becomes noticeably louder and more active.
2:27	*Remitte mihi, prius quam abeam et amplius non ero.*	Look away from me, that I may know gladness, before I depart and be no more. Ps. 39: 12–13 (RSV)	From this point on, the choir sings continuously, although the texture of the orchestral accompaniment shifts several times.

anything but a 20th-century composition, just as there is no chance of mistaking a skyscraper for a cathedral spire. The short, detached chords at the opening, the percussive timbres of the pianos used in combination with the orchestral winds, the dissonant harmonies, and the sudden shifts and changes heard throughout the piece all mark it as a product of its own time.

Focus On
Igor Stravinsky (1882–1971)

Igor Stravinsky (1882–1971). Stravinsky moved from Russia to France, Switzerland, and finally the United States. *(Library of Congress Prints and Photographs Division Washington, DC 20540 USA)*

Russian composer, later of French (1934) and American (1945) nationality. One of the most widely performed and influential composers of the 20th century, he remains also one of its most multifaceted. A study of his work automatically touches on almost every important tendency in the century's music. To some extent the mobile geography of his life is reflected in his work, with its complex patterns of influence and allusion. In another sense, however, he never lost contact with his Russian origins and, even after he ceased to compose with recognizably Russian materials or in a perceptibly Slavonic idiom, his music maintained an unbroken continuity of technique and thought. (Stephen Walsh, *Grove Music Online.*)

Grove Music Online.

Igor Stravinsky lived a long life, and throughout most of it he was the virtual emblem of modern music, even after most of his music was no longer particularly modern. Stravinsky's early ballets remain his best-known works—*The Rite of Spring* caused a famous riot when it was premiered at the Théâtre des Champs-Elysées in Paris in 1913—but his longest creative period, Neoclassicism, began after the First World War and continued until the early 1950s.

The *Symphony of Psalms* falls in the middle of this period and exemplifies it with its international character: Written by a Russian composer in Latin for an American orchestra, it was actually premiered in Brussels. It is a deeply sacred work that eschews the somewhat showy emotionalism of much Romantic choral music in favor of the detachment, and permanence, of ritual.

Across the Arts
Of Cathedrals and Skyscrapers—Architecture that Joins Earth and Sky

What do they have in common? Both are examples of architecture that seeks to defy gravity and reach into the sky, conveying in the process the aspirations of the builders. In the latter case, those aspirations were religious: in the former, commercial. Thus, they provide a great deal of insight into the societies that built them. The skyscraper can be seen as an updated version of the cathedral spire. Notice that both thrust upward through most of their length, beginning to taper noticeably toward the top and culminating in a small and separate spire. The Empire State

Building, though, presents a strikingly continuous surface, with many windows indicating an abundance of office space within. The church spire, on the other hand, is closed and somewhat forbidding, with its age contributing to the unevenness of its surface details. Inside is a winding, narrow staircase leading to the top, where the bells are situated. Nobody works inside this tower, whose main function is to bridge the gap between earth and heaven.

Like much art from the early 20th century, the Empire State Building is based on

The Empire State Building in New York and **The Church of St. Mary the Virgin at Oxford University.** Have you looked at a skyscraper lately? If not, examine the picture on this page closely, then compare it to the spire of a Gothic church. *(Library of Congress Prints and Photographs Division Washington, DC 20540 USA & Courtesy of Robin Wallace)*

something from the past, but presents that thing in a pared-down, functional way. This kind of art is often called Neoclassical—although in this case Neo-Gothic, after the Gothic architecture of the late Middle Ages, would be more accurate—or simply "Modern."

Still Life with a Guitar, **by Pablo Picasso (1881–1973).** This example of modernist art is from 1924. Like the skyscraper pictured here, it is a pared-down version of a much older prototype—in this case a still-life painting combining food with everyday objects. © *2013 Estate of Pablo Picasso/Artists Rights Society (ARS), New York, Kunsthaus, Zurich, Switzerland / Giraudon / The Bridgeman Art Library*

Debussy's Sonata for Flute, Viola, and Harp

Listen now to the first movement of the *Sonata for flute, viola, and harp* by Claude Debussy (1862–1918). Debussy's music is often associated with the artistic movement known as Impressionism. This particular piece, however, has no specific connection with visual art. Instead, it combines the different sounds of these three instruments to create moments of varying tone color. Notice how, at the very beginning, the viola, a bowed string instrument, seamlessly takes over the melody from the flute, a woodwind, and then passes it back again as the harp begins to play gentle, plucked chords. As we will see in Chapter 6, Debussy vigorously explored the musical possibilities of timbre. This reliance on sound qualities gives the work a sensuous feeling. These timbres are the subject of this music, just as the story of Šárka was the subject of Smetana's.

LEARNING TO LISTEN GUIDE

TAKE NOTE OF TIMBRE AND METER

What to Listen For: The sonically effective contrasts between three very different-sounding instruments.

Streaming audio track 60.
Interactive Listening Guide ILG-16.

Debussy: Sonata for flute, viola, and harp
I: Pastorale—Lento, dolce rubato, beginning
Date: 1915
Instrumentation: Flute, viola, and harp
Key: F major
Meter: $\frac{9}{8}$ (a compound meter with three groups of three notes per measure), with several changes of meter
Form: Ternary (ABA)
Core Repertory Connections: Debussy's Sonata for flute, viola, and harp will be discussed again in Chapters 7, 8, and 9.

TIME	PROGRESSION	COMMENT
0:09	Opening	The flute is featured prominently, with a light accompaniment in the harp.
0:26	Exchange	The flute almost imperceptibly gives way to the viola.
0:44	Faster section	The flute returns to prominence as the music briefly accelerates.
1:00	Harp and viola	The harp plays slowly changing chords with a barely audible viola accompaniment.
1:09	Flute solo	The flute enters with much faster notes as the other two instruments remain largely stationary.
1:23	Full ensemble	All three instruments interact in the passage that begins here.

As you listen to the remainder of the movement, pay attention to the continuing rapid changes in the sound and tempo (speed) of the music. As noted above, these are the main subject of the music.

Not all Modern composers rejected Romanticism. On a superficial level, the Violin Sonata no. 4 by Charles Ives also sounds "Modern," primarily because of the high level of dissonant harmony: a feature it has in common with the Debussy and the Stravinsky. As we will see in Chapter 5, though, Ives has a very different

Focus On
Claude Debussy (1862–1918)

French composer. One of the most important musicians of his time, his harmonic innovations had a profound influence on generations of composers. He made a decisive move away from Wagnerism in his only complete opera, *Pelléas et Mélisande*, and in his works for piano and for orchestra he created new genres and revealed a range of timbre and color that indicated a highly original musical aesthetic. (François Lesure and Roy Howat, *Grove Music Online*.)

Claude Debussy (1862–1918). Debussy composed many volumes of colorful and evocative music for piano, as well as ensemble and vocal music. (© *adoc-photos/Lebrecht Music & Arts*)

Grove Music Online.

In 1948, 30 years after the death of Claude Debussy, American composer Virgil Thomson wrote, "Modern music, the full flower of it, the achievement rather than the hope, stems from Debussy. Everybody who wrote before him is just an ancestor and belongs to another time. Debussy belongs to ours." Thomson's essential insight still applies today. All great composers have broken rules, but Debussy was one of the few who have been able to reinvent the language of music. Like the Impressionist painters to whom he is often compared, he worked with colors, both instrumental and harmonic, in ways that defied traditional expectations. While his music has become "classical," it has not lost its edge; it still surprises and delights us.

Landscape at Vétheuil, c. 1890, by Pierre-Auguste Renoir. This painting by the French impressionist master shows the same experimentation with color effects and blurring of traditional lines that are widely associated with Debussy's music. (*Ailsa Mellon Bruce Collection*)

trick up his sleeve: by the end of the second movement, many American listeners, at least, will recognize the underlying refrain of *Jesus Loves Me*, on which the entire movement is built. By quoting a familiar tune that is quite likely to have strong sentimental associations for many people, and was even more likely to do so in the less culturally diverse America of his own time, Ives seeks to make exactly the sort of personal connection that Stravinsky and Debussy sought to avoid.

What all of these works have in common, and what makes them Modern, is their highly distinctive combination of progressive and conservative traits. All three composers were writing in forms with long historical pedigrees, and called attention to that fact in the titles of their works. Pieces called "sonata" and "symphony" had been written since the Baroque period. Although the meaning of the terms changed—"sonata" certainly didn't mean the same thing for Debussy as it did for Monteverdi—the very fact that 20th-century composers continued to use them is an indication of their strong sense of connection with the musical past. The sense of a permanent repertory—a **canon**, to use the academic term—came later to music than it did to the other arts. Paradoxically, therefore, a burgeoning sense of being connected with the canon and its traditions was a strong sign of musical modernity.

All of these works, though, are also aggressively challenging for listeners accustomed to those older traditions. The unusual sonorities of the Debussy and Stravinsky, and the pungent harmonic language of all three pieces, mark them as Modern, as do their flexibility in rhythm and meter: all traits that we will examine again in later chapters. The music of the early 20th century can be challenging to listen to, but it is also uniquely rewarding.

Canon: Literally, "rule" or "law." In music, the term refers to the idea of a permanent body of musical masterpieces determined by an established set of criteria. It also refers to a type of composition in which a part is imitated or repeated before its completion, resulting in a multipart texture built out of a single melodic line.

TABLE 4.1 **Major Composers of the Modern Period**

Claude Debussy (French—1862–1918): The most important Impressionist composer, whose style encompasses most other aspects of Modern music as well
Igor Stravinsky (Russian—1882–1971): A virtual emblem of Modern music, who continued to write challenging new works well into the 1960s
Arnold Schoenberg (Austrian—1874–1951): The inventor of atonal and 12-tone music and one of the 20th century's most influential composers
Béla Bartók (Hungarian—1881–1945): Worked to create a style of concert music based on the styles of Eastern European folk music
Charles Ives (American—1874–1954): Composed in virtual isolation and produced music with a uniquely American voice

Contemporary Music

Symbolic Meaning: Numerical or other relationships not audible in the music but incorporated through musical devices. Especially prevalent in early music.

In the latter part of the 20th century, music continued to change and develop in ways that often defied expectation. We need to look no further than George Crumb's *Black Angels*, which we first examined in Chapter 1, for an example. Like the Josquin Mass discussed in Chapter 2, the Crumb work also contains **symbolic meanings** having to do with numerical relationships that cannot possibly be discerned by the listener without prior knowledge. It also features a traditional ensemble—the string quartet—used in ways that drastically violate listener expectations. Compare the sound of this music with that of the Haydn quartet we examined in the last chapter and you will realize that Crumb is asking us to "hear outside the box." The familiar aural calling cards of Romantic music— mellow strings, soft lighting—are absent here, so the listener is forced to come to terms with this music without any familiar stylistic context. Crumb's musical language is unique, in a way that would have been inconceivable before the late 20th century.

The same is true of other works and styles from this most recent historical period, which is sometimes called "Postmodern" and often simply "**Contemporary**." It has produced music of baffling complexity—as in much of the work of **serialists** like Milton Babbitt (1916–2011) and Pierre Boulez (b. 1925), who based their music on rows of independent notes that are repeated, combined, reversed, and turned upside-down according to strict formulas, as are other stylistic features in their works. It has also produced music of stunning simplicity—as in the music of **minimalists** like Steve Reich (b. 1936) and Philip Glass (b. 1937), who constructed their works around very brief ideas that repeat over long stretches of time and change only extremely gradually. It has seen experiments with new ways of producing sound through technology—an approach pioneered in the work of Edgard Varese (1883–1965) and popularized by Wendy Carlos (b. 1939) on recordings made in the late 1960s and early 1970s using the Moog synthesizer. Contemporary music also experiments with novel ways of playing instruments that have existed for a long time—as in the works of John Cage (1912–1992) for "prepared piano": a piano on which various objects have been inserted between the strings in order to alter the sound.

Contemporary: In music, a term whose meaning shifts along with our constantly changing perspective on what is "contemporary." In the broadest sense, it refers to music written since the end of the Second World War (1945). In churches, the term is often used to designate music in a popular and accessible style. Classical music in contemporary styles, on the other hand, can be difficult and challenging for many listeners.

Serialism (Serialists): A method of composition employing series of pitches (and sometimes rhythms, dynamics, and timbres) that are repeated, combined, and reversed or inverted according to strict formulas. Serialist compositions typically ignore traditional or expected relationships between notes and chords.

Minimalism (Minimalists): A style of composition that uses brief musical ideas repeated over long stretches of time and changed only very gradually.

***Einstein on the Beach*, by Philip Glass (b. 1937).** Works by this American composer have often become multimedia events, attracting the kind of crowds normally associated with the popular music scene. *(© Marion Kalter/ Lebrecht Music & Arts)*

TABLE 4.2 **Major Late 20th-Century Composers**

Pierre Boulez (French—b. 1925): An important conductor and composer of complex, challenging works

Olivier Messiaen (French—1908–1992): Expressed a uniquely personal religious faith through music rich in meaningful associations

Karlheinz Stockhausen (German—1928–2007): An innovator in the use of technology to produce novel musical sounds

Milton Babbitt (American—1916–2011): Also known for technological innovations and for complex music in high Modern styles

George Crumb (American—b. 1929): Composer of music that experiments with instrumental and vocal sonorities, with unusual notation that is often visually appealing

Steve Reich (American—b. 1936): Helped to popularize the minimalist style of composition, which features long stretches of near-repetition with subtle shifts and changes

Krzysztof Penderecki (Polish—b. 1933): Uses novel notation to produce new instrumental effects, including "stochastic" or probabilistic ones that mirror the discoveries of modern physics

John Corigliano (American—b. 1938): Author of music whose wide appeal reflects its often harrowing emotional content

Listening to Jazz: Sophisticated Music with Popular Roots

In previous chapters, we listened to excerpts from a wide range of music, including works from different times and using different styles. We will now take some time to listen in depth to a single piece of music. In doing so, all of the fundamental elements of music will be examined within the context of a single work. Each of these individual elements—form, timbre, rhythm, meter, melody, harmony, and texture—will then be explored in depth in the chapters that follow.

The music we will listen to is the jazz work *Lester Leaps In*. In this recording, it is performed at the Montreux Jazz Festival in 1975 by a group of six virtuoso musicians under the leadership of William "Count" Basie (1904–1984). Basie is the pianist; the other members of the ensemble are Milt Jackson, vibraphone (vibes), Johnny Griffin, tenor saxophone, Roy Eldridge, trumpet, Niels Pedersen, string bass, and Louis Bellson, drums.

Jazz is complex yet highly accessible. Its complexity stems from its sophisticated and often dazzling use of basic musical elements such as rhythm, melody, and harmony. Its accessibility springs from the way that jazz seamlessly integrates many aspects of popular music with which we are already familiar. Add to these the factors of improvisation and the technical proficiency required to play the music and you can see why closely examining a work of jazz is a superb exercise in active listening.

The Story Behind *Lester Leaps In*

During the swing era, jazz was one of America's most popular forms of music. But by the time of this Basie performance in 1975, jazz had become a much more specialized idiom with many competing sub-genres. It now had its "technicians" and "connoisseurs." Basie performed at the Montreux Jazz Festival—a Swiss celebration of this once-uniquely American music. Still, jazz remains close to popular styles with which many Americans feel at home, as *Lester Leaps In* demonstrates.

Focus On

William "Count" Basie (1904–1984)

American jazz bandleader and pianist. He was a leading figure of the swing era in jazz and, alongside Duke Ellington, an outstanding representative of big-band style. Like all bands in the Kansas City tradition, the Count Basie Orchestra was organized about its rhythm section, which supported the interplay of brass and reeds and served as a backdrop for the unfolding of solos. Using an elliptical style of melodic leads and cues, Basie was able to control his band firmly from the keyboard while blending perfectly with his rhythm section. This celebrated group, consisting of Basie, Walter Page, Jo Jones and, from 1937, Freddie Green, altered the ideal of jazz accompaniment, making it more supple and responsive to the wind instruments and helping to establish four-beat jazz (with four almost identically stressed beats to a bar) as the norm for jazz performance. (J. Bradford Robinson, *Grove Music Online.*)

William "Count" Basie (1904–1984). Basie was one of the most prominent figures of the swing era. *(Library of Congress Prints and Photographs Division Washington, DC 20540 USA)*

Grove Music Online.

The **swing era** of the 1930s and 1940s emphasized arrangements for large groups of musicians. Count Basie's sparer style was a contrast to the rich arrangements of Duke Ellington (1899–1974). Ellington has increasingly been recognized as one of the most significant American composers. Basie, on the other hand, is remembered mostly for his recordings. These included piano solos, piano duets, and even some distinctive performances at the organ, as well as his work in larger groups.

Basie recorded this version of *Lester Leaps In* toward the end of his life, with a group of jazz superstars. By then, his status as an elder statesman of jazz allowed him to perform around the world. Basie can be heard at the piano throughout. However, unlike the other performers, he does not play a solo and does not call attention to himself. At this point in his life, he did not need to.

Swing Era: The period in the 1930s and 40s when jazz was dominated by big bands playing a dance-based repertory. Although he lived until the 1980s, Count Basie first rose to prominence during this time.

The title may already have you wondering about the story behind this piece. The work is named after Lester Young (1909–1959), an American saxophonist and one of the most important figures in early jazz. *Lester Leaps In* was his signature piece. Its tune was based on *I Got Rhythm*, from the musical *Girl Crazy*, by George Gershwin (1898–1937), an American popular songwriter. As Young's biographer Douglas Henry Daniels has put it:

> *Lester Leaps In* was not merely the trademark tune of Lester Young and a standard of the swing era; it was also a classic example of the exchange

Lester "Pres" Young (1909–1959). Young was the influential jazz musician behind *Lester Leaps In*. *(Library of Congress Prints and Photographs Division Washington, DC 20540 USA)*

Grove Music Online.

Lester Young first recorded his composition *Lester Leaps In* with Count Basie in 1939. The original 78 rpm recording, which can be purchased in digital form from iTunes, makes an interesting contrast with the one we will hear. Young's tenor saxophone can be heard throughout, often in "conversation" with the other performers. Basie himself takes a prominent role. The many exchanges between the instruments and other subtle details reward the active listener. Even so, there are no extended solos and the entire recording clocks in at barely over three minutes—less than a fifth the length of the 1975 version. This is a "pop" song, intended for a large audience. The 1975 performance, by contrast, runs more than seventeen minutes and features lengthy solos. It *demands* an audience who will give it sustained attention.

that took place between jazz and popular-music traditions, each one influencing and being influenced by the other in a cycle . . . that is the heartbeat of African American and American culture. The African American swing stylist reclaimed [what] the Russian American composer had borrowed.

By the time Count Basie and his ensemble played this music at Montreux, Young had been dead for 16 years and Gershwin for 38. In every sense, this music was already a classic. More than 100 versions have been recorded over the years. For his arrangement, Basie plays supportively in the background while each member of the band takes a solo turn. The result is a monumental performance of a jazz classic.

First Impressions of *Lester Leaps In*

Lester Leaps In may be a classic, but it is also quite accessible in style. It still makes audiences want to tap their feet and dance. The high energy of the work is further magnified because the musicians accentuate the spaces in between the natural beats of the music: an effect that is still common in much popular music.

Listening for the beat: You will recall that rhythms are usually divided into strong and weak beats, and that meter is the intrinsic pattern of beats that recurs throughout a work. In a measure in $\frac{4}{4}$ time—the most common meter in popular

The rhythm of a jazz piece is typically articulated by the drums, with an assist from the piano and bass. *(AP Photo/Robert Spencer)*

music—the strong beats are the first and third of the four. When listening to a classic song like The Beatles' *Yesterday*, for example, it is possible to count slowly to four repeatedly; "one" and "three" consistently correspond to the important words and major divisions of the text.

Music with a **backbeat**—a characteristic of much popular music—puts constant emphasis on the second and fourth beats. In the case of *Lester Leaps In*, there is a similar emphasis on the cracks between the beats. Try counting "one, and, two, and, three, and, four, and" while listening to the music, and notice the constant rhythmic emphasis on the "and." This kind of rhythmic displacement, known as **syncopation**, will be discussed when we return to this piece in Chapter 7.

Listening for the melodies and chords: *Lester Leaps In* also features melodies that contemporary audiences can easily recognize. In addition to frequent references to *I Got Rhythm*, it contains a portion of *Dixie*, and hints of other familiar tunes as well.

Many listeners may notice the familiarity of the chord sequence heard in *Lester Leaps In*. This sequence from Gershwin's *I Got Rhythm* has become so standard that jazz musicians can play it in their sleep. A version of it even appears in the theme from *The Muppet Show*. In musical jargon, this sequence of chords is often called the **rhythm changes**. Repeated over and over throughout the performance, it provides audible form to the music.

Similar patterns can be found in any form of popular music, from alternative to urban soul, and they are common in classical music as well. Another well-known example is from the song *Heart and Soul*, perhaps the most universally recognizable piece played on the piano by amateur musicians. The series of chords that accompanies this familiar tune, together with its characteristic rhythm, simply repeats over and over as the music continues. Any pianist who is familiar with the pattern can play the accompaniment, leaving somebody else free to play the melody.

Backbeat: Regular emphasis of the second and fourth beats, in common time, which are otherwise generally the unaccented, weaker ones. The backbeat gives much popular music its rhythmic kick.

Syncopation: The displacement of notes so that they fall on beats not normally accented, or between the beats, and thus contradict the meter. This is a common feature of jazz, although it can be heard in much classical music as well.

Rhythm Changes: The series of chords used in Gershwin's *I Got Rhythm*. It quickly took on a life independent of that song and became a standard progression of chords all jazz musicians know and use.

Listening for the form: *I Got Rhythm* is based on a series of chords that is just as easy to recognize, although it is considerably longer than, that of *Heart and Soul*. The music of the first two lines . . .

> I got rhythm, I got music,
> I got my man, who could ask for anything more?

. . . is repeated to the next two:

> I got daisies, in green pastures
> I got my man, who could ask for anything more?

The two lines that follow . . .

> Old man trouble, I don't mind him,
> You won't find him 'round my door.

. . . are set to new chords and a new melody. The opening music then returns for the concluding lines:

> I got starlight, I got sweet dreams,
> I got my man, who could ask for anything more?

AABA: A standard construction in popular music and jazz, in which a musical statement (A) is repeated, followed by a contrasting statement (B), after which A returns. The entire AABA unit repeats throughout the piece. In jazz, each AABA unit is known as a chorus.

Chorus: In jazz, a single repetition of the basic underlying pattern. Typically, this pattern is repeated multiple times as a piece progresses, allowing for improvisation within a carefully structured framework.

The structure of the music can thus be described as **AABA**, with A representing the first strain of the melody and its corresponding harmonies, and B the contrasting strain that is heard beginning with the words "Old man trouble." In our recording of *Lester Leaps In*, this underlying AABA pattern is heard exactly 33 times (including the initial statement). In jazz, each repetition is called a **chorus**, and comprises a restatement of the theme, with variations.

Note that the words of the B strain also introduce a contrasting idea into the text: all the other lines speak of satisfaction, while these lines present the alternative. Likewise, the continuing series of images in the text prevents the musical repetitions from making the song monotonous. Because it works so well, many other popular songs—*Yesterday* can again serve as an example—follow the same pattern, although it might be defined differently: A chorus in a pop song is the same thing as a refrain.

Listening Closely to *Lester Leaps In*

It is time now to begin listening to *Lester Leaps In*. You might want to start by playing just the first 31 seconds of the recording several times. This is the length of the initial chorus, and it establishes the pattern that you will need to remember as the music becomes more complex later on.

Of course, Count Basie's version of this music has no text. The lyrics of *I Got Rhythm* can provide much of the variety heard in the song. But for *Lester Leaps In*, only the music can do that. In fact, while we can describe the form as AABA, the music never repeats itself exactly, even after 17 minutes. To a casual listener, it moves seamlessly, punctuated only by an unremitting sequence of one instrumental solo after another. Music this complex can be challenging, but it rewards those who listen more closely.

If you can learn to recognize the patterns on which this music is built, and the ways they interact with individual details, you will be able to do everything required in the later chapters as well, building your listening skills as you go.

The sections of *Lester Leaps In*: The secret of listening actively to *Lester Leaps In* is an awareness of the underlying chorus structure, which repeats the pattern AABA 33 times in all. Each repetition lasts around 30 seconds, and each follows the previous one with absolute regularity. Thus, once you are aware of the pattern, you should be able to focus on its reoccurrence as the music progresses.

LESTER LEAPS IN

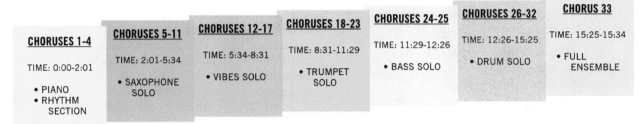

FIGURE 4.1 **The Chorus Sequence of *Lester Leaps In*.**

How the pattern works: repetition and contrast: Each time the AABA pattern is repeated, the musicians articulate it in clearly audible ways. If this were not the case, the pattern would be only an intellectual convenience with no importance to the listener. It is clear, though, that the musicians *intend* for you to hear the pattern.

Why, then, does the pattern become confusing at times? During the drum solo, for example, you may find it impossible to follow, even after repeated hearings. One answer is that music is in many ways like spoken language. There are rules—grammar—that must be followed, but speakers often decide to break them in order to make their language more colorful or effective. In the same way, musicians often set up rules and patterns only to break them, making their performances as colorful as spontaneous conversation. (See box.)

Across the Arts
A Jazz Pattern in the Poetry of E.E. Cummings

Examine the poem *All in green went my love riding*, by E.E. Cummings, a well-known poet of the jazz age. Cummings became famous for his innovative writing style and avoidance of capital letters, leading many to believe that he spelled his own name without them (he didn't). Cummings's meticulous control of poetic form is comparable to the mastery of musical form shown by Basie's musicians.

All in green went my love riding
on a great horse of gold
into the silver dawn.

four lean hounds crouched low and smiling
the merry deer ran before.

Fleeter be they than dappled dreams
the swift sweet deer
the red rare deer.

(continued)

Across the Arts (continued)

Four red roebuck at a white water
the cruel bugle sang before.

Horn at hip went my love riding
riding the echo down
into the silver dawn.

four lean hounds crouched low and smiling
the level meadows ran before.

Softer be they than slippered sleep
the lean lithe deer
the fleet flown deer.

Four fleet does at a gold valley
the famished arrows sang before.

Bow at belt went my love riding
riding the mountain down
into the silver dawn.

four lean hounds crouched low and smiling
the sheer peaks ran before.

Paler be they than daunting death
the sleek slim deer
the tall tense deer.

Four tall stags at a green mountain
the lucky hunter sang before.

All in green went my love riding
on a great horse of gold

into the silver dawn.

four lean hounds crouched low and smiling
my heart fell dead before.

One of the intriguing things about this poem is that it contains repeated patterns while also avoiding strict repetition. Thus, the opening five lines, consisting of a three-line stanza and a two-line stanza, are mirrored by the last five lines, which begin like a literal repetition—a device not uncommon in poetry. Only the final line is different. The poem alternates throughout between three-line and two-line stanzas. All of the two-line stanzas end with the word "before." The concluding lines of these stanzas, though, vary from six to eight syllables. While the three-line stanzas all begin with eight-syllable lines, they continue with lines of either six or four syllables, in an alternating pattern.

This poem thus contains elements that are also important in music: *repetition*, represented by the recurring stanza forms and textual images; *variation*, represented by the subtle changes among the stanzas; and *contrast*, represented by the sudden shifts in imagery that the first two elements allow. Much music works in the same way.

Lester Leaps In features a regular underlying pattern that is dressed up so as to avoid absolute regularity. As at the conclusion of the E.E. Cummings poem (see Across The Arts), there are moments when a musician's personal voice seems to break through. Examples of this are the extended bass solo toward the end and the quotation of *Dixie* by the saxophone at the end of its long solo heard earlier. Both of these briefly call attention to the ingenuity of an individual musician and away from the repeated pattern. In both the poem and the music, the amount of underlying regularity and sheer repetition only become apparent after careful examination.

The first chorus: The music begins with piano alone. We might expect this to continue at least through the repeat of A, or perhaps through the entire AABA section. Instead, the drums begin playing quietly halfway through the second A.

This somewhat sneaky entry is followed by an audible shift at the beginning of the B section. The bass now enters and begins playing a fast-paced line that will be heard throughout much of the rest of the piece. At the final A, the bass slows down and the piano returns to prominence; it is especially noticeable at the conclusion, when it repeats some of the melodic phrases heard in the first two A sections.

The audible entry of the bass serves to establish the appearance of the B section as the most important point of arrival so far. Meanwhile, the more subtle changes just described mark the various A sections as being less important, but significant nonetheless.

LEARNING TO LISTEN GUIDE

TAKE NOTE OF MUSICAL FORM

What to Listen For: The repeated AABA chorus structure as the piece unfolds; the solos by all instruments except the piano.

William "Count" Basie: *Lester Leaps In*, the first chorus
Date: 1975; first recorded 1939
Instrumentation: Saxophone, trumpet, vibraphone, piano, drums, and string bass
Key: B-flat major
Meter: $\frac{4}{4}$, also known as common time (four rapid beats per measure)
Core Repertory Connection: This music will be discussed again in Chapter 7.

Streaming audio track 72.
Interactive Listening Guide ILG-18
will help you follow both the
structure and individual
details of *Lester Leaps In*.

TIME	PROGRESSION	COMMENT
First Chorus		
0:00	A section	Piano
0:08	Repeat of A section	Piano, with drums entering halfway through
0:16	B section	Bass enters
0:24	A section again	The bass plays harmonic support while the piano solos above.

The pattern continues: The same three performers continue to play throughout choruses two and three. In subtle ways, they also continue to call attention to the beginning of the B in each pattern. In both cases, though, it is actually the final return of A that receives the strongest emphasis. That emphasis is particularly noticeable because, compared to the first chorus, there is little musical variety here. In the second chorus (beginning at 0:31), the return of A is prepared by a burst of activity in the pianist's left hand (descending low notes), which seems to communicate that something important is about to happen. In the third chorus, the piano part actually thins out during the B section, playing for the most part only isolated, emphatic chords. At the return of A, though, it picks up and moves even more quickly than before.

LEARNING TO LISTEN GUIDE

TAKE NOTE OF MUSICAL FORM AND TEXTURE

What to Listen For: The repeated AABA chorus structure, the changing prominence of the piano.

Streaming audio track 72.
Interactive Listening Guide ILG-18.

William "Count" Basie: *Lester Leaps In*, the pattern continues
Date: 1975; first recorded 1939
Instrumentation: Saxophone, trumpet, vibraphone, piano, drums, and string bass
Key: B-flat major
Meter: $\frac{4}{4}$, also known as common time (four rapid beats per measure)
Core Repertory Connection: This music will be discussed again in Chapter 7.

TIME	PROGRESSION	COMMENT
Second Chorus		
0:31	A section	Piano still soloing
0:39	Repeat of A	
0:46	B section	Listen to the descending low notes in the pianist's left hand at 0:52
0:54	A section	
Third Chorus		
1:01	A	The piano continues to play solo.
1:09	A	
1:16	B	The piano thins out, drawing attention to the bass.
1:23	A	The piano returns to prominence.

Johnny Griffin (1928–2008). This extraordinary Chicago-born saxophonist, featured on our recording of *Lester Leaps In*, was also a regular member of pianist Thelonious Monk's quartet. (© *JazzSign/Lebrecht Music & Arts*)

The fourth chorus (up to 2:01) is a distinct musical unit. Both the saxophone and the vibes (vibraphone) enter at the beginning, meaning that everyone but the trumpeter is now playing. The saxophone is the most audible, since it has the melody most of the time. The vibes, though, also play the melody, backing up the saxophone but continuing to play even when the saxophonist pauses for breath. The difference between the sections this time is primarily melodic. All three As feature the same phrase of melody, while the B section is a clearly audible contrast.

The saxophone solo: With the fifth chorus (starting at 2:01), the long saxophone solo begins, and with it what might be considered the main "body" of the music. The saxophone solo lasts for seven complete choruses (nos. 5–11), or slightly more than three and a half minutes (up to 5:33). The beginning of each B section is marked, not only by the familiar harmonic shifts, but by some other musical articulation as well. In one way or another, you can always tell that the B section is a contrasting passage.

In the fifth chorus, for example, the saxophone plays much faster notes in the B section, and then returns to the slower, but still fast pace of the first two parts for the return of A, though with a distinctive rhythmic kick that makes this passage sound as though the music has arrived at a goal. The B section of the sixth chorus

LEARNING TO LISTEN GUIDE

TAKE NOTE OF MELODY

What to Listen For: The repeated AABA chorus structure as the piece unfolds; continuation of the melody by all instruments except the piano.

Streaming audio track 72.
Interactive Listening Guide ILG-18.

William "Count" Basie: *Lester Leaps In*
Date: 1975; first recorded 1939
Instrumentation: Saxophone, trumpet, vibraphone, piano, drums, and string bass
Key: B-flat major
Meter: $\frac{4}{4}$, also known as common time (four rapid beats per measure)
Core Repertory Connection: This music will be discussed again in Chapter 7.

TIME	PROGRESSION	COMMENT
Fourth Chorus		
1:31	A	The saxophone and vibes enter, playing melodic content. Listen to how the vibes continue to play even when the saxophonist pauses for breath.
1:38	A	
1:46	B	
1:54	A	

does the same thing, but also goes in another direction; the saxophone line is broken up by a few isolated notes that stand apart from the rest. In the seventh chorus, the piano marks the B section by playing a series of highly audible chords. These chords are particularly noticeable because the piano has been largely silent since the beginning of the fifth chorus, a fact that you may not have fully realized, since there is so much else going on. When the piano does enter, it sounds as if Count Basie is conversing with the soloist. His carefully timed interjections serve, though, here and elsewhere, to articulate the beginning of a new portion of the AABA pattern.

Like E.E. Cummings in the poem quoted above, the musicians continue to articulate that pattern in subtle and irregular ways. There is actually much more to this articulation than the above description can even suggest. The more you listen to this music, the more you become aware of those barely perceptible gradations of sound that mark off and call attention to the absolutely regular underlying pattern.

The vibraphone solo: Following the ear-catching conclusion of the saxophone solo, the vibes emerge circuitously, near the beginning of the second A of chorus 12. The vibe solo lasts nearly six full choruses until it quietly diminishes during the initial A of chorus 18. The overall pattern of the musical form remains the same; B sections are still emphasized by musical contrast, with the return of A also receiving frequent emphasis. Since the vibes are quieter than the saxophone, though, this pattern may be harder to hear.

LEARNING TO LISTEN GUIDE

TAKE NOTE OF MELODY, HARMONY, AND MUSICAL FORM

What to Listen For: The repeated AABA chorus structure and the way it plays out during the extended saxophone solo.

Streaming audio track 72.
Interactive Listening Guide ILG-18.

William "Count" Basie: *Lester Leaps In*

Date: 1975; first recorded 1939

Instrumentation: Saxophone, trumpet, vibraphone, piano, drums, and string bass

Key: B-flat major

Meter: $\frac{4}{4}$, also known as common time (four rapid beats per measure)

Core Repertory Connection: This music will be discussed again in Chapter 7.

TIME	PROGRESSION	COMMENT
Fifth Chorus		
2:01	A	The saxophone solo begins, with the vibes in an accompaniment role.
2:09	A	
2:17	B	Listen to the faster notes in the saxophone.
2:24	A	
Sixth Chorus		
2:32	A	
2:39	A	
2:47	B	
2:54	A	
Seventh Chorus		
3:02	A	Saxophone still soloing
3:09	A	
3:17	B	Listen to the chords in the piano.
3:25	A	
Eighth Chorus		
3:32	A	
3:40	A	
3:47	B	
3:55	A	
Ninth Chorus		
4:03	A	
4:10	A	
4:17	B	
4:25	A	
Tenth Chorus		
4:32	A	
4:40	A	
4:48	B	
4:55	A	

TIME	PROGRESSION	COMMENT
Eleventh Chorus		
5:02	A	
5:10	A	
5:18	B	
5:25	A	*Dixie* marks the end of the saxophone solo.

LEARNING TO LISTEN GUIDE

TAKE NOTE OF MUSICAL FORM AND TEXTURE

What to Listen For: The repeated AABA chorus structure and changing textures and timbres as the solo shifts from the saxophone to the vibes.

Streaming audio track 72.
Interactive Listening Guide ILG-18.

William "Count" Basie: *Lester Leaps In*

Date: 1975; first recorded 1939

Instrumentation: Saxophone, trumpet, vibraphone, piano, drums, and string bass

Key: B-flat major

Meter: $\frac{4}{4}$, also known as common time (four rapid beats per measure)

Core Repertory Connection: This music will be discussed again in Chapter 7.

TIME	PROGRESSION	COMMENT
Twelfth Chorus		
5:33	A	Bass, piano, and drums continue playing.
5:40	A	Vibraphone solo begins.
5:48	B	
5:55	A	
Thirteenth Chorus		
6:03	A	
6:10	A	
6:17	B	
6:25	A	
Fourteenth Chorus		
6:32	A	
6:40	A	The saxophone reenters with two exclamatory notes, then drops out again.
6:47	B	
6:55	A	
Fifteenth Chorus		
7:02	A	
7:10	A	
7:17	B	
7:24	A	

TIME	PROGRESSION	COMMENT
Sixteenth Chorus		
7:32	A	
7:39	A	
7:46	B	
7:54	A	
Seventeenth Chorus		
8:01	A	
8:09	A	
8:16	B	
8:23	A	
Eighteenth Chorus		
8:31	A	Vibe solo fades.

The remaining choruses: As the work continues at a frenetic pace, the trumpet solo follows the pattern set by the vibes, beginning with the second **A** of chorus 18 (8:38). It stops immediately, though, at the beginning of chorus 24 (11:28), to be followed by the two-chorus bass solo. In this solo, bassist Niels Pedersen audibly marks the **A″** passages of choruses 24 and 25 by shifting the sound quality of his notes. He achieves this effect by plucking the string at different points both near and far from the instrument's bridge.

Chorus 26 is articulated in a way not heard so far in the piece. The full ensemble re-enters for the first half of the initial A, to be followed by a short drum solo in a pattern that jazz musicians call "trading twos"—that is, they play two-measure passages (eight beats in performance) in quick succession. This pattern is repeated for A′. In the B section, the drums play alone throughout, but the "trading twos" effect returns for the final A″. Thus, the B section is effectively set off, while the entire chorus is highlighted, leading the listener to expect something of heightened interest to follow.

Listening to the concluding drum solo is the ultimate challenge to your active listening skills, since the AABA form is more difficult to recognize here than anywhere else. The piano continues to play along through the next two choruses, largely so it can provide occasional harmonies to remind the listener—and musicians—of the pattern. The new chords at 13:08, for example, let you know that this is the B section; the A″ begins at 13:14. Prominent piano chords at 13:34 announce that another B section has begun, while the extended drum rolls beginning at 13:41 mark another A″.

Beginning with chorus 29 (13:47), the piano drops out, leaving the drummer to articulate the pattern by himself. Notice the change in the color of the sound from 14:06 to 14:09, which marks the A″ section of the chorus. A similar effect begins at 14:17 to articulate the second A section of chorus 30. The piano joins in briefly at 14:22 to mark the B section. Chorus 31, beginning at 14:35, consists of a series of unusual sounds. Once again, though, they follow the usual AABA pattern; you can hear the audience's heightened excitement during the B section and the beginning of the final A. Chorus 32 starts at 15:01 and is underscored by an extended drum roll, which grows louder and louder, heightened by a series of emphatic drumbeats in the B section (starting at 15:13).

When the full ensemble reenters, with lightning precision, it is at the beginning of the A section of chorus 33. Obviously, the musicians have been carefully following the pattern, even if only active listeners are always fully aware of it!

Taking It All In

This exercise in listening attentively to *Lester Leaps In* provides many excellent opportunities to explore the elements of form, timbre, rhythm, meter, melody, harmony, and texture in music. As with the works first explored in Chapter 1, each repeated listening of *Lester Leaps In* will probably reveal new aspects of the music that you may not have noticed before. Music contains patterns and elements that are not self-explanatory, but that musicians may assume you can recognize. Active listening helps you enjoy music more fully by listening with a more informed ear.

You have now been introduced to the tools that are required to listen carefully to a new piece of music in any style. In the chapters that follow, you will have a chance to practice active listening skills by exploring repertories of music that may be much less familiar to you.

If You Liked This Music . . .
Other Classic Jazz Selections

If you enjoyed *Lester Leaps In*, you might want to spend some time listening to the many recordings left behind by Count Basie and other great musicians of the swing band era, who include:
- **Duke Ellington** (1899–1974), pianist and bandleader
- **Benny Goodman** (1909–1986), clarinettist and bandleader
- **Artie Shaw** (1910–2004), clarinettist and bandleader
- **Louis Armstrong** (1901–1971), trumpeter and singer
- **Ella Fitzgerald** (1917–1996), singer

All of these musicians, and many others from the period, performed and recorded in different styles and with ensembles of different sizes. Nevertheless, in listening to virtually anything they recorded, you will hear both similarities to *Lester Leaps In* and distinctive qualities that mark these performers as individuals. In the process of learning to recognize these, you will also hear a great deal of wonderful music.

In History

Basie's *Lester Leaps In*

To modern listeners, jazz may be just a musical style, with a rich history all its own. To African Americans, it can also be a point of pride, as a unique contribution to American music. In its earliest years, jazz also helped contribute to a rapid transformation of society—in what has come to be known as the "jazz age."

While jazz first came to national prominence during the "Roaring 20s," by the time Count Basie and his band first recorded *Lester Leaps In* in 1939, the Great Depression had gripped the nation for a decade. Many people turned to new forms of entertainment—particularly popular music and the movies—in order to take their minds off the disappointments of everyday life. This in turn helped to bring people together in new ways.

African Americans from the South moved to northern cities such as Chicago and New York in large numbers in the early 20th century. Among them were musicians who performed in musical styles such as jazz, ragtime, and the blues. These were provocative, challenging styles that Northerners had never heard before, because they had been limited to black performers and to the South. In large cities, black musicians would often perform for entirely white audiences with whom they were not allowed to mix socially. The dancing that took place at such performances, while perhaps mild by today's standards, was considered daring and overtly sexual, creating rifts between young people and their scandalized parents.

Jazz also reached a broader audience than would have been possible a generation earlier through the revolutionary medium of recording. Previously, the only people who could enjoy music in their homes were those who could play it themselves, or the rich who could afford to pay others to do so. Now, for a modest investment, anyone could purchase a phonograph and a collection of recordings, and this helped jazz win new listeners and transcend social barriers. The early version of *Lester Leaps In* was not only short and catchy, it was just the right length to fit on one side of an early 78. The later, much longer version is scaled for the long-playing records that first emerged in the 1950s. Recordings like these helped to make jazz a household word, and to pave the way for the more culturally and socially integrated society of today.

SUMMARY

- Much of the music of the early 20th century, which is still usually called Modern, is rooted in a rejection of Romantic assumptions about music. Like other Modern art, this music often reinterprets forms and styles from the past in functional, efficient terms.
- Not all Modern composers rejected Romantic expressivity, but their music is marked by their increasingly self-conscious relationship with the past.
- Contemporary music, written from the mid-20th century to the present, often breaks the rules established by the classical music canon. As such, it enriches the musical experience by offering sounds that can be interesting and unexpected, and that richly reward the active listener.
- Jazz combines great musical sophistication with elements of popular styles that are still familiar to most listeners from their own experience. Thus, Count Basie's *Lester Leaps In* is an ideal piece on which to practice your attentive listening skills.

KEY TERMS

AABA	p. 108	Minimalism		Swing Era	p. 105
Backbeat	p. 107	(Minimalists)	p. 103	Symbolic Meaning	p. 102
Canon	p. 102	Rhythm Changes	p. 107	Syncopation	p. 107
Chorus	p. 108	Serialism (Serialists)	p. 103		
Contemporary	p. 103	Staccato	p. 96		

REVIEW QUESTIONS

1. What are the main characteristics of Modernism, and how are they represented in the pieces by Stravinsky and Debussy discussed in this chapter?
2. What is the canon, and how has it affected our musical tastes and preferences?
3. In what ways is jazz complex and in what ways is it accessible to the average listener?
4. How did jazz change and develop from its beginnings in the early 20th century to 1975, when this version of *Lester Leaps In* was recorded?
5. How did *Lester Leaps In* go from being a song in a hit Broadway musical to becoming the elaborate piece of sophisticated music heard in this chapter?
6. Which instruments are heard on this performance of *Lester Leaps In*? Which ones play the most important roles?

REVIEW CONCEPTS

1. What are some familiar examples of Modern art and architecture? How do they resemble the Modern music discussed in this chapter? Are there any differences?
2. What is a **chorus** in jazz? How can the repeated chorus structure of *Lester Leaps In* be compared to the structure of a poem like E.E. Cummings's *All in green went my love riding*? Which elements of these structures are obvious, and which are hidden?
3. How do the solos for the saxophone, vibraphone, trumpet, bass, and drums in *Lester Leaps In* fit into the underlying **AA'BA"** chorus structure? What musical cues do the performers use to let the audience know what is going on?
4. List some details that you noticed only after listening to *Lester Leaps In* repeatedly.

LISTENING EXERCISES

1. Listen to Stravinsky's most famous work, *The Rite of Spring*. (You may already have heard sections of it in Disney's *Fantasia*). Why do you think this work caused a riot at its first performance in 1913? Does it still sound shocking and modern nearly a century later?
2. Listen to some other works by George Crumb, e.g. his *Makrokosmos* for piano, and pay particular attention to his use of unusual sonorities. Does this aspect of Crumb's music grow on you with repeated exposure?
3. Listen to some other jazz recordings, perhaps by other "classical" jazz musicians like Duke Ellington or Benny Goodman. Do you notice similar patterns in the music? In particular, do you hear examples of backbeat, repeated chorus structure, and successive solos for various instruments? If necessary, listen repeatedly before answering these questions.
4. Listen to some popular songs and see if you can pick out structural patterns, like the AABA chorus discussed in this chapter. Make some notes about what

you hear, so you can come back and revise and expand them later.

5. Listen to one of the shorter classical works on the listening list and see if you can recognize such patterns. Make some notes on these pieces as well.

6. Listen to some of the other versions of *Lester Leaps In* available on iTunes or elsewhere. Do you recognize the musical connections between them, despite the often considerable differences in length, instrumentation, and the degree to which the performers elaborate the material?

7. Listen to some recordings by pianist Robert Levin, who improvises while playing classical music, much as its creators did, and as jazz musicians do today. It would be particularly instructive to compare Levin's recordings of Mozart's piano concertos with those made by jazz legend Chick Corea (with Bobby McFerrin and the Saint Paul Chamber Orchestra). Does either of these pianists' performance of Mozart sound "jazzy?" How can you tell?

Chapter

5

Form

TAKE NOTE

Form defines the way a piece of music begins, continues, develops, and ends. It is the way in which other musical elements such as melody, harmony, timbre, and texture are combined through the passage of time to create a complete work of music.

Previous chapters introduced the major styles and periods in classical music. Our discussion returns now to the fundamental elements of music introduced in Chapter 1. Learning how to understand each element of a work contributes immensely to the rewards of active listening. Normally, we do not listen to a piece

Chapter Objectives

- Recognize the basic structural principles of musical form.

- Explore repetition-based forms, as represented in strophic form, modified strophic form, and variation form.

- Discover contrast and return-based forms, as represented in ternary form, rondo form, and sonata form.

- Understand how composers may combine forms to increase the complexity of a work.

- Compare two different approaches to constructing a multimovement work—those of the Classical symphony and the dance suite.

- Understand the musical development that characterizes an arch form.

- Identify distinguishing elements of musical form in an Indian raga and a piece from the Middle Ages.

of music by isolating its components. We usually respond to the whole without thinking about the individual elements. But listening carefully to the smaller things that make up a work can heighten our awareness and greatly enrich the experience. Each of the next five chapters explores what goes into a piece of music by focusing on these individual elements. This chapter considers the element of form, which provides both the structure of a musical work and the "glue" that holds it together.

Form is a composer's plan for combining musical elements in time to create a complete musical work. Form provides the blueprint for organizing elements including the timbre, rhythm, meter, melody, harmony, and texture of music. You cannot hear "form" as an individual element of a work, like the flourish of a French horn or the clashing of a cymbal. But what you perceive as the beginning, middle, and end of a work is the embodiment of its form. Form is the device that enables a listener to recognize and follow the main ideas of a piece of music.

Form is often called the architecture of music. When you look at a building, you may be unaware of all the bricks, planks, and nails that go together to produce the finished structure, but you recognize its broader elements: It has one or more

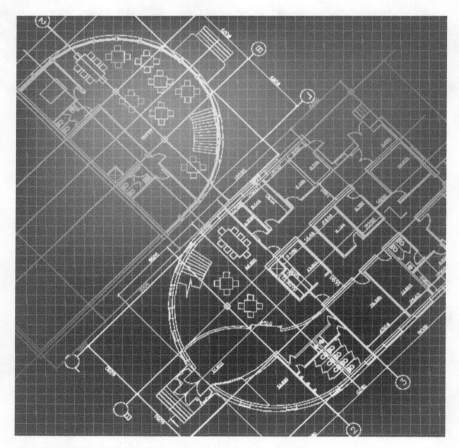

An architectural blueprint. Similarly, musical form lays out the structure of a piece.
(© *nahariyani/ShutterStock*)

stories; it is square, round, or rectangular; it has windows and doors arranged in a pattern evident when viewed from a distance. These are all part of the building's form, its overall plan. If you want to construct a building, you will need a detailed plan—a blueprint—showing its design.

An architectural plan for a building is analogous to the score of a piece of music. The written music lays out the plan, or form of a work. This form is then realized by individual musicians playing their separate parts of the composition. The score provides the shape and organization of a work, just as an architectural blueprint provides the overall plan for a building. Composers and performers can relate to this comparison to architecture, but does this comparison also have meaning for the listener? Yes, it does, and this chapter will explore the ways in which an understanding of the architecture of a piece of music enriches the listening experience.

Building Blocks of Musical Form

Even with the many ways that a work can be organized, every musical form imaginable is merely a variant of three basic structural principles known as repetition, contrast, and variation.

Repetition in music enables the active listener to detect structure and enjoy its development. Because music unfolds in real time, repetition is a composer's tool for reinforcing main ideas and underscoring the most important themes of a work so that the listener will take notice. Repetition also instills balance and resolution to a work of music, returning to familiar components, such as a melody or chorus. In this way, repetition reminds the listener of what has come before and anticipates what may follow. One familiar example of repetition is the refrain, which consists of one or more lines of words and melody repeated at intervals throughout a song, typically at the end of a verse. Refrains are easy to detect in popular songs. Some examples:

> "Who's gonna save my soul, now?"—Gnarls Barkley (*Who's Gonna Save My Soul?*)
> "'Cause I may be bad, but I'm perfectly good at it."—Rihanna (*S&M*)
> "I'm in the war of my life."—John Mayer (*War of My Life*)

Repetition emphasizes the familiar, while **contrast** introduces the new. The introduction of changes in a piece of music may take many forms. Contrast is most evident when a piece changes sharply in tempo, mood, instrumentation, or structure. These opposing forces grab the attention of the listener and signal that something important is happening in the work.

Variation, the third principle of form, integrates elements of repetition and contrast. Variation takes a familiar component of the music and changes some elements of it while retaining others. In most cases, the element upon which the variation is based is still recognizable but different. Composers often create works that explore variations of a given melody or harmonic structure. Earlier we saw how jazz artists can produce variations on a given theme while improvising.

Chronology Continued

1828
Franz Schubert
Winterreise: Die Post p. 126;
Der Lindenbaum p. 129

1906–16
Charles Ives p. 145
Sonata no. 4 for violin and piano, 2nd movement

1975
William "Count" Basie p. 130
Lester Leaps In (1939), recorded at the 1975 Montreux Jazz Festival

Traditional (recorded Late 20th Century)
Ustad Vilayat Khan p. 150
Raga Bhanka, for sitar

Repetition: A composer's tool for reinforcing main ideas and underscoring the most important themes of a work, enabling the listener to detect structure and enjoy its development. Repetition also instills balance and resolution to a piece of music.

Contrast: Change of tempo, mood, instrumentation, or structure in a piece of music.

Variation: A principle of form that integrates the other two principles, namely, repetition and contrast. It takes a familiar component of the music and changes some elements of it while retaining others.

How do repetition, contrast, and variation contribute to form? We have already looked at two simple examples of musical form. We explored the AABA structure shared by many popular songs. In this case, two basic structures—verses (A) and chorus (B)—are repeated in a familiar song sequence. Meanwhile, a repeated chorus pattern underlies much jazz. It would be a mistake, however, to assume that all popular music and jazz adhere to such forms. The astounding thing about music is that it often shatters the rules governing our expectations. For every straight-ahead rock song that conforms strictly to the AABA structure—such as *Great Balls of Fire* by Jerry Lee Lewis or *The Suburbs* by Arcade Fire—there are endless variations that add, shorten, repeat, contrast, or reorganize parts of a song.

Bridge: An instrumental section between the verse and chorus.

It is common for a song to add an extra part, called a **bridge**, between the verses and choruses, as in *This is the House that Jack Built* by Aretha Franklin or *Every Breath You Take* by the Police. Some songs begin with the chorus before the first verse, as in *Anytime At All* by the Beatles. Sometimes songwriters even blur the parts of a song by making the parts so similar that it is difficult to hear when a verse ends and a chorus begins, as with *Australia* by the Shins. As a result, form should not be thought of as a strict set of rules but as a collection of proven techniques with which the composer may work.

In the remainder of this chapter, we will examine some musical forms used in classical music, which are not fundamentally different from the examples given above from popular songs. Many of these forms originated in the Classical period. Thus, we will begin with music from the late 18th and early 19th centuries, before looking at some examples from other periods and other cultures.

Repetition-Based Forms

The most fundamental device for constructing musical forms is simple repetition. That can mean literal repetition or variations on what we have already heard.

Strophic Form

Strophic Form: A poetic structure in which successive verses, or strophes, of text follow the same rhyme scheme and metrical pattern. In music, it refers to a form of vocal music in which each verse, or strophe, of text is sung to the same tune.

One of the most basic musical forms is **strophic form**, a vocal song structure in which the same melody is repeated for each verse. Examine the text of the familiar song *Clementine*.

In a cavern, in a canyon,
Excavating for a mine,
Dwelt a miner, forty-niner,
And his daughter Clementine.

Refrain:
Oh my darling, oh my darling,
Oh my darling Clementine
You are lost and gone forever,
Dreadful sorry, Clementine.

Light she was, and like a fairy,
And her shoes were number nine,
Herring boxes without topses,
Sandals were for Clementine.
Walking lightly as a fairy,
Though her shoes were number nine,
Sometimes tripping, lightly skipping,
Lovely girl, my Clementine.

Later verses make it clear that, despite the death of the heroine, this is no senti-mental love song, but a light-hearted parody. Even if you knew only the first verse and the refrain, however, it would be clear that they are both written with the same rhyme scheme; the second and fourth lines rhyme. They also share the same me-ter. The odd-numbered lines have eight syllables, the even-numbered lines seven, and all lines alternate stressed and unstressed syllables. This pattern is continued in the later verses. The second and fourth lines of *all* the verses contain the same rhyme, but that is not an essential part of the strophic structure. The continuity of the meter, though, *is* essential. It means that all the verses, including the refrain, can be sung to the same tune.

Strophic form uses the same music for each stanza. If you have ever sung a hymn, you are familiar with strophic form. *(© posztos/ShutterStock)*

Song Cycle: A set of art songs that share a common idea or central theme and that are intended to be performed as a unit. This form originated in the Romantic period and remained popular in the 20th century.

Art Song: A song in the classical tradition (as opposed to a folk or popular song) that is typically written on a poetic text and features a prominent instrumental accompaniment (usually piano). Art songs often add an extra dimension to the text or reinterpret it in significant and sometimes surprising ways. In German, *Lied* (pl. *Lieder*); in French, *mélodie*.

Lied (pl. Lieder): An art song. Because of the tremendous number produced in the 19th century by German-speaking composers, it became standard to use the German term.

Strophic poems are easy to set to music. The melody for the first stanza can be used for every other stanza as well. Music using the strophic form could be described simply as AAAA (etc. for each stanza).

A more complex example of strophic form is Franz Schubert's (1797–1828) song *Die Post*, from his **song cycle** *Winterreise* (*Winter's Journey*). Schubert was an early Romantic composer whose career intersected with the late Classical period. Despite his brief lifetime, he is remembered as perhaps the most significant com-poser of **art songs**, an artful combination of music and poetry. Known also as **lieder** (sing. **lied**; in the original German, the words would be capitalized), these are short settings of poetic texts, usually for a solo singer accompanied by piano. Understanding the text and its relationship to the music is usually crucial to ex-periencing an art song. We will examine how music and poetry work together in another chapter. For now, though, we will focus on the musical form of two of Schubert's art songs.

Listen to *Die Post* carefully. It is easy to grasp the idea that, in this song, the same music is presented twice, repeated virtually note for note. You may have to listen several times, though, before you really *hear* this repetition and experience it as an important fact about the music. See if you can find the exact point at which it begins. Can you tell that the music is stopping and starting over again? Does Schubert call attention to this repetition, or does he try to disguise it?

Focus On
Franz Schubert (1797–1828)

Franz Schubert (1797–1828). In this famous contemporary depiction of a "Schubertiade," Schubert sits at the piano among patrons, artists, and friends gathered in an intimate space to enjoy an evening of his music as well as other artistic performances. *(Erich Lessing/Art Resource, NY)*

Austrian composer. The only canonic Viennese composer native to Vienna, he made seminal contributions in the areas of orchestral music, chamber music, piano music, and, most especially, the German lied. The richness and subtlety of his melodic and harmonic language, the originality of his accompaniments, his elevation of marginal genres, and the enigmatic nature of his uneventful life have invited a wide range of readings of both man and music that remain among the most hotly debated in musical circles. (Robert Winter, *Grove Music Online.*)

Grove Music Online.

Franz Schubert is the model of the Romantic artist. Living on the fringes of society, misunderstood by all but a close circle of friends, he died at the age of 31 before reaching what might have been his full potential. Nevertheless, he left behind an astonishing body of work, including over 600 songs for voice and piano that have virtually defined the genre of the art song ever since.

What makes his music clearly Romantic, rather than Classical, is his distinctive and imaginative use of the musical language he inherited. Schubert's harmonies, in particular, tend to go in surprising directions. Thus, they upset, or at least confuse, the classically based expectation that music will be universally comprehensible. Do you encounter any surprises in listening to *Die Post*?

LEARNING TO LISTEN GUIDE

TAKE NOTE OF FORM

What to Listen For: The repeat of the music of the first stanza during the second stanza; the expressive change that occurs halfway through each.

Streaming audio track 41.
Interactive Listening Guide ILG-11
will allow you to follow the
strophic form of *Die Post* visually.

Schubert: *Winterreise, Die Post*
Date: 1828
Instrumentation: Baritone and piano
Key: B major (transposed)
Meter: $\frac{6}{8}$ (a compound meter with two fairly rapid groups of three notes per measure)
Form: Strophic
Core Repertory Connection: Schubert's *Winterreise* is also discussed in Chapter 10.

TIME	SECTION	ORIGINAL TEXT	TRANSLATION	COMMENT
0:00	First stanza	*Von der Straße her ein Posthorn klingt.* *Was hat es, daß es so hoch aufspringt,* *Mein Herz?*	From the street a posthorn sounds. What is it that makes you spring up so eagerly, My heart?	The singer enters after a short piano introduction.
0:36	Change in tone	*Die Post bringt keinen Brief für dich.* *Was drängst du denn so wunderlich,* *Mein Herz?*	The post brings no letter for you. Why, then, are you feeling these strange urges, My heart?	The mood of the music shifts dramatically.
1:05	Second stanza	*Nun ja, die Post kommt aus der Stadt,* *Wo ich ein liebes Liebchen hat,* *Mein Herz!*	Well, then, the post comes from the city, Where I had a dear beloved, My heart!	The initial music is repeated.
1:41	Change in tone	*Willst wohl einmal hinüberseh'n,* *Und fragen, wie es dort mag geh'n,* *Mein Herz?*	Do you want to take just a look across, And ask how things are going there, My heart?	The shift in mood is repeated as well.

If You Liked This Music. . .
Strophic Songs by the Troubadours

Many popular songs and folk songs are in strophic form. Perhaps the oldest repertory to follow this form consistently—and the model for all later ones—is the *troubadour* songs of the late Middle Ages. Some of the best-known troubadours are the following:
- **Bernart de Ventadorn** (fl. ca. 1130-40–1190-1200)—The most famous of all the troubadours, equally celebrated for both poetry and music
- **Jaufre Rudel** (fl. 1120–1147)—Known for expressing the pain and devotion of love for a distant—and hence unattainable—object: an important troubadour theme
- **Beatriz de Dia** (fl. late 12th century)—One of the few women troubadours, also called a *trobairitz*

The songs of these and other troubadours have been performed and recorded in a wide variety of ways. Listening to several such recordings will give you a good understanding of the different approaches to interpreting music in which the same melody is repeated while the words change. A great deal of information about the troubadours can be found at the website *The Medieval Lyric* (see companion website), which also includes several audio links.

Modified Strophic Form

Die Post is just one example of strophic form. The composer working in strophic form writes these songs so that the same music is repeated for each stanza. As we have seen, this is the same structure found in many folk songs, ballads, and popular music. A variation on strophic form is **modified strophic form**. Modified strophic form is a song structure for which the composer changes the music for some stanzas of the work. For example, the opening and closing stanzas may use the same music while others may introduce changes to the melody, key, or rhythm to set them apart. A talented performer may make such changes as well, so technically any strophic form may be modified.

Modified strophic form allows a text to be set to music in a way that brings each stanza to life. An example of this is Franz Schubert's song *Der Lindenbaum* (like *Die Post*, from the song cycle *Winterreise*). Even without understanding the German text, you can hear the modified strophic form. After an introductory prelude on the piano, the singer enters with a melody that is so straightforward and memorable it sounds almost like a folk song. When the singer repeats the melody, after an interlude on the piano, it sounds different—darker and more somber. While keeping the same melody, Schubert has moved it from a major into a minor key. In the next section, the music becomes more dramatic and contrasts significantly from the opening melody. Finally, that melody returns exactly as it sounded at the beginning but with different words.

Modified Strophic Form: A form of vocal music in which each verse, or strophe, of the text is sung to a different, although related, section of music.

A Pastoral Scene, 1858, by Asher Brown Durand (1796–1886).
(Gift of Frederick Sturges, Jr.)

The music of this song follows the changing emotional state of the singer, from a gentle, melodious beginning of calm to agitation and back to a state of composure. The modified strophic form successfully conveys this evolving emotional state by repeating the same melody but changing it from one appearance to the next.

LEARNING TO LISTEN GUIDE

TAKE NOTE OF FORM

What to Listen For: The shifts in the music that mark the three stanzas and make each different from the others.

Schubert: *Winterreise, Der Lindenbaum*
Date: 1828
Instrumentation: Baritone and piano
Key: D major (transposed)
Meter: $\frac{3}{4}$ (three moderately-paced beats per measure)
Form: Modified strophic
Core Repertory Connection: Schubert's *Winterreise* is also discussed in Chapter 10.

Streaming audio track 40.
Interactive Listening Guide ILG-10
will allow you to follow
the modified strophic form
of *Der Lindenbaum* visually.

TIME	SECTION	ORIGINAL TEXT	TRANSLATION	COMMENT
0:00	Piano introduction			The piano plays an extended prelude before the singer begins.
0:25	First stanza	*Am Brunnen vor dem Thore* *Da steht ein Lindenbaum;* *Ich träumt' in seinem Schatten* *So manchen süßen Traum.* *Ich schnitt in seine Rinde* *So manches liebes Wort;* *Es zog in Freud' und Leide* *Zu ihm mich immer fort.*	At the well by the gate There stands a linden tree; I dreamed in its shadow So many a sweet dream. I carved in its bark So many loving words; It drew me, in joy and sorrow Back to it always.	The singer introduces a lyrical, highly memorable tune.
1:27	Piano interlude			The opening music in the piano returns, but with a shift to the minor, which makes it sound more serious. This reflects a change in the text.
1:39	Second stanza	*Ich mußt' auch heute wandern* *Vorbei in tiefer Nacht,* *Da hab' ich noch im Dunkel* *Die Augen zugemacht.*	Today I again had to wander By in deepest night, And in the dark I once again Closed my eyes.	The singer repeats the melody but remains in the minor, confirming the change in mood.

TIME	SECTION	ORIGINAL TEXT	TRANSLATION	COMMENT
2:08	Shift to major	*Und seine Zweige rauschten,* *Als riefen sie mir zu:* *Komm her zu mir, Geselle* *Hier find'st du deine Ruh!*	And its branches rustled As if they were calling to me: "Come here to me, fellow, Here you will find your rest."	Halfway through the stanza, the music returns to major, once again changing the mood. This is a reflection of the text as well.
2:39	Interlude	*Die kalten Winde bliesen* *Mir grad' in's Angesicht,* *Der Hut flog mir vom Kopfe,* *Ich wendete mich nicht.*	The cold winds blew Straight into my face, My hat flew from my head, I did not turn away.	There is no piano introduction this time. The interlude begins with music that is louder and more emphatic than anything heard previously. This once again reflects a change in the text.
3:16	Third stanza	*Nun bin ich manche Stunde Entfernt von jenem Ort,* *Und immer hör' ich's rauschen:* *Du fändest Ruhe dort!*	Now I am many hours Distant from that place, And I still hear the rustling: "You would have found rest there!"	The music of the first stanza returns for the final lines of text.
4:35	Piano postlude			The piano repeats its introductory music to conclude the song.

Variation Form

Variation Form: Also known as theme and variations. A form of (usually instrumental) music that first presents a theme and then presents that theme in a series of alterations that typically retain the length and harmonic structure of the original theme but change some of its other characteristics.

Coda: Literally "tail," in Italian. Used to describe the final added measures of a composition that do not fit into the standard form of the piece but follow logically from the preceding material.

Variation form, also known as theme and variations, is one of the most commonly used musical forms. This may be because it offers a distinct pattern that is easily heard: variety unfolds within a series of repetitions.

You have already heard an example of variation form. In Count Basie's *Lester Leaps In*, the AABA pattern is repeated 33 times, each time sounding different but with the underlying pattern intact. Thus, *Lester Leaps In* can be considered a theme and variations without the theme.

In most variation forms, the theme is explicitly stated at the beginning and is sometimes repeated at the end as well. An example is the sixth movement of Mozart's *Gran Partita*, which the composer titled *Tema con variazioni* (theme with variations). The movement consists of a melody, which is stated only at the beginning, six variations, and a **coda**. This term, which means "tail" in Italian, is used to describe a short conclusion that does not fit into the form of the rest of the piece, even though it follows logically from what comes before.

Perhaps the first thing to note about this piece is that the theme and six variations last 10 minutes and 26 seconds, compared to 16 minutes and 32 seconds

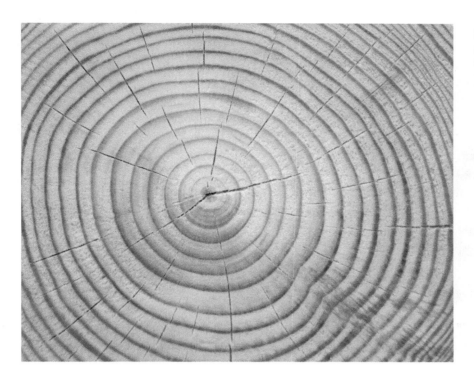

A repetitive pattern in nature.
We typically crave a certain amount of repetition in music.
(© sspopov/ShutterStock)

for the entire 33 variations in *Lester Leaps In*. Obviously, the individual sections are longer, which makes the form more difficult to follow. However, clear signposts also show when one variation has ended and another is beginning. Mozart signals this in a variety of ways. He may change the tempo—the rate at which the music moves—as between variations 4 and 5. He may alter the meter—the way beats are grouped together—as between variations 5 and 6. He may change the **articulation**—the extent to which the notes are joined together or separated. Some important, highly audible features of the music change each time a new variation begins. Notice, for example, the smooth, **legato** phrases that begin variation 2. Thus, the form is also much less seamless than that of *Lester Leaps In*, where the beginning of a new variation is frequently marked by none of these changes.

The easiest way to follow the music is to become familiar with the form of the melody, since that form is repeated in each of the variations. Mozart's melody, like many pop songs, has two sections, which can be labeled A and B, and the first section is repeated (AA). Unlike that in *I Got Rhythm*, however, the B section is not followed by a repeat of the A section but by its own repeat. Thus, the overall form is AABB.

The difference between the A and B sections is the same as that between a question and an answer, or between what are sometimes called an antecedent and a consequent statement.

      A—Don't you think that it's a fine day?
      B—Yes, I think it is quite fine.
Notice that this example is carefully constructed. If it read
      A—Don't you think that it's a fine day?
      B—Yes, I think that it's a fine day.

Articulation: In musical performance, the extent to which notes are joined together or separated.

Legato: An articulation mark directing the performer to play the affected notes in a smooth, connected style. (Contrast **staccato**).

The Juilliard String Quartet in performance. Today's string quartets still tend to play the music exactly as written—which the audience expects, as well. *(Library of Congress Prints and Photographs Division Washington, D.C. 20540 USA)*

Classical musicians often appear formal and reserved when compared to their counterparts in the pop music world. When an ensemble like the Juilliard String Quartet performs a piece with repeats marked by the composer, they generally play the music the same way both times. That doesn't necessarily mean that this is what Mozart and other classical composers expected. Eighteenth-century musicians, at least, felt free to add to the music in much the way jazz musicians do today, especially when sections were repeated. Today's classical performers may feel more comfortable doing this than those of a generation ago. In most cases, however, repeats marked by the composer are still observed literally.

it would be needlessly repetitious. On the other hand, if it read

> A—Don't you think that it's a fine day?
> B—Yes, I like fried chicken too.

it would be incoherent. To make an interesting exchange, the two statements have to relate to one another yet preserve something of their own identity. The same is often true for the two halves of a melody. If you listen carefully, you will also hear that each half of the melody divides into two halves. To better appreciate what Mozart is doing, consider the following examples.

Too repetitious:

> A—Don't you think that it's a fine day? Don't you like this fine, fine weather?
> B—Yes, I think that it's a fine day. Yes, I like this fine, fine weather.

Incoherent:

> A—Don't you think that it's a fine day? Where did you put my keys just now?
> B—Yes, I like fried chicken too. I want a new refrigerator.

Just right:

> A—Don't you think that it's a fine day? Wouldn't a picnic be quite nice?
> B—Yes, I'll bring some delicious fried chicken. What a fine day to eat outside!

It isn't Shakespeare, of course, but it makes good sense, while avoiding needless repetition. The final phrase does repeat some words from the initial question, making it clear that speaker B has heard what speaker A said earlier. The conversation "hangs together."

Now look at this exchange:

> A—Don't you think that it's a fine day? Wouldn't a picnic be quite nice?
> B—Yes, I'll bring some delicious fried chicken. What a fine day to eat outside and have a picnic on the grass!

Note how the last sentence has been extended, setting up a rhythm of accented syllables that makes it sound quite final: What a fine day to *eat* out-*side* and *have* a *pic*-nic *on* the *grass*! This little conversation is constructed so as to take full advantage of the rhythms and patterns inherent in spoken language. These patterns should also be clearly audible in any restatement of the same ideas, even if the wording is changed significantly. This is essentially what musical variation does; it changes the wording while retaining the ideas and the order in which they are presented.

Mozart's theme and variations do exactly the same thing, but their content consists of notes, not words. Each variation, however different it sounds from the original melody, follows the same pattern. Once you grasp it, you can follow its repetitions through the entire piece, just as you can in *Lester Leaps In*.

As you listen to the theme of Mozart's *Tema con variazioni* movement, pay particular attention to the following signposts:

 A—First half: A melodic phrase is stated by the clarinet with a light accompaniment.

  ("Don't you think that it's a fine day?")

 A—Second half: The full ensemble enters with a faster moving phrase, as though supplying a sudden inspiration that also completes the thought.

  ("Wouldn't a picnic be quite nice?")

 B—First half: The clarinet begins again tentatively and is joined by the other instruments as though in agreement.

  ("Yes, I'll bring some delicious fried chicken.")

 B—Second half: Accompanied by a smaller group of instruments, the clarinet plays another phrase that complements the very beginning.

  ("What a fine day to eat outside...")

 But it then extends the phrase as the full ensemble joins in for an emphatic conclusion.

  ("...and have a picnic on the grass.")

Focus On
The Clarinet

Generic term for a wind instrument sounded by a single beating reed; in the system of Hornbostel and Sachs such an instrument is classified as an aerophone. The clarinet of Western art music (from which the generic term is taken) is of essentially cylindrical bore and is made in a variety of sizes and tonalities; the soprano instrument pitched in B♭, with the Boehm system of keywork and fingering, is the most widely used today. The tube is usually cylindrical, but occasionally funnel-shaped or ending in a bell. (Janet K. Page, *Grove Music Online*.)

Basset horn. (© *Museum of Fine Arts, Boston /Lebrecht*)

Grove Music Online.

The clarinet, which is featured prominently in the *Gran Partita* along with its now obsolete cousin the basset horn, was a

(continued)

relatively new instrument in Mozart's time. Unlike the oboe and bassoon, which are also used in the *Gran Partita*, these are single-reed instruments. The reed, which is actually made of cane, vibrates against the opening of the mouthpiece, setting up a vibrating column of air within the instrument.

Like other wind instruments, the clarinet can also be overblown to produce higher pitches. The difference is particularly audible on the clarinet, which has two distinct registers—pitch ranges—that sound very different from each other. These registers, at the high and low ends of the clarinet's total range, can be thought of as roughly equivalent to female and male human voices. They are also very different in timbre, making them almost sound like two different instruments. Mozart frequently takes advantage of this fact in his writing for the clarinet; listen for examples as you become familiar with the *Gran Partita*.

The pattern, which is repeated in each variation, is this: An opening, question-like phrase is followed by a more emphatic phrase of equal length, as though to round out the thought and finalize it. The entire "question" is then repeated. The "answer" begins with a more tentative phrase, followed by a more final-sounding one that recalls the opening, and finally by an emphatic, highly rhythmic conclusion. The entire "answer" is then repeated as well. The full theme thus presents a repeated question followed by a repeated answer.

These variations work because the underlying pattern is consistently repeated. As you listen several times and become familiar with the pattern, you will find yourself hearing more in the music, just as you did with *Lester Leaps In*. This is how musical form works; it organizes the events in a piece of music so that those events appear to unfold logically, thus making the music easy to follow. See Table 5.1 highlighting key elements of form in this Mozart piece.

TABLE 5.1 Highlights of the Variations in Mozart's *Gran Partita*

Progression	Comment
Variation 3	Variation 3 is a double variation. Instead of repeating the A and B parts, Mozart writes what amounts to a new variation each time, so that the AABB form becomes AA'BB'. In fact, in both cases, the new variation is so different from the first one that you may hear the form as ABCD. The broader pattern continues, though, because not only is the second half of C reminiscent of the beginning of B, but D is reminiscent of A as well. Thus, the entire variation is like a sandwich, in which a larger conversation surrounds a smaller one.
Variation 4	Variation 4 is in the minor, making it sound more serious. (For more on this, see Chapter 9.) It is as though the conversation has shifted from commenting on the fine weather to observing that it has started to rain.
	Variation 4 is followed by a sustained chord played by all the instruments in the ensemble (as though to say: "Enough of that").
Variation 5	Variation 5 is played much more slowly, so it lasts much longer than the other variations. As though to make up for this, Mozart omits the repeat of the A section (but not the B).
Variation 6	Variation 6 is much faster and concludes with the short coda mentioned above.

LEARNING TO LISTEN GUIDE

TAKE NOTE OF FORM

What to Listen For: The parallel AABB construction that links all the variations, despite the strong contrasts between them.

Streaming audio track 27.
Interactive Listening Guide ILG-6
will take you through the six
variations of this movement
from the *Gran Partita*.

Mozart: *Gran Partita*, K. 361
VI: *Tema con variazioni*
Date: 1781
Instrumentation: Two oboes, two clarinets, two basset horns, four horns, two bassoons, and bass
Form: Theme and variations
Key: B-flat major
Meter: $\frac{2}{4}$ (two fairly rapid beats per measure), final variation in $\frac{3}{4}$ (three quite rapid beats per measure)
Core Repertory Connection: Mozart's *Gran Partita* is also discussed in chapters 3, 6, and 8.

TIME	PROGRESSION	COMMENT
	THEME	
0:00	A—First half	The clarinet plays the opening phrase. ("Don't you think that it's a fine day?")
0:08	A—Second half	The full ensemble completes the thought. ("Wouldn't a picnic be quite nice?")
0:15	Repeat	Everything heard so far is repeated.
0:31	B—First half	The clarinet begins and is joined by the other instruments. ("Yes, I'll bring some delicious fried chicken.")
0:40	B—Second half	The clarinet complements the first phrase, then extends it with the full ensemble. ("What a fine day to eat outside and have a picnic on the grass!")
0:55	Repeat of B	
	VARIATION 1	
1:17	A—First half	
1:25	A—Second half	
1:33	Repeat of A	
1:48	B—First half	
1:57	B—Second half	
2:12	Repeat of B	
	VARIATION 2	
2:36	A—First half	
2:44	A—Second half	
2:52	Repeat of A	
3:08	B—First half	
3:16	B—Second half	
3:32	Repeat of B	

TIME	PROGRESSION	COMMENT
	VARIATION 3	**(SANDWICH)**
3:57	A—First half	
4:06	A—Second half	
4:14	A'—First half	This is a completely new variation of the A part of the theme.
4:21	A'—Second half	The new variation continues.
4:29	B—First half	This sounds like a continuation of A'.
4:38	B—Second half	
4:53	B'—First half	This, in turn, mirrors the initial A of the third variation.
5:01	B'—Second half	
	VARIATION 4	**(MORE SERIOUS)**
5:18	A—First half	Despite the change in mood, the pattern continues. ("Don't you think that it's a rainy day?")
5:27	A—Second half	("Hadn't we better get inside?")
5:35	Repeat of A	
5:52	B—First half	("Yes, I'll gather up what's left.")
6:00	B—Second half	("It's a good thing we got inside before it really started to pour.")
6:16	Repeat of B	
6:30	Sustained chord by the full ensemble.	("Enough of that!")
	VARIATION 5	**(SLOW)**
6:52	A—First half	Now the mood becomes more relaxed and intimate. ("Come sit a little closer.")
7:19	A—Second half	("OK; I think I will, sweetie!")
7:37	B—First half	(Adjusting seating arrangements.)
7:55	B—Second half	("You know, I really like spending time with you." "Yeah, I'm having a good time, too.")
8:33	Repeat of B	
	VARIATION 6	**(FAST, TRIPLE METER)**
9:29	A—First half	This perky conclusion is a complete contrast. ("Hey! The sun's back out!")
9:33	A—Second half	("Aw, shucks! You're right.")
9:38	Repeat of A	
9:46	B—First half	("Maybe we should get going.")
9:51	B—Second half	("Sounds good to me." "Let's do this again sometime.")
10:00	Repeat of B	
10:13	Short coda	("The end!")

Contrast and Return-Based Forms

So far, we have looked only at musical forms based on the principles of repetition and variation. The same music is repeated over and over (strophic form), or it is repeated with changes, either small or large (modified strophic and variation

In History
Mozart's *Gran Partita*

In 1781 Mozart made a fateful decision: He would take up permanent residence in Vienna and attempt to support himself as a freelance musician. For the next ten years, until his death in 1791, he experienced the ups and downs that still plague independent musicians today. It is now widely recognized, though, that he did not die in poverty as commonly believed; he earned enough to keep a horse and carriage and occupy apartments that would be large even by today's standards.

He was able to do so because Vienna was the capital of a large and thriving state—not yet officially an empire—that included much of Eastern Europe and had diplomatic ties throughout the world. The Viennese public was used to hearing the best of Italian music as well as that of German-speaking composers. While there was not yet a standing civic orchestra—the Vienna Philharmonic was not founded until 1842—there were large numbers of musicians for hire and multiple performance spaces for public concerts.

For Mozart, as for most successful composers in the 18th century, opera was the center of his creative universe. He was also greatly in demand as a pianist, and he frequently appeared in piano concertos, a form to which he contributed more masterworks than any other composer. At the subscription concerts he gave yearly, he typically performed a concerto and some symphonic and chamber music, and also improvised.

Music for wind ensemble, however, was not as popular in Vienna as it had been in Salzburg, where Mozart grew up. Thus, the *Gran Partita*, written shortly after his arrival in the capital, was one of the last such works he composed. It thus stands on the dividing line between the concert life of an earlier world and that of today. Because it contains no part for strings apart from the double bass that supports the rest of the ensemble, it is unlikely to be heard at an orchestral concert. There is no modern equivalent, however, for the informal, largely outdoor occasions at which wind music was often heard in Mozart's lifetime. The changes that were taking place in late 18th-century Vienna—changes that Beethoven later capitalized upon—have shaped the world of classical music ever since.

form). Many musical forms, though, are based on contrast and **return**; after the introduction of music that differs distinctly from what has come before, the original music is brought back, producing a rounded form with a satisfying sense of completion. The opening of a piece of music may lead to something different, after which the beginning may then reassert itself. The degree of contrast varies. The contrasting section may be only slightly different from the first, or it may be drastically different. The repeat of the initial music may be literal, or it may present a different version of the initial music: a variant of it. Something extra may be added at the end. The pattern may also continue, with new contrasting sections and further returns of the initial music. We will look now at examples of each of these possibilities.

Return: A compositional technique in which, after the introduction of music that differs distinctly from what has come before, the original music is brought back, producing a rounded form with a satisfying sense of completion.

Ternary Form

The simplest possible return-based form is **ternary form**, in which two contrasting sections are followed by a repeat of the first section. This is also sometimes called ABA form.

Ternary Form: Also known as ABA. A musical structure, either vocal or instrumental, in which an initial section (A) is followed by a significantly contrasting section (B) and a repeat of the original A section, either in its original form or in an easily recognizable variation of it (A').

Minuet: A graceful, triple meter dance popular in the 18th century. Many composers, including later ones, adopted its style and ternary form for independent compositions or the third movement of such works as symphonies and string quartets.

Like most pieces called **minuet** (*menuetto* in Italian), the third movement of Franz Joseph Haydn's (1732–1809) String Quartet in B-flat major, op. 64, no. 3, is in ternary form. The minuet is a dance that was popular in the 18th century and was frequently imitated by composers. In its original form, it was moderate in tempo and very formal; a series of prescribed dance steps was executed within a pattern of eight three-beat measures. Most minuets by classical composers are actually stylized minuets, unintended for dancing since they have phrases of irregular lengths, and the composers often make it hard to find the beat.

The Minuet, **by Giandomenico Tiepolo (1727–1804).** The minuet was a graceful, dignified dance in triple meter with very specifically prescribed steps. (*Scala/Art Resource,* NY)

Thus, minuets written in the Classical period were not necessarily intended for scenes such as the social gathering shown in the photo. The sophisticated and largely undanceable music in the minuets of Haydn and Mozart illustrates the separation of concert music from popular entertainment.

The form of this piece consists of an A section about two minutes long, a B section of the same length (known, confusingly enough, as the trio), and a repeat of the A section. That repeat is literal; at the end of the B section, the composer simply wrote the words *Menuetto da capo.* **Da capo** ("from the head" or, as we would say in English, "from the top") is a way of telling the performers to start over again. Haydn then instructed *Fine* (conclusion) at the end of the A section, indicating that this was where the performers should stop.

Da Capo: Literally, "from the head" or, in English parlance, "from the top." These Italian words instruct the performer to return to the beginning of the piece and play to a specified point.

In listening to this music, you will notice that when the A section is repeated, it is shorter the second time around. This is because both the A and B sections are themselves divided into two parts, each of which is repeated. On the repeat of the A section, the performers usually omit the repeats, as on this recording. Thus, the overall form can be described as AABBCCDDAB. (See Learning to Listen Guide.) For obvious reasons, it is simpler just to call this form ABA, and to refer to the smaller sections as a, b, c and d. As with the other forms we have examined, you may need to listen to this one more than once before you can recognize the beginnings and ends of the sections on your own.

The fifth movement of Mozart's *Gran Partita*, titled *Romanze,* is an example of ABA form with a coda. It begins much more slowly than the Haydn minuet we just listened to. In this case, though, the B section is a striking contrast. The music is much faster, and the meter changes from the first section. Much of the

LEARNING TO LISTEN GUIDE

TAKE NOTE OF FORM

What to Listen For: The large-scale ternary form; the division of each of the three sections into complementary halves.

Haydn: String Quartet in B-flat major, op. 64, no. 3
III: Menuetto: Allegretto
Date: 1790
Instrumentation: Two violins, viola, and cello
Key: B-flat major
Meter: $\frac{3}{4}$ (three fairly rapid beats per measure)
Form: Ternary (ABA)
Core Repertory Connection: Haydn's String Quartet in B-flat major is also discussed in chapters 3, 6, and 7.

Streaming audio track 20.
Interactive Listening Guide ILG-4
will show you through the ABA
structure of the Haydn minuet.

TIME	PROGRESSION	COMMENT
	BIG A	
0:00	First half (little a)	The first violin plays the melody. The conclusion (BUM-bah-BUM-bah-BUM!, etc.) is stated repeatedly for comic effect.
0:18	Repeat of little a	Everything heard so far is played again.
0:36	Second half (little b)	The "ending" of the last section continues into this one.
0:58	Return of the opening	In the middle of little b, the opening returns, creating a small-scale ternary form within this first section of the movement.
1:31	Repeat of little b	The entire second half (little b) is played again.
	BIG B	
2:27	First half (little c)	A new melody is heard.
2:42	Repeat of little c	
2:57	Second half (little d)	The melody is extended further.
3:12	Return of the opening	The middle section is also "rounded off."
3:34	Repeat of little d	
	BIG A	
4:13	Repeat of Big A	The entire first part is played again, but without the internal repeats.
4:31	Second half (little b)	
4:53	Return of the opening	

B section also features a smaller ensemble, with only basset horns, bassoons, and double bass. The A section then returns, and with it, the original tempo, meter and instrumentation.

The coda, unlike the B section, is not a contrast. It simply extends the material of the A section to complete the piece. Thus, the three sections of the piece are approximately equal in length, but Mozart avoids the monotony that might arise from a literal repeat of a long, slow passage.

LEARNING TO LISTEN GUIDE

TAKE NOTE OF FORM AND RHYTHM

What to Listen For: The large-scale ternary construction; the subtle differences between the first and second A sections.

Streaming audio track 26.

Mozart: *Gran Partita*, K. 361
V: Romanze, Adagio—Allegretto—Adagio
Date: 1781
Instrumentation: Two oboes, two clarinets, two basset horns, two horns, two bassoons, and bass
Key: E-flat major
Meter: A section $\frac{3}{4}$ (three slow beats per measure), B section $\frac{2}{4}$ (two rapid beats per measure)
Form: Ternary (ABA) with coda
Core Repertory Connection: Mozart's *Gran Partita* is also discussed in chapters 3, 6, and 8.

TIME	PROGRESSION	COMMENT
0:00	A section	The opening "romance" is slow and lyrical.
3:01	B section	The middle section is a complete contrast: faster and more serious. The meter of the music changes as well.
4:51	A section	The opening returns, and with it, the relaxed mood.
6:25	Coda	The movement concludes with an extension of the A section.

Rondo Form

Rondo: A form popular in the late Baroque and Classical periods in which a first section (A) recurs following alternate sections of music (ABACA, etc).

A **rondo** (*rondeau* in French) is a form based on the same principle as ternary form, that of a contrasting section and a return of the opening. A rondo differs from a piece in ternary form in that the A section returns repeatedly, each time preceded by new material. Thus, a rondo can be described schematically as ABACA etc. The last movement of the Mozart *Gran Partita* is a short and straightforward example of rondo form in which the A section returns twice, the first time note-for-note and the second time in a somewhat different form. A coda follows. The entire movement can therefore be described as ABACA'coda. The first time it is stated, the A section is repeated, and the B and C sections also contain short repeated passages. Because there is so much repetition, and because the piece as a whole is so short, it is very easy to follow.

TAKE NOTE OF FORM

What to Listen For: The multiple returns of the **A** section; the contrasting music that separates them.

Streaming audio track 28.

Mozart: *Gran Partita*, K. 361
VII: Rondeau: Allegro
Date: 1781
Instrumentation: Two oboes, two clarinets, two basset horns, four horns, two bassoons, and bass
Key: B-flat major
Meter: $\frac{2}{4}$ (two rapid beats per measure)
Form: Rondo (ABACA) with coda
Core Repertory Connection: Mozart's *Gran Partita* is also discussed in chapters 3, 6, and 8.

TIME	PROGRESSION	COMMENT
0:00	A section—First half	The movement opens with a perky melody.
0:07	A section—Second half	The second phrase is almost a mirror of the first, but it ends more conclusively.
0:14	Repeat	The entire A section is played again.
0:28	B section—First part	A contrasting idea follows directly after the repeat of A.
0:34	Repeat	It is immediately played again.
0:41	B section—Second part	Another contrasting phrase follows.
0:49	Repeat	It is also played again.
0:56	B section—Third part	Yet another phrase follows, this time in a minor key.
1:03	Repeat	It is also played again.
1:10	A section	The entire section is played again exactly as it was heard before, but it is not repeated.
1:24	C section—First part	Another contrasting idea follows.
1:32	Repeat	It is played again.
1:39	C section—Second part	The music again turns to a minor key.
1:46	Repeat	This phrase is played again as well.
1:54	C section—Third part	The minor key continues.
2:01	Repeat	
2:16	C section—Fourth part	
2:16	Repeat	
2:23	A section	The A music returns, but with different instrumentation and harmony.
2:38	Coda	This emphatic concluding section rounds off the movement and the work.

Sonata Form

Sonata form (also called sonata-allegro form) is one of the most important musical forms ever devised—and also one of the most misunderstood. Sonata form is a type of musical construction often used in the first movement of a multipart

Sonata Form: Also called sonata-allegro form. A flexible form, normally applying to the first movement of a sonata, symphony, or other multimovement instrumental composition, that allows for the exposition of two or more themes, their subsequent development, and then a recapitulation and resolution.

Exposition: In sonata form, the first section, in which two or more themes are presented.

Development: In sonata form, the second section, in which the themes presented in the exposition are taken apart, transformed, and tried out in new keys.

Recapitulation: In sonata form, the third and final section, in which the themes reappear in their original versions but all in the same key, creating a feeling of resolution.

instrumental work, for example a sonata, symphony, concerto, or other composition. Sonata "form" should not be confused with an entire work that may be called a "sonata." It is also not as straightforward as the forms just described, because composers treat it with considerable flexibility, adding or omitting freely.

Sonata form as usually described incorporates three sections:

- **Exposition** (First theme, transition to new key, second theme);
- **Development** (thorough exploration of the main theme and of the central conflicts);
- **Recapitulation** (First theme, transition modified so as to stay in the main key, Second theme).

To understand the logic behind this complex formula, let us return to the first movement of Mozart's Symphony no. 40 and see how Mozart uses it to tell a kind of musical story. In this movement, as in a good story, we meet a musical idea (theme, motive) that will be the central character in what follows. We do not at first see this musical idea in all its fullness and complexity. That must await the unfolding of the plot.

As in most sonata form movements, the statement of the central musical idea is followed by elements that serve to continue the story. In the most basic terms, this means that the music changes key. This is not something that you will easily be able to hear, however. What you will notice is that Mozart follows the initial thematic statement with something different. Thus, the music seems to be leading somewhere rather than settling into rounded phrases and regular stops and starts.

Then comes a major point of arrival, and a new musical idea is introduced. This is the complication in the story, analogous to the love interest, practical obstacle, or unusual situation that makes the rest of the plot necessary. Like the

Across the Arts
How Music Tells a Story

What are the basic elements in a good story and how can music express them? Take a few minutes to write down some ideas. Did your list include the following?
- A central character
- Conflict (either with other character(s) or with a situation)
- Complications that arise as the character faces the conflict
- Resolution of the conflict, either happily or unhappily

Nearly every story, when stripped to its core, can be reduced to these elements.

Why do people buy so many murder mysteries when they already know that somebody will be murdered and that the

crime will be solved? The answer is that this seemingly formulaic plot structure allows for an almost infinite variety of complications and of interactions between characters. Musical form operates in much the same way. People do not listen to music written in standard forms because they want to hear the same forms over and over again. They listen because they are interested in the variety and novelty of the music that those forms may contain. A good composer develops musical "ideas" in much the same way an author develops a character. The question is always this: "What will happen in this music that I don't expect, making me see new possibilities that I had not anticipated?"

initial section of a story, this section of sonata form, consisting of a main theme, a transition, and a contrasting theme, is called the exposition. This is where we meet the music that we will be hearing for the remainder of the piece.

There is one significant difference between this section of sonata form and the plot of a typical story. The composer usually asks for the exposition to be repeated note for note. This is why, as we observed earlier, the first two minutes of the opening movement of Mozart's symphony are heard twice. Not all performers follow this direction. Musical themes are often harder to fix in our minds than human characters, though, since they don't have the distinguishing qualities we expect: sex, age, hair color, marital status, etc. It helps if we are introduced to them more than once.

In a story, the plot and characters are then developed, and in sonata form, the section that follows is likewise called the development. This is the most dramatic and unpredictable part of the form. Just about anything can happen. The development section may last anywhere from less than a minute to five minutes or more—Mozart's lasts barely over a minute. In almost every case, however, it will focus on the main musical theme, just as the development of a story focuses on the central character.

Every story contains a point at which all the central threads in the narrative come together in some kind of resolution. In sonata form, the corresponding point is called the recapitulation. It provides musical resolution, restating the material of the exposition without the change of key. When it is over, you are ready for the piece to conclude, just as you are ready for a story to be over when the central conflicts have been resolved.

Since the recapitulation largely repeats the material of the exposition, the sonata form is like a large-scale ternary structure. However, it is considerably more flexible. The exposition, for example, may contain more than two themes. Almost anything can happen in the development section. The whole movement may be preceded by an introduction, usually in a slower tempo. It may conclude with a coda (remember this means "tail"), which may be quite short or rather lengthy; sometimes the tail actually wags the dog!

Haydn, Mozart, and Beethoven were not following a blueprint. In fact, sonata form was described in writing only after its most famous practitioners were dead. Haydn, the first of these, rarely followed the form exactly. What is surprising is that so many movements by Mozart, Beethoven, and later composers do follow it so closely. The reason is that it works.

As you listen to the first movement of the Mozart symphony, you will see that its structure is close to the "textbook" description of sonata form. After listening to it several times, you should be able to hear—and not just understand intellectually—that this entire eight-minute piece is based on the first three notes played by the violins at the very beginning. Think of this motive as a memorable pair of eyes belonging to the lead actor in a movie. You may notice the actor's eyes the first time he appears on screen. As the story develops, you may then see those eyes register a wide range of emotions, providing access to the character's soul.

Mozart's three-note motive functions much the same way. You understand that it is part of a longer melody. You know that you will continue to hear that melody at crucial points in the form. It is the "eyes," though, that Mozart wants you to notice. As he lets you "see" them over and over again, he virtually forces you to care about them and to become involved in the story. When that story concludes, you may have a sense that something tragic has happened to the central character. At the very least, Mozart has piqued your interest.

LEARNING TO LISTEN GUIDE

TAKE NOTE OF FORM AND MELODY

What to Listen For: The large-scale sonata construction; the many occurrences of the three-note opening motive.

Mozart: Symphony no. 40 in G minor, K. 550
I: Molto Allegro
Date: 1788
Instrumentation: Small orchestra
Key: G minor
Meter: $\frac{4}{4}$ (four rapid beats per measure)
Form: Sonata form
Core Repertory Connection: This music is also discussed in Chapters 1 and 9.

Streaming audio track 35.

TIME	PROGRESSION	COMMENT
	EXPOSITION	
0:00	First theme	After a short introduction, the strings play the opening theme.
0:23	Restatement	The first theme is played again but changed so it leads into what follows.
0:33	Transition	A passage at a louder dynamic level forms the bridge to the next theme.
0:52	Second theme	The contrasting theme is introduced.
1:02	Restatement	This theme is also played again, once again leading to a bridge to the next section.
1:20	Closing section	An emphatic conclusion rounds out the exposition.
1:28	Opening motive	The opening three-note motive is featured in this passage, but without the rest of the theme of which it originally formed a part.
2:02	Repeat	The entire exposition is played again.
	DEVELOPMENT	
4:07	First theme	After some transitional chords, the first theme returns, but it sounds less stable than before.
4:21	Dramatic section	The dynamic level rises, and the music becomes more intense.
4:49	Preparation	The music becomes quieter and seems to be preparing for the return of the first theme. The opening motive (minus the theme) is heard over and over.
5:06	Dramatic outburst	In a surprise move, the orchestra bursts out with several impassioned statements of the opening motive. It eventually subsides.
	RECAPITULATION	
5:21	First theme	Notice how Mozart sneaks the theme in when you are no longer really expecting it.
5:46	Restatement	Once again, the theme is restated. This time, though, it is rewritten in a different way.
5:55	Transition	This passage is rewritten as well and is much longer than it was in the exposition.
6:37	Second theme	The contrasting theme returns.
6:48	Restatement	
7:12	Closing section	This dramatic passage now sounds very final.
7:20	Opening motive	The passage based on the three-note motive is heard again.
7:50	Short coda	A final passage based on the three-note motive rounds out the movement.

These descriptions of musical forms are only generalizations, based on patterns that composers follow over and over. Not all music fits one of these forms. In some cases, a piece that *does* fit may also have something else going on that is equally important. One such piece is the second movement of the Violin Sonata no. 4 by Charles Ives (1874–1954).

Like many 20th-century composers, Ives frequently borrowed established forms from the past and used them in novel ways. The first thing you may notice is that this music is vastly different in style from the pieces we have examined so far in this chapter. Like much modern music, it is highly dissonant—full of challenging harmonic clashes—and disjunctive, with few of the straightforward thematic statements found in the music of earlier composers like Mozart. Singing along to Ives's music might seem difficult.

If you listen carefully, though, you may recognize that this music falls into an ABA ternary form. The movement begins with a slow, quiet section that lasts approximately four minutes. It is followed by a B section that is fast, loud, and disruptive, but that lasts less than a minute. The original tone then returns, even though the music is not identical to what was heard earlier.

However, Ives also had a secret up his sleeve, one that American audiences of his time were particularly prepared to recognize. Just like the Mozart movement discussed above, this one is based primarily on a single theme. The difference is that, in the Ives, the theme is not stated in its entirety until the end of the movement. It is the refrain of the Christian hymn *Jesus Loves Me*. If you know this tune, see if you can pick out the fragments of it that permeate the entire movement. Listen also for the complete statement of the tune that begins at 5:34. (It is foreshadowed by a partial statement in the piano beginning at 4:50.)

The experience of listening to this music is much like that of reading an essay in which the thesis is only presented at the very end. Until that point, you are not sure you know what the work is about. You might then be inspired to go back and reread it in light of your new understanding of its topic. Likewise, someone who is hearing this piece for the first time will only realize in retrospect that *Jesus Loves Me* was the subject of the entire movement. You may wish to listen again to this movement until the fragments of *Jesus Loves Me* imbedded throughout the music become more audible.

LEARNING TO LISTEN GUIDE

TAKE NOTE OF FORM

What to Listen For: The large-scale ABA construction; the gradual clarification of the tune *Jesus Loves Me* as the subject of the music.

Streaming audio track 59.

Ives: Violin Sonata no. 4 ("Children's Day at the Camp Meeting")
II: Largo–Allegro (conslugarocko)–Andante con spirito–Adagio cantabile–Largo cantabile
Date: 1906–1916
Instrumentation: Violin and piano
Key: This movement has no central key.

Meter: This movement has no consistent meter.
Form: Ternary (ABA)

TIME	PROGRESSION	COMMENT
0:00	A section	The slow introductory section contains brief references to the refrain of *Jesus Loves Me*, but they are unlikely to be recognized on first hearing.
3:58	B section	Ives whimsically marked the middle section "Allegro (conslugarocko)," since it is meant to depict boys throwing rocks in a stream. *Jesus Loves Me* is still present.
4:50	A section, highly modified	This is not so much a return of the original music as of the original mood. *Jesus Loves Me* is now heard clearly in the piano part.
5:34	Complete tune	The violin plays the entire refrain of *Jesus Loves Me* at a very slow tempo, marking the emotional high point of the movement.

Multimovement Forms

We have spoken repeatedly of movements within longer works. A movement by Mozart or Haydn is a self-contained musical form, but many works of music have more than one such movement. For example, Mozart's entire Symphony no. 40 consists of four separate movements, and the entire Ives violin sonata consists of three. Each movement can be listened to on its own, but the movements making up each work also belong together. Despite these peculiarities, composers generally organize long works in one of two ways, using the symphonic or suite models.

The Symphonic Model

Think back to the descriptions of the murder mystery or of sonata form earlier in this chapter. These patterns are structural archetypes. They work because they appeal to the human mind's need for adventure and variety on the one hand, and for structure and closure on the other.

Another such archetype is the four-movement pattern found in many classical works. It can be described as beginning with a fast, vigorous movement followed by a slower, more introspective one. This leads to a lighter, dance-like movement and, finally, to a fast and conclusive finale.

Why does this pattern occur so frequently? Probably because it represents a sequence of thoughts or emotions with which most people can easily identify. Have you ever hit upon a new idea, only to be struck by doubts and insecurities, then made a conscious effort to lighten your mood in order to recover your original resolve? If so, you have had "symphonic thoughts."

You have also had "string-quartet thoughts." As an example, let us look at the entire quartet in B-flat major by Haydn (whose third movement we examined earlier as an instance of ternary form). Like many composers, Haydn marked each movement with a designation in Italian. These designations not only tell the performers approximately how fast to play but also often give additional information about how to perform the music. Audience members not already "in the know" may find these designations confusing. For example, on a concert program, this quartet would be listed as follows:

String Quartet in B-flat major, op. 64, no. 3   Joseph Haydn (1732–1809)

Vivace assai
Adagio
Menuetto: Allegretto
Finale: Allegro con spirito

What is the listener to make of this? It helps to know that composers and/or publishers have often grouped their works by opus numbers. The word "opus" (abbreviated op., plural opp., for "opera") means "work" in Latin. It can refer either to a single work or to a group of works published together. Haydn, for example, typically published his string quartets in groups of six.

There may be more in the opus number than meets the eye. While opus numbers are usually in roughly chronological order, it is important to understand that they indicate order of publication, not composition. For example, a work with an opus number over 100 is likely to have been written relatively late in a composer's lifetime. It is always possible, though, that such a work was written earlier and not published until the composer's growing reputation created an increased demand for new works. Within an opus number, composers generally feel free to arrange the individual works in whatever order they wish. Thus, while it appears that op. 64, no. 3 was in fact the third of the op. 64 quartets to be composed, this should not necessarily be taken for granted.

Individual movements within a work are usually referred to by their **tempo marking**: a designation by the composer, usually in Italian, indicating how fast the music is to be played. These tend to fall somewhere on a continuum ranging from very fast to extremely slow. (See Table 5.2.)

Tempo Marking: A designation by the composer, usually in Italian, indicating how fast the music is to be played.

TABLE 5.2 Some Typical Tempo Designations

Prestissimo—As fast as possible

Presto—Extremely fast

Allegro—Fast (literally "lively")

Allegretto—Only moderately fast

Moderato—Neither particularly fast nor particularly slow

Andante—A bit slow (literally "walking")

Adagio—Slow (literally "at ease")

Largo—Very slow (literally "broad")

These terms have no absolute meaning. Since the early 19th century, a composer who wants to indicate precisely how fast a piece should go has had the option of providing a metronome marking, showing how the beats in the music should correspond to the ticking of that notorious musical taskmaster, the metronome.

The traditional mechanical metronome. Johann Nepomuk Maelzel introduced this device in 1815. (© Platslee/ShutterStock)

Many composers, however, have preferred not to do so. For one thing, tempo in classical music usually needs to be more flexible than a ticking metronome will allow. "Metronomic" is actually a term of disapproval among classical musicians. For another, the choice of tempo is often the most distinctly personal decision that a performer makes. Different performers will "feel" the same piece of music very differently and hence perform it at very different speeds. The space in which the music is being played may also affect the choice of tempo: the more resonant the environment, for example, the slower the music may need to go.

The same terms have also had different meanings at different points in history. In the early 18th century, the term *presto* simply meant "fast." By the 19th century, it had come to mean, in Peter Schickele's elegant phrase, "*come un pipistrello fuori dall' inferno*" ("like a bat out of hell").

Taken together, the four movements of the Haydn quartet present the predictable pattern: Fast–Slow–Moderate and Dancelike–Fast. Typically, the first movement is in a slightly irregular sonata form. Much slower and more serious, the *Adagio* is in ternary form, as is the minuet, which we have already examined. The last movement, even lighter in tone than the first, is also in sonata form.

If a performance were to stop after the first two movements, many listeners—especially those accustomed to the typical four-movement structure—might sense that the performance was incomplete. An extroverted piece like the first movement, when followed by an introverted one like the second movement, seems to require a more extroverted conclusion, a kind of emotional ternary form, in fact. While this could be achieved by simply adding a fast-paced finale and omitting the third movement, this lightweight dance piece has long been seen as an important element of the structure as well, a moment of comic relief after the intensity of the slow movement.

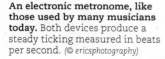

An electronic metronome, like those used by many musicians today. Both devices produce a steady ticking measured in beats per second. (© ericsphotography)

Countless works follow the symphonic model, but a good place to start would be the symphonies of Haydn, since there are so many of them. Although nearly all are outstanding, the following are recommended as a sample:

- No. 44 in E minor—One of the so-called *Sturm und Drang* ("storm and stress") symphonies of Haydn's early maturity, this work is packed with dramatic intensity.
- No. 77 in B-flat major—This delightful work from Haydn's middle years is a good example of the lighter style of the mature Classical period.
- No. 92 in G major ("Oxford")—This incredibly rich work, written less than a decade later, represents what is often called the high Classical style.
- No. 102 in B-flat major—One of the symphonies that Haydn wrote for his visits to London in the early 1790s, this work combines the mature Classical style with some of the power and drama of the *Sturm und Drang* years.

The Suite Model

Mozart's *Gran Partita* presents a more complicated case. Generically, this piece is classified as a serenade. As a piece for wind instruments, it follows a different set of conventions than those for orchestra. Such pieces are often longer, with more individual movements. Thus, the work as a whole has not four movements but seven. They are arranged as follows:

First movement—*Molto allegro* (very lively) sonata form with a slow introduction (almost long enough to constitute a separate movement)
Second movement—Minuet with two trios (ABACA rather than ABA)
Third movement—*Adagio* slow movement
Fourth movement—Another minuet, also with two trios
Fifth movement—*Adagio* slow movement in ternary form, with an *Allegretto* B section
Sixth movement—Theme with six variations, with the theme and first four variations marked "*Andante*," the fifth variation marked "*Adagio*," and the sixth variation marked "*Allegro*"
Seventh movement—Fast, lighthearted finale in rondo form

Compared to the tight structure of the Haydn quartet and of the other works just mentioned, this one offers a veritable banquet of variety. It is a multi-course feast that invites the listener to linger and to remember individual details rather than the experience as a whole.

Thus, although they both come from the Classical period, the Haydn and the Mozart represent seemingly opposite approaches to writing a multimovement piece. The composer can keep the structure relatively simple and predictable, so that it articulates a clearly perceptible formal archetype. He can also make it loose and expansive, inviting the listener to linger and relax.

Composers in the 18th century and earlier frequently exercised the second option. Works put together this way are often called **suites** and may consist entirely of stylized dance pieces. Often, like the theme of the variation movement in Mozart's *Gran Partita* discussed earlier, those pieces are in **binary form**, consisting of two halves of approximately equal length that mirror each other.

Later composers usually followed the first option, often tightening it even more, so that the relationship between the movements became clearer, even as the movements themselves expanded. We will see this process in action when we study Beethoven's Symphony no. 5 in C minor, op. 67, in Chapter 12. First, though, let us take a closer look in the intervening chapters at some of the basic elements of music out of which large-scale forms are put together.

Other Approaches to Form

All of the forms described so far depend on sections that can be easily heard—labeled with capital letters, if you will. Such sections are distinguished from one another by new melodies or by other easily perceived changes in the surface of the music. Form can also be created, though, by changes that are more gradual in nature.

Suite: A set of dances or dance-like pieces, which developed as a genre in the early Baroque era (elements of it go back to the Renaissance). A suite typically has more movements, and is hence less compact, than a multimovement composition from the Classical period or later (e.g., a symphony).

Binary Form: A form, often found in Baroque dance suites, that consists of two approximately equal halves, each usually repeated. The two halves often share thematic material, but it is not necessarily repeated exactly.

Ustad Vilayat Khan playing the sitar. Notice the frets on the long fingerboard; unlike guitar frets, these can be moved, allowing the instrument to play a wide variety of pitches. *(© AP Photo/file)*

Streaming audio track 74.

Steady Growth—Arch Form

Listen to *Raga Bhankar*, performed by the great Indian sitar player Ustad Vilayat Khan, accompanied by Akram Khan on tabla, a pair of small, tuned hand drums.

A **raga** by definition consists of a limited arrangement of pitches similar in nature but not identical to the Western concept of melody. Most Indian ragas do not contain melodic contrasts. As the performance progresses, though, the pace of the melodic activity increases almost imperceptibly. In this example, this activity

Raga: A musical term from India referring not only to a specific series of pitches but also to motivic patterns, specific ornaments, and the general emotional character that should be applied to music based on those pitches.

culminates with a burst of very fast notes at 4:31 and then slows down a bit, but the tempo and volume of the music continue to accelerate. Indian musicians have technical terms for what happens in this piece, but to Western ears what results is a steady increase in musical activity. In such a form, the musical intensity gradually grows toward a high point at or near the end.

A similar **crescendo**, or steady increase in volume, can be heard throughout the famous *Bolero* by Maurice Ravel (1875–1937), a piece from the 20th century. The same thing happens in the "Et in terra pax" section of Bach's Mass in B minor, a piece from the Baroque era. Some pieces of music follow an **arch form**, in which the musical intensity gradually grows toward a high point near the end and then fades away. An example, written in the Romantic period, is the Prelude to *Lohengrin* by Richard Wagner (1813–1883). Wagner's music illustrates musically the descent of the Holy Grail from heaven, concluding with its re-ascent.

The pieces just mentioned originated in different centuries and on different continents. They suggest, then, that the concept of development by steady, incremental growth, with or without a falling away at the end, is close to being a musical universal.

> **Crescendo:** A steady increase in volume.

> **Arch Form:** A form defined not by discrete musical sections or themes but by gradually growing and diminishing musical intensity, with a climax somewhere past the midpoint of the piece.

Forms for Music with Text

The medieval composer Guillaume de Machaut (ca. 1300–1377) is virtually the only person in history widely remembered as both a poet and a composer of the first rank. That this should be so is no coincidence: Machaut worked within a long tradition of poet-musicians, which included the legendary troubadours of a few centuries earlier, as well as their successors, the trouvères. By Machaut's time, the forms in which a poet or composer worked had been standardized into a number of predictable patterns known as ***formes fixes***. Three dominated: the ballade, the rondeau, and the virelai. Unlike the forms described above, these depended on both text and music for their definition. It is thus not surprising that the same person typically wrote both. Let us examine the text of Machaut's virelai *Foy porter*, given here in medieval French and in English translation.

The stanza form of the virelai, in which this song is cast, has been described as ABbaA. This means that a section of text and music, A, is followed by new text and new music, B. The music of B is then repeated with new text, b. The A music is then also repeated with new text, a, followed by the original A music *and* text.

> ***Formes Fixes:*** Forms widely practiced during the 14th and 15th centuries, particularly by French-speaking musicians like Guillaume de Machaut, that required both poetic and musical devices for their articulation. They frequently featured one or more stanzas with an AAB structure and a refrain. The best-known examples are the ballade, the virelai, and the rondeau.

LEARNING TO LISTEN GUIDE

TAKE NOTE OF FORM

What to Listen For: The internal repeats in the text and their coordination with the musical structure.

Streaming audio track 2.

Machaut: *Foy porter*, virelai
Mid-14th century
Instrumentation: Solo soprano
Key: Like all medieval music, this piece is not written in a key in the modern sense.

Meter: Duple
Form: Virelai (ABbaA)

TIME	SECTION	ORIGINAL TEXT	TRANSLATION	COMMENT
0:00	A	*Foy porter,* *honneur garder,* *et pais querir,* *oubeïr,* *doubter, servir* *et honnourer* *vous vueil jusques ou morir,* *dame sans per.*	I will stay loyal, Preserve your honor, Seek peace with you, Obey, Fear, serve And honor you Until I die, Peerless lady.	The first section of the melody is sung to a text that introduces the theme of service and devotion.
0:19	B	*Car tant vous aim, sans mentir,* *qu'on porroit avant tarir* *la haute mer*	For I love you so much, in truth, That one could sooner dry up The deep sea	A new, shorter melody is sung.
0:29	b	*Et ses ondes retenir* *que me peüsse alentir* *de vous amer,*	And hold back its waves Than I could restrain myself From loving you	The shorter melody is repeated, but with a more conclusive ending.
0:40	a	*Sans fausser;* *car mi penser,* *mi souvenir,* *mi plaisir* *et mi desir* *sont sans finer* *en vous que ne puis guerpir* *n'entroublier.*	Without deceit; For my thoughts, My memories, My pleasures And my desires Are continually Of you, whom I cannot leave Or forget even for a while.	The opening melody returns with a new text.
0:58	A	*Foy porter,* *honneur garder,* *et pais querir,* *oubeïr,* *doubter, servir* *et honnourer* *vous vueil jusques ou morir,* *dame sans per.*	I will stay loyal, Preserve your honor, Seek peace with you, Obey, Fear, serve And honor you Until I die, Peerless lady.	The original text **and melody** are repeated.
1:17	B	*Il n'est joie ne joïr* *n'autre bien qu'on puist sentir* *n'imaginer*	There is no joy or pleasure Or any other good that one might feel Or imagine	The shorter melody returns with a new text.
1:27	b	*Qui ne me samble languir,* *quant vo douceur adoucir* *vuet mon amer:*	Which does not seem vain to me, Whenever your sweetness deigns To sweeten my bitterness.	It is repeated, once again with a more conclusive ending.
1:37	a	*Don't loer* *et aourer* *et vous cremir,* *tous souffrir,* *tout conjoïr,* *tout endurer* *vueil plus que je ne desir* *guerredonner.*	Therefore I want to praise And adore And fear you, Suffer everything, Accept everything, Endure everything, More than I desire Reward.	The opening melody is set to yet another new text.

TIME	SECTION	ORIGINAL TEXT	TRANSLATION	COMMENT
1:55	A	*Foy porter,* *honneur garder,* *et pais querir,* *oubeïr,* *doubter, servir* *et honnourer* *vous vueil jusques ou morir,* *dame sans per.*	I will stay loyal, Preserve your honor, Seek peace with you, Obey, Fear, serve And honor you Until I die, Peerless lady.	Once again, the original text and melody are repeated.
2:14	B	*Vous estes le vray saphir* *qui puet tous mes maus garir* *et terminer,*	You are the true sapphire Which can cure And end all my woes,	The shorter melody returns with another new text.
2:25	b	*Esmeraude a resjoïr,* *rubis pour cuers exclarcir* *et conforter.*	The emerald which cheers, The ruby to brighten And invigorate every heart.	Again, it is repeated with a more conclusive ending.
2:36	a	*Vo parler,* *vo regarder,* *vo maintenir* *font fuïr* *et enhaïr* *et despiter* *tout vice et tout bien cherir* *et desirer.*	Your speech, Your look, Your bearing Make one flee And hate And detest All vice and cherish And desire all that is good.	For the final time, a new text appears to the opening melody.
2:55	A	*Foy porter,* *honneur garder,* *et pais querir,* *oubeïr,* *doubter, servir* *et honnourer* *vous vueil jusques ou morir,* *dame sans per.*	I will stay loyal, Preserve your honor, Seek peace with you, Obey, Fear, serve And honor you Until I die, Peerless lady.	The opening text and melody are repeated, also for the final time.

Overall, then, this song is in a multistanza strophic form similar to the most rudimentary ballad. It is also much more, though—a finely coordinated combination of text and music that plays on the subtleties available to a skilled writer of both.

SUMMARY

- Musical form defines the way that a piece of music begins, continues, develops, and ends. It is the overall structural plan of a piece of music as conceived by the composer.

- The most fundamental musical forms are those based on repetition: strophic form, in which the repetition is literal, modified strophic form, in which it is not, and variation form, in which the repeated material is changed in a variety of ways.

- More complex musical forms are often contrast and return-based, with one or more repetitions separated by contrasting material. Examples include ternary form, in which a contrasting middle section is followed by a literal or varied repeat of the opening, rondo form, in which there are two or more contrasting sections, and sonata form, in which the structure of the music resembles that of a story or of an expository essay.
- There are many other options for musical organization, not all of which depend on the perception of discrete sections. Arch forms, in which the music gradually grows and then often fades away, can be found in music throughout the world and from widely diverse periods in Western music.
- The structure of multimovement works may be either tight and compact, as in the four-movement structure of the typical symphony, or loose and more varied, as in the suite and serenade (e.g., Mozart's *Gran Partita*).

KEY TERMS

Arch Form	p. 151	Exposition	p. 142	Return	p. 137
Articulation	p. 131	*Formes Fixes*	p. 151	Rondo	p. 140
Art song	p. 125	Legato	p. 131	Sonata Form	p. 141
Binary Form	p. 150	Lied (pl. Lieder)	p. 125	Song Cycle	p. 125
Bridge	p. 124	Minuet	p. 138	Strophic Form	p. 124
Coda	p. 130	Modified Strophic		Suite	p. 150
Contrast	p. 123	Form	p. 128	Tempo Marking	p. 147
Crescendo	p. 151	Raga	p. 150	Ternary Form	p. 137
Da Capo	p. 138	Recapitulation	p. 142	Variation	p. 123
Development	p. 142	Repetition	p. 123	Variation Form	p. 130

REVIEW QUESTIONS

1. What is strophic form? Why is this, strictly speaking, a poetic form and not a musical one?
2. What is modified strophic form? How does Schubert use this form in his song *Der Lindenbaum*?
3. What is variation form? How does it differ from strophic form?
4. What is a contrast and return-based form, and how does it differ from a form based solely on repetition?
5. How does rondo form differ from ternary form?
6. What is sonata form, and why is it often misunderstood?
7. What are some other ways in which an extended composition can be put together?
8. What are the two most important ways of putting together a multimovement composition? How does each reflect a different understanding of the nature and function of multimovement form?

REVIEW CONCEPTS

1. How can the structure of a piece of music be compared to that of a building? What are the limitations of such a comparison?
2. How does a set of theme and variations like the sixth movement of Mozart's *Gran Partita* differ from Count Basie's *Lester Leaps In*, which is also based on the principle of variation?
3. In what ways is sonata form like a story or an essay? What are some of the limitations of such a comparison?
4. How do composers successfully reuse the same basic musical forms to produce a wide variety of works? Why are listeners willing to listen to these forms again and again?
5. What are the advantages and limitations of each of the approaches to multimovement composition discussed in this chapter?

LISTENING EXERCISES

1. Think of some strophic songs with which you are familiar. (Examples are *America the Beautiful*, *Amazing Grace*, and *Home on the Range*.) Listen to a recording of one or more of them, or try singing them yourself. Do you notice the performer(s) (or yourself) making musical distinctions among the verses, even though they are all sung to the same tune?

2. List some ways in which Schubert either calls attention to the strophic repetition in *Die Post* and/or disguises it. Then listen to *Gute Nacht*, also from the song cycle *Winterreise*, while following the words carefully. Like *Der Lindenbaum*, this song is written in modified strophic form. What changes does the composer make from one stanza to another to reflect the changes in the text? Describe these changes as precisely as you can using the musical vocabulary you have acquired, but feel free to use other terms that occur to you. (Does the music sound "dark," "happy," or "confused?" Feel free to say so. Writing about music is an imprecise art, but, like listening, it can be developed with practice and experimentation.)

3. Listen to the fourth movement of Schubert's "Trout" Quintet, one of the best-known examples of theme and variation form. Can you identify the theme when it recurs in the variations? How does Schubert change it from one variation to the next? (As in the previous exercise, feel free to use a combination of technical and nontechnical vocabulary as you see fit.)

4. Find another piece from the listening list (other than the ones discussed in this chapter) that is in simple ternary (**ABA**) form. How easy, or difficult, is it to recognize this form when you hear it?

5. Listen to a symphony or string quartet by Mozart. The first movements of these works are typically in sonata form, and the last movements are often rondos. Is this true of the work you listened to? How can you tell? How easy are these forms to recognize when you hear them? (Feel free to listen repeatedly if you need to. You may even want to listen to the first 30 seconds of each movement several times before proceeding, to help you remember what the main musical material sounds like.) Can you tell what form(s) the middle two movements are written in?

6. Listen to Ives's Violin Sonata no. 4, Bach's Concerto in D minor for harpsichord and strings, Stravinsky's *Symphony of Psalms*, Crumb's *Black Angels*, and Debussy's Sonata for flute, viola, and harp, each of which has a three-movement structure, in their entirety. (You will need to find a complete recording for the Ives, Bach, and Stravinsky.) Are there patterns that all or most of them follow in the arrangement of movements, at least in regard to tempo? Which one(s) differ(s) from the pattern?

6

Timbre: The Character of a Sound

TAKE NOTE

Timbre, or tone color, is the quality of sound that makes one instrument or voice distinguishable from another. Composers and musicians work with timbre as an expressive tool, much in the way that a visual artist works with colors in a painting. Timbre can greatly affect the mood and atmosphere of a piece of music.

Timbre refers to the sound quality or tone color of a musical instrument or voice. As a basic building block of sound, timbre is one of the most interesting and flexible means of musical expression.

The properties of sound that account for timbre are explained by the science of acoustics. A single musical note played on an instrument is composed of sound waves that create the vibrations detected by the ear. Any note contains several sympathetically vibrating waves that determine the nature or color of the sound. The predominant part of the sound is called the **fundamental**; this is the lowest frequency vibration, which we recognize as the note being played. However, the fundamental is not alone. It is accompanied by related vibrations, or **harmonics**, above the pitch of the fundamental. Harmonics are also known as overtones and partials. The timbre of a sound relies on the intensity, order, and number of harmonics. Every musical instrument, including the human voice, exhibits its own unique mixture of harmonics that help to account for its distinct timbre.

This chapter will help you learn to recognize the contribution of timbre to the active listening experience.

Timbre and Design of Musical Instruments

Most musical instruments contain a sound source and something to make the sound louder. Each helps shape the tone color of the instrument. The violin, the most prominent instrument in the symphony orchestra, is a good example. Its sound is produced by strings and then amplified by the hollow, wooden body of the instrument. The vibrating action of the violin strings produces a given timbre that is further refined by the resonating features of the instrument's sound chamber. When the sound waves produced by the vibrating strings resonate in the body of the instrument, they not only become louder, they become considerably more complex through the addition of overtones that color the sound even more.

The violin is unique, even though similar designs appear in many cultures. The Indian sitar heard in *Raga Bhankar* is also a stringed instrument, but we would never confuse it with a violin. The violin's timbre depends, for example, on the distinctive f-shaped sound holes and on the strings, which may be made out of a variety of materials including pure gut (as was typical until fairly recently), gut wound with metal wire (which produces a "bigger" sound), various types of metal, or entirely synthetic materials that imitate gut. The design of the bow (which uses

Elizabeth Pitcairn with the Red Mendelssohn violin by Stradivari. This instrument may have inspired *The Red Violin*. (© AP Photo/Richard Drew)

Chapter Objectives

⬤ Understand how timbre functions as a basic building block of music and how different instruments produce different timbres.

⬤ Recognize different vocal ranges and how these may interact in a choir and with an orchestra.

⬤ Recognize the way in which music for large orchestras and smaller ensembles takes advantage of instrumental timbres.

⬤ Recognize the performer's role in the production of timbre.

Fundamental: The lowest-frequency vibration of a sounding tone, and the predominant part of the sound.

Harmonics: Related vibrations above the pitch of the fundamental. Also known as overtones or partials.

Vibrato: A subtle pulsating quality, caused by very slight pitch change recurring in a rapid pattern, that is said to increase the expressiveness of a tone.

stretched horsehair) also contributes to the timbre of the violin, and it, too, has changed over time. So have such subtle factors as the height of the bridge (the wooden piece over which the strings are stretched) and the size of the sound post, a small wood dowel providing structural support inside the body of the instrument.

Famous violin makers such as Antonio Stradivari (1644–1737) designed instruments that produced exceptionally rich and beautiful sounds that have lasted for centuries. Intriguingly, there is no widespread agreement as to why Stradivari's violins sound so good. One recent scientific examination of old and new violins showed that the wood used to make the Stradivari models was of a higher density than that found in modern violins, which could account for differences in their resonating properties. But because so many aspects of violin construction affect the tone, holding any single attribute chiefly accountable is probably ill-advised.

Just as significantly as the construction of an instrument, the timbre of the violin is affected by the player, who draws the bow across the strings to produce the sound. Players practice for years to develop a good "tone," which is the product of various, mostly elusive, factors. Sufficient pressure must be applied to the string, but not too much. The pressure needs to be even, but not monotonously so. The bow can be drawn either downward or upward, along its entire length or along only a portion of it, and at varying rates of speed. The fingers of the player's left hand, which "stop" the strings at different points along their length, may oscillate back and forth to produce a trembling quality known as **vibrato**. The production of vibrato may also involve the wrist and the arm. The vibration may be wide or narrow, fast or slow.

The example of the violin points out how its timbre is affected by an incredibly complex set of factors. There is an equally complicated science behind the design, and consequently the timbre, of every instrument. Nevertheless, we can easily learn to recognize the sound of the violin and of other instruments as well.

Sounds of the Voice

The most basic of all musical instruments is the human voice. As far as we know, people have always used their voices to make music. The voice meets the description of a musical instrument given above: sounds produced by the vocal cords are amplified and enriched by resonating through the singer's throat and mouth. The singer can, of course, vary the pitch and change the timbre of the sound in a variety of ways. You may experiment, for example, by pronouncing successively the words "see," "sit," "chaotic," "set," and "cat." The initial vowel sounds in these words are all produced in the front of your mouth. As you speak them, you will notice your tongue moving to progressively lower positions, altering the shape of the space in which the sounds resonate. Now say the words "boot," "book," "obey," "jaw," and "father." The initial vowel sounds in these words are all produced at the back of your mouth, but once again your tongue moves progressively lower while your lips become less rounded and more open. You have learned to change the structure of your "instrument" to produce these sounds without giving the process much conscious thought. Singers knowingly do the same.

Across the Arts
The Painter's Art

What composers and performers do with timbre, or tone color, is often compared directly to the use of color by painters. J.M.W. Turner's painting *Light and Colour: The Morning After the Deluge*, for example, is built on the contrast between different shades of blue and brown, with hints of yellow, red, and black.

The painting, itself inspired by Johann Wolfgang von Goethe's theories of color, represents Moses writing the book of Genesis. In a sense, though, color is itself the subject of the painting, in the same way that tone color is often the most immediately noticeable feature of a work of music.

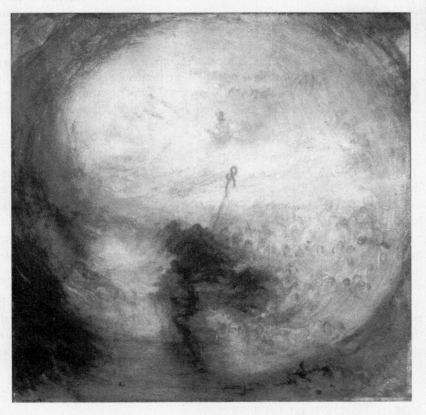

Light and Colour (Goethe's Theory): The Morning After the Deluge, **by William Turner (1775–1851).** This painting is also subtitled *Moses Writing the Book of Genesis.* (Tate, London/Art Resource, NY)

Frank Sinatra (1915–1998). Sinatra was one of the great crooners. (Library of Congress Prints and Photographs Division Washington, DC 20540 USA)

Soprano: The highest-pitched female voice. In operas, sopranos usually play the leading female roles.

Alto: The lowest female singing voice.

Tenor: The highest male singing voice. In operas, tenors usually play the romantic lead.

Bass: The lowest male singing voice. It is commonly used for authority figures in opera, and sometimes for villains

SATB Choir: A choir that follows the standard division into sopranos, altos, tenors, and basses.

Countertenor: A man who sings in a falsetto voice.

Mezzo-soprano: The female vocal range between alto and soprano.

Baritone: The male vocal range falling between tenor and bass.

Voices and Vocal Ranges

Singers speak of three distinct modes of vocal production: chest voice, in which the resonance begins in the chest and is supported by the full power of the singer's lungs; head voice, in which the resonance occurs primarily in the singer's head; and middle voice, which lies between these two extremes. Pitches produced using head voice are higher than those produced using chest voice. Someone who sings falsetto is using head voice exclusively. A singer who yodels moves back and forth between the ranges of head and chest voice. In modern classical vocal technique, though, singers are usually taught to blend all three registers so that the transition between them is as seamless as possible.

There are many other singing styles, of course. Popular singers often "croon," relying to some extent on the microphone to amplify their voices while singing in a more flexible, speech-like manner. Arena rock singers often use a powerful chest voice through a wide part of their register. Classical singers are trained to be highly adaptable to the setting. They must be able to project their voices over the powerful competition of a full orchestra when singing opera but also perform in more intimate styles like the art song.

Every voice is unique. If you have sung in a choir, though, you know that voices are generally grouped into four vocal ranges: **soprano**, **alto**, **tenor**, and **bass** (SATB). A choir that uses all four of these voice types is called an **SATB choir**. In order, these terms refer to high and low women's voices (soprano and alto) and high and low men's voices (tenor and bass). You can hear an SATB choir, both with and without instrumental accompaniment, in the second movement of our core repertory selection, Stravinsky's *Symphony of Psalms*. Some men can sing alto and even soprano, primarily by singing falsetto or relying primarily on the head voice; **countertenors** sing this way exclusively. Some women can also sing tenor. The ranges of **mezzo-soprano**, or second soprano, and **baritone**, or first bass, can be added to fill in the gaps between (first) soprano and alto, and tenor and (second) bass, respectively. Actually, there are very few true alto voices; most choral altos are mezzo-sopranos. Thus, a six-part choir might consist of high and low sopranos, altos, tenors, and high and low basses.

Vocal Timbre in Opera

In most operas, the romantic leads have usually been given to soprano and tenor voices. The higher range of sopranos and tenors may give them enormous power and intensity, especially when they reach for the high notes. Altos and basses, on the other hand, project a darker and less intense timbre. Altos and mezzo-sopranos thus generally fill the role of "supporting actress," while baritones and basses may also portray villains, authority figures (e.g., kings and emperors), and comic roles. There are, of course, exceptions, since great composers often refuse to play

The Tallis Scholars, a much smaller choir that specializes in performance of early music. Much Renaissance choral music was written for a group about this size, although the original performances would have used boys or male falsettists, not women. (© 2004 Jack Vartoogian/Front Row Pictures.)

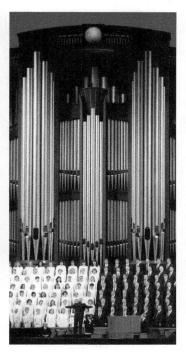

The Mormon Tabernacle Choir, with women in white and men in black. The big, lush sound of this group is appropriate to the large size of a modern concert hall. (© AP Photo/Steve C. Wilson)

by the rules. For example, the male romantic lead in Mozart's *The Marriage of Figaro*, which we will examine in Chapter 11, is a baritone, just like the villain, Count Almaviva. The female romantic lead, Susanna, and the Countess Almaviva are both sung by sopranos, and even a pubescent boy named Cherubino is sung by a mezzo-soprano. (We listened to the Countess's aria *"Dove sono"* in Chapter 3.)

An example of the romantic pairing of soprano and tenor voices can be heard in the love duet that concludes Act I of Giuseppe Verdi's (1813–1901) opera *Otello*. Otello, the military governor of Cyprus, and Desdemona, his wife, are enjoying a brief moment of peace and quiet after a fateful and dramatic scene. In this memorable duet, we look briefly into the souls of both characters. We learn of Otello's early struggles and of the violent emotions that lie just beneath the surface of his commanding presence. We also learn of Desdemona's deep empathy and inner tranquility, so we are all the more surprised when that tranquility is shattered later in the opera. Most importantly, this music encourages us to care deeply about what happens to both of them as the tragedy unfolds. Both soprano and tenor voices fulfill their standard roles in this scene, but an active listener may also be aware of a darker edge to some of Otello's music that foreshadows the events to come.

A very different pairing of soprano and tenor can be heard in the duet "Domine Deus, rex coelestis" from Bach's Mass in B minor. The writing here is comparatively light, with lots of rapid notes and ornaments, and the voices are accompanied only by a small ensemble of flute, violins, viola, and basso continuo. The voices and the instruments blend together, so the singers are not highlighted like Verdi's lovers—who sing primarily one at a time. This piece, by contrast, is a true ensemble.

LEARNING TO LISTEN GUIDE

TAKE NOTE OF TIMBRE

What to Listen For: The strongly contrasting timbres of the tenor and soprano voice, and the way that Verdi uses them to draw contrasts between, but also to unite, the characters.

Streaming audio track 55.

Verdi: *Otello*, Act II, Già nella notte densa

Date: 1887

Instrumentation: Soprano, tenor, and orchestra

Key: G-flat major, changing to D-flat major

Meter: $\frac{4}{4}$, also known as common time (4 slow beats per measure)

Form: Through-composed, with continuous music divided into contrasting sections reflecting the major divisions of the text

Core Repertory Connection: Verdi's *Otello* is also discussed in Chapter 11.

TIME	ORIGINAL TEXT	TRANSLATION	COMMENT
0:00			A subdued orchestral introduction features the timbres of the strings.
0:34	***Otello:*** *Già nella notte densa* *s'estingue ogni clamor.* *Già il mio cor fremebondo* *s'ammansa in quest'amplesso* *e si rinsensa.*	**Othello:** Now in the dark night All noise is quiet. Now my pounding heart Is soothed and calmed in this embrace.	Otello's opening words highlight the romantic qualities of the tenor voice.
1:07	*Tuoni la guerra e s'inabissi il mondo* *se dopo l'ira immensa* *vien quest'immenso amor!*	Let war rage and the world be engulfed, If after great rage Comes this great love!	At the mention of war, the music momentarily becomes more dramatic, but the romantic tenor style returns when Otello speaks of the greatness of his love.
1:36	***Desdemona:*** *Mio superbo guerrier! quanti tormenti,* *quanti mesti sospiri e quanta speme* *ci condusse ai soavi abbracciamenti!* *Oh! com'è dolce il mormorare insieme:* *te ne rammenti?* *Quando narravi l'esule tua vita* *e i fieri eventi e i lunghi tuoi dolor,* *ed io t'udia coll'anima rapita* *in quei spaventi e coll'estasi in cor.*	**Desdemona:** My proud warrior! How many torments, How many sorrowful sighs and how much hope Have led to these sweet embraces! Oh! How sweet to murmur together: Do you remember? When you told of your life as an exile And your brave deeds and long suffering And I listened with my soul enraptured By those fears, and with my heart in ecstasy.	Desdemona's soprano voice contrasts with Otello's tenor, which it follows without break.

TIME	ORIGINAL TEXT	TRANSLATION	COMMENT
3:01	*Otello:* *Pingea dell'armi il fremito, la pugna* *e il vol gagliardo alla breccia mortal,* *l'assalto, orribil edera, coll'ugna* *al baluardo e il sibilante stral.*	**Othello:** I described the clash of arms, the fighting And the vigorous flight into the deadly breach, The assault, when like ivy we clung to the ramparts By our nails, the arrows whistling by.	As Otello describes the clash of arms, the orchestra again surges with drama. This passage showcases the heroic quality of the tenor voice.
3:20	*Desdemona:* *Poi mi guidavi ai fulgidi deserti,* *all'arse arene, al tuo materno suol;* *narravi allor gli spasimi sofferti* *e le catene e dello schiavo il duol.* *Otello:* *Ingentilia di lagrime la storia* *il tuo bel viso e il labbro di sospir;* *scendean sulle mie tenebre la gloria,* *il paradiso e gli astri a benedir.*	**Desdemona:** Then you led me to the shining deserts, To the burning sands, to your native soil; There you told of the torments you suffered And of the chains and the misery of slavery. **Othello:** Your beautiful face ennobled the story With tears, and your lips with sighs; On my darkness there descended glory, Paradise, and the stars to bless.	Desdemona's gentle soprano provides a clearly marked contrast, and Otello's tenor responds in kind.
4:27	*Desdemona:* *Ed io vedea fra le tue tempie oscure* *splender del genio l'eterea beltà.* *Otello:* *E tu m'amavi per le mie sventure* *ed io t'amavo per la tua pietà.* *Desdemona:* *Ed io t'amavo per le tue sventure* *e tu m'amavi per la mia pietà.*	**Desdemona:** And from your dark temples I saw The ethereal beauty of your soul shine forth. **Othello:** And you loved me for my misfortunes, And I loved you for your pity. **Desdemona:** And I loved you for your misfortunes, And you loved me for my pity.	Desdemona's brief comment is followed by words taken directly from Shakespeare. The two voices blend together, showcasing the compatibility of the tenor and soprano timbres.
5:33	*Otello:* *Venga la morte! e mi colga nell'estasi di quest'amplesso* *il momento supremo!* *Tale è il gaudio dell'anima che temo,* *temo che più non mi sarà concesso* *quest'attimo divino* *nell'ignoto avvenir del mio destino.*	**Othello:** Let death come! And in the ecstasy Of this embrace Let the supreme moment take me! Such is the joy in my soul that I fear, I fear that never again will I be granted Such a divine moment In the unknown future of my destiny.	Otello expresses his deepest (and prophetic) fears in a passage of great lyricism.

TIME	ORIGINAL TEXT	TRANSLATION	COMMENT
6:27	**Desdemona:** *Disperda il ciel gli affanni* *e Amor non muti col mutar degli anni.*	**Desdemona:** Let heaven dispel these fears, And may love not change with the changing years.	In a long, descending melodic arc, Desdemona seeks to reassure him.
6:45	**Otello:** *A questa tua preghiera* *"Amen" risponda la celeste schiera.* **Desdemona:** *"Amen" risponda.*	**Othello:** To this your prayer May the heavenly host reply "amen." **Desdemona:** May it reply "amen."	Otello responds with an appeal that is immediately echoed by Desdemona.
7:12	**Otello:** *Ah! la gioia m'innonda* *si fieramente . . . che ansante mi giacio.* *Un bacio . . .* *Un bacio . . . ancora un bacio.* *Già la pleiade ardente in mar discende.* **Desdemona:** *Tarda è la notte.* **Otello:** *Vien . . . Venere splende.* **Desdemona:** *Otello! . . .*	**Othello:** Ah! Such fierce joy overwhelms me . . . That I lie gasping. A kiss . . . A kiss . . . yet another kiss. Already the bright Pleiades sink into the sea. **Desdemona:** The night is late. **Othello:** Come . . .Venus shines forth. **Desdemona:** Othello! . . .	Otello's kiss is followed by a final blending of the two voices.

LEARNING TO LISTEN GUIDE

TAKE NOTE OF TIMBRE

What to Listen For: The contrast in timbre between the soprano and tenor voices, and the ways in which they interact with the accompaniment.

Streaming audio track 13.

Bach: Mass in B Minor, Gloria, "Domine Deus, rex coelestis"

Date: 1723–1733

Instrumentation: Soprano and tenor solo, with light orchestral accompaniment

Key: G major

Meter: $\frac{4}{4}$, also known as common time (four rapid beats per measure)

Form: Concerted duet with ritornellos

Core Repertory Connection: Bach's Mass in B Minor is also discussed in chapters 2 and 9.

TIME	ORIGINAL TEXT	TRANSLATION		COMMENT
0:00				A flute solo introduces this charming duet for a soprano and a tenor.
0:52	*Domine Deus,* *Rex coelestis,* *Deus Pater omnipotens.* *Domine fili unigenite,* *Jesu Christe altissime.* *Domine Deus,* *Agnus Dei,* *Filius Patris.*	Lord God, king of heaven, God the almighty Father. The only begotten Son of God, Jesus Christ most high. Lord God, Lamb of God, Son of the Father.		The flute continues to play, and to interject occasional solos, as the voices sing the text.

Focus On
Countertenors

A male high voice, originally and still most commonly of alto range, though the title is increasingly employed generically to describe any adult male voice higher than tenor. Historically, it derived in England from the contratenor line in late medieval and Renaissance polyphony, via *contratenor altus* ("high contratenor"), which—used interchangeably—became "countertenor" and "altus," then alto (as in Italian nomenclature) and, later still, even "male" alto. (Peter Giles and J.B. Steane, *Grove Music Online*.)

Alfred Deller (1912–1979). This English countertenor contributed significantly to a revival of interest in early music. (© *Lebrecht Music and Arts Photo Library/Alamy*)

David Daniels (b. 1966). This American countertenor began his musical studies as a tenor. (© *2007 Jack Vartoogian/Front Row Pictures.*)

Although the countertenor is considered an emblem of early music, the prominence of this voice type in today's classical performance world is actually unprecedented. Countertenors have performed and recorded repertory ranging from Gregorian chant and troubadour songs from the Middle Ages to lieder and operatic roles that were clearly written for other kinds of voices. This was true of the earliest generation of countertenors, like Russell Oberlin (b. 1928) and Alfred Deller (1912–1979), and has become even more so with the emergence of the latest generation, represented by David Daniels (b. 1966). Stephen Foster, the composer of *Camptown Races* and *Oh! Susanna*, has been recorded by countertenor Jeffrey Dooley.

Many Voices, One Timbre: The Choir

Choral timbres vary from one work and performance to the next. The recording of the Bach B minor Mass heard here, by the English Baroque Soloists and the Monteverdi Choir conducted by John Eliot Gardiner, uses a choir of 26 singers (enlarged to 32 later in the work). This same music has also been recorded, however, with much larger choirs, and also with only one singer on each part. Not surprisingly, the size of the choir makes a vast difference in its sound. A large choir produces a lush, sensuous sound, while a small one produces a lean, clear one. A big choir can make a fast piece, like the opening chorus of Bach's Gloria, sound mushy, while a small choir can leave a slower work, like the "Gratias agimus tibi" section of the Gloria, sounding a bit thin.

Even choirs of comparable size can sound very different. For one thing, directors often fill places in the choir by audition, so they can select not only the best singers but the ones whose voices best suit the kind of choral sound they desire. A good director can also explain to choir members how to produce different timbres in different pieces.

Choirs often sing a cappella—without instrumental accompaniment. Regardless of the composition of the choir and its accompaniment, though, choir directors prize the "blend" of a good ensemble, in which the individual voices lose themselves in the sound of the whole. A good choir, like a string orchestra but unlike, say, a marching band, presents a continuous timbre from the high to the low end of its range.

John Eliot Gardiner's Monteverdi Choir has a distinctive sound because Gardiner uses women for the soprano part and countertenors for the alto part. This does not correspond to any historical precedent. Bach used boys to sing the upper parts. As Gardiner himself has explained, he simply became convinced that women could handle the demands of the difficult upper part better. The fact that the age of puberty has dropped significantly since Bach's time is also a contributing factor. Prior to puberty, a boy's voice has a higher range. Bach and other

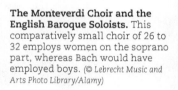

The Monteverdi Choir and the English Baroque Soloists. This comparatively small choir of 26 to 32 employs women on the soprano part, whereas Bach would have employed boys. *(© Lebrecht Music and Arts Photo Library/Alamy)*

Baroque composers worked with 16- and 17-year-old boy sopranos who had not yet undergone puberty, but who had considerable musical experience. Boys of that age today, regardless of their interest in music, are already tenors and basses.

Listen to Josquin's *Missa "L'homme armé" super voces musicales*, which was written for a four-part choir. The uppermost part stays in a relatively low range, making it easier to perform this work with a choir consisting entirely of adult males, which is how it would have been sung in Josquin's time. The Tallis Scholars, directed by Peter Phillips, is a modern group that uses women for the upper parts. Like many Renaissance choirs, though, it is very small by modern standards, generally using only two singers per part. The result is a clear and sonically appealing ensemble that, paradoxically, conforms to contemporary ideas about what Renaissance music should sound like.

Voice and Orchestra: Berlioz's *Roméo et Juliette*

Hector Berlioz, composer of *Roméo et Juliette*, is widely considered to have been a wizard with the orchestra. Using a larger orchestra than most of his contemporaries, Berlioz experimented widely with instrumental timbres, with often stunning effects. We will look at an example of his orchestral writing later in this chapter. *Roméo et Juliette*, though, shows that Berlioz was also an expert at manipulating vocal timbres and combining them with those of the orchestra.

In this work, Berlioz calls for two large STB (soprano, tenor, and bass) choirs, representing the Montagues and the Capulets, a small choir consisting of four altos, four tenors, and four basses, a solo alto, a solo tenor, and a solo bass, the latter representing Friar Lawrence. The small choir is used as a narrator; it tells portions of the story, singing in a manner resembling recitative in opera (see Chapter 11).

After the instrumental introduction, titled *Combats—Tumulte—Intervention du Prince* (*Fights—Tumult—Intervention of the Prince*), the *Récitatif choral* begins with the small choir, supplemented by the solo alto and tenor, describing the situation:

LEARNING TO LISTEN GUIDE

TAKE NOTE OF TIMBRE AND TEXTURE

What to Listen For: The use of the choir as narrator, resulting in some unusual choral sonorities with minimal orchestral accompaniment.

Streaming audio track 46.

Berlioz: *Roméo et Juliette, Récitatif choral*

Date: 1839

Instrumentation: Alto and tenor solo, small choir, and orchestra

Key: Variable keys

Meter: Variable meters

Form: Varied

Core Repertory Connection: Berlioz's *Roméo et Juliette* was also discussed in Chapter 3.

TIME	ORIGINAL TEXT	TRANSLATION	COMMENT
0:00	*D'anciennes haines endormies* *Ont surgi comme de l'enfer;* *Capulets, Montagus, deux maisons* *ennemies,* *Dans Vérone ont croisé le fer.* *Pourtant de ces sanglants désordres* *Le Prince a réprimé le cours,* *En menaçant de mort ceux qui malgré* *ses ordres* *Aux justices du glaive auraient encore* *recours.* *Dans ces instants de calme une fête est* *donnée* *Par le vieux chef des Capulets.*	Old hatreds that had fallen asleep Have re-emerged as if from hell. The Capulets and the Montagues, two rival houses, Have come to blows in Verona. Yet the prince has stopped These bloody conflicts in their tracks, Threatening those who, against his orders, Have sought out violent justice, with death. At this moment of calm the aged leader Of the Capulets gives a party.	The choir sings *a cappella*, but its words are punctuated by chords in the harp and in the brass section of the orchestra.
1:12	*Le jeune Roméo, plaignant sa destinée,* *Vient tristement errer à l'entour du* *palais;* *Car il aime d'amour Juliette, la fille* *Des ennemis de sa famille.*	The young Romeo, lamenting his destiny, Sadly wanders outside the palace; For he is deeply in love with Juliet, The daughter of his family's enemies.	The solo alto then sings the words that follow without accompaniment of any kind.
1:41	*Le bruit des instruments, les chants* *mélodieux* *Partent des salons où l'or brille,* *Excitant et la danse et les éclats joyeux.*	The noise of the instruments, the melodious singing Drift from the gleaming, golden chambers, Where they arouse both dancing and joyous applause.	Another chord in the harp signals the re-entry of the choir.
1:56	*La fête est terminée et quand tout* *bruit expire,* *Sous les arcades on entend* *Les danseurs fatigués s'éloigner* *en chantant.*	The party is over, and when all the noise dies down, Under the arcades the tired dancers Can be heard singing their way home.	There follows a brief orchestral interlude, suggestive of dancing. The orchestra quickly diminishes, though, to the string section alone, followed by the choir's statement.
2:54	*Hélas! et Roméo soupire,* *Car il a dû quitter Juliette.* *Soudain pour respirer encore* *Cet air qu'elle respire* *Il franchit les murs du jardin.* *Déjà sur son balcon la blanche Juliette* *Paraît et se croyant seule jusques* *au jour* *Confie à la nuit son amour.* *Roméo, palpitant d'une joie inquiéte,* *Se découvre à Juliette* *Et de son coeur les feux éclatent à leur* *tour.*	Alas! Romeo sighs, For he has had to leave Juliet. Suddenly, in order to breathe The air that she breathes again He leaps into the garden. Juliet, pale and already on her balcony, Appears and, believing herself alone until morning Confides her love to the night. Romeo, trembling with restless joy, Reveals his presence to Juliet And the flames burst forth from her heart in turn.	The choir blends with a solo flute, clarinet, and the cellos from the orchestra, with the upper strings eventually joining in. Finally, with the lines describing Romeo revealing himself to Juliet, strings and winds join the choir in proclaiming the theme of the later *Scène* *d'amour*, or love scene. The entire section highlights the shifting timbres of the choir and orchestra.

TABLE 6.1 Dynamic Markings

Dynamics are the intensity of volume at which notes are played. Although dynamics are not the same thing as timbre, they play an important role in the way timbre is perceived. Dynamics may be marked by the composer but can be added or interpreted by the performer as well. Some standard dynamic marking are listed here.

Pianissimo (*pp*)—Very quiet (soft)

Piano (*p*)—Quiet (soft)

Mezzo-piano (*mp*)—Somewhat quiet (soft)

Mezzo-forte (*mf*)—Somewhat loud

Forte (*f*)—Loud

Fortissimo (*ff*)—Very loud

Composers who want the music to be extremely soft or loud may also write triple or even quadruple *pianos* and *fortes*. As mentioned earlier, a crescendo (designated by <) is a steady change from quieter to louder dynamics; a **diminuendo** (designated by >) is a change in the opposite direction.

In the following discussion, the dynamic levels are frequently noted. You should get accustomed to listening for contrasts of dynamics as well as for those of timbre.

Dynamics: The loudness or softness of music. Dynamics are typically indicated by markings in the score, although they can be added by the performer as well.

Diminuendo: A steady decrease in volume.

Timbres of the Orchestra

The instruments of the orchestra provide the composer with an unlimited variety of timbres. These are first organized into groups of instruments with similar sounds, such as the strings, winds, brass, percussion, and keyboard instruments. A considerable range of tone colors is achievable even within a single group of instruments, such as a string quartet. Consider, then, the enormous timbral possibilities when you combine instruments from different groups. Using these individual building blocks of timbre along with variety in the dynamics of each instrumental group, the composer is able to create limitless new tone colors that individual instruments are not able to produce on their own.

The String Section

Of all the instruments in the classical orchestra, the ones that most clearly parallel the ranges of the human voice are the strings. In fact, the violin, viola, cello, and bass correspond to the soprano, alto, tenor, and bass ranges of the human voice. This correspondence is not exact. The cello, for example, can actually play notes lower than even a vocal bass is expected to sing. What do correspond, though, are the roles that composers normally assign to these instruments in orchestral writing. The violins and, to a lesser extent, the cellos, are the lyrical leaders. The violas provide a darker, supporting voice, while the basses, when they do emerge in their own right, often sound either weighty or comical.

The sound of orchestral strings can be heard clearly in the first movement of J. S. Bach's Harpsichord Concerto in D minor. The orchestra consists exclusively of string instruments and is much smaller than the orchestras used by many

The String Family. From left to right: violin, viola, cello, and bass (Courtesy of Robin Wallace)

later composers. The recording by harpsichordist Gustav Leonhardt and the Collegium Aureum uses original instruments, ones modeled on actual instruments that existed during Bach's lifetime.

A characteristic exploration of string timbre within an orchestra can be heard at the beginning of Mozart's Symphony no. 40. The first sound in the symphony is from the lower strings: The cellos and basses play single notes while the violas play a running accompaniment. This continues through the first several phrases of the melody, which are played by the violins. Although the dynamic level is *piano*, meaning quiet, the strings are perfectly suited to conveying both the dramatic urgency and the lyricism of this opening melodic statement.

A very different use of the orchestral strings is heard at the beginning of the *Scène d'amour* from Berlioz's *Roméo et Juliette*. Instead of Mozart's vigorous, pulsing ensemble, we hear long sustained chords marked "*pppp*" (barely audible), with occasional quiet interjections from the horns and flutes. Later in the scene, after the choir disappears, the string section becomes even more prominent, providing a magical, undulating background to the unfolding nocturnal love scene. As the main theme of the work is repeated, it becomes louder and the sound richer because it engages all the orchestral cellos and violas, doubled by the first bassoon and English horn. These timbral effects and the mood they produce are entirely separate from the effect of the pitches themselves.

LEARNING TO LISTEN GUIDE

TAKE NOTE OF TIMBRE

What to Listen For: The full lyrical potential of the cellos heard in this scene.

Streaming audio track 48.

Berlioz: *Roméo et Juliette*
Scène d'amour, beginning
Date: 1839
Instrumentation: Large orchestra
Key: A major
Meter: $\frac{6}{8}$ (a compound meter with two slowly moving groups of three beats per measure)
Core Repertory Connection: This music has been previously discussed in Chapter 3.

TIME	PROGRESSION	COMMENT
0:00	Beginning	After the choral introduction, which is tracked separately (see Chapter 3), the strings play gently rocking music with sustained notes in the flutes, clarinets, English horn, bassoons, and French horns.
1:38	Halting introduction	The cellos and violas play a rising introduction to the love theme, punctuated by stops.
1:45	Love theme	The main melody of the love scene is played by half of the cello section and a single French horn.
2:19	Interlude	The rocking music from the beginning returns.
3:22	Halting introduction	As before, the cellos play a rising introduction to the love theme, punctuated by stops and, this time, by interjections from the winds.
3:33	Love theme	The melody is now played by all the cellos and violas, one bassoon, and one English horn. It is marked *appassionato assai* (very impassioned).

The Woodwind Section

The wind, or woodwind, section of the orchestra can reproduce a greater diversity of timbres than the strings. Each type of wind instrument can occupy many different ranges, but the oboes and bassoons are usually assigned the soprano and bass ranges, flutes are heard in the soprano range, and the clarinet, the most prominent orchestral single-reed instrument, has two distinct ranges that can be compared to the soprano and tenor voices.

The sound of the flute can be heard clearly in the Debussy Sonata for flute, viola, and harp. As we saw in Chapter 4, one of the most interesting features of this music is its systematic use of the contrasting timbres of three kinds of instruments: wind, bowed string, and plucked string. Debussy's writing for all of these instruments is highly specialized, showcasing their unique timbres and capabilities. The flute frequently moves quickly from the high to the low end of its range. The viola plays melodies that stay within a narrower range, allowing its understated lyricism to be heard clearly. The sounds of the harp, which, like all plucked notes, fade very quickly, contrast strongly with the longer notes frequently played by the other instruments, the duration of which is limited only by the flutist's ability to sustain a breath and by the length of the violist's bow.

The clarinet is featured prominently in Smetana's *Šárka*, where it represents the warrior maiden throughout the work. A prominent clarinet solo, which shows something of the instrument's range and variety of timbre, becomes audible after 2:20, and, since the clarinet actually represents the character Šárka, returns at various other points. Some orchestral works feature a bass clarinet, which plays even lower than the standard clarinet and is usually heard at the low end of its range. Not found in modern orchestras, the basset horn, which Mozart used in the *Gran Partita*, is a single-reed instrument related to the clarinet but with a slightly lower range (not nearly as low as the bass clarinet).

It is the clarinet, in its soprano register, that is heard most prominently in the statement of the theme in the sixth movement in Mozart's *Gran Partita*. It can also be heard clearly at the beginning of the *Gran Partita*, where a single clarinet plays the faster passages in between the chords of the full ensemble. Both clarinets in the ensemble then state the opening motive of the fast part of the movement. When that motive is repeated, it is played by the two basset horns. The first trio of the first minuet, meanwhile, is scored solely for clarinets and basset horns. Using such combinations, Mozart successfully varies the use of timbre as a major expressive element throughout the work. The same piece also extensively explores the contrasting timbres of the oboe and clarinet.

LEARNING TO LISTEN GUIDE

TAKE NOTE OF TIMBRE

What to Listen For: Different groups of featured winds, such as the first trio written only for clarinets and basset horns.

Mozart: *Gran Partita*, K. 361
II: Minuet with two trios

Streaming audio track 23. Interactive Listening Guides ILG-5 and ILG-6 will show you exactly where the clarinets and other instruments are playing in these movements.

Date: 1781
Instrumentation: Two oboes, two clarinets, two basset horns, four horns, two bassoons, and bass
Key: B-flat major
Meter: $\frac{3}{4}$ (three moderately paced beats per measure)
Form: ABACA
Core Repertory Connection: Mozart's *Gran Partita* is also discussed in chapters 3, 5, and 8.

TIME	PROGRESSION	COMMENT
Minuet		
0:00	First half	The theme is stated by the first oboe, accompanied by the full ensemble. At 0:30, the oboes and second clarinet drop out, leaving the first clarinet to conclude the section, supported by sustained chords in the lower winds.
0:39	First half, repeat	
1:18	Second half	The oboe once again takes the lead, with the clarinet emerging at 1:59.
2:08	Second half, repeat	
Trio I		
2:57	First half	Only clarinets and basset horns—four instruments in all—play in this section. Each occasionally emerges into prominence or retreats into the background.
3:27	First half, repeat	
3:57	Second half	
4:44	Second half, repeat	
Minuet		
5:31	First half	Notice the five introductory notes that were not heard earlier.
6:07	Second half	
Trio II		
6:53	First half	Notice the bubbling bassoon part at the start of this section and the exchange between the first oboe and first clarinet that begins at 5:28. The horns are also featured briefly at 5:39.
7:22	First half, repeat	
7:51	Second half	The bassoon is heard more extensively in this half, in an exchange with the first clarinet. The oboe/bassoon dialog is repeated at 6:26, and the horn passage at 6:35.
8:31	Second half, repeat	
Minuet		
9:12	First half	
9:48	Second half	

The Brass Section

The sonorities of the brass instruments can be heard clearly in the two pieces for band included in your listening list: Sousa's *The Stars and Stripes Forever* and *An American Salute,* by the 20th-century American composer Morton Gould (1913–1996). Like the orchestra, the band has been a flexible ensemble, with no completely standard scoring. Gould's piece uses two instruments that are more likely to be found in band music than in an orchestra: the baritone, a brass instrument with, as its name implies, a relatively low pitch often used for harmonic support, and the cornet, a higher-pitched instrument similar to the trumpet.

After two measures of **tutti** (Italian for "all"), in which all the instruments play, the majority of the horns in the band can be heard alternating with an ensemble consisting of a few horns, trombones, and baritone, which state in alternation a short motive reminiscent of the familiar tune *When Johnny Comes Marching Home*. Ultimately, all of these instruments are combined, with the timpani joining in, followed by a repeat of the opening tutti, whose rhythm is also derived from *When Johnny Comes Marching Home*. There is then another exchange between horns and low brass, followed by a solo on the side drum repeating the rhythm of the tutti. The full tune is then played by the bassoons, echoed by muted horns. The distinctive sound of the three bassoons, playing close together, continues to be heard as the English horn then plays the melody. Finally, the entire melody is proclaimed *fortissimo* by the low brass (tubas, baritones, horns, and saxophones) with a concluding, fanfare-like echo by the trumpets and cornets. The full range of brass instruments is thus heard within the first minute of the piece.

Tubas in a brass band. (Lee Yiu Tung)

Tutti: Italian for "all." A designation used to indicate that all instruments in an orchestra should play (as opposed to only solo instruments). A passage in which the full orchestra plays (e.g., the opening of a classical concerto) is also called a tutti.

Timbres of Percussion Instruments

The percussion section of the orchestra is the most diverse of all when it comes to timbre. Twentieth-century composers have often used percussion instruments

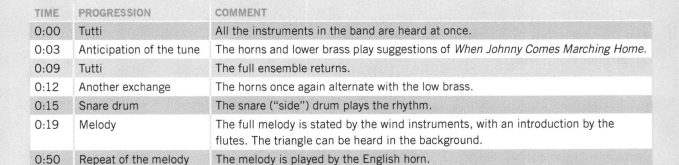

LEARNING TO LISTEN GUIDE

TAKE NOTE OF TIMBRE

What to Listen For: Distinctive groups of instruments featured in quick succession.

Streaming audio track 68.

Gould: *An American Salute*, beginning
Date: 1943
Instrumentation: Large concert band
Key: G minor
Meter: $\frac{12}{8}$ (a compound meter with four rapid groups of three beats per measure)
Form: Varied repetition

TIME	PROGRESSION	COMMENT
0:00	Tutti	All the instruments in the band are heard at once.
0:03	Anticipation of the tune	The horns and lower brass play suggestions of *When Johnny Comes Marching Home*.
0:09	Tutti	The full ensemble returns.
0:12	Another exchange	The horns once again alternate with the low brass.
0:15	Snare drum	The snare ("side") drum plays the rhythm.
0:19	Melody	The full melody is stated by the wind instruments, with an introduction by the flutes. The triangle can be heard in the background.
0:50	Repeat of the melody	The melody is played by the English horn.
1:05	Another repeat	The melody is played by the low brass, concluding the opening section of the piece.

inventively. *Canti di prigionia* by Luigi Dallapiccola (1904–1975), for example, is written for SATB choir, two pianos, two harps, six timpani, xylophone, vibraphone, bells, cymbals (including one that is suspended and two that are crashed together in the usual way, though one of them also needs to be attached to the bass drums), three tam-tams (gongs) at different pitches, triangle, bass drum, snare drum, tenor drum, and muffled drum (*tamburo coperto*). Since the piano is technically a percussion instrument, the harp is the only non-percussion instrument heard in this entire piece. The contrast among the sounds of this distinctive ensemble and the very different timbres of the choir make this music a feast for the ears.

The first movement sets a prayer written by Mary, Queen of Scots, shortly before her execution. This movement begins with an *Introduzione* in which the *Dies irae*—a highly recognizable tune from the traditional Roman Catholic funeral liturgy that describes the Day of Judgment—is stated *pianissimo* by the first harp and timpani. (You can verify this, since the *Dies irae* is also on your listening list; see Chapter 2.) Meanwhile, the second harp and first piano play, in their very lowest registers, the melodic motive that will serve as the basis for much of the succeeding music. Four of the timpani have been tuned, unusually, to play successive pitches, and the resulting sound, backed up by barely audible (*ppp*) tones from the bass drum, tam-tam, and cymbals, may sound eerily unsettling.

The second piano quickly joins the ensemble, but an even greater timbral contrast occurs when the choir enters, whispering the words "*O Domine Deus*" (O Lord God). Dallapiccola directs that they should sing "*assolutamente senza timbro*" (absolutely without timbre). They then sing a wordless, sustained chord *a bocca chiusa* (with mouths closed). In a passage of extraordinary beauty, the sounds of the choir then mingle with those of the instruments as both present similar melodic material. As the choir reiterates the words "*O Domine Deus*," the music grows louder, punctuated with startling, sharp, isolated notes from the cymbals, vibraphone, xylophone, second harp, and both pianos. At the high point of this passage, every instrument but the vibraphone and xylophone plays at once, and the dynamic level rises to *fortissimo*. The choir then returns to wordless vocalization as the instruments slowly drop out.

LEARNING TO LISTEN GUIDE

TAKE NOTE OF TIMBRE

What to Listen For: The astounding richness of percussion sonorities and the ways that they complement the choir.

Streaming audio track 65.

Dallapiccola: *Canti di prigionia*
1st movement: "Preghiera di Maria Stuarda," beginning
Date: 1938–1941
Instrumentation: Four-part mixed choir, two pianos, two harps, and percussion
Key: This music has no key in the traditional sense.
Meter: $\frac{4}{2}$ (four very slow beats per measure)
Core Repertory Connection: Dallapiccola's *Canti di prigionia* is also discussed in Chapter 10.

TIME	SECTION	ORIGINAL TEXT	TRANSLATION	COMMENT
0:00	Beginning			Two harps, two pianos, and tuned timpani present the *Dies irae* theme. A few other percussion instruments are barely audible.
0:38	Entry of the choir	*O Domine Deus!*	Oh Lord God!	The choir sings the words and then continues wordlessly, with mouths closed.
1:55	Dynamic growth			The choir sings the text again, and the dynamic level quickly rises.
2:19	Fadeout			The choir returns to singing wordlessly, and the dynamic level falls again. Finally, the choir drops out completely.

Percussion Timbres in Non-Western Music

Orchestral works that showcase percussion like the Dallapiccola piece are very much the exception in Western music; the percussion instruments usually play only a supporting role in classical ensemble music. Many other cultures, however, have produced large bodies of music for percussion ensemble. Listen now to the performance by a **gamelan** ensemble from the village of Sukawati in Bali, an island that is part of the vast nation of Indonesia. Larger gamelans use a variety of instruments such as tuned gongs, drums, flutes, and single- and multi-octave metallophones, mallet-struck instruments tuned to specific pitches, much like the xylophone. This small ensemble uses only two pairs of similar instruments.

If you listen carefully to the long note at the beginning of the recorded selection, you will hear the beats, or quick oscillations of volume level, that arise from the same note being played simultaneously on two pitched metallophones, known as gender wayang, slightly out of tune with each other. Because the vibration rates of the notes they produce are slightly different, their sounds cycle in and out of sync. Though often obscured by the rapidity of the notes, the resulting beats can in fact be heard throughout the recording.

This is indeed a virtuoso performance, as writer Michael Tenzer observes:

> Many visitors to Bali hear their first Balinese music played on a pair or quartet of gender wayang, placed off to the side in the hotel lobby. Being relegated to background accompaniment is too often the status quo for this elite chamber gamelan. But its players, over the generations, have slyly exacted their revenge by concocting the most complex, technically difficult, and respected music in all of Bali.

The complex interactions of the metallic, yet delicate, timbres of the four percussion instruments, so different from anything we have examined so far in this chapter, provide eloquent testimony both to the range of sonorities within the percussion family and to the nearly infinite variety of musical timbres.

Chamber Ensembles

In addition to the full orchestra, instrumental timbres play an important role in smaller groups known as chamber ensembles. While composers have always been

Gamelan: A general term for various types of Indonesian orchestras. These orchestras consist of mostly percussion instruments, including tuned gongs, xylophones, drums, chimes, etc., and occasionally flutes, stringed instruments, and even vocalists.

LEARNING TO LISTEN GUIDE

TAKE NOTE OF TIMBRE

What to Listen For: The rapid contrast of different timbres and tempos produced by this small group of instruments.

Streaming audio track 76.

Gender wayang, *Sukawati* (*Sulendro*)
No Date
Key: This music is not in a key in the Western sense
Meter: Duple but without the regular grouping into measures characteristic of Western music
Instrumentation: A small group of paired, metallic percussion instruments.

TIME	PROGRESSION	COMMENT
0:00		The small ensemble, consisting of two pairs of instruments, is featured in a variety of ways right at the beginning.
0:04	Single, sustained note	Listen to the "beats" (rapid oscillations) produced by two instruments slightly out of tune with each other.
0:10	Short melodic phrase	Like all melodies in this music, this one is pentatonic, using a traditional scale of only five notes, a smaller range of pitches than are found in most of the other music discussed in this book.
0:16	Repeated notes	This section highlights the contrasting timbres that can be produced on the same pitch.
0:23	Very short melodic phrases	
0:31	More repeated notes	As the music continues, these effects are heard again, but new complexity is added as well. Note, for example, the effects described below.
0:36	Longer melodic section	Having shown the range of effects they can produce, the musicians play melodically for a longer stretch that no longer resembles the short "phrases" heard earlier. Note the very audible beats on the final, sustained note, which results from the simultaneous use of two instruments slightly out of tune with each other.
1:33	Short, isolated phrases	A series of very short, very fast four-note phrases is heard. Several variations on this effect follow.
2:42	Extended melodic activity	A long section begins here where the extended pauses featured earlier are not heard, giving the music a feeling of greater continuity. The melodic material is also very repetitive, but listen carefully to the often subtle ways in which the players vary the timbre. The performance ends with a burst of faster notes and a final, sustained sound at 7:07.

able to write chamber music for any combination of instruments they wish—an example of a highly unusual combination is Debussy's Sonata for flute, viola, and harp—the vast majority of chamber music has been written for one of the standard ensemble configurations (see table).

These ensembles have been widely accepted in part because they offer timbral combinations that have proven over time to be both logical and highly flexible.

TABLE 6.2 Common Chamber Music Forms

- Trio sonata (common in the Baroque period)—two melodic instruments (often two violins or violin and flute) and basso continuo, making a total of four instruments

- String quartet (common from the Classical period on)—two violins, viola, and cello

- String quintet (common in the Classical period: less common later)—a string quartet plus either an extra viola or an extra cello

- Piano trio (common from the Classical period on)—piano, violin, and cello

- Piano quartet (common in the Classical period; less common later)—piano, violin, viola, and cello

- Piano quintet (most common in the 19th century)—piano, two violins, viola, and cello, or (as in Schubert's "Trout" Quintet) piano, violin, viola, cello, and double bass

- Woodwind quintet (most common in the late 18th and early 19th centuries, though there are many 20th-century examples as well)—flute, clarinet, oboe, French horn, and bassoon

- Chamber orchestra (used from the Baroque period on: *all* baroque orchestras were technically chamber orchestras by modern standards)—loosely defined as a small orchestra of 30 or fewer players, often containing only string instruments, or strings and a few winds

The string quartet, for example, offers not just one soprano instrument, but two, allowing them to play off of one another and share thematic material. Although the bass member of the string family is omitted, the cello can play low enough to provide a bass line while also emerging from time to time as a lyrical voice in its own right. Even the viola is occasionally featured in a solo role.

The second movement of Haydn's String Quartet in B-flat major, op. 64, no. 3, for example, opens at a *forte* dynamic level with an extended conversation between the first and second violins that makes up the entire A section of this rounded binary form. Although the viola and cello largely accompany them, the viola does get a brief phrase of its own. In the first part of the third movement (as you can see by following interactive listening guide no. 4) the cello then emerges much more prominently, both in combination with the viola and all by itself.

LEARNING TO LISTEN GUIDE

TAKE NOTE OF TIMBRE AND MELODY

What to Listen For: The interactions between the two violins, which present most of the melodic material.

Streaming audio track 19.

Haydn: String Quartet in B-flat major, op. 64, no. 3, 2nd movement
Date: 1790
Instrumentation: Two violins, viola, and cello
Key: E-flat major
Meter: $\frac{2}{4}$ (two slow beats per measure)
Form: ABA (ternary)
Core Repertory Connection: Haydn's String Quartet in B-flat major is also discussed in chapters 3, 5, and 7.

TIME	PROGRESSION	COMMENT
0:00	A section	The theme is presented as an extended dialog between the first and second violins. When the second violin is playing, the first violin plays sustained notes in a higher register. Listen for the short viola solo at 1:18.
2:45	B section	The middle section, in a minor key, is dominated by the first violin nearly throughout. A series of brief interjections by the second violin begins at 4:03.
4:43	A' section	The dialog between the first and second violins returns. Beginning at 5:00, the dotted rhythms of the earlier A section are replaced by triplets (see Chapter 7).
6:51	Coda	The coda begins with a rising scale in the solo cello. The first violin then returns to prominence.

Twentieth-century composers have used standard chamber ensembles in ways that differ from the norm, thus demonstrating the flexibility of these ensembles and their timbres. *Genesis II*, by the contemporary American composer Janika Vandervelde (b. 1955), is written for violin, cello, and piano—the traditional piano trio. This is a genre, though, that has undergone considerable historical change. When it originated in the 18th century, works like this would have been considered piano sonatas accompanied by violin and cello. The term "piano trio" originated more recently, in order to indicate greater equality among the instruments in trios written by composers like Schubert and Brahms. Vandervelde goes further, though. At the beginning of *Genesis II*, the instruments are not featured in a typical chamber music "conversation." Instead, they fit together in what has been described as a "clockwork": a continuous pattern in which all the instruments play very similar, repetitive music.

Later, though, the violin and the cello share an extended solo passage—a **cadenza**—in which the piano remains silent. Vandervelde at times calls on the string players to play *sul ponticello*—near the bridge of the instrument—and at one point she asks the violinist to remain quieter than the cello, even though it is higher in pitch. The pianist is asked to produce sonorities that are "dry, detached" and "sharp, metallic"; in these passages, the timbres of the string instruments blend with those of the piano in intriguing ways. Toward the end of the piece, Vandervelde asks the pianist to use his or her forearms to produce a loud, percussive sound at the low end of the piano's range; in combination with the seemingly random **pizzicato** (plucked) notes heard in the strings, this produces a surprising and highly disruptive effect.

Timbre in Performance

Performers know that the production of timbre is a crucial part of the very substance of what they play and sing. Perhaps you have been to a performance by a pianist and have observed the many different sounds that can be produced from this instrument—far more than simply the loud and soft indicated by the term "pianoforte." Pianists are often told not to "bang," but they can certainly do so for special effects. They can also "sing," an effect facilitated by the fact that the individual strings on each piano note are just slightly out of tune with each other, producing reverberatory beats that make the notes literally throb with intensity. Pianists may also use the pedals. The right pedal, known as the damper pedal, actually prevents the dampers from returning to the strings, resulting in more sustained and

Cadenza: A solo passage, often intended to be improvised, usually indicated by a fermata (hold mark) in the score. Many concerto movements call for a cadenza toward the end, although this practice fell into disuse in the later 19th century. Short cadenzas are also called for in many vocal pieces.

Pizzicato: In string instrument technique, this refers to plucking the strings rather than bowing them.

LEARNING TO LISTEN GUIDE

TAKE NOTE OF TIMBRE

What to Listen For: The often surprisingly unconventional ways in which the instruments are used.

Streaming audio track 73.

Vandervelde: *Genesis II* for piano trio
Date: 1983
Instrumentation: Piano, violin, and cello
Key: Variable
Meter: Irregular
Core Repertory Connection: This music is also discussed in chapters 7 and 12.

TIME	PROGRESSION	COMMENT
0:00	First "clockwork" section	The three instruments combine in repeated but irregular rhythms. The music gradually becomes louder.
0:54	More clockwork	After a disruption, the repeated rhythms begin again.
2:32	Increased activity	The violin part becomes faster, although the underlying meter is the same.
3:15	Greater prominence of the cello	The cello begins to take a more active role. The level of activity gradually increases in both the cello and the violin.
5:49	New section	The clockwork begins to slow down.
6:20	Cadenza for violin and cello	The piano is not heard in this section.
8:41	The piano re-enters	The other instruments gradually join back together with the piano.
12:04	Sudden contrast	The sounds of the instruments become more isolated and aggressive. The level of activity gradually increases.
14:18	Crash	The music is suddenly punctuated by a low, dissonant chord in the piano. This is followed by confused, "scratchy" sounding music in the strings, concluding with a section in pizzicato.
14:41	Silence	There is a long pause.
14:54	More clockwork	The regular rhythms begin again but faster and more urgent-sounding than earlier. They gradually slow as the piece concludes.

blurry sonorities. The left pedal, known as the una corda pedal, shifts the hammers to a position where not all the strings for each note are struck, resulting in a thinner, less complex timbre.

Most instruments can also be muted. With a grand piano, this can be done simply by closing the lid. In the case of strings, a small piece of metal or other material can be clamped onto the bridge, "damping" the vibration. Wind and brass instruments can be muted by inserting something into the end of the instrument from which the air emerges. Perhaps you have seen a jazz trumpeter pull out the business end of a bathroom plunger and place it inside the bell of the trumpet to produce a very different sound. This is only one example of the ingenuity that performers have often shown in experimenting with timbre. As we saw in Chapter 4, the 20th-century American composer John Cage (1912–1992) even

The interior of a prepared piano. Composers in search of novel sounds may use traditional instruments in imaginative ways. (© Pierre BRYE/Alamy)

wrote a number of pieces for "prepared piano," in which the timbre of the instrument is changed dramatically by placing nuts and bolts, pieces of rubber, and other objects between the strings.

Players also vary the articulation of the sounds they produce. A group of notes may be played staccato, legato, or in a combination of the two. At the same time, staccato notes may be very short or merely detached from one another, while legato notes may be merely connected without spaces or seem almost to blur together. Good performers make use of an infinite number of shadings.

Timbre as Structural Division: Stravinsky's *Symphony of Psalms*

Timbres can also be manipulated by the composer, and an awareness of the shifting "colors" that result is one of the most fascinating aspects of listening to ensemble music, in which different instrumental timbres can be combined ingeniously. We have already seen how Mozart does this throughout the *Gran Partita*. Listen now to the second movement of Stravinsky's *Symphony of Psalms*, in which the composer uses his altered orchestra in a variety of ways. In fact, the juxtaposition of "blocks" of sound that are dramatically different from each other is the primary means by which he articulates the music's form.

The first sound you hear is that of a solo oboe, joined successively by a solo flute, another flute, and another oboe. Stravinsky particularly liked the sounds of wind instruments, but he had an unusual reason for this preference. As he said in his commentary on the *Symphony of Psalms*: "It is exactly the breathing of wind instruments that is one of their greatest attractions for me." He also earned the enmity of organists by stating that he disliked their instrument because "the monster never breathes." Thus, in the melody with which each of the four instruments enters, he called specifically for the players to take a breath between each of the first five notes. These breaths are not necessary. Any experienced oboist or flutist has enough breath control to be able to play through much longer phrases without running out of air. Stravinsky, though, wanted the breaths between the notes to be an audible part of the music. Don't misunderstand; unless you are sitting very close to the player, you will not actually hear him or her breathe. You will, however, hear each note as an isolated musical event separated by silence. The distinctive articulation that results is a part of the music's timbre.

Later in the melody, Stravinsky creates contrasting articulations by indicating that the shorter notes that follow are to be joined together in groups of two, three, or more notes; in fact, the groupings get longer as the melody progresses. This, along with the distinctive profile of the melody's opening motive, allows each new instrument to be clearly heard when it first enters, repeating the isolated-note articulation of the opening oboe solo. When the oboes drop out and are replaced by the fourth flute and the piccolo, though, the result is a large mass of legato flute sound that contrasts markedly with the opening.

In a stunning transition, the choral sopranos then enter, accompanied by two oboes, English horn, bassoon, two French horns, cellos, and basses. At exactly the same point, the flutes simply drop out. As the music continues, the choral parts enter one by one, much as the oboes and flutes did at the beginning, while the accompanying ensemble shifts, with trumpet, tenor and bass trombones, and the first two flutes being heard from as well. The net effect of this sudden shift is to create a timbral contrast just as strong as that between the contrasting themes that we have already observed in Mozart and Haydn. The orchestra continues to play the opening melody, and the music sung by the choir is also closely related to what has been sung before—the primary change is one of sonority, of timbre.

Another very noticeable shift occurs when the entire orchestra suddenly drops out, leaving the SATB choir to sing *a cappella* for an extended stretch. Notice that the text at this point reads: "And [He] set my feet upon a rock, making my steps secure." Equally suddenly, the choir then stops singing—Stravinsky is careful to write a breath mark at this point, as though they had a choice!—to be replaced by a shifting orchestral ensemble that prominently features both trombones.

In another timbral shift whose effect is easy to overlook, Stravinsky then marks a full measure of silence. The complete absence of sound during this time is itself an important event in the music's structure. After this, the full choir and most of the orchestra enter *fortissimo*. In the final section, on the words "and put their trust in the Lord," Stravinsky reverts to a *piano* dynamic level and removes all but the flutes, oboes, piccolo trumpet, and low strings from the orchestra.

The movement as a whole is thus made up of six large blocks of sound, with a measure of silence between what would otherwise be the final two blocks. Each has its own distinct timbre, while the flutes and oboes at the conclusion mirror the sound of the beginning, thus suggesting, though just barely, a sort of timbral ABA effect.

LEARNING TO LISTEN GUIDE

TAKE NOTE OF TIMBRE AND FORM

What to Listen For: The large, contrasting timbral blocks of which the movement is constructed.

Streaming audio track 64.
Interactive Listening Guide 17
will highlight the timbral
changes in the second movement.

Stravinsky: *Symphony of Psalms*

II: *Expectans expectavi*

Date: 1930

Instrumentation: Large orchestra

Key: C minor

Meter: $\frac{2}{4}$ (two slow beats per measure)

Form: Fugal (See Chapter 9), with contrasting sections

Core Repertory Connection: Stravinsky's *Symphony of Psalms* is also discussed in chapters 4 and 9.

TIME	PROGRESSION	ORIGINAL TEXT	TRANSLATION*	COMMENT
0:00	First block: Instrumental introduction			Instruments enter one at a time as the texture becomes more and more dense.
1:50	Second block: Entrance of the choir	*Expectans expectavi Dominum, et intendit mihi.* *Et exaudivit preces meas; et exudit me da lacu miseriae, et de lato faecis.*	I waited patiently for the Lord; he inclined to me and heard my cry. He drew me up from the desolate pit, out of the miry bog,	Beginning with the sopranos, the parts of the choir enter one by one, making a double fugue (see Chapter 9) in combination with the orchestra.

TIME	PROGRESSION	ORIGINAL TEXT	TRANSLATION	COMMENT
3:27	Third block: a cappella choir	*Et statuit super petram pedes meos: et direxis gressus meos.*	and set my feet upon a rock, making my steps secure.	The orchestra drops out, illustrating the text "and set my feet upon a rock, making my steps secure" by showing that the choir can sing without any accompaniment.
4:06	Fourth block: Orchestral interlude			Listen to the prominent trombone parts in this section.
4:46	Fifth block: A measure of silence			Though short, this passage of silence plays an important role in the music's structure, setting the stage for the conclusion.
4:48	Sixth block: Conclusion	*Et immisit in os meum canticum novum, carmen Deo nostro.* *Videbunt multi, videbunt et timabunt: et spe aperabunt in Domino.* Ps. 40: 1–3 (RSV)	He put a new song in my mouth, a song of praise to our God. Many will see and fear, and put their trust in the Lord.	The concluding lines of the text are proclaimed loudly by the full ensemble. The dynamics fade only at the very end.

Timbre as Sonic Experiment: Crumb's *Black Angels*

Some most intriguing timbres are found in George Crumb's *Black Angels*. Crumb is a master of using traditional instruments in nontraditional ways. At the very beginning of *Black Angels*, he provides unusually specific instructions pertaining to timbre. In place of a traditional tempo marking, the entire first section of Part I, *Threnody I: Night of the Electric Insects,* is marked "Vibrant, intense!" It begins with all four members of the string quartet playing notes at the extreme high end of their ranges. Crumb indicates that these notes are to be played *sempre sul ponticello e glissando,* meaning that the players should hold their bows as close as possible to the bridge and slide their fingers up and down the fingerboard instead of playing discrete pitches. He further states that "the tremolo [backward and forward motion of the bow] should be extremely rapid." Later points in the movement are marked *piangendo* (crying). In combination with the electronic amplification of the instruments, these effects produce some startling sonorities.

The second section, "Sounds of Bones and Flutes," calls for the performers to play *col legno*—with the wooden part of the bow—to throw the bow onto the strings and to make their instruments sound like Tibetan prayer stones. They are also asked to click their tongues and whisper the syllables "ka-to-ko to-ko to-ko to-ko to-ko to-ko!" Despite what you may think you hear, there are no flutes in this movement; the flute-like sounds are produced by the first violinist playing on the G string (the lowest on the instrument) with the wooden part of the bow. At several points in this and the succeeding movements, the players are also asked to touch the string carefully so that it divides into smaller portions that vibrate more quickly, producing very high pitches.

In the fourth section, *Devil-Music,* Crumb calls for an excruciating sound to be "produced by moving bow very slowly while exerting great pressure." The resulting "fingernails-on-the-blackboard" sonority sends shivers of revulsion up some peoples' spines. These and other unusual effects foreground the timbre of the musical experience to a rare degree.

[See Learning to Listen Guide on Crumb in Chapter 1.]

In History
Crumb's *Black Angels*

When George Crumb completed *Black Angels*, he signed the manuscript *in tempore belli* (in time of war). This was in 1970 at the height of America's involvement in Vietnam, when the war and protests against it dominated the news. Crumb did not connect his work with Vietnam, however, until it was almost finished. When he began writing, he acknowledged, it was simply an experimental work for string quartet. Crumb himself may have entertained different, even conflicting, ideas about its meaning.

It is not surprising, though, that Crumb ultimately associated his work with contemporary political events. Composers have often done so. Beethoven originally named his "Eroica" (heroic) symphony for Napoleon, whereas later generations, understandably disillusioned with Napoleon, tended to see Beethoven himself as the hero of the work. In this view, the composer's struggle with deafness and other adversities was a heroic endeavor that continued to dignify the lives of countless listeners as well.

Most students in college today were born long after the Vietnam War. For you, that may make Crumb's intended meaning a pressing question. If the work's subject is Vietnam, is its appeal limited to those who lived through that experience? Or is it instead about broader themes, suggested in the titles of the movements and sections of the work—good vs. evil, God vs. the devil? If so, its appeal may transcend its historical origins, making it a work for the ages.

Either way, this music is a product of the late 1960s. The use of electrically amplified string instruments stems from the popularity of the electric guitar in pop music. Although it might not have occurred to a composer 20 years earlier to use such sounds, within another few decades electronic instruments had become commonplace. They no longer had the novelty that sparked Crumb's experiment.

The international references—including the use of Russian and Swahili—are also linked with the work's historical moment. The relationship of the United States with Russia was the central foreign policy challenge of the time, and the Civil Rights movement had elevated awareness of African culture.

Crumb's *Black Angels* and Beethoven's "Eroica" symphony are partly defined—but clearly not limited—by the times in which they were written.

SUMMARY

- Timbre, or tone color, one of the most important components of music, is also one of the most difficult to define.
- Complex physical factors affect the timbres of different instruments, and the performer also plays a crucial role in producing them.

- Related issues include dynamic level (loudness) and articulation.
- The most basic instrument is the human voice. Vocal timbres are classified in a variety of ways, but one of the most familiar, and useful, classifications divides

- them into soprano, alto, tenor, and bass: the standard components of a mixed choir.
- Families of instruments often follow this classification as well.
- Percussion timbres can be featured in unique ways in non-Western music.

- In works like Stravinsky's *Symphony of Psalms*, the contrasts of timbres are at least as important in defining the structure of the music as are thematic contrasts. Earlier composers like Mozart and Bach also use timbre very effectively.

KEY TERMS

Alto	p. 160	Dynamics	p. 169	SATB Choir	p. 160
Baritone	p. 160	Fundamental	p. 157	Soprano	p. 160
Bass	p. 160	Gamelan	p. 175	Tenor	p. 160
Cadenza	p. 178	Harmonics	p. 157	Tutti	p. 173
Countertenor	p. 160	Mezzo-soprano	p. 160	Vibrato	p. 158
Diminuendo	p. 169	Pizzicato	p. 178		

REVIEW QUESTIONS

1. What elements do all musical instruments have in common?
2. Why is the voice the most basic musical instrument? In what ways do other instruments resemble the voice?
3. What are the four main ranges of the human voice?
4. How are string instruments constructed? Which instruments correspond to which vocal ranges described in question 3?
5. What is unusual about George Crumb's approach to the timbres of the string quartet in *Black Angels*?

REVIEW CONCEPTS

1. What can the performer add to the timbre of music?
2. How can the makeup of a choir affect its sound? What other factors may make one choir sound different from another?
3. How did the orchestra change from the time of Mozart to the time of Stravinsky, as represented by the examples described in this chapter? How are those changes put to use by the composers of those examples?
4. Why have standard chamber music ensembles like the string quartet proven to be so durable?
5. How is timbre used as an important element of music by Stravinsky and Crumb in the pieces discussed in this chapter?

LISTENING EXERCISES

This chapter is written as a series of listening exercises designed to acquaint you with the distinctive sounds of different voices and instruments. The focus has been on picking out these instruments from a larger ensemble. You can continue to practice this skill any time you listen to ensemble music. Ask yourself: What instruments or voices are performing? Don't hesitate to use the program notes or, in the case of a live performance, your eyes to answer this question. In addition, you may find the following exercises helpful:

1. Listen carefully to the performance of Chopin's Ballade no. 1 in G minor by Vladimir Horowitz and note

some of the ways in which Horowitz varies the timbre of the piano. Use your imagination to find ways to describe in writing the different sounds he produces.

2. Compare some other recordings on original instruments (often also called historical or authentic instruments) with recordings of the same music on standard instruments. Which do you prefer, and why? (A recording of Mozart's Symphony no. 40 on original instruments by Les Musiciens du Louvre, directed by Marc Minkowski, is available on iTunes, as are several modern instrument recordings of Bach's Mass in B Minor.)

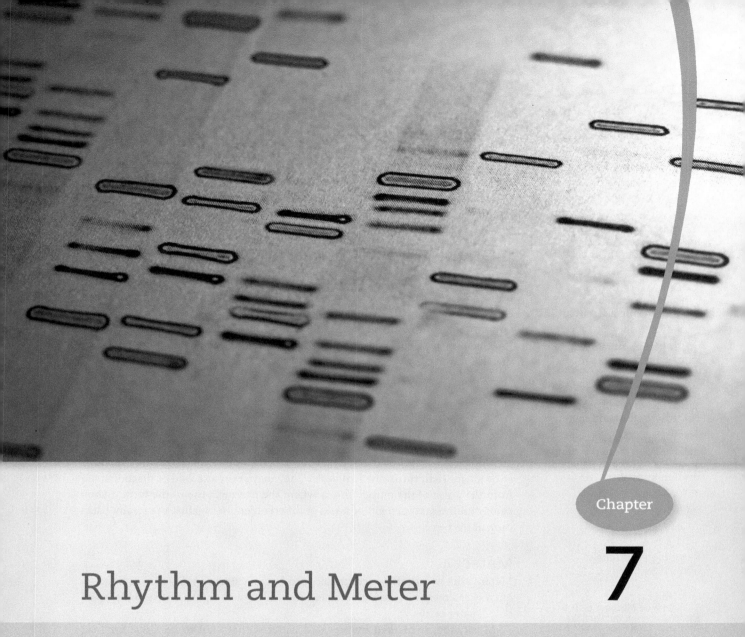

7

Rhythm and Meter

TAKE NOTE

Rhythm is the organization of music through time. The term *rhythm* may refer in a general way to the element of time in music, but more specifically to the patterns of long notes, short notes, and rests. Musical rhythms—patterns of notes and rests of varying durations—can exist only on a supporting framework created by the collaboration of beat, meter, and tempo.

Chapter Objectives

🔘 Understand the difference between rhythm and meter.

🔘 Compare rhythm and meter in music to rhythm and meter in poetry.

🔘 Familiarize yourself with the most commonly used musical meters, moving from the simplest to the most complex.

🔘 Learn to recognize syncopation, backbeat, and other rhythmic alterations.

🔘 Observe the use of flexible meter (tempo rubato) for expressive purposes in performance.

🔘 Investigate how a composer may purposefully obscure rhythm and meter.

🔘 Recognize how Western music differs from the music of other cultures in its use of rhythm and meter.

Life is often defined by the rhythm of the day: how fast it seems to go by, or how slowly it unfolds. Sometimes, by evening, you feel like the day just disappeared behind you. Other times, the day passes more slowly, and you are able to attend to every necessary detail. A day's rhythm often seems beyond our control.

Music, similarly, moves forward in time, but composers and performers have specific rhythmic tools available for controlling the way it unfolds, ebbs, and flows. Musicians employ a variety of techniques to create a satisfying experience in which the listener senses that each musical detail has been allotted just the right amount of time.

Components of Rhythm

Rhythm is the most physical element of music and often the most immediately noticeable. How many times have you heard somebody say, "It's not music if you can't tap your foot to it"? That may not always be true, but music often makes us tap our feet, drum our fingers, or move rhythmically. Rhythm results from the interrelationship of note duration with beat, meter, accent, and tempo, which we'll discuss now in turn.

Beat

The beat of the day is made of the minutes that divide the day into equal parts of time. In a piece of music, the beat is a regular pulse, an invisible grid on which the composer places musical notes.

Not every beat is heard, but it must be felt. The notes themselves may be shorter or longer than the individual beats. They may seem attached or disconnected from the pulse of the music. This is where the narrower use of the term *rhythm* comes in: the arrangement of notes of different lengths against the steady backdrop of the beat.

Meter

Meter is the way beats are combined into larger patterns. A day may seem to go quickly or slowly, but the regular alternation of day and night never stops. It is part of the meter of life.

Music, too, is marked by repeated patterns that tend to continue for long stretches. Depending on the musical style, the meter may be easy or hard to hear. In much popular music, the pulse of the drums, or rhythm section, puts the meter in the foreground. In other cases, the meter may be much harder to hear. Like the alternation of day and night, though, it is always present. Learning to hear and recognize it is an important skill for the active listener.

Accent

Some days are more important than other days. Fridays, weekends, holidays, birthdays, and other special occasions stand out from the relentless pattern of one day following another.

Likewise, some musical notes are **accented** to make them seem more important. In simple terms, this usually means they are played louder than the notes around them. These accented notes may correspond with the beat and the meter, or, intriguingly, they may contradict it, in the effect known as syncopation. In most music, though, beats are regularly accented, creating a sense that some beats are strong and others weak, and that they alternate in regular patterns.

Tempo

Of course, the actual rate at which time passes does not change. No matter how long it may seem to take, every day is 24 hours long. Music, though, may go quickly, slowly, or somewhere in between. The speed at which music moves is its tempo. Tempo can be described as the framework in which rhythm, meter, and accent unfold. Without recognizing the tempo of the music, it is hard to perceive these other patterns and how they operate.

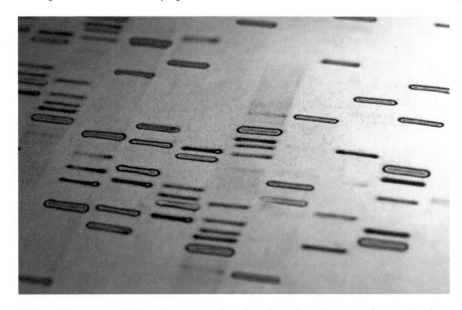

DNA coding, represented here by a succession of marks and empty spaces, is an example of a rhythmic pattern that can be found in nature.

Chronology Continued

1831-1835
Frédéric Chopin p. 201
Ballade no. 1 in G minor,
op. 23, for piano solo

1886
Antonín Dvořák p. 191
Slavonic Dance in E minor, op.
72, no. 10, for piano four-hands

1897
John Philip Sousa p. 187
The Stars and Stripes Forever

1915
Claude Debussy p. 202
Sonata for flute, viola, and harp,
1st movement; 2nd movement;
3rd movement

1906-1916
Charles Ives p. 207
Violin Sonata no. 4, 2nd
movement

1975
William "Count" Basie p. 194
Lester Leaps In , recorded at
the Montreux Jazz Festival
(first recorded 1939)

1983
Janika Vandervelde
Genesis II, p. 209

(no date)
Traditional
Jumping Dance Drums, p. 210

Exploring Meter

Rhythm and meter are also central to poetry, where they help communicate content. In music, however, the rhythm often *is* the most important content. Rhythm's physical, emotional, and intellectual impact is only increased by careful, active listening.

As we saw in Chapters 2, 3, and 4, different historical periods introduced new forms, new instruments, and other building blocks of music. Most meters, though, were used in music from many different periods. As we examine these meters, moving from the simple to the complex, we'll explore some history along the way.

Accented: Played louder. Individual notes are accented to make them seem more important than the notes around them. Accents may correspond with the beat, or they may contradict it.

Duple Meter: Sousa and Count Basie

Classical music tends to be marked by very regular meters. Yet its rhythms often change from moment to moment, making the meter less easy to identify.

Time Signature: The numbers at the beginning of a musical score indicating how many beats there are in a measure (top number) and what kind of note gets one beat (bottom number). The top number is significant for the meter: duple, triple, or compound.

Duple Meter: A simple pattern of regularly alternating stressed and unstressed beats. It can be counted either as ONE-two-ONE-two, known as $\frac{2}{4}$ meter, or as ONE-two-THREE-four, known as common time or $\frac{4}{4}$ meter.

John Philip Sousa (1854–1932). America's March King was born to immigrant parents (Portuguese and German). *(Library of Congress Prints and Photographs Division Washington, D.C. 20540 USA)*

TABLE 7.1: Common Musical Meters

Listed below are some of the most common meters, all of which are featured in the examples discussed in this chapter. One repetition of any of these patterns constitutes a measure, a basic unit of musical time. The numbers that look like fractions are called **time signatures**. The top number tells us how many beats are in each measure, and the bottom tells us what kind of note (quarter note, eighth note, half note, etc.) gets one beat. For our purposes, the top number is the significant one. To get a feel for these meters, try tapping, clapping, or stomping your feet while counting the numbers aloud using the emphasis given.

$\frac{2}{4}$ or $\frac{2}{2}$ (duple)—ONE-two (etc.)

$\frac{3}{4}$ (triple)—ONE-two-three

$\frac{4}{4}$ (common time; a kind of duple meter)—ONE-two-THREE-four

$\frac{6}{8}$ or $\frac{6}{4}$ (compound duple)—ONE-two-three TWO-two-three (or, ONE-two-three-FOUR-five-six)

$\frac{5}{8}$ or $\frac{5}{4}$ (irregular)—ONE-two-three ONE-two OR ONE-two ONE-two-three

$\frac{9}{8}$ or $\frac{9}{4}$ (compound triple)—ONE-two-three TWO-two-three THREE-two-three

$\frac{12}{8}$ (compound quadruple)—ONE-two-three TWO-two-three THREE-two-three FOUR-two-three

$\frac{7}{8}$ (irregular)—ONE-two-three TWO-two THREE-two OR ONE-two TWO-two-three THREE-two OR ONE-two TWO-two THREE-two-three

---

In contrast, the underlying metrical pattern of most popular music stands out right away. Thus, it makes sense to begin listening for meter with a piece of popular music.

John Philip Sousa's *The Stars and Stripes Forever*, a popular march from the late 19th century, has a regular, emphasized beat designed to make people step in an organized way: "LEFT-right-LEFT-right." Thus, there are two beats per measure: "ONE-two ONE-two." Since marching demands regularity, the measures are grouped in pairs, so that you can also count "ONE-two-THREE-four" to this music. Like most current popular music—and like much classical music as well—this piece is in **duple meter**. Such music has either two or four beats per measure.

Many of Sousa's marches were used for popular dances like the two-step or were performed at outdoor concerts. Today, jazz has also become a form of concert music, although audiences may behave much more informally at jazz concerts than at classical performances. Listen again to Count Basie's *Lester Leaps In*. This music has the foot-tapping rhythm that one expects from a jazz performance. Its rhythm serves a purpose, too: It lets you dance. Much of the music in this book would be very difficult to dance to. Not so the Basie!

As you listen this time, pay attention to the beat and the accents. Try counting "one-two-three-four" rapidly as you listen. Depending on how fast you are counting, you may find that the strongest accents fall either on beats two and four or on the "cracks" between the beats. This pattern, characteristic of much current popular music, resembles the familiar iambic meter of poetry (see box). Both have a regular da-DUM-da-DUM pattern. Musical meter works differently than poetic meter, though. Nobody would suggest that iambic meter in poetry is particularly exciting. The musical equivalent, on the other hand—commonly called backbeat, when it occurs on the second and fourth beats of the measure—is the foundation of the stirring rhythms found in both jazz and rock music.

Iambic is the most common meter in English poetry. What makes its musical equivalent so powerful and effective? *Lester Leaps In* has four beats per measure, a duple meter known as "common time" or $\frac{4}{4}$. Thus, it would be most natural to step on beats one and three, which are considered the strong beats—particularly on beat one, known as the **downbeat**. Backbeat accents on beats two and four, or emphasis on notes in the cracks between the beats, encourage people to move in more spontaneous and less predictable ways.

Triple Meter: Dvořák's *Slavonic Dance*

Dvořák's *Slavonic Dance* in E minor, op. 72, no. 10, as its title suggests, also evokes dancing. In its own day, in fact, it would have been considered popular music; it belongs to the somber folk genre known as *dumka* (plural *dumky*). It is an unusual dumka, though, by virtue of its **triple meter**, or three beats per measure. It is also a great deal slower than our earlier pieces, which contributes to its melancholy feeling. Slower music is often perceived as being more serious than fast, sprightly music. Each beat in the Dvořák lasts about twice as long as the beats in the Sousa or the Basie.

Listening carefully to this piece reveals something else important about musical meter: we can recognize it by counting. Pieces in duple meter, like those we have discussed so far, contain strong and weak beats. Pieces in triple meter might be expected to have two unstressed beats for each stressed one, much like dactylic meter in poetry ("higgledy, piggledy"). Musical rhythm offers some fundamentally

Downbeat: The first beat of the measure, or of any regular metrical pattern. It is typically stressed.

Triple Meter: A regular pattern of three beats, with the first one being stressed. It normally features a secondary stress on the third beat, in the pattern ONE-two-THREE, ONE-two-THREE, etc. It is also possible for the secondary stress to be placed on the second beat, giving music in triple meter an inherent metrical flexibility.

Iambic Pentameter: In poetry, an alternation of five stressed and five unstressed syllables.

Across the Arts
Shakespeare's Rhythm

When to the sessions of sweet silent thought
I summon up remembrance of things past,
I sigh the lack of many a thing I sought,
And with old woes new wail my dear time's
    waste:
Then can I drown an eye, unused to flow,
For precious friends hid in death's dateless
    night,
And weep afresh love's long since cancelled woe,
And moan the expense of many a vanished
    sight:
Then can I grieve at grievances foregone,
And heavily from woe to woe tell o'er
The sad account of fore-bemoanèd moan,
Which I new pay as if not paid before.
But if the while I think on thee, dear friend,
All losses are restored and sorrows end.

Shakespeare's Sonnet XXX, which we examined in Chapter 2 for its meaning and structure, is in **iambic pentameter**: an alternation of five unstressed and five stressed syllables—_ / _ / _ / _ / _ / —forms the basis of every line. The term "iambic" refers to the iambs, units of two syllables in the pattern "unstressed, stressed." Pentameter, meanwhile, literally means a metrical pattern of five units. Of course, Shakespeare, as a skilled poet, varies this pattern. The first line, for example, begins with a stressed syllable, followed by two unstressed syllables in a row. However, the underlying pattern remains regular and discernable throughout. In musical terms, we could say that Shakespeare alters the rhythm of the poetry while keeping the underlying meter the same.

Focus On

Antonín Dvořák (1841–1904)

Dvořák had a strong musical feeling for the folk dances of his native country, a trait he shared with many Romantic composers. Chopin, for example, wrote mazurkas and polonaises, based on the folk dances of Poland. Schubert wrote many ländler (sing. and pl.), an Austrian folk dance familiar to us from *The Sound of Music*. Dvořák's *Slavonic Dances* feature the distinctive styles of such Czech dances as the furiant, odzemek, skočna, and starodávný, which would have been immediately recognizable to his compatriots. He also featured the dumka in his "Dumky" Trio, op. 90, for piano, violin, and cello.

For a biographical profile of Antonín Dvořák, see p. 8.

different possibilities, however. In English poetry, most rhythms are defined entirely by stressed and unstressed syllables. Music, on the other hand, works with note duration as well. The Dvořák begins with an intriguing combination of short notes and longer ones. The longest notes often fall on beat one and extend over beat two, leading us to count more like ONE-two-THREE, rather than a simple ONE-two-three (as in higgledy, piggledy). We actually place a lighter accent on the third beat, so the pattern is best described as ONE-two-THREE ONE-two-THREE. Although not as strong as ONE, THREE is nevertheless an accented beat, not an unaccented one. This is a beat pattern that frequently appears in music in triple meter, making it fun to dance to. Since an unstressed beat seems to be missing in every measure, some fancy footwork is required.

Listening Closely for Meter

That fancy footwork is also a challenge for the composer. Like a good dancer, Dvořák accepts the challenge by working both *with* and *against* the meter as he devises his rhythms. Let us take up the same challenge by listening closely to the rhythmic complexity of this seemingly simple piece. Stop and start the music as necessary to make sure you can follow all of its subtleties.

In the A section, the accompaniment often underscores the long-short pattern by pausing on the last beat of the measure. A musician counting this part in perfect time would say, steadily, "one-and-two-and-three-rest, one-and-two-and-three-rest." Here the "ands" represent notes on the half-beats, and the "rest" represents a half-beat on which no note is played. But by taking just a little extra time with the final beat—stretching out the "three-rest" ever so slightly—the musician gives the third beat added emphasis. This contributes to our hearing "ONE-two-THREE."

At the same time, Dvořák confuses the issue. Rather than beginning on beat one, the melody begins on the "and" of the first beat, called an **upbeat**. Because this note is between beats and unaccented, we hear a natural emphasis on the beat immediately following it. But that beat is beat two, a beat we expect to be weak! It may

Upbeat: An unstressed beat that comes before the downbeat and thus precedes the beginning of the metrical pattern. Pieces, sections of pieces, and phrases often begin on an upbeat, forcing the listener to concentrate to find where the regular meter actually begins.

therefore take a few measures before you can securely identify where the down-beat, beat one, actually is. Each time a new phrase of the melody begins, every four measures, it begins on this upbeat. As though to compensate for this and strengthen the regular beat pattern, Dvořák places a similar upbeat before the third beat in the third measure of each phrase. Take some time to listen repeatedly to just the first minute or so of this music until you can clearly hear how this occurs. Then read on.

In the second half of the A section, beginning at 1:08, the phrases are shorter, temporarily placing a weak-beat accent at the beginning of every other measure. The rhythm now feels unstable. The A section concludes with two four-measure phrases (beginning at 1:23—the whole pattern repeats beginning at 1:42). Here the rhythmic pattern is even more regular, with a clear long-short in nearly every measure. As often in music, a period of instability is followed by greater stability.

How Dvořák Shifts the Rhythm

Thus far, Dvořák has used a typical accent pattern for music in triple meter. In the B section, he changes the pattern—from long-short (ONE-two-THREE) to short-long (ONE-TWO-three). (Robert Browning does something analogous in the opening stanza of his poem "Home-Thoughts, from Abroad"—see box.) To make

Trochaic Meter: In poetry, a meter that begins with a stressed syllable and then alternates with an unstressed one.

Across the Arts
How Meter Shifts in Poetry

Oh, to be in England
Now that April's there,
And whoever wakes in England
Sees, some morning, unaware,
That the lowest boughs and the brushwood
  sheaf
Round the elm-tree bole are in tiny leaf,
While the chaffinch sings on the orchard
  bough
In England—now!

In the moving lyric of "Home-Thoughts, from Abroad," Robert Browning uses an underlying **trochaic meter**, which begins with a stressed syllable and then alternates with an unstressed one (the opposite of iambic). None of the first four lines, though, has the same number of syllables as any of the others, and lines 2 and 4 end in stressed syllables, thus disrupting the regular flow of the pattern. The next three lines repeat the stress pattern _ _ /_ / six times:

That__the__low/est__boughs/and__the__ brush/wood__sheaf/
  Round__the__elm/tree__bole/are__in__ti/ ny__leaf/
  While__the__chaf/finch__sings/on__the__ or/chard__bough/

Since these patterns begin with relatively insignificant words—"that," "and," "round," "are," "while," "on"—the natural tendency is to pronounce those words without stress, making the meter of these lines appear to be a modified iambic. This metrical shift is completed in the final line, where the dash before the final word and the exclamation point that follows it emphasize the strong iambic meter: "In England—now!" These also create a sense of extra metrical space, as though the poem were slowing down, an effect also commonly found in music.

the transition, the opening measures of the B section, beginning at 2:16, briefly have a more complicated placement of accents.

The fourth measure (2:22; 2:38 on the repeat) helps resolve the ambiguity. Here Dvořák inverts the pattern of the A section by stressing the second beat of the measure and leaving the third beat unstressed. The stress on beat two is inten-sified by a **dotted rhythm**. By placing a dot after the first note, Dvořák lengthens it and shortens the note that follows. To understand dotted rhythm, consider this: a measure of three beats, counted evenly as "one-and-two-and-three-and," would be counted "one—a-two—a-three—a" in dotted rhythm, with the numbers lengthened and the "a" syllables made short. The short note after beat one serves as an upbeat to beat two, highlighting the long note that begins there.

The arrival of a new melody halfway through the B section confirms this shift of accent (2:49 and following). This melody repeats three times the pattern "one-two-three one—a-TWO." It concludes on a sustained note on beats two and three of the final measure, preceded by a melodic **triplet**: three short notes of equal value. When the A section returns, so does the original rhythm (4:10 and following). The coda, beginning at 5:23, then briefly restores some of the metrical ambiguity of the B section.

Dotted Rhythm: A rhythm consisting of notes of unequal duration, in which one (usually the first) is lengthened by means of a dot in the score, and the other shortened.

Triplet: Three notes of equal value that subdivide a beat.

LEARNING TO LISTEN GUIDE

TAKE NOTE OF RHYTHM AND METER

What to Listen For: The shifts in rhythmic emphasis within the over-all $\frac{3}{4}$ meter.

Streaming audio track 53.
Interactive Listening Guide ILG-13.

Dvořák: *Slavonic Dance* in E minor, op. 72, no. 10
Date: 1886
Instrumentation: Piano four-hands
Key: E minor
Meter: $\frac{3}{4}$ (three moderately paced beats per measure)
Form: Ternary (ABA)
Core Repertory Connection: Dvořák's *Slavonic Dance* is also discussed in Chapters 1, 8, and 12.

TIME	PROGRESSION	COMMENT
0:00	A section, first half	The rhythm of the melody places the main emphasis on beat 1 and a secondary emphasis on beat 3.
1:08	Rhythmic instability	A series of short phrases makes the beat a bit harder to find.
1:23	Return to stability	This section features very regular rhythms.
1:42	Repeat	Both the rhythmically unstable section and the stable one that follows are repeated.
2:16	B section, beginning	The B section starts with music that is rhythmically active and somewhat confusing.
2:22	Resolution	The fourth measure, though, places a firm secondary accent on beat 2. More rhythmically confusing measures follow.
2:32	Repeat	The entire pattern is heard again.

TIME	PROGRESSION	COMMENT
2:49	New melody	With the arrival of a new melody, the shift of the secondary accent to beat 2 is confirmed.
4:10	A section	The first section returns, and with it the original rhythms.
5:23	Coda	The concluding section returns to some metrical ambiguity.

Syncopation: Where's the Beat?

As you can see, comparisons between poetic and musical meter are sometimes misleading. Nowhere is this truer than in *Lester Leaps In*. Like most jazz, it uses syncopation, rhythmic accents that do not correspond exactly to the underlying meter. Notes don't have to come right on the beat; they can come slightly in between. In Gershwin's *I Got Rhythm,* for example—the song on which Basie's *Lester Leaps In* is based—the distinctly syncopated rhythms make it clear exactly what kind of rhythm the singer has "got." The first note of the melody comes in on beat 2, the weak beat. The second note occurs on the crack between beats 3 and 4. The song proceeds as follows:

```
Beat: 1 and 2 and 3 and 4 and | 1 and 2 and 3 and 4 and | 1 and 2 and 3 and 4 and |
Text:      I       got  rhyth-  m                            I       got
Beat: 1 and 2 and 3 and 4 and | 1 and 2 and 3 and 4 and | 1 and 2 and 3 and 4 and |
Text: mus-  ic                   I       got     my       man  who  could
Beat: 1 and 2 and 3 and 4 and | 1 and 2 and 3 and 4 and |
Text: ask   for  an- y thing   more?
```

Listen to a recording or video of the song, and see if you can pick out the syncopated syllables from those relatively few ones that fall directly on the beats. Notice how the rhythm seems to be constantly shifting.

Swing: *Lester Leaps In*

In *Lester Leaps In*, this shifting rhythm is the music's most significant content. It provides the "swing" that makes jazz fun and exciting. Syncopation still depends on a strong beat. Unless the beat is clear, often literally "drummed in," we cannot hear just how flexible rhythm can be. Picture a brick wall, broken by uneven cracks in the bricks. The pattern is regular, but the cracks can fall anywhere. Listen again to the beginning of *Lester Leaps In*, and think of the regular beats as the brickwork. How many irregular cracks can you hear?

Syncopation in Classical Music: Bach's Concerto in D Minor for Harpsichord and Strings

Much classical music also features syncopation, although it may seem less spontaneous than the syncopations of jazz. A good example is the main theme in the first

LEARNING TO LISTEN GUIDE

TAKE NOTE OF RHYTHM AND METER

What to Listen For: The way Count Basie (the pianist) plays with the underlying beat in the first two choruses.

Streaming audio track 72.
Interactive Listening Guide ILG-18.

William "Count" Basie: *Lester Leaps In*
Date: 1975; first recorded 1939
Instrumentation: Saxophone, trumpet, vibraphone, piano, drums, and string bass
Key: B-flat major
Meter: $\frac{4}{4}$, also known as common time (four rapid beats per measure)
Form: Repeated AABA choruses
Core Repertory Connection: *Lester Leaps In* is also discussed in Chapter 4.

TIME	PROGRESSION	COMMENT
First Chorus		
0:00	A	Even the first piano notes don't occur exactly where you expect to hear them.
0:08	A	Basie's left hand, though, plays on the beat.
0:16	B	Listen to the isolated piano chords here. They are slightly but exquisitely "off."
0:24	A	
Second Chorus		
0:31	A	The piano part grows more complicated.
0:39	A	
0:46	B	Once again, there are many off-beat chords.
0:54	A	The notes may seem regular, but they have a subtle long-short pattern unlike the even alternation of stressed and unstressed beats that we heard in the Sousa march.

movement of the Bach Harpsichord Concerto in D minor. As with the Basie, we first have to follow the basic metrical pattern before we can hear the syncopation. The movement is in common time. The first three notes (short-short-long) take up one beat, as do the two notes that follow them. These are followed by another note of the same value, taking up half of the third beat. The next note, though, which is longer than any of those heard so far, extends over the beat. As a result, there is no note played, and hence no rhythmic emphasis, on the beginning of the fourth beat. The measure concludes with a single note that takes up the second half of that beat.

In the next measure, the first three beats are occupied by a long-short-short rhythm, which inverts the first beat of the previous measure. This time, the fourth beat concludes with a note extending over the beat. In fact, it extends over the beginning of the next measure, which therefore begins with no rhythmic emphasis at all. The same thing happens on the second and fourth beats of that next measure.

By this time, the chain of syncopations actually seems to shift the rhythm forward half a beat. The effect is to add rhythmic urgency to the music. And since this theme is repeated many times in the course of the movement, that sense of urgency frequently returns. Listen carefully several times to this theme and its first several repetitions. Then keep listening to the rest of the movement and try to pick up the syncopations as they occur.

LEARNING TO LISTEN GUIDE

TAKE NOTE OF RHYTHM AND METER

What to Listen For: The syncopation of the opening measures recurring throughout the movement.

Bach: Concerto in D minor for harpsichord and strings, BWV 1052

I: Allegro

Date: Early 18th century

Instrumentation: Harpsichord and string orchestra

Key: D minor

Meter: $\frac{4}{4}$, also known as common time (four rapid beats per measure)

Form: Orchestral ritornellos alternating with solo passages

Core Repertory Connection: This music was also discussed in Chapter 1.

Streaming audio track 8.

TIME	PROGRESSION	COMMENT
0:00	Opening statement by the orchestra	The orchestra states the main theme of the movement. The harpsichord is heard in the background. This orchestral statement is known as a *ritornello*, from the Italian word for "return," because it will return at various points within the movement. It contains the prominent syncopations discussed in the text, which are thus a defining feature of the ritornello at each of its appearances.
0:16	First harpsichord solo	The harpsichord takes the spotlight as the orchestra assumes an accompanimental role.
0:31	Orchestral passage	The orchestra repeats the *ritornello*, but the harpsichord occasionally comes to the fore.
0:55	Second harpsichord solo	The harpsichord dominates, but it often seems to converse with the orchestra.
2:23	Orchestral passage	The orchestra again states the *ritornello* theme.
2:39	Third harpsichord solo	This solo begins by featuring fast repeated notes in the harpsichord. Later the harpsichord part ranges more widely.
3:52	Thematic statement	The orchestra repeats the opening *ritornello* quietly, then alternates with the harpsichord.
4:26	Orchestral passage	The orchestra powerfully restates the *ritornello* theme.
4:43	Cadenza	The *ritornello* concludes with a showy passage for the harpsichord.
5:01	Dialog	An extended passage features both the harpsichord and the orchestra.
7:58	Orchestral passage	There is a final statement of the main ritornello theme by the orchestra.

Haydn the Beat

Joseph Haydn's music can sound deceptively simple, hiding the extent to which the composer plays with the beat and our perception of it. Haydn was particularly devious in his minuets—a kind of in-joke, since the minuet was originally a

Focus On
Joseph Haydn (1732–1809)

Like many 18th-century composers, Joseph Haydn worked closely with the aristocracy for most of his life. His primary patrons were the Esterházys, a fabulously wealthy family of Austro-Hungarian princes. As a servant of the Esterházys, Haydn had the advantage of a steady salary and a standing orchestra, but he was obliged to write music on demand to suit the princes' taste. By all accounts, Prince Nikolaus Esterházy, who held the family title from 1762 until his death in 1790, deeply appreciated both Haydn's music and his rich sense of humor.

Haydn wrote a large number of works in virtually every genre prominent in his lifetime. His symphonies and string quartets, in particular, virtually define the Classical style. However, he also wrote important vocal works like the oratorio *The Creation*. Haydn's music still offers abundant riches to today's listeners.

For a biographical profile of Joseph Haydn, see p. 70.

The Esterházy concert hall in the palace at Fertőd, Hungary. Haydn's patrons had a lot of money to spend on music. *(© F1online digitale Bildagentur GmbH / Alamy)*

formal dance, in triple meter. Haydn's minuets seem designed to make self-conscious aristocrats fall flat on their faces, should they be foolish enough to attempt to dance to them. The listening guide highlights some of those effects in the minuet of the String Quartet in B-flat major, op. 64, no. 3, a prime example of Haydn's use of musical humor.

LEARNING TO LISTEN GUIDE

TAKE NOTE OF RHYTHM AND METER

What to Listen For: The various ways in which Haydn tricks the listener by making the beat very difficult to find.

Streaming audio track 20.
Interactive Listening Guide ILG-4.

Haydn: String Quartet in B-flat major, op. 64, no. 3
III: Menuetto: Allegretto
Date: 1790
Instrumentation: Two violins, viola, and cello
Key: B-flat major
Meter: $\frac{3}{4}$ (three rapid beats per measure)
Form: Ternary with binary repeats in each section (ABA, or aabb ccdd ab)
Core Repertory Connection: Haydn's Quartet in B-flat major is also discussed in Chapters 3, 5, and 6.

TIME	PROGRESSION	COMMENT
Big A		
0:00		The first violin plays a four-measure phrase, beginning with an upbeat ("three" of an incomplete introductory measure) and concluding on the downbeat of the fourth complete measure.
0:05		The second phrase starts out the same way, but the other instruments, which served to articulate the beat in the first phrase, drop out, leaving the violin to conclude the phrase on its own.
0:10		The three accompanying instruments then mimic the final three notes played by the first violin, with the distinctive beat pattern "two-three-ONE." It is possible to hear this either as a continuation of the previous phrase or as an extended upbeat to the next phrase.
0:14		That phrase concludes as expected. The first violinist, however, continues playing for another two measures, all alone, as though oblivious to the fact that the other instruments have dropped out. The pattern is a repeated "ONE-two ONE-two," which contradicts the prevailing triple meter.
0:18	Repeat of little a (the first half of the big A section)	
0:36		After the repeat, Haydn has the viola and cello echo the violin's characteristic "ONE-two ONE-two ONE-two" rhythm. He also inserts a beat of rest (silence), so that the implied duple meter of the echo does not simply continue that heard before.
0:38		Beginning with an upbeat, the original triple meter is finally reestablished.
1:13		An even more confusing passage, combining shifts to duple meter and strategically inserted rests, concludes the big A portion of the minuet.
1:31	Repeat of little b (the second half of the big A section)	
Big B		
2:27		Note how the upper instruments keep coming in before the beat, which the cello reminds them of with its plodding downbeats.

TIME	PROGRESSION	COMMENT
2:33		Things get straightened out.
2:42	Repeat of little c (the first half of the big B section)	
2:57		The rhythmic displacement returns, and continues much longer than before.
3:17		It is finally straightened out again.
3:26		After a rest, however, the displacement returns, and the section concludes with a kind of rhythmic seesaw.
3:34	Repeat of little d (the second half of the big B section)	
Big A		
4:13		The big A section is heard again, but without the internal repeats.

In History

Haydn's String Quartet in B-flat major, op. 64, no. 3

By the time Haydn wrote the six string quartets published in 1791 as op. 64, he had already lived a long and musically fruitful life. However, he was just entering what was in many ways the most satisfying part of his career. His longtime employer, Prince Nikolaus Esterházy, had died in September of the previous year. Nikolaus's son, Anton, who succeeded him, was no music lover, but that proved to be to the composer's benefit. Pensioned off, Haydn took up permanent residence in Vienna, where Mozart was living and where Beethoven would shortly move as well.

Mozart had come to know Haydn during the older composer's frequent sojourns in Vienna in the 1780s. Mozart was deeply impressed by the six quartets published in 1782 as op. 33. He responded with his own set of six quartets, which he dedicated to Haydn. Beginning in 1787, Haydn wrote several more sets in quick succession, producing what is considered the foundation of the string quartet repertory. In these works, he employed the high Classical style. Tightly organized around a few musical motives, this style proved to be at once sophisticated and popular.

Haydn soon made two highly profitable trips to London, for which his last 12 symphonies were written. Back in Vienna, he continued to write quartets and piano trios, along with highly successful choral works, including the oratorios *The Creation* and *The Seasons*. Rarely has a composer produced so much great music at such an advanced age.

The op. 64 quartets thus stand on the borderline between Haydn's years as a working musician and as a fully autonomous artist. Before, he drew a paycheck, had regular duties, and was treated as a servant. Now he was about to be celebrated throughout the world and could compose on his own terms.

Mozart died soon afterward, having left his own mark on Haydn's style, and it was natural that Beethoven, who moved to Vienna in 1792, should go to Haydn for instruction. Haydn's music strongly influenced his pupil as well. If you listen carefully to this quartet, you will hear sudden dramatic contrasts, elaborate working out of short motives, and quirky humor. All these mark Beethoven's Symphony no. 5, too. A work that may seem simple and unpretentious is actually much more: It sums up four creative decades and is a harbinger of the music to come.

Compound Meters

A significant amount of classical music—and a much smaller amount of popular music—uses **compound meters**: metrical patterns in which the measure is subdivided into either two or three smaller units.

Compound Meters in the Middle Ages: Machaut

In the late Middle Ages, the time of Guillaume de Machaut, all musical meters were considered compound, simply by convention. The musical notation of the time described as many as four different levels. In duple meter, for example, each measure might be paired with another measure. These pairs might make up regular groups of two, and these groups might in turn be paired to make up blocks of four. It sounds complicated, but fortunately the pattern, once established, rarely changed.

Listen again to Machaut's motet *Lasse! comment oublieray/Se j'aim mon loyal/Pour quoy me bat mes maris?*, which we first encountered in Chapter 2. In Chapter 10, we will explore how this piece sets three different texts simultaneously. For now, listen to the rhythm of this beautiful 14th-century work. It falls into a regular duple-meter pattern: groups of four short notes are heard throughout. You can count either "one-two-three-four" or "one-and-two-and" from beginning to end.

```
1 2 1 2 1 2 1 2 1 2 1 2 1 2 1 2 1 2 1 2 1 2 1 2 1 2 1 2 1 2 1 2 1 2 1 2 1 2 1 2 1 2 1 2 1 2 1 2
1   2   1   2   1   2   1   2   1   2   1   2   1   2   1   2   1   2   1   2   1   2   1   2
1       2       3       1       2       3       1       2       3       1       2       3
1                       2                       1                       2
```

FIGURE 7.1 Machaut's motet presents a complex layer cake of interlocking rhythms.

It is easy to miss, but these four-note groups are themselves joined in groups of three (see Figure 7.1). If you count "one-two-three" slowly, with one count for each group of four notes, you will find that a regular pattern emerges that is maintained throughout the piece. That pattern is most clearly articulated by the lowest—and slowest—of the three voices. Much of the time, it begins with one long note, occupying four counts in the upper voices, and continues with an even longer note, occupying eight such counts. The voice thus moves in an extremely slow triple meter, in a short-long rhythm: "ONE-TWO-three." The slow but regular unfolding of this triple meter governs the movement of the music as a whole.

For most listeners, this grouping is not conspicuous enough to be perceived as either a rhythm or a meter. Musical rhythm is not just a matter of foot-tapping beats or danceable patterns, however. Rhythm can also be a primarily intellectual experience that rewards careful listening. This kind of rhythmic layering was very much in keeping with medieval thought (see "Across the Arts: The Medieval Worldview").

By now, you will probably not be surprised to learn that the piece has an even bigger rhythmic pattern. The large-scale triple-meter units just described are themselves grouped together in pairs that proceed with absolute regularity. This little piece thus has a fourfold compound meter: duple at the largest, and slowest, level; triple at the next largest; and duple at the two smallest.

Compound meter: A regular pattern in which the beat is subdivided at two or more different levels. Typical compound meters are compound duple (ONE-two-three-TWO-two-three, designated as $\frac{6}{8}$ or $\frac{6}{4}$) and compound triple (ONE-two-three-TWO-two-three-THREE-two-three, designated as $\frac{9}{8}$ or $\frac{9}{4}$).

Streaming audio track 3. Interactive Listening Guide ILG-1 will help you see how the voices and rhythmic layers in Machaut's motet fit together.

Across the Arts
The Medieval Worldview

The rhythm of *Lasse! comment oublieray/Se j'aim mon loyal/Pour quoy me bat mes maris?* is difficult for us to understand, but it made perfect sense to medieval listeners. In the medieval world-view, the universe itself was built in interlocking layers, thought to operate according to musical proportions. If you have trouble perceiving Machaut's rhythms, consider that the proportions of the universe cannot be seen or heard either, at least in ordinary terms. Yet in the medieval cosmology they dictate the terms on which life is lived in the visible world.

In this photo, Music is personified in the panels on the left, while the panels on the right illustrate the three levels of the musical universe. On top is *musica mundana,* better known as the "music of the spheres," showing that the universe is constructed according to musical proportions. In the middle is *musica humana,* the "music of human life." *Musica instrumentalis,* sounding music, appears only in the bottom panel, and the female figure of Music points at it reprovingly, as though to remind it that it is only a pale imitation of the higher levels.

This view of music was most notably expressed by Boethius (ca. 480–524), the late Roman philosopher who also provided the text for the second movement of Dallapiccola's *Canti di prigionia.* Though it was based on ideas from the ancient world, Boethius's musical worldview helped to define the way the universe was understood for centuries after his death.

This famous illustration shows the medieval view of the world as consisting of three different kinds of music.
(© *Lebrecht Music and Arts*)

Most later music also has multiple rhythmic layers, even if they are not as predictable as Machaut's. In Dvořák's *Slavonic Dance,* for example, the measures are grouped in pairs, and the pairs of measures are grouped in pairs as well, as are the pairs of pairs, resulting in regular phrases (a term used to describe musical thoughts, which are much like phrases in language) of four and eight measures and even regular groups of such phrases. Such large-scale metrical patterns are often called hypermeter, and if you listen carefully, you can hear them in most of the music on your listening list. The shift in the secondary accent from beat three to beat two and back again just described can also be considered a rhythmic alternation in the large-scale structure of the music.

If You Liked This Music...
More Late Medieval Music

Machaut's music and that of other late medieval composers has been widely recorded. A recent album by Ensemble Musica Nova contains all of Machaut's motets. David Munrow's *Music of the Gothic Era*, from which this recording was taken, features motets from the 13th and 14th centuries and other early polyphonic music. The rhythms can sound deceptively simple to modern ears, but there is often a great deal going on beneath the surface.

Compound Meter in Romantic Music: A Chopin Ballade

Let us now look at some later instances of musical rhythm at its most sophisticated. A good modern example of compound duple meter is Chopin's Ballade in G Minor, op. 23. After a brief duple-meter introduction, the music settles into a slow $\frac{6}{4}$ meter, with two groups of three beats in each measure ("ONE-two-three-FOUR-five-six," or "ONE-two-three TWO-two-three"). As we noted in Chapter 3, this piece has two main themes, stated repeatedly as the music unfolds. Both themes illustrate compound duple meter, but in very different ways. The first theme—the refrain, which is stated immediately after the introduction—actually sounds like a continuation of that introduction, as though answering a question posed by the sustained, dissonant chord with which it ends.

The $\frac{6}{4}$ meter of this answer is not immediately easy to identify, after the duple meter introduction. An isolated bass note enters on "TWO" of the "ONE-two-three TWO-two-three" rhythmic pattern (0:33), and five melodic notes continue with the remaining "and-two-and-three-and" of this extended upbeat. The first sustained note falls on ONE of the next measure and occupies three successive beats—you can hear the two and three as repeated chords in the accompaniment. Two more notes of the same length follow, on the "TWO-two-three" of that measure and the "ONE-two-three" of the next measure. The entire pattern is then repeated five times, always with this half-measure displacement.

At the beginning of the second theme (the stanza), Chopin confuses the issue in a different way. First, after a passage marked *ritenuto* (literally, "held back," or, by implication, gradually slowing down), he marks the music *meno mosso* (slower) at the exact point at which the second theme begins. The theme itself starts with an accented note on the sixth beat of the measure that extends to the first three beats of the next measure as well. The downbeat of that measure is thus marked solely by a low, staccato, pianissimo note in the left hand (3:10). Only as the theme continues does the $\frac{6}{4}$ meter become clearly audible once again.

Tempo Rubato: "Stolen time," in Italian. As it is used today, the term simply means a flexible, expressive approach to tempo. It is rarely marked by the composer, so its use—particularly common in music from the Romantic period—is at the performer's discretion.

One more factor may complicate your perception of rhythm in this piece. Romantic music is often played with the technique called **tempo rubato** (literally, "stolen time"). In this a highly flexible approach to tempo—the opposite of "metronomic"—the beats are hurried forward and held back according to what is happening in the music. The virtuoso Vladimir Horowitz (1903–1989), who performs this ballade on your recording, epitomized Romantic piano playing. Listen carefully to the way he bends the beat, frequently lingering on notes for extra expressive emphasis. At the second statement of the second theme, beginning at 4:54, he holds back the tempo considerably for several full measures. He then accelerates quite audibly with the repetition beginning at 5:13. For many listeners, this intensifies the emotional content.

LEARNING TO LISTEN GUIDE

TAKE NOTE OF RHYTHM AND METER

What to Listen For: The use of flexible meter (tempo rubato) for expressive purposes by the performer.

Chopin: Ballade no. 1 in G minor, op. 23 beginning.
Date: 1831–1835
Instrumentation: Piano solo
Key: G minor
Meter: $\frac{4}{4}$, also known as common time (four fairly slow beats per measure)—$\frac{6}{4}$ (a compound meter with two groups of three beats per measure, treated in this performance with considerable flexibility)—$\frac{2}{2}$, also known as cut time (two very rapid beats per measure rather than four)
Form: Stanza and refrain, with introduction and conclusion
Core Repertory Connection: This music was also discussed in Chapter 3.

Streaming audio track 43.
Interactive Listening Guide ILG-12 will help you follow the subtleties of Horowitz's interpretation of the Chopin Ballade.

TIME	PROGRESSION	COMMENT
0:00	Introduction	The piece begins with a section in duple meter.
0:33	Refrain	The bass note that begins this section falls on beat TWO of a compound duple meter.
3:10	Stanza	This section also begins with a bass note, but this time it falls on ONE. As before, the meter is gradually clarified as the theme continues.
4:54	Rubato	Vladimir Horowitz holds back the tempo as the stanza theme returns.
5:13	Accelerando	He then speeds up dramatically as it repeats.

Disguising the Meter: Debussy and Impressionism

Rubato varies from one performance, or performer, to another. Sometimes, however, composers themselves disguise the meter. Claude Debussy, for example, blurs the meter in a variety of ways in his Sonata for flute, viola, and harp. First, like many 20th century composers, he often shifts the meter briefly but repeatedly over the course of a single movement. He also uses very complicated rhythms that defy regular patterns and may shift constantly between duple and triple divisions of the beat and half-beat. He frequently calls for the tempo to speed up (*accelerando*) or slow down (*ritardando*). Most importantly, he often obscures the meter so that it is almost impossible to discern.

The last movement of the sonata is the most straightforward rhythmically, and thus a good place for us to start. It is in common time nearly throughout, and Debussy begins by making this meter quite audible. The harp plays fast rocking notes at a rate of four per beat, with a pronounced accent on the first beat of every measure. Having drawn this clear outline, Debussy has the harpist back off a bit after the other instruments enter. However, partly because of Debussy's careful framing and partly because of the regular, emphatic accents in the melodic lines of the other instruments, the beat remains easy to hear. The meter also remains mostly the same throughout. Listen carefully to this movement, making sure you can follow the beat and the meter.

LEARNING TO LISTEN GUIDE

TAKE NOTE OF RHYTHM AND METER

What to Listen For: The consistent $\frac{4}{4}$ meter, which is sometimes disguised by the composer but never actually changes.

Streaming audio track 62.

Debussy: Sonata for flute, viola, and harp
III: Final—Allegro moderato ma risoluto
Date: 1915
Instrumentation: Flute, viola, and harp
Key: F minor/major
Meter: $\frac{4}{4}$, also known as common time (four rapid beats per measure)
Core Repertory Connection: Debussy's Sonata for flute, viola, and harp is also discussed in Chapters 4 and 8.

TIME	PROGRESSION	COMMENT
0:00	Opening section	Throughout this passage, a strong downbeat can be heard in the harp.
0:32	The harp backs off	The other instruments are more prominent in this section, but the beat remains quite audible.
0:46	Opening tempo	After a passage marked *poco rubato* (a little flexibility with the meter), the strong opening beat returns, though it is less dynamically emphasized.
1:09	Strong beat in harp	In a section marked *agitato* (agitated), the harp firmly emphasizes each beat, even though the dynamic level is mostly pianissimo.
1:42	The viola takes over	In a section marked *un poco più mosso* (a bit faster), the viola takes over the articulation of the beat. It begins playing pizzicato (plucked) to mimic the sound of the harp, which eventually joins back in.
2:04	The tempo speeds up again	In a section marked *accelerando poco a poco* (gradually speeding up), all three instruments take turns with the melody.
2:21	Backing off	The motion of the previous section quickly subsides.

TIME	PROGRESSION	COMMENT
2:36	Flexible tempo	In this section marked *tempo rubato*, the beat is still clearly articulated by the harp.
2:56	Opening tempo returns	Although this section is marked *tempo giusto* (the right tempo)—that is, without the previous rubato—the beat can be hard to hear because of the amount of rhythmic activity in all three instruments.
3:19	The tempo slows down	Despite the marking of *meno mosso* (slower), the level of rhythmic activity remains high.
3:41	The rhythm of the opening movement returns	For the first time in the movement, the meter briefly changes—to the $\frac{9}{8}$ of the opening movement.
4:03	Conclusion	It quickly changes back to $\frac{4}{4}$, though, to bring the movement to a rousing conclusion.

The second movement in Debussy's sonata is a bit more complicated, as it alternates two conflicting meters—triple and duple—and the tempo is also quite variable. The movement begins with a sustained low note in the viola, while the flute plays a triple meter melody. This passage is marked *tempo di minuetto*, meaning that, like Haydn's minuet, it should resemble the formal 18th-century dance. The beat may be hard to find, however, since there is usually not an emphasized note on the first beat of the measure.

The first of the contrasting passages is a short one marked *poco animando* (animating, or speeding up a little); the meter remains the same but the tempo quickens (0:36 and following). A concluding *ritardando* (slowing down) leads to a passage marked *au mouvement*, indicating a return to the original tempo (0:52 and following). This is followed by another faster passage, in which the flute plays very short notes (beginning at 1:09), making the music seem to accelerate even more. After a series of fluctuations, the original tempo returns for the conclusion of the first part of the movement (1:40 and following). So far, though, the original triple meter has persisted throughout.

In the next section (2:05 and following), the meter shifts to duple, and the tempo to *poco più animato* (a little faster). The change in meter is at first very hard to perceive, as this section begins with barely audible fast rocking notes marked *pp murmurando* (very quietly murmuring). Unlike the similar passage at the beginning of the finale, this one has no strongly articulated accent. When the other instruments enter playing slow, sustained notes, the beat remains unclear. It falls to the harp to articulate it, and it does so, once again, with music that repeatedly fails to emphasize the downbeat. Only after a striking harp glissando (2:18) do we encounter a passage with real rhythmic definition.

These metrical changes are one of the most distinctive surface features of this music. In effect, they divide the movement into five smaller movements in an overall pattern of ABA'B'A". Stravinsky used timbre to articulate the form of the second movement of the *Symphony of Psalms*; Debussy uses meter here for a similar purpose. Although they contrast in other ways—note the sweeping harp passages at the beginning of B'—these short sections of the movement also share similar timbres and melodic material. It is the meter that most clearly sets them apart.

LEARNING TO LISTEN GUIDE

TAKE NOTE OF RHYTHM AND METER

What to Listen For: The highly flexible rhythm, which this time involves actual changes in the underlying meter.

Streaming audio track 61.

Debussy: Sonata for flute, viola, and harp
II: Interlude, Tempo di Minuetto
Date: 1915
Instrumentation: Flute, viola, and harp
Key: F minor
Meter: $\frac{3}{4}$ (three moderately slow beats per measure), with several changes of meter
Form: ABA'B'A"
Core Repertory Connection: Debussy's Sonata for flute, viola, and harp is also discussed in Chapters 4 and 8.

TIME	PROGRESSION	COMMENT
A Section		
0:00	Opening	The beginning of the movement has a steady $\frac{3}{4}$ meter, even though the beat can be hard to pick out.
0:36	First contrasting passage	In this section, the meter remains the same but the tempo speeds up.
0:52	Cadence and harp solo	The original tempo returns.
1:09	Prominent flute passage	Notice the series of fast notes in the flute. Although they make the music sound faster, the tempo actually remains the same.
1:23	Variable tempos	The tempo first speeds up, then slows down.
1:40	Original tempo	The original minuet tempo returns to conclude this section of the movement.
B Section		
2:05	Meter change	Here the meter changes to $\frac{4}{4}$, but this is hard to hear due to the lack of strong accents.
2:18	Emphasized meter	Following a striking glissando in the harp, the $\frac{4}{4}$ meter becomes more audible. Strong downbeats are still missing, though, so you have to listen carefully to discern this.
2:32	Shift in emphasis	In a section marked "rubato," the meter remains the same, but the downbeats become more audible.
2:39	Faster tempo	Almost imperceptibly at first, the tempo begins to increase, with the meter remaining $\frac{4}{4}$.
2:50	Slower again, at first	The slower, rubato tempo returns, only to accelerate again, then slow for the conclusion of this section.
A' section		
3:16	Return	The harp plays the opening theme of the movement in the original $\frac{3}{4}$ time and at the original tempo. It is then joined by the other instruments.
B' section		
3:40	$\frac{4}{4}$ meter	Swirling runs in the harp and sustained notes in the flute help disguise the fact that the meter has shifted again.
A" section		
4:26	$\frac{3}{4}$ meter	The original meter and theme return once more at a slightly slower tempo to conclude the movement.

The first movement of the sonata is the hardest to follow metrically, a prime example of the subtlety and flexibility of Debussy's artistry. The main meter of the movement is $\frac{9}{8}$ (compound triple). At the end of the first section, though, Debussy shifts briefly to $\frac{7}{8}$ and $\frac{8}{8}$. These are highly unusual meters, since they involve irregular divisions of the beat. In the case of $\frac{7}{8}$, this is unavoidable, since seven, a prime number, cannot be divided into regular groupings. There are thus three different ways to count $\frac{7}{8}$ meter: "ONE-two-three TWO-two THREE-two," "ONE-two TWO-two-three THREE-two," and "ONE-two TWO-two THREE-two-three." Debussy chooses the first of these options. For the measures in $\frac{8}{8}$, he divides the beat not as "one-and-two-and-three-and-four-and," as one might expect, but as "ONE-two-three TWO-two-three THREE-two," another irregular grouping. Debussy then switches back to $\frac{9}{8}$ for three measures before changing to $\frac{18}{16}$ for the middle section of the movement.

At this point, you may be asking yourself, "$\frac{18}{16}$—what kind of meter is that?" Don't worry. For most listeners, the details are academic. The general impression is that this music has no regular meter. Debussy creates a feeling of almost infinite rhythmic flexibility through a variety of means. Any effort to tap your foot or dance to this music would seem almost to violate Debussy's intentions in composing it.

LEARNING TO LISTEN GUIDE

TAKE NOTE OF RHYTHM AND METER

What to Listen For: The way Debussy makes the underlying meter all but unrecognizable at times.

Streaming audio track 60.
Interactive Listening Guide ILG-16
will show you where the metrical
changes occur in the first movement
of the Debussy sonata.

Debussy: Sonata for flute, viola, and harp
I: Pastorale—Lento, dolce rubato
Date: 1915
Instrumentation: Flute, viola, and harp
Key: F major
Meter: $\frac{9}{8}$, with several changes of meter
Form: ABA'
Core Repertory Connection: Debussy's Sonata for flute, viola, and harp is also discussed in Chapters 4 and 8.

TIME	PROGRESSION	COMMENT
A section		
0:09	Metrically ambiguous opening	The $\frac{9}{8}$ meter is virtually impossible to hear throughout the first section of the movement.
1:43	First meter change	As the tempo picks up, the meter changes briefly to $\frac{7}{8}$.
1:53	Second meter change	Two measures of $\frac{8}{8}$ follow.
1:58	Original meter	The $\frac{8}{8}$ measures are followed by a return to $\frac{9}{8}$.
B Section		
2:16	Tempo and meter change	A faster section in $\frac{18}{16}$ provides a strong contrast. Despite the complex meter, three beats per measure can usually be heard.

TIME	PROGRESSION	COMMENT
A' section		
3:12	Meter change	The original meter returns, and with it the metric ambiguity of the opening.
4:23	Tempo and meter change	A brief passage at a faster tempo switches to $\frac{7}{8}$ for two measures before returning to $\frac{9}{8}$.
4:35	Original tempo	The music slows down again.
5:45	Conclusion	There are two measures of $\frac{6}{8}$ before the meter shifts back to $\frac{9}{8}$ to end the movement.

Clearly, this is not music meant to suggest or encourage dancing, marching, or any activity dependent on regular, clearly articulated rhythms. In fact, much classical music, while it may have more regular meters than this piece, also varies those meters by means both subtle and obvious. The only way to gain an appreciation of this fact is to listen to a lot of music, taking care to pay attention to the rhythm and meter as one of its most potentially interesting features.

The 20th Century: Rhythmic Freedom

In the 20th century, it became common to compose music with no regular meter at all. In some cases, as in many works by Igor Stravinsky, the composer changes time signatures so often that no regular pattern emerges. In other cases, there simply is no time signature, allowing the composer infinite flexibility in arranging the rhythms.

Irregular Meters: Ives's Violin Sonata no. 4

Ives uses both approaches in the second movement of his Violin Sonata no. 4. Unlike the Debussy sonata, this one often has very audible, accented beats. As in the Debussy, though, the metrical pattern is very hard to pick out. In this case, it's because for the first three minutes, there actually isn't one!

Ives's compositional strategy has to do with musical rhetoric, which is often similar to the rhetoric of speech. As we learned in Chapter 5, Ives weaves into the movement a quotation from the song *Jesus Loves Me*. The earliest presentation of it is fragmented, and obscured by the lack of clear meter. The first measure, as marked by Ives, technically contains eleven and a half beats in slow tempo, while the second contains thirty and a half! Even though Ives eventually introduces a $\frac{4}{4}$ time signature, irregular meter continues to prevail, with the last $\frac{4}{4}$ measure actually containing only three beats.

The middle, faster section of the movement, beginning at 3:58, contains time signatures throughout, but they change so frequently that the effect is the same. There appears to be no regular metrical pattern, even though the rhythms of this section are much firmer and more emphatic than those of the opening. Fragments of the tune are played throughout by both the pianist and the violinist, and it is heard in its entirety only at the end, first in somewhat distorted form in the piano, then more clearly in the piano, and finally, with the greatest clarity, in the violin. At that moment, the meter becomes completely regular as well, conforming to the common time of the original tune. The effect is similar to the conclusion of

President Kennedy giving his famous "Ich bin ein Berliner" speech. The speech was Kennedy's response to the building of the Berlin Wall, which separated West from East and transformed West Berlin into a kind of island within a hostile state. (© *Sipa via AP Images*)

Grove Music Online.

John F. Kennedy's famous speech in Berlin in 1963, when he proclaimed, "All free men, wherever they may live, are citizens of Berlin, and, therefore, as a free man, I take pride in the words 'Ich bin ein Berliner.'" The intense effect of this phrase, delivered in highly accented German, moved the audience deeply. It has become one of the most famous sound bites of the 20th century. An audience that did not speak German would have missed the point of Kennedy's speech, just as one who did not know *Jesus Loves Me* would miss the point of Ives's music. Ives frequently wrote pieces in which a familiar tune, implied or partially stated throughout, is only played in completely recognizable form at the very end, thereby strengthening its expressive impact when it emerges in all its simplicity.

Focus On
Charles Ives (1874–1954)

American composer. His music is marked by an integration of American and European musical traditions, innovations in rhythm, harmony, and form, and an unparalleled ability to evoke the sounds and feelings of American life. He is regarded as the leading American composer of art music of the 20th century. (J. Peter Burkholder, *Grove Music Online*.)

Ives's Violin Sonata no. 4 is titled "Children's Day at the Camp Meeting." Although composers' explanations always have to be taken with a grain of salt, Ives's commentary on the second movement is interesting enough to be worth quoting in its entirety.

The Second Movement is quieter and more serious except when Deacon Stonemason Bell and Farmer John would get up and get the boys excited. But most of the Movement moves around a rather quiet but old favorite Hymn of the children, while mostly in the accompaniment is heard something trying to reflect the out-door sounds of nature on those Summer days—the west wind in the pines and oaks, the running brook—sometimes quite loudly—and maybe towards evening the distant voices of the farmers across the hill getting in their cows and sheep.

But as usual even in the quiet services, some of the deacon-enthusiasts would get up and sing, roar, pray and shout but always fervently, seriously, reverently—perhaps not "artistically"—(perhaps the better for it)—"We're men of the fields and rocks, not artists," Farmer John would say. At times these "confurorants" would give the boys a chance to run out and throw stones down on the rocks in the brook! (Allegro conslugarocko!)—but this was only momentary and the quiet Children's Hymn is sung again, perhaps some of the evening sounds are with it—and as this Movement ends, sometimes a distant Amen is heard—if the mood of the Day calls for it—though the Methodists and Baptists seldom called for it, at the end of their hymns, yet often, during the sermon, an "Amen" would ring out as a trumpet call from a pew or from an old "Amen-Seat." The Congregationalists sometimes leaned towards one, and the Episcopalians often.

One can only imagine where most of the events described by Ives (see box) take place in the music. However, the fast middle section, marked *Allegro* (*conslugarocko*)—a typically Ivesian blend of Italian and English—clearly depicts the boys throwing stones in the brook. The conclusion, meanwhile, represents the final singing of the hymn, mingling with the sounds of evening. Only during this final section does a regular meter—common time—establish itself, as though to indicate that the passions of the day are subsiding.

Irregular Compound Meters: Vandervelde's *Genesis II*

Composers sometimes sustain irregular compound meters, like the $\frac{7}{8}$ and $\frac{8}{8}$ in the Debussy discussed earlier, for long stretches and even entire compositions. An example of this is Janika Vandervelde's *Genesis II*, which begins with an extended passage in which $\frac{5}{8}$ meter predominates.

LEARNING TO LISTEN GUIDE

TAKE NOTE OF RHYTHM AND METER

What to Listen For: The unusual $\frac{5}{8}$ meter and the ways in which it is both established and disrupted.

WEBSITE

Streaming audio track 73.

Vandervelde: *Genesis II* for piano trio, beginning
Date: 1983
Instrumentation: Piano, violin, and cello
Key: Variable
Meter: Irregular
Core Repertory Connection: *Genesis II* is also discussed in Chapters 6 and 12.

TIME	PROGRESSION	COMMENT
0:00		The pattern at the beginning can be counted "ONE-TWO-three-FOUR-five."
0:19		Here it shifts to "ONE-two-THREE-four-five."
0:27		The regular clockwork subsides and the meter becomes much harder to follow.
0:42		The music becomes more animated and a fast triple meter becomes audible.
0:54		The $\frac{5}{8}$ meter returns, but in much more irregular patterns. The tempo also slows.

Polymeters: Global Music

More than one meter may also run at the same time, although this effect rarely occurs in European-influenced Western music. Listen to *Jumping Dance Drums*, a recording made in the Bahamas in the 1950s of a native drumming ensemble. The music begins with the sound of the *claves*, a Latin American instrument consisting of short sticks that are struck together. The *claves* are gradually joined by three drums and a saw, the latter played by scraping a knife along its teeth.

Claves. *(merthuroglu)*

At first, the meter of the music is relatively easy to pick out. Somewhere in the second minute of the track, though, you may realize that you have entered uncharted rhythmic territory. This is because the meters played by the various drums in the ensemble do not mesh like those of the ensembles we have encountered previously. This is an example of **polymeters**: literally, more than one meter running simultaneously.

Although the combination of different meters is second nature to many African and Middle Eastern musicians—and to those in the New World who, like those on this recording, are influenced by them—they present a unique challenge to nearly everybody else. Even if you are used to the strong, percussive, emphasized rhythms of rock music, you have probably never heard drums used in this way before.

Polymeters: Multiple meters used simultaneously. This effect is rarely heard in Western music but is common in the music of Africa, the Caribbean, and the Middle East.

LEARNING TO LISTEN GUIDE

TAKE NOTE OF RHYTHM AND METER

What to Listen For: The often surprising subdivisions of the audible beat, due to the simultaneous use of different metric patterns.

Streaming audio track 75.

Jumping Dance Drums
No Date
Instrumentation: *Claves*, three drums, and saw
Meter: Polymetric

TIME	PROGRESSION	COMMENT
0:00	Beginning	The claves are heard first and are almost immediately joined by one of the drums and the saw. If you listen carefully, you will hear that notes emphasized by the saw do not correspond to those played by the drums.
1:14	The second drum enters	The first sounds from the second drummer immediately complicate the rhythmic texture. Rather than the regular emphasized beat heard from a jazz or pop rhythm section, you can hear a profusion of drum strokes that seem to defy such expectations. Note how the *claves* complicate the picture even further.
1:37	The third drum enters	The first sounds from the third drum are even more confusing. Beats seem to be raining from all directions. As the piece continues, the instruments continue to mix in interesting ways. Listen carefully to the ways they merge and yet remain distinct until the fadeout at the end.

This music also differs significantly from other examples we have heard in what might be called its sense of direction. It may sound strangely circular. You might think that it is simply repeating the same things over and over, rather than going anywhere. If you listen carefully, though, you will hear that this music allows for a complex interplay among its different rhythmic levels.

If You Liked This Music...
Caribbean and African Drumming

Many field recordings of Caribbean and African drumming ensembles are available. These differ from studio recordings by virtue of being made on location rather than in an artificial studio environment. The one heard here is from a Smithsonian Folkways recording released in the 1950s under the title *African and Afro American Drums*. Polymeters can also be heard in music from Middle Eastern cultures: that of Afghan Pashtuns, for example.

Intriguingly, the same effect can be heard in much Western classical music of the 20th century and the late Middle Ages. Polymeters were used by Stravinsky in *The Rite of Spring*, one of the most widely performed early 20th-century works, and by mannerist French composers of the late 14th century. Examples of the latter can be found on the album *Ars magis subtilior* by Ensemble Project Ars Nova.

In short, polymeters are a widespread musical phenomenon and a unique challenge to your active listening skills.

Not all meters can be classified as easily as those we have been discussing. For example, the first variation in the sixth movement of Mozart's *Gran Partita* is written in $\frac{2}{4}$. For most of the variation, though, the melody moves in triplets. If you try to count "one-and-two-and," you will find that each half beat is divided into three notes instead of the expected two ("one-and-a-two-and-a"). The music thus *sounds* as if it is in a compound meter. Twice, however, at the beginning of the second phrase of the melody, it returns briefly to a duple division, as though the implied compound meter had suddenly disappeared.

As this exceptional passage reminds us, most music depends on regular metrical patterns. Because of its fundamentally physical impact, regular rhythm is frequently music's most noticeable feature. It is as essential to music as the rhythms of breathing and the beating of the heart are essential to life. Yet sometimes even rhythm can be trumped by a good tune. In the next chapter, we turn to melody.

SUMMARY

- Rhythm plays an even more defining role in our experience of music than it does in that of poetry.
- Rhythm is organized as meter, whose changes, like those in timbre, can serve to articulate the structure of music.
- The most widely used meters in Western music are duple and triple—which include, respectively, two or three beats per measure—and common time— which has four beats per measure, or unit of musical time.
- Composers and performers articulate meter in a variety of ways. It can be made considerably more complex through the use of syncopation, which displaces the beat, tempo rubato, which renders it more flexible, and backbeat, which emphasizes what would normally be the spaces between the beats.

- Compound meters subdivide the measure further at as many as four different levels, as in some late medieval music.

- Non-Western music, by contrast, often features more complex meters, including polymeters, which use different metrical patterns simultaneously.

KEY TERMS

Accented	p. 186	Iambic pentameter	p. 189	Triplet	p. 192
Compound meter	p. 199	Polymeters	p. 210	Trochaic meter	p. 191
Dotted rhythm	p. 192	Tempo rubato	p. 202	Upbeat	p. 190
Downbeat	p. 189	Time signature	p. 188		
Duple meter	p. 188	Triple meter	p. 189		

REVIEW QUESTIONS

1. What is meter and how does it relate to rhythm?
2. What is duple meter? What pattern of stressed and unstressed beats is typically found in duple-meter music?
3. What is triple meter? How does the pattern of stressed and unstressed beats in triple-meter music differ from that in duple-meter music?
4. What are compound meters? What are some typical compound meters found in recent Western music?

5. What are some ways in which composers and performers can alter the rhythm and meter of music?
6. How does Debussy's and Ives's use of meter differ from those of earlier composers?
7. What are polymeters, and in what kinds of music are they likely to be found?

REVIEW CONCEPTS

1. Why does rhythm play an even more fundamental role in music than it does in poetry?
2. How does syncopation, as used by Bach in his Concerto in D minor for harpsichord and strings, differ from that found in jazz pieces like Basie's *Lester Leaps In*?
3. How did the Medieval approach to meter differ from that found in more recent music? How is the Medieval approach represented in the Machaut motet discussed in this chapter?

4. What is distinctive about the use of meter in Vandervelde's *Genesis II*? Why does the meter of this piece sound so unusual?
5. How can our perception of meter be altered by the composer? By the performer? Give some examples from the listening list other than those discussed in the chapter.

LISTENING EXERCISES

1. Listen to some of the examples from the listening list not discussed in this chapter. Can you determine the meter? Does the meter change at any point? Try counting out loud if you have trouble finding the beat.
2. Listen carefully to some recordings of works by Chopin. Chopin's music is often played with considerable use of *tempo rubato.* Can you identify the meter, and then find places where the performer is altering it for expressive purposes?

3. Listen to some other recordings of African or Caribbean music featuring drumming ensembles. Can you hear the use of polymeters? What challenges does this music pose for listeners not accustomed to its rhythmic complexity?
4. Listen to some recordings of current popular music. How does the approach to rhythm differ from that in the classical music you have been hearing? Try to use the vocabulary introduced in this chapter as precisely as possible in answering this question.

Melody

TAKE NOTE

Melody is the sequence of individual notes that make up the tune of either a section or an entire piece of music. It is defined by rhythm, pitch range, distance between each note, and length of individual notes. A motive is a short melodic fragment crafted to be especially memorable. Melody is the element of music that many listeners find easiest to recognize and remember.

Chapter Objectives

⬤ Identify melodic lines and recognize the pervasiveness of melody in virtually all music.

⬤ Learn the characteristics of melody in Western music, and their historical roots.

⬤ Understand what characterizes a good melody and what makes some melodies "lyrical."

⬤ Describe how composers build melodies from shorter musical phrases.

⬤ Distinguish motive from melody, and motivic development from thematic development.

Drone: A sustained low note.

When you think of your favorite music, melody is what probably comes to mind first. Everybody loves a good tune, and most people think they know one when they hear one. But what exactly constitutes a good tune? Melody can be used in many ways. Some melodies are instantly memorable, and you find yourself humming along. Songwriters of popular music are skilled at saving their best melodies for the most dramatic moments in a song. Likewise, classical composers often do not present the most memorable tune at the beginning of a piece but prefer to save it for later. Melodies can be more subtle as well. As we have already observed, they may also be disguised, varied, or developed. They are often the most convenient building blocks for constructing musical forms and the most convenient signposts for recognizing them.

This chapter examines how to listen for melody in any kind of music. We will consider the characteristics of melodies, the ways in which composers construct them, and their role in the overall structure and success of a piece of music.

Melodic Lines in a Non-Western Melody

Virtually all music contains melody. Listen, for example, to the beginning of *Raga Bhankar*, which we examined in Chapter 5 as an example of an arch-shaped form. This piece begins with seemingly random sounds: a **drone** (or sustained low note) and a group of descending notes. At about 0:10, though, the sitar begins playing notes that are melodic. The series of pitches forms what is often described as a **melodic line**. This familiar visual metaphor implies that melodies have both continuity and direction. You can think of traditional musical notation as a graph, with the vertical dimension showing changes in pitch and the horizontal dimension showing the progress of time from left to right. The interactive listening guides also use graphs to show the shape of some of the melodic lines that we discuss in this chapter and elsewhere.

Actually, most melodic lines are complicated shapes more appealing to the ear than to the eye. This is particularly true of *Raga Bhankar*, since, unlike most Western musicians, Indian sitar players "bend" pitches—they hover around them rather than playing them discretely. Rock and blues guitarists often do the same thing. Traditional music notation does not show this bending of pitches. If you want to understand how pitch bending affects your perception of melody, compare the music you just listened to with the beginning of the second movement of the Ives violin sonata, which also begins slowly with what sound like fragments of melody. Contrast the pitches played by the violin with those played by the sitar. Although violinist Gregory Fulkerson uses vibrato in this performance, the underlying pitches he plays remain stable enough that your ears hear them as distinct and separate. Sitarist Ustad Vilayat Khan, on the other hand, frequently slides between pitches, treating the notes more like momentary resting places. While some of the pitches remain steady for short periods, others wobble audibly, and the entire progression feels unstable to ears accustomed to Western music.

Listen now to the rest of *Raga Bhankar* and pay careful attention to the unfolding of the melodic line. You may notice that certain patterns are repeated at various points. This is because the piece is based on a raga, which can be thought of as a collection of melodic materials rather than a melody in the Western sense. All seven minutes are really one continuous melody worked out in a variety of ways that make the music interesting.

Melody in Western Music

In Western music, melody—contrary to what you may think—is often not the focal point. This is because it has to compete with other elements of music, particularly form and harmony. A Western piece with a strong, memorable melody, such as the Dvořák *Slavonic Dance* or a three-minute pop song, tends to be short and uncomplicated. A long and highly developed composition, like the Mozart and Bach pieces we already examined, may be built on a surprisingly small amount of melodic material.

But what is it that makes a melody like the one used by Dvořák so memorable? One quality that defines a memorable tune is **lyricism**, a term derived from "lyrical," which stems from an ancient type of poetry meant to be sung to the accompaniment of the lyre. (*Lyric* refers to the words coupled with a melody to reinforce the emotional story of a song.) What makes a singable, lyrical melody—and what communicates emotion and meaning, so that we remember it?

Musical Intervals

One answer to the question of what makes music lyrical is its **intervals**: the way the melody moves from one note to another. Intervals also exist in harmony, where they sound simultaneously rather than in succession. Melodic motion, in musical terminology, is often **conjunct**: one pitch tends to follow another one that is either directly above it or directly below it. In the opening of *Row, Row, Row Your Boat*, for example, the words "gently down the stream" are set entirely to conjunct pitches. However, in the next line—"merrily, merrily, merrily, merrily, life is but a dream"—each repetition of "merrily" is followed by a melodic leap over one or more notes to reach the next one. We call this a **disjunct** progression. Now think of the beginning of the song *Somewhere Over the Rainbow*. The two syllables of the opening word, "somewhere," are set to a clearly disjunct interval, requiring a jump from the low end to the high end of the singer's range.

On the piano, it is no more difficult to play the beginning of *Somewhere Over the Rainbow* than to play the beginning of *Row, Row, Row Your Boat*. You just have to know which keys to press. A singer, however, has to find the second note: no easy task for a beginner, as anyone who has struggled to sing *The Star-Spangled Banner* will attest. It is no accident that schoolchildren are usually taught *Row, Row, Row* and similar songs first. The opening theme of the Bach concerto, like *Somewhere Over the Rainbow* and *The Star-Spangled Banner*, contains large, disjunct intervals. In fact, unlike those two melodies, which alternate disjunct intervals with conjunct passages, Bach's melody is made up almost entirely of intervals that are much easier to play on an instrument than to sing. This melody would not be described as lyrical.

Dvořák, on the other hand, has chosen almost exclusively conjunct intervals. The few small melodic jumps he includes become quite noticeable. Conjunct melodies are lyrical because they are easy to sing. The voice, the first and most basic

Chronology Continued

1915
Claude Debussy p. 225
Sonata for flute, viola, and harp, 1st movement

late 20th century
Ustad Vilayat Khan p. 217
Raga Bhankar, for sitar

Melodic Line: A visual metaphor for a succession of musical tones arranged in a shape perceived as unified and conveying a sense of movement or direction.

Lyricism: The quality of being singable.

Interval: The distance between two pitches.

Conjunct: Melodic motion that features intervals consisting primarily of successive pitches. (Contrast **disjunct**).

Disjunct: Melodic motion that features large intervals, requiring the performer to jump between nonconsecutive pitches. (Contrast **conjunct**).

LEARNING TO LISTEN GUIDE

TAKE NOTE OF MELODY AND FORM

What to Listen For: The continuous melodic line whose individual pitches are bent by the performer but which nevertheless unfolds steadily throughout the music.

Streaming audio track 74.

Raga Bhankar
Date: Late 20th century
Instrumentation: Sitar and tabla
Meter: Duple meter, with the tempo gradually accelerating
Form: Raga, arch-shaped form with a peak at the end
Core Repertory Connection: This music is also discussed in Chapter 5.

TIME	PROGRESSION	COMMENT
0:00	Introduction	Only a steady drone (sustained pitch) and descending notes in the sitar are heard.
0:10	The melody begins	The sitar begins playing pitches that our ear can join together as a melody, even if it doesn't behave like most melodies we have heard.
0:18	Entrance of the tabla	The tabla, or hand drums, become audible and begin their highly rhythmic accompaniment.
		The sitar melody continues to unfold in irregular sections. Listen carefully for the points of rest when one ends and another begins.
4:31	Faster pace	The sitar begins playing faster notes than have been heard so far.
5:15	More fast notes	The pace of the sitar picks up again. The speed and volume of the music continue to increase.

In History

Raga Bhankar

The classical music of India is often compared to classical music of the West for its richness, depth, and variety. But there is one important difference: as in many non-Western societies, this music is not written down. What you hear in *Raga Bhankar* is an example of a musical repertory that has been passed on by oral tradition and performance practice.

Raga Bhankar can be precisely placed within Indian culture as a raga in the North Indian, or Hindustani, style. Because the piece is not a written composition, however, *Raga Bhankar* cannot be tied to a specific historical moment.

Its historical associations are of a very different kind. Unlike Western music, which is often heard in concert halls, this music plays a much more concrete role in everyday life.

Its main instrument, the sitar, assumed its present form during the last two centuries. The common concert sitar has a long fret board and a half-gourd for its main body. The instrument has five main strings, two drone strings, and about a dozen sympathetic strings. The main strings and drone strings are plucked with the fingers, and the instrument creates a deep, resonating sound. Sympathetic strings are not plucked or played directly but vibrate in harmony with the plucked strings.

During the late 20th century, sitar music was popularized in the West by charismatic performers including Pandit Ravi Shankar (1920–2012) and the Beatles, particularly George Harrison (1943–2001). Shankar wrote concertos combining the instrument with a Western orchestra, but he also played in more traditional formats. The Beatles featured the instrument in the song *Norwegian Wood (This Bird Has Flown)* (1965) and several subsequent recordings, as did many other rock groups.

Indian performers typically sit directly on a rug, rather than standing or sitting in chairs. Not simply decorative, this rug is traditionally associated with prayer, giving the music itself a quasi-sacred role. Ironically, some critics have suggested that the isolation of the Western concert stage has the same effect, but with different implications. Religion in India is not separated from everyday life to the extent that is common in the West, and neither is music—even classical music. The reverent hush of the concert stage thus imparts a kind of sacredness that is fundamentally antithetical to the raga.

For all their differences, however, Indian and Western music have certain historical connections. The sitar is widely believed to have originated in Western Asia, which also produced the lute—a standard instrument in Europe for centuries. The rhythmic patterns that complement the melodic ragas are called *talas*. Late medieval European composers often wrote motets—short, polytextual vocal pieces like Machaut's *Lasse! comment oublieray/Se j'aim mon loyal/Pour quoy me bat mes maris?*—supported by elaborate rhythmic patterns called *taleas*.

In short, there are many different ways of placing this music in history and society. As with Western music, these are most valuable if they cause you to think more deeply about what you are hearing.

If You Liked This Music. . .
Indian Classical Music

Recordings of Indian classical music are widely available. Ustad Vilayat Khan and Pandit Ravi Shankar were both Hindustani, or North Indian, sitar players. In addition to their many traditional performances, both recorded their own compositions in more eclectic styles. Some of Khan's music for the 1958 Indian film *Jalsaghar* can be heard in the more recent film *The Darjeeling Limited*. Shankar recorded his first concerto for sitar and orchestra with the London Symphony Orchestra.

There are also many recordings of music in the Carnatic, or South Indian, tradition. Much of this music features vocalists, as well as performers who have adapted the violin from Western music. Well-known artists include singer R.K. Srikanthan (b. 1920) and violinist Lalgudi Jayaraman (1930–2013).

musical instrument, tends to be a point of reference for all others. A lyrical melody also seems amenable to lyrics, which typically accompany vocal music.

Rhythm and Melody

Rhythm also affects the accessibility of a melody, and this can be illustrated again by a comparison between the Dvořák and the Bach. The Bach melody is

Judy Garland (1922–1969) sings
Somewhere Over the Rainbow **in the**
1939 movie *The Wizard of Oz.*
The song, with music by Harold
Arlen and lyrics by E.Y. Harburg,
won an Academy Award.
(© Moviestore collection Ltd/Alamy)

rhythmically complicated. It presents a chain of syncopations, with notes frequently falling between the beats rather than on them. This kind of complex rhythm is also easier to play on an instrument than to sing. In contrast, the more regular rhythm of Dvořák's melody makes it easier both to sing and to remember.

Phrase Structure

Dvořák's melody strikes most listeners as good shower-humming material for yet a third reason. It consists of absolutely regular phrases that mirror one another like the lines in much familiar poetry (see box). The successive phrases alternate open and closed endings—lines that sound incomplete and lines that sound more final. The endings are marked by **cadences**, harmonic and melodic stops. The first phrase (through 0:08) is less final sounding than the second one (through 0:16), which concludes exactly one note lower. The harmony at the end of the second phrase, though, is still inconclusive, making the ending of the fourth phrase at 0:32 sound even more final.

Cadence: A harmonic and melodic stop, found at the end of a phrase of a melody, of a section of a piece, or of an entire piece.

Roots of Modern Melody

Balanced phrase structure—musical phrases of equal length grouped together in pairs—seems so intuitive and universal that it is important to recognize this feature as virtually unique to Western culture. It originated in the late Middle Ages, as the Western music we studied in Chapters 2, 3 and 4 was developing.

The troubadours, who flourished in what is now southern France in the 12th and 13th centuries, were not the wandering vagabonds of popular imagination. They were highly educated, often aristocratic, poet-composers, steeped in a rich tradition that provided many of the foundations of modern poetry. Their language

LEARNING TO LISTEN GUIDE

TAKE NOTE OF MELODY

What to Listen For: The exact beginning and ending of each phrase of the melody.

Dvořák: *Slavonic Dance* in E minor, op. 72, no. 10, opening melody
Date: 1886
Instrumentation: Orchestra
Key: E minor
Meter: $\frac{3}{4}$ (three moderately slow beats per measure)
Core Repertory Connection: This music is also discussed in Chapters 1, 7, and 12.

Streaming audio track 53.
Interactive Listening Guide
ILG-13 helps visualize the melodic
structure of the *Slavonic Dance*
by showing only melody and
accompaniment.

TIME	PROGRESSION	COMMENT
0:00		The first phrase ends inconclusively.
0:08		The second phrase has a more final-sounding conclusion, but the harmony is still unstable.
0:16		The third phrase mirrors the first one, although it is not identical to it.
0:24		The fourth phrase ends with both melodic and harmonic stability, concluding the first melodic statement. Its ending is marked by a slowdown in the tempo (tempo rubato).

Across the Arts
Dvořák, Dance, and Poetry

The way Dvořák constructs his melody in the *Slavonic Dance* in E minor is exactly analogous to what the poet A.E. Housman does in the following stanzas of *With Rue My Heart Is Laden*:

> With rue my heart is laden
> For golden friends I had,
> For many a rose-lipt maiden
> And many a lightfoot lad.
>
> By brooks too broad for leaping
> The lightfoot boys are laid;
> The rose-lipt girls are sleeping
> In fields where roses fade.

Each stanza of Housman's poem contains four lines that rhyme in the pattern ABAB. The odd-numbered lines conclude with no punctuation, indicating that they are incomplete (an open ending), while the second lines conclude with nonfinal punctuation (a comma and a semicolon, respectively) and the fourth lines conclude with periods.

Dvořák does precisely the same thing musically. The first and third phrases "rhyme," in that they contain similar music, as do the second and fourth phrases. In fact, if you listen carefully, you will hear that the first half of the first phrase has the same rhythm and melodic shape as the first half of the second phrase; they match, as do the second halves of these phrases. This melody works in part due to its balanced and harmonious proportions that remind us of the structure of a simple poem.

Troubadours, in a 13th-century manuscript. Most of what we know about the use of instruments in the Middle Ages comes from illustrations such as this one. (© *The Bridgeman Art Library Ltd./Alamy*)

***The Last Judgment,* by Giotto (1266/7–1337).** Giotto painted this dramatic fresco on the Arena Chapel in Padua, Italy. (*Scala/Art Resource, NY*)

Sequence: A Medieval form consisting of pairs of textual lines, each pair set to a new line of music played twice.

(Occitan) and imagery—frequently based on what is now often called courtly love—may be remote from modern experience, but their songs sound notes of introspection and romantic despair still echoed in popular songs of today.

Although often anthologized as poetry, troubadour lyrics were not poetry in the modern sense. Just like the work of any current singer-songwriter, they were a combination of poetry and music. Unlike the songs of Bob Dylan or Joni Mitchell, though—which most people learn through recordings—they were composed and transmitted orally, and generally not put in writing until many years later. The music for many troubadour songs has been lost because it was never written down.

The technical characteristics of troubadour poetry also began to appear prominently in the music of the same period, influenced in part by a shift in common language usage. The writing of poetry shifted from Latin to vernacular languages such as Occitan. This transformed the quantitative rhythms and meters of classical Latin poetry, based on syllable length rather than stress, to the accentual meters that have prevailed ever since. So profound was this change that, by the late Middle Ages, Latin poetry was also being written using accentual meters, and Latin was probably being pronounced that way as well.

Balanced Phrase Structure: The *Dies irae*

The transition to accentual meters in Latin pronunciation carried over to music with Latin texts. An example is the *Dies irae*, a 13th-century composition that we first encountered in Chapter 2, and that is used by Luigi Dallapiccola throughout his *Canti di prigionia* and also by George Crumb in *Black Angels*. The text of this piece—which takes the Medieval form of the **sequence**, consisting of pairs of textual lines, with each pair set to a new line of music sung twice—was written by Thomas of Celano, based on Zephaniah 1:15–16. Dallapiccola and Crumb chose it because of its subject matter—it deals with the Judeo-Christian concept of the Day of Judgment—but also because its tune is probably the most easily recognizable melody from the Middle Ages. See the listening guide for the text of the *Dies irae*.

The First Two Stanzas

Notice that this poem (in the Latin) has the plodding, monotonous quality that we associate today with doggerel: the kind of poetry seen in advertising or greeting cards. Because every stanza has the exact same rhythm and rhyme scheme, the poem might seem to lack variety, suggesting to modern readers that the poet was unoriginal or unskilled. Medieval readers, however, may simply not have had the same concept of originality. And the matching rhythms and rhymes make the text well suited to melodic treatment.

Every other stanza, a new melody appears. If you listen carefully, you will notice that the melodies are shaped very differently. Stanzas one and two, along with stanzas seven and eight and thirteen and fourteen, are set to the tune used by Dallapiccola and Crumb, a distinctive melodic line beginning with descending intervals that are disjunct but interlocking. All three lines of the stanza are set within a relatively narrow range: the distance between the highest and the lowest notes is quite small. In the first line, the text-setting is entirely **syllabic**, meaning one note

LEARNING TO LISTEN GUIDE

TAKE NOTE OF MELODY, FORM, and TEXT

What to Listen For: Every second stanza of the text is set to the same music as the previous stanza. There are three main sections of the melody, labeled A, B, and C, each of which is repeated several times.

Streaming audio track 1.

Thomas of Celano: *Dies irae*
Date: 13th century
Instrumentation: Unaccompanied male voices
Meter: No regular meter: the musical accents are shaped by those of the text.
Form: Sequence, with paired stanzas of poetry set to identical music

TIME	SECTION	ORIGINAL TEXT	TRANSLATION	COMMENT
0:00	A	1. *Dies irae, dies illa solvet saeclum in favilla,* *teste David cum Sibylla.*	Day of wrath, day that will dissolve the world into burning coals, as David bore witness with the Sibyl.	This opening section of the melody, which is sung twice, is the one that most people associate with the *Dies irae.*
		2. *Quantus tremor est futurus, quando iudex est venturus cuncta stricte discussurus!*	How great a tremor is to be, when the judge is to come briskly shattering every grave.	
0:34	B	3. *Tuba mirum spargens sonum* *per sepulcra regionum, coget omnes ante thronum.*	A trumpet sounding an astonishing sound through the tombs of the region drives all men before the throne.	Like the A section, this part of the melody is sung twice, once for each three lines of the text.
		4. *Mors stupebit et natura,* *cum resurget creatura iudicanti responsura.*	Death will be stunned and so will Nature, when arises man the creature responding to the One judging.	
1:12	C	5. *Liber scriptus proferetur,* *in quo totum continetur* *unde mundus iudicetur.*	The written book will be brought forth, in which the whole record of evidence is contained whence the world is to be judged.	The next section of the melody is also repeated.
		6. *Iudex ergo cum sedebit, quidquid latet apparebit; nil inultum remanebit.*	Therefore when the Judge shall sit, whatever lay hidden will appear; nothing unavenged will remain.	
1:50	A	7. *Quid sum miser tunc dicturus, quem patronum rogaturus, cum vix iustus sit securus?*	What am I the wretch then to say, what patron I to beseech? when scarcely the just man be secure?	All three sections of the melody are repeated—each sung twice—to new text.
		8. *Rex tremendae maiestatis, qui salvandos salvas gratis, salva me, fons pietatis.*	King of tremendous Majesty, who saves those-to-be-saved free, save me, Fount of piety.	

TIME	SECTION	ORIGINAL TEXT	TRANSLATION	COMMENT
2:26	B	9. *Recordare, Iesu pie,* *quod sum causa tuae viae,* *ne me perdas illa die.*	Remember, faithful Jesus, because I am the cause of your journey: do not lose me on that day.	
		10. *Quaerens me sedisiti lassus,* *redemisti crucem passus;* *tantus labor non sit cassus.*	Thou hast sat down as one wearied seeking me, Thou has redeemed me having suffered the Cross: so much labor let it not be lost.	
3:03	C	11. *Iuste iudex ultionis,* *donum fac remissionis* *ante diem rationis.*	Just judge of the avenging-punishment, work the gift of the remission of sins before the Day of the Reckoning.	
		12. *Ingemisco tamquam reus,* *culpa rubet vultus meus;* *supplicanti parce Deus.*	I groan, as the accused: my face grows red from my fault: spare this supplicant, O God.	
3:39	A	13. *Qui Mariam absolvisit* *et latronem exaudisti,* *mihi quoque spem dedisti.*	Thou who absolved Mary, and favorably heard the good thief, hast also given me hope.	The melody is repeated again, but the C section is only sung once.
		14. *Preces meae non sunt* *dignae,* *sed tu, bonus, fac benigne* *ne perenni cremer igne.*	My prayers are not worthy, but do Thou, Good God, deal kindly lest I burn in perennial fire.	
4:14	B	15. *Inter oves locum praesta* *et ab haedis me sequestra,* *statuens in parte dextra.*	Among the sheep offer me a place and from the goats sequester me, placing me at Thy right hand.	
		16. *Confutatis maledictis,* *fl ammis acribus addictis,* *voca me cum benedictis.*	After the accursed have been silenced, given up to the bitter flames, call me with the blest.	
4:51	C	17. *Oro supplex et acclinis,* *cor contritum quasi cinis,* *gere curam mei fi nis.*	Kneeling and bowed down I pray, my heart contrite as ashes: do Thou, my End, care for my end.	
5:09	D	18. *Lacrimosa dies illa,* *qua resurget ex favilla* *iudicandus homo reus:* *huic ergo parce, Deus.* *Pie Jesu Domine,* *dona eis requiem. Amen.*	That sorrowful day, on which will arise from the burning coals man accused to be judged: therefore, O God, do Thou spare him. Faithful Lord Jesus, Grant them rest. Amen.	The concluding section of the text stands by itself, although there are clear melodic connections to what has come before.

of music for each syllable of text. In the second and third lines, though, several syllables are set to groups of two notes, making the music a bit more expansive. All three lines end on the same note, providing a sense of cohesion and finality.

Stanzas Three and Four

The melody of the third and fourth stanzas begins very differently; its first phrase, corresponding to the first line of each stanza, contains much higher pitches, a much wider range from the first to the last notes, and syllables set to as many as three notes. The music of the second phrase repeats the music for the opening line of stanzas one and two. The third phrase then seems to mirror the second line of those stanzas, though with a wider range.

As you listen to the rest of the sequence, you will notice that all melodic phrases continue to end on the same note, but the variety of shapes in the melodic line prevents any monotony. Though each phrase of the melody except the last is ultimately heard six times, this is far from musical doggerel; it displays the inventiveness of a composer unburdened by harmony or by the need to create strong contrasts in rhythm or timbre.

Melodic Phrase Structure: From Celano to Chopin and Debussy

Later composers reinforced the power of melody by enlivening it with other musical elements. Chopin's melodies had a broader range, more disjunct intervals, and more rhythmic variety than any of the melodies we have examined so far. Composers may also disguise the phrase structure, as we shall see with Debussy, or give the impression of continuous motion across phrases.

Internal Repetition: A Chopin Nocturne

Listen to the beginning of the Nocturne in A-flat major, op. 32, no. 2, by Chopin. After a brief introduction, the melody begins with a clearly defined phrase that concludes at 0:28 with an open ending: one that, like the odd-numbered lines in the A.E. Housman poem, sounds inconclusive and thus demands a continuation. The next phrase of the melody mirrors the first one, beginning—after an upbeat—with the same eight notes but concluding with a more stable, closed ending at 0:46. These two phrases are exactly the same length and balance one another perfectly, just like the opening lines of the poem. They are followed by two more phrases of exactly the same length that also conclude with open and closed endings, respectively. The latter phrase, ending at 1:22, is an exact repetition of the second phrase heard earlier. So far, then, the melody has the structure of a poetic stanza with the rhyme scheme ABAB. The two Bs not only rhyme but are identical. The melody is subsequently rounded out by a repetition of phrases three and four (the final AB), concluding at 1:57.

Like many melodies, including the *Dies irae*, Chopin's contains a good deal of internal repetition. Indeed, this is one of the important differences between the structure of a melody and that of a poem. A poem has a subject: It is about something, and that subject matter gives it unity and makes it hang together. In music, though, the melody itself is the subject and thus needs to provide its own coherence. Even in compositions with words, the melody tends to contain more repetition than the text. In the *Dies irae*, for example, there is one new melody for every two stanzas. On the even-numbered stanzas, the melody of the previous stanza repeats.

Syllabic: A style of text setting where each musical note is assigned one syllable of text.

LEARNING TO LISTEN GUIDE

TAKE NOTE OF MELODY

What to Listen For: The regular melodic phrases resembling the structure of a simple poetic stanza.

Streaming audio track 44.

Chopin: Nocturne in A-flat major, op. 32, no. 2, beginning
Date: 1836–1837
Instrumentation: Piano solo
Key: A-flat major
Meter: $\frac{4}{4}$, also known as common time (four slow beats per measure)
Form: Ternary (ABA)
Core Repertory Connection: This music is also discussed in Chapters 9 and 12.

TIME	PROGRESSION	COMMENT
0:00	Introduction	A few sustained chords seem to pose a question as the piece begins. Since they are heard again at the end (5:24ff), they also constitute a frame.
0:13	First phrase	This phrase, longer than those in the Dvořák, divides into two halves, with the second beginning at 0:21. Note both the melodic flourish and the inconclusive harmony at the end of the entire phrase.
0:28	Second phrase	The second phrase, after an upbeat, begins like the first but ends more stably. In a sense, the first two phrases rhyme.
0:46	Third phrase	The third phrase begins with a new melodic idea and ends inconclusively.
1:05	Fourth phrase	Again beginning with an upbeat, the fourth phrase mirrors the third but ends more conclusively.
1:22	Third phrase, repeat	The third phrase is heard again, exactly as before.
1:41	Fourth phrase, repeat	The fourth phrase is heard again as well, bringing the A section of the piece to a conclusion.

Ornamentation: Extra notes not written in the music, added by the performer for decorative or expressive purposes.

Many popular songs also follow the principle of melodic repetition. Think of *Yesterday*, by the Beatles. The opening verse ("Yesterday, all my troubles...") is set to a highly memorable tune and then repeated ("Suddenly, I'm not...").

Only with the next words ("Why she had ...") does a new melody appear. The opening melody returns, though, for the words "Yesterday, love was ..." In short, this song, like so many others, follows the AABA melodic pattern that we observed in *Lester Leaps In.* The internal repetitions in the melody compensate for the lack of clear story or details, making the tune easy to grasp and memorable.

Chopin's melody, although written in a very different style, with complicated **ornamentation**—fast, decorative notes that are not essential to the melodic line—is repetitive enough to make it clear that all the different phrases belong together and have not been chosen arbitrarily. At the same time, the ornamentation helps disguise the simplicity of the melodic structure, perhaps making this melody sound more complicated than it actually is.

Melodic Disguise: Debussy

Not all melodies are so well-behaved, of course. The melody of *Raga Bhankar* also contains internal repetition, but it does not divide into regular phrases like the other melodies we have examined. Some melodies, like those in the Debussy Sonata for flute, viola, and harp, have a clear phrase structure but much more ambiguous organization. The beginning of the first movement has regular stops and starts, like the Chopin nocturne. Because of the constant changes in instrumentation, tempo, and meter, though, it is difficult to hear these phrases as balancing or complementing one another. This is not to say that such relationships do not exist; they are simply hard to discern and thus require listening with particular attentiveness and imagination.

LEARNING TO LISTEN GUIDE

TAKE NOTE OF MELODY AND TIMBRE

What to Listen For: The sonically effective contrasts between the three very different-sounding instruments.

Debussy: Sonata for flute, v___ ___d harp
I: Pastorale—Lento, dolce ___ ___ning
Date: 1915
Instrumentation: Flut
Key: F major
Meter: $\frac{9}{8}$ (a comp ___ ___s per measure), with several changes of meter
Form: Ternary (
**Core Reperto ___ ___n is also discussed in Chapters 4 and 7.

Streaming audio track 60.
Interactive Listening Guide ILG-16
will show you how the melodic
parts in the three instruments fit
together in the first movement of
the Debussy sonata.

TIME	
0:0?	___cked up by the flute.
0:?	___otes (or are they just false starts?), followed by a ___ viola.
	___ in fast notes.
0:5?	___rase comes to a satisfying conclusion.
	___ck out where other phrases begin and end. As the above ___ys clear.

Musical Motives

In some music, particularly from the Classical and Romantic periods, melodies are less important than motives, even if these musical fragments don't by themselves constitute a tune. Sometimes a motive is only the very beginning of a longer melody. In Chapter 1 we saw that the opening three notes of the melody in the first movement of Mozart's Symphony no. 40 are repeated over a hundred times. These three notes—not the melody as such—are the true subject of the music.

The Gardener Vallier, by Paul
Cézanne (1839–1906). Like
Debussy's *Sonata for Flute, Viola, and
Harp,* Cézanne's work is made up
of multiple disparate fragments.
(Gift of Eugene and Agnes E. Meyer)

Fermata: A marking indicating
that a note should be held for an
indefinite length of time. It may
also indicate that a cadenza is
expected to be performed.

**Self-portrait of E.T.A. Hoffmann
(1776–1822).** Hoffmann was one of
the most important figures of the
early Romantic movement. *(© Mary
Evans Picture Library/Alamy)*

The Opening Notes as Motive:
Beethoven's Fifth Symphony

Perhaps the most famous motive in all music is the opening four notes of
Beethoven's Symphony no. 5 in C minor, op. 67. Unlike the opening notes of the
Mozart, these four notes are not presented as the beginning of a longer melody.
Instead, they are stated by themselves. The final note is marked with a **fermata**,
indicating that it is to be held for an indefinite length of time. The motive is then
repeated one note lower, again with a concluding fermata. Clearly, Beethoven
wants you to hear these four notes as particularly important. If he were writing a
story, we could say that he begins with the main character's name and then says
it again.

When the music continues after the opening fermatas, these four notes remain
at the forefront of the listener's awareness. In fact, many music students learn the
following words to characterize the opening: "Beethoven's Fifth! It goes like this!
And then like this, and then like this, and then like this! And then like this, and
then like this, and then like this! And then like this (and then like this), and then
like this (and then like this), and then it goes—like—this!!"

Listen now to the first movement of Beethoven's Fifth Symphony, up to
1:26 (the end of the exposition). Then read the following excerpt from E.T.A.
Hoffmann's review of the symphony, which first appeared in 1810, a year and a
half after the first performance. This highly influential review, virtually unprecedented in length and level of detail, forcefully articulated the Romantic concep-
tion of art and argued that instrumental music, in particular, was the best vehicle
for Romantic expression.

> There is no simpler idea than that which the master laid as the foundation
> of this entire *Allegro* and one realizes with wonder how he was able to
> align all the secondary ideas, all the transitional passages with the rhyth-
> mic content of this simple theme in such a way that they served continu-
> ally to unfold the character of the whole, which that theme could only
> suggest. All phrases are short, consisting of only two or three measures,
> and are divided up even further in the ongoing exchanges between the
> string and the wind instruments. One might believe that from such
> elements only something disjointed and difficult to comprehend could
> arise; nevertheless, it is precisely this arrangement of the whole, as well
> as the repetitions of the short phrases and individual chords that follow
> continually upon one another, which hold the spirit firmly in an unname-
> able longing.

Notice that Hoffmann is describing how the music makes its powerful, emotional impression. After the two opening statements of the motive, and a few more
fitful stops and starts, it finally seems to flow more continuously. Under the surface, though, the opening four notes repeat again and again.

At 0:44, for example, the French horn introduces the movement's second
theme. One of the defining characteristics of sonata form, as it is usually described, is the contrast between the two main themes. In the first movement of
Mozart's Symphony no. 40 in G minor, that contrast is pronounced. Compare
the beginning of Mozart's movement with its second theme, which enters at 0:52.

Focus On
E.T.A. Hoffmann (1776–1822)

German writer and composer. His fantastic tales epitomize the Romantic fascination with the supernatural and the expressively distorted or exaggerated. As a critic, he placed his sharp mind at the service of a consistent (if partial) view of Romanticism and wrote vivid and forceful reviews of the music of his time. His work as a composer, which he himself regarded highly, has been neglected but shows a certain verve and originality. (Gerhard Allroggen. *Grove Music Online.*)

Grove Music Online.

Ernst Theodor Amadeus Hoffmann was one of the central figures of the early Romantic movement. You may know him as the author of the story on which Tchaikovsky's ballet *The Nutcracker* was based. Romantic composers drew heavily on Hoffmann's writings, and the results included an opera, *Tales of Hoffmann*, by Jacques Offenbach, and Robert Schumann's *Kreisleriana* for piano. Schumann's work is based on Hoffmann's archetypal musician Kapellmeister Kreisler, who may in turn have been based on Beethoven. The cross-fertilization went both ways; Hoffmann was also an accomplished musician and composer, and his reviews of Beethoven's music contributed substantially to that composer's growing reputation.

Perhaps Hoffmann's most accomplished literary work is his novel *The Life and Opinions of the Tomcat Murr* (*Lebensansichten des Katers Murr*). The title character is an accomplished cat who has taught himself to write and pens his own biography. He then tears out random pages from a fictional biography of Kapellmeister Kreisler, which he uses as blotting paper between the pages of his manuscript. Due to a colossal mistake, the publisher prints everything exactly as received. The result is that the cat's autobiography, which appears in its entirety, is interrupted—frequently in the middle of a sentence—by random fragments of Kreisler's life, which never appears in its entirety.

Hoffmann's elaborate literary construction reinforces the idea of dual identities, which was an important Romantic literary device for suggesting that a character may be more complex than appearances suggest. You can see the same kind of fanciful thinking at work in his description of Beethoven's Fifth Symphony, which pulses with imagination but is grounded in a thorough study of the score.

Illustration of Hoffman's short story *The Sandman.* Although he was a musician and music critic, Hoffmann is most famous for his stories, which influenced many composers (Tchaikovsky's *Nutcracker* was based on a story by Hoffmann). (*© Mary Evans Picture Library/Alamy*)

Note that the contrast between the two melodies is strong. The opening melody is centered on the three-note motive with which it begins, while the new theme is more lyrical and contains no trace of that motive, although it also begins with two conjunct, descending notes.

Motivic Cohesiveness: The Second Theme of Beethoven's Fifth Symphony

The second theme of the Beethoven begins with the same rhythm of three shorts and a long that was heard at the opening of the movement. While the music that follows is, perhaps, more relaxed than the earlier music, if you listen carefully to the bass line, you will hear continuous, and ultimately more and more urgent, repetitions of that rhythm. It is then hurled out triumphantly and repeatedly by the full orchestra at the close of the exposition, beginning at 1:17. If the exposition is repeated, as Beethoven instructed, the motivic cohesiveness of this music becomes all the more apparent.

By this point, the motive has not simply been stated—it has been developed. You have heard it in various incarnations: as an ominous pronouncement at the beginning of the movement; as a mounting crescendo beginning at 0:29; as an accompaniment figure at 0:48ff; and finally, from 1:17, as a kind of culmination. Beethoven is busy transforming the way you think about four notes, and he will continue to do so throughout the rest of the movement, not just in the section usually called the development.

Melody and Thematic Development: The Development Section

The development section begins at 2:55 with a repetition of the opening motive in something like its original form. Listen carefully to the music that follows. In place of the fitful stops and starts at the beginning of the movement, there is now continuous music, the three-shorts-and-a-long rhythm repeated over and over. At 3:10 you will notice something else interesting—the same rhythm continues, but the primary melodic motion is now upward rather than downward. Beethoven has done two things: First, he has evened out the motive so that the three repeated notes followed by a downward jump are replaced by conjunct notes. Then, beginning at 3:10, he turns it upside down. In musical terminology, he **inverts** the motive so that the conjunct notes move in the opposite direction. If you listen really carefully, though, you may also notice that the lower strings (violas and cellos) are still playing the notes in the original direction, downward.

> **Inversion:** To play a melody "upside down," with the same intervals going in opposite directions.

This is thematic development in full swing. The motive forming the kernel of the main melody is being combined with itself, smoothed out, and stretched in both directions simultaneously. Finally, at 3:24, the full orchestra unites and issues a climactic statement—not the original three shorts and a long, but eight shorts and a long, all on the same pitch. After a rest, eleven shorts follow and a long on an even higher pitch. Beethoven is letting us know that we have arrived somewhere.

Binding It All Together: The Recapitulation

Just where we might have arrived is clarified at 3:31, when the first and second violins together play the version of the motive first stated by the horn at 0:44. Beethoven is demonstrating once again the powerful link that binds together all the material of this movement. Then he seemingly breaks the motive apart until it consists of only two notes (at 3:42ff), then of only one (at 3:52ff). Finally, after what seems an eternity, the orchestra begins to pound out the motive in its original form, leading to the beginning of the recapitulation at 4:18.

LEARNING TO LISTEN GUIDE

TAKE NOTE OF MELODY AND FORM

What to Listen For: The many developmental strategies applied to the opening four notes in the course of the movement.

Beethoven: Symphony no. 5 in C minor, op. 67
I: Allegro con brio
Date: 1807–1808
Instrumentation: Symphony orchestra
Key: C minor
Meter: $\frac{2}{4}$ (two fast beats per measure)
Form: Sonata form
Core Repertory Connection: Beethoven's Symphony no. 5 is also discussed in Chapters 3 and 12.

Streaming audio track 36.
Interactive Listening Guide ILG-9 will help you follow the structure and motivic content of this work, also highlighting the inversion of the motive.

TIME	PROGRESSION	COMMENT
Exposition		
0:00	First theme	The opening motive is stated twice. It is then developed into a theme.
0:19	First theme repeats	The opening motive is restated, then extended into a transitional passage.
0:44	Second theme	The horn states a version of the opening motive that is extended to form the contrasting second theme.
1:07	Concluding section	The full orchestra proclaims that the first section of the piece has ended, apparently on a positive note.
1:28	Exposition repeat	Everything heard so far is literally repeated.
Development		
2:55	Opening motive	The opening motive is repeated emphatically, marking the beginning of the development section.
2:59	Motive development	A short section mirrors the theme heard at the beginning of the movement, but with a more open-ended continuation.
3:17	Heightened intensity	The motive is worked up through repetition at higher and higher pitches, leading to a series of repeated notes that recall the opening.
3:31	Major thematic statement	The horn theme from 0:44 returns in the violins.
3:42	Breakup of the theme	The motive begins to appear in smaller and smaller units.
4:04	Dramatic contrast	The full orchestra enters with a more complete statement of the theme, followed by more pianissimo single chords.
4:12	Definitive return	The opening theme returns in the full orchestra, preparing for the recapitulation.
Recapitulation		
4:18	First theme	The opening motive returns in the original key.
4:35	Oboe solo	This short cadenza in the oboe is one of the most audible differences between the recapitulation and the exposition.
5:13	Second theme	The second theme returns in the major rather than the expected minor.
Coda		
5:59	Extension	Instead of ending where expected, the music continues to build in intensity.
6:30	New theme	Beethoven surprises the listener by introducing thematic material not previously heard.
7:06	Final statement of the opening motive	After this summation, the movement ends quickly.

Motive and Melody

The subject of this chapter is melody, but you may well think that the music you have been listening to is not particularly melodic. Certainly, it does not pass the shower-humming test that we alluded to earlier. But then, neither does the Debussy sonata or the Indian raga. Of the items on your listening list, many others would not pass that test either: not the *Jumping Dance Drums*, with their exclusively percussive timbres; not most portions of *Lester Leaps In*, with its free-wheeling improvisation; certainly not the pieces by Dallapiccola, Crumb, and Vandervelde, with their experimental sonorities and unusual combinations of instruments. In fact, it is often the shortest pieces—ones like the Dvořák *Slavonic Dance*, the Schubert lieder, the Chopin nocturne, the Machaut virelai—that have the most accessible melodies.

Of course, there are exceptions. The lengthy love scene from Berlioz's *Roméo et Juliette* features a very lyrical melody, full of clear melodic lines and regular phrases. In this music, though, Berlioz is not as interested in thematic development as he is in telling a story and manipulating orchestral timbres. The melody serves as the prop that allows him to do these things.

While the melodic material of Beethoven's fifth symphony may not be lyrical, it is certainly memorable. In fact, of all the melodies in all the music we have examined, Beethoven's three-shorts-and-a-long motive may be the easiest to remember—even virtually impossible to forget. This makes it perfectly suited to the kind of developmental processes that Beethoven preferred to use. In the music of Beethoven and many of his successors—Brahms, Wagner, Richard Strauss—thematic development is really motivic development.

If You Liked This Music. . .

More Explorations of Motivic Development

If you enjoyed this music, you might also want to listen to the following:

- The four symphonies of Johannes Brahms (1833–1897). Brahms wrote only four symphonies because, by his time, the bar had been raised so high by Beethoven that any new symphony made a statement. Each of the Brahms symphonies exemplifies motivic development in its most concentrated form. Robert Schumann's four symphonies also provide an interesting contrast with those of Beethoven, his predecessor, and with those of Brahms, his successor.
- The tone poems of Richard Strauss (1864–1949). A tone poem, also known as a symphonic poem, is an orchestral work that is based on a narrative, image, or mood and usually takes a freer form than a symphony. The composer often writes what is called a *program* to accompany the musical work, outlining dramatic events or reinforcing other associations. Though Strauss lived well into the 20th century, most of his tone poems were written in the final decades of the 19th. Each uses the processes of motivic development to narrate a specific story. Examples include *Don Juan, Don Quixote, Till Eulenspiegels lustige Streiche* (*Till Eulenspiegel's Merry Pranks*), and *Also Sprach Zarathustra* (*Thus Spake Zarathustra*), which provided some of the familiar music in Stanley Kubrick's *2001: A Space Odyssey*.

Thematic Development in Mozart

Not all music that uses thematic development, though, is so single-mindedly concentrated on a short, memorable motive. We have already seen how Mozart, in the first movement of his Symphony no. 40, combines such a motive with a longer melodic line that is memorable in its own right. The first movement of the *Gran Partita* also shows a typically Mozartian balance between the short motive and the longer line.

Listen to the beginning of the *Molto Allegro* section of the first movement (2:09ff.). You will notice that the first theme begins with a self-contained five-note motive just as short and nearly as memorable as Beethoven's famous four-note salvo. Mozart's motive, too, is immediately repeated at a different pitch level. In this case, though, the repetition is not literal, and it serves as the second half of a complete melodic phrase. It is answered by another phrase more melodically continuous and more fully scored—Mozart thus uses contrasting timbres to emphasize the change in the nature of the melodic material. After a repetition of this sequence, the more melodic answering phrase leads to the transition to the second theme.

Technically speaking, Mozart's exposition is monothematic; when you expect the second theme to appear (at 2:53), the initial motive returns instead. This time, however, the basset horns, rather than the clarinets, play the motive and then repeat it literally on a higher pitch. The real contrast comes in the passage that follows (3:01ff): the basset horns continue with the melody while a walking bass line (steady beats and mostly conjunct motion) in the bassoons steals the attention. Mozart is again playing with instrumental timbres. In the section that follows, he features the oboes with the opening motive (from 3:12 to 3:18, after which they are joined by the bassoons), the clarinets (from 3:23 to 3:35, where the first bassoon briefly grabs the melody), and then the full ensemble (from 3:42 until, with brief interruptions, the end of the exposition).

LEARNING TO LISTEN GUIDE

TAKE NOTE OF MELODY AND TEXTURE

What to Listen For: The motivic unity of the fast section of the movement, partially disguised by the varied instrumentation.

Streaming audio track 22.

Mozart: *Gran Partita*, K. 361
I: Largo: Molto Allegro, beginning
Date: 1781
Instrumentation: Two oboes, two clarinets, two basset horns, four horns, two bassoons, and bass
Key: B-flat major
Meter: $\frac{4}{4}$, also known as common time (four fast beats per measure)
Form: Sonata form
Core Repertory Connection: Mozart's *Gran Partita* is also discussed in Chapters 3, 5, and 6.

TIME	PROGRESSION	COMMENT
0:00	Slow introduction	A leisurely slow introduction begins the *Gran Partita* and prepares the listener for the long, complex fast section of the movement.
2:09	First theme	The clarinets and bassoons state the main motive of the Allegro section. The full ensemble enters at 2:16.
2:28	Repetition and transition	The clarinets and bassoons play the main motive again. At 2:35 the full ensemble enters again and begins the transition to the second theme.
2:53	Second theme area	Mozart has prepared for a new theme, but instead the opening motive is restated by the basset horns, with horns and bassoons accompanying.
3:01	Walking bass	As the basset horns and horns continue to play, they are accompanied by a walking bass line, a series of fast, staccato passages in the bassoons.
3:12	Restatement	The motive is played again, this time by oboes and basset horns.
3:19	Walking bass	This time the basset horns play the walking bass, with the oboes and then the clarinets above them. Finally, it returns to the bassoons at 3:25 as the full ensemble enters.
3:29	Start of the concluding section	Clarinets and bassoons alone are heard.
3:42	Continuation	The full ensemble enters and, except for a few brief passages, plays until the end of the exposition.

As is usually the case with Mozart, the melody has to compete with the ingenious scoring and constant changes of texture for the listener's attention. As you continue to listen to the movement, though, you will find that it contains a balance of short motives and longer, more continuous melodic lines, with neither really gaining the upper hand. This is the Classical style at its most democratic: a true musical conversation, in which the topic often seems to be the suppleness and variety of the music itself.

As you can see, melody, timbre, and rhythm are not always easy to separate. Mozart's melodic contrasts are heightened by ingenious use of timbre. The main motive in Beethoven's Fifth Symphony is memorable primarily for its distinctive rhythm, which Beethoven often uses without reference to the melodic shape it originally took. Everybody thinks they know a good tune when they hear one, but the issue may actually be more complicated than most people realize. The more music you listen to, the more you will learn about melody, and the more you will understand its relationship to the other elements of music. The listening exercises at the end of this chapter are designed to help you cultivate this skill.

In the next chapter, we will explore how melody, timbre, and rhythm can all be brought together by the great musical unifier: harmony.

SUMMARY

- Melody is not easy to define but is present in some form in virtually all music.
- The distinctive melodic characteristics of Western music have their origins in the musical-literary conventions of the Middle Ages.

- To Western ears, a good tune (a lyrical one) is one that has regular phrases and is easy to sing, even if it is played on an instrument.

- Motives (short, memorable musical fragments) have been a distinctive characteristic of Western music since the 18th century.

- Motives may be part of a longer melody, or they may become the musical subject.

KEY TERMS

Cadence	p. 218	Fermata	p. 226	Melodic Line	p. 214
Conjunct	p. 215	Interval	p. 215	Ornamentation	p. 224
Disjunct	p. 215	Inversion	p. 228	Sequence	p. 220
Drone	p. 214	Lyricism	p. 215	Syllabic	p. 220

REVIEW QUESTIONS

1. How does the performance of the melody in *Raga Bhankar* differ from the performance of most Western music?
2. What are the distinctive characteristics of Western melody?
3. How do these qualities of melody relate to the musical-poetic traditions of the Middle Ages?
4. What is a motive, and how is it different from a melody? What does it mean for a motive to be developed apart from the melody to which it belongs?

REVIEW CONCEPTS

1. What makes a melody lyrical? What are some examples of lyrical melodies you know?
2. What does it mean to say that all music contains melody, even when it is not lyrical?
3. How are the melodies of the Dvořák *Slavonic Dance*, the *Dies irae*, and the Chopin nocturne discussed in this chapter similar to each other? In what ways are they different?
4. How does Debussy's use of melody in the Sonata for flute, viola, and harp differ from that of Dvořák and Chopin?
5. How is the thematic development in Beethoven's Fifth Symphony different from that in Mozart's *Gran Partita*?

LISTENING EXERCISES

1. Compare the two examples just discussed (the first movement of Beethoven's Fifth Symphony and Mozart's *Gran Partita*) with the first movement of Haydn's String Quartet in B-flat major, op. 64, no. 3. How does Haydn's use of melody compare with that of the other two composers? Is he more like Mozart or Beethoven in his use of motives?
2. Compare the first movement of Bach's Concerto in D minor for harpsichord and strings with the selections from the Gloria of the Mass in B minor. Is Bach's melodic writing different when he writes for voices rather than for instruments? Try to explain the reasons for your answer.
3. Compare the rhythms of the Caribbean *Jumping Dance Drums* with the rhythms of Basie's *Lester Leaps In*. How do they differ from each other, and how do they interact with the melodic content of the music?
4. What is the most memorable melody from the selections you have heard so far? How does it compare to other melodies you already knew?
5. What is the most unconventional melody from the selections you have heard so far? In what sense is it different from what you expect? What does this suggest about the nature of melody?

9 Harmony and Texture

TAKE NOTE

Harmony and texture are related concepts crucial to understanding the way music affects the listener. Harmony is the combination of notes to produce chords, and a way of understanding the progression of chords throughout a piece. Texture refers to the number of pitches or melodies that sound at the same time, and the way they operate together.

When two people are in harmony, they understand each other and cooperate. When we say that an opinion harmonizes with reality, we mean that it is consistent with what we know to be true. On the other hand, if we turn on the television, and two commentators are speaking in point-counterpoint, we can expect an argument. We know that we will be hearing different voices and different opinions, which often cause disharmony.

In each case, we are using metaphors taken from music. Perhaps you have heard someone refer to an important idea as key, or you have heard that someone is delivering a keynote address. You may not have realized that these, too, are musical metaphors. Most music we hear is written in a key, meaning that the piece consistently returns to a few familiar chords and to a central note, known as the keynote, or **tonic**.

Chords, two or more notes sounded simultaneously, are a way of explaining what is going on harmonically in a piece of music. If we consider music on a grid, as we did in Chapter 7 when thinking about beats, melody is the horizontal element and harmony is the vertical element. What occurs when two or more tones sound simultaneously? Is the sound pleasant or unpleasant? Do we feel increasing tension, or are we heading toward relaxation or resolution? These are questions about harmony. *Texture* also describes the way notes sound together, but it pertains to the number of notes and their relationship to each other. Does each note belong to an independent melody, or do some notes play an accompanying role? It is common for music to feature one melody accompanied by subordinate lines combined into chords. Counterpoint, on the other hand, is a method for crafting separate, equally valid melodies that make sense when they are played or sung at the same time. When two or more melodies are heard together, they give music a more complex texture. The historical development of harmony in Western music began with the combination of different melodic lines through the use of counterpoint.

Listen to virtually any piece on the listening list, and harmony will be front and center. This does not mean that harmony always plays the same role—far from it! The way Josquin des Prez uses harmony is vastly different from the way Beethoven uses it. Beethoven's harmony, in turn, is not at all like that of Debussy, or Stravinsky, or Crumb. This chapter will look at harmonic practices throughout the history of Western music.

The Middle Ages: Texture

In the Middle Ages, harmony as we understand it today was in its earliest stages. In fact, the harmonic aspects of much early music can be best understood in terms of texture—the level of complexity—rather than chords. At this point, texture, not harmony, was in the driver's seat.

Monophonic Texture

In monophonic music, only one note is played or sung at a time. This is the simplest, most basic, and most widespread musical texture. Any time you sing by yourself, you are singing monophonic music. A group of singers all singing the same notes are also singing in monophony. There is no accompaniment and, hence, no harmony.

Chapter Objectives

- Define texture and harmony, and learn how their relationship has evolved through various musical periods.

- Distinguish between monophonic and polyphonic textures, as well as dissonance and consonance.

- Understand counterpoint as a significant musical development of the Middle Ages and Renaissance.

- Recognize and distinguish between major and minor chords, and identify the way functional harmony serves as a building block for musical form.

- Hear how harmonic elements have evolved from the Romantic period to the present.

Tonic: The main note and/or chord of a key, or of a piece written in that key.

Not surprisingly, monophonic texture seems to have appeared first in the history of Western music.

Listen again to Machaut's *Foy porter*, a 14th-century work we discussed in Chapter 5 as a medieval approach to form. Only one person is singing. Since we are accustomed to hearing some type of backup to a singer, this music may first strike you as strangely thin, as though something is missing. If you listen carefully, however, you may realize that no accompaniment is necessary. This piece has a melody that is not only catchy but also imaginative and rhythmically engaging. Extra notes would just get in the way. Adding an accompaniment, say a guitar or a piano, would only weigh the piece down.

Guillaume de Machaut (ca. 1300–1377), from an early manuscript. The composer, shown standing on the right, was perhaps the first to oversee production of a compendium of his own collected works. (© *Photos 12/Alamy*)

Monophonic music was widely written and performed in the Middle Ages; most music heard even into the Renaissance was probably monophonic. This includes the most important musical repertory of the Roman Catholic Church, Gregorian chant.

Focus On
Gregorian Chant

A 17th-century painting by Carlo Saraceni showing the traditional, and now discredited, view of the composition of Gregorian chant. The dove represents the Holy Spirit, who dictates to Pope Gregory I. *(Alfredo Dagli Orti/The Art Archive at Art Resource, NY)*

Grove Music Online.

A term conventionally applied to the central branch of Western Plainchant. Though not entirely appropriate, it has for practical reasons continued in use. Gregorian chant originated as a reworking of Roman ecclesiastical song by Frankish cantors during the Carolingian period; it came to be sung almost universally in medieval western and central Europe, with the diocese of Milan the sole significant exception. (James W. McKinnon, *Grove Music Online*.)

"Gregorian" is actually a misnomer for the vast body of liturgical chant preserved by the Roman Catholic Church. It is not clear exactly what role, if any, the 6th-century pope for whom it is named actually played in its creation. He certainly did not write it, though, as was once believed; in its earliest years, this music was transmitted orally. When the Church decided, in the 9th century, that the repertory needed to be standardized, musical notation was born. Thus, later chants like the *Dies irae* were actually written down at the time of composition, in a manner that would have been impossible in Gregory's time.

Gregorian chant was traditionally sung without instrumental accompaniment. In more recent times, instruments have often been used. Chant continues to grow and develop. Remnants of the old chant are still present, alongside newer chant compositions, in widely used liturgies—Protestant as well as Catholic.

Polyphonic Texture

The most important musical development during the Middle Ages may have been polyphonic music, in which more than one note sounds at a time. Everything on the listening list except the *Dies irae* and *Foy porter* contains polyphony. In polyphony, the simultaneous statement of different pitches produces a more complex texture than that of simple monophony. Polyphony technically includes any texture that involves a melody and an accompaniment. Often, though, independent melodic lines will be stated simultaneously through the use of counterpoint.

You can produce a polyphonic texture of this kind simply by singing a round. *Row, Row, Row Your Boat*, for example, can be sung by four voices entering at different times. Although they are all singing the same melody and the same text, the resulting music sounds as though four different melodies and four different texts are being sung at any one point.

Streaming audio track 3. Interactive Listening Guide ILG-1 will allow you to see the complex interaction of the three melodic lines in Machaut's motet.

Dissonant/dissonance: The result of a combination of notes with strongly clashing overtones, as when two adjacent notes on a keyboard are played simultaneously. (Contrast **consonant/consonance**).

Consonant/consonance: The sound produced by a combination of notes that harmonize well because their overtones are compatible. (Contrast **dissonant/dissonance**).

A more complex use of polyphony can be heard in Machaut's *Lasse! comment oublieray/Se j'aim mon loyal/Pour quoy me bat mes maris?*, sung by three solo voices. As we will see in the next chapter, it also has three different texts, each sung to a different melody. All the melodies begin and end at the same point; there are no staggered voice entries like in *Row, Row, Row Your Boat*.

Almost immediately, Machaut presents some striking clashes between the three melodic lines. In the section extending from about 0:13 to 0:18, for example, a strong, almost painful **dissonance** is produced when two harmonically incompatible notes are heard at the same time. The voices then come to rest together and continue.

Consonance, the opposite of dissonance, occurs when two harmonically compatible notes form into chords. A consonant chord may contain two notes or many, but they will sound together in a way that the ear finds pleasing and resolved. A dissonant combination, on the other hand, may be perceived as being less stable and unresolved. Playing two adjacent notes on a piano keyboard simultaneously will produce such a sound. The impression that the harmony is unfinished or unresolved can elicit a feeling of expectation or even anxiety in the listener, but that may very well be the point in some music.

It is an oversimplification to suggest that dissonance sounds "bad" and consonance "good." All polyphonic music actually contains both, in proportions that have shifted throughout history. *Lasse! comment oublieray/Se j'aim mon loyal/ Pour quoy me bat mes maris?* features much more dissonance, and less consonance, than *Row, Row, Row Your Boat*. This is not because Machaut was careless, but because he was more interested in his melodic lines than in the harmony between them. He may even have enjoyed the pungent sounds created when melodies intersect.

The Renaissance: Counterpoint Comes to the Fore

In the Renaissance, monophonic music became increasingly uncommon as composers such as Josquin des Prez focused on cultivating the complex, polyphonic textures produced by writing counterpoint. The art of combining independent melodic lines so that they fit together with only a limited number of clashes—to produce polyphonic music both pleasing and provocative—had become essential in the education of musicians.

A Masterpiece of Polyphonic Texture: Josquin's *Missa "L'homme armé"*

Josquin des Prez (see box) lived about a century and a half after Machaut. Josquin's *Missa "L'homme armé" super voces musicales*, probably written in the late 1480s, is a remarkable illustration of the ways in which polyphonic texture could be used by this point in history. The piece is a setting of the Ordinary of the Mass, meaning those texts that are sung every time the Mass is celebrated, rather than just for a particular occasion. The entire piece is based on a cantus firmus (see Chapter 2), a kind of melodic scaffolding: in this case, the tune *L'homme armé*, which was well known to Josquin's contemporaries and whose use here had deep symbolic significance.

The Kyrie: Josquin's Mass is written for a four-part, originally all-male, choir. In the opening setting of the text "Kyrie eleison" (Lord, have mercy)—approximately the first minute of music—the tenors sing the first part of the tune in slow notes. A few extra notes are added, especially at the end. All of the other voices sing portions of the tune as well, often at faster speeds.

This piece, like much polyphonic music from the Renaissance, sounds something like a supercharged version of *Row, Row, Row Your Boat*. As with a round, it contains staggered voice entries, though they are often widely separated. It also has passages where the voices follow one another very closely. The prominent features of the cantus firmus melody often stand out clearly. For example, the melody begins with a large ascending interval that is then filled in, in the other direction. Then comes an even larger descending interval, immediately repeated in a filled-in version. Both of these melodic jumps are heard repeatedly in Josquin's music, the latter both with and without the filler notes. Recorded versions of the *L'homme armé* tune are easily accessible on YouTube if you want to verify this for yourself and compare the original to Josquin's more elaborate polyphonic setting.

LEARNING TO LISTEN GUIDE

TAKE NOTE OF MELODY

What to Listen For: The melodic nature of each independent vocal part.

Josquin: *Missa "L'homme armé" super voces musicales*, Kyrie
Date: ca. 1480s
Instrumentation: Four-part men's choir
Meter: Triple meter (Kyrie I), Duple meter (Christe), Triple meter (Kyrie II)
Core Repertory Connection: Josquin's *Missa "L'homme armé" super voces musicales* is also discussed in Chapters 2 and 12.

Streaming audio track 4. Interactive Listening Guide ILG-2 will allow you to see the complex interactions between the four melodic parts in Josquin's Kyrie.

TIME	SECTION	ORIGINAL TEXT	TRANSLATION	COMMENT
0:00	Kyrie I	*Kyrie eleison*	Lord have mercy	Listen to the interaction of the voices, each of which contains fragments of the melody on which the mass is based.
1.22	Christe	*Christe eleison*	Christ have mercy	This section is based on a different part of the melody, but the interaction between the voices continues.
3.36	Kyrie II	*Kyrie eleison*	Lord have mercy	See if you can hear the melodic connections between this music and that of the first Kyrie.

The Agnus Dei: Music that relies on counterpoint is called **contrapuntal**, and an even more rigorous example can be found in the second of the three Agnus Dei sections of the Mass. This music, which sets the text *"Agnus Dei, qui tollis peccata mundi, miserere nobis"* (Lamb of God, who takes away the sins of

Contrapuntal: Music relying on counterpoint.

2:34 - 3:48

the world, have mercy on us), lasts barely more than 30 seconds (~~2:08 to 2:45~~). Nevertheless, it is incredibly complex. It is scored for soprano, alto, and bass, all three of which sing the same adaptation of the *L'homme armé* tune but at differing rates of speed. The alto sings it at half the speed of the bass, and the soprano sings it at one and a half times the speed of the bass. As the fastest voice, the soprano is the only one to sing all the notes Josquin wrote. The others simply stop at the same time.

The concluding Agnus Dei is nearly five minutes long and substitutes the concluding plea *"Dona nobis pacem"* (Grant us peace). Here Josquin places the *L'homme armé* tune in the soprano voice in extremely slow note values, while the lower voices weave a contrapuntal web around it. This is some of Josquin's most brilliant and emotionally affecting music, and it richly rewards active listening.

LEARNING TO LISTEN GUIDE

TAKE NOTE OF MELODY

What to Listen For: The intricate part writing, the three-voice canon in Agnus Dei II, and the presentation of the *L'homme armé* tune in slow note values in the upper voice of Angus Dei III.

Streaming audio track 5.

Josquin: *Missa "L'homme armé" super voces musicales*, Agnus Dei
Date: ca. 1480s
Instrumentation: Four-part men's choir
Meter: Triple meter (Agnus Dei I), duple meter (Agnus Dei II), triple meter (Agnus Dei III)
Core Repertory Connection: Josquin's *Missa "L'homme armé" super voces musicales* is also discussed in Chapters 2 and 12.

TIME	SECTION	ORIGINAL TEXT	TRANSLATION	COMMENT
0:00	Agnus Dei I	*Agnus Dei, qui tollis peccata mundi, miserere nobis*	Lamb of God, who takes away the sins of the world, have mercy on us	The text is set in a style similar to that of the Kyrie.
2:36	Agnus Dei II	*Agnus Dei, qui tollis peccata mundi, miserere nobis*	Lamb of God, who takes away the sins of the world, have mercy on us	The same text is set as a three-part canon. All the voices sing the same melody, but on different pitches and at different rates.
3:55	Agnus Dei III	*Agnus Dei, qui tollis peccata mundi, dona nobis pacem*	Lamb of God, who takes away the sins of the world, grant us peace	In an extended final section, the cantus firmus (the *L'homme armé* tune on which the entire mass is based) appears in the top voice in very slow notes.

Focus On

Josquin des Prez (ca. 1450–1521)

French composer. He was one of the greatest composers of the Renaissance, whose reputation stands on a level with those of Du Fay, Ockeghem, Palestrina, Lassus, and Byrd. His music spans the transition between the sound world of the late Middle Ages and that of the High Renaissance, and served as a model for much of the 16th century. "Josquin" is the diminutive of Josse (Lat. Judocus), the name of a Breton saint active in northern France and Flanders in the 7th century; an uncommon name in recent times, it was widespread in that region during the 15th and 16th centuries. (Patrick Macey, Jeremy Noble, Jeffrey Dean, and Gustave Reese, *Grove Music Online*.)

Josquin des Prez (ca. 1450–1521). He is referred to as "Josquin" because "des Prez" was not actually his surname. (© *Lebrecht Music & Arts*)

Grove Music Online.

With the revival of early music in the 20th century, Josquin des Prez emerged as the most celebrated musician of his time—an evaluation that today's scholars and performers share with his contemporaries. During his lifetime, Josquin was seen as the prince of music. Martin Luther, who was very musically knowledgeable, observed that Josquin was the master of the notes, which must do as he wished, unlike other composers, who must do as the notes wished.

Josquin spent much of his life in Italy, where he worked for a series of aristocratic patrons. Although most of his music was written for the church and in Latin, he also wrote secular music in various languages. In short, Josquin was what is now known as a "Renaissance man."

The Baroque: Counterpoint Yields to Harmony

With the beginning of the Baroque period in the late 16th century, musicians began to understand harmony the way we do today: as a form of accompaniment to a single melodic line. In this period, while texture continued to be important, harmony emerged as a defining force in the development of musical style.

In its most basic form, harmony consists of a series of chords that back up a melody, making it more expressive and musically interesting. The basso continuo, hallmark of the Baroque sound, consisted of a bass line and chords expressed as numbers on the page—much like the symbols now printed with popular songs to guide a keyboardist or guitarist in creating accompaniment for the singer.

Dave Grohl with the Foo Fighters. Popular musicians often refer to chord symbols not unlike those used by basso continuo players. (© *James Arnold/The Hell Gate/Corbis/APImages*)

Chordal harmony is evident in *Row, Row, Row Your Boat* despite its contrapuntal texture. If you pause on any beat, you will hear it. (In between the beats, musicians have always allowed themselves more leeway.) In fact, there is really only one chord in the entire piece, which explains why the parts fit together so well.

Homophonic Texture

In the simplest version of melody plus accompaniment, two or more parts move together in harmony, to the same rhythm, forming chords at each step. Typically, a **homophonic** piece has one melodic line with other parts acting as accompaniment. If you have ever sung a traditional hymn, you know what this texture sounds like. There may be multiple voices singing multiple parts, but everybody harmonizes to form the chords. Most often, that means they sing at the same rate and in the same rhythm, so that all the chord notes are in step. A solo singer can do the same thing by playing one chord on the guitar or piano for each note of melody.

Purely homophonic textures are rare. Even when harmonizing a simple melody, composers and performers naturally try to make their accompaniment interesting in its own right. Homophony and its variants appeared during the Baroque period and became even more common in the Classical and Romantic periods. You can hear examples in the Schubert songs we examined earlier.

This does not mean that polyphony disappeared. Quite the contrary: Bach, in particular, is often considered the greatest master of polyphonic writing in history. Bach's music, though, like virtually all Western music from the Baroque period until the 20th century, is centered on what has come to be called functional harmony.

Homophonic: Consisting of a melody accompanied by chords moving at the same speed, as in a hymn.

Functional Harmony

In **functional harmony**, chords follow one another to build larger units, much like the words in a sentence. In English, the subject of a sentence usually comes before the verb, and adjectives come before the words they modify. Sense differently would a not make sentence constructed. Likewise, harmony is said to be functional if the chords are arranged according to well-defined patterns.

A complete harmonic sentence begins and ends on the tonic chord of the piece, which is the chord built on the keynote. If the piece is in C major, for example, this is a C major chord. In between, the piece may move to other chords, but our ear will always try to relate them to C major. Since C major can be played using only the white keys on the piano, these other chords may also consist only of white keys. This harmonically sound conclusion to a phrase, movement or piece is called a cadence.

The familiar accompaniment to *Heart and Soul* contains the four most commonly used chords in functional harmony, in the appropriate order. If you listen to one repetition only, you will find that your ear expects something else to follow. The return of the opening chord is a given; the music cannot stop until that chord has been reached.

More complicated chord progressions, like the "rhythm changes" (the sequence of chords in Gershwin's *I Got Rhythm* and *Lester Leaps In*), introduce chords that are farther afield. The rhythm changes cannot be played, even in C major, without using some of the black keys. As in *Heart and Soul*, though, the changes inexorably lead back to the tonic chord. This repeated drive back to the starting point controls and articulates the AABA structure of a piece like *Lester Leaps In*.

The same principle applies in large-scale forms like those we discussed in Chapter 5. A piece in sonata form, such as the first movement of Mozart's Symphony no. 40, also begins and ends in the tonic. In between lie seven minutes of music. Like most long pieces, this one is far-ranging in its harmonies. Just as predictably as *Heart and Soul* or *Lester Leaps In*, though, it moves back to the chord it started on. If it did not do this, the music would not sound complete.

This view of harmony as a defining feature of musical form emerged during the Baroque period and is one of the key traits of the **common practice period**: the time between approximately 1680 and 1875 when virtually all European music shared a common style. In fact, the use of the word "key" in the previous sentence reflects its absorption by the broader culture. This musical metaphor is widely used to mean that something is central, crucial, and extremely significant, and that we will return to it again and again.

You can actually hear the development of the concept of key by comparing the Monteverdi and Bach pieces, written more than a century apart, that we first encountered in Chapter 2. Unless you listen carefully to the text, the ending of Monteverdi's *Io son pur vezzosetta*, from the early 1600s, sounds almost arbitrary. We know the piece is over because there is no more text to sing. The music, however, could just as easily continue.

At the conclusion of the "Cum sancto spiritu" of Bach's Mass in B minor, written in the 1730s, on the other hand, there is no doubt that the music is over. This has nothing to do with the text, which by this time has been repeated a few dozen times. We might note the increased pace and volume of the music during the final 20 seconds. Primarily, though, we rely on the harmony, which settles firmly into the final chord. This is functional harmony at work.

Functional Harmony: The use of harmonic progressions that have a syntax comparable to that of language. It is characteristic of the music of the common practice period.

Common Practice Period: The time from about 1680 to about 1875, when virtually all Western music shared a common language. One of the most important features of that language was its use of functional harmony.

Focus On

Johann Sebastian Bach (1685–1750)

A statue of Bach in front of the Thomaskirche in Leipzig, Germany. Bach worked here as cantor from 1723 until his death in 1750. *(Vanni/Art Resource, NY)*

From reading a book like this, you might get the impression that Bach and his music have always been widely heard and enjoyed. Actually, the picture is more complicated. Bach is now the most famous member of a large family of musicians who played prominent roles in German musical life for generations. Several of his sons also became famous composers, and for a while, his fame was almost eclipsed by that of Carl Philipp Emmanuel Bach (1714–1788) and Johann Christian Bach (1735–1782). Johann Sebastian's music was not forgotten, though; it simply became old-fashioned and was rarely performed in the late 18th and early 19th centuries.

That began to change in the mid-19th century. Felix Mendelssohn (1809–1847) revived Bach's monumental *St. Matthew Passion* in 1829, and interest in his music grew as the century progressed. The "Bach revival," one of the most significant musical phenomena of the Romantic period, contributed greatly to establishing the idea of a permanent repertory of classical music.

In the early 20th century, Bach was, in a sense, rediscovered again, his music serving as an important source of inspiration to many early modern composers, including Igor Stravinsky (1882–1971). As we shall see shortly, many features in Stravinsky's *Symphony of Psalms* are reminiscent of Bach.

For a biographical profile of Johann Sebastian Bach, see p. 56.

Fugal Texture

Fugal: Making use of polyphonic texture to develop (usually) a single melody, which is stated successively by different voices (in instrumental music the term is metaphorical), each of which continues as in a round.

Despite Bach's strong and effective use of functional harmony, his music is also highly polyphonic. The passages from 1:01 to 1:47 and from 2:15 to 3:09 introduce the melody in a single voice part with only minimal accompaniment. This melody is memorable in its own right for its large melodic leaps and contrasting rhythms; these make it easy to follow through the increasingly complex textures to come. After the entrance of the tenor part at 1:01, the alto part joins in at 1:09, the first soprano at 1:21, and the second soprano and bass in quick succession beginning at 1:30, resulting in an extremely rich texture that continues for the next 17 seconds. A similar process occurs in the later passage, beginning with the first soprano part and working downward. Both of these passages are examples of Bach's justly celebrated **fugal** writing: his use of polyphonic texture to develop a single melody stated successively by different voices.

The **fugue** is sometimes considered a musical form, but it is really a technique. A piece called a fugue simply uses that technique from beginning to end. A familiar example is Bach's famous Toccata and Fugue in D minor, for organ. The fugue section, which begins about two and a half minutes into the piece, is based entirely on a single melody, known as a **subject**, stated first without accompaniment and then imitated in different registers of the organ, much like a round. Similar passages occur throughout the section, separated by alternate passages called **episodes**, which feature contrasting textures and an absence of the subject. The piece concludes with a reprise of the opening toccata.

As with all of Bach's fugues, this music is also extremely harmonic; even the most complex textures are supported by functional harmony. In the passage from the Mass in B minor, fugal sections also alternate with more homophonic ones, like the one beginning at 1:47. Since this is Bach, there is more going on here than simple chords. Still, you can hear sustained chords in both the melody and the accompaniment. This music thus presents an artful blending of harmony and counterpoint, with harmony firmly in control.

Fugue: An extended composition using fugal technique.

Subject: The single melody on which a fugue is based.

Episode: A passage in a fugue that features contrasting texture and in which the subject is absent.

LEARNING TO LISTEN GUIDE

TAKE NOTE OF MELODY AND TEXTURE

What to Listen For: The increasingly complex texture resulting from the staggered entries of the various voice parts, each stating the musical subject in turn.

Streaming audio track 17. Interactive Listening Guide ILG-3 will show you the full complexity of the musical textures used by Bach.

Bach: Mass in B minor, "Cum Sancto Spiritu," fugal sections
Date: 1723–1733
Instrumentation: Five-part choir and orchestra
Key: D major
Meter: $\frac{3}{4}$ (three rapid beats per measure)
Core Repertory Connection: Bach's Mass in B minor is also discussed in Chapters 2 and 6.

TIME	SECTION	ORIGINAL TEXT	TRANSLATION	COMMENT
0:00	Full Choir	*Cum Sancto Spiritu, in gloria Dei Patris.*	With the Holy Spirit, in the glory of God the Father.	The complete text is stated repeatedly by the full choir and orchestra.
1:01	First fugal section begins			The texture thins out, and the tenors of the choir sing the fugue subject, accompanied only by continuo.
1:09	Alto entry			The altos take up the subject while the tenors continue to sing; their line is a counterpoint to the main melody.
1:21	1st soprano entry			The first sopranos of the choir take up the subject, while the tenors and basses continue in counterpoint.

TIME	SECTION	ORIGINAL TEXT	TRANSLATION	COMMENT
1:30	2nd soprano and bass entry			The second sopranos take up the theme, followed about a second later by the basses. Bringing two voices in with the theme in quick succession is a technique called **stretto**. All five choral parts are now singing, but the orchestra is silent, leaving only the continuo to accompany them.
1:47	Re-entry of the orchestra			As soon as the choir stops singing, the orchestra begins again.
1:54	Re-entry of the choir	*Amen, cum Sancto Spiritu, Amen, in gloria Dei Patris.*	Amen, with the Holy Spirit, Amen, in the glory of God the Father.	The choir joins in, singing homophonically.
2:15	Second fugal section begins			Before the full choir stops singing, the first sopranos begin the fugue subject again. This time the first violins and winds play along with them.
2:23	Stretto entry of the other parts			The second sopranos, altos, tenors, and basses enter in quick succession. If you listen carefully, you will hear other sets of stretto entries in the passage that follows. Bach is letting the music pick up momentum.
3:09	Concluding section	*In gloria Dei Patris. Amen.*	In the glory of God the Father. Amen.	The choir drops out, and re-enters a few seconds later with the text in homophony. The contrapuntal texture then returns as the music drives to the conclusion.

The Classical Period: Functional Harmony Reigns

Stretto: A passage in a fugue that features multiple entrances of the subject in quick succession.

In the Classical period, the dominance of harmony that had been established during the Baroque period became even more pronounced. Polyphony is not absent from late 18th-century music, but it takes a back seat. The texture of Mozart's and Haydn's music is predominantly one of melody and accompaniment, clearly distinguished from each other.

Major and Minor: The Exposition of Mozart's Symphony no. 40

At the start of Mozart's Symphony no. 40, written in 1788, for example, the orchestra begins by playing a pulsing accompaniment that sets the stage for the entrance of the melody. The first statement of the melody is followed, at 0:18, by a series of highly rhythmic chords played by the full orchestra. The accompaniment then returns, and the melody is restated beginning at 0:23. Further melodic and rhythmic activity follow, leading to the appearance of the second theme at 0:52.

Unlike the music heard so far in the piece, this theme is in a major key. A comparison of the first and second themes thus illustrates one of the most important harmonic principles in the music of the common practice period: the contrast between major and minor. Despite being part of a Mass in B minor, the Bach piece we just examined is in a major key, which contributes to its bright, upbeat sound. The Mozart, on the other hand, is in a minor key, which helps make it sound darker and more dramatic.

You can play a major chord by starting with middle C on the piano and using only white keys (see figure 9.1). You can play a minor chord by simply shifting the middle note from the white key to the black key below it (see figure). Either of these chords can serve as the tonic for a key, and hence either can be the point of return for a piece of music. For a list of listening selections in major and minor keys, see Table 9.1.

It is often said that major keys are happy and minor keys are sad. Yet a great deal of sad music is written in major keys and even some quite perky music in minor keys. What is unquestionably true is that composers often use the contrast between major and minor as a means of musical expression. We saw an example of this when we looked at the modified strophic form of Schubert's "Der Lindenbaum" in Chapter 5; a transition to minor underscores the more serious tone of the beginning of the second stanza. The shift in tone in the middle of each of the two stanzas of Schubert's "Die Post," also discussed in Chapter 5, is likewise marked by a temporary change from major to minor.

When a piece begins in a minor key, it almost always changes keys, or **modulates**, to major as the music progresses. In a movement in sonata form, this change typically occurs with the second theme. In ABA form, it often occurs at the start of the B section. Many key changes in classical music are difficult to hear, but not these! Listen to the Mozart Symphony no. 40 from 0:52 (the beginning of the second theme) to the end of the exposition at 2:00. When the repeat of the exposition begins, you will have been listening for over a minute to major-key music, but now the minor key has reappeared. The move back to major occurs at 2:53. These shifts provide a highly audible contrast.

Polyphony in the Development

So far, the texture of the Mozart symphony has consisted of melody and accompaniment. In the development section, though (beginning at 4:07), Mozart uses polyphony to make the music sound more exciting, beginning at 4:21 and continuing until 4:44. Thus, the expressive effects of shifting from minor to major and back again, which we saw in the exposition, are now intensified by the addition of a richer, more complex texture. The main theme from the beginning of the movement is played *forte* by the lower strings and bassoons. Meanwhile the upper strings play a rising **countersubject**, a separate melody that complements the main theme. At 4:26 the roles are reversed, and the upper strings take the melody while the lower strings and bassoons play the countersubject. The same exchange then occurs two more times; the subject plunges into the bass at 4:30 and re-emerges at 4:35, while

C Major Chord   C Minor Chord

FIGURE 9.1 **Major and Minor Chords.**

Modulate: To change keys. This happens repeatedly in most extended compositions from the common practice period.

Countersubject: A melody that is combined contrapuntally with another melody, so both are heard at once, but is clearly subordinate to it.

Learning to recognize and distinguish between major and minor is an important active listening skill, and it is largely a matter of practice. To get you started, here is a list of some minor- and major-key pieces from our listening list. Note that pieces that begin in the major may contain sections in minor keys, while pieces that begin in the minor almost always contain sections in major keys. You will find, however, that the pieces on the first list have an overall major sound distinctively different from those on the second list. That sound is established within the first few seconds and forms a lasting impression.

TABLE 9.1 **Major vs. Minor**

Major:	
	All the selections from the Bach Mass in B minor except the "Qui tollis" and the "Qui sedes" (which are in minor keys)
	All four movements of the Haydn String Quartet in B-flat major, op. 64, no. 3
	All seven movements of the Mozart *Gran Partita*, with the exception of the second trio of the first minuet, the first trio of the second minuet, the B section of the fourth movement, and the fourth variation in the fifth movement (all of these are in minor keys)
	The second and fourth movements of Beethoven's Symphony no. 5, as well as the B section of the third movement
	Der Lindenbaum and *Die Post* from Schubert's *Winterreise* (but note that the second strophe of *Der Lindenbaum* shifts to minor)
	Ich grolle nicht from Schumann's *Dichterliebe*
	Chopin's Nocturne in A-flat major, op. 32, no. 2
	Sousa's *The Stars and Stripes Forever*
Minor:	
	The first movement of Bach's Concerto in D minor for harpsichord and strings, BWV 1052
	The first movement of Mozart's Symphony no. 40
	The first and third movements of Beethoven's Symphony no. 5
	Der Leiermann from Schubert's *Winterreise*
	Die alten, bösen Lieder from Schumann's *Dichterliebe* (which nevertheless ends in a major key)
	Chopin's Ballade in G minor, op. 23
	Dvořák's *Slavonic Dance* in E minor, op. 72, no. 10 (except for the B section, which is in a major key)
	Smetana's *Šárka*

When you listen to any music written from the late Baroque through at least the mid-Romantic period, you should get in the habit of asking whether it is in major or minor. Often this information is printed in the concert program or in the playlist for a recording. Even if it does not appear, accept the challenge and figure it out for yourself.

the countersubject goes to the bass. In the context of the movement, this entire section sounds extremely dramatic and powerful. The music seems to be heating up: entirely appropriate for a development section.

Recapitulation: The Original Texture Returns

The recapitulation sneaks in, beginning at 5:21. Now the texture of melody and accompaniment reasserts itself. Furthermore, when the second theme reappears at 6:37, after another brief polyphonic interlude, it is now also in a minor key. Compare this passage with the one beginning at 0:52 until you are sure you can hear the difference. This shift of the second theme from major to minor is standard practice in minor-key movements in sonata form. It emphasizes that the dramatic conflicts in the movement have now been resolved: the minor key has won.

LEARNING TO LISTEN GUIDE

TAKE NOTE OF MELODY AND TEXTURE

What to Listen For: The shifts between major and minor keys and between simple and complex textures.

Streaming audio track 35.

Mozart: Symphony no. 40 in G minor, K. 550
I: Molto Allegro
Date: 1788
Instrumentation: Small orchestra
Key: G minor
Meter: $\frac{4}{4}$ (four rapid beats per measure)
Core Repertory Connection: This is the same listening guide that appeared in Chapter 5 to illustrate the form of the movement. Additions pertaining to the harmony are presented in parentheses. Mozart's Symphony no. 40 in G minor was also discussed in Chapter 1.

TIME	PROGRESSION	COMMENT
Exposition		
0:00	1st theme (minor key)	After a short introduction, the strings play the opening theme.
0:23	Restatement (minor key)	The first theme is played again but changed so it leads into what follows.
0:33	Transition (major key)	A passage at a louder dynamic level forms the bridge to the next theme.
0:52	2nd theme (major key)	The contrasting theme is introduced.
1:02	Restatement (major key)	This theme is also played again, once again leading to a bridge to the next section.
1:20	Closing section (major key)	An emphatic conclusion rounds out the exposition.
1:28	Opening motive (major key)	The opening three-note motive is featured in this passage, but without the rest of the theme of which it originally formed a part.
2:02	Repeat	The entire exposition is played again.
Development		
4:07	1st theme	After some transitional chords, the first theme returns, but it sounds less stable than before. (Much of this is due to shifting chords in the harmony.)
4:21	Dramatic section	The dynamic level rises, and the music becomes more intense. The harmony also continues to shift, and the texture becomes more complex with the addition of a countersubject.
4:49	Preparation	The music becomes quieter and seems to be preparing for the return of the first theme. The opening motive (minus the theme) is heard over and over. (The changes that occur here are in the harmony.)
5:06	Dramatic outburst	In a surprise move, the orchestra bursts out with several impassioned statements of the opening motive. It eventually subsides. (In the process, it leads back to the minor key with which the symphony began.)
Recapitulation		
5:21	1st theme (minor key)	Notice how Mozart sneaks the theme in when you are no longer really expecting it.
5:46	Restatement (minor key)	Once again, the theme is restated. This time, though, it is rewritten in a different way.

TIME	PROGRESSION	COMMENT
5:55	Transition	This passage is rewritten as well and is much longer than it was in the exposition. (It also leads back to the minor key, making it sound darker as well.)
6:37	2nd theme (minor key)	The contrasting theme returns.
6:48	Restatement (minor key)	
7:12	Closing section (minor key)	This dramatic passage now sounds very final.
7:20	Opening motive (minor key)	The passage based on the three-note motive is heard again.
7:50	Short coda (minor key)	A final passage based on the three-note motive rounds out the movement.

The Romantic Period: Harmony Begins to Change

Romantic composers were often more adventurous in their use of harmony. The harmonic language of the Classical period is both limited and clear; that is one of the things that make it classical. This is not to say that composers of this period never used more complicated harmonies. Mozart's harmony, in fact, can be as rich and surprising as anything to be found before the 20th century (as can Bach's). Mozart generally saves such effects, though, for times when they can be particularly effective. A Romantic composer such as Chopin may use such harmonies more frequently.

Harmonic Enrichment: Chopin's Nocturne in A-flat Major

Listen, for example, to the B section of the Chopin Nocturne in A-flat major, op. 32, no. 2, written in 1836 and 1837. The texture throughout this piece is one of melody and accompaniment. Beginning at 2:01, the music switches from major to minor. This in itself is not unusual, but the harmony also becomes increasingly rich, as in the passage that starts at 2:31 and continues to 2:45. The same richness is evident in the parallel passage from 3:15 to the return of the A section at 3:31.

Chromatic: Making use of the notes in between the given notes of a key.

Diatonic: Using only the notes belonging to a particular key.

The melody in these passages is primarily **chromatic**: Unlike most melodies from the Classical period, it cannot be played entirely, or even primarily, on the white keys of the piano. Such a melody would be known as **diatonic**. The scales we are most familiar with, major and minor, are diatonic, because it is possible to play them using only white keys of the piano if one begins in the right spot: C for a major scale, and A for a minor scale. Chopin uses the notes in between as well. You can verify this by sitting at a keyboard. Start with the C above middle C, and play each successive note below it, including the black keys, until middle C is reached. Then listen to the passages from the Chopin just cited, and you will realize that Chopin is building his melody from note combinations like the ones you just played. If you think of the black keys as the "cracks" between the familiar sounds of the C major scale, then Chopin has filled in the cracks.

Such a melody cannot be harmonized with the four chords of *Heart and Soul*, which, as you will recall, can be played on the white keys alone. A melody that makes so much use of the black keys needs to be harmonized with different chords. This explains the passage's harmonic richness. Chopin makes that richness more prominent by using an exclusively homophonic texture, a rarity in piano music. It makes an effective contrast with the A section, in which the left-hand accompaniment generally moves faster than the melody.

LEARNING TO LISTEN GUIDE

TAKE NOTE OF MELODY AND HARMONY

What to Listen For: The increased harmonic richness of the B section, which distinguishes it from the A sections that precede and follow it.

Streaming audio track 44.

Chopin: Nocturne in A-flat major, op. 32, no. 2
Date: 1836–1837
Instrumentation: Piano solo
Key: A-flat major
Meter: Common time
Form: Ternary (ABA)
Core Repertory Connection: This music is also discussed in Chapters 8 and 12.

TIME	PROGRESSION	COMMENT
0:00	A section	The first main section of the piece is in a major key and has relatively simple harmonies.
2:01	B section, beginning	After a quick change of key, the B section starts with darker, minor-key harmonies. The melody in the right hand is chromatic, meaning it cannot be played on the white keys of the piano.
2:31	Harmonic enrichment	The harmonies in this part of the B section are particularly rich.
2:45	B section, repeat	The B section is heard again, with the pitch a half-step (one key on the keyboard) higher than before. The dynamic level is also louder than before.
3:15	Harmonic enrichment	The harmonically rich section is repeated in the new key.
3:31	A section	The music of the A section returns, but the dynamic level is now forte.

Harmonic Revolution: Wagner's *Tristan und Isolde*

By the later 19th century, harmony like Chopin's had become the norm for many composers. In his opera *Tristan und Isolde*, completed in 1859, Richard Wagner used such harmonies almost constantly. We shall listen to the instrumental prelude that begins its first act.

If you listen carefully to the first few minutes of this music, you will hear that most of the melodic motion is chromatic. The cracks occupied by the black keys have now become essential to even the most basic melodic statement. In fact, when a melody emerges at 1:26 that can be played on the white keys alone, it stands out as a contrast.

Grove Music Online.

Focus On
Richard Wagner (1813–1883)

German composer. One of the key figures in the history of opera, Wagner was largely responsible for altering its orientation in the 19th century. His program of artistic reform, though not executed to the last detail, accelerated the trend towards organically conceived, through-composed structures, as well as influencing the development of the orchestra, of a new breed of singer, and of various aspects of theatrical practice. (Barry Millington, *Grove Music Online*.)

Wagner's *Tristan und Isolde* appeared in 1859, the same year as Charles Darwin's *On the Origin of Species*. Both works were revolutionary—and unsettling. Darwin's work contradicted the traditional Judeo-Christian view of the Creation, by showing that life forms change in ways governed by the struggle for survival. Wagner's work brought about a similar revolution in the world of music: the laws of harmony could change and develop as well. One hundred fifty years later, Darwin's conclusions have been proven by science, but many people still find them difficult to understand and accept. In a similar way, Wagner's harmony anticipated the development of modern music, which many traditional listeners can still find disturbing. Wagner's music may mark the end of the very idea of a universal language of music, which the early 19th century had emphatically affirmed.

Charles Darwin (1809–1882). Darwin developed the principle of natural selection and is buried in Westminster Abbey near Isaac Newton, who developed the theory of gravity. *(Library of Congress Prints and Photographs Division Washington, DC 20540 USA)*

Richard Wagner (1813–1883). Wagner sought a unification of the arts on the ancient Greek model and wrote extensively on the subject. *(Library of Congress Prints and Photographs Division Washington, DC 20540 USA)*

The harmony has become more chromatic, too. The opening chord, known as the "Tristan" chord because of the way Wagner uses it to represent that character, is difficult to analyze according to harmonic rules developed over the preceding centuries. In some ways, it might be considered the beginning of the end of functional harmony. The music that follows is fundamentally different from the earlier examples by Bach, Mozart, and even Chopin. Here there is no "home," no moment of repose or cadence, no sense that the music can comfortably stop at some particular point. Instead, a restless sea of shifting harmonies creates a perfect musical metaphor for the unresolved love that is the opera's subject.

LEARNING TO LISTEN GUIDE

TAKE NOTE OF MELODY AND HARMONY

What to Listen For: The lack of harmonic resolution, which makes this music sound restless and unsettled.

Streaming audio track 51.

Wagner: *Tristan und Isolde*, Prelude, beginning
Date: 1859
Instrumentation: Large orchestra
Key: A minor
Meter: $\frac{6}{8}$ (two slowly moving groups of three beats per measure)

TIME	PROGRESSION	COMMENT
0:00	Opening motive	The motive representing Tristan is stated by the cello, with the winds adding the harmonies that make up the famous "Tristan chord" progression.
0:21	Repetition	The opening is repeated at a higher pitch.
0:41	Repetition and continuation	It is repeated on yet a higher pitch and then extended.
1:35	Love theme	The theme representing the love between Tristan and Isolde is played by the cellos. This is the first music heard so far that can be played on the white keys alone.

If You Liked This Music . . .
A Quick Listen to Wagner

Wagner's operas are long and daunting, but for a quick glimpse at his dramatic genius, the following are recommended:

- Wotan's Farewell from *Die Walküre*—The scene in which the king of the gods leaves his daughter Brünnhilde defenseless except for the ring of magic fire with which he surrounds her is deeply affecting, especially if you listen to the duet that precedes it (approximately the last 40 minutes of Act III).
- The song contest from *Die Meistersinger von Nürnberg*. The conclusion of Act III of Wagner's only mature comic opera contrasts Walther von Stolzing's stunning prize song

with a very funny misreading of it by his rival Beckmesser.
- The *Liebestod* from *Tristan und Isolde*—Isolde's "love death," with which the opera concludes, is frequently paired with the prelude in performance.
- After listening to these examples, you might also consider watching the *Star Wars* movies and paying particular attention to John Williams's music. Williams deliberately imitated many of Wagner's techniques, particularly the use of pregnant motives to represent characters and ideas in the plot.

In technical terms, the harmony now contains more dissonance than consonance. Traditional musical syntax dictates that a dissonant chord be followed by a consonant one. To follow a dissonance with another dissonance, and then another—as Wagner does here—is like writing a sentence consisting almost entirely of verbs.

(I ran, ran, ran to escape what loomed and threatened, forcing me to struggle to flee.) Such a sentence would be all action and momentum. This music is too.

The Modern Period: Dissonance is Set Free

In the 20th century, composers continued to break the rules of harmony. Early modern composers including Debussy, Ives, Stravinsky, and Schoenberg often made use of a level of dissonance that would have been unthinkable even for Wagner. Remember that nearly all music contains dissonance, but that in a functional harmonic context it is immediately resolved by consonant harmonies. One of the rules Debussy broke was this requirement that a dissonance should be followed by a consonance. Even Wagner's harmony depends on our perception that dissonance needs to go somewhere. When we do not arrive on schedule, the music can sound turbulent and unstable.

Harmony as an Adjective: Debussy's Sonata for Flute, Viola, and Harp

If Wagner's harmonies are like verbs, Debussy's are like adjectives: They provide music with its color. Wagner's harmonies, compared earlier to a sentence consisting almost entirely of verbs, describe continuous action. A sentence consisting almost entirely of adjectives, by contrast, would be rich in descriptive evocation. (The lush, warm, verdant solitude was welcome, relaxing, and enveloping.) It might imply some action but of a more indirect kind. This is how Debussy's harmonies work.

Listen again to the opening of the Sonata for flute, viola, and harp, written in 1915, and focus this time on Debussy's use of harmonic color. Like the prelude

Autumn woods. A piece of music, like a photograph, might be more about color and texture than about action. *(Taiga)*

to *Tristan und Isolde*, this piece begins with a dissonant chord. The harp plays its notes one by one for emphasis, before a string of other dissonances. When the viola emerges by itself after 0:25, it plays a melody that, once again, cannot be harmonized by functional chords like those in *Heart and Soul*. It implies dissonance even when we hear only one note at a time. The first consonant harmony in the piece appears at 0:57. Its seeming finality, though, immediately gives way to more dissonances in the harp.

As you listen to the rest of the movement, you will find that this pattern continues. Occasional consonances appear, usually at points of rest. Most of the time, however, the harmony is dissonant without being particularly disruptive or urgent. Debussy is simply enjoying experimenting with these sounds and hoping that you will enjoy listening to them as well.

The texture of this music, meanwhile, is largely one of melody and accompaniment, with the flute and viola taking turns with the melody, and the harp doing most of the accompanying. Yet the contrasting color of the harp is so much a part of the music that one hesitates to describe it simply as an accompanying instrument. Debussy uses the timbres of the harp much the way he uses harmony—to enrich the sound of the music and give it sensuous appeal.

Streaming audio track 60. Interactive Listening Guide ILG-16 will show you how the instruments interact in the first movement of Debussy's sonata.

Across the Arts
Color and Suggestion

When impressionist painters such as Claude Monet (1840–1926) set out to capture an object, they were less intent on rendering an accurate, realistic image than on portraying the particular light and color surrounding it in any given moment. The label "impressionist" had initially been applied pejoratively, by a critic, to describe the paintings' apparent unfinished quality, but Monet and others soon adopted it as a way to explain their methods. In order to convey subjective impressions of moments in time, the artists gave color preference over line, applying large and small dabs of paint corresponding to their perceptions of an object as opposed to the way they knew the object was supposed to look. Although Debussy rejected the label of impressionist, the richly suggestive images Monet and others created find parallels in his music. Debussy used harmonies rather like dabs of color—instead of placing them in traditional straight-line progressions—to suggest moods, sensations, and even places or figures.

Monet's many paintings of the water lilies in the pond at his country home at Giverny show the impressionist concern for texture and color over more traditional qualities like clarity of line and form. (© *The Bridgeman Art Library Ltd. / Alamy*)

If You Liked This Music . . .

More Debussy

Debussy's use of instrumental color to complement his unusual harmony is particularly evident in his orchestral works.

- The *Prelude à l'après-midi d'un faune* brilliantly evokes the shimmering heat of a summer afternoon and the increasing sensual arousal of its subject, the mythical faun.

- *La Mer*, a set of three "symphonic sketches," is one of the most important orchestral works of the early 20th century.
- The three *Images* for orchestra show Debussy at his most extroverted.

Stravinsky's *Symphony of Psalms*: Echoing Bach

Debussy's music was very forward-looking; many later 20th-century composers are indebted to his experiments with harmony and tone color. Stravinsky's music, on the other hand, often shows how a composer can reach backward and forward simultaneously. The second movement of the *Symphony of Psalms*, written in 1930, uses fugal techniques like those we encountered in the "Cum Sancto Spiritu" from Bach's Mass in B minor.

In Chapter 6 we examined this movement for its use of instrumental and vocal timbres. Now listen again to the beginning of the movement, but this time concentrate on hearing the entry of the instrumental voices as Stravinsky builds up a rich polyphonic texture. The opening thematic statement by the oboe is answered by the flute at 0:20. Further statements of the theme occur at 0:47 and 1:07. When the choir enters at 1:50, it introduces a new theme, making this a **double fugue**. In the passage that follows, the instruments continue to play the opening theme contrapuntally, while successive choral parts enter with the new one. By three minutes into the piece, the sound has become bafflingly complex. For any connoisseur of classical music, however, the reference to Bach is obvious.

Double Fugue: A fugue with two subjects instead of one.

TAKE NOTE OF MELODY

What to Listen For: The opening of this movement features a series of fugal entries, first in the orchestra and then in the choir.

Stravinsky: *Symphony of Psalms*

II: "Expectans expectavi," beginning

Date: 1930

Instrumentation: Four-part choir and large orchestra

Key: C minor

Meter: $\frac{2}{4}$ (two slow beats per measure)

Core Repertory Connection: Stravinsky's *Symphony of Psalms* is also discussed in Chapters 4 and 6.

Streaming audio track 64. Interactive Listening Guide ILG-17 will show you which instruments are playing and which vocal parts are singing at each point during the second movement.

TIME	SECTION	ORIGINAL TEXT	TRANSLATION	COMMENT
0:00	Oboe			The theme is played by the first oboe without accompaniment.
0:20	Flute			The first flute plays the theme while the oboe continues to play in counterpoint.
0:47	Second flute			The second flute enters with the theme while the other two instruments continue.
1:07	Second oboe			The second oboe now takes up the theme. Four individual instruments are now playing, each with an independent musical line.
1:27	Thinner texture			There is no new thematic statement, but two oboes and the first flute suddenly drop out, while two more flutes begin playing simultaneously.
1:38	Five flutes			The first flute comes in again, followed quickly by the piccolo, so that five flutes are now playing at once.
1:50	Entry of the choir	*Expectans expectavi Dominum, et intendit mihi.*	I waited patiently for the Lord; he inclined to me and heard my cry.	The choral sopranos enter with a new theme. Simultaneously, the flutes drop out and the other winds and horn begin playing. If you listen carefully, you can also hear the cellos and basses playing the original theme, making it a countersubject to the theme in the choir. The wind instruments play additional counterpoints, resulting in a rich, Bach-like texture.
2:07	Alto entry			The choral altos take up the theme.
2:31	Tenors			The choral tenors begin singing the theme, with the other two voices in counterpoint. The orchestration thins out, so the choir can be clearly heard.
2:48	Basses			The choral basses enter, complicating the texture even further.

While the texture of this music recalls Bach, Stravinsky's harmony is more like Debussy's. Paradoxically, it is also more like Machaut's, which can be quite dissonant because it was written before the development of tonal harmony as practiced in the Baroque, Classical, and Romantic periods. Stravinsky's parts clash at least as often as they blend. Rather than being in control, as it is in the Bach, the harmony here is a by-product of the counterpoint. For the instrumental opening, Stravinsky wrote a jagged melody full of large intervals. He wanted it to stand out every time it appeared rather than blend into the harmonic background. Rarely do you get the sense that this music could stop and produce a pleasant-sounding chord—as could happen at virtually any point in *Row, Row, Row Your Boat* and at most points in Bach as well. The consistent level of dissonance is one of this music's most noticeable features.

In History
Stravinsky's *Symphony of Psalms*

Like almost anyone who lived through so much of the turbulent 20th century, Igor Stravinsky had a complex life. He was Russian by birth, but he never lived in Russia after the Bolshevik Revolution in 1917, returning only briefly in his 80s. He spent much of his young adulthood in Western Europe, particularly France, and much of his later life in the United States. His musical style was thus international in nature, and yet it is the distinctly Russian elements of his music that helped shape an international style adopted by others.

Stravinsky is still a dominant figure among classical composers of the modern period. His reputation was cemented early, with the blockbuster ballets that he wrote before the First World War—*The Firebird*, *Petrushka*, and *The Rite of Spring*. Yet he continued to write new and challenging works well into the 1960s.

The *Symphony of Psalms* was completed in 1930, in the middle of his long life and almost exactly halfway between the two world wars. It epitomizes the composer's international approach both to life and to music. Although he was living in France, where many of his earlier works had been premiered, Stravinsky wrote the piece on commission for the Boston Symphony Orchestra. The orchestra, too, was notably multinational, then conducted by his fellow Russian expatriate Serge Koussevitzky. Like much of the art and music of the 1920s and 30s, the *Symphony of Psalms* refers to styles of the past, including a Bach fugue and Gregorian chant. The symphony is in Latin, still the language of the Catholic Mass, even though Stravinsky had recently reconfirmed his commitment to the Russian Orthodox Communion of his birth. Less obvious is that the work makes extensive use of the exotic octatonic scale, commonly found in the music of Russian composers but utilized by others as well.

In many ways, the work recalls the age-old role of music in religious ritual. At the same time, references to past styles produce a very different effect, sometimes called "emotional distancing." By avoiding showy effects, this music reacts against what many at the time perceived as the emotional excesses of late Romanticism, widely associated with the savagery of the First World War. Yet the rising tide of totalitarianism held new perils as well.

Is the musical style of this work, then, mired in the struggles and contradictions of its times? Music can be—and often is—bigger than its historical context. Stravinsky's music has survived the tumultuous period when it was written, along with much of the late Romantic music that preceded it and at least some of the postmodern music that followed. A familiarity with context is nevertheless an important part of the active listener's equipment. Our understanding of this work grows with our knowledge of the man who produced it and of his times.

The Later 20th Century and Beyond: Anything Can Happen

As with so many other things in the complex postwar world, no general formula can describe what has happened to harmony since the latter part of the 20th century. Most popular music still uses functional harmony. Some classical composers, including George Crumb, have continued to write highly dissonant music, while others, like his fellow American Steve Reich (b. 1936), have returned to consonance while experimenting with other aspects of their music.

Focus On
Janika Vandervelde (b. 1955)

American composer. She received the BME degree from the University of Wisconsin, Eau Claire, and postgraduate degrees in composition from the University of Minnesota (MA 1980, PhD 1985), where she studied with Eric Stokes and Dominick Argento, among others. Her work first drew wide interest when the musicologist Susan McClary championed *Genesis II*, later the subject of a chapter in *Feminine Endings* (Minneapolis, 1991). She has

Janika Vandervelde. *(Photo of Janika Vendervelde by Larry Fuchsberg)*

since received commissions from such organizations as the Minnesota Orchestra and the St. Paul Chamber Orchestra. In 1990 she accepted teaching positions at the Minnesota Center for Arts Education and the University of Minnesota's Department of Independent Study. The *Genesis* cycle, a series of seven chamber works, reveals a minimalistic technique guided by a feminist concept of life's cycles. In *Genesis III* a medieval-sounding theme, scored for the flute, viola, and harp, generates concentric circles of variation, twice broken by free cadenzas that contrast sharply with surrounding material. *Ancient Echoes Across the Stara Planina* is less strictly minimalist and more postmodern in approach, employing strikingly contrasting timbres of a full orchestra, a Bulgarian women's folk choir, and soloistic instrumental lines. The opera *Seven Sevens* merges a variety of popular idioms and uses both acoustic and electronic sounds. Constantly changing meters and cross-rhythms, as well as the juxtaposition of additive rhythms and freely lyrical lines, are regular features of her style. (Karin Pendle, *Grove Music Online.*)

Grove Music Online.

Beginning with Beethoven, composers' careers have frequently been divided into three periods, a division appropriate to Janika Vandervelde's work so far. While the three periods of Beethoven's career are usually called simply "early," "middle" and "late," those that Vandervelde imagines for herself are "post-minimalist," "post-modernist," and "post-postmodern fusionist." One of her earliest works, *Genesis II*, written in 1983, dates from her post-minimalist period. It is one of seven works in her *Genesis* cycle, which she describes as "an extended exploration of life cycles and cycles of change, rooted in the contrapuntal flow of expanding palindromes and clockworks."

While Vandervelde's career has subsequently gone in other directions, her choice of words to describe these works clearly connects them with the minimalist movement, widely associated with Steve Reich and Philip Glass (b. 1937). In this music, small segments of harmonically simple material are repeated with subtle changes over long stretches of time.

In Janika Vandervelde's *Genesis II*, most of the harmony is quite consonant compared to the music by Debussy and Stravinsky that we just examined. Occasionally, more dissonant passages intrude and contrast strongly with the rest of the music. Passages in Count Basie's *Lester Leaps In*, on the other hand, are as dissonant as anything in Stravinsky.

Crumb's *Black Angels*: Part II: Absence

Crumb's *Black Angels*, written in 1970, is perhaps the most dissonant piece on the listening list. Of course, this piece has many other unusual features as well: the electronic amplification, the nontraditional playing techniques and the unusual timbres they produce, and the use of spoken words. Crumb's treatment of dissonance may seem less significant by comparison. In fact, the sounds of *Black Angels* are so unusual that it might not even occur to you that this music has harmony at all.

That is why the opening of Part II, titled Absence, is so disconcerting but evocative. The beginning of this section is scored for cello, second violin, and viola (listed in that order in the score). Here Crumb quotes the accompaniment to Schubert's song *Der Tod und das Mädchen* (*Death and the Maiden*). Schubert himself used this theme as the subject of the second movement of a string quartet (D. 810 in D minor). Crumb further complicates matters by directing the players to bow using the wrong side of their hand, making their instruments sound more like violas da gamba (a Renaissance and Baroque instrument that is hardly appropriate to Schubert). Occasionally, the first violin interjects high-pitched notes that sound like distractions. Apart from this, though, the texture is homophonic and mostly consonant—Crumb has even thinned out Schubert's harmonies so that they, too, sound almost Renaissance-like.

When this section ends abruptly at 1:20, we realize that we had been only momentarily transported into the past: for just a moment, harmony had operated according to principles more familiar to Western ears. Those same principles emerge again at 4:03 in the section that Crumb titled *Sarabanda de la Muerta Oscura* (*Sarabande of Dark Death*)—an original composition this time, but in Renaissance style. This, too, submerges at 6:04. Both these passages are marked "Trio," a reference to their scoring for (primarily) three instruments but perhaps also a play on words, since the "trio," or B, section of a minuet or scherzo is an interjection within the form.

LEARNING TO LISTEN GUIDE

TAKE NOTE OF MELODY AND HARMONY

What to Listen For: The contrast created in the context of this piece by the relatively ordinary harmonies of the "Pavana Lachrymae" and "Sarabanda de la Muerte Oscura."

Streaming audio track 70.

Crumb: *Black Angels*
II: Absence
Date: 1970
Instrumentation: Electronically amplified string quartet
Key: Largely undefined
Meter: Irregular
Core Repertory Connection: Crumb's *Black Angels* is also discussed in Chapter 1.

TIME	PROGRESSION	COMMENT
0:00	"Pavana Lachrymae"	This section is based on the second movement of Schubert's "Death and the Maiden" quartet, which in turn is based on one of Schubert's songs. The first violin interjects insect sounds. Otherwise, the harmony here is strangely archaic.
1:20	"Threnody II: Black Angels!"	This section, in many ways the heart of the piece, features a variety of experimental sounds from the string instruments, as well as brief chants in several different languages. Here it may sound like there is no harmony at all, at least as we have described it in this chapter.
4:03	"Sarabanda de la Muerte Oscura"	This original composition also makes use of an archaic harmonic style, once again with interjections from the first violin.
5:43	"Lost Bells (Echo)"	This section overlaps with the Sarabanda and begins with a first barely audible bowed note on the tam-tam, or gong. The same effect concludes the section and the second part as a whole.

Crumb's *Black Angels*: Part III: Return

Something like traditional harmony appears again in the extended "God-Music" section that begins Part III and continues to 3:00. Here, though, the effect is hardly old-fashioned. This harmony is more like Charles Ives's in the second movement of his Violin Sonata no. 4: it includes a high level of dissonance while maintaining clear references to traditional harmony. More unusual timbres follow, including a reprise of "Night of the Electric Insects," with which the first movement began. The quartet then concludes, beginning at 5:34, with a blending of the "Sarabanda" and the insect music. The two worlds meet.

LEARNING TO LISTEN GUIDE

TAKE NOTE OF MELODY AND HARMONY

What to Listen For: The reconciliation of traditional harmony with the more advanced techniques that have been heard throughout the quartet.

Streaming audio track 71.

Crumb: *Black Angels*
III: Return
Date: 1970
Instrumentation: Electronically amplified string quartet
Key: Largely undefined
Meter: Irregular
Core Repertory Connection: Crumb's *Black Angels* is also discussed in Chapters 1.

TIME	PROGRESSION	COMMENT
0:00	"God-Music"	This section, in which the lower three instrumentalists play on crystal glasses, contains clear but highly dissonant harmonic writing. The first violin, labeled here Vox Dei (voice of God), is separated from the rest of the ensemble, so the texture can be described as melody and accompaniment.
3:48	"Ancient Voices"	Only the two violins play in this section, and they use some unusual techniques, so harmony in the traditional sense is much harder to perceive.
4:29	"Ancient Voices (Echo)"	The unusual textures of the previous section are reflected in this one, but the texture is even thinner.
5:00	"Threnody III: Night of the Electric Insects"	The transition to the last section is nearly imperceptible. Once it is under way, however, you will hear echoes of the music with which the quartet began.
7:00	Conclusion	In the conclusion of this section, the insect music and the more harmonic "Sarabanda de la Muerte Oscura" are combined.

Harmony, Texture, and Meaning

Harmony and texture invite active listening. Music that highlights polyphonic writing, like the Josquin Mass or most movements of the Bach Mass in B minor, is astoundingly rich and rewarding. Since there is so much going on at once, you cannot possibly take these pieces in at a single hearing.

Richness of harmony may also take repeated hearings to grasp. Music with no dissonance would be unbearably boring, and the deeply dissonant harmonies of composers such as Ives and Stravinsky can reward an active listener. This music— to say nothing of that by Crumb and Dallapiccola—deserves to be heard again and again to be understood and enjoyed.

In the last five chapters, you have acquired a vocabulary for active listening, and pieces like these may be growing on you. There is more to music, though, than even what you hear. As we shall see in the following chapters, in order to listen actively, you also need to think about meaning—what music and musicians are trying to communicate, and why.

SUMMARY

- Texture and harmony are related concepts crucial to understanding the unique developments in Western music of the last several centuries. Texture refers to the number of pitches or melodies that sound at the same time. In harmony, the notes form chords that can be either consonant or dissonant and whose interaction provides harmonic interest.
- In monophonic music, only one note and one melody are heard at a time, though it may be sung by multiple voices or played by multiple instruments. A monophonic texture was prominent in early music.
- Polyphony is the combination of multiple simultaneous melodic lines. Counterpoint is a method for creating combinations with minimal clashing sounds. Notes sounding together may produce dissonances or consonances. During the Middle Ages and Renaissance, these were still heard primarily in the context of the respective melodies.

- During the Baroque, the chords themselves took on greater significance. Musicians began to understand harmony in terms of a melodic line accompanied by chords (homophony). Baroque composers like Bach were still masters of counterpoint, but they used what is called functional harmony to give music its form.
- The control of musical forms by harmonic progressions is a defining trait of music from roughly 1680 to 1875, known as the common practice period.
- Music from the Classical and Romantic periods is often primarily harmonic, but composers like Mozart still used counterpoint effectively. Romantic composers began to expand the harmonic vocabulary to include richer and more unusual chords, with more dissonance. The chromaticism of Richard Wagner is often seen as marking the beginning of modern music.
- Early 20th-century composers expanded the harmonic vocabulary even further. Their music may contain a high level of dissonance, making it uniquely challenging. In the later 20th century, this process has continued, but composers have also felt free to draw on harmonies of the past and to expand music in other directions as well.

KEY TERMS

Chromatic	p. 250	Diatonic	p. 250	Homophonic	p. 242
Common Practice Period	p. 243	Dissonant/Dissonance	p. 238	Modulate	p. 247
Consonant/consonance	p. 238	Double Fugue	p. 256	Stretto	p. 246
Contrapuntal	p. 239	Episode	p. 245	Subject	p. 245
Countersubject	p. 247	Fugal	p. 244	Tonic	p. 235
		Fugue	p. 245		
		Functional Harmony	p. 243		

REVIEW QUESTIONS

1. What is meant by texture in music? How does it differ from harmony?
2. What is monophonic texture? When was monophonic music most prominent historically?
3. What is polyphonic texture? What is counterpoint, and how do the two terms relate to each other?
4. What is meant by functional harmony, and when did it come to prominence?
5. How does Bach's use of counterpoint differ from that of Josquin?
6. What are the harmonic characteristics, respectively, of the music of the Classical and early Romantic periods?
7. How did Richard Wagner expand the harmonic vocabulary of the late Romantic period?
8. How does the harmony of early 20th-century composers like Debussy and Stravinsky differ from that of Wagner?
9. What is the role of harmony in the music of late 20th-century composers like George Crumb and Janika Vandervelde?

REVIEW CONCEPTS

1. How did the relationship between counterpoint and harmony change from the Middle Ages to the Baroque period? Give some examples from the listening list for this chapter.
2. How does Bach use counterpoint within the context of functional harmony in the selections from the Mass in B minor?
3. How did composers in the Classical period make their music interesting despite its relatively limited harmonic vocabulary? Be sure to consider other factors like use of timbre, rhythm, and melody.
4. How did Romantic composers like Chopin expand on the harmonic vocabulary of past music?
5. What does it mean to describe Wagner's harmonies as verbs and Debussy's as adjectives? How would this analogy apply to some of the other works on the listening list (e.g., Berlioz, Chopin, Smetana, Ives, Basie)?
6. What different kinds of harmonic possibilities are represented by Vandervelde's *Genesis II* on the one hand and by Crumb's *Black Angels* on the other?

LISTENING EXERCISES

1. Listen carefully to some of the works on the listening list not described in this chapter (e.g., the Bach harpsichord concerto, the Mozart *Gran Partita*, Beethoven's Fifth Symphony, the Schubert and Schumann songs, Berlioz's *Roméo et Juliette*). Do these works confirm or contradict what has been said in this chapter about the use of harmony and counterpoint by these particular composers, and about the periods in which these works were written?

2. Listen to some fugues by Bach. There are many written for organ, often paired with other pieces so that they appear as "Prelude and Fugue," "Toccata and Fugue," or "Fantasy and Fugue." *The Well-Tempered Clavier* is a collection of 48 preludes and fugues in all 24 keys. See if you can get used to hearing the contrapuntal statements of the fugal subjects and their alternation with contrasting material.

3. Tune in to a classical radio station and see if you can identify the period of the music being performed. You should listen primarily to the harmony, but other factors, such as instrumentation and melodic writing, may help to reinforce your decision. Wait until the announcer identifies the piece and composer and see if you were correct. Repeat.

4. Listen to some atonal compositions by Arnold Schoenberg—for example, his song cycles *Pierrot lunaire* and *Book of the Hanging Gardens*. In these works, traditional tonality is deliberately dissolved, leading them to be called *atonal*, a term of which Schoenberg disapproved but which has become common. You will still hear some tonal-sounding progressions in this music, but they do not resolve as expected, and no key is ever established. This music is difficult and challenging, but many have found it uniquely rewarding as well. Do you agree? Why or why not?

10

Music and Text

TAKE NOTE

In listening to music with a text, one must take into account the ways these elements communicate alone and in combination to amplify the emotion and meaning of a work.

Popular song, art song, folk song, hymn, rock and roll anthem—although these genres may differ significantly in many ways, they all share the basic challenges of effectively combining music with lyrics. In classical music, the words that accompany music are often drawn from literature or poetry and are simply referred

Chapter Objectives

● Describe the different ways music and text can work together.

● Consider what happens when a composer makes the text deliberately hard to understand, or when the music seems to subvert the text.

● Distinguish among semantic, phonetic, and syntactic qualities of text, and understand how they may all be reflected in a musical setting.

● Indicate how music can suggest meanings that are less evident when one simply reads the words.

● Recognize the different voices (personas) from which music texts can be interpreted.

Chronology of Music Discussed in this Chapter

Mid-14th century
Guillaume de Machaut p. 271
Lasse! comment oublieray/Se j'aim mon loyal/Pour quoy me bat mes maris?, motet

1828
Franz Schubert p. 266, 280
Winterreise: Der Lindenbaum; Die Post; Der Leiermann

1840
Robert Schumann
Dichterliebe: Ich grolle nicht, p. 278; *Die alten, bösen Lieder* p. 282

1938–1941
Luigi Dallapiccola p. 284
Canti di prigionia (3 movements).

to as the *text*. In opera, the lyrics are part of the libretto, which may contain both spoken text and words to be sung (see Chapter 11).

When music has words, the active listener is faced with some interesting questions. What is the relationship between the music and text? What options does a composer have for combining these elements? Should music illustrate or mimic the text? Is it possible for music and text to contradict each other intentionally? How might the skillful combination of music and text communicate meaning more effectively than either of these elements alone?

In this chapter, we will see how text and music work together to paint pictures in our mind and arouse emotional responses. We will also see how music can respond to the sounds and structure of a text, and how it can even alter our perception of the text's meaning, perhaps by contradicting what it seems to say. All these techniques were common in the Romantic period, the historical high point of the art song. Therefore, we will concentrate on songs by Romantic composers, while also looking at some music from other periods to explore different ways in which music with text may challenge our expectations.

Fitting Music and Text Together

Some music is so elaborate that the text is difficult to understand. Yet it is hard to think of a well-known song in which the music doesn't fit the mood of the text. In many cases, the music also enhances the text in an almost pictorial way, a technique commonly known as **text painting** or word painting. In *Twinkle, Twinkle, Little Star*, for example, the phrase "up above the world so high" is set to a tune that begins on a high note before it descends. In *Somewhere Over the Rainbow*, the large melodic jump at the opening also illustrates the text: the melody immediately ascends far above the note it started on, then arches down and back again in a manner that resembles an inverted rainbow. Songwriters may even turn text painting upside down by having the music move in a direction opposite to that indicated by the text. When Johnny Cash, for example, sings "down, down, down" in *Ring of Fire*, the notes are rising, whereas the word "higher" is sung with the notes dropping down.

Creating a purposeful connection between music and text is at the heart of many art songs from the Romantic period. As we saw in Chapter 5, an art song is a work from the classical music repertory that is not part of a larger staged work and often provides a musical setting for an existing work of poetry. These pieces typically feature a singer and piano accompaniment, and the accompaniment plays a crucial role in reinforcing and interpreting the text.

Schubert: *Winterreise, Der Lindenbaum*

We have already examined one song in the *Winterreise* cycle, *Der Lindenbaum*, as an example of modified strophic form. Its text, like those of the other *Winterreise* songs, was written by Wilhelm Müller, a minor German poet and contemporary of Schubert. Despite the text's predictable structure, the music shifts along with Müller's imagery to create vivid emotions. The text helps us to understand the musical images, and Schubert's music adds meanings at which the text alone only hints.

If You Liked This Music . . .

Creating Musical Pictures

Composers have delighted in creating musical pictures since the 16th century. They are particularly common in the madrigals of the late Renaissance. Semantic text painting is easy to hear in these two late 16th-century English madrigals:

- *April Is in My Mistress' Face*, by Thomas Morley (ca. 1557–1602), draws sharp contrasts between textual images like September, which is in the mistress' bosom, and December, which is in her heart.
- *Fair Phyllis*, by John Farmer (ca. 1570–1601), contains striking musical illustrations of nearly every image in the text. When Phyllis is sitting "all alone," just one voice sings. When the shepherds search for her "up and down," the voices seem to chase each other through the hills, with rapid descending lines entering in quick succession.

Sometimes composers created musical pictures for the pleasure of the performers. In his enduringly popular work *O occhi manza mia*, the Franco-Flemish (but very international) Orlando di Lasso (ca. 1532–1594) set the word "occhi" (eyes) to two notes of equal duration. In the musical notation of the 16th century, these were written as open circles (breves) that resembled a pair of eyes.

Detail from *The Journey of Moses*, c. 1481-3 (fresco), by Pietro Perugino. This painting shows the kind of idealized pastoral scene frequently described in the texts of late Renaissance madrigals.

Text Painting: The deliberate imitation of pictorial images suggested by the text in the musical setting.

Even before the singer comes in, the piano begins to paint a picture. Images may form in your mind, but you can't be sure what is intended. Once the words enter, though, the picture readily coalesces into the branches of a tree rustling in the wind. Text and music together complete an image that neither could create by itself.

When this music returns, to prepare for the third and fourth stanzas, it is transformed. This time it is in the minor, producing a much darker and more somber image. Once again, for an explanation we can look to the text, whose imagery has become distinctly darker. This is especially clear if we understand that for many Romantic poets, "rest" was a metaphor for death. The tree is inviting the traveler to lie down and to welcome death beneath its branches.

Grove Music Online.

Focus On

The Piano

A keyboard instrument distinguished by the fact that its strings are struck by rebounding hammers rather than plucked (as in the harpsichord) or struck by tangents that remain in contact with the strings (as in the clavichord). (Edwin M. Ripin/ Stewart Pollens, *Grove Music Online*.)

Early piano. A fortepiano by Conrad Graf, a Viennese manufacturer of Schubert's time. (© *The Metropolitan Museum of Art. Image source: Art Resource, NY*)

The modern piano was invented by the Italian instrument maker Bartolomeo Cristofori around 1700, and three of his instruments dating from the 1720s survive to this day. The Cristofori piano was a huge technological innovation—the first instrument to allow hammers to strike the strings and bounce off, leaving them free to vibrate—but was quiet in comparison to today's instruments. Bach was shown an early piano but disliked it. Viennese pianos made during Mozart's time in the late 1700s were quite different from the more dynamic English pianos, which were also widely played. All of these instruments were still much smaller than today's pianos, with fewer keys and a less penetrating sound. By the 1820s, when Schubert wrote the songs discussed in this chapter, the piano was going through a period of rapid changes.

Improvements in manufacturing technology now made it possible for many more people to own pianos than before. This made the partnership between voice and piano a practical one that inspired the writing of many Romantic art songs. These works were not so much intended for public performance as for private enjoyment. The piano was the home entertainment system of choice for the rising middle class, and composers such as Schubert and Schumann were two of the most popular songwriters of the day.

Early pianos such as the one pictured here are often called *fortepianos*, to distinguish them from today's instruments, which are technically called *pianofortes*.

LEARNING TO LISTEN GUIDE

TAKE NOTE OF MUSIC AND TEXT

What to Listen For: The close but subtle interactions between the text and the music.

Schubert, *Winterreise*, *Der Lindenbaum*
Date: 1828
Instrumentation: Baritone and piano
Key: D major (transposed)
Meter: $\frac{3}{4}$ (three moderately-paced beats per measure)
Form: Modified strophic form
Core Repertory Connection: Schubert's *Winterreise* is also discussed in Chapter 5.

Streaming audio track 40.
Interactive Listening Guide ILG-10 will allow you to follow the text carefully while also watching the song's structure and melodic content unfold.

TIME	ORIGINAL TEXT	TRANSLATION	COMMENT
0:00			A piano prelude introduces the song.
0:25	*Am Brunnen vor dem Tore* *Da steht ein Lindenbaum;* *Ich träumt' in seinem Schatten* *So manchen süßen Traum.*	At the well by the gate There stands a linden tree; I dreamed in its shadow So many a sweet dream.	The first four lines of the text are set to a repeated line of the melody.
0:53	*Ich schnitt in seine Rinde* *So manches liebe Wort;* *Es zog in Freud' und Leide* *Zu ihm mich immer fort.*	I carved in its bark So many loving words; It drew me, in joy and sorrow Back to it always.	The melody continues through the next four lines.
1:27			The piano prelude reappears in a minor key.
1:39	*Ich mußt' auch heute wandern* *Vorbei in tiefer Nacht,* *Da hab' ich noch im Dunkel* *Die Augen zugemacht.*	Today I again had to wander By in deepest night, And in the dark I once again Closed my eyes.	The first half of the melody also returns in the minor, including the repeated phrase.
2:08	*Und seine Zweige rauschten,* *Als riefen sie mir zu:* *Komm her zu mir, Geselle,* *Hier find'st du deine Ruh'!*	And its branches rustled As if they were calling to me: "Come here to me, fellow, Here you will find your rest."	The music shifts back to major for the second half of the melody.
2:39	*Die kalten Winde bliesen* *Mir grad' ins Angesicht,* *Der Hut flog mir vom Kopfe,* *Ich wendete mich nicht.*	The cold winds blew Straight into my face, My hat flew from my head, I did not turn away.	A musical interlude underscores this dramatic episode.
3:16	*Nun bin ich manche Stunde* *Entfernt von jenem Ort,* *Und immer hör' ich's rauschen:* *Du fändest Ruhe dort!*	Now I am many hours Distant from that place, And I still here the rustling: "You would have found rest there!"	The entire opening melody is repeated to the final four lines of text.

Wilhelm Muüller (1794–1827). He wrote the texts for *Winterreise* and for Schubert's earlier song cycle *Die schöne Müllerin* (The Beautiful Maid of the Mill). *(© INTERFOTO/Alamy)*

The fifth stanza introduces even more dramatic imagery, describing the bitter winter wind blowing directly into the traveler's face. By this time, Schubert has established a relationship between the piano part and the text. He can now dispense with an introduction, so that the text is accompanied by a powerful new version of the "rustling" music. This music combines forte dynamics with a dramatic plunge into a lower register. These effects reinforce the picture of an icy winter wind violent enough to blow the hat from the singer's head, while underscoring his determination not to be distracted from his goal.

However, after the line *"Ich wendete mich nicht"* (I did not turn away), the piano does indeed turn away from this powerful image and once again becomes seductive. The last stanza is sung twice, covering all of the music of the first two stanzas, followed by a final return of the rustling piano. The image of death is thus made doubly attractive. The music adds a layer of meaning not necessarily present in the original poem but consistent with it.

This little song, then, is not as simple as it sounds. Text and music combine to amplify each other and accomplish what neither could alone.

Text as Drama: *Winterreise, Die Post*

Now listen again to the song *Die Post*, which we examined previously as an example of simple strophic form. In this text, the singer listens hopefully to the sound of the posthorn, a signal that mail is being delivered—but alas, no letters have arrived for him.

LEARNING TO LISTEN GUIDE

TAKE NOTE OF MUSIC AND TEXT, RHYTHM, AND TIMBRE

What to Listen For: The way Schubert uses melody, rhythm, and harmony to dramatize elements of the text.

Streaming audio track 41.
Interactive Listening Guide ILG-11.

Schubert, *Winterreise, Die Post*
Date: 1828
Instrumentation: Baritone and piano
Key: B major (transposed)
Meter: $\frac{6}{8}$ (a compound meter with two fairly rapid groups of three notes per measure)
Form: Simple strophic form
Core Repertory Connection: Schubert's *Winterreise* is also discussed in Chapter 5.

TIME	ORIGINAL TEXT	TRANSLATION	COMMENT
0:00	*Von der Straße her ein Posthorn klingt.* *Was hat es, daß es so hoch aufspringt,* *Mein Herz?*	From the street a posthorn sounds. What is it that makes you spring up so eagerly, My heart?	The vigorous rhythms, which begin in the piano introduction, and rising dynamic level dramatize the singer's expectant agitation.
0:36	*Die Post bringt keinen Brief für dich.* *Was drängst du denn so wunderlich,* *Mein Herz?*	The post brings no letter for you. Why, then, are you feeling these strange urges, My heart?	A dramatic pause, followed by more even rhythms and minor key harmonies, underscores his disappointment.

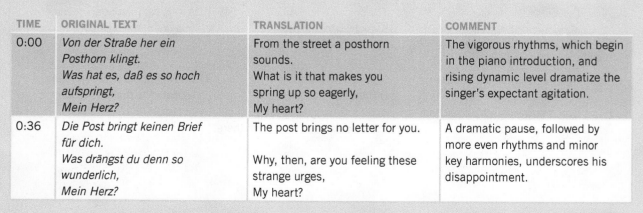

TIME	ORIGINAL TEXT	TRANSLATION	COMMENT
1:05	*Nun ja, die Post kommt aus der Stadt,* *Wo ich ein liebes Liebchen hat,* *Mein Herz !*	Well, then, the post comes from the city, Where I had a dear beloved, My heart!	The same music is repeated for the second stanza of text.
1:41	*Willst wohl einmal hinüberseh'n* *Und fragen, wie es dort mag geh'n,* *Mein Herz?*	Do you want to take just a look across, And ask how things are going there, My heart?	The dramatic effect is repeated as well, even though the text is different.

Schubert's music evokes the sounds of both the posthorn and the singer's pounding heart, and it links these sounds as the poem alone could not. The piano part, before the voice enters, imitates the fanfare of a valveless natural horn. The meter is $\frac{6}{8}$, and the repeated dotted rhythm (a prolonged note followed by a shortened one) also suggests the pounding of a heart. The piano continues to pound anxiously after the singer comes in. By the end of the phrase *"Was hat es, daß es so hoch aufspringt, mein Herz?"* (What is it that makes you spring up so eagerly, my heart?), the rising dynamics make the singer's anticipation and excitement palpable.

Schubert saves his most dramatic stroke, though, for the repetition of this line. At its conclusion, the music simply stops for a measure, and then it continues with minor key chords and without the dotted rhythm. The singer's disappointment thus becomes inescapably real, even before the next line of the text: *"Die Post bringt keinen Brief für dich"* (The post brings no letter for you). This dramatic device shows the extent to which a skilled composer like Schubert can coordinate musical and textual meaning.

There are other possibilities, however, and we will now take a historical detour to the Middle Ages in order to examine one of them. We have seen how Schubert, a Romantic composer, drew on many of the same assumptions about music and text that we still make today. Medieval composers, we will see, drew on completely different assumptions, producing music that can both challenge and reward us.

Polytextuality

We have already examined Machaut's *Lasse! comment oublieray/Se j'aim mon loyal/Pour quoy me bat mes maris?* for its use of rhythm and counterpoint. We now return to this selection as an illustration of **polytextuality**: the use of more than one text at the same time in a piece of music. In this example, the relationship between the music and words presents challenges we have not encountered previously. Not only is it difficult to make out some of the words and the musical imagery, we also have to listen for the relationship between three musical settings and three different texts.

Like Palestrina's *Sicut cervus,* this piece is a motet. For Machaut, though, a motet meant something different than it did for Palestrina more than two centuries

Polytextuality: The simultaneous use of more than one text. It occurs frequently in operatic ensembles, where different characters may be singing different things at the same time. Medieval motets are also frequently polytextual, often using parts in two different languages, such as Latin and French.

In History
Schubert's *Winterreise*

Winterreise (Winter's Journey), written only months before Schubert's death in 1828, was the second of his two genuine song cycles. Both it and the earlier *Die Schöne Müllerin (The Beautiful Maid of the Mill)* deal with unrequited love, one of the favorite subjects of the Romantics. They both consist of settings of a series of poems told from the point of view of a rejected lover and implicitly ending with his death. *Winterreise*, however, is particularly severe. The lover has already been rejected when the cycle begins, and his love is described only in retrospect. The images in the poetry are unrelentingly somber, and Schubert's music follows suit.

It is something of a cliché to say that this subject is an expression of the alienation and loneliness so frequently expressed in modern art of all kinds. In fact, similar images of isolation from a beloved occur in the troubadour poetry of the late Middle Ages. These songs can be linked in many ways, however, to their historical moment.

One is their abundance of nature images, including the linden tree with its rustling leaves and the fierce winter wind. In his poems, Müller treats nature as a place to escape the pressures of modern urban life. Readers of English literature often find this theme in the writing of the early Romantics, such as the poetry of William Wordsworth.

Rest as a metaphor for death and release was also a favorite theme of the Romantics. In *Ode to a Nightingale*, for example, John Keats yearns "to cease upon the midnight with no pain," much as Schubert's singer-hero longs to lie down beneath the tree and its sheltering branches.

The idea of the rootless wanderer as a heroic figure is also typical of Schubert's time; his own

Wanderer Above the Sea of Fog, by Caspar David Friedrich (1774–1840). Restlessness, longing, and the power of nature were primary components of the Romantic spirit. *(bpk/Berlin, Art Resource, NY)*

song *The Wanderer* served as the basis of one of his most famous piano works, the *Wanderer Fantasy*. German artists such as Caspar David Friedrich (1774–1840) often depicted this figure as well.

So if there is such a thing as the *Zeitgeist*, or "spirit of the times," these songs convey it in a particularly poignant and powerful way. Schubert's music, which does so much to amplify Müller's texts, is a uniquely suitable vehicle for the outlook of the Romantic period.

LEARNING TO LISTEN GUIDE

TAKE NOTE OF MUSIC AND TEXT, AND TEXTURE

What to Listen For: The impossibility of following all three texts at the same time.

Machaut: *Lasse! comment oublieray/Se j'aim mon loyal/Pour quoy me bat mes maris?*
Date: Mid-14th century
Instrumentation: Three solo voices
Core Repertory Connection: This music is also discussed in Chapters 2, 7, and 9.

Streaming audio track 3.
Interactive Listening Guide ILG-1
will allow you to follow all
three texts in real time and
link them to the voice parts.

TEXT 1 (FRENCH)	TEXT 1 (ENGLISH TRANSLATION)	TEXT 2 (FRENCH)	TEXT 2 (ENGLISH TRANSLATION)	TEXT 3 (FRENCH)	TEXT 3 (ENGLISH TRANSLATION)
Lasse! comment oublieray le bel, le bon, le dous, le gay	Alas! How can I forget that handsome, kind, sweet and charming man?	Se j'aim mon lyal ami	If I love my faithful lover	Pour quoy me bat mes maris?	Why does my husband beat me?
A qui entierement donnay Le cuer de mi Pour le sien que j'ay sans demi	In return for the fullness of his love I gave him all my heart.	Et il mi si loyaument	and he loves me so faithfully	Lassette! Ay mi! Dieus!	God have pity on me!
Et le retins pour mon ami einssois qu'eüsse mon mari, qui me deffent et me gaite mult durement que ne voie son corps le gent,	I took him as my lover before I was married to this man who guards me and watches over me so jealously that I may not see my lover's fair body.	Qu'il est tous miens sans nul si,	that he is all mine without any ifs or buts,	Pour quoy me bat mes maris?	Why does my husband beat me?
Don't li cuers en deux pars me fent?	As a result my heart is broken in two.	Et je aussi entierement,	and I give myself to him just as completely,	Lassette!	Poor me!
Car il m'estuet malgré mien faire ce qu'il wet, don't durement li cuers me duet.	Despite myself I must do what he wants and this gives my heart grievous pain.	Sans nul vilein pensement,	with no base thought,	Jen e li ay riens meffait,	I have done him no wrong,

TEXT 1 (FRENCH)	TEXT 1 (ENGLISH TRANSLATION)	TEXT 2 (FRENCH)	TEXT 2 (ENGLISH TRANSLATION)	TEXT 3 (FRENCH)	TEXT 3 (ENGLISH TRANSLATION)
Mais pour ce drois ne se remuet ne bonne foy;	Yet, for all this, what is right and pledged between us cannot change.	Bonnement A li m'ottri, pour ce qu'il m'a longuement, liément de cuer servi,	simply because he has long and gladly given me the service of his love,	Jen e li ay riens meffait,	I have done him no wrong,
Car puis que certeinnement voy qu'il wet et quiert l'onneur de moy Et qu'il m'aimme asses plus que soy,	Since I see for a fact that he only wants and seeks of me what is honorable, and that he loves me far more than himself,	Ay me pour ce desservi, lasse! ay mi!	have I for this— the pity of it!—	Fors qu'a mon ami parlay,	apart from having spoken to my lover.
Et se le truis Si bon qu'il prent tous ses deduis eh moy servir, je ne le puis laissier, se mauvaise ne suis,	And when I find him so loyal that all his pleasure lies in serving me, I cannot leave him without giving offense.	Que tellement m'en demeinne mon mari	deserved to be so treated by my husband	Seulette! Ai mi! Dieus!	God have pity on a hapless one!
Eins le puis bien amer par honneur et par bien, quant j'ay son cuer et il le mien, Sans ce que je mespreingne en rien, ce m'est avis.	No, rather can I love him honorably and virtuously, since I have his love and he mine, without any wrong whatsoever, as far as I can see.	Que de li n'ay fors tourment?	that I get nothing but torture from him?	Fors qu'a mon ami parlay,	I only spoke to my lover.
Mais j' eüsse trop fort mespris se j' eüsse l'amer empris, depuis que j'eus a marit pris.	Of course, it would have been very wrong of me if I had begun to love him after my marriage.	Nennil, car certeinnement,	No, I say, for there is no doubt	Seulette!	Poor girl!
Lasse! Celui qui tant me fait peinne et annuy qu'en tous cas toute joie fui,	Alas, he gives me such pain and sorrow that I know no joy:	Mortelment peche celi,	that any man is in mortal sin	Pour quoy me bat mes maris?	Why does my husband beat me?

TEXT 1 (FRENCH)	TEXT 1 (ENGLISH TRANSLATION)	TEXT 2 (FRENCH)	TEXT 2 (ENGLISH TRANSLATION)	TEXT 3 (FRENCH)	TEXT 3 (ENGLISH TRANSLATION)
N'en ce monde n'a moy n'autrui qui me confort, car mi gieu, mi ris, mi deport, mi chant, mi revel, mi confort, mi bien et mi bon jour sont mort.	I can find consolation neither in myself nor in anybody else in the world, for my sport, my laughter, my joys, my singing, my pleasures, my consolations, my happiness and my happy days are gone for ever.	Qui pour bien faire mal rent.	who gives evil for good.	Lassette! Ay mi! Dieus!	God have pity on me!
Et nuit et jour accroist li ruissiaus de mon plour, quant le plus bel et le millour de tous ne voy; c'est ma dolour!	By night and day a stream of tears ever grows within me now that I am forbidden to see the finest and fairest man in the world: Such is my pain.	Or m'apprent a faire einssi	Now he teaches me to behave in this way	Pour quoy me bat mes maris?	Why does my husband beat me,
Mais soit certeins que, comment que mes corps lonteins li soit, mes cuers li est procheins, d'amour et de loyauté pleins.	But let him be reassured on one point: However much my body is far from him, my heart is near to him, filled with true love.	Qu'il wet que mette en oubli celui qui m'a humblement doubté, celé, obeï et cheri a mon talent.	because he wants me to forget the man who humbly revered me, concealed and obeyed me, and cherished me as I desired.	Lassette!	a poor wretch like me?

later. Machaut's understanding of the term was more closely related to its literal meaning: a piece with words.

Machaut certainly does use a lot of words. In fact, three sets of words are sung at the same time. Here they are, in the original medieval French with English translations. After you have read all three texts, listen to the music. Note that the texts do not actually align as shown in the listening guide.

This elaborate little gem reminds us that not all of our seemingly intuitive ideas about music are universally shared—not even one so basic as having only a single text presented at any one time. We do not have to go back to the Middle Ages to find examples of polytextuality. In Chapter 11, we will look at examples from operas by Mozart and Verdi. This piece, however, is different. No characters are specified as in an opera. No dramatic context helps us understand what is going on. There are simply three texts, each with its own melody.

Actually, as you will have noticed, the texts are closely related. All three are written from the perspective of a married woman with a lover. In the first, she laments that she can no longer see her lover since her marriage—no doubt one arranged by her family, as was typical at the time. In the second, she complains about her husband, who objects to her continued association with her lover. In the third, she states that she has spoken to her lover since her marriage, and her husband has beaten her as a result.

Each text is shorter and more direct than the previous one. On first hearing, though, this is far from evident. In fact, the uppermost voice has so many words and moves so quickly that the lower voices are almost buried. If you had not read the texts in advance, you might be able to understand the top voice on first hearing if you listened carefully. The middle voice, however, is already much more difficult to hear, since it tends to emerge only at certain points, when the upper voice is silent. As for the lower voice, it is experienced primarily as a part of the music, its provocative text nearly inaudible. The only way to understand them all is to read them, either before or after listening to the music.

You may wonder whether the music really does reflect the meaning of these two lower texts. A casual listener is unlikely even to ask! If you are reading the words *while* listening to the music, you are forced to choose; you can concentrate on only one of the texts, since the human mind is incapable of following three texts simultaneously. (Try listening to three TVs tuned to three different channels if you doubt this.) In the process, you end up focusing on one of the musical voices and paying less attention to the others. Paying more attention to the words actually distracts you from hearing the music in its entirety. Machaut sought primarily to create an artful and complex piece with different layers of meaning, not communicate a single text.

Although many other late medieval composers wrote similar works, their complexity is uncommon. Most music with text presents only one set of words. Let us look more closely now at some of the techniques composers use to link music and text together.

How Music and Text Communicate

Semantic: Having to do with textual meaning and how it is communicated.

Phonetic: Having to do with the way a text sounds.

Syntactic: Having to do with a text's structure.

Texts can communicate with us in music in three different ways. **Semantic** content deals with the meaning of the words. This is what we normally expect when we hear text matched with music. We ask ourselves, what *sense* does it make? It is also true that the aural, or **phonetic**, quality of the text may communicate another dimension of meaning through its sound alone. Finally, just as musical form is important to active listeners, the meaning of a text may depend in part on its structure, or **syntactic** qualities. These three aspects of textual content provide the composer with a powerful set of communication tools.

Semantic Content: The Sense

When we say that music reflects the text to which it is set, we generally mean that it matches the semantic content, or what the text is about. All texts convey semantic meaning, and poetic texts often suggest strong emotions. Since music is such an expressive art form, it seems reasonable to expect that the music set to a text should reflect those emotions—or at least not contradict them. As we have seen with Schubert, texts also often suggest images, which music can reinforce.

The active listener will naturally ask whether, and to what extent, the mood and imagery of the text are reflected in the music. Feel free to use your imagination in answering this question. This is exactly what composers like Schubert did in creating the moods and images in their music, so they must have expected their listeners to bring their imaginations to bear as well.

Phonetic Quality: The Sound

Texts—particularly poetry—can also have a significance beyond their literal meaning, found instead in their phonetic qualities, or their sound. These phonetic qualities may correspond closely to some of the elements of music that we have discussed in previous chapters. Music touches us through its melodic shapes, timbres, dynamics, and rhythms. Words may do so as well.

Returning to Schubert, we find an example of the composer's response to the phonetic qualities of text in *Der Lindenbaum*. As we saw in Chapter 3, this poem is strophic: each of the six stanzas follows the same metrical and rhyme scheme. This allows them all to be set to the same music, should the composer choose to do so. The stresses of those stanzas can be indicated as follows, using the first as an example:

     _   /   _   /   _   /   _
1. Am Brunn-en vor dem Tor-e

     _   /   _   /   _   /
2. Da steht ein Lin-den-baum;

     _   /   _   /   _   /   _
3. Ich träumt' in sein-em Schatt-en

     _   /   _   /   _   /
4. So manch-en süß-en Traum

Lines 1 and 3 have seven syllables, while lines 2 and 4 have six. Each line alternates unaccented syllables with accented ones. The odd-numbered lines end on an unaccented syllable, traditionally called a feminine ending, whereas the even-numbered ones end with an accented syllable, a masculine ending. These endings emphasize the meaning of the words, and because the lines concluding in unaccented syllables are incomplete, the lines that follow them continue the thought.

We can analyze any number of diverse poems in very much the same way. Counting the syllables and marking the stresses of verse is a practice known as scansion. In simple four-line stanzas like these, the lines often have a similar number of syllables, and the even-numbered lines generally sound more final than the odd-numbered ones. The text of *Der Lindenbaum* has some irregularities, though, which Schubert goes out of his way to accommodate. The second and fourth lines of stanza 1 do not correspond exactly. In the second, there is a strong accent on the third syllable from the end (LIN-den-baum), while in the fourth, the accent on the final syllable is stronger (süß-en TRAUM). Stanza 3 is set to a minor-key version of the same melody, and the situation is reversed. The second line places the stress on the final syllable (tief-er NACHT), while the fourth line places it on the third syllable from the end (ZU-ge-macht).

Such variations in stress do not mean that the poet was careless or unskilled. Quite the contrary: they keep the poem from sounding monotonous, and they may suggest feelings or meanings of their own. These syllables pose a special challenge to the composer, though. Schubert solved it by placing the highest note of the melody on the third syllable from the end of both lines, thus creating a secondary accent. The final syllable of these lines, meanwhile, appears on the downbeat, beat 1 of the measure. Thus, the melody fits both lines and both stanzas equally well.

In short, a composer may take care to match the distinctive sound qualities of a text. This is a reflection not so much of the text's literal meaning as of its phonetic content.

Syntax: The Structure

Third and last, every text has sentence structure, or syntax. It may not make much difference whether you say, "I had a whole chapter assigned by my music teacher this week" or "This week, my music teacher assigned me a whole chapter." Often, however, the *way* we say something is as expressive as *what* we say—especially in music.

Musical syntax may correspond very closely to textual syntax. You may have noticed, for example, that the kind of poetic structure discussed above corresponds to similar qualities of a good melody. The phrases parallel one another, and incomplete endings alternate with more final sounding ones. It is obvious what kind of a melodic structure is best suited to the text of *Der Lindenbaum*, and Schubert is happy to oblige. Often, though, composers set texts that suggest more complex musical responses.

Listen to *Ich grolle nicht* (*I won't complain*), from the song cycle *Dichterliebe* (*A Poet's Love*) by Robert Schumann. The text is by Heinrich Heine (1797–1856), an eminent German poet. It is given below as Heine wrote it to clarify its structure, which Schumann complicated by repeating the opening words at some points where Heine did not.

This is a much more sophisticated poem than the one Schubert set in *Der Lindenbaum*, and Schumann pays close attention in his musical setting. Listen to how the second stanza picks up from the first without a break. Schumann incorporates the line *"Das weiß ich längst"* (I've known that for a long time), which begins the second stanza, into the music of the first stanza. In so doing, he follows the poem's syntax, as these words conclude the thought expressed by the previous lines.

Heinrich Heine (1797–1856), author of the texts for ***Dichterliebe*** **and many other songs by Schumann.** Unlike Müller, Heine is considered a major poet in his own right.
(*© The Bridgeman Art Library Ltd./Alamy*)

LEARNING TO LISTEN GUIDE

TAKE NOTE OF SEMANTICS, PHONETICS AND SYNTAX IN MUSIC AND POETRY

What to Listen For: The way the music brings out the poet's use of irony.

Streaming audio track 49.

Schumann, *Dichterliebe, Ich grolle nicht*
Date: 1840
Instrumentation: Tenor and piano
Key: C major
Meter: $\frac{4}{4}$, also known as common time (four rapid beats per measure)

TIME	ORIGINAL TEXT	TRANSLATION	COMMENT
0:00	*Ich grolle nicht, und wenn das Herz auch bricht,* *Ewig verlor'nes Lieb! Ich grolle nicht.* *Wie du auch strahlst in Diamantenpracht,* *Es fällt kein Strahl in deines Herzens Nacht.*	I won't complain, even though my heart is breaking, Love lost forever! I won't complain. Though you may shine with the splendor of diamonds, No light falls within your heart's night.	The piano begins with pounding chords that call attention to the harsh content of the text.
0:34	*Das weiß ich längst. Ich sah dich ja im Traume,* *Und sah die Nacht in deines Herzens Raume,* *Und sah die Schlang', die dir am Herzen frißt,* *Ich sah, mein Lieb, wie sehr du elend bist.*	I've known that for a long time. Indeed, I saw you in a dream, And saw the night within your heart. And saw the serpent that gnaws at your heart, I saw, my love, how miserable you are.	The opening words of the second stanza are linked musically with the first stanza, to which they also belong grammatically.

Can These Qualities Conflict?

In the Schumann piece, the text by Heinrich Heine relies on all three kinds of expression—semantic, phonetic, and syntactic. We have already looked at its syntax. Semantically, the poem says that the speaker willingly relinquishes his beloved, since she is truly unhappy. At the same time, though, his bitter descriptions of her and his repeated denials that he is complaining make it sound like he is doing just that. Semantically, the poem undermines itself, showing the irony for which Heine was famous.

If there could be any question about the poem's double meaning, its phonetic qualities leave no doubt about what the poet is up to. Pronunciation is especially brutal in some parts of the text: for example, in the lines *"Wie du auch strahlst in Diamantenpracht, Es fällt kein Strahl in deines Herzens Nacht. Das weiß ich längst."* The abundance of "s," "t," "st," and "ch" sounds makes it impossible to pronounce these words without hissing and spitting, signs of disrespect and contempt. Thus, the sound of the poem—its phonetic quality—supports an ironic reading of its apparent semantic meaning.

Musically, Schumann is happy to pick up on Heine's irony. From the beginning, the piano sets the mood for a pulsing, highly accentuated reading of the words. The emphatic first chord is followed on beat 3 by firm support in the left hand. After the voice enters, the piano continues to throb relentlessly with chords on every half beat. In the climactic phrase, the singer describes the serpent gnawing at his beloved's heart. By this time, Schumann has added rich dissonances to the already pounding rhythm of the accompaniment. He makes it clear that the speaker's attitude toward his beloved is marked by pain and defiance. Furthermore, Schumann's frequent repetition of the words *"Ich grolle nicht"* reinforces a reading of the text as whiny and repetitive, thus stressing the irony even more. Note that the entire first line is repeated before the text *"Ich sah dich ja im Traume,"* even though Heine did not write it there, and that the opening words are repeated at the end of the song as well.

In short, both the meaning of the text and its actual sound have influenced the music. And this is by no means unusual. In the process, the composer helps to reinterpret the text. Once again, as we saw for Schubert, the music can suggest meanings that are less evident when one simply reads the words.

Interpreting Persona

So far in this chapter, we have explored how listening actively for melodies, forms, textures, and other musical complexities can contribute immensely to the interpretation of music with text. Furthermore, it is evident that text content has its own special semantic, phonetic, and syntactic qualities. An active listener needs to study all of these aspects to gain a full understanding of a work.

Persona: The character who is understood to be speaking the words.

Another critical element of music with text can inform active listening. The presence of a text naturally suggests the point of view of a character, or **persona**, behind the words. Whether listening to Machaut's polytextuality or simply to a piano and singer together, we may wonder whose metaphorical voice we are really hearing. The answer to this question provides yet another dimension of a work for active listeners to interpret. The voice they hear may be the composer's, another person's, the singer's, or even their own.

The Composer's Persona: Schubert's *Der Leiermann*

Listen to *Der Leiermann* (*The Hurdy-Gurdy Man*), the final song from Schubert's *Winterreise*. The text describes a devastating image of human helplessness and isolation.

LEARNING TO LISTEN GUIDE

TAKE NOTE OF MUSIC AND TEXT AND TEXTURE

What to Listen For: The way the minimal accompaniment emphasizes the starkness of the poetic image.

Streaming audio track 42.

Schubert: *Winterreise, Der Leiermann*
Date: 1828
Instrumentation: Baritone and piano
Key: F minor (transposed)
Meter: $\frac{3}{4}$ (three slow beats per measure)
Core Repertory Connection: Schubert's *Winterreise* was discussed previously in Chapter 5.

TIME	ORIGINAL TEXT	TRANSLATION	COMMENT
0:00			The simple piano introduction imitates the sound of a hurdy-gurdy.
0:23	*Drüben hinterm Dorfe* *Steht ein Leiermann,* *Und mit starren Fingern* *Dreht er, was er kann.* *Barfuß auf dem Eise* *Wankt er hin und her* *Und sein kleiner Teller* *Bleibt ihm immer leer.*	There behind the village Stands a hurdy-gurdy man, And with stiff fingers He grinds out what he can. Barefoot on the ice He staggers here and there And his little plate Always remains empty.	The voice sings a similar melody to that played by the piano, which provides occasional punctuation.
1:34	*Keiner mag ihn hören,* *Keiner sieht ihn an,* *Und die Hunde knurren* *Um den alten Mann.* *Und er läßt es gehen* *Alles, wie es will,* *Dreht und seine Leier* *Steht ihm nimmer still.*	None want to hear him, None look at him, And the dogs growl At the old man. And he lets it go by, Everything, as it will, Grinds, and his hurdy-gurdy Is never quiet.	The music of the previous stanza is repeated.
4:26	*Wunderlicher Alter,* *Soll ich mit dir geh'n?* *Willst zu meinen Liedern* *Deine Leier dreh 'n?*	Strange old man, Shall I go with you? Do you want to grind your hurdy-gurdy To my songs?	The final four lines of the text are set to different but related music. The simplicity of this conclusion intensifies the starkness of the image and the suffering it represents.

Schubert's setting of this text is what might be termed minimalist. A simple piano accompaniment imitates the sound of the hurdy-gurdy. Its repetition vividly evokes the pathos of a helpless old man alone in winter. The singer stays within a narrow range, on just the sort of tune that the old man might play on his primitive instrument. With the final line, the identification between the singer and this enigmatic figure seems complete.

Many, though, also find it meaningful to know that Schubert, when he wrote this song, was near death. He had spent most of his short life in poverty, writing music that would largely remain unknown until many years later. Is the composer himself speaking? Answering this question is less important than asking it. As so often with active listening, knowing the music's context deepens our understanding. The pathos of the music seems all the greater if we realize its close connection with the tragedy of the composer's life.

The Character's Persona: Schumann's *Die alten, bösen Lieder*

Composers frequently suggest voices other than their own, primarily for the purpose of telling a compelling story. It can be difficult to separate today's rock and pop singer-composers from their imaginary song characters. When Bono of U2 wrote the songs for the group's 2009 album *No Line on the Horizon*, he decided to write stories from the point of view of imaginary characters—a sharply different approach from the highly personal one he took on the group's previous recordings. As a result, in songs such as *White As Snow*, listeners often have difficulty adjusting to the fact that Bono isn't singing about himself. In this instance, Bono trades his own perspective and experience for the persona of a soldier dying from an improvised explosive device in Iraq. Once the active listener is aware of this fact, however, the meaning of the song becomes crystal clear.

In *Die alten, bösen Lieder* (The old, wicked songs), the final song from *Dichterliebe*, Schumann seems to wrestle with the question of which persona will best communicate his meaning. The text states that the poet is burying all of his songs, dreams, and sorrows in the sea in an extremely large coffin.

LEARNING TO LISTEN GUIDE

TAKE NOTE OF MUSIC AND TEXT AND FORM

What to Listen For: The extraordinary piano postlude, which almost overwhelms the rest of the song while concluding the cycle as a whole.

Streaming audio track 50.

Schumann: *Dichterliebe*, "Die alten, bösen Lieder"
Date: 1840
Instrumentation: Tenor and piano
Key: A minor/major, transposed
Meter: $\frac{4}{4}$, also known as common time (four moderately paced beats per measure)

TIME	ORIGINAL TEXT	TRANSLATION	COMMENT
0:00			A stark, simple piano introduction begins the song.
0:10	*Die alten, bösen Lieder,* *Die Träume bös' und arg,* *Die laßt uns jetzt begraben,* *Holt einen großen Sarg.*	The old, wicked songs The dreams naughty and mischievous, Let us now bury them, Fetch a big coffin.	The first stanza of text is sung with a simple piano accompaniment.

TIME	ORIGINAL TEXT	TRANSLATION	COMMENT
0:29	*Hinein leg' ich gar Manches, / Doch sag' ich noch nicht was; / Der Sarg muß sein noch größer / Wie's Heidelberger Faß.*	In it I will place a great deal, / But I will not yet say of what; / The coffin must be yet bigger / Than the Heidelberg keg.	In the second stanza, the accompaniment becomes more forceful to emphasize the final two lines.
0:47	*Und holt eine Totenbahre, / Und Brettern fest und dick; / Auch muß sie sein noch länger / Als wie zu Mainz die Brück'.*	And fetch a bier, / Of boards firm and thick: / It must also be even longer / Than the bridge at Mainz	The second two lines of this stanza receive a similar emphasis.
1:06	*Und holt mir auch zwölf Riesen, / Die müssen noch stärker sein / Als wie der starke Christoph / Im Dom zu Köln am Rhein.*	And fetch me also twelve giants, / They must be even stronger / Than Saint Christopher / In the cathedral at Cologne on the Rhine	As do the second two lines of this one.
1:25	*Die sollen den Sarg forttragen, / Und senken ins Meer hinab, / Denn solchem großen Sarge / Gebührt ein großes Grab.*	They must carry the coffin forth / And sink it into the sea, / For such a big coffin / Deserves a big grave.	The piano accompaniment is reduced to simple chords.
1:53	*Wißt ihr, warum der Sarg wohl / So groß und schwer mag sein? / Ich senkt' auch meine Liebe / Und meinen Schmerz hinein.*	Do you know why the coffin / Must be so big and heavy? / I want to sink my love / And my suffering into it as well.	The last stanza ends on an inconclusive harmony, making a continuation of the music necessary.
2:33			The piano then continues to play for nearly two minutes: nearly as long as the rest of the song has lasted.

From whose perspective are we hearing all this? Notice that while this text is being sung, the piano part is limited to a supportive background role. During this section of the work, the accompaniment is much less prominent than in the three previous songs we have examined.

As the final note of the melody is sung, however, we hear a harmony that is inconclusive. After that, the piano continues to play for another minute and a half. In this postlude, the piano plays strikingly lyrical music that is completely different from what has been sung up to this point. The singer is not heard from again. In a sense, the pianist has the last word.

Schumann seems to be suggesting that he has something deeper and more significant to say than what the words suggest, and the pianist waits until the singer is silent to say it. This could mean that Schumann himself has the final word, since his primary instrument was the piano. Perhaps, though, the piano does not represent a human voice at all. It could be understood as the voice of music, the ocean, or even death. Listeners who have heard the entire song cycle

Mary, Queen of Scots. She was executed in 1587 for plotting against Queen Elizabeth I of England. *(Library of Congress Prints and Photographs Division Washington, DC 20540 USA)*

will also recognize the beginning of the postlude as belonging to the earlier song *Am leuchtenden Sommermorgen*, in which the singer is addressed by the flowers in his garden. The active listener might imagine this as another possible voice—perhaps a conciliatory one.

The Listener's Persona: Dallapiccola's *Canti di prigionia*

In some cases, the composer's life is less important to understanding the music than the general cultural, religious, economic, or political context in which it was written. The composer's own circumstances are often intimately connected to those of the intended audience. Understanding the background of such music is critical to its interpretation.

The composer Luigi Dallapiccola (see box), living in fascist Italy during the dark time just before the Second World War, discovered a short Latin prayer written by Mary, Queen of Scots, shortly before her execution.

Dallapiccola completed his setting of this text as the European war was beginning in 1939. Over the next two years, he set two further texts to music, one by the late Roman philosopher Boethius and one by the 15th-century Florentine monk Girolamo Savonarola. Like Mary, both of these texts' authors were in prison awaiting their deaths. "In those days," Dallapiccola observed, "I was far from imagining that, only a few years later, various works created in that gloomy period or in that which followed would be defined as 'protest music.'"

LEARNING TO LISTEN GUIDE

TAKE NOTE OF MUSIC AND TEXT, RHYTHM, AND TIMBRE

What to Listen For: How the unusual percussion timbres that we studied in Chapter 6 personalize the message in the text, making it resonate with 20th- and 21st-century listeners.

Streaming audio track 65.

Dallapiccola: *Canti di prigionia*
1st movement: Preghiera di Maria Stuarda
Date: 1938–1939
Instrumentation: Four-part mixed choir, two pianos, two harps, and percussion
Core Repertory Connection: Dallapiccola's *Canti di prigionia* is also discussed in Chapter 6.

TIME	ORIGINAL TEXT	TRANSLATION	COMMENT
0:00			Two harps, two pianos, and tuned timpani present the *Dies irae* theme. A few other percussion instruments are barely audible.
0:37	*O Domine Deus!*	Oh Lord God!	The choir sings the words and then continues wordlessly, with mouths closed.
1:54			The choir sings the text again, and the dynamic level quickly rises. The full percussion ensemble accents the change in dynamics.
2:17			The choir returns to singing wordlessly, and the dynamic level falls again. Finally, the choir drops out completely.

TIME	ORIGINAL TEXT	TRANSLATION	COMMENT
2:52	*O Domine Deus! Speravi in Te.* *O care mi Jesu! Nunc libera me.*	Oh Lord God! I have hoped in Thee. Oh my dear Jesus! Now set me free.	The choir sings this next section a cappella (without instrumental accompaniment).
4:40			The piano and harps quietly re-enter, followed by the bells, xylophone and tam-tams.
5:14			The bass drum and timpani enter, the latter playing melodically.
5:59	*In dura catena, in misera poena, desidero Te.*	In harsh chains, In miserable punishment, I long for you.	One piano, one harp, timpani, and bass drum introduce the next section.
6:54			Both pianos and harps are now playing. The harps play glissandos (continuous series of notes played by sweeping along the strings) as the dynamic level rises.
7:14	*Languendo, gemendo et genuflectendo,*	Languishing, moaning, and kneeling,	Piano dynamics return with the next phrase of text, and the accompaniment thins out to slow-moving notes in the pianos, harps and vibraphone.
8:10	*Adoro, imploro, ut liberes me.*	I adore Thee, I implore Thee, To set me free.	The accompaniment is reduced to a sustained, pianissimo timpani roll to introduce the last phrases of the text.
8:33			The dynamic level returns to forte, and the full ensemble briefly enters on the final "me."
8:55	*O Domine Deus!*	O Lord God!	The first words of the text return, along with the piano dynamics. The music concludes with the sounds of the tam-tams and bass drum.

The Eternal City, **by Peter Blume (1906–1992).** Mussolini and others are caricatured against the backdrop of the Roman forum, which they are seen as desecrating. *(Digital Image © The Museum of Modern Art/ Licensed by SCALA/Art Resource, NY)*

He certainly knew, though, that he was setting texts of deep expressive signifi-cance. His *Songs of Imprisonment* continue to move us because each of the authors speaks with a distinctive voice, discernible even in the brief Latin texts. Mary's poetry speaks of personal suffering. In the next selection, Boethius, author of *The Consolation of Philosophy*, speaks with more detachment, without mentioning his personal circumstances.

LEARNING TO LISTEN GUIDE

TAKE NOTE OF TEXT, RHYTYM, AND TIMBRE

What to Listen For: How the unusual percussion timbres that we studied in Chapter 6 help emphasize the composer's personal voice.

Streaming audio track 66.

Dallapiccola: *Canti di prigionia*
2nd movement: Invocazione di Boezio
Date: 1939–1941
Instrumentation: Four-part mixed choir, two pianos, two harps, and percussion
Core Repertory Connection: Dallapiccola's *Canti di prigionia* was discussed previously in Chapter 6.

TIME	ORIGINAL TEXT	TRANSLATION	COMMENT
0:00			The fast-moving instrumental introduction prominently features the two pianos. If you listen carefully, you can hear the harps and vibraphone play the *Dies irae*.
1:03	*Felix qui potuit boni fontem visere lucidum,*	Happy is he who has been able To see the clear spring of goodness,	The choir erupts fortissimo with the first lines of the text. Only the women are heard in this movement.
1:38			The repetition of the text is emphasized by the timpani and tam-tam, with the *Dies irae* sounding in the bells.
1:55			The xylophone joins the ensemble, adding its metallic sound to the accompaniment.
2:15	*felix qui potuit gravis terrae solvere vincula.*	Happy he who has been able To unloose the heavy earth's chains.	The sudden cessation of movement leaves a sonic vacuum, out of which the choir emerges quietly with the remainder of the text, which is sung by the choir in imitation.
2:59			A sudden shift to forte dynamics is emphasized by the full percussion ensemble.
3:30			The music and scoring of the introduction return as the choir quietly repeats the final lines of the text.

Across the Arts
Painters Against Fascism

In his painting *The Eternal City* (1934–37), American Peter Blume challenged fascism with specific imagery. Mussolini and others are caricatured against the backdrop of the Roman forum, which they are seen as desecrating. Blume spent the year 1932 in Italy on a Guggenheim grant and, after returning to the United States, was able to produce his painting safely ensconced in his home country. It would have been considerably less safe for the Italian Dallapiccola to compose an overtly antifascist work, which perhaps partly explains why he gravitated to texts about imprisonment in order to express the general atmosphere of oppression. Musical meaning can be much less direct than meaning in figurative art. At the very least, precise meaning in music is much more difficult for authorities to identify, even if that meaning resonates on an intuitive level with its listeners. On the other hand, the movement known as surrealism produced paintings whose meanings could be arguably as difficult to identify as musical ones. Max Ernst, a German residing in France between the wars, painted a grim caricature of the fascist menace sweeping Europe

The Angel of Hearth and Home. 1937. By Max Ernst

in *The Angel of Hearth and Home* (1937). Whatever was left unclear by the monstrous image itself, Ernst clarified with the title, borrowed directly from a fascist slogan describing the role of the Italian woman in society. Max Beckmann's *Departure* triptych (1932–33) also contains apparent commentaries on human brutality along with the possibility of redemption.

Savonarola, meanwhile, prays in terms both personal and universal:

LEARNING TO LISTEN GUIDE

TAKE NOTE OF TEXT, RHYTHM, AND TIMBRE

What to Listen For: How the unusual percussion timbres that we studied in Chapter 6 help emphasize the composer's personal voice.

Streaming audio track 67.

Dallapiccola: *Canti di prigionia*
3rd movement: Congedo di Gerolamo Savonarola
Date: 1939–1941
Instrumentation: Four-part mixed choir, two pianos, two harps, and percussion
Core Repertory Connection: Dallapiccola's *Canti di prigionia* was discussed previously in Chapter 6.

TIME	ORIGINAL TEXT	TRANSLATION	COMMENT
0:00	*Premat mundus, insurgant hostes, nihil timeo*	Though the world may oppress, the enemy attack, I fear nothing	A fast crescendo by the percussion ensemble precedes the entry of the choir.

TIME	ORIGINAL TEXT	TRANSLATION	COMMENT
0:20			The *Dies irae* theme is played by the pianos and harps. After a timpani roll, the choir repeats the first two words of the text. The *Dies irae* theme continues.
0:48			The bass drum and then the snare drum introduce the image of an enemy attack.
1:19			The entire text so far is repeated, with accompaniment of the full percussion ensemble. Quiet repetitions of "*nihil timeo*" continue with a reduced accompaniment.
3:04	*Quoniam in Te Domine speravi,*	For in Thee, oh Lord, have I hoped,	The next lines of text are sung very quietly. If you listen carefully, you can hear canonic imitations (like a round) among the parts.
4:05	*Quoniam Tu es spes mea,*	For Thou art my hope,	The music continues seamlessly with the next phrase of text, but the dynamic level gradually increases at the end of this section.
5:40	*Quoniam Tu altissimum posuisti refugium tuum.*	For the refuge Thou hast established is the highest of all.	The final phrase of text begins forte with accompaniment by the harps and pianos.
7:04			The dynamics fall off drastically as the concluding text is repeated. Nevertheless, all the instruments in the ensemble can be heard during this section.

Focus On
Luigi Dallapiccola (1904–1975)

Luigi Dallapiccola (1904–1975). He was a leading Italian composer of the 20th century.
(© Lebrecht Music and Arts Photo Library/Alamy)

Italian composer. He grew up in a disputed territory (then part of the Austrian empire), a circumstance that seems to have had a significant effect on his character in later life. Immediately after the war, Dallapiccola came to know the music of Debussy (the opera *Pelléas* in particular impressed him) and he developed an enthusiasm (shared by many leading Italian composers of the day) for early Italian music, notably that of Monteverdi. Through the examples of Berg and, during the 1940s and 50s, Webern, he gradually forged a language of his own, amalgamating Germanic serial and developmental procedures with a characteristically Italian feel for melody. He became the principal pioneer of dodecaphony in Italy and also encouraged other Italian composers. (Anthony Sellors, *Grove Music Online.*)

Grove Music Online.

In Chapter 6 we examined Dallapiccola's *Canti di prigionia* as an example of the effective use of percussion timbres. The Italian composer had the misfortune to live through both world wars of the 20th century. He was only 10 years old when the First World War began. Dallapiccola

(continued)

Focus On (continued)

lived near the border between Italy and Austria, in what had long been disputed territory. Many in this area were viewed with particular suspicion by the Austrian authorities. In March 1917 the composer and his family were deported to the Austrian city of Graz, where they lived under close supervision. In Dallapiccola's own words:

"We did not suffer any violence. My father had no particular duty other than to report to the police periodically. But the change from the quiet rhythm of my first 10 years of life and the events described, which took place within such a short time, had been too abrupt for my sensitivity. I felt in my soul that something unjust had befallen my family (and therefore me). Considering that the injustice of man had hit my father more than anyone else, and that I could do nothing to redress its offenses, I felt very deeply humiliated."

More than 20 years later, just before the start of World War II, the fascist Italian government under Mussolini released an anti-Semitic "race manifesto" modeled on the policies of Hitler. Like many Italians, Dallapiccola was appalled. It was at this time that he conceived of writing a work of music based on the experience of imprisonment.

At the time Dallapiccola set these texts he was not, like the three authors, awaiting execution. He had, however, experienced confinement during World War I, and he was now experiencing a hostile regime, as the authors had. His *Canti* soon came to be seen as a musical protest against fascism. Dallapiccola used the words of three writers who lived centuries apart, and drew on his own experience as well, yet he gave voice to something that many of his European contemporaries also felt in very personal terms.

The Performer's Persona: Bob Dylan and His Covers

In vocal music it is possible to hear voices other than that of the singer. This is not to say that the performer does not also contribute something of vital importance. The performer's role is perhaps most obvious in popular music. We remember the timbre—the twang of a country singer or the soulful quality of a blues artist. Jazz and rock singers can also alter the rhythm or even the melody, changing the way you think about the text and its relationship to the music.

Consider Bob Dylan, whom many consider the foremost singer-songwriter of our time. Like the medieval troubadours, Dylan is more than just a musician or a poet; he writes songs that combine both arts. In addition, he is known for his performance style. In his early years, he used only acoustic instruments, alternating his distinctive, raspy voice with an equally recognizable style of harmonica playing. After Dylan began to use electric instruments in 1965, he was widely imitated by rock musicians.

We can hear the importance of a performer's persona in different interpretations of Dylan's songs, by himself and

Bob Dylan at the 1965 Newport Festival. His songs have been covered by numerous other artists. *(Photo by David Gahr/ Getty Images)*

others. The songs of the troubadours were probably not written down until long after they were composed, and the art of the performer became an important part of their identity. In turn, a song's strophic structure left others free to change musical nuances from one stanza to the next. The same is true for Dylan's songs.

Dylan's *Blowin' in the Wind* became a hit thanks to the folk trio Peter, Paul and Mary. Their performance is much more polished than his—and considerably more in tune. In his own performance, Dylan's voice, in both the literal and metaphorical senses of the word, gives the song a distinctive stamp that may be impossible to reproduce. At the same time, though, other performers can reveal aspects of the song that Dylan himself conceals.

Dylan's song *Like a Rolling Stone* is considered something of a meeting point between the rock and singer-songwriter traditions. The text, about a woman who has gone from riches to being "a complete unknown," has been interpreted in a variety of ways, as is often the case with Dylan's lyrics. Although the song was a huge success, he was criticized at the time for deserting his roots in folk music and protest songs. *Like a Rolling Stone* was soon covered by other singers and bands, notably Jimi Hendrix, who performed it live at the Monterey Pop Festival in 1967. Hendrix's performance lacks the organ solo that was a distinctive feature of Dylan's original. Instead, his signature electric guitar playing can be heard throughout. His rendition of the lyrics, while different, is highly effective. Listening to Hendrix, we are reminded that not even the composer's interpretation of a song or its text is the last word.

The combination of text and music is a unique form of expression. Not all composers excel at setting texts, and not all poets can write music. At its most profound, however, music can clarify, complicate, elucidate, or amplify the written word. As this chapter has demonstrated, neither the words nor the music alone tell the whole story.

If You Liked This Music . . .
Bob Dylan Covers

- Other early Bob Dylan covers can be heard on Peter, Paul and Mary's album *In the Wind* (*Don't Think Twice, It's All Right, Quit Your Low Down Ways*) and on the album *Farewell Angelina* by Joan Baez (*A Hard Rain's a-Gonna Fall, It's All Over Now, Baby Blue*, and the title track).

- Later Dylan songs that have been extensively covered include *Just Like a Woman* (Richie Havens, Judy Collins, the Byrds), *Lay Lady Lay* (Cher, the Everly Brothers, Neil Diamond), and *Knockin' on Heaven's Door* (Eric Clapton, Guns N' Roses, Avril Lavigne), among many others.

In the next chapter, we will look at some practical applications of this principle. When composers add music to a poem (as in the examples in this chapter), it may grow and develop. When they add music to a drama, the sky is the limit. The result is opera, which one author has called "the extravagant art." It is one of the most exciting multimedia experiences ever created.

SUMMARY

- Music with words can be found in all genres, from popular song to the art song. An art song is a work from the classical music repertory that is not part of a larger staged work and often provides a musical setting for an existing work of poetry.
- We often assume that text and music should work together, but that can mean many different things. Perhaps the music should fit the mood of the text or even illustrate what the text is about. Songs from Schubert's *Winterreise* show how a skilled composer can use text and music with unexpected subtlety.

- The relationship between music and text must take into account the different ways the text alone communicates with us. Words have familiar meanings, or semantic content, and music can reflect that. Music also responds to the text as phonetics (how it sounds) and as syntax (how it is constructed).
- The voice or persona of a song is also critical to its interpretation. The voice may represent the composer or poet, another person or character, or the audience.

KEY TERMS

Persona	p. 280	Polytextuality	p. 271	Syntactic	p. 276
Phonetic	p. 276	Semantic	p. 276	Text Painting	p. 268

REVIEW QUESTIONS

1. What are some of the ways in which text and music are expected to correspond?
2. How are these principles represented by the text-music relationship in Schubert's *Der Lindenbaum*?
3. In what way(s) is the style of text-setting found in Machaut's *Lasse! comment oublieray/Se j'aim mon loyal/Pour quoy me bat mes maris?* different from your answers to the first two questions?
4. What do the terms *semantic*, *phonetic*, and *syntactic* mean? How do they apply to the relationship of music and text?

5. How are the phonetic qualities of Müller's *Der Lindenbaum* and Heine's *Ich grolle nicht* reflected in Schubert's and Schumann's settings of these poems?
6. How does Schumann's setting further reflect the syntactic qualities of Heine's poem?
7. How does Schumann's setting of Heine's *Die alten, bösen Lieder* add an extra dimension of meaning to the poem?
8. How does the question of persona—who is understood to be speaking—affect your understanding of these and other musical settings of texts?

REVIEW CONCEPTS

1. In what ways are your answers to Review Question 1 supported by songs (or other vocal pieces) with which you are familiar?
2. Can you find other examples of the principles discussed in this chapter in the Schubert and Schumann songs we have examined?
3. How would you interpret the question of persona in these songs? Can the persona of the composer be distinguished from that of the poet or the singer?

4. How does the question of persona apply to Machaut's *Lasse! comment oublieray/Se j'aim mon loyal/Pour quoy me bat mes maris?* Does the relative prominence of the first text, and the difficulty of hearing the third one, affect the way you answer this question?

LISTENING EXERCISES

1. Listen to some of the other songs from *Winterreise* and *Dichterliebe* after carefully examining their texts. To what extent do you find that the music reflects the text at the semantic, phonetic, and syntactic levels?

2. Examine some other medieval motets, being sure to read through all the texts carefully. Do you find any consistent principles guiding the ways the texts are combined?

3. Listen to some popular songs and examine their texts carefully. Do you find the same principles at work that you did in answering question 1?

4. Review the discussion of Dallapiccola's *Canti di prigionia* in Chapter 6. Does knowledge of the circumstances in which the piece was written affect your understanding of the unusual timbres used in this music and their significance? Why or why not?

5. Listen to some other songs by Bob Dylan, both his interpretations and versions by other performers. What do you learn about the role of the performer in interpreting the text musically?

Music and Drama

TAKE NOTE

Music plays a crucial role in our experience of drama, clarifying and reinforcing the action that you see and the words that you hear. Opera composers pioneered many of the basic ways to combine music and drama that are also used in motion pictures, television, and musical theater.

Before you read this chapter, try doing an experiment. Watch a show or a movie on television or your computer with the sound turned off. Turn on closed captioning if you wish, and read the text, but make certain that all dialog, sound effects, and especially music are inaudible.

Chapter Objectives

● Assess how music and drama fit together.

● Distinguish between music drama and number opera, and describe how each is constructed.

● Recognize how elements of music drama and number opera may be integrated.

● Explain the role of a libretto in transforming a play into an opera.

● Identify ways music can develop plot and character.

Chronology of Music Discussed in this Chapter

1786
Wolfgang Amadeus Mozart p. 302, 322
The Marriage of Figaro (Le nozze di Figaro)

1887
Giuseppe Verdi p. 298, 311
Otello

Now that you have performed this exercise, what did you notice about the experience of silent drama? If you followed the dialog using closed captions, were they adequate? Or did you find yourself looking for other cues as to what was going on? You may have found yourself paying more attention, for example, to the actors' body language and facial expressions.

Chances are, too, that you sensed something important was missing. Most television shows rely heavily on aural cues in the music track. So do movies. You may not notice how important those cues are until you try to watch without them.

How Music Contributes to Drama

Music can support the plot of a TV show, movie, or stage drama in a wide variety of ways:

- *The characters.* It may let you know when a particular character is approaching. You might hear the same notes whenever that character is on or near the scene. (Think of *Star Wars* and the Darth Vader theme.) It may also help you understand what a character is like.

- *Their emotions.* It may fill in the gaps between spoken lines to help explain a character's emotions. Suppose a character has just poured out her heart. The music may reinforce her heightened emotional state by inviting you to share it.

- *The action.* It may describe nonverbal actions. The score is likely to become even more prominent in scenes that do not allow for extensive dialog. Rousing music usually accompanies chase scenes, for example. Or the music may anticipate action. (Think of the shark music in *Jaws*.)

- *The scene.* It may mark the transition from one scene to another, letting you know when a new scene is beginning.

- *The genre.* It can help you identify what kind of show you are watching. Cartoon music would not fit a horror movie, for example.

Music may convey strong feelings about the story as well:

- *Emotional support.* It may encourage you to feel a certain way about what you are seeing. A strong, pounding beat may cause you to feel fear, while a lush string sound may enhance a romantic scene.

- *Expressive unity.* The repetition of familiar music may help unify the movie.

- *Popular appeal.* Music may appeal to listeners outside the context of the movie, television program, or stage musical and become popular as part of a soundtrack or cast recording.

You can see that music is vital to the success of many motion picture, television, and stage productions—as important as any of the characters. Whether you are watching a drama, a comedy, a horror film, an action movie, or even a cartoon, you are likely experiencing a union of music and drama. As we saw in Chapter 10, short texts can interact with music in ways that make them stronger as a unit than either would be alone. The same is true for longer stories as well.

Cinematic Opera

You may be surprised to know that music was used in ways that resemble today's soundtracks long before television or movies existed. Composers like Beethoven

Across the Arts
What's Up With Cartoon Music?

Rhapsody Rabbit (1947). This cartoon features Bugs Bunny playing Liszt's Hungarian Rhapsody no. 2. (© AF *archive/Alamy*)

Wagner's music provides the soundtrack to the classic Warner Brothers cartoon *What's Opera, Doc?* Many other cartoons have featured classical music, often in stereotypical ways that show how broadly that music's expressive language is still understood. For example, another Looney Tunes classic, *Rabbit of Seville*, uses music from Rossini's overture to *The Barber of Seville* with comic dialog added. One of the funniest things about the cartoon is how well this dialog fits the music—which was, after all, taken from a comic opera.

The use of music in cartoons is significant enough that one of the classic techniques of movie music—using music to mimic a character's actions—has come to be called "Mickey Mousing."

and Schubert wrote music to accompany dramatic performances. This **incidental music** was meant to augment the audience's experience of a stage play.

By far the most important interactions between music and drama, though, have taken place in opera, which was invented at the beginning of the Baroque period.

Incidental Music: Music meant to augment the audience's experience of a stage play.

As we saw in Chapter 2, this era heavily emphasized dramatic expression. Surviving across four centuries of changing taste and style, opera has evolved, adapted, and proven to be one of the most enduring of musical genres. In pioneering effective ways of combining drama and music, opera composers anticipated all the soundtrack devices later developed by movie composers (many of whom have been strongly influenced by opera). It is not surprising, therefore, that opera is becoming more popular once again in our multimedia age. Live simulcasts of performances at the Metropolitan Opera can now be seen in movie theaters throughout the world, and television and DVDs have brought opera to home audiences, including many who have never seen a live performance.

Music Drama: An opera in which the music is continuous throughout each act or scene.

Number Opera: An opera in which musical numbers, very much like songs, are separated by other text, which may or may not be set to music.

Composers have adopted two primary formats for effectively transforming a play into an opera. In a **music drama**, the music is continuous throughout each act or scene; in a **number opera**, musical numbers very much like songs are separated by other text, which may or may not be set to music at all. In a music drama, the music and text always work closely together, whereas in a number opera they are to some extent separated. In order to understand how these two formats work, we will look closely at two beloved and widely performed operas. *Otello*, by Giuseppe Verdi, first performed in 1887 at the famous La Scala opera house in Milan, is our example of a music drama. Mozart's *Le nozze di Figaro* (*The Marriage of Figaro*, in English), written and first performed in Vienna in 1786, is our example of a number opera.

A Literary Link

One thing these two operas have in common is that both are based on well-known plays that are more than capable of holding an audience's attention without the addition of music. *Otello* is based on Shakespeare's tragedy *Othello*, and *The Marriage of Figaro* is based on *La folle journée, ou Le mariage de Figaro*, a comedy by the 18th-century French playwright Pierre-Augustin Caron de Beaumarchais (1732–1799). Not all opera stories can boast such auspicious origins. For example, Mozart based his famous opera *The Magic Flute* (*Die Zauberflöte*, in German) on a short story of only minor literary interest: *Lulu oder die Zauberflöte*, by J. A. Liebeskind. In the process of being transformed into an opera, the story was altered extensively from its original version, a case of an opera elevating pedestrian literary material to much greater heights.

A scene from Mozart's opera *The Magic Flute*, composed in 1791. This modern interpretation shows music's ability to soothe the savage beast. *(© epa european pressphoto agency b.v./Alamy)*

Both *Otello* and *The Marriage of Figaro* remain fairly faithful to their literary sources. In each, the original play gives the opera much of its musical and dramatic strength. Neither Mozart nor Verdi, however, simply set the original text to music. For one thing, because music tends to slow down the action, a literal setting of a two-hour play could easily produce an unbearably long opera. For another, as you probably realize by now, the nature of music is unique. Music has its own forms, techniques, and styles that differ from other arts. Thus, a drama must undergo significant transformations when it is set to music. The result is the libretto, the actual text with which the composer works.

Lorenzo Da Ponte (1749–1838). Mozart's librettist later became the first professor of Italian literature at Columbia University in New York. *(© World History Archive/Alamy)*

Because drama is so different from music, composers do not usually write their own librettos. (An exception was Wagner; see Chapter 9.) Mozart's libretti for *Le nozze di Figaro* and for two other major operas, *Don Giovanni* and *Così fan tutte*, were written by Lorenzo Da Ponte (1749–1838), an Italian (and later naturalized American) who wrote in his native language. *Figaro* is an opera by a German-speaking composer, written in Italian, and based on a French play set in medieval Spain! Verdi's libretto for *Otello* was by a fellow composer, Arrigo Boito (1842–1918). Boito also wrote in Italian, his and Verdi's native tongue. Since Shakespeare's *Othello* takes place in Cyprus and Venice, *Otello* returns to its characters' original language. Boito's 19th-century poetic Italian, however, is still far removed from the Venetian dialect of Shakespeare's time.

Music Drama

In his book *Opera and Drama* (1851) Richard Wagner outlined his revolutionary ideas about musical theater. The term "music drama," which is widely associated with him, suggests that the music and the action onstage can and should work closely together. In a music drama, the orchestra plays continuously, and the music spells out important dramatic events.

The ideas that produced the music drama did not necessarily originate with Wagner, and they were so influential that modern audiences often take them for granted. (See box, In History: Verdi's *Otello*.) Many composers have written music dramas—including Verdi, whose *Aida* may be the most widely performed example.

Arthur Rackham's (1867–1939) depiction of the Ride of the Valkyries, from Wagner's music drama *Die Walküre*. Wagner was unusual in that he wrote his own librettos. (© *Lebrecht Music and Arts Photo Library/Alamy*)

Focus On

Giuseppe Verdi (1813–1901)

Giuseppe Verdi (1813–1901). When Italy finally became a state in 1861, Verdi served in its parliament. (*Lebrecht Music . . . Arts*)

Italian composer. By common consent he is recognized as the greatest Italian musical dramatist. By the time of his death, Verdi had established a unique position among his fellow countrymen: although many of his operas had disappeared from the repertory, he had nevertheless become a profound artistic symbol of the nation's achievement of statehood. Parts of his operatic legacy had entered into a kind of empyrean, divorced from the checks and balances of context and passing fashion. The fact that *Va, pensiero*, written some 60 years earlier, could express contemporary Italians' feelings for their departed hero demonstrated the extent to which Verdi's music had been assimilated into the national consciousness. (Roger Parker, *Grove Music Online.*)

Giuseppe Verdi was one of the most important people in 19th-century Italy. This was the country where opera was born, and opera remained the most popular form of entertainment. Verdi was the most successful opera composer of his day, making him a Steven Spielberg–like figure with vast sway over the public imagination. But he was more than that. Although the extent of Verdi's involvement in, and influence over, Italian nationalism has been disputed, his music was written at a time when the Italian people were longing to shake off foreign domination and emerge as a modern nation. It is no surprise that he has become a national symbol as well.

Like other Romantics, Verdi admired Shakespeare. By the time he came out of retirement to write *Otello*, his status as a musical elder statesman allowed him almost unlimited creative freedom. In this work, and in his next opera, *Falstaff* (based mainly on *The Merry Wives of Windsor*), he used that freedom to fulfill his lifelong goal of interpreting Shakespeare musically. Thus, this opera represents a confluence of his personal goals, his artistic maturity, the musical history of his people, and the literary aspirations of his time. It is a rich and extraordinary work.

Grove Music Online.

So did Giacomo Puccini (1858–1924), Richard Strauss (1864–1949), and other composers of the late 19th and 20th centuries.

Listen to the opening scene of Verdi's *Otello*. As the curtain goes up, the people of Cyprus anxiously await the arrival of the ship carrying their new governor, Otello. A violent storm rages, and the ship is saved only after great struggle. Coming ashore, Otello proclaims that the enemy has been defeated. Meanwhile, in a second scene, Roderigo talks with Iago, the villain of the story. Roderigo, who is in love with Otello's wife, Desdemona, asks Iago how he may win her love. As he and Iago

LEARNING TO LISTEN GUIDE

TAKE NOTE OF FORM AND METER

What to Listen For: The continuity of the music, which mirrors the fast-paced action.

Streaming audio track 54.

Verdi, *Otello*, beginning of Act I
Date: 1887
Instrumentation: Soloists, choir, and large orchestra
Key: Many keys are touched on, creating a sense of tonal instability.
Meter: Begins and ends in $\frac{4}{4}$, also known as common time. with a section in $\frac{6}{8}$.
Core Repertory Connection: Verdi's *Otello* is also discussed in Chapter 6.

TIME	ORIGINAL TEXT	TRANSLATION	COMMENT
0:00	*Ciprioti:* Una vela! Una vela! Un vessillo! Un vessillo!	**Cypriots:** A sail! A sail! A standard! A standard!	The opera begins without an overture, plunging the audience immediately into the midst of the action.
	Montano: È l'alato Leon!	**Montano:** It's the winged lion.	
	Cassio: Or la folgor lo svela.	**Cassio:** Now a lightning flash reveals it.	
	Ciprioti: Uno squillo! Uno squillo!	**Cypriots:** A trumpet blast! A trumpet blast!	
	Tutti: Ha tuonato il cannon!	**All:** The cannon has sounded.	
	Cassio: È la nave del Duce.	**Cassio:** It's the General's ship.	
	Montano: Or s'affonda. Or s'inciela. . .	**Montano:** First it sinks. Then it rises. . .	

TIME	ORIGINAL TEXT	TRANSLATION	COMMENT
	Cassio: *Erge il rostro dall'onda.*	**Cassio:** The prow emerges from the waves.	
	Metà del coro: *Nelle nubi si cela e nel mar,* *e alla luce dei lampi ne appar.*	**Half of the chorus:** She is hidden by the clouds and the night But appears in the flashes of lightning.	
1:08	**Tutti:** *Lampi! Tuoni! Gorghi!* *Turbi tempestosi e fulmini!* *Treman l'onde! Treman l'aure!* *Treman basi e culmini.* *Fende l'etra un torvo* *e cieco spirto di vertigine.* *Iddio scuote il cielo bieco,* *come un tetro vel.* *Tutto è fumo! Tutto è fuoco!* *L'orrida caligine* *si fa incendio, poi si spegne più funesta.* *Spasima l'universo, accorre a valchi* *l'aquilon fantasima,* *i titanici oricalchi squillano nel ciel.*	**All:** Lightning! Thunder! Whirlpools! Stormy winds and flashing lightning! The waves tremble! The winds tremble! Foundations and summits tremble. A ghastly, blind spirit of vertigo seems to cleave the air. God shakes the angry heavens like a dark curtain. All is smoke! All is fire! The horrid darkness catches fire, then grows darker still. The universe is in torment, through the mountain passes rushes the ghostly north wind, powerful trumpets blare in the heavens.	
2:32	*Dio, fulgor della bufera!* *Dio, sorriso della duna!* *Salva l'arca e la bandiera* *della veneta fortuna!* *Tu, che reggi gli astri e il Fato!* *Tu, che imperi al mondo e al ciel!* *Fa che in fondo al mar placato* *posi l'àncora fedel.*	God, the lightning of this storm! God, the smile of the sand dunes! Save the ship and the flag of Venice's fortune! You, who control the stars and Fate! You, who command the world and sky! Grant that at the bottom of a calmed sea the faithful anchor may rest.	
	Iago: *È infranto l'artimon!*	**Iago:** The mainsail is broken!	
	Roderigo: *Il rostro piomba su quello scoglio!*	**Roderigo:** The prow is crashing onto that rock!	
	Coro: *Aita! Aita!*	**Chorus:** Help! Help!	
	Iago (a Roderigo): *L'alvo frenetico del mar sia la sua* *tomba!*	**Iago** (*to Roderigo*): May the frenzied belly of the sea be its tomb!	
	Coro: *È salvo! è salvo!*	**Chorus:** It's saved! It's saved!	
3:48	**Voci interne:** *Gittate i palischermi!* *Mano alle funi! Fermi!*	**Voices within:** Send out the lifeboats! Hands on the ropes! Steady!	

TIME	ORIGINAL TEXT	TRANSLATION	COMMENT
	Prima parte del coro: *Forza ai remi!*	**First part of the chorus:** Give the oars a push!	
	Seconda parte: *Alla riva!*	**Second part of the chorus:** To the shore!	
	Voci interne: *All'approdo! allo sbarco!*	**Voices within:** To land! Get ashore!	
	Altra voci interne: *Evviva! Evviva! Evviva!*	**Other voices within:** Hurrah! Hurrah! Hurrah!	
4:13	***Otello:*** *Esultate! L'orgoglio musulmano sepolto è in mar; nostra e del ciel è gloria! Dopo l'armi lo vinse l'uragano.*	**Othello:** Rejoice! The pride of the Moslem is buried in the sea; the glory belongs to us and to heaven! After our arms, he was defeated by the storm.	
	Tutti: *Evviva Otello! Evviva! evviva! evviva! Vittoria! Vittoria!*	**All:** Long live Othello! Hurrah! Hurrah! Hurrah! Victory! Victory!	
	Coro: *Vittoria!* *Stermino, dispersi, distrutti, sepolti nell' orrido tumulto piombâr. Avranno per requie la sferza dei flutti. Avranno per requie la sferza dei flutti, la ridda dei turbini, l'abisso del mar.*	**Chorus:** Victory! Slaughtered, dispersed, destroyed, fallen and buried in the horrible tumult. Their requiem will be the whipping of the waves. Their requiem will be the whipping of the waves, the whirling of the winds, the abyss of the sea.	
	Coro: *Si calma la bufera.*	**Chorus:** The storm is ending.	
6:30	***Iago*** (*indisparte a Roderigo*): *Roderigo, ebben, che pensi?* ***Roderigo:*** *D'affogarmi . . .* ***Iago:*** *Stolto è chi s'affoga per amor di donna.* ***Roderigo:*** *Vincer nol so.*	**Iago** (*aside to Roderigo*): So, Roderigo, what are you thinking about? **Roderigo:** Drowning myself . . . **Iago:** He is a fool who drowns himself over a woman's love. **Roderigo:** I don't know how to win her.	The conversation between Iago and Roderigo is set in recitative, which contrasts with the elaborate scene that precedes it. Occasionally, as when Iago speaks of Desdemona's "fragile vow," he breaks into mocking fragments of melody.

TIME	ORIGINAL TEXT	TRANSLATION	COMMENT
	Iago:	**Iago:**	
	Suvvia, fa senno, aspetta	Come now, be reasonable, wait	
	l'opra del tempo.	for time to do its work.	
	A Desdemona bella,	To fair Desdemona,	
	che nel segreto dei tuoi sogni adori,	whom in the privacy of your dreams you adore,	
	presto in uggia verranno i foschi baci	that swollen-lipped savage's dismal kisses	
	di quel selvaggio dalle gonfie labbra.	will soon become tedious.	
	Buon Roderigo, amico tuo sincero	Good Roderigo, I consider myself	
	mi ti professo, nè in più forte ambascia	a true friend of yours, nor could I help you	
	soccorrerti potrei. Se un fragil voto	in a more painful situation. If a woman's	
	di femmina non è tropp'arduo nodo	fragile vow be not too difficult	
	pel genio mio ne per l'inferno, giuro	for my wits or for hell to unravel, I promise	
	che quella donna sarà tua. M'ascolta:	that woman shall be yours. Listen to me:	
	Benchè finga d'amarlo, odio quel Moro	Though I may pretend to love him, I	
		hate that Moor.	
	. . .E una cagion dell'ira, eccola, guarda.	. . .There is a reason for my anger; look, there he is.	
	(Indicando Cassio)	*(Pointing to Cassio)*	
	Quell'azzimato capitano usurpa	That preening captain usurps	
	il grado mio, il grado mio che in cento	my rank, the rank I have won	
	ben pugnate battaglie ho meritato;	through a hundred well-fought battles;	
	tal fu il voler d'Otello, ed io rimango	that's how Othello wanted it, and I remain	
	di sua Moresca Signoria l'alfiere!	His Moorish Lordship's ensign!	
	Ma, come è ver che tu Roderigo sei,	But, as true as it is that you are Roderigo,	
	così è pur vero che se il Moro io fossi	it is just as true that if I were the Moor	
	vedermi non vorrei d'attorno un Iago.	I wouldn't want to have an Iago around.	
	Se tu m'ascolti. . .	If you'll just listen. . .	

In History

Verdi's *Otello*

When Giuseppe Verdi wrote his second-to-last opera, he was in his 70s and a venerated figure in Italy and much of the rest of the musical world. It had been 16 years, though, since he had produced his last opera, *Aida*. Many, perhaps even the composer, believed that he had retired from composition after that powerful and spectacular work.

Yet he did return to opera—and to Shakespeare, whose works he had long revered. Only once before had he written an opera based on a Shakespeare play, the 1847 *Macbeth*. Opera, he knew, had been developing rapidly since then toward a newer, late Romantic style. The librettist, Arrigo Boito, helped the composer understand the new attitudes toward music and drama held by his younger contemporaries. Verdi must have found it irresistible to contribute to those developments himself.

He did not, as has sometimes been suggested, imitate his German counterpart Richard Wagner, whose work he admired with reservations.

(continued)

In History (continued)

It would be more accurate to say that Wagner and Verdi were both inspired, in different ways, by the French operas of the early 19th century.

Paris was the cultural capital of Europe, and the most famous Romantic composers—among them Chopin, Rossini, Wagner, and Verdi himself—were irresistibly drawn there. French opera had long differed significantly from that of Italy. Yet the city's operatic life was controlled by a succession of foreign-born composers, including Luigi Cherubini (1760–1842), Johann Simon Mayr (1763–1845), and Giacomo Meyerbeer (1791–1864). These composers, along with many others whose works are only rarely performed today, drew on the traditions of French opera to produce a new and powerful style. It featured a more extensive use of the orchestra and chorus, greater dramatic and musical continuity, and less emphasis on individual songs set off from the rest of the music.

Since Paris was a cultural crossroads, the impact of this new operatic style was felt throughout Europe. This is not to say that either Verdi or Wagner simply imitated what he heard in France. It does mean, though, that their later styles have a common ancestor.

We have labeled this style music drama. However, to call *Otello* a music drama—a term Wagner himself never fully endorsed—is not to call it Wagnerian. It means, rather, that Verdi found his own personal solution to a widely felt problem: He sought to adapt opera, with its many rules and conventions, to a new dramatic realism.

converse, a fire is lit and a celebration begins. On first hearing, the music appears to flow seamlessly through these two very different scenes and naturally fit the changes in the dramatic action.

Number Opera

A much older concept than music drama, number opera originated in the 17th century and dominated opera composition until well into the 19th, when music drama began to replace it. It has been revived by 20th-century composers, including Igor Stravinsky, who rejected many aspects of musical Romanticism and found the concept of music drama outdated. Most Broadway musicals can be compared to number operas, since the songs are separated by spoken lines, even though those lines play a much more important role than in a typical opera.

The premise of the number opera is that music and drama need to be carefully separated for each to achieve its full effect. Thus, in addition to musical numbers, like songs, ensembles, or sections for the orchestra alone, all number operas contain something like the spoken sections in Broadway musicals.

Recitative: A Useful Convention

Often, as in Mozart's *The Magic Flute*, the lines between musical numbers are actually spoken. In other operas, though, like *Le nozze di Figaro*, they are presented as recitative, an adaptation of the Italian *stile recitativo* (reciting style). In a

Focus On
Wolfgang Amadeus Mozart (1756–1791)

Mozart's signature. Note that he spelled his middle name Amadè, not Amadeus. *(© Friedrich Saurer/Alamy)*

Opera was at the center of Mozart's creative life, as it was for most 18th-century composers. Since opera was known as an Italian form, having originated in Italy during Monteverdi's time, German composers who wanted to learn to write opera often went to study in Italy. Mozart traveled to Italy three times as a child, spending about two years there, and became thoroughly familiar with the traditions and styles of Italian opera. Thus, it is not surprising that most of his best-known operatic works (including *Le nozze di Figaro*, *Don Giovanni*, and *Così fan tutte*) were written in Italian, even though they were intended for German-speaking audiences. Italian was the international language of opera, no matter where it was performed.

For a biographical profile of Wolfgang Amadeus Mozart, see p. 12.

recitative, the text is sung quickly, as though spoken. Mozart's recitatives are usually accompanied only by harpsichord.

With relatively rare exceptions (e.g., the orchestrally accompanied recitative that precedes the aria *"Dove sono"*—see Chapter 3), the recitatives in Mozart's operas were not meant to be as musically interesting as the arias (songs by individual characters; see the following section) and **ensembles** (numbers featuring multiple characters), even though they were written with great care and attention to the text. Usually, recitative serves to facilitate the dramatic action without interfering musically. Listen to Figaro and his bride-to-be, Susanna, discuss their new living arrangements.

Don't feel stupid if you are wondering, "Why don't they just speak the lines?" That's a very good question. The music at this point is so simple that its necessity is far from obvious. The singers pronounce the lines quickly. There is no melody to speak of, and the accompaniment consists of only an occasional "plunk" on the harpsichord.

The answer has to do with the origins of opera in the late 16th century. Musicians, artists, and philosophers were on a quest to rediscover the mythic perfect union of music and words they believed the ancient Greeks had employed in their dramas. No detailed evidence remained, but from descriptions, they gathered that it was something in between speech and song. The earliest operas contained long

Ensemble: Broadly, any performing group. In opera, specifically, an extended section in which two or more people sing, either one at a time or simultaneously. Like an aria, it can be a number in a number opera, or it can emerge from the seamless flow of a music drama.

LEARNING TO LISTEN GUIDE

TAKE NOTE OF FORM AND TEXTURE

What to Listen For: The way the minimal musical accompaniment focuses attention on the text.

Streaming audio track 30.

Mozart: *Le nozze di Figaro*, K. 492, recitative from Act I ("Cosa stai misurando")
Date: 1786
Instrumentation: Soprano, baritone, and harpsichord
Key: Constantly changing
Meter: $\frac{4}{4}$, also known as common time
Core Repertory Connection: Mozart's *Le nozze di Figaro* is also discussed in Chapter 3.

TIME	ORIGINAL TEXT	TRANSLATION	COMMENT
0:00	*Susanna:* *Cosa stai misurando,* *caro il mio Figaretto?*	Susanna: What are you measuring, Figaro my dear?	
	Figaro: *Io guardo se quell letto* *che ci destina il Conte* *farà buona figura in questo loco.*	Figaro: I'm seeing if this bed which the Count intends for us will look good in this spot.	
	Susanna: *In questa stanza?*	Susanna: In this room?	
	Figaro: *Certo, a noi la cede* *generoso il padrone.*	Figaro: Certainly, our master has generously granted it to us.	
	Susanna: *Io per me te la dono.*	Susanna: It's yours, for all I care.	
	Figaro: *E la ragione?*	Figaro: What's gotten into you?	
	Susanna (**tocandosi la fronte***):* *La ragione l'ho qui.*	Susanna (***tapping her forehead***): My reason is here.	
	Figaro (**facendo lo stesso***):* *Perchè non puoi* *far che passi un po' qui?*	Figaro: (***doing the same***): Why can't you share it with me a bit?	
	Susanna: *Perchè non voglio.* *Sei tu mio servo, o no?*	Susanna: Because I don't want to. Are you my servant, or aren't you?	
	Figaro: *Ma non capisco* *perchè tanto ti spiace* *la più comoda stanza del palazzo.*	Figaro: But I don't understand why you are so unhappy with the most comfortable room in the palace.	
	Susanna: *Perchè io son la Susanna e tu sei pazzo.*	Susanna: Because I'm Susanna and you're nuts.	
	Figaro: *Grazie, non tanti elogi! guarda un poco* *se potria meglio stare in altro loco.*	Figaro: Thanks, don't overdo it! Just take a look to see if there's any better place for us.	

passages in this "reciting style," designed to stir emotion while moving the story along. As arias and other operatic numbers developed and took precedence, recitative remained a useful convention for relaying dialog and sometimes narration fairly quickly.

Arias: The Music that Provides the Magic

In between the recitatives, number operas also contain many arias: sustained solos that allow us to experience the dramatic situation in greater depth. Arias are essentially like the songs sung in Broadway musicals that help develop the character. Often, not much actually happens, yet these songs allow you to understand something about that character in a way that spoken lines could not possibly convey. It is the music that provides the magic.

In these musical numbers, you really get to know and even identify with the individuals onstage. You share their emotions and their innermost thoughts. Without these solos, the action might seem more realistic, but you would not care nearly as much. The same could be said about Shakespeare's soliloquies. Hamlet's famous "To be or not to be" soliloquy is not realistic: sane people don't usually talk out loud to themselves at such length. Yet this dramatic form develops Hamlet's character and increases our sympathy for him.

Meet Cherubino

Listen now to another scene from *The Marriage of Figaro*. In this scene, we are introduced to Cherubino, a supporting character who will nevertheless play a considerable role in the action. Cherubino represents another operatic convention: he is a "pants role" (a term derived from the German *Hosenrolle*), a male character whose part is written to be sung by a woman.

The decision to have this part sung by a woman was not made by Mozart. He was simply following the precedent set by Beaumarchais, who explained in his preface to the play that there were no male actors young enough to fit the part and simultaneously act it with the degree of maturity it required. Cherubino's high voice is also appropriate because he is a confused boy going through puberty. Every time he sees a woman, he is overwhelmed by strange feelings that he doesn't understand.

LEARNING TO LISTEN GUIDE

TAKE NOTE OF MELODY AND RHYTHM

What to Listen For: The way the music brings the character of Cherubino to life.

Streaming audio track 31.

Mozart: *Le nozze di Figaro*, K. 492, "*Non so più cosa son, cosa faccio*"
Date: 1786
Instrumentation: Soprano and orchestra
Key: E-flat major
Meter: $\frac{2}{2}$, also known as cut time (two quick beats per measure)
Core Repertory Connection: Mozart's *Le nozze di Figaro* is also discussed in Chapter 3.

TIME	ORIGINAL TEXT	TRANSLATION	COMMENT
0:00	***Cherubino:***	**Cherubino:**	Cherubino pours out his confusion in fast-paced music whose constant pulsing energy reflects the unsettled emotions he feels in his heart.
	Non so più cosa son, cosa faccio,	I don't know what I am or what I'm doing any more,	
	or di foco, ora sono di ghiaccio,	now I'm made of fire, now of ice,	
	ogni donna cangiar di colore,	every woman makes me blush,	
	ogni donna mi fa palpitar,	every woman makes me throb,	
	ogni donna mi fa palpitar,	every woman makes me throb,	
	ogni donna me fa palpitar.	every woman makes me throb.	
	Solo ai nomi d'amor, di diletto,	At the mere words love or beloved	
	mi si turba, mi s'altera il petto	my breast becomes agitated and disturbed,	
	e a parlare mi sforza d'amore	and when I talk about love,	
	un desio, un desio ch'io non posso spiegar,	I am overcome by inexplicable desire,	
	un desio, un desio ch'io non posso spiegar!	I am overcome by inexplicable desire!	
	Non so più cosa son, cosa faccio,	I don't know what I am or what I'm doing any more,	
	or di foco, ora sono di ghiaccio,	now I'm made of fire, now of ice,	
	ogni donna cangiar di colore,	every woman makes me blush,	
	ogni donna mi fa palpitar,	every woman makes me throb,	
	ogni donna mi fa palpitar,	every woman makes me throb,	
	ogni donna me fa palpitar.	every woman makes me throb.	
	Parlo d'amor vegliando,	I talk about love when I'm awake,	
	parlo d'amor sognando,	I talk about love when I'm dreaming,	
	all'acqua, all'ombra, ai monti,	to the waters, to the shadows, to the mountains,	
	ai fiori, all'erbe, ai fonti,	to the flowers, to the grass, to the fountains,	
	all'eco, all'aria, ai venti,	to the echo, to the air, to the winds,	
	che il suon dei vani accenti	which carry the sound of my empty words	
	portano via con sé,	away with them,	
	portano via con sé.	away with them.	
	Parlo d'amor vegliando,	I talk about love when I'm awake,	
	parlo d'amor sognando,	I talk about love when I'm dreaming,	
	all'acqua, all'ombra, ai monti,	to the waters, to the shadows, to the mountains,	
	ai fiori, all'erbe, ai fonti,	to the flowers, to the grass, to the fountains,	
	all'eco, all'aria, ai venti,	to the echo, to the air, to the winds,	
	che il suon dei vani accenti	which carry the sound of my empty words	
	portano via con sé,	away with them,	
	portano via con sé.	away with them.	
	E se non ho chi m'oda,	And if there's nobody to listen to me,	
	e se non ho chi m'oda,	and if there's nobody to listen to me,	
	parlo d'amor con me, con me,	I talk about love to myself, to myself,	
	parlo d'amor con me.	I talk about love to myself.	

We encounter this aspect of Cherubino in his first solo. Listen to the aria, in which Cherubino shares his consternation with Susanna, one of the two main female characters in the opera. The melody Mozart writes for him pulses with the same sexual urgency suggested in the words, alternately rising to new heights and falling back again over a throbbing orchestral accompaniment.

Integrating Music Drama and Number Opera

Most operas cannot be pigeonholed into the strict category of either music drama or number opera; what occurs in practice often resists the tidy definitions presented in theory. Even *Otello*, our music drama example, contains many arias and other musical numbers that are integrated seamlessly into the music, which moves without stopping from the beginning to the end of each act. Other passages in *Otello* resemble recitative, including the earlier conversation between Iago and Roderigo in the listening guide.

In *The Marriage of Figaro*, many numbers surpass the limitations of an aria. Ensembles, such as duets and trios, allow different characters to interact extensively. At their most sophisticated, Mozart's ensembles can be quite complex; the second and fourth act finales of *The Marriage of Figaro* ring down the curtain with nearly 20 minutes of continuous music. These ensembles are like small-scale music dramas integrated into a number opera.

The better your active listening skills become, the more you will be able to discern both paradigms operating within a work. There are other possibilities as well; early Baroque operas, for example, like those by Monteverdi, used recitative for the most expressive and musically powerful moments, while in Mozart these are saved for the arias and ensembles. Mozart's recitatives, as we have seen, are usually the least musically interesting sections of his operas.

Mozart's *Le nozze di Figaro*, in a 2011 production by Opera Holland Park in London, directed by Liam Steel. Elizabeth Llewellyn plays the Countess and Hannah Pedley plays Cherubino. (© *Laurie Lewis/Lebrecht Music & Arts*)

An ensemble scene from *The Marriage of Figaro*. Mozart is particularly skilled at creating complex and interesting interactions between characters. (© *Mark Alexander/Alamy*)

If You Liked This Music . . .
More Music for Stage and Screen

You may be intrigued by the comparisons with film music and Broadway musicals in this chapter. If so, here are some suggestions for further listening:

- Many classical composers wrote film scores, often for films that are also considered classics. These include the Russian Sergey Prokofiev (1891–1953) (*Alexander Nevsky*) and the Americans Aaron Copland (1900–1990) (*The Red Pony, Of Mice and Men*), Leonard Bernstein (1918–1990) (*On the Waterfront*), and Virgil Thomson (1896–1989) (*The Plow that Broke the Plains*).

- The musicals of Stephen Sondheim often skirt the music drama/number opera distinction made in this chapter (which, like all such distinctions, is a generalization rather than a rule). *Into the Woods*, an imaginative updating of classic fairy tales, is notable for being sung throughout, while *Sweeney Todd: The Demon Barber of Fleet Street* has relatively little spoken dialog and uses Wagnerian techniques of motivic signification. Like Wagner, Sondheim also generally writes his own texts.

The Role of the Libretto

In the rest of this chapter, we'll listen more closely to selected scenes from *Otello* and *Le nozze di Figaro*. However, to understand how music transforms the text, we need to look first at how the librettos have transformed the plays. Let's start with the stories of each of these operas.

Stories of the Operas

Otello is the story of a Moor, which in Shakespeare's Europe probably referred to a dark-skinned person of African or Arab descent. Although he is of lowly birth, he has risen to the highest levels of Venetian society thanks to his military prowess. Othello (known in Italian as Otello) falls in love with and marries a high-born Venetian woman named Desdemona (in Italian pronounced Dez-DEH-moh-na, with the accent on the second syllable). He also earns the fierce enmity of Iago, who feels slighted professionally and yearns for greater recognition for himself.

The story centers on Iago's revenge, which exploits Othello's "tragic flaw" of jealousy. Iago pretends to aid Roderigo, a rival for Desdemona's love, but his real goal is to destroy Otello's love for her. He makes Otello suspect Desdemona of having an affair with his own lieutenant, Cassio. Enraged, Otello looks for proof and seems to find it in a fateful handkerchief that has been carefully planted by Iago. To keep Desdemona from further betrayals, he murders her. When Iago's scheme is revealed, Otello takes his own life.

While *Otello* is a tragedy, *The Marriage of Figaro* is a comedy, and a provocative one at that. Beaumarchais first introduced Figaro as the title character in an earlier play, *The Barber of Seville*, which the composer Giovanni Paisiello (1740–1816) then turned into a popular opera. (The better-known *Barber of Seville* by Gioacchino Rossini (1792–1868), still performed widely today, was not composed until after Mozart's death.) Figaro, a servant turned barber turned valet, has a way of outwitting and outmaneuvering the members of the upper class and nobility who surround him. In *The Barber of Seville*, he successfully foiled an engagement between the important doctor Don Bartolo and his ward Rosina, engineering a marriage between this young woman and Figaro's former master Count Almaviva instead. Now, a few years later, Figaro is engaged to Susanna, a maid to the Countess Almaviva (a more mature Rosina). Susanna suspects the Count, rightly, it turns out, of having designs on her. In fact, he wishes to revive the medieval custom of *droit du seigneur*, which allowed a nobleman to sleep with the bride of any of his vassals on their wedding night. (Whether such a right ever actually existed has been the topic of considerable debate.) An elaborate ruse is contrived to humiliate the Count and frustrate his schemes. This leads to considerable confusion and incidents of mistaken identity along the way. Finally, the Count recognizes his errors and begs the Countess for forgiveness.

When it appeared in 1784, Beaumarchais's *Le mariage de Figaro* was considered scandalous. Not only was it open about sex, but it was also a daring portrayal of the nobility. The Count had been the romantic hero of *The Barber of Seville*. Here he is arrogant and conniving, and brought down to Earth by a couple of commoners. He must even ask forgiveness of his wife, and by granting it, she asserts a power rarely attained by women in her time. In pre-Revolutionary France, this was both politically incorrect and vastly appealing. Mozart and Da Ponte adapted the play almost immediately, which was equally daring; the opera was to be performed in cosmopolitan but highly conservative Vienna.

Why the Libretto Is Important

An opera composer could simply set a play to music, word for word. Neither Verdi nor Mozart, however, would have dreamed of doing this. They knew that success depended on having a good libretto and adapting the original to their special needs. Composers often work closely with their librettists to do just that.

What makes the **libretto** so important? Strangely enough, it is the role of the music. In opera, the development of the story is entrusted to the music. A novel or stage play, in contrast, entrusts the story to the text alone. In each case, that means finding the right details to bring the bare outlines of the story to life. Because in opera, the music tells us what the characters are like, how they are feeling at each moment, and why we should care about them, the job of the librettist is to strip down the text to a form the composer can work with.

Libretto: A text written for an opera or oratorio. It may be based on a play or story, or it may be written just to be set to music. In either case, a good libretto is very different from a good stage play.

The Libretto and the Music Drama: Transforming *Othello*

Consider the character of Iago in Shakespeare's *Othello*. He is one of the most complex characters in fiction, since he works upon the other characters indirectly by playing on their suspicions. Let us see how Boito adapts Iago's role for opera.

What Shakespeare Tells Us about Iago

Early in the play, Roderigo threatens to drown himself because of his unrequited love for Desdemona. Here is how Shakespeare's Iago responds:

> Come, be a man. Drown thyself? Drown cats and blind puppies. I have professed me thy friend, and I confess me knit to thy deserving with cables of perdurable toughness. I could never better stead thee than now. Put money in thy purse. Follow thou these wars; defeat thy favour with an usurped beard. I say, put money in thy purse. It cannot be that Desdemona should long continue her love to the Moor—put money in thy purse—nor he his to her. It was a violent commencement, and thou shalt see an answerable sequestration—put money in thy purse. These Moors are changeable in their wills—fill thy purse with money. The food that to him now is as luscious as locusts shall be to him shortly as acerbe as the coloquintida. She must change for youth: When she is sated with his body she will find the error of her choice. Therefore put money in thy purse. If thou wilt needs damn thyself, do it a more delicate way than drowning. Make all the money thou canst. If sanctimony and a frail vow betwixt an erring barbarian and a super-subtle Venetian be not too hard for my wits and all the tribe of hell, thou shalt enjoy her—therefore make money. A pox of drowning thyself! It is clean out of the way. Seek thou rather to be hanged in compassing thy joy than to be drowned and go without her.

Ewan McGregor as Iago in Shakespeare's _Othello_. McGregor played the part in a 2007–8 London stage production. (© _Geraint Lewis/Alamy_)

This speech shows Iago's powers of persuasion. Notice how much he relies on repetition ("put money in thy purse") and insinuation. He plays on Roderigo's prejudices, for example, when he talks of Desdemona as "super-subtle," or open to sexual advances, and Otello as an "erring barbarian." He hints that their relationship had a "violent commencement"—in other words, sex before marriage. In fact, Iago's careful language is part of why you may have difficulty following it all today; among other things, Shakespeare's audience would have known that the coloquintida plant is a bitter ("acerbe") medicine. In this way, Iago manages to encourage Roderigo to hope for something that he had given up for lost. Roderigo believes that his friend has his best interests at heart, when in reality Iago is seeking only revenge. Someone who can play on other people's weaknesses is a force to be reckoned with.

What Boito Tells Us about Iago

In the scene of the opera that you listened to earlier, Iago's speech comes out rather differently:

> Iago: So, Roderigo,
> What are you thinking about?
> Roderigo: Drowning myself . . .
> Iago: He is a fool who drowns himself over a woman's love.
> Roderigo: I don't know how to win her.
> Iago: Come now, be reasonable, wait for time to do its work. To fair Desdemona, whom in the privacy of your dreams you adore, that swollen-lipped savage's dismal kisses will soon become

tedious. Good Roderigo, I consider myself a true friend of yours, nor could I help you in a more painful situation. If a woman's fragile vow be not too difficult for my wits or for hell to unravel, I promise that woman shall be yours. Listen to me: though I may pretend to love him, I hate that Moor. . . .There is a reason for my anger; look, there he is. (*Pointing to Cassio*) That preening captain usurps my rank, the rank I have won through a hundred well-fought battles; that's how Othello wanted it, and I remain His Moorish Lordship's ensign! But, as true as it is that you are Roderigo, it is just as true that if I were the Moor I wouldn't want to have an Iago around. If you'll just listen . . .

The librettist Boito's Iago says almost the exact same things as in the play. Gone, though, is his subtlety and psychological nuance. You may find this easier to read than Shakespeare's language, because *this* Iago says what he means. He also directly proclaims his hatred for Otello and the selfishness of his own motives. This is a black and white villain, and the music accords with this stark characterization without really developing it. Most of the scene is set in the barest recitative, not unlike the conversation between Figaro and Susanna we examined earlier. For a few brief passages, Iago breaks into melody to parody the frailness of Desdemona's vow and his own unctuous servitude. Verdi is already establishing Iago as a sneaky, manipulative character whose resentments are only thinly disguised by a more polished exterior.

What Verdi Tells Us about Iago

Verdi and Boito expand on this characterization dramatically at the beginning of the second act, when Iago makes a speech that has no parallel in Shakespeare's play. Here he parodies the Nicene Creed, the sacred statement of faith of the Christian Church: "I believe in a cruel God who created me like unto himself and whom I invoke in anger." Boito takes advantage of the fact that the word for "I believe" (*credo*) is the same in Italian as in the Latin of the Creed. The result is one of the most powerful monologues in opera. Because it lacks a regular musical form, it is usually not called an aria. Listen to the way it emerges from, yet contrasts strikingly with, the short conversation with Cassio that precedes it.

LEARNING TO LISTEN GUIDE

TAKE NOTE OF MELODY

What to Listen For: The subtle details of Iago's character that are brought out by the music.

Verdi, *Otello*, Iago's monologue from Act II
Date: 1887
Instrumentation: Baritone and orchestra
Key: F major, changing to F minor
Meter: $\frac{4}{4}$, also known as common time
Core Repertory Connection: Verdi's *Otello* is also discussed in Chapter 6.

Streaming audio track 56.
Interactive Listening Guide ILG-14
will help you see how Verdi
develops Iago's character
in this scene.

TIME	ORIGINAL TEXT	TRANSLATION	COMMENT
0:00			A lengthy orchestral introduction begins the second act and introduces this scene.
0:52	**Iago:** *Non ti crucciar.* *Se credi a me, tra poco* *farai ritorno ai folleggianti amori* *di Monna Bianca,* *altiero capitano,* *coll'elsa d'oro* *e col balteo fregiato.*	**Iago:** Don't get upset: If you put your faith in me, Miss Bianca's frivolous love will soon be yours again, proud captain, with your golden hilt and ornate sword-belt.	In his dialogue with Cassio, Iago is subtle and insinuating, keeping his anger and jealousy well under control.
	Cassio: *Non lusingarmi. . .*	**Cassio:** Don't flatter me. . .	
	Iago: *Attendi a ciò ch'io dico.* *Tu dêi saper che Desdemona* *è il Duce* *del nostro Duce, sol per essa ei vive.* *Pregala tu, quell'anima cortese* *per te interceda e il tuo perdono* *è certo.*	**Iago:** Listen to what I say. Surely you know that Desdemona is the general of our general; he lives for her alone. Plead with that kind soul to intercede for you and your pardon is assured.	
	Cassio: *Ma come favellarle?*	**Cassio:** But how can I talk to her?	
	Iago: *È suo costume* *girsene a meriggiar fra quelle fronde* *colla consorte mia.* *Quivi l'aspetta.* *Or t'è aperta la via di salvazione.* *Vanne. (Cassio s'allontana.)*	**Iago:** She often takes a walk at midday to rest under those trees with my wife. Wait for her there. Now the path to salvation is open to you. Go. (*Cassio departs.*)	
2:19	**Iago:** *Vanne; la tua meta già vedo.* *Ti spinge il tuo dimone,* *e il tuo dimon son io.* *E me trascina il mio, nel quale io credo, inesorato Iddio.* *Credo in un Dio crudel che m'ha creato* *simile a sè e che nell'ira io nomo.* *Dalla viltà d'un germe o d'un atòmo* *vile son nato.* *Son scellerato*	**Iago:** Go: I already see your goal. Your are driven by your demon, and I myself am that demon. And I am drawn on by the inexorable God in whom I believe. I believe in a cruel God who created me like unto himself and whom I invoke in anger. I was born from the baseness of a germ Or from a lowly atom. I am a scoundrel	In Iago's monologue, Iago's suppressed emotions come pouring forth, as does his contempt for the other characters. Interactive listening guide no. 13 will help you see how Verdi links this music to the orchestral introduction.

TIME	ORIGINAL TEXT	TRANSLATION	COMMENT
	perchè son uomo;	Because I am human;	
	e sento il fango originario in me.	And I feel within me the slime from which I sprang.	
	Si! Questa è la mia fè!	Yes! This is my faith!	
	Credo con fermo cuor, siccome crede la vedovella al tempio,	I believe with a firm heart, just as a young widow does in church,	
	Che il mal ch'io penso e che da me procede,	that the evil I think and that proceeds from me,	
	per il mio destino adempio.	is a fulfillment of my destiny.	
	Credo che il giusto è un istrion beffardo,	I believe that the just man is a foolish clown,	
	e nel viso e nel cuor,	and in my face and in my heart,	
	che tutto è in lui bugiardo:	that everything is inherently false:	
	lagrima, bacio, sguardo,	tears, kisses, glances,	
	sacrificio ed onor.	sacrifice and honor.	
	E credo l'uom giuoco d'iniqua sorte	And I believe that man is the plaything of unjust fate	
	dal germe della culla	from the germ of the cradle	
	al verme dell'avel.	to the decay of the tomb.	
	Vien dopo tanta irrision la Morte.	After all this folly comes Death.	
	E poi? E poi? La morte è il nulla.	And then? And then? Death is nothingness.	
	È vecchia fola il Ciel.	Heaven is an old fable.	

One reason this scene is so powerful is that Verdi makes use of motives to unify the scene and underscore changes in Iago's thinking. A motive does not have to be a good melody; it simply has to be memorable. One of the most famous examples of a motive is the "shark" theme from *Jaws*, which contains only two notes, insistently repeated.

The motive that underscores the beginning of this scene is not all that different. It consists of a rapid turn, with three fast ascending notes followed by a longer note that repeats the central pitch and thus conveys a sense of solidity. On interactive listening guide no. 13, this motive is designated A. As the scene opens, A is stated forcefully eight times in succession, first by the cellos and bassoons in the bass and then by the violas and clarinets an octave higher, making it sound very much like *Jaws*. A further statement of A by the violins, oboes, and horns is followed by what sounds like the beginning of a melody, but the melody is not completed; it is merely echoed by the cellos. The insistent repetitions of A then return, only much more quietly, and with a minor key harmonization. The effect of this opening is to suggest a many-sided character, who is at once aggressive, conciliatory, and sneaky.

Verdi then develops the sneakiness further by presenting A imitatively, first in the violins and continuing down to the violas and cellos, followed each time by just a few notes of melody. If the audience members have been listening carefully,

Carlos Álvarez as Iago in Verdi's Otello. The Spanish baritone has played the part in productions around the world. *(HERWIG PRAMMER/ Reuters/Landov)*

they may find the resulting music reminiscent of that by which Iago urged Cassio to "*beva, beva*" (drink, drink) in the previous act, ultimately getting him drunk and resulting in his demotion by Otello. Finally, a complete melodic phrase emerges. Unlike his victims, Iago seems to have himself under control.

Appearances can be deceiving, though. As the curtain rises, Verdi presents a new version of A with a different continuation, consisting of anxious, rising staccato notes. This is repeated at higher and higher pitch levels, only to descend again and give way once more to the beguiling melodic phrase heard earlier. Clearly, Iago is putting on an act, struggling to appear in control while underneath his emotions are still churning. Appropriately, his first words to Cassio are "*Non ti crucciar*": roughly, "don't get upset."

Follow the opening of this scene using the interactive listening guide to see how clearly Verdi has painted a complex personality and a dramatic scene of deception, using only a few notes, a short phrase of melody, and contrasting registers, dynamics, and instrumentation. Pause the listening guide after Iago's first line, and read the description of what follows.

The *Credo* Monologue

The conversation between Iago and Cassio that opens the second act of *Otello* is set as recitative. Here the orchestra repeats various versions of motive A. There is also a brief, seductive phrase when Iago states that Desdemona is the "general of our general." As soon as Cassio leaves, though, the full orchestra proclaims the A motive four times in a row, *fortissimo*. This leads to Iago's contemptuous repetition of the word "*Vanne*" (Go). The effect is to convey Iago's utter disdain for Cassio before he says a word. Over a fierce crescendo in the strings, he then invokes his terrible God.

In this scene, Verdi uses two new motives, designated B and C, along with the A motive, to punctuate Iago's speech. This is not all that Verdi does, however. As we have seen, motives are extremely malleable. The same few notes can suggest very different emotional states while also indicating that they belong to the same individual. The powerful B motive, hurled out fortissimo and in unison by every single instrument in the orchestra except the timpani, accompanies Iago's bold opening line. Restated with harmony, it later accompanies the line "after all this folly comes Death" and the mocking question "*E poi?*" (And then?). At this point, it almost resembles a religious chorale. The following line ("Heaven is an old fable!") is backed up by the same C motive that had earlier mocked the devotion of a widow praying in church. Then it had a gentler form, but now it is pounding.

In short, Verdi takes the black and white villain sketched by Boito and develops him into a character every bit as complex as Shakespeare's, only different. Our insight into the shifting and volatile nature of Iago's personality is derived almost entirely from Verdi's music. A more complex and nuanced text might have gotten in the way of this musical development.

The Trio from Act III

Not all operatic characterizations are this rich. When he wrote this opera, Verdi was over 70 years old and still at the height of his powers. He could draw on a lifetime of experience. The amazing flexibility of the music for this opera is evident in almost every moment of the score, but a particularly good and concentrated example can be found in the trio from Act III.

Before listening to the trio, read the same scene from Shakespeare (Act IV, scene 1). At Iago's urging, Otello listens in secret while Iago teases Cassio about his love for his mistress, Bianca. Because Iago has firmly planted the seed of suspicion, Otello is convinced that Cassio is really speaking of Desdemona. When Bianca enters and enquires about "that same handkerchief you gave me even now," he thinks of Desdemona's handkerchief. His asides, which Cassio cannot hear, express his growing fury.

> Iago: Now I will question Cassio of Bianca,
> A housewife, that by selling her desires
> Buys herself bread and clothes. It is a creature
> That dotes on Cassio—as 'tis the strumpet's plague
> To beguile many and be beguiled by one.
> He, when he hears of her, cannot refrain
> From the excess of laughter. Here he comes:
> *Enter Cassio*
> As he shall smile, Othello shall go mad;
> And his unbookish jealousy must construe
> Poor Cassio's smiles, gestures and light behaviour,
> Quite in the wrong. How do you now, lieutenant?
> Cassio: The worser that you give me the addition
> Whose want even kills me.
> Iago: Ply Desdemona well, and you are sure on't.
> *Speaking lower*
> Now if this suit lay in Bianca's power,
> How quickly should you speed!
> Cassio: Alas, poor caitiff!
> Othello: (*aside*) Look, how he laughs already!
> Iago: I never knew woman love man so.
> Cassio: Alas, poor rogue! I think i'faith she loves me.
> Othello: (*aside*) Now he denies it faintly, and laughs it out.
> Iago: Do you hear, Cassio?
> Othello: (*aside*) Now he importunes him
> To tell it o'er: go to; well said, well said.
> Iago: She gives it out that you shall marry her.
> Do you intend it?
> Cassio: Ha, ha, ha!
> Othello: (*aside*) Do you triumph, Roman? Do you triumph?
> Cassio: I marry her! What? A customer! Prithee, bear some charity
> to my wit: do not think it so unwholesome. Ha, ha, ha!
> Othello: (*aside*) So, so, so, so: they laugh that win.
> Iago: Faith, the cry goes that you shall marry her.
> Cassio: Prithee, say true.
> Iago: I am a very villain else.
> Othello: (*aside*) Have you scored me? Well.
> Cassio: This is the monkey's own giving out. She is persuaded I will
> marry her out of her own love and flattery, not out of my promise.

Othello: (*aside*) Iago beckons me; now he begins the story.

Cassio: She was here even now; she haunts me in every place. I was the other day talking on the sea-bank with certain Venetians, and thither comes the bauble and, by this hand, falls me thus about my neck.

Othello: (*aside*) Crying "O dear Cassio!" as it were. His gesture imports it.

Cassio: So hangs and lolls and weeps upon me, so hales and pulls me. Ha, ha, ha!

Othello: (*aside*) Now he tells how she plucked him to my chamber. O, I see that nose of yours, but not that dog I shall throw it to!

Cassio: Well, I must leave her company.

Iago: Before me! Look, where she comes.

Cassio: 'Tis such another fitchew! Marry, a perfumed one.

Enter Bianca

What do you mean by this haunting of me?

Bianca: Let the devil and his dam haunt you! What did you mean by that same handkerchief you gave me even now? I was a fine fool to take it. I must take out the work! A likely piece of work, that you should find it in your chamber, and not know who left it there! This is some minx's token, and I must take out the work? There, give it your hobby-horse, wheresoever you had it. I'll take out no work on't.

Cassio: How now, my sweet Bianca! How now, how now!

Othello: (*aside*) By heaven, that should be my handkerchief!

Bianca: If you'll come to supper to-night, you may. If you will not, come when you are next prepared for.

  Exit

Iago: After her, after her!

Cassio: Faith, I must: she'll rail in the street else.

Iago: Will you sup there?

Cassio: Faith, I intend so.

Iago: Well, I may chance to see you: for I would very fain speak with you.

Cassio: Prithee come, will you?

Iago: Go to; say no more.

  Exit Cassio

Now listen to the corresponding scene from Verdi's opera.

This time, the two scenes are about equal in length, at least when read as text. Bianca does not appear, here or anywhere else in the opera, so Boito's Iago taunts Otello with the handkerchief directly. Otherwise, the action is similar in both scenes.

Verdi's version, however, shows how opera is unlike any other form of dramatic expression. For one thing, he writes in a polyphonic texture, enabling multiple characters to speak simultaneously in counterpoint. Superficially, this resembles the polytextuality we saw in the Machaut motet (Chapter 10). Yet although we may not be able to hear everything that is said at the climax of this trio, we fully understand the dramatic context. Also, the music is so vivid that we do not have to follow every word of the text.

LEARNING TO LISTEN GUIDE

TAKE NOTE OF MELODY AND TEXTURE

What to Listen For: The interaction between the characters, whom the music lets speak not only successively but simultaneously as well.

Verdi, *Otello*, trio from Act III
Date: 1887
Instrumentation: Two baritones, tenor, and orchestra
Key: Variable, ending in C major
Meter: Starts in $\frac{4}{4}$, also known as common time, changes to $\frac{6}{8}$
Core Repertory Connection: Verdi's *Otello* is also discussed in Chapter 6.

Streaming audio track 57.
Interactive Listening Guide ILG-15 will allow you to follow who is speaking at all times during this fast-moving scene.

TIME	ORIGINAL TEXT	TRANSLATION	COMMENT
0:00	**Iago:** *Vieni, l'aula è deserta.* *T'inoltra, o Capitano.*	Iago: Come, the chamber is empty. Advance, o Captain.	
	Cassio: *Questo nome d'onor suona ancor vano per me.*	Cassio: That name of honor still rings hollow to me.	
	Iago: *Fa cor, la tua causa è in tal mano che la vittoria è certa.*	Iago: Take courage; with your cause in my hands it is sure to prevail.	
	Cassio: *Io qui credea di ritrovar Desdemona.*	Cassio: I expected to meet Desdemona here.	
	Otello (nascosto): *Ei la nomò!*	Othello (aside): He named her!	
	Cassio: *Vorrei parlarle ancora,* *per saper se la mia grazia è profferta.*	Cassio: I was hoping to talk to her again, to learn if I have been pardoned.	
0:42	**Iago:** *L'attendi.* *E intanto, giacchè non si stanca mai la tua lingua nelle fole gaie, narrami un po' di lei che t'innamora.*	Iago: Wait for her. In the meantime, since never does your tongue get tired of idle talk, tell me something about her whom you love.	As Iago leads Cassio on, the tempo speeds up and the meter changes to $\frac{6}{8}$.
	Cassio: *Di chi?*	Cassio: Of whom?	
	Iago (sotto voce): *Di Bianca.*	Iago (*in an undertone*): Of Bianca.	
	Otello: *Sorride!*	Othello: He laughs!	
	Cassio: *Baie!*	Cassio: Nonsense!	
1:10	**Iago:** *Essa t'avvince coi vaghi rai.*	Iago: She vanquishes you with her radiance.	

TIME	ORIGINAL TEXT	TRANSLATION	COMMENT
	Cassio: *Rider mi fai.*	**Cassio:** You make me laugh.	
	Iago: *Ride chi vince.*	**Iago:** He who wins laughs.	
	Cassio: *In tai disfide, per verità,* *vince chi ride—Ah! Ah!*	**Cassio:** In truth, faced with such challenges, whoever laughs wins—Ha! Ha!	
	Iago: *Ah! Ah!*	**Iago:** Ha! Ha!	
	Otello: *L'empio trionfa, il suo scherno m'uccide.* *Dio, frena l'ansia che in core mi sta!*	**Othello:** The scoundrel is triumphant, his scorn is killing me. God, help me control my anxious heart!	
	Cassio: *Son già di baci sazio e di lai.*	**Cassio:** I'm already fed up with kisses and laments.	
	Iago: *Rider mi fai.*	**Iago:** You make me laugh.	
	Cassio: *O amor' fugaci!*	**Cassio:** O fleeting love!	
	Iago: *Vagheggi il regno d'altra beltà.* *Colgo nel segno?*	**Iago:** You long for another conquest. Am I right?	
	Cassio: *Ah! Ah!*	**Cassio:** Ha! Ha!	
	Iago: *Ah! Ah!*	**Iago:** Ha! Ha!	
	Otello: *L'empio m'irride, il suo scherno m'uccide.* *Dio, frena l'ansia che in core mi sta!*	**Othello:** The scoundrel is mocking me, his scorn is killing me. God, help me control my anxious heart.	
	Cassio: *Nel segno hai côto.* *Si, lo confesso.* *M'odi. . .*	**Cassio:** You're exactly right. Yes, I admit it. Listen to me. . .	
	Iago: *Sommesso parla. T'ascolto.*	**Iago:** Keep it quiet. I hear you.	
	Cassio: *Iago, t'è nota la mia dimora. . .*	**Cassio:** Iago, you know where I live. . .	
	Otello: *Or gli racconta il modo,* *il luogo e l'ora. . .*	**Othello:** Now he is telling him how, where and when. . .	
	Cassio: *. . .da mano ignota. . .*	**Cassio:** . . .from an unknown hand. . .	

TIME	ORIGINAL TEXT	TRANSLATION	COMMENT
	Otello (ascolto): *Le parole non odo. . .* *Lasso! E udir le vorrei!* *Dove son giunto!*	**Othello** (*aside*): His words are inaudible. . . Alas! I want to hear them! What have I come to?	
	Cassio: *. . .Un vel trapunto. . .*	**Cassio:** . . .a piece of embroidering. . .	
	Iago: *È strano! È strano!*	**Iago:** How strange! How strange!	
	Otello (**nascosto***):* *D'avvicinarmi Iago mi fa cenno.*	**Othello** (*aside*): Iago signals me to come closer.	
	Iago (**sotto voce***):* *Da ignota mano?* *(molto forte) Baie!*	**Iago** (*quietly*): From an unknown hand? (*aloud*) Nonsense!	
	Cassio: *Da senno.* *Quanto mi tarda saper chi sia. . .*	**Cassio:** That's right. How I long to know whose. . .	
	Iago (**fra sè***):* *Otello spia.* *(a Cassio ad alta voce) L'hai teco?*	**Iago** (*quietly*): Othello is watching. (*aloud*) You have it with you?	
	Cassio: *Guarda.*	**Cassio:** Look.	
	Iago (**predendo il fazzoletto***):* *Qual meraviglia!* *(a parte) Otello origlia.* *Ei s'avvicina con mosse accorte.* *(a Cassio) Bel cavaliere,* *nel vostro ostello perdono gli angeli* *l'aureola e il vel.*	**Iago** (*taking the handkerchief*): How marvelous! (*aside*) Othello is listening. He is approaching discreetly. (*to Cassio*) You fine gentleman, around you angels lose their halos and their veils.	
	Otello: *È quello! È quello!* *Ruina e morte!*	**Othello:** That's enough! That's enough! Ruination and death!	
	Iago (**fra sè***):* *Origlia Otello.*	**Iago** (*aside*): Othello is listening.	
	Otello: *Tutto è spento! amore e duol.* *L'alma mia nessun più smuova.*	**Othello:** It's all over! love and pain. My soul can no longer be stirred.	
3:41	*Iago* (**a Cassio***):* *Questa è una ragna* *dove il tuo cuor* *casca, si lagna,* *s'impiglia e muor.* *Troppo l'ammiri,* *troppo la guardi;* *badi ai deliri* *vani e bugiardi.* *Questa è una ragna, ecc.*	**Iago** (*to Cassio*): This is a web into which your heart stumbles, complains, is caught and dies. You admire it in excess, look at it in excess; Beware of deceptive and vain raptures. This is a web, etc.	In the final section, the tempo speeds up even further and all three characters sing simultaneously much of the time.

TIME	ORIGINAL TEXT	TRANSLATION	COMMENT
	Cassio: *Miracolo vago* *dell'aspo e dell'ago* *che in raggi tramuta* *le fila d'un vel,* *più bianco, più lieve* *che fiocco di neve,* *che nube tessuta* *dall'aure del ciel.*	**Cassio:** Beautiful miracle of the loom and thread which transforms into sunbeams the weave of a fabric, whiter, lighter, than a flake of snow, than a cloud spun out by heavenly breezes.	
	Iago: *Questa è una ragna* *dove il tuo cuor. . .*	**Iago:** This is a web into which your heart. . .	
	Cassio: *Miracolo vago. . .*	**Cassio:** . . .beautiful miracle. . .	
	Iago: *. . .casca, si lagna,* *s'impiglia e muor. . .* *Questa è una ragna* *Dove il tuo cuor* *Casca, si lagna* *S'impiglia e muor.* *Troppo l'ammiri. . .*	**Iago:** . . .stumbles, complains, is caught and dies. . . This is a web into which your heart stumbles, complains, is caught and dies. You admire it in excess. . .	
	Otello: *Tradimento, tradimento!*	**Othello:** Betrayal! Betrayal!	
	Cassio: *. . .più bianco, più lieve. . .*	**Cassio:** Whiter, lighter. . .	
	Iago: *. . .troppo la guardi;. . .*	**Iago:** . . .look at it in excess. . .	
	Cassio: *. . .che fiocco di neve. . .*	**Cassio:** . . .than a flake of snow. . .	
	Otello: *Tradimento, la tuo prova. . .*	**Othello:** Betrayal! Your proof. . .	
	Iago: *. . .bada ai deliri,* *vani e bugiardi.*	**Iago:** . . .beware of deceptive and vain raptures.	
	Cassio: *. . .che nube tessuta* *dall'aure del ciel.*	**Cassio:** . . .than a cloud spun out by heavenly breezes. . .	
	Otello: *. . .la tua prova spaventosa*	**Othello:** . . .your frightening proof. . .	
	Iago: *Ah, bada. . .*	**Iago:** Ah! Beware. . .	
	Cassio: *Miracol. . .*	**Cassio:** Miracle. . .	

TIME	ORIGINAL TEXT	TRANSLATION	COMMENT
	Otello: . . .mostri al sol.	**Othello:** . . .show it forth in the sunlight. . .	
	Iago: Questa è una ragna dove il tuo cuor casca, si lagna, s'impligia, e muor.	**Iago:** This is a web into which your heart stumbles, complains, is caught and dies.	
	Cassio: . . .miracolo vago. . .	**Cassio:** . . .beautiful miracle. . .	
	Otello: Tradimento!	**Othello:** Betrayal!	
	Iago: Troppo l'ammiri.	**Iago:** You admire it in excess.	
	Otello: Tradimento!	**Othello:** Betrayal!	
	Iago: Bada, bada!	**Iago:** Beware, beware!	

The scene begins with musical "prose," as Iago and Cassio greet each other. Their melodic phrases of unequal length do not balance to form a single line. When Iago begins to speak of Bianca, the music changes dramatically and becomes flirtatious. The dialog after this has a rocking accompaniment in compound $\frac{6}{8}$ meter. This music is devious, since Otello's asides lead into a minor key. The change in key shows his frustration without disrupting the rhythmic flow. At the words *"É quello"* (It is the one), Otello's anger finally bursts out uncontrollably, and so does the music.

Now begins the most musically fascinating section of the piece. Like Iago's *Credo*, it has no parallel in Shakespeare. In a fast section marked *Allegro brillante*, Iago warns Cassio about his excessive fascination with the handkerchief. Cassio responds with an enraptured speech praising its beauty and delicacy. When Cassio speaks, the tempo slows, but both characters return to the $\frac{6}{8}$ meter of the previous section. Cassio's lush legato phrases, though, are the polar opposite of Iago's light but ominous patter. It is as if each man is revealing his unique perspective on the scene we have just witnessed.

Iago and Cassio then sing sections of their text simultaneously, while Otello joins in with his own comments, imploring that the evidence of his betrayal be brought to light. Otello is heard by himself only briefly, and he has become nearly inarticulate. He sings an ominous, ascending chromatic scale (requiring both the black and white keys on a keyboard instrument) on the "to" syllable of the word *spaventosa* (literally, "frightening"). In all, the time the characters sing together lasts less than 30 seconds, and you may not understand all the words. During that time, though, the music conveys the drama in concentrated form. In fact, it offers a degree of realism not available in a spoken play. Each of these characters, although sharing the stage with others, is in his own emotional world. For a brief moment, we can hear and experience this truth through the magic of music.

The Libretto and the Number Opera: Transforming *Le Nozze di Figaro*

Now let us compare some scenes from Mozart and Da Ponte's *Le nozze di Figaro* with the corresponding scenes from Beaumarchais's play. The number opera format affords its own unique expressive possibilities for combining music and drama.

What Beaumarchais Tells Us about Cherubino

Earlier we examined Cherubino's *Non so più*. Actually, it corresponds almost exactly to a speech that Beaumarchais's Chérubin makes to Suzanne in the play. Here is Beaumarchais's version:

> I have no idea what's come over me. These last few days, I've felt my heart pound every time I see a woman. The words "love" and "tender" make it race. The need to tell someone "I love you" has become so strong that when I'm by myself, running through the grounds, I shout it out loud to her Ladyship, to you, to the trees, the clouds, to the wind that blows the clouds away and my words with them.

This speech is so straightforward that it was unnecessary for librettist Da Ponte to do what Boito would later do with Shakespeare's Iago. The character does not need to be simplified in order to facilitate musical development. Chérubin's lines practically beg to be sung just as they are!

What Da Ponte Tells Us about the Countess

Da Ponte would have been challenged only if playwright Beaumarchais had not written such a speech for Chérubin. Then he would have had to invent one. And that is exactly what Da Ponte did for the character of the Countess. Beaumarchais introduces this character casually, in the midst of a scene in the first act of his play. Da Ponte, however, crafts a *cavatina*, or introductory aria, for her.

As the curtain rises on the second act, the Countess sings a memorable solo. In this beautiful piece, she laments that she has apparently lost the love of the Count. Only a few years ago, he had courted her so ardently as Rosina in *The Barber of Seville*! Beaumarchais knew that his audience would understand *Le nozze di Figaro* as a sequel to his earlier play. Similarly, Mozart and Da Ponte knew that their opera would be seen as a sequel to the popular opera by Paisiello.

What Mozart Tells Us about the Countess

Mozart's music tells us things about the Countess that are, at most, only implied by Da Ponte's text. First, as audiences of the time would have recognized, her aria marks her as a character from *opera seria*, or serious Italian opera. Unlike Cherubino's fast-moving comic aria, this one is slow and stately. It is also preceded by an orchestral ritornello that carefully sets the mood. The Countess is an aristocrat, so she complains only indirectly, in music containing almost no hint of the turmoil that must be raging within her soul. In fact, the entire aria is in a major key.

LEARNING TO LISTEN GUIDE

TAKE NOTE OF HARMONY AND FORM

What to Listen For: The musical illustration of the Countess's nobility of character.

Mozart, *Le nozze di Figaro*, K. 492, beginning of Act II
Date: 1786
Instrumentation: Soprano and orchestra
Key: E-flat major
Meter: $\frac{2}{4}$ (two slow beats per measure)
Core Repertory Connection: Mozart's *Le nozze di Figaro* is also discussed in Chapter 3.

Streaming audio track 32.

TIME	ORIGINAL TEXT	TRANSLATION	COMMENT
0:00			The orchestral introduction establishes the nobility of the Countess's character.
1:18	*Contessa:* *Porgi amor qualche ristoro* *al mio duolo, a'miei sospir.* *O mi rendi il mio tesoro,* *o mi lascia almen morir.*	Countess: Grant, love, some consolation to my sorrow, to my sighs. Either give me back my treasure Or at least let me die.	The Countess sings in a restrained manner that gives little hint of the passions suggested by the text.

Has Mozart failed to rise to the challenge? Actually, he has surpassed it. He has produced a piece of music of such pure, poignant beauty that passion seems somehow beside the point. In this way, Mozart tells us that this is a truly exceptional person, capable of self-control and understatement. Two and a half acts later, at the very end of the opera, the Countess bestows her forgiveness on her cheating husband with the same crystalline elegance and simplicity. There is rarely a dry eye in the house. Only music can reach so directly into our souls and make us understand so much.

The Opening Duet

Already in the opening duet, the number opera does something that a spoken play could not. Indeed, the most interesting passages in *The Marriage of Figaro* often come in the ensembles. Here Mozart uses musical numbers to present miniature tableaus, much as Verdi did in the trio from *Otello* discussed above. Once again, Da Ponte adapted this scene directly from the opening lines of Beaumarchais's play. Figaro is measuring the room that he and Suzanne will use as their bedroom:

> Figaro: Nineteen foot by twenty-six.
> Suzanne: Look, Figaro, my wedding bonnet. Do you reckon it looks better like this?
> Figaro: [*holding both her hands*]: My pet, it's perfect. Ah! What sight could be better calculated to enslave a doting bridegroom than a dainty, virginal garland on the head of this pretty wife-to-be on the morning they are to be married?

This is not much of a scene. Indeed, it is really a mere pretext to bring the characters on stage so that Suzanne can tell Figaro of her suspicions about the Count, who has the room next door. Now listen to the corresponding scene from the opera, in which Suzanne's garland has become Susanna's new hat.

LEARNING TO LISTEN GUIDE

TAKE NOTE OF MELODY AND FORM

What to Listen For: The way the music mirrors the interaction between the characters.

Mozart: *Le nozze di Figaro*, K. 492, opening duet
Date: 1786
Instrumentation: Baritone, soprano, and orchestra
Key: G major
Meter: $\frac{4}{4}$, also known as common time (four rapid beats per measure)
Core Repertory Connection: Mozart's *Le nozze di Figaro* is also discussed in Chapter 3.

Streaming audio track 29.
Interactive Listening Guide ILG-7
will help you understand
the thematic structure
of the opening duet.

TIME	ORIGINAL TEXT	TRANSLATION	COMMENT
0:00			The orchestra introduces a theme (A) which is associated with the words sung by Figaro at the beginning.
0:16			It then continues with another theme (B) that is associated later with Susanna.
0:33	*Figaro* (**misurando la camera**): Cinque. . .dieci. . .venti. . .trenta. . . Trentasei. . .quarantatre. . .	Figaro (*measuring the room*): Five. . .ten. . .twenty. . .thirty. . . Thirty-six. . .forty-three. . .	As the orchestra returns to play the A theme, Figaro calls out measurements.
0:54	*Susanna* (**fra se, guardendosi nello specchio**): Ora sì ch'io son contenta, sembra fatto inver per me.	Susanna (*to herself, gazing into the mirror*): How happy I am just now, it truly seems made for me.	As soon as Susanna begins to sing, the B theme returns.
1:05	*Guarda un po', mio caro Figaro, guarda adesso il mio cappello.* (seguitando a guardarsi)	Just look, my dear Figaro, look right now at my hat. (*continuing to gaze at herself.*)	The A theme reasserts itself as Figaro continues his measurements, but Susanna continues to sing as well, ending with a small temper tantrum demanding his attention.
1:29	*Figaro:* Sì, mio core, or è piu bello, sembra fatto inver per te.	Figaro: Yes, my sweet, it does look prettier, it truly seems made for you.	Figaro responds with the B theme, showing that he is now giving Susanna his full attention.

TIME	ORIGINAL TEXT	TRANSLATION	COMMENT
2:05	**Susanne e Figaro:** *A, il mattino alle nozze vicino* *quanto è dolce al mio (tuo) tenero sposo,* *questo bel cappellino vezzoso* *che Susanna ella stessa si fe'.*	**Susanna and Figaro:** Ah, the morning of our wedding day how delightful to my (your) beloved spouse, is this charming little hat which Susanna herself has made.	Both now sing the B theme together, showing that they are now in complete unity. The A theme never returns.

These lines took only a few seconds to speak in the play. Solely through Mozart's music, which involves a great deal of repetition, they have been extended to nearly three minutes. This gives the audience a real chance to meet these characters before the action begins. How will they relate to each other, you may be asking? Is Figaro the boss, or does Susanna influence him in ways he may not be entirely aware of? Though you may not realize it at first, Mozart gives us the answers.

As the music of the duet begins, the orchestra introduces a theme (A on the interactive listening guide), which continues as Figaro begins to call out his measurements. Clearly, this is *his* music. Susanna sings a more melodic theme (labeled B), which had also been introduced by the orchestra, and which expresses her satisfaction with the new hat. At first Figaro ignores her and keeps measuring. His music returns as well, even as Susanna, off in her own world, continues to sing. Finally, though, she forces Figaro to pay attention to her, by repeating *"il mio cappello"* over and over until he drops what he is doing and joins in. From this point on, Figaro's theme is never heard again. Susanna's music has completely supplanted it.

Susanna has won this little skirmish! Mozart shows us how she might control her fiancé as the opera progresses. Nothing of the sort is even hinted at in the text.

The Sextet in Act III

A more intricate ensemble occurs in the third act of the opera. In this "comic opera moment," the various strands of the complex plot come together all at once. The housekeeper Marcellina has lent Figaro money on the condition that he will marry her if he is unable to repay it. Meanwhile, Doctor Bartolo, has been hoping to avenge himself for Figaro having deprived him of Rosina in *The Barber of Seville*. Now Bartolo sees an opportunity, and the Count also seeks to frustrate Figaro's plans because he is pursuing Figaro's wife-to-be Susanna.

When hauled before a magistrate to settle the matter, the ever-resourceful Figaro comes up with an ingenious ploy. He believes that he was born a nobleman and so cannot marry without his parents' consent. As proof, he points out a birthmark on his arm. Here is what happens next in Beaumarchais's play:

Marcellina [*jumping to her feet*]: A spatula? On your right arm?
Figaro: How do you know that?
Marcellina: Merciful heaven! It's him!
Figaro: Yes, it's me.
Bartolo [*to Marcellina*]: Who? Who's this "him"?
Marcellina [*euphoric*]: Emmanuel!
Bartolo [*to Figaro*]: Were you stolen by gypsies?

Figaro [*excited*]: Near a chateau. Good Doctor Bartolo, restore me
to my noble family and you can name your price. Ask a mountain
of gold, and my illustrious parents would not quibble . . .
Bartolo [*pointing to Marcellina*]: There's your mother.
Figaro: You mean, my old nursemaid.
Bartolo: Your own mother.
Figaro: Explain yourself.
Marcellina [*pointing to Bartolo*]: He's your father.

Wisely, Da Ponte and Mozart left this scene in recitative. Equally wisely, though,
they also left out much of the following scene. In the play, Marcellina makes a series
of impassioned speeches about the degradation of women. Instead, they followed
the revelation of Figaro's identity with a complex sextet. Now the various strands
are presented and partially resolved. Don Curzio is the magistrate.

LEARNING TO LISTEN GUIDE

TAKE NOTE OF FORM

What to Listen For: The close correspondence between the music and
the dramatic action.

Mozart: *Le nozze di Figaro*, K. 492, sextet from Act III
Date: 1786
Instrumentation: Soprano, mezzo-soprano, tenor, two baritones, bass, and orchestra
Key: F major
Meter: $\frac{4}{4}$, also known as common time (four rapid beats per measure)
Core Repertory Connection: Mozart's *Le nozze di Figaro* is also discussed in Chapter 3.

Streaming audio track 34.
Interactive Listening Guide ILG-8
will show you exactly who is
singing throughout this
complex piece.

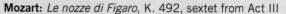

TIME	ORIGINAL TEXT	TRANSLATION	COMMENT
0:00	**Marcellina:** *Riconosci in questo amplesso* *una madre, amato figlio!*	**Marcellina:** Recognize a mother in this embrace, dear son!	The bewildered characters all react to Marcellina's revelation about Figaro's parentage.
	Figaro: *Padre mio, fate lo stesso,* *non mi fate più arrossir.*	**Figaro:** My father, do likewise, don't make me blush any longer.	
	Bartolo: *Resistenza la coscienza* *Ffar non lascia al tuo desir.*	**Bartolo:** Resistance, conscience, will not let you have your wish.	
	Don Curzio: *Ei suo padre, ella sua madre,* *l'imeneo non può seguir.*	**Don Curzio:** He his father, she his mother, the marriage can't go forward.	
	Il Conte: *Son smarrito, son stordito,* *meglio è assai di qua partir.*	**The Count:** I'm bewildered, I'm stunned, it's much better just to leave.	
	Marcellina e Bartolo: *Figlio amato!*	**Marcellina and Bartolo:** Dear son!	

TIME	ORIGINAL TEXT	TRANSLATION	COMMENT
	Figaro: *Parenti amati!*	**Figaro:** Dear parents!	
0:49	*Susanna:* *Alto, alto, signor Conte,* *mille doppie son qui pronte,* *a pagar vengo per Figaro,* *ed a porlo in libertà.*	**Susanna:** Wait, wait, lord Count, I have a thousand doubloons, I've come to pay for Figaro, and set him at liberty.	The music becomes more agitated as Susanna returns and finds Figaro and Marcellina embracing.
	Il Conte e Don Curzio: *Non sappiam com' è la cosa,* *Osservate un poco là!*	**The Count and Don Curzio:** We don't know what's going on, Take a look over there!	
	Susanna: *Già d'accordo ei colla sposa;* *giusti Dei, che infedeltà!* *Lascia iniquo!*	**Susanna:** He's already reconciled to having her as a wife; just gods, what infidelity! Give her up, you wretch!	
	Figaro: *No, t'arresta!* *Senti, o cara!*	**Figaro:** No, hold on! Listen, sweetheart!	
	Susanna (dà uno schiaffo a Figaro): *Senti questa!*	**Susanna (slapping Figaro):** Listen to this!	
1:52	*Marcellina, Bartolo e Figaro:* *È un effetto di buon core,* *tutto amore è quel che fa.*	**Marcellina, Bartolo and Figaro:** It's the result of having a good heart, love is as love does.	The characters react in different ways to what they believe is happening.
	Il Conte: *Fremo, smanio dal furore,* *il destino a me la fa.*	**The Count:** I shudder, I'm mad with fury, destiny has it in for me.	
	Don Curzio: *Freme e smania dal furore,* *il destino gliela fa.*	**Don Curzio:** He shudders, he's mad with fury, destiny has it in for him.	
	Susanna: *Fremo, smanio dal furore,* *una vecchia a me la fa.*	**Susanna:** I shudder, I'm mad with fury, An old woman has it in for me.	
2:35	*Marcellina:* *Lo sdegno calmate,* *mia cara figliuola,* *sua madre abbracciate* *che or vostra sarà.*	**Marcellina:** Calm your anger, my dear girl, embrace his mother who will now be yours as well.	Marcellina's explanation leads to a musical resolution and a repetition of the earlier banter.
	Susanna: *Sua madre?*	**Susanna:** His mother?	
	Bartolo: *Sua madre!*	**Bartolo:** His mother!	
	Susanna: *Sua madre?*	**Susanna:** His mother?	
	Il Conte: *Sua madre!*	**The Count:** His mother!	

TIME	ORIGINAL TEXT	TRANSLATION	COMMENT
	Susanna: *Sua madre?*	**Susanna:** His mother?	
	Don Curzio: *Sua madre!*	**Don Curzio:** His mother!	
	Susanna: *Sua madre?*	**Susanna:** His mother?	
	Marcellina: *Sua madre!*	**Marcellina:** His mother!	
	Susanna: *Tua madre?*	**Susanna:** Your mother?	
	Figaro: *E quello è mio padre* *che a te lo dirà.*	**Figaro:** And this is my father as he will tell you himself.	
	Susanna: *Suo padre?*	**Susanna:** His father?	
	Bartolo: *Suo padre!*	**Bartolo:** His father!	
	Susanna: *Suo padre?*	**Susanna:** His father?	
	Il Conte: *Suo padre!*	**The Count:** His father!	
	Susanna: *Suo padre?*	**Susanna:** His father?	
	Don Curzio: *Suo padre!*	**Don Curzio:** His father!	
	Susanna: *Suo padre?*	**Susanna:** His father?	
	Marcellina: *Suo padre!*	**Marcellina:** His father!	
	Susanna: *Tuo padre?*	**Susanna:** Your father?	
	Figaro: *E quella è mia madre* *che a te lo dirà.*	**Figaro:** And this is my mother, as she will tell you herself.	
3:40	**Susanna, Marcellina, Bartolo e Figaro:** *Al dolce contento* *di questo momento,* *quest'anima appena* *resister or sa.*	**Susanna, Marcellina, Bartolo and Figaro:** To the sweet contentment of this moment, this soul can hardly offer any resistance.	The ensemble ends with contrasting reactions among the two groups of characters.
	Don Curzio e Il Conte: *Al fiero tormento* *di questo momento,* *quell'/quest'anima appena* *resister or sa.*	**Don Curzio and the Count:** To the fierce torments of this moment, this soul can hardly offer any resistance.	

Mozart shows how music can artfully weave together the different strands of a drama and present them all at once. He contrasts the long melodic phrases of Marcellina, Figaro, and Bartolo with the short, astonished queries of Don Curzio and the Count. At first these appear in succession, then simultaneously. After this, as if it were possible, things grow even more complicated. Susanna, who has been absent, searching for the money to pay off Figaro's debt, enters. When she sees Figaro and Marcellina embracing, she naturally jumps to the wrong conclusion. Mozart presents her initial appeal to the Count as a separate musical statement, followed by a return of the complex ensemble. And that's not all. As if seeing this scene at the same time the ensemble music returns, Susanna bursts into a rage, confronts Figaro, and angrily slaps him.

In what follows, all six characters sing at once. The graceful ensemble of Marcellina, Bartolo, and Figaro contrasts with the jumpy, uncertain phrases of the Count and Susanna, who answer one another musically, and those of Curzio, which largely blend with them. For a brief moment, the sextet divides into two equal parties—the newly reconciled family and the angry outsiders. In the conclusion of the ensemble, after everything is explained, the balance is shifted. Susanna's rapid, far-ranging phrases throw her into prominence. She now leads the newly reunited family, while Don Curzio and the Count briefly vent their frustration in a minor key.

If You Liked This Music . . .
A Sampling of Other Operas

There are so many operas that it is hard to pick just a few to recommend for further listening. The following is thus a highly selective list. (Suggestions for further listening from Wagner's operas are found in Chapter 9.)

- *The Magic Flute* (*Die Zauberflöte*) is a delightful *Singspiel* (a German-language opera with spoken dialogue) whose fairy-tale plot masks hidden depths of meaning and characterization.
- Mozart's *Don Giovanni*, for which Da Ponte also wrote the libretto, is a tragicomic version of the Don Juan story.
- Verdi's *Rigoletto*, one of his most popular works, tells the melodramatic story of a court jester whose protectiveness of his daughter Gilda leads directly to her tragic death.
- *Aïda*, also by Verdi, is one of the grandest of grand operas. Set in ancient Egypt, it has vast crowd scenes, stunning ensembles, and a tragic story of an impossible love that is fulfilled by the heroine's self-sacrifice.
- *Carmen*, by Georges Bizet (1838–1875), is one of the most popular French operas. It tells a vivid, provocative story of seduction and jealousy.
- *La Bohème*, by Giacomo Puccini (1858–1924), is based on the same story that inspired the Broadway musical *Rent*. It is full of memorable tunes and characters.
- *Wozzeck*, by Alban Berg (1885–1935), is probably the most frequently performed early modern opera. It tells the tale of a hapless soldier driven to murder and suicide by forces outside his control. The music is largely atonal and vividly expressive.
- *Einstein on the Beach*, by Philip Glass (b. 1937), is an experimental work that deliberately pushes the limits of the genre. It takes nearly five hours to perform. There is no intermission and no real story, and the audience is encouraged to enter and leave at any point, as though they were viewing an artwork in a museum.

Mozart ties these threads together with exceptional grace and elegance. The structure of the music resembles a return-based musical form, like a sonata—which, as we saw in Chapter 5, contains contrasting material, a development section, and at last a return to the original idea and the original key. Similarly, in this sextet, Susanna's entrance is presented as a contrasting musical idea. It is followed by a kind of miniature development section, the unstable-sounding episode in which Susanna confronts Figaro. When she recognizes what is really going on, some of the opening material returns, along with the opening key. Here the characters return to the "*Sua madre? Sua padre?*" exchange, voiced earlier by Don Curzio and the Count. Finally, in a coda, the larger group is pitted against the smaller one, and the situation is stabilized, at least for now.

Mozart could not have done all this with just any text. Da Ponte expertly crafted the scene to conform to musical logic, and the composer responded in kind. *The Marriage of Figaro* is collaborative artistry at its best.

Some Final Thoughts

Opera is one of the most overwhelming musical performance experiences. These examples give some sense of the variety of operatic expression. Sometimes composers keep dramatic aims and musical aims separate, and sometimes they integrate them. Needless to say, we have barely scratched the surface.

While you can get some idea of an opera by listening to a recording or watching a video, nothing can substitute for seeing it live. Imagine the combination of magnificently trained voices, a soaring orchestra, and the spectacle that goes with them. A scene often involves ballet, choral singing, and elaborate stagecraft. At most opera houses today, running translations are available, either above the stage or on the back of individual seats. These present a continuous translation of the text so that you can follow everything that happens onstage. If you live in a large city, you will have many chances to see an opera performed live, but if you don't, take advantage of the opportunity whenever it comes along; it will be worth it.

SUMMARY

- Because of its widespread use on television and in the movies, music plays a crucial role in our experience of drama. Opera pioneered many of the ways of combining music and drama used in today's art and entertainment media.

- Two broad categories of opera are music drama and number opera. In the music drama, which originated more recently, music and drama work closely together. In the number opera, music and drama are carefully separated. This approach survives not only in Broadway musicals but also in the work of some recent opera composers.

- Verdi's *Otello* (a music drama) and Mozart's *The Marriage of Figaro* (a number opera) are both based on major works of literature. To help transform such works into operas, a good libretto lets the composer tell more of the story than words could alone. By studying the transformation, we can learn about the unique demands of the musical stage.

KEY TERMS

Ensemble   p. 303   Libretto   p. 309   Number Opera   p. 296
Incidental Music p. 295   Music Drama   p. 296

REVIEW QUESTIONS

1. What did you learn from listening to a TV show or movie without the sound? What are some of the things music contributes that you may have taken for granted?
2. What is a music drama, and how is such an opera constructed?
3. What is a number opera, and how is such an opera constructed?
4. What is a libretto? Why is it crucial to the success of an opera?
5. How is music in an opera like plot development in a story, novel, or play?
6. What is Shakespeare's *Othello* about? How are the story and the major characters transformed by Verdi and Boito?
7. What is Beaumarchais's *Le nozze di Figaro* about? How are the story and the major characters transformed by Mozart and Da Ponte?

REVIEW CONCEPTS

1. In what ways is the music of an opera similar to the music of a movie or TV show? In what ways is opera different?
2. What is character development, and how does the music of these operas contribute to it?
3. What are some of the limitations on the distinction between music drama and number opera? What are some examples from your listening for this chapter?

LISTENING EXERCISES

1. Listen to (or watch) *Otello* and *The Marriage of Figaro* in their entirety. Be sure to follow the text carefully. Either read the libretto included with the recording or the subtitles if you are watching a video. (Many opera companies offer subtitles, but you can also bring the libretto with you to a live performance.) Find some other examples of the principles discussed in this chapter.
2. If you have read the original plays, find your own examples of how they have changed.
3. Listen to Mozart's *The Magic Flute* and/or Verdi's *Il trovatore*. Although major operas, they are not known for the literary value of their stories. Do you find the same principles of musical dramatization at work? Does a good opera need a good story? Can a story actually get in the way?
4. Listen to one of Wagner's music dramas, such as *Die Walküre*, the second opera of his huge tetralogy *Der Ring des Nibelungen*. What differences do you notice between Wagner's and Verdi's approaches to writing music drama?
5. Listen to another opera based on a major work of literature, such as Verdi's *Falstaff* (based on Shakespeare's *The Merry Wives of Windsor*), Britten's *The Turn of the Screw* (based on a Henry James short story), or Tchaikovsky's *Eugene Onegin* (based on the verse novel by Pushkin). How does the music of the opera enhance the literary original?
6. Listen to an early Baroque opera like Monteverdi's *L'incoronazione di Poppea* (*The Coronation of Poppea*). These operas were written before either the music drama or the number opera paradigm had been formulated. What other possibilities do they suggest for the interaction of drama and music?

12 Instrumental Music and Meaning

TAKE NOTE

Program music is intended to tell a story, but music without a program may also suggest meaning in various ways. Whether it should suggest meaning or not, and what the possible meanings are, remain interesting subjects for debate.

A young woman, having been rejected by her lover, swears revenge on all men. She and her band of female warriors contrive a plot. Šárka is tied to a tree, and left to be discovered and "rescued" by the warrior Citrad and his men. Citrad falls in love with her. She summons the other members of her band, and there is general rejoicing. Unknown to the men, though, they have been given a sleeping potion. As soon as they are asleep, the women descend on them and massacre them all.

You may recall this as the story behind Smetana's orchestral tone poem *Šárka*. In Chapter 3, you listened to the music and wrote some notes about the story *you* thought it might be telling. You may have thought of dancing, a love scene, and a battle.

At the same time, though, you probably did not imagine anything like the real story. Dancing and love scenes are usually considered happy events. Not in this case! And in conventional military stories, the hero is usually a man. If he is defeated, it is certainly not by a woman. Other parts of the Šárka story are not even narrated by the music. You would have to know that, before the story begins, Šárka has been rejected by her lover.

Program Music: Telling a Story

At a concert, the story of a piece like this is usually printed in the program. Otherwise, most audiences would have trouble understanding it. Smetana gives us a great deal of help, of course. He begins with a powerful chord played by every instrument in his large orchestra except the piccolo, triangle, and cymbals. The music that follows paints a perfect picture of a warlike people impatient for action. Listen to its jerky, inconsistent rhythms and its wide melodic range.

An abrupt transition leads to a new section. Now Citrad and his men ride in. Here the music is much more predictable. The tempo slows down, and the dynamic level changes to *piano*, with the additional marking *a la marcia* (like a march). As the men approach, the dynamic level gradually increases. Still, the beat remains steady, with a fanfare of triplets followed by dotted rhythms. If you listen carefully to the bass line, played *pizzicato* at first, you will hear a pattern in nearly every other $\frac{4}{4}$ measure—one-two-three-rest. It gives the impression of a stolid band of men on horseback.

Then the clarinet solo (described in Chapter 6) begins. Evidently, something has disturbed Citrad's progress, and he has given up all pretense of advancing. He responds with an urgent, questioning motive, played by half the cellos and the first bassoon. The motive is too short even to be called a melody. In response, the clarinet is heard all by itself, answered by an equally extended phrase in the cellos. The rest of the orchestra is silent. It couldn't be clearer that a woman and a man are speaking to each other alone.

In the following passage, the love scene is under way. We can sense it in the lush string scoring, with its undulating cellos and soaring violins. The violins are doubled by the flutes, first oboes, and first clarinet—virtually the entire soprano contingent of the wind section. The orchestra no longer represents either group of warriors. Now the focus is entirely on Šárka and Citrad.

Then the dance begins, heralded by a martial rhythm in the brass and percussion. The irregular meter of this section suggests the dancing of increasingly sedated men. If you try dancing to this music, you can sense for yourself their awkwardness and the comedy. You will find that a predictable beat is

Chapter Objectives

● Identify ways program music can help to tell a story.

● Distinguish between program music and absolute music, and consider whether music really can communicate concrete meanings.

● Discuss several types of musical meaning, including symbolic meaning, the use of musical gestures, social meaning, and personal interpretation.

● Recount how different musical forms, such as ternary, theme and variations, and sonata, may convey meaning.

● Closely examine Beethoven's Fifth Symphony from the standpoints of meaning and musical legacy.

● Consider some of the implications of gender, sex, and sexuality in music.

Chronology of Music Discussed in this Chapter

ca. 1480s
Josquin des Prez p. 337
Missa "L'homme armé" super voces musicales

1781–1788
Wolfgang Amadeus Mozart
Serenade no. 10, Gran Partita K. 361 (1781), p. 339;
Symphony no. 40 in G minor, K. 550 (1788), p. 342

1807–1808
Ludwig van Beethoven p. 343
Symphony no. 5

1831–1835
Frédéric Chopin p. 340
Nocturne in A-flat major, op. 32, no. 2

often very hard to locate, and finally it disappears entirely. In the most comical effect in the piece, Smetana uses an extremely low bassoon note: the men are now snoring.

Šárka's clarinet is heard again, only now it is playing the impulsive music with which the tone poem began. Šárka is ready to take her revenge! In this section, the lush scoring of violins and upper winds returns to the enthusiastic accompaniment of the rest of the orchestra. Again, however, the opening music is heard, evened out into a regular, warlike $\frac{4}{4}$ meter. Several passages include trombones: The men are vigorously fighting back. Ultimately, though, they are vanquished, and the piece concludes with emphatic chords played triple forte by every single instrument in the orchestra.

Use the listening guide to follow the story described in the piece, or try to follow it on your own. It's really not that hard, because the changes are so cinematic. The standard cues are all there, and the composer expects his audience to hear them.

Types of Musical Meaning

Can music really tell a story? Some influential music critics have suggested that it cannot. One of the first was the 19th-century critic Eduard Hanslick (1825–1904) in his treatise *On the Beautiful in Music* (*Vom Musikalisch-Schönen*, 1854). Hanslick adamantly criticized composers who used their music to narrate. Music, he said, was about music, and its meaning was limited by its very nature to musical subjects and musical development. Composers who attempt to have music exceed its capabilities, he argued, diminish music rather than expand it. In this view, music unencumbered by story is superior, and it requires a greater intellectual commitment.

Hanslick's ideas are clearly a product of their time. He was reacting against what he saw as the excesses of Richard Wagner (1813–1883) and Franz Liszt (1811–1886), among others. In the early 20th century, music with no specified meaning—known as **absolute music**—attained an unprecedented degree of intellectual prestige. Narrative and programmatic music became correspondingly unfashionable, even though they remained popular with the public—perhaps because they provide something obvious to listen for, thus making music more immediately comprehensible.

Should music try to tell a story? A typical modern answer to this question might be that music can tell only musical stories, because music's subject is always music itself. Musical themes and ideas may indeed occupy roles like characters in stories, but what happens to them can only be understood in musical terms. No external references are required.

While many will be satisfied with this answer, it can also be argued that a great deal of what is called absolute music can be understood more richly and deeply by venturing beyond it. Such a view is supported by the writings of musicians from the 19th century, when much of this music was composed. These writers often suggested that music could convey meaning more directly than a written text, without resorting to pictorial representations like those found in *Šárka*.

This view rests to some extent on the very nature of musical expression. Music can seem to be about something—to tell a story—while avoiding many of the

Absolute Music: Instrumental music without a story, or program, specified by the composer.

The statue of Citrad and Šárka in Vyšehrad park in Prague. There is also a nature reserve outside of Prague named for the young woman alleged to have thrown herself from a cliff there. (© *Profimedia.CZ a.s./Alamy*)

LEARNING TO LISTEN GUIDE

TAKE NOTE OF FORM, MELODY, AND TEXTURE

What to Listen For: The musical cues that alert you to the central events in the story.

Streaming audio track 52.

Smetana: *Šárka*, from *Má vlast* (*My Homeland*)
Date: 1875
Instrumentation: Large orchestra
Key: A minor
Meter: $\frac{4}{4}$, also known as common time (four rapid beats per measure)
Core Repertory Connection: This music is also discussed in Chapter 3.

TIME	PROGRESSION	COMMENT
0:00	Introduction	The full orchestra plays the theme that represents the aggressive warrior maidens.
0:58	Contrasting section	A very different passage follows, with long, sustained notes in the strings suggesting love and tenderness.
1:12	Return	A return to the more aggressive tone heard earlier quickly follows.
1:21	Citrad rides in	This rocking music, which gradually grows louder, suggests the approach of Citrad and his horsemen.
2:22	Entry of the clarinet	The clarinet that represents Šárka throughout the piece is heard for the first time.
2:45	Interruption	The solo is punctuated by loud, full orchestral chords.
2:54	Solo	The clarinet is heard with no accompaniment.
3:13	Answer	The cello section is heard by itself, representing Citrad's response to Šárka's entreaty.
3:34	Love scene	A lush, fully orchestrated section shows Citrad falling for Šárka's charms.
5:12	Dance	A loud fanfare announces the start of the dance section.
7:00	Snore	A low bassoon note represents Citrad snoring as the dance music winds down.
7:20	Call to arms	A subdued but ominous summons marks the beginning of Šárka's revenge.
7:34	Šárka's battle cry	Over a quiet string tremolo, Šárka's clarinet is heard playing the ominous music with which the tone poem began.
8:07	Response	The full orchestra joins in, initiating the frenetic scene of slaughter with which the piece concludes.
8:58	Trombones	The men try to fight back . . .
9:14	Conclusion	. . . but they are relentlessly crushed.

specific associations that might limit that story's appeal. To put it a bit differently, many musical forms can be said to have a narrative contour, content less specific than that found in program music but inherent in the music rather than external to it. We will look at several examples of narrative contour later in this chapter. First, though, let us examine some of the ways in which the association of music with meaning has grown and developed.

Focus On
The Orchestra

Grove Music Online.

"Orchestra" has been used in a generic sense to mean any large grouping of instrumentalists. The word "orchestra," which in ancient Greece and Rome referred to the ground level of an amphitheatre, was revived in the Renaissance to designate the area immediately in front of the stage. In the early 17th century this became a favourite spot to place the instrumentalists who accompanied singing and dancing, and "orchestra" began to mean "the place where the musicians sit" (E. Phillips, *The New World of English Words*, London, 1658). By the 18th century the meaning of the word had been extended to the instrumentalists themselves and to their identity as an ensemble (J.-J. Rousseau, *Dictionnaire de musique*, Paris, 1768). (John Spitzer and Neal Zaslaw, *Grove Music Online*.)

The orchestra is used differently by different composers. Smetana uses a larger orchestra in *Šárka* than Beethoven does in his Fifth Symphony, which we shall examine later in this chapter. However, in the last movement of the Fifth Symphony, Beethoven adds some instruments, including piccolo, trombone, and contrabassoon, that were not used earlier in the piece. Thus, changing orchestral timbre becomes one of the features that articulate the Fifth Symphony's expressive content. Smetana, on the other hand, uses specific instruments to represent characters in the story, clearly linking timbre and narrative. Smetana's use of the orchestra thus strikes many listeners as more colorful than Beethoven's, which seems more classical and restrained.

A performance of Má vlast. The large orchestra, including extra percussion and harp, is typical of those used to perform late 19th-century orchestral works. (© *Pavel L Photo and Video*)

Symbolic Meaning

For hundreds of years, composers, too, have believed that music can have inherent meanings. Before the late Renaissance, that meaning was most often conveyed symbolically through commonly used melodies and procedures.

Josquin's *Missa "L'homme armé" super voces musicales* is based on a common Renaissance tune. The "armed man" was widely understood as a metaphor for Christ and his struggles with evil. Josquin does not simply quote the melody, though. Rather, he uses it as a musical scaffold in ways that are nearly impossible to hear. In the Gloria and Credo, he uses it this way and then repeats it in retrograde—backwards! In the Credo, it then appears once more in the correct direction. Over the course of the Mass, the melody moves upward in pitch, starting one note higher for each successive section. In the opening Kyrie and most of the other sections of the Mass, it appears, as was typical at the time, in the tenor voice, but allusions to it appear in the other voices as well. In the final Agnus Dei, however, it appears in the soprano voice. Here the very slow note values make it prominent but also quite hard to recognize.

In these ways, Josquin subtly illustrates an upward progression suggesting the ascendancy of Christ. The passages in retrograde, meanwhile, indicate that Christ both descends and ascends. Renowned scholar Craig Wright suggests that Josquin also refers to the "harrowing of hell," when virtuous souls from pre-Christian times are rescued and taken up to heaven. As with the Smetana, you have to be "in the know" to be fully aware of this meaning. But the symbolism is inherent in the music's structure.

Eduard Hanslick (1825–1904). He was an influential music critic and aesthetician, and a friend of Brahms—who did not compose program music. *(© INTERFOTO/Alamy)*

LEARNING TO LISTEN GUIDE

TAKE NOTE OF MELODY AND RHYTHM

What to Listen For: The very slow statement of the *L'homme armé* tune in the upper voice. (See Chapter 2 for the text and translation of the *L'homme armé* tune.)

Streaming audio track 5.

Josquin: *Missa "L'homme armé" super voces musicales*, Agnus Dei III
Date: ca. 1480s
Instrumentation: Four-part choir
Meter: Triple meter
Core Repertory Connection: Josquin's *Missa "L'homme armé" super voces musicales* is also discussed in Chapters 2 and 9.

TIME	SECTION	ORIGINAL TEXT	TRANSLATION	COMMENT
3:52	Phrase 1	*L'homme, l'homme, l'homme armé,*	The man, the man, the armed man,	Melodic activity in the lower voices largely obscures the melody and the division between the phrases.
4:47	Phrase 2	*L'homme armé,*	The armed man,	
4:59	Phrase 3	*L'homme armé doibt on doubter, doibt on doubter.*	The armed man is a fearsome sight, is a fearsome sight.	

TIME	SECTION	ORIGINAL TEXT	TRANSLATION	COMMENT
5:42	Phrase 4	*On a fait partout crier*	It has been proclaimed everywhere	
6:18	Phrase 5	*Que chascun se viengne armer*	That each person needs to be armed	
6:54	Phrase 6	*D'un haubregon de fer.*	With a suit of iron mail.	
7:30	Phrase 7	*L'homme, l'homme, l'homme armé,*	The man, the man, the armed man,	
8:34	Phrase 8	*L'homme armé,*	The armed man,	
9:00	Phrase 9	*L'homme armé doibt on doubter, doibt on doubter.*	The armed man is a fearsome sight, is a fearsome sight.	

Meaning Through Musical Gesture

In later music, composers often conveyed meaning in more obvious ways. As we saw in Chapter 2, Baroque composers like Monteverdi and Bach used strong contrasts and vivid musical imagery to communicate the content of their texts. In the Romantic period, Chopin used contrast and the repetition of a few central ideas to suggest an unfolding story in his Ballade in G minor, though no text was present.

Since the late 16th century, then, composers have often simply assumed that music can convey meanings very much like words and phrases in language. Once people started thinking this way, there was no going back. If you look hard enough at virtually any piece written in the last 400 years, you can find analogies between music and speech. These analogies can be just as evident in instrumental music as they are in the vocal music we discussed in the last two chapters.

Personal and Accrued Meaning

Many listeners also project meanings of a still more personal nature. Music, like literature and art, lends itself to a variety of interpretations. What is *Hamlet* about, and what, if anything, does it teach? The answers depend, in part, on us. The person performing the music may have completely different ideas about its meaning and expressive content than did the composer. Members of the audience, in turn, may bring their own ideas and hear something different in the music as it speaks to each of them in seemingly personal terms.

Even commonly shared interpretations of a piece of music may have nothing to do with the composer or the original context. For example, Aaron Copland (1900–1990) wrote *Fanfare for the Common Man* during World War II as a statement of resistance to European fascism. Used later as the theme for televised broadcasts of the Olympic games, this music has lost its original association for most listeners. This is an example of meaning that music can accrue through uses not intended by the composer. That doesn't mean that the composer would not have approved. The Olympics, which stand for international cooperation and harmony, are also a symbol of the "common man."

Across the Arts
Movies and Famous Music

One of the most famous examples of accrued meaning stems from director Stanley Kubrick's use of the opening music of Richard Strauss's tone poem *Also Sprach Zarathustra* (*Thus Spake Zarathustra*) in his film *2001: A Space Odyssey*. The music accompanies the sunrise over a black monolith, after which an ape uses a primitive tool, apparently for the first time. This scene has been imitated countless times.

While Strauss's music may not originally have been associated with apes and monoliths, it was composed to represent a sunrise and a revelation from God, which marks the beginning of Zarathustra's journeys. Thus, the accrued meaning is not that different from the composer's intended meaning. What Strauss did not intend is for the scene to be funny—as it becomes, for example, when the Kubrick scene is parodied in *Charlie and the Chocolate*

Factory and *The Simpsons Movie*. The humor in these later movies, though, depends on the expectation that the audience will associate this music with the familiar scene in *2001*.

The monolith scene from Kubrick's *2001: A Space Odyssey*. Kubrick used music by two composers named Strauss: *On the Beautiful Blue Danube*, used for long space sequences, was written by Viennese waltz composer Johann Strauss (no relation). (© *AF archive/Alamy*)

Musical Form and Meaning

Regardless of how we understand and interpret musical meaning, our perception of it is often closely related to music's form. Form, as we have seen, brings together every other aspect of the music. It may therefore suggest an overall narrative contour in pieces whose meaning is not specified, by the composer or by anybody else. Let's see how this works for some of the common musical structures introduced in Chapter 5.

Ternary Form: Mozart, Chopin, and Dvořák

The fifth movement of Mozart's *Gran Partita* uses ternary form to carry the work's narrative contour. This movement is titled *Romance* to suggest a fairy tale quality. Listen especially closely to the A section, which is extremely slow, with mostly conjunct melodic lines and major key harmonies. For the first three minutes, reality seems under restraint.

Then the B section begins, the key switches to minor, and the bubble is burst. The bustling bassoon part, combined with staccato articulations in the other instruments, calls forth the constant activity of the workaday world. This two-minute interlude doesn't sound like a new section of the same piece, but rather an intrusion that leaves its mark on the fairy tale world it disrupts.

When the A section returns, the original air of romance seems to reappear with it. Things are not so simple, though. As noted in Chapter 5, Mozart has omitted the repeats from the original A section. This removes our sense of a long, uninterrupted idyllic mood. It also allows room for a lengthy coda.

In the coda, which begins at 6:25, something intriguing happens. A steady, throbbing pulse in the double bass slowly moves upward in pitch. In the process, it creates dissonant harmonies that were simply not heard in the initial romance. This mood of insecurity continues for just over 30 seconds: long enough for it to lodge in the listener's mind. In fact, it is sufficient to overshadow the return of the previous mood in the movement's final measures. If you listen carefully, you will hear an undulating clarinet part in these measures that would have been completely out of place in the initial A section.

Mozart uses the ternary form here not just to suggest a disrupted idyll. He also seems to be hinting that the view of life represented by the A section has been permanently altered by the intrusion of a different reality. This use of the ternary form may have originated with Mozart. His biographer Maynard Solomon has even termed it "Trouble in Paradise." Many later composers have repeated the formula. On your listening list, for example, it also appears in Chopin's Nocturne in A-flat major, op. 32, no. 2. (See Learning to Listen Guide).

Not every piece in ternary form should be heard this way. Often, though, the contrasts between the sections are so pronounced that even a casual listener senses the presence of narrative; anyone can tell that the situation is changing.

LEARNING TO LISTEN GUIDE

TAKE NOTE OF HARMONY AND TEXTURE

What to Listen For: The simple narrative contour traced by the three sections of the piece, and the way the B section both disrupts and enriches the story.

Streaming audio track 44.

Chopin: Nocturne in A-flat major, op. 32, no. 2
Date: 1836–37
Instrumentation: Piano solo
Key: A-flat major
Meter: $\frac{4}{4}$, also known as common time (4 slow beats per measure)
Core Repertory Connection: This music is also discussed in Chapters 8 and 9.

TIME	PROGRESSION	COMMENT
0:00	A section (Paradise)	The major key harmonies and slow tempo make this section sound relatively happy and relaxed. Notice how the section is framed by the sustained chords at the beginning.
2:01	B section (Trouble)	A change to minor and the increasing harmonic richness (see Chapter 9) make this section more serious and dramatic.
3:31	A section (Paradise, but with a difference)	When the A section returns, the dynamic level is much louder than before, making the music sound passionate rather than relaxed. The sustained chords from the beginning of the piece reappear at the end, finishing the frame of the entire piece.

Dvořák's *Slavonic Dance*, for example, also presents a strong contrast—this time in the opposite direction.

Compared to the minor-key A section, the B section (see Chapter 5) sounds bright and perky, with much more pronounced dance rhythms. The mood seems to shift from somber to happy. The A section then returns, and with it the original mood. The coda briefly revives the music of the B section, only to have it submerge in a final recollection of the A material. This is not "trouble in paradise" but an opposite kind of scenario—which could perhaps be seen as "encouragement that fails."

Still, the material of the B section has not entirely gone away. The narrative contour is not a simple return but rather a progression of emotional states. We are left in flux, even if transformation is never quite achieved.

LEARNING TO LISTEN GUIDE

TAKE NOTE OF FORM

What to Listen For: A kind of inverse version of ternary form, from the point of view of expression.

Streaming audio track 53.
Interactive Listening Guide ILG-13.

Dvořák: *Slavonic Dance* in E minor, op. 72, no. 10
Date: 1886
Instrumentation: Originally for piano four-hands, arranged here for orchestra
Key: E minor
Meter: $\frac{3}{4}$ (three moderately slow beats per measure)
Form: Ternary (ABA) with coda
Core Repertory Connection: This music is also discussed in Chapters 1, 7, and 8.

TIME	PROGRESSION	COMMENT
0:00	A section	The first part of the piece is wistful, with its minor-key melody and moderately slow tempo.
2:16	B section (Encouragement)	The B section presents a strong contrast. It moves to a major key with faster and more vigorous rhythms. As a result, the music seems to cheer up.
4:10	A section (Failure)	The original music then returns. Expressively, the music of the middle section is overshadowed, since the music of the A section both precedes and follows it.
5:23	Coda (Final struggle)	In the last section, the B music briefly returns, only to disappear in a final statement of the A music. Whatever encouragement was suggested by the middle section has clearly not succeeded.

Variation Form: A Character's Many Moods

Variation form, discussed in Chapter 5, can be compared to a modified strophic form, only without a text. Can a series of variations, then, like a strophic song,

Don Quixote attacking a flock of sheep (which he perceives as a hostile army), by Gustave Doré (1832–1883). Richard Strauss illustrated the bleating of the sheep with tone clusters: highly dissonant combinations of notes that violated the traditional rules of harmony. Effects like this struck commentators like Hanslick as unmusical. (© *INTERFOTO/Alamy*)

tell a story? Some composers have thought that it could. Richard Strauss (1864–1949) wrote an orchestral work titled *Don Quixote*, which, in essentially a series of variations, tells the story of the legendary Spanish knight errant. Vincent d'Indy (1851–1931) wrote orchestral variations narrating the Assyrian legend of Istar descending to the underworld. These works, however, are program music and as such exceptions to the form. Most sets of variations tell no explicit story. Hanslick might have argued that Strauss and d'Indy stretched the variation form beyond recognition.

Nevertheless, many sets of variations, like pieces in ternary form, suggest a standard underlying plot, with an imagined human actor. When the theme appears, this character is introduced. We then see the character in a variety of moods that may progress from lighthearted to more serious, culminating in a slow variation that takes much longer to perform than any of the others. At last the character shrugs off solemnity and ends up even more cheerful than before.

In the fifth movement of Mozart's *Gran Partita*, for example, one could easily imagine a story like this. Perhaps two friends of the opposite sex set out for a picnic on a pleasant day. Chapter 5 already described their imagined conversation. The day is so lovely that at first they are overcome by enthusiasm (variation 1). They then find a nice spot and settle down to eat (variation 2). Taking out their food, they enjoy a succession of different items (variation 3). It suddenly starts to rain, and they must quickly seek shelter (variation 4). Finding a safe place (the sustained chord at the end of variation 4), they begin to notice how much they are enjoying each other's company (variation 5). The sun comes back out, though, and they decide that they are having too much fun to "get serious" (variation 6).

Perhaps Mozart never did have such a story in mind. Without a doubt, however, he wrote music suited to its outline. And many listeners want to hear some kind of story when they listen to sustained pieces of instrumental music. The ternary form and theme and variations suggest a limited range of narratives and, in this way, encourage an imaginative listener to interpret the music.

Sonata Form: The Musical Essay

Sonata form is especially broad and flexible. As we saw in Chapter 5, this form, too, can be understood as a narrative in which a character is introduced (exposition), complications ensue (development), and the complications are resolved (recapitulation). Sonata form also resembles a common essay form. Maybe you received this advice on writing, at some point: "Tell them what you're going to say, say it, and then remind them of what you've said." If that advice still makes sense, you can see why many composers are drawn to write in sonata form.

Consider the first movement of Mozart's Symphony no. 40. The minor key tonality helps create a deeply serious mood. So do the dynamic and timbral contrasts and the incessant development of the opening motive. In the first movement of the *Gran Partita*, on the other hand, the mood is much more relaxed. Here the major tonality and the more expansive thematic material convey a leisurely discussion among the instruments. The slow introduction carefully prepares us. It is easy to imagine social interactions leading to the picnic in the fifth movement. The first movement of Haydn's B-flat major quartet, Op. 64, no. 3, is even lighter in tone, with scarcely a serious moment.

Of course, it is not necessary to imagine a story to enjoy these pieces. With the beginning of the Romantic period, though, came a new awareness of how musical forms can narrate. We'll look next at a single, powerful example, one of the best-known and most frequently performed pieces of music ever written.

Beethoven's Symphony No. 5

With Beethoven's Symphony no. 5 in C minor, op. 67, we encounter something new. Now musical meanings forge connections between the movements in a large-scale composition. The idea of this symphony as the record of a triumphant struggle goes back so far in history that it has become a part of the work. Without it, many would have had trouble knowing how to listen to a piece of music this long and so full of dramatic contrasts.

In History
Beethoven's Symphony no. 5

Ludwig van Beethoven's Symphony no. 5 marks a unique moment in history. Completed in 1808, it premiered in Vienna in December of that year at a concert arranged by the composer. Just over four years before, in May 1804, Napoleon became emperor of France, and war still raged. The recent French and American revolutions stirred awe and fear, and so did the vast political changes that came in their wake.

Rarely has a composer been so closely associated with important historical events. Beethoven, an early admirer of Napoleon, lived through the French occupation of Vienna in 1805 and invasion of Austria in 1809. He was also an active bystander at the Congress of Vienna in 1814, which celebrated Napoleon's defeat. (This was the high point of Beethoven's public success, much of which centered on a notorious potboiler—now little known—called *Wellington's Victory at the Battle of Victoria*.) He did not live, however, to see the next round of revolutions and the subsequent reforms. His own political views have often been seen as progressive—and even revolutionary. He had dedicated his Symphony no. 3, the "Eroica," to Napoleon. When Napoleon had himself crowned emperor, Beethoven angrily scratched his name from the title page.

He did, nevertheless, use aristocratic patronage to his advantage. Without the friendship and financial support of wealthy and influential friends, Beethoven might not have had the freedom to forge his style. He might never have created the large-scale works that have cemented his reputation. Works like the Symphony no. 5 and the "Eroica" baffled traditional audiences but appealed strongly to those who saw themselves as progressive, modern artists and connoisseurs. Among the latter were E.T.A. Hoffmann, a key figure in the German Romantic movement, and the Archduke Rudolph, younger brother of the Austrian emperor.

Hoffmann, writing in 1810 in the *Allgemeine musikalische Zeitung*—the most widely read music journal of its time—described the Symphony no. 5 as "one of the most important works of that master who no one will now deny belongs among the first rank of instrumental composers." Hoffmann's words, his glowing descriptions of Beethoven's music and its emotional power, were often repeated and helped it gain broad recognition. This symphony's primal strength and optimistic trajectory both frightened and inspired its first hearers, many of whom stood either to gain or to lose from the revolutionary change that was sweeping their world.

Perhaps the most important thing to understand about Beethoven's Fifth Symphony is that it reveals the extent of the composer's mastery of musical form. That mastery is not simply a matter of following rules and fleshing out established frameworks. Leonard Bernstein, one of the greatest all-around American musicians of the 20th century, put it this way:

> Many, many composers have been able to write heavenly tunes and respectable fugues. Some composers can orchestrate the C-major scale so that it sounds like a masterpiece, or fool with notes so that a harmonic novelty is achieved. But this is all mere dust—nothing compared to the magic ingredient sought by them all: *the inexplicable ability to know what the next note has to be* [emphasis in original]. Beethoven had this gift in a degree that leaves them all panting in the rear guard . . . Form is only an empty word, a shell, without this gift of inevitability; a composer can write a string of perfectly molded sonata-allegro movements, with every rule obeyed, and still suffer from bad form. Beethoven broke all the rules, and turned out pieces of breathtaking rightness.

Bernstein's description, extravagant as it is, may seem to suggest that Beethoven's music is self-contained, referring to nothing beyond itself. As we have seen in this chapter, though, the way that a piece of music is put together is often a key to its meaning. If ever there was a piece that shows the use of expressive contour, it is this symphony. This music, said Hoffmann:

> Opens up to us the kingdom of the gigantic and the immeasurable. Glowing beams shoot through this kingdom's deep night, and we become aware of shadows that surge up and down, enclosing us more and more narrowly and annihilating everything within us, leaving only the pain of that interminable longing, in which every pleasure that had quickly arisen with sounds of rejoicing sinks away and founders, and we live on . . . only in this pain, which, consuming love, hope, and joy within itself, seeks to burst our breast asunder with a full-voiced consonance of all the passions.

Although Hoffmann speaks here of Beethoven's instrumental music in general, the tone of these words is almost perfectly suited to a description of the Fifth Symphony, which was the subject of his review. Listen to the first movement, in particular, and you will hear violent contrasts and music of painful intensity. This experience was apparently so overwhelming for Hoffmann that it didn't matter that the emotions he experienced were primarily negative ones: pain, longing, annihilation.

There is another aspect of the music, though, that also struck listeners almost from the beginning. This is the fact that the symphony as a whole shows not just tragedy but triumph, not just painful emotions but victorious ones as well. Furthermore, it illustrates a transition between these opposing worlds. This contour is so powerful precisely because it is universal. Not everyone can identify with Beethoven's struggle with his deafness; in fact, of all possible human struggles, this is perhaps the one that active music listeners are least likely to understand in personal terms. Everyone, though, can understand what Beethoven faced in being confronted with the irretrievable loss of his most precious possession—watching it gradually being taken away from him and knowing that he would never get it back. For some, this will resonate personally as a love story, for others, as a confrontation with spiritual doubt. However, the human need to overcome adversity and emerge victorious resonates deeply in each individual soul. Everybody can read his or her life story into Beethoven's Fifth Symphony.

Beethoven's Fifth: A Guided Tour

Like so many symphonies, the Fifth consists of four movements: fast-slow-moderate-fast. The first and last movements are in sonata form. The second movement is a combination of rondo and variation form, and the third is in the expected ternary form. Yet closer examination reveals features that place the symphony "outside the box." The third and fourth movements are joined together without a break. Part of the third movement briefly returns in the course of the fourth, as though the two movements were a single extended piece.

The third movement, furthermore, is not quite in the expected ABA form of a minuet or scherzo. Rather, the A section returns drastically transformed. If you saw the film *Howards End*, you may recall that this movement is played on a piano at a public lecture. In the film, the speaker compares the A section of the movement to goblins. By the same analogy, the B section could be a circus performance—"elephants dancing," in E.M. Forster's own words! The return of the A, though, suggests that the sinister goblins are sneaking back. What was loud and fully orchestrated before becomes quiet and furtive. This is neither "trouble in paradise" nor "encouragement that fails." It is more like "Boo! Ha ha, just kidding! Scared you! No, wait a minute, there really *is* something scary here."

What is really going on in this symphony? We have already examined the process of motivic development in the first movement (see Chapter 8). Let us now take a movement-by-movement trip through this remarkable work, as recorded by George Szell and the Cleveland Orchestra. We will use all the active listening skills that we have developed in the preceding chapters.

The First Movement

The first movement of Beethoven's Fifth Symphony shows the drama and passion that music's narrative contour makes possible. Its pattern of alternating restraint and mounting intensity outstrips the contour of sonata form. It is hard to listen to this music passively; it all but demands active listening, which generates a more deeply emotional response as well. If you *really* listen to this music, you may well find the experience overwhelming.

Exposition: As E.T.A. Hoffmann recognized, two outstanding features of the Fifth Symphony's first movement help define it for the listener. First, the opening motive—about which Beethoven is supposed to have said, "Thus fate pounds at the gate"—is insistently repeated. The rhythm, three shorts and a long, is heard so often that it is part of the atmosphere of this music. Second, despite this obsessive rhythm, the music alternates between passages of stagnation and passages of mounting intensity. Each statement of the "fate" motive at the beginning of the movement concludes with a fermata, a long held note. Fitful stops and starts mark the following passage, which terminates in a sustained note in the violins. The opening motive and the fermata are then repeated.

In this scene from the film *Howard's End.* E. M. Forster's description of the powerful effect of Beethoven's 5th symphony from the original novel is presented as a public lecture, to which these two characters listen intently. (© Moviestore collection Ltd/Alamy)

Next begins a crescendo, leading to a dramatic pause followed by the second theme. The orchestration and the minor key intensify the powerful rhythm. The crescendo is not merely a transition: it grinds the rhythm deeply into the listener's consciousness. This is perhaps what Hoffmann meant by shadows annihilating everything within us.

The second theme, although in the expected major key, is only a momentary contrast. It begins by repeating the opening rhythm, this time played by the horns. Soon the orchestra builds up again until a triumphant major-key tutti (a passage for full orchestra) and a final barrage of three shorts and a long conclude the exposition. George Szell observes Beethoven's repeat, so this whole succession of events is heard again.

Development: As we saw in Chapter 8, the development section starts with another fitful, isolated statement of the opening motive. The orchestra then begins another lengthy buildup that peaks about halfway through the movement. Now the music once again seems to bog down. A long passage of isolated chords marked *sempre più p* seems to support Hoffmann's image of pleasure sinking away and foundering. In fact, Beethoven extends this passage for so long that he achieves a seemingly impossible feat: When the recapitulation arrives, the fitful opening motive sounds like a new beginning.

Recapitulation: As we expect, the recapitulation repeats the events of the exposition with minor changes. Most notably, instead of the sustained note in the violins heard earlier, the first oboe plays a brief solo. When the second theme reappears, though, it does not, as in Mozart's Symphony no. 40, shift into the prevailing minor key. Instead, it remains in the major. Perhaps the conflicts are not yet resolved after all. Otherwise, everything proceeds as expected until what should be the final barrage of three shorts and a long.

Coda: So far, Beethoven has followed sonata form. At this point, however, he throws away the script. By superimposing a series of crescendos, he has already given the familiar plot outline a deeper structure. Each of those crescendos has held something in reserve; there was always the sense that the music could go even further. And in the coda, it does just that. You might say that the tail (*coda* in Italian) ends up wagging the dog! Despite a few fits and starts, the pounding intensity of the movement sounds unstoppable.

Furthermore, it seems evident now that the movement is going to end tragically, in C minor; the change to C major suggested earlier will have to wait until the finale for its fulfillment. Indeed, the only thing the music needs to continue its tragic intensity is some new thematic material—and that is just what Beethoven provides. All that can stop this inexorable momentum is a return of the fitful beginning. Now, reappearing for the last time, it punctuates a story that has us gasping for breath. But the punctuation is not final.

Not every listener will agree on what this movement means. Unlike Smetana's *Šárka*, this is not program music, with a specified story line. It does seem clear, though, that the subject is tragedy rather than comedy, struggle rather than acceptance. Beethoven establishes this outline by using a minor key, pounding rhythms, strong contrasts, and wide-ranging dynamics. At the end of the first movement,

LEARNING TO LISTEN GUIDE

TAKE NOTE OF FORM

What to Listen For: The continuous, mounting dynamism of the music as it flows through the formal divisions.

Streaming audio track 36.
Interactive Listening Guide ILG-9.

Beethoven: Symphony no. 5 in C minor, op. 67
I: Allegro con brio
Date: 1807–8
Instrumentation: Orchestra
Key: C minor
Meter: $\frac{2}{4}$ (two rapid beats per measure)
Form: Sonata form with coda
Core Repertory Connection: Beethoven's Symphony no. 5 is also discussed in Chapters 3 and 8.

TIME	PROGRESSION	COMMENT
EXPOSITION		
0:00	First theme	The opening motive announces the subject of the symphony: "Thus fate pounds at the gate." The passage that follows culminates with a dramatic pause; the violins continue to play a sustained note after the other instruments drop out.
0:19	First theme repeats	The opening motive is restated, then extended into a transitional passage. This time, all the instruments stop together at the end.
0:44	Second theme	The horn states a version of the opening motive, which is extended to form the contrasting second theme. A steady orchestral buildup follows.
1:07	Concluding section	A barrage from the full orchestra concludes the exposition triumphantly.
1:28	Exposition repeat	Everything heard so far is literally repeated.
DEVELOPMENT		
2:55	Opening motive	The opening motive is repeated emphatically, marking the beginning of the development section.
2:59	Motivic development	A short section mirrors the theme heard at the beginning of the movement, but with a more open-ended continuation.
3:17	Heightened intensity	The motive is worked up through repetition at higher and higher pitches, leading to a series of repeated notes that recall the opening.
3:31	Major thematic statement	The horn theme from 0:44 returns in the violins.
3:42	Breakup of the theme	The motive begins to appear in smaller and smaller units.
4:04	Dramatic contrast	The full orchestra enters with a more complete statement of the theme, followed by more pianissimo single chords. The music seems to bog down.
4:12	Definitive return	The opening theme returns in the full orchestra, preparing for the recapitulation.
RECAPITULATION		
4:18	First theme	The opening motive returns in the original key.
4:35	Oboe solo	This short cadenza in the oboe replaces the sustained violin note that marked the parallel spot in the exposition.
5:13	Second theme	The second theme returns in the major rather than the expected minor.

TIME	PROGRESSION	COMMENT
CODA		
5:59	Extension	The buildup continues past the point where it stopped in the exposition.
6:30	New theme	Beethoven surprises the listener by introducing thematic material not previously heard.
7:06	Final statement of the opening motive	After this summation, the movement ends quickly.

a possibly life-threatening struggle is under way, and it has not yet concluded. At best, fate has been beaten into temporary submission. Unlike the first movements of many earlier symphonies, this one could not really stand as an independent composition. It is more like an overture: the introduction to a drama as yet unresolved.

The Second Movement

The second movement continues the story, but with a much more relaxed approach. After the dramatic beginning, the curtain now seems to have risen on a pleasant outdoor scene. (Beethoven's next symphony, the Pastoral, actually provides images of country life; its slow movement is titled "Scene by the Brook.") The violas and cellos play a lyrical, major-key melody unlike anything that has been heard so far in the symphony. Indeed, you may now realize that, except for a few brief passages in the first movement, you have not previously heard anything that could really be described as a tune.

Very soon, though, the picture grows more complicated. This movement cannot stand alone either. The orchestra begins to play echoes of the first movement. Then, suddenly, the full orchestra enters *fortissimo*, and the horns and trumpets, doubled by the oboes—all traditionally outdoor instruments—convert the rhythm of three shorts and a long into a military-sounding fanfare. The battle is joined!

This movement only hints at the struggle suggested in the first movement. Following the fanfare, a mysterious, hovering *pianissimo* passage leads to the return of the melody that began the second movement. Once again, it is played by the violas and cellos. This time, though, the jerky rhythm of the opening statement is smoothed out into a stream of flowing sixteenth notes. Thus, the form of the movement so far can be described as ABA'. Something seems to be happening to the melody, suggesting an ongoing story rather than a simple ternary or rondo form.

Then the military fanfare returns, but with a more active accompaniment in the strings. This leads in turn to a faster version of the opening melody, played this time by the first violins in 32nd notes. The form is now ABA'B'A", as though Beethoven were combining the rondo form with the theme and variations form. Why not? Remember Leonard Bernstein's statement: "Beethoven broke all the rules, and turned out pieces of breathtaking rightness." Rightness is the only standard here—rightness both within this movement and within the narrative contour of the symphony as a whole, to which it so clearly refers.

This time, accordingly, the military fanfare does not arrive when expected. Instead, the music briefly seems to lose its way. It is as though the hero or heroine of the story has temporarily lost resolve. Furthermore, when that resolve does return (call it B″), it just as quickly disappears, and the music appears lost once again. Finally, after much aimless wandering, the A theme triumphantly reemerges, hurled out *fortissimo* by the full orchestra (A‴).

This is a cathartic moment, and you may feel at this point that the course of the music so far finally makes sense. It is more than simply a rondo or a theme and variations; it is like the gradual assembling of a human soul. Now, its resolve rediscovered and thoroughly assimilated, that soul proclaims itself ready for the struggle still to come. Beethoven then lingers over the theme in the coda, as though

---

LEARNING TO LISTEN GUIDE

TAKE NOTE OF MELODY

What to Listen For: How the opening theme gradually acquires more weight and significance by returning repeatedly in new and different forms.

Streaming audio track 37.

Beethoven: Symphony no. 5 in C minor, p. 67
II: Andante con moto
Date: 1807–8
Instrumentation: Orchestra
Key: A-flat major
Meter: $\frac{3}{8}$ (three moderately slow beats per measure)
Form: ABA'B'A"B"A‴Coda
Core Repertory Connection: Beethoven's Symphony no. 5 is also discussed in Chapters 3 and 8.

TIME	PROGRESSION	COMMENT
A		
0:00	First theme	The lyrical main theme is stated, beginning in the violas and cellos.
0:52	Transition	The theme is extended, leading to a sudden change in dynamics.
B		
1:13	Second theme	The powerful second theme recalls the "three shorts and a long" rhythm of the first movement.
1:30	Transition	A muted echo of the second theme concludes the first part of the movement.
A'		
1:57	Restatement of the first theme	A more flowing version of the theme appears, once again beginning in the violas and cellos.
2:48	Transition	The passage at 0:52 is repeated, with a more active accompaniment.
B'		
3:09	Restatement of the second theme	The second theme is repeated, also with a more active accompaniment.
3:25	Transition	Even the muted echo of the theme now has a more active accompaniment, making it sound tenser.

TIME	PROGRESSION	COMMENT
A″		
3:51	Second restatement of the first theme	A faster flowing version of the first theme begins, again in the violins and cellos.
4:27	Counterstatement	Instead of the expected transition, the flowing version of the theme is restated, forte, by the cellos and basses.
4:54	Uncertainty	The music bogs down, seemingly uncertain about what will happen next.
B″		
5:50	Surprise!	The second theme suddenly appears yet again, along with the fortissimo dynamics that accompany it. But then the uncertainty returns.
6:36	Another surprise	A minor key version of the opening theme emerges.
A‴		
7:17	Final restatement of the first theme	After a dramatic buildup, the main theme emerges triumphantly from the full orchestra.
CODA		
8:08	Breakup of the theme	In a concluding section, the theme seems to be disassembled, so that only small sections of it are heard.

reluctant to let go. You can trace these steps by following the *Learning to Listen* guide through this mini-epic of a movement.

The Third Movement

The third movement reintroduces the full intensity of the struggle heard in the first. This time, the main theme emerges in the A section, like one of Hoffmann's surging shadows (see above). The first phrase is played by cellos and basses alone, answered by the upper strings and lower winds. This process is then repeated with a longer version of the opening phrase. Then, fate once again pounds at the gate. The horns repeatedly proclaim, *fortissimo*, the three-shorts-and-a-long rhythm, with the long note emphasized by chords in the strings. This is not an exact quotation from the first movement. The rhythm is heard at first on a single note, and because the meter is now $\frac{3}{4}$, it is able to plod along doggedly (one-two-three one-two-three, etc.) without the fitful stops and starts heard before. The reference, though, is clear. As the full orchestra takes up the theme, it is easy to imagine that Beethoven wants you to recall the most dynamic sections of the first movement.

Such powerful music in a third movement is quite extraordinary. In a classical symphony, this movement was traditionally a minuet, a stylized dance movement of courtly elegance or gentle humor cast in ternary form. At this point, Beethoven often wrote a somewhat more substantial but still light-hearted movement titled **scherzo**, which means "joke" in Italian. The third movement of the Fifth Symphony, like a scherzo or minuet, follows a ternary form and triple meter—but it is titled simply *Allegro*. Could this be because it is more serious than either of the other two designations imply?

Scherzo: "Joke," in Italian. A movement in ternary form and triple meter that sometimes takes the place of the minuet in multimovement works such as symphonies or sonatas.

As the movement continues, its seriousness only intensifies. The initial phrase in the cellos and basses continues to be extended, alternating with pounding statements by the full orchestra. Then the music grows ominously quiet as the two ideas mix. A double, *fortissimo* restatement of three shorts and a long, followed by an eerie *piano* extension, concludes the A section. For now, fate seems not only to have pounded at the gate but also to have gained access to the fortress.

The B section that follows can be heard as comic relief. Beethoven gives an exposed solo to the double basses, something that was extremely rare in orchestral music up to this time. The cellos and bassoons join in, followed by the rest of the string section and, eventually, the winds and brass. The basses then begin again . . . and again and again. These rapid, repeated passages are meant to sound as if the bass players are struggling with their parts. (It's actually difficult for a modern orchestra ever to sound this way, because of the high level of technical proficiency, greatly increased since Beethoven's time.) Eventually, the full orchestra once again joins in, and the crisis is resolved.

As we have seen (Chapter 5), a typical minuet and trio movement is written in ABA form with two internal repeats in each section. It might perhaps be more accurately described as aabbccddaabb, with the lowercase letters representing smaller, repeated sections within the overall form. Beethoven at this point does something unusual. (As you should realize by now, the unusual was usual with him.) He writes out the repeat of the second half of the B section (small d) rather than simply placing repeat marks around it. Once again, the basses play their introduction. This time, however, they grow quieter with each repetition, as though afraid of being heard too clearly. As if to spare them further embarrassment, Beethoven then rescores the passage that follows for the winds. The dynamic level is *pianissimo*, and for several measures, the strings drop out entirely. This sounds like a fitful, uncertain echo of the earlier statement of this passage. The first time, the passage ended with a strong, affirmative conclusion. Now the passage simply peters out, with a few disoriented-sounding *pizzicato* notes in the cellos and basses. These instruments then repeat their shadowlike theme from the beginning of the movement, and the return of the A section is under way.

Yet here in the A' section, things do not go according to script either. What had been sustained notes in the A section are now separated by rests. Instead of being answered, as before, by the upper strings and lower winds, the opening phrase is answered only by the clarinets, bassoons, and horns. When the cellos and basses repeat their phrase, they play it pizzicato, doubled by the first bassoon and answered by the upper strings, likewise playing pizzicato. When the rhythm of three shorts and a long appears, it is not played fortissimo by the horns but pianissimo by a single clarinet.

Fate is no longer pounding at the gate, only tapping at the shutter. The effect is not so much funny, as in the B section, as uncanny—what German writers at the time called *unheimlich*. The entire repeat of the A section unfolds as a kind of ghastly parody of its bold first appearance. It finally ends on an inconclusive harmony—it sounds as though the music will return to the tonic, but the harmony moves to a chord two notes down instead, leaving the listener's expectations in suspense. The anticipated final resolution is denied, and for close to a minute, the music hangs suspended in time, as if uncertain how to proceed.

LEARNING TO LISTEN GUIDE

TAKE NOTE OF TIMBRE AND TEXTURE

What to Listen For: Beethoven's manipulation of the standard ABA third-movement form to produce unusual and disturbing effects.

Streaming audio track 38.

Beethoven: Symphony no. 5 in C minor, op. 67
III: Allegro
Date: 1807–8
Instrumentation: Orchestra
Key: C minor
Meter: $\frac{3}{4}$ (three rapid beats per measure)
Form: Ternary (ABA') with coda
Core Repertory Connection: Beethoven's Symphony no. 5 is also discussed in Chapters 3 and 8.

TIME	PROGRESSION	COMMENT
A SECTION		
0:00	First theme	The opening musical idea is stated by the cellos and basses, pianissimo, and answered by the upper strings and winds.
0:19	Contrasting idea	A motive reminiscent of the "three shorts and a long" from the first movement is stated fortissimo by the horns.
0:40	Restatement	The cellos and basses restate the first theme at a lower pitch than before, making it sound even darker.
1:03	Contrasting idea	"Three shorts and a long" is now hurled out forte by the full orchestra, powerfully recalling the first movement.
1:24	Development	In this section, the two musical ideas stated so far work together.
1:38	Concluding theme	A faster, running idea in the violins concludes the first section of the movement.
1:52	Summation	There is a final series of statements of "three shorts and a long."
B SECTION		
1:58	Contrasting idea	A strongly contrasting theme in C major is introduced by the double basses alone, then imitated by the other strings, with support from the winds.
2:14	Repeat	The previous section is repeated note for note, plus a concluding flourish.
2:30	Continuation	The basses again begin and are imitated by the other strings, leading to a rousing climax by the full orchestra.
2:57	Varied repeat	The previous section is repeated, but this time the repeat is not literal. Can you hear the difference?
A SECTION VARIED		
3:29	Repeat of the opening	The opening of the entire movement returns, but once again, the repeat is not literal. Can you hear the difference?
CODA		
4:46	Coda	This hovering, concluding passage, in which the harmony doesn't resolve as expected, prepares the transition to the finale.

What has happened in this movement? It would not be too much of a stretch to say that fate has been engaged by the resources of the human spirit. As you will recall, in the A section, the struggle was directly joined for the first time. In the B section, attempts at humor and defiance ultimately failed. Now fate seems to be licking its wounds. As suggested earlier, though, deeper and scarier implications are even more evident than before. The outcome of the struggle hangs in the balance. For close to a minute, with the timpani pounding away on an increasingly dissonant C (the tonic of the entire symphony), the music remains dark, tense, and uncertain. Then there is a dramatic crescendo, and the finale begins.

The Fourth Movement: Finale

The start of the finale of Beethoven's Fifth Symphony is one of the most stunning moments in all of music. The orchestra is now joined by piccolo, contrabassoon, and three trombones, and every instrument plays fortissimo. The C minor tonality that dominated the first and third movements of the symphony yields to C major, and the theme sounds like a military fanfare, this time proclaiming victory. As the music continues, the violins soar triumphantly into their uppermost range, doubled by the upper winds and backed up by powerful, repeated rhythms in the brass. The contrast with the end of the previous movement could not be more complete. Even the most casual listener can hear that something momentous has occurred. If you have identified with the soul oppressed by fate, you can now experience a sense of release and rejoice in the power of the human spirit. The expressive contour of the symphony as a whole is one of affirmation and victory over fate.

As the finale continues, the central rhythm of three shorts and a long is heard once again, but this time it is fast-paced and affirmative. Beethoven chose, though, to write a full-scale sonata form movement, and in the development section, things get a bit dicier. Abundant minor key sonorities are heard again, and the brass instruments begin to sound ominous rather than affirmative. It seems that dark fate has not been entirely vanquished.

The dark side never does disappear, of course. Beethoven seems to suggest here that the battles of the human spirit are not easily won, as he was personally all too aware. Surprisingly, the "uncanny" portion of the third movement returns, too— only to be defeated once again as the finale reaches its recapitulation. And from this point on, the rejoicing continues until the end.

Beethoven extends the conclusion in another "tail wagging the dog" coda. He seems to be thumbing his nose at the menacing powers that had loomed so large earlier. For over two minutes—the length of the development section—the coda surges on, becoming faster and faster until the force of the music appears unstoppable. Only then does the symphony conclude.

Legacy

It is hard to imagine a clearer example of narrative contour. The struggle against fate presented in the opening movement and continued in the next two is resolved in the brilliant affirmation of the finale. In fact, the effect established in Beethoven's Fifth Symphony is so powerful that many later composers have

LEARNING TO LISTEN GUIDE

TAKE NOTE OF MELODY AND HARMONY

What to Listen For: The way the finale, which contrasts strongly with the preceding movements, provides a triumphant conclusion to the entire symphony's narrative contour.

Streaming audio track 39.

Beethoven: Symphony no. 5 in C minor, op. 67
IV: Allegro
Date: 1807–8
Instrumentation: Orchestra
Key: C major
Meter: $\frac{4}{4}$, also known as common time (four rapid beats per measure)
Form: Sonata form with an interpolation and coda
Core Repertory Connection: Beethoven's Symphony no. 5 is also discussed in Chapters 3 and 8.

TIME	PROGRESSION	COMMENT
EXPOSITION		
0:00	First theme	The finale begins without a break from the previous movement and with a powerful fanfare theme stated fortissimo by the full orchestra. This includes trombones, which have not been heard so far in the piece.
0:33	Second theme	Though the music is still in the home (tonic) key, a new theme is introduced that is, in many ways, a continuation of the first.
0:58	Contrasting third theme	Now in a new, but closely related, key, this theme once again recalls the "three shorts and a long" rhythm, at a very fast tempo.
1:25	Concluding fourth theme	A more final-sounding theme rounds off the exposition.
DEVELOPMENT		
2:00	Contrasting theme	The development section begins with a repeat of the "three shorts and a long" contrasting theme. It quickly becomes more dramatic, recalling the emotional world of the first movement.
2:58	Preparation	This long section on a stable harmony seems to prepare the return of the first theme.
3:30	Surprise	Instead, the music of the third movement returns—right in the middle of the finale!
RECAPITULATION		
4:09	Return	When the recapitulation does arrive, it closely parallels the exposition.
CODA		
6:09	A familiar rhythm	To kick off a tail-wagging-the-dog conclusion, Beethoven returns once again to three shorts and a long.
6:40	Another surprise	And you thought the piece was over!
7:08	Growing impetus	This time for sure?
7:32	Thematic statement	The concluding theme from the exposition returns, apparently to round off the piece.
7:47	Repeat of the opening	The opening fanfare returns for the final time, at twice its original speed.
7:55	Concluding chords	Nearly a minute of powerful orchestral chords serves to conclude the movement, and the symphony as a whole.

imitated it. The pattern of *per aspera ad astra* (through bitterness to the stars) appears again in symphonies by Robert Schumann (1810–1856), Johannes Brahms (1833–1897), Anton Bruckner (1824–1896), Gustav Mahler (1860–1911), and countless others. In some of their symphonies, Berlioz, Brahms, and Tchaikovsky even offer a backhanded tribute by deliberately contradicting the scenario and ending on a tragic note. One can hear versions of a musical struggle in many other works as well, including Ives's Violin Sonata no. 4 and Stravinsky's *Symphony of Psalms.* The former concludes with a short movement based on a hymn (*Shall We Gather at the River?*), while the latter ends with a setting of Psalm 150, in which the composer portrayed a vision of Elijah's chariot ascending to the heavens.

Narrative Contour and Gender

Not all nonprogrammatic music uses narrative contour so clearly. As we saw earlier, in fact, many see lack of concrete meaning as a strength of music, not a weakness. For them, the less defined the narrative contour, the more musical the results. Beethoven's musical language may seem clear-cut, but it, too, is open to different interpretations. Even his shattering climaxes can be seen as a metaphor for a wide range of experiences—including, of course, sex. The influential musicologist Susan McClary suggests that metaphors of sexuality are imbedded in much Western tonal music. That may sound surprising, and plenty of others disagree with her ideas. Popular performers like Elvis Presley and Rihanna may flaunt their sexuality on stage, but classical music has often been seen as above all that.

But is it? If musical themes are like characters in a story, then we can certainly ask about the gender of those characters. In the early 19th century, when the outlines of many musical forms were first put in writing, it was not uncommon to refer to the first theme in sonata form as "masculine" and the second as "feminine." That's because often the first theme is strong and more dynamic, and the second relaxed and more lyrical, corresponding to prevailing generalizations about gender at the time.

The "masculine" first theme is not only the primary subject of most sonata movements; it is the victor as well. The "feminine" second theme rarely gets as much attention. In the first movement of the Haydn string quartet we have examined, it does not return in the recapitulation at all. One might even conclude that the feminine element has been suppressed in most movements in sonata form. The pounding climaxes of Beethoven's Fifth Symphony would then have to be heard very differently.

Indeed, much of the music of the Romantic period pulses with sexuality; a particularly striking example is the overture to Richard Strauss's opera *Der Rosenkavalier,* which describes a sexual act, after which the curtain goes up to show the characters in bed together. Strauss thus drew back the literal as well as the metaphorical curtain that often conceals the highly charged sexual content of much Romantic music.

What does it mean, though, that these composers—like most composers in the common practice period—were men? Machaut wrote all three texts of *Lasse! comment oublieray/Se j'aim mon loyal/Pour quoy me bat mes maris?* from a female perspective, but might a woman who had actually suffered spousal abuse have written these texts—and the music—differently? Might a woman describe sex musically in different terms as well?

Elvis Presley onstage. Rock is often explicitly sexual, while meanings in classical music are much less overt.
(© Bettmann/Corbis/AP Images)

Janika Vandervelde's *Genesis II* for piano trio (piano, violin, and cello) has often been cited as an alternative to the musical "quest" or "struggle" forms developed and touted by primarily male composers and critics over the last few centuries in the West. As you listen again to this work, let all of these ideas be food for thought. According to the notes from the original recording, "*Genesis II* is one of a series of pieces exploring life cycles and cycles of change. It is based on a crystalline, rotating body of pitches and rhythms in the piano—a 'clockwork' over which are layered free-flowing melodies in the violin and cello. Thus as the work evolves, both circular and linear models of time are presented."

In other words, not all music has to "go somewhere." In the "clockwork" sections of *Genesis II*, musical ideas are repeated rather than developed, and contrast is kept to a minimum. We heard something similar in Javanese gamelan music (Chapter 6) and Caribbean drumming (Chapter 7). This music can be frustrating for Western listeners because it seems so stable and repetitive. Music that develops and grows over time, however, might seem equally strange to Javanese or Caribbean ears. Susan McClary has also asserted that men and women may react to *Genesis II* in very different ways.

A linear model of time implies a goal, meaning that the music's narrative contour advances toward a particular point. This is clearly what happens, again and again, in Beethoven's Fifth Symphony. In *Genesis II*, however, Janika Vandervelde begins with circular music. Almost immediately, a more linear, goal-oriented music begins, reaching a quite audible high point. The clockwork then returns for several minutes. As the piece continues, there are longer and longer linear sections, the last of them followed by a long pause. Finally, the clockwork returns to conclude the piece. Thus, circular music is affirmed as normative, and goal-oriented music becomes the exception rather than the rule.

LEARNING TO LISTEN GUIDE

TAKE NOTE OF FORM

What to Listen For: How the more dynamic sections are presented as contrasts to the more circular norm, instead of dominating as in Beethoven's Fifth Symphony.

Streaming audio track 73.

Vandervelde: *Genesis II* for piano trio
Date: 1983
Instrumentation: Violin, cello, and piano
Meter: Variable
Core Repertory Connection: This music is also discussed in Chapters 6 and 7.

TIME	PROGRESSION	COMMENT
0:00	First clockwork section	The first music heard in the piece is circular, repeating the same basic ideas, although it gradually gets louder.
0:41	Disruption	Although it's not clear exactly where this began, the music has now become faster, more urgent, and no longer circular.
0:54	More clockwork	The earlier circular music reasserts itself.

TIME	PROGRESSION	COMMENT
2:32	Increased activity	The violin part becomes faster, although the underlying meter is the same.
3:15	Greater prominence of the cello	The cello begins to take a more active role. The circular, clockwork feeling remains, although the level of activity gradually increases.
5:49	New section	The clockwork begins to slow down.
6:20	Disruption	The violin and cello play an extended cadenza that gradually becomes more intense.
8:41	The piano reenters	The rate of activity slows down again, with the circular feeling reasserting itself.
12:05	Sudden contrast	The music suddenly becomes more dynamic, disrupting the circular feeling once again.
14:18	Crash	The disruption culminates in this one-time event, followed by confusion and silence.
14:54	Final clockwork section	The circular music returns but sounds more urgent than before. It gradually slows down as the piece comes to an end.

If traditional sonata form shows a masculine first theme vanquishing a contrasting, feminine second theme, then this piece shows something close to the opposite. The less dynamic music is heard first and last, and the more dynamic, aggressive music appears more as an interruption.

If You Liked This Music . . .

Music by Women Composers

Until recently, women composers have been poorly represented in concerts and recordings of classical music. Recent research, and the emergence of composers such as Vandervelde with a distinctive view of what it means to write music as a woman, have begun to change that. If you want to explore the issue further, here are some recommendations:

- Hildegard von Bingen (1098–1179), all but unknown a generation ago, is now widely represented in recordings. Her music, written in monophonic chant forms, is often heard as distinctively individual. Her *Ordo virtutum*—for which she wrote both the words and the music—is a fully developed liturgical drama, a play set to music and designed for use in church.
- Fanny Mendelssohn Hensel (1805–1847), the sister of Felix Mendelssohn (1809–1847), was for years virtually unrecognized as a composer. It is now understood that, in addition to the substantial body of instrumental and vocal works she composed under her own name, she wrote a few of the works published under that of her brother.
- Joan Tower (b. 1938) has gained recognition as a strikingly original composer of instrumental music. In *Made in America*, one of her best-known works, she is more concerned with establishing an American musical voice than a feminine one.
- Ellen Taaffe Zwilich (b. 1939) was the first woman composer to receive a Pulitzer Prize in music. She favors traditional forms, and has written five symphonies and a large number of concertos, including a *concerto grosso* (multi-instrument concerto) based on a trio sonata by Handel.

SUMMARY

- The most obvious way composers can convey meaning is by writing program music, with a story that is spelled out for the audience to follow.
- Even instrumental music without a program—often called absolute music—can follow patterns that suggest certain types of meaning. Such patterns constitute the music's narrative contour. Recognizing narrative contour is the key to understanding why music may seem to convey profound meaning; however, the meaning is still unspecified and may be interpreted differently by different people.
- Examples of narrative contour can be found in ternary form and in theme and variations. Sonata form—one of the most widely used musical forms—resembles a kind of musical essay, and it, too, can convey a great variety of content.

- Beethoven's Fifth Symphony combines different musical forms in a large-scale narrative contour that includes all four movements. Many listeners have intuitively sensed this that music tells a story that involves them in deeply personal ways.
- Because he was able to employ the expressive resources of music so effectively, Beethoven revolutionized people's perception of what music could communicate. Many later composers have tried to imitate him. Some, though, have rebelled against this idea. Like Hanslick, they conceive of music more in terms of beauty than of narrative content.
- Janika Vandervelde's *Genesis II* provides another interesting challenge. Some see it as presenting a woman's voice, in contrast to the masculine narrative found in much other music of the last few centuries.

KEY TERMS

Absolute Music	p. 334	Scherzo	p. 350

REVIEW QUESTIONS

1. What is program music, and how does it differ from absolute music? Why did Eduard Hanslick oppose program music?
2. What musical techniques does Smetana use to tell the story of *Šárka*?
3. What are some distinctive ways in which music can convey meaning?
4. What does it mean for music to have an inherent narrative contour? What are some notable examples?

5. What did E.T.A. Hoffmann and Leonard Bernstein think about Beethoven's music?
6. Why is Beethoven's Fifth Symphony often considered a uniquely meaningful piece of absolute music?
7. In what ways might Janika Vandervelde's *Genesis II* present a woman's voice, in contrast to much earlier music?

REVIEW CONCEPTS

1. Can you imagine other ways of discussing the expressive or narrative content of the pieces discussed in this chapter?
2. Do you agree that everybody can read his or her life story into Beethoven's Fifth Symphony? Why or why not?

3. In what ways can gender influence narrative contour and/or be expressed by it?

LISTENING EXERCISES

1. Listen to the second movement of the Haydn String Quartet in B-flat major, op. 64, no. 3. Pay particular attention to the composer's use of ternary form. What kind of narrative contour does the piece suggest?

2. Listen to some other sets of variations. Do they seem to follow the same pattern as the one in the variations from Mozart's *Gran Partita*?

3. Listen to Strauss's *Don Quixote* or d'Indy's *Istar* variations. Do you recognize the profile of the theme and variations form? How does the composer adapt it to the requirements of telling a specific story?

4. Listen to some other Beethoven symphonies—the Third and Seventh are particularly recommended. Do you hear a narrative contour, either within the movements or between them? What about in the Sixth Symphony, which has a brief program supplied by the composer? Does the program deepen your understanding of the music or detract from it?

5. Listen to Beethoven's Ninth Symphony, which shares the *per aspera ad astra* profile of the Fifth Symphony but includes a text in the last movement that makes it more explicit. Does the text (make sure to read it carefully) help or hinder Beethoven's communication of a message in this music?

6. Listen to all three movements of Crumb's *Black Angels* using the listening guides in Chapters 1 and 9. What kind of narrative content does this music seem to suggest, and why?

APPENDIX I: *Take Note* Guide to Streaming Music Tracks and Interactive Listening Guides (ILGs)

Accessed on the Dashboard site for *Take Note* at **www.oup.com/wallace**

TRACK	COMPOSER	TITLE	ARTIST(S)	PAGE(S)	ILG	SOURCE
1	Thomas of Celano	*Dies Irae*	Capella Antiqua Munchen; Konrad Ruhland, director	221		(P) 1982 Sony Music Entertainment
2	Machaut	*Foy porter*, virelai	Emma Kirkby	151, 236		(P) 1987 Hyperion Records Ltd. Courtesy of Hyperion Records Ltd.
3	Machaut	*Lasse! comment oublieray/Se j'aim mon loyal/Pour quoy me bat mes maris?*	Early Music Consort of London; David Munrow, director	200, 273	ILG-1	(P) 1976 Deutsche Grammophon, under license from Universal Music Enterprises
4	Josquin	*Missa "L'homme armé" super voces musicales*, Kyrie	Tallis Scholars; Peter Phillips, director	42, 239	ILG-2	(P) 1989 Gimell Records Ltd. Courtesy of Gimell Records Ltd.
5	Josquin	*Missa "L'homme armé" super voces musicales*, Agnus Dei	Tallis Scholars; Peter Phillips, director	240, 337		(P) 1989 Gimell Records Ltd. Courtesy of Gimell Records Ltd.
6	Palestrina	*Sicut cervus*	Westminster Choir; Joseph Flummerfelt, director	44		Courtesy of Chesky Records [chesky.com], from 'Westminster Choir – Like As A Hart: Psalms and Spiritual Songs' [CD 138]
7	Monteverdi	*Io son pur vezzosetta*, from Madrigals, Book 7	La Venexiana; Claudio Cavina, director	52		(P) 2004 Glossa Music, S.L. Courtesy of Glossa Music, S.L.
8	Bach	Concerto in D minor for harpsichord and strings, BWV 1052 I: Allegro	Gustav Leonhardt, harpsichord, and Collegium Aureum	14, 28, 195		Originally released 1965. All rights reserved by Sony Music Entertainment
9	Bach	Bach Mass in B minor, BWV 232 Gloria in excelsis Deo	The Monteverdi Chorus and Orchestra; John Eliot Gardiner, conductor	54		(P) 1985 Deutsche Grammophon Courtesy of Deutsche Grammophon, under license from Universal Music Enterprises
10	Bach	Bach Mass in B minor, BWV 232 Et in terra pax	The Monteverdi Chorus and Orchestra; John Eliot Gardiner, conductor	54		(P) 1985 Deutsche Grammophon Courtesy of Deutsche Grammophon, under license from Universal Music Enterprises
11	Bach	Bach Mass in B minor, BWV 232 Laudamus Te	The Monteverdi Chorus and Orchestra; John Eliot Gardiner, conductor	54		(P) 1985 Deutsche Grammophon Courtesy of Deutsche Grammophon, under license from Universal Music Enterprises
12	Bach	Bach Mass in B minor, BWV 232 Gratias agimus tibi	The Monteverdi Chorus and Orchestra; John Eliot Gardiner, conductor	54		(P) 1985 Deutsche Grammophon Courtesy of Deutsche Grammophon, under license from Universal Music Enterprises
13	Bach	Bach Mass in B minor, BWV 232 Domine Deus	The Monteverdi Chorus and Orchestra; John Eliot Gardiner, conductor	164		(P) 1985 Deutsche Grammophon Courtesy of Deutsche Grammophon, under license from Universal Music Enterprises

TRACK	COMPOSER	TITLE	ARTIST(S)	PAGE(S)	ILG	SOURCE
14	Bach	Bach Mass in B minor, BWV 232 Qui tollis peccata mundi	The Monteverdi Chorus and Orchestra; John Eliot Gardiner, conductor	54		(P) 1985 Deutsche Grammophon Courtesy of Deutsche Grammophon, under license from Universal Music Enterprises
15	Bach	Bach Mass in B minor, BWV 232 Qui sedes ad dexteram Patris	The Monteverdi Chorus and Orchestra; John Eliot Gardiner, conductor	54		(P) 1985 Deutsche Grammophon Courtesy of Deutsche Grammophon, under license from Universal Music Enterprises
16	Bach	Bach Mass in B minor, BWV 232 Quoniam tu solus sanctus	The Monteverdi Chorus and Orchestra; John Eliot Gardiner, conductor	54		(P) 1985 Deutsche Grammophon Courtesy of Deutsche Grammophon, under license from Universal Music Enterprises
17	Bach	Bach Mass in B minor, BWV 232 Cum sancto spiritu	The Monteverdi Chorus and Orchestra; John Eliot Gardiner, conductor	245	ILG-3	(P) 1985 Deutsche Grammophon Courtesy of Deutsche Grammophon, under license from Universal Music Enterprises
18	Haydn	String Quartet in B-flat major, op. 64, no. 3 I: Vivace assai	Kodály Quartet	69		(P) 1993 HNH International Ltd. Courtesy of Naxos of America
19	Haydn	String Quartet in B-flat major, op. 64, no. 3 II: Adagio	Kodály Quartet	177		(P) 1993 HNH International Ltd. Courtesy of Naxos of America
20	Haydn	String Quartet in B-flat major, op. 64, no. 3 III: Menuetto. Allegretto	Kodály Quartet	139, 197	ILG-4	(P) 1993 HNH International Ltd. Courtesy of Naxos of America
21	Haydn	String Quartet in B-flat major, op. 64, no. 3 IV: Allegro con spirito	Kodály Quartet	71		(P) 1993 HNH International Ltd. Courtesy of Naxos of America
22	Mozart	*Gran Partita*, K. 361 I: Largo. Molto Allegro	Music from Marlboro; Marcel Moyse, conductor	231		(P) 1975 Sony Music Entertainment
23	Mozart	*Gran Partita*, K. 361 II: Minuetto	Music from Marlboro; Marcel Moyse, conductor	171	ILG-5	(P) 1975 Sony Music Entertainment
24	Mozart	*Gran Partita*, K. 361 III: Adagio	Music from Marlboro; Marcel Moyse, conductor	66		(P) 1975 Sony Music Entertainment
25	Mozart	*Gran Partita*, K. 361 IV: Menuetto. Allegretto	Music from Marlboro; Marcel Moyse, conductor	66		(P) 1975 Sony Music Entertainment
26	Mozart	*Gran Partita*, K. 361 V: Romanze. Adagio	Music from Marlboro; Marcel Moyse, conductor	140		(P) 1975 Sony Music Entertainment
27	Mozart	*Gran Partita*, K. 361 VI: Tema con variazioni	Music from Marlboro; Marcel Moyse, conductor	135	ILG-6	(P) 1975 Sony Music Entertainment
28	Mozart	*Gran Partita*, K. 361 VII: Rondeau. Allegro	Music from Marlboro; Marcel Moyse, conductor	141		(P) 1975 Sony Music Entertainment
29	Mozart	*Le nozze di Figaro*, K. 492 Act I, "Cinque... dieci... venti"	Alan Titus; Helen Donath; Bavarian Radio Symphony Orchestra; Colin Davis, conductor	324	ILG-7	(P) 1991 Sony Music Entertainment

TRACK	COMPOSER	TITLE	ARTIST(S)	PAGE(S)	ILG	SOURCE
30	Mozart	*Le nozze di Figaro*, K. 492 Act I, "Cosa stai misurando"	Alan Titus; Helen Donath; Bavarian Radio Symphony Orchestra; Colin Davis, conductor	304		(P) 1991 Sony Music Entertainment
31	Mozart	*Le nozze di Figaro*, K. 492 Act I, "Non so più cosa son, cosa faccio"	Alan Titus; Helen Donath; Bavarian Radio Symphony Orchestra; Colin Davis, conductor	305		(P) 1991 Sony Music Entertainment
32	Mozart	*Le nozze di Figaro*, K. 492 Act II, "Porgi amor"	Alan Titus; Helen Donath; Bavarian Radio Symphony Orchestra; Colin Davis, conductor	323		(P) 1991 Sony Music Entertainment
33	Mozart	*Le nozze di Figaro*, K. 492 Act III, "E Susanna non vien-Dove sono"	Alan Titus; Helen Donath; Bavarian Radio Symphony Orchestra; Colin Davis, conductor	68		(P) 1991 Sony Music Entertainment
34	Mozart	*Le nozze di Figaro*, K. 492 Act III, "Riconosci in questo amplesso"	Alan Titus; Helen Donath; Bavarian Radio Symphony Orchestra; Colin Davis, conductor	326	ILG-8	(P) 1991 Sony Music Entertainment
35	Mozart	Symphony no. 40 in G minor, K. 550, I: Molto Allegro	Cleveland Orchestra; George Szell, conductor	11, 144, 249		Originally released 1964. All rights reserved by Sony Music Entertainment
36	Beethoven	Symphony no. 5 in C minor, op. 67, I: Allegro con brio	Cleveland Orchestra; George Szell, conductor	75, 229, 347	ILG-9	Originally released 1964. All Rights reserved by Sony Music Entertainment
37	Beethoven	Symphony no. 5 in C minor, op. 67 II: Andante con moto	Cleveland Orchestra; George Szell, conductor	349		Originally released 1964. All Rights reserved by Sony Music Entertainment
38	Beethoven	Symphony no. 5 in C minor, op. 67 III: Allegro	Cleveland Orchestra; George Szell, conductor	352		Originally released 1964. All Rights reserved by Sony Music Entertainment
39	Beethoven	Symphony no. 5 in C minor, op. 67 IV: Allegro	Cleveland Orchestra; George Szell, conductor	354		Originally released 1964. All Rights reserved by Sony Music Entertainment
40	Schubert	*Winterreise*, "Der Lindenbaum"	Thomas Quasthoff, baritone; Charles Spencer, piano	129, 269	ILG-10	(P) 1998 Sony Music Entertainment
41	Schubert	*Winterreise*, "Die Post"	Thomas Quasthoff, baritone; Charles Spencer, piano	126, 270	ILG-11	(P) 1998 Sony Music Entertainment
42	Schubert	*Winterreise*, "Der Leiermann"	Thomas Quasthoff, baritone; Charles Spencer, piano	281		(P) 1998 Sony Music Entertainment
43	Chopin	Ballade No. 1 in G minor, Op. 23	Vladimir Horowitz	82, 202	ILG-12	Originally released 1965 Sony Music Entertainment
44	Chopin	Nocturne in A-flat major, op. 32, no. 2	Arthur Rubinstein	224, 340		Originally recorded 1965. All rights reserved by Sony Music Entertainment

TRACK	COMPOSER	TITLE	ARTIST(S)	PAGE(S)	ILG	SOURCE
45	Berlioz	*Roméo et Juliette* Introduction: Combats-Tumeltes	Rosalind Elias, Giorgio Tozzi; New England Conservatory Chorus; Charles Munch, conductor	81		Originally released 1961. All rights reserved by Sony Music Entertainment
46	Berlioz	*Roméo et Juliette* Recitatif Choral	Rosalind Elias, Giorgio Tozzi; New England Conservatory Chorus; Charles Munch, conductor	167		Originally released 1961. All rights reserved by Sony Music Entertainment
47	Berlioz	*Roméo et Juliette* Ohé, Capulets!	Rosalind Elias, Giorgio Tozzi; New England Conservatory Chorus; Charles Munch, conductor	84		Originally released 1961. All rights reserved by Sony Music Entertainment
48	Berlioz	*Roméo et Juliette* Scene d'amour	Rosalind Elias, Giorgio Tozzi; New England Conservatory Chorus; Charles Munch, conductor	170		Originally released 1961. All rights reserved by Sony Music Entertainment
49	Schumann	*Dichterliebe*, "Ich grolle nicht"	Thomas Quasthoff, baritone; Robert Szidon, piano	279		(P) 1993 Sony Music Entertainment
50	Schumann	*Dichterliebe*, "Die alten, bösen Lieder"	Thomas Quasthoff, baritone; Robert Szidon, piano	282		(P) 1993 Sony Music Entertainment
51	Wagner	*Tristan und Isolde*, Prelude, beginning	Cleveland Orchestra; George Szell, conductor	253		Originally released 1965. All rights reserved by Sony Music Entertainment
52	Smetana	*Šárka* from *Má vlast* (My Homeland)	Milwaukee Symphony Orchestra; Zdenek Macal, conductor	86, 335		(P) 1992 Telarc International Corp. Courtesy of Concord Music Group
53	Dvořák	*Slavonic Dance* in E minor, Op. 72, no. 10	Cleveland Orchestra; George Szell, conductor	8, 192, 219, 343	ILG-13	Originally released 1963. All rights reserved by Sony Music Entertainment
54	Verdi	*Otello* Act I, "Una vela!" and "Esultate!"	Placido Domingo, Renata Scotto; Ambrosian Opera Chorus; National Philharmonic; James Levine, Conductor	298		(P) 1978 Sony Music Entertainment
55	Verdi	*Otello* Act II, "Gia nella note densa"	Placido Domingo, Renata Scotto; Ambrosian Opera Chorus; National Philharmonic; James Levine, Conductor	162		(P) 1978 Sony Music Entertainment
56	Verdi	*Otello* Act II, "Non ti crucciar" and "Credo in un dio crudel"	Placido Domingo, Renata Scotto; Ambrosian Opera Chorus; National Philharmonic; James Levine, Conductor	311	ILG-14	(P) 1978 Sony Music Entertainment

TRACK	COMPOSER	TITLE	ARTIST(S)	PAGE(S)	ILG	SOURCE
57	Verdi	*Otello* Act III, "Vieni l'aula e deserta" and "Questa e una ragna"	Placido Domingo, Renata Scotto; Ambrosian Opera Chorus; National Philharmonic; James Levine, Conductor	317	ILG-15	(P) 1978 Sony Music Entertainment
58	Sousa	*The Stars and Stripes Forever*	US Marine Band; Lt. Colonel Albert Schoepper, conductor	188		Originally released 1962. All rights reserved by Sony Music Entertainment
59	Ives	Violin Sonata no. 4 ("Children's Day at the Camp Meeting") II: Largo	Gregory Fulkerson, violin; Robert Shannon, piano	145		(P) 1993 Bridge Records, Inc.
60	Debussy	Sonata for flute, viola, and harp I: Pastorale. Lento. dolce rubato	Melos Ensemble	100, 206, 225	ILG-16	(P) 1988 The Decca Record Company Ltd. Courtesy of Decca Classics, under license from Universal Music Enterprises
61	Debussy	Sonata for flute, viola, and harp II: Interlude. Tempo di Minuetto	Melos Ensemble	205		(P) 1988 The Decca Record Company Ltd. Courtesy of Decca Classics, under license from Universal Music Enterprises
62	Debussy	Sonata for flute, viola, and harp III: Finale. Allegro moderato ma risoluto	Melos Ensemble	203		(P) 1988 The Decca Record Company Ltd. Courtesy of Decca Classics, under license from Universal Music Enterprises
63	Stravinsky	Symphony of Psalms, I: Exaudi orationem	Columbia Symphony Orchestra; Igor Stravinsky, conductor	97		Originally released 1964. All rights reserved by Sony Music Entertainment
64	Stravinsky	Symphony of Psalms II: Expectans expectavi	Columbia Symphony Orchestra; Igor Stravinsky, conductor	181, 256	ILG-17	Originally released 1964. All rights reserved by Sony Music Entertainment
65	Dallapiccola	*Canti di prigionia* I: Preghiera di Maria Stuarda	Members of the Swedish Radio Symphony Orchestra and Choir; Esa-Pekka Salonen, conductor	174, 284		(P) 1995 Sony Music Entertainment
66	Dallapiccola	*Canti di prigionia* II: Invocazione di Boezio	Members of the Swedish Radio Symphony Orchestra and Choir; Esa-Pekka Salonen, conductor	286		(P) 1995 Sony Music Entertainment
67	Dallapiccola	*Canti di prigionia* III: Congedo di Gerolamo Savonarola	Members of the Swedish Radio Symphony Orchestra and Choir; Esa-Pekka Salonen, conductor	287		(P) 1995 Sony Music Entertainment
68	Gould	*American Salute*	United States Marine Band	173		Courtesy of Altissimo
69	Crumb	*Black Angels* I: Departure	New York String Quartet	17		Courtesy of Recorder Anthology of American Music, under license from New World Records

TRACK	COMPOSER	TITLE	ARTIST(S)	PAGE(S)	ILG	SOURCE
70	Crumb	*Black Angels* II: Absence	New York String Quartet	260		Courtesy of Recorder Anthology of American Music, under license from New World Records
71	Crumb	*Black Angels* III: Return	New York String Quartet	261		Courtesy of Recorder Anthology of American Music, under license from New World Records
72	Basie	*Lester Leaps In*	Count Basie	111, 194	ILG-18	(P) 1975 Fantasy Records, Inc., Courtesy of Concord Music Group
73	Vandervelde	*Genesis II* for piano trio	Mirecourt trio	179, 209, 356		(P) 1984 Cinnabar Records Courtesy of Cinnabar Records
74	Traditional	*Raga Bhankar*	Ustad Vilayat Khan	216		Courtesy of Saregama Records
75	Traditional	*Jumping Dance Drums*	Bahamian drumming ensemble	210		Courtesy of Smithsonian Folkways Recordings
76	Traditional	*Gender wayang, Sukawati* (Sulendro)	Sukawati gamelan ensemble	176		Produced under license from Nonesuch Records

APPENDIX II: *Take Note* Video Guide to Musical Instruments

Accessed on the Dashboard site for *Take Note* at **www.oup.com/wallace**

Videos Copyright ©Tristan Arts (TristanArts.com)

VIDEO #	INSTRUMENT	TITLE	PAGE(S)
V1	Violin	All Notes Bowed	22
V2	Violin	Pizzicato	22
V3	Violin	Prokofiev – Peter's Theme (*Peter & The Wolf*)	22
V4	Violin	Tremolos	22
V5	Viola	All Notes Bowed	22
V6	Viola	Pizzicato	22
V7	Viola	Mendelssohn – Melody (Sym. 4)	22
V8	Viola	Tremolos	22
V9	Cello	All Notes Bowed	22
V10	Cello	Pizzicato	22
V11	Cello	Elgar – Cello Concerto	22
V12	Cello	Tremolos	22
V13	Double-Bass	All Notes Bowed	22
V14	Double-Bass	Pizzicato	22
V15	Double-Bass	Mahler – Symphony No. 9	22
V16	Double-Bass	Tremolos	22
V17	Flute	Melody	24
V18	Flute	Prokofiev – Bird Theme (*Peter & The Wolf*)	24
V19	Flute	Stravinsky – Rite of Spring	24
V20	Flute	Trills I	24
V21	Clarinet	Melody	24
V22	Clarinet	Prokofiev – Cat Theme (*Peter & The Wolf*)	24
V23	Clarinet	Mendelssohn – Staccato Melody (*Midsummer Night's Dream*)	24
V24	Clarinet	Trills	24
V25	Oboe	Melody	25
V26	Oboe	Wagner – Solo Melody (*Gotterdammerung*)	25
V27	Oboe	Oboe – Prokofiev – Duck Theme (*Peter & The Wolf*)	25
V28	Oboe	Oboe – Rossini Tongued Melody (*La Scal di Seta*; Sinfonia)	25
V29	Bassoon	Melody	25
V30	Bassoon	Prokofiev – Grandfather Theme (*Peter & The Wolf*)	25
V31	Bassoon	Stravinsky – *Rite of Spring* (I, opening)	25
V32	Bassoon	Trills I	25
V33	French Horn	Romantic Melody with Mute	26
V34	French Horn	Prokofiev – Wolf Theme (*Peter & The Wolf*)	26
V35	French Horn	Strauss – Prankster Theme (*Till Eulenspiegel*)	26
V36	French Horn	Glissandos	26
V37	Trumpet	Melody	26

VIDEO #	INSTRUMENT	TITLE	PAGE(S)
V38	Trumpet	*Firebird* - Stravinsky	26
V39	Trumpet	Tremolos	26
V40	Trumpet	Trills	26
V41	Trombone	Melody	27
V42	Trombone	Strauss – Prankster Melody (*Till Eulenspiegel*)	27
V43	Trombone	Glissandos	27
V44	Trombone	Trills	27
V45	Tuba	Melody	27
V46	Tuba	Strauss – Prankster I (*Till Eulenspiegel*)	27
V47	Tuba	Flutter Tongue	27
V48	Tuba	Trills	27
V49	Drums	Timpani: Melody Medium Mallet	30
V50	Drums	Snare Drum: Long Roll	29
V51	Drums	Snare Drum: Mahler – Solo	29
V52	Drums	Bass Drum: Roll Loud	29
V53	Percussion	Crash Cymbals: Loud	30
V54	Percussion	Suspended Cymbal: Rolls	30
V55	Percussion	Tam Tam: Medium Stroke	30
V56	Percussion	Triangle: Medium Beater	30

GLOSSARY

Note: The number in parenthesis following each definition indicates the chapter in which the term is first discussed. For additional mentions of these terms within the book, see the Index.

ABA A way of identifying the sections of ternary (three-part) form. After an opening section (A), a contrasting section (B) follows, and then the opening section (A) returns. (3)

AABA A standard construction in popular music and jazz, in which a musical statement (A) is repeated, followed by a contrasting statement (B), after which A returns. The entire AABA unit repeats throughout the piece. In jazz, each AABA unit is known as a chorus. (4)

Absolute Music Instrumental music without a story, or program, specified by the composer. (12)

A cappella A performance style in which a singer or, usually, a choir sings without instrumental accompaniment. (2)

Accented Played louder. Individual notes are accented to make them seem more important than the notes around them. Accents may correspond with the beat, or they may contradict it. (7)

Active listening A way of paying attention to music at multiple levels of complexity for a richer, more rewarding experience. The active listener builds a framework for listening by learning to recognize, analyze, and interpret the fundamental elements all works of music share. (1)

Alto The lowest female singing voice. The term is also used for instruments with a comparable range (e.g., viola). (6)

Arch form A form defined not by discrete musical sections or themes but by gradually growing and diminishing musical intensity, with a climax somewhere past the midpoint of the piece. (5)

Aria An extended solo in an opera, oratorio, or cantata, intended to show musically how a character reacts to a situation. It is analogous to a song in a Broadway musical or to a monologue in a play. (3)

Articulation In musical performance, the extent to which notes are joined together or separated. (5)

Art song A song in the classical tradition (as opposed to a folk or popular song) that is typically written on a poetic text and features a prominent instrumental accompaniment (usually piano). Art songs often add an extra dimension to the text or reinterpret it in significant and sometimes surprising ways. In German, *Lied* (pl. *Lieder*); in French, *mélodie*. (5)

Backbeat Regular emphasis of the second and fourth beats, in common time, which are otherwise generally the unaccented, weaker ones. The backbeat gives much popular music its rhythmic kick. (4)

Ballade A character piece that gives the impression of telling a story. (3)

Baritone The male vocal range falling between tenor and bass. Baritones commonly sing supporting roles in operas, although they occasionally sing the lead. The term is also used for a brass instrument with a corresponding range. (6)

Bass The lowest male singing voice. It is commonly used for authority figures in opera, and sometimes for villains (either of these may also be baritones). The term is also used for instruments with a comparable range (e.g., double bass, bass tuba). (6)

Basso continuo A form of accompaniment that is often the most recognizable feature of music in Baroque style. It usually makes use of both a melodic bass instrument (e.g., cello or viola da gamba) to play the bass line and a harmonic instrument (e.g., harpsichord or organ) to play chords. Both are traditionally written on a single line of music, with numerical symbols used to indicate the chords. (Hence, this part is often called a *figured bass* line.) (2)

Beat The regular pulse of the music. (1)

Binary form A form, often found in Baroque dance suites, that consists of two approximately equal halves, each usually repeated. The two halves often share thematic material, but it is not necessarily repeated exactly. (5)

Bridge An instrumental section between the verse and chorus. (5)

Cadence A harmonic and melodic stop, found at the end of a phrase of a melody, of a section of a piece, or of an entire piece. (8)

Cadenza A solo passage, often intended to be improvised, usually indicated by a fermata (hold mark) in the score. Many concerto movements call for a cadenza toward the end, although this practice fell into disuse in the later 19th century. Short cadenzas are also called for in many vocal pieces. (6)

Canon Literally, "rule" or "law." In music, the term signifies a permanent body of musical masterpieces determined by an established set of criteria. It also refers to a type of composition in which a part is imitated or repeated before its completion, resulting in a multipart texture built out of a single melodic line. (4)

Cantus firmus A tune, or melody, from Gregorian chant or another composition used as the structural basis for a new composition. This was a very important practice in the Middle Ages and Renaissance. (2)

Chamber music Music written for a small ensemble. In modern usage, it usually refers only to instrumental music. Historically, it indicated music meant to be performed in chambers: i.e., in private homes. (1)

Character piece A short, Romantic work for piano solo that reflects a scene, idea, or personality, or is simply written in a characteristic genre like the nocturne or mazurka. (3)

Chords Two or more notes sounding simultaneously; the foundation of harmony. (1)

Chorus In jazz, a single repetition of the basic underlying pattern. Typically, this pattern is repeated multiple times as a piece progresses, allowing for improvisation within a carefully structured framework. (4)

Chromatic Making use of the notes in between the given notes of a key. On a piano, chromatic motion can be identified by playing every black and white key, moving up or down the keyboard, without skipping any. (Contrast **Diatonic**.) (9)

Classical music A general category for music that continues to be heard from one generation to the next, commonly broken down into chronological periods known as Medieval, Renaissance, Baroque, Classical, Romantic, and Modern. (2)

Coda Literally "tail," in Italian. Used to describe the final added measures of a composition that do not fit into the standard form of the piece but follow logically from the preceding material. (5)

Common practice period The time from about 1680 to about 1875, when virtually all Western music shared a common language. One of the most important features of that language was its use of functional harmony. (9)

Common time A duple meter consisting of four beats per measure. It can also be designated as $\frac{4}{4}$. (1)

Compound meter A regular pattern in which the beat is subdivided at two or more different levels. Typical compound meters are compound duple (ONE-two-three-TWO-two-three, designated as $\frac{6}{8}$ or $\frac{6}{4}$) and compound triple (ONE-two-three-TWO-two-three-THREE-two-three, designated as $\frac{9}{8}$ or $\frac{9}{4}$). (7)

Concerto A genre built on the contrast between a solo instrument or group of instruments and a larger ensemble. (1)

Conjunct Melodic motion that features intervals consisting primarily of successive pitches. (Contrast **disjunct**.) (8)

Consonant/consonance The sound produced by a combination of notes that harmonize well because their overtones are compatible. (Contrast **dissonant/dissonance**.) (9)

Contemporary In music, a term whose meaning shifts along with our constantly changing perspective on what is "contemporary." In the broadest sense, it refers to music written since the end of the Second World War (1945). In churches, the term is often used to designate music in a popular and accessible style. Classical music in contemporary styles, on the other hand, is frequently difficult and challenging. (4)

Contrapuntal Music relying on counterpoint. (9)

Contrast Change of tempo, mood, instrumentation, or structure in a piece of music. (5)

Counterpoint The art of combining melodies to produce a polyphonic texture. (2)

Countertenor A man who sings in a falsetto voice. This allows him to sing higher pitches that those normally associated with the male voice. (6)

Countersubject A melody that is combined contrapuntally with another melody, so both are heard at once, but is clearly subordinate to it. (9)

Crescendo A steady increase in volume. (5)

Da capo Literally, "from the head" or, in English parlance, "from the top." These Italian words instruct the performer to return to the beginning of the piece and play to a specified point. (5)

Development In sonata form, the second section, in which the themes presented in the exposition are taken apart, transformed, and tried out in new keys. (5)

Diatonic Using only the notes belonging to a particular key. On a piano, depending on the starting note, a diatonic scale will include a certain combination of black and white keys that produce the desired sound. Or, it may include all white keys, for the major scale beginning on C or the minor scale beginning on A. It will NOT include all black and all white keys, however, but only a selection of them. (Contrast **chromatic**.) (9)

Diminuendo A steady decrease in volume. (6)

Disjunct Melodic motion that features large intervals, requiring the performer to jump between nonconsecutive pitches. (Contrast **conjunct**.) (8)

Dissonant/dissonance The result of a combination of notes with strongly clashing overtones, as when two adjacent notes on a keyboard are played simultaneously. (Contrast **consonant/consonance**.) (9)

Dotted rhythm A rhythm consisting of notes of unequal duration, in which one is lengthened by means of a dot in the score, and the other shortened. (7)

Double fugue A fugue with two subjects instead of one. (9)

Downbeat The first beat of the measure, or of any regular metrical pattern. It is typically stressed. (7)

Drone A sustained low note. (8)

Duple meter A simple pattern of regularly alternating stressed and unstressed beats. It can be counted either as ONE-two-ONE-two, known as $\frac{2}{4}$ meter, or as ONE-two-THREE-four, known as common time or $\frac{4}{4}$ meter. (7)

Dynamics The loudness or softness of music. Dynamics are typically indicated by markings in the score, although they can be added by the performer as well. (6)

Early music A term widely used for music from the 17th century or earlier. Its meaning has shifted over the years, and it refers as much to a style of performance as to a style of music. Even music from the 19th century can be "early music" when played on original instruments by performers who pay close attention to historical performance practice. (2)

Emotional listening Listening to music primarily for the emotional responses it evokes. Such a listener will be most comfortable with short, uncomplicated pieces that do not stretch the limits of the human attention span. (1)

Ensemble Broadly, any performing group. In opera, specifically, an extended section in which two or more people sing, either one at a time or simultaneously. Like an aria, it can be a number in a number opera, or it can emerge from the seamless flow of a music drama. (11)

Episode A passage in a fugue that features contrasting texture and in which the subject is absent. (9)

Exposition In sonata form, the first section, in which two or more themes are presented. (5)

Fantasy A musical genre meant to sound like improvisation. (3)

Fermata A marking indicating that a note should be held for an indefinite length of time. It may also indicate that a **cadenza** is expected to be performed. (8)

Form The way musical material is organized. It is the way in which other musical elements such as melody, harmony, timbre, and texture are combined through the passage of time to create a complete work of music. (1)

Formes fixes Forms widely practiced during the 14th and 15th centuries, particularly by French-speaking musicians like Guillaume de Machaut, that required both poetic and musical devices for their articulation. They frequently featured one or more stanzas with an AAB structure and a refrain. The best-known examples are the ballade, the virelai, and the rondeau. (5)

Fugal Writing that uses polyphonic texture to develop (usually) a single melody, which is stated successively by different voices (in instrumental music the term is metaphorical), each of which continues as in a round. (9)

Fugue An extended composition using fugal technique. (9)

Functional harmony The use of harmonic progressions that have a syntax comparable to that of language. It is characteristic of the music of the common practice period. (9)

Fundamental The lowest-frequency vibration of a sounding tone, and the predominant part of the sound. (6)

Gamelan A general term for various types of Indonesian orchestras. These orchestras consist of mostly percussion instruments, including tuned gongs, xylophones, drums, chimes, etc., and occasionally flutes, stringed instruments, and even vocalists. (6)

Genre A musical category, such as concerto, art song, or character piece. (1)

Glissando A series of very rapid notes sliding up or down. On a keyboard, it is produced by sliding the thumb or forefinger along the keys, and on a string instrument, it is produced by sliding the finger up or down the string on the fretboard or fingerboard. Glissandos may also be played on the harp by sweeping across the strings. (1)

Gregorian chant A body of monophonic church music standardized in the early Middle Ages. It was long attributed to Pope Gregory I (r. 590–604), but it was likely neither written nor standardized by him, nor even by Pope Gregory II (r. 715–731). (2)

Harmonics Related vibrations above the pitch of the fundamental. Also known as overtones or partials. (6)

Harmony The combination of notes to produce chords, and a way of understanding the progression of chords throughout a piece. (1)

Homophonic Consisting of a melody accompanied by chords moving at the same speed, as in a hymn. (9)

Iambic pentameter In poetry, an alternation of five stressed and five unstressed syllables. (7)

Incidental music Music meant to augment the audience's experience of a stage play. (11)

Interval The distance between two pitches. (8)

Invert To play a melody "upside down," with the same intervals going in opposite directions. (8)

Key The note (named by letter) and mode (major or minor) on which a piece of music is based. (1)

Keynote See **Tonic**. (9)

Legato An articulation mark directing the performer to play the affected notes in a smooth, connected style. (Contrast **Staccato**.) (5)

Libretto A text written for an opera or oratorio. It may be based on a play or story, or it may be written just to be set to music. In either case, a good libretto is very different from a good stage play. (10)

Lied (pl. **Lieder**) An art song. Because of the tremendous number produced in the 19th century by German-speaking composers, it became standard to use the German term. (5)

Liturgical Written for a specific function in a church service. (2)

Lyricism The quality of being singable. The word stems from ancient poetry sung to accompaniment by the instrument called a lyre. (8)

Major The sound of a melody based on the eight sung syllables "do-re-mi-fa-sol-la-ti-do," or the notes sounded by playing only white keys on the piano between one C and the next. It is typically thought of as having a brighter, happier sound than **minor**. (1)

Mazurka A character piece evoking the Polish dance of the same name. (3)

Measure One unit of the regular metrical pattern repeated throughout a piece of music (three beats, four beats, six beats, as the case may be). (1)

Melodic line A visual metaphor for a succession of musical tones arranged in a shape perceived as unified and conveying a sense of movement or direction. (8)

Melody A succession of musical notes arranged as a recognizable unit. (1)

Meter The repeated pattern of stronger and weaker beats. (1)

Mezzo-soprano The female vocal range between alto and soprano. Mezzo-sopranos usually have a darker tone color than straight sopranos, and are used for supporting roles in operas. Most choral altos are actually mezzo-sopranos. (6)

Minimalism (Minimalists) A style of composition that uses brief musical ideas repeated over long stretches of time and changed only very gradually. (4)

Minor The sound of a melody based on the eight sung syllables "la-ti-do-re-mi-fa-sol-la," or the notes sounded by playing only white keys on the piano from one A to the next. It is typically thought of as having a darker, sadder sound than **major**. (1)

Minuet A graceful, triple meter dance popular in the 18th century. Many composers, including later ones, adopted its style and ternary form for independent compositions or the third movement of such works as symphonies and string quartets. (5)

Modified strophic form A form of vocal music in which each verse, or strophe, of the text is sung to a different, although related, section of music. (5)

Modulate To change keys. This happens repeatedly in most extended compositions from the common practice period. (9)

Monophonic Consisting of a single melodic line with no accompaniment. (2)

Motet One of the most significant genres of the Middle Ages and Renaissance. In the Middle Ages, at the time of Machaut, it was a secular, polyphonic genre that often featured a different text for each voice, sometimes even in different languages. By Palestrina's time, the motet was returning to its religious roots, and it was cultivated by both Catholic and Protestant composers in the Baroque and afterward. (2)

Motive A memorable melodic fragment significant to the structure of a piece of music. (1)

Movement A self-contained section of a longer piece. The most common number of movements is four, although there may be only two, and in some cases as many seven, or even more, movements in a single work. (1)

Music drama An opera in which the music is continuous throughout each act or scene. (11)

Narrative contour A formal trajectory in music that can suggest a story. It may be contained within a single piece or movement, or it may embrace all the movements of a multimovement piece. (3)

Nationalist Designation for composers who actively seek to reflect some aspect of their national identity in their music. There was a resurgence of nationalism in the late 19th century, as composers from Eastern Europe, Scandinavia, and other countries outside of the musical mainstream appeared in large numbers. (3)

Nocturne "Night piece." A genre of character piece featuring elegant melodic lines. (3)

Number opera An opera in which musical numbers very much like songs are separated by other text, which may or may not be set to music. (11)

Oratorio A dramatic composition often based on a religious subject and featuring extensive choral writing. It has similar musical content (arias, recitative, etc.) to a secular opera but lacks staging, costumes, and scenery. (3)

Orchestra The most common instrumental performing ensemble in Western classical music. There is no completely standard orchestra, although all orchestras have things in common—a preponderance of string instruments, for example—that distinguish them from other large instrumental ensembles like the band. (1)

Ordinary The parts of the Mass that are the same for every service and do not change week to week. (2)

Ornamentation Extra notes not written in the music, added by the performer for decorative or expressive purposes. (8)

Overtone See **Harmonics**. (6)

Persona The character who is understood to be speaking the words. (10)

Phonetic Having to do with the way a text sounds. (10)

Phrase A section of a melody. (3)

Pitch The highness or lowness of a sound. It is measured relative to other pitches and also to absolute standards like 440 megahertz (the standard orchestral A). (1)

Pizzicato In string instrument technique, this refers to plucking the strings rather than bowing them. (6)

Polymeters Multiple meters used simultaneously. This effect is rarely heard in Western music but is common in the music of Africa, the Caribbean, and the Middle East. (7)

Polyphonic Consisting of multiple parts or voices, allowing more than one note to sound at a time. Use of the term often implies that more than one melody is stated simultaneously, although technically, even the simplest chordal accompaniment is polyphonic. (2)

Polytextuality The simultaneous use of more than one text. It occurs frequently in operatic ensembles, where different characters may be singing different things at the same time. Medieval motets are also frequently polytextual, often using parts in two different languages, such as Latin and French. (10)

Prelude (1) A short piece that introduces another composition, such as a fugue. (2) A character piece in an improvisatory style. (3)

Program music A musical composition based on or alluding to a nonmusical program, usually a pictorial or literary idea, specified by the composer. (3)

Raga A musical term from India referring not only to a specific series of pitches but also to motivic patterns, specific ornaments, and the general emotional character that should be applied to music based on those pitches. (5)

Recapitulation In sonata form, the third and final section, in which the themes reappear in their original versions but all in the same key, creating a feeling of resolution. (5)

Recitative A style of singing usually associated with opera or oratorio. Typically sparsely accompanied, sometimes with only continuo, it is intended to move along the plot of the story by quickly presenting key text or dialogue. (The term is derived from the Italian for "reciting style.") (3)

Refrain A section of music that recurs at predictable intervals. Another word for it is *chorus*. (3)

Register A specific range of low, medium, or high pitches on an instrument or in a voice. (1)

Repetition A composer's tool for reinforcing main ideas and underscoring the most important themes of a work, enabling the listener to detect structure and enjoy its development. Repetition also instills balance and resolution to a piece of music. (5)

Return A compositional technique in which, after the introduction of music that differs distinctly from what has come before, the original music is brought back, producing a rounded form with a satisfying sense of completion. (5)

Rhythm The organization of music through time. The term may refer in a general way to the element of time in music, but more specifically to the patterns of long notes, short notes, and rests. Rhythm results from the interrelationship of note duration with beat, meter, accent, and tempo. (1)

Rhythm changes The series of chords used in Gershwin's *I Got Rhythm*. It quickly took on a life independent of that song and became a standard progression of chords all jazz musicians know and use. (4)

Ritornello A section of music to which the entire ensemble returns after sections played by a smaller ensemble. (2)

Rondo A form popular in the late Baroque and Classical periods in which a first section (A) recurs following alternate sections of music (ABACA, etc.). (5)

SATB choir A choir that follows the standard division into sopranos, altos, tenors, and basses. Much choral music is written for this combination, although some adds extra parts, often designated as second soprano, first bass or baritone, etc. (6)

Scale The series of pitches, arranged from low to high or high to low, on which a melody is based. Major and minor, the most common scales, have eight. (1)

Scherzo "Joke," in Italian. A movement in ternary form and triple meter that sometimes takes the place of the minuet in multimovement works such as symphonies or sonatas. (12)

Semantic Having to do with textual meaning and how it is communicated. (10)

Sequence 1. A Medieval form consisting of pairs of textual lines, each pair set to a new line of music played twice. The *Dies irae* was written in this form. 2. (Not capitalized.) A melodic fragment repeated at successively higher or lower pitches. (8)

Serialism (Serialists) A method of composition employing series of pitches (and sometimes rhythms, dynamics, and timbres) that are repeated, combined, and reversed or inverted according to strict formulas. Serialist compositions typically ignore traditional or expected relationships between notes and chords. (4)

Sonata form Also called sonata-allegro form. A flexible form, normally applying to the first movement of a sonata, symphony, or other multimovement instrumental composition, that allows for the exposition of two or more themes, their subsequent development, and then a recapitulation and resolution. (5)

Song cycle A set of art songs that share a common idea or central theme and that are intended to be performed as a unit. This form originated in the Romantic period and remained popular in the 20th century. (5)

Soprano The highest-pitched female voice. In operas, sopranos usually play the leading female roles. The designation is also used to describe the member(s) of each instrument family with a similar range (e.g., violin, flute). (6)

Staccato An articulation mark directing the player to perform the affected notes in a light and detached manner. (Contrast **Legato**.) (4)

Stretto A passage in a fugue that features multiple entrances of the subject in quick succession. (9)

Strophic form A poetic structure in which successive verses, or strophes, of text follow the same rhyme scheme and metrical pattern. In music, it refers to a form of vocal music in which each verse, or strophe, of text is sung to the same tune. (5)

Subject The single melody on which a fugue is based. (9)

Suite A set of dances or dance-like pieces, which developed as a genre in the early Baroque era (elements of it go back to the Renaissance). A suite typically has more movements, and is hence less compact, than a multimovement composition from the Classical period or later (e.g., a symphony). (5)

Swing era The period in the 1930s and 40s when jazz was dominated by big bands playing a dance-based repertory. Although he lived until the 1980s, Count Basie first rose to prominence during this time. (4)

Syllabic A style of text setting where each musical note is assigned one syllable of text. (8)

Symbolic meaning Numerical or other relationships not audible in the music but incorporated through musical devices. Especially prevalent in early music. (4)

Symphonic poem A program music genre common in the late 19th century, consisting of a single, often lengthy, movement written for a large orchestra. (3)

Syncopation The displacement of notes so that they fall on beats not normally accented, or between the beats, and thus contradict the meter. This is a common feature of jazz, although it can be heard in much classical music as well. (4)

Syntactic Having to do with a text's structure. (10)

Tempo The speed of a piece of music. (1)

Tempo marking A designation by the composer, usually in Italian, indicating how fast the music is to be played. (5)

Tempo rubato "Stolen time," in Italian. As it is used today, the term simply means a flexible, expressive approach to tempo. It is rarely marked by the composer, so its use—particularly common in music from the Romantic period—is at the performer's discretion. (7)

Tenor The highest male singing voice. In operas, tenors usually play the romantic lead. The term is also used for instruments with a comparable range (e.g., cello, tenor trombone). (6)

Ternary form Also known as **ABA**. A musical structure, either vocal or instrumental, in which an initial section (A) is followed by a significantly contrasting section (B) and a repeat of the original A section, either in its original form or in an easily recognizable variation of it (A'). (5)

Text painting The deliberate imitation of pictorial images suggested by the text in the musical setting. (10)

Texture The relationship between melodic and harmonic elements in a piece of music, especially how many layers of notes occur at the same time. (1)

Theme and variations See **Variation form**. (5)

Timbre The distinctive sound of a particular instrument or voice. (1)

Time signature The numbers at the beginning of a musical score indicating how many beats there are in a measure (top number) and what kind of note gets one beat (bottom number). The top number is significant for the meter: duple, triple, or compound. (7)

Tone poem See **Symphonic poem**. (3)

Tonic The main note and/or chord of a key, or of a piece written in that key. For example, the tonic of Mozart's Symphony no. 40 is G minor. (9)

Triple meter A regular pattern of three beats, with the first one being stressed. It normally features a secondary stress on the third beat, in the pattern ONE-two-THREE, ONE-two-THREE, etc. It is also possible for the secondary stress to be placed on the second beat, giving music in triple meter an inherent metrical flexibility. (7)

Triplet Three notes of equal value that subdivide a beat. (7)

Trochaic Meter In poetry, a meter that begins with a stressed syllable and then alternates with an unstressed one. (7)

Tutti Italian for "all." A designation used to indicate that all instruments in an orchestra should play (as opposed to only solo instruments). A passage in which the full orchestra plays (e.g., the opening of a classical concerto) is also called a tutti. (6)

Upbeat An unstressed beat that comes before the downbeat and thus precedes the beginning of the metrical pattern. Pieces, sections of pieces, and phrases often begin on an upbeat, forcing the listener to concentrate to find where the regular meter actually begins. (7)

Variation A principle of form that integrates the other two principles, namely, repetition and contrast. It takes a familiar component of the music and changes some elements of it while retaining others. (5)

Variation form Also known as theme and variations. A form of (usually instrumental) music that first presents a theme and then presents that theme in a series of alterations that typically retain the length and harmonic structure of the original theme but change some of its other characteristics. (5)

Vibrato A subtle pulsating quality, caused by very slight pitch change recurring in a rapid pattern, that is said to increase the expressiveness of a tone. Vibrato is used by most wind instrumentalists as well as string players to enhance their sound. There is some aesthetic debate as to whether vibrato should be employed in the performance of older music, since it has only been a fixture in performance practice for a little over a century. (6)

Word painting See **Text painting**. (10)

SOURCE NOTES

Chapter 1

P. 9 The social context of four-hand piano music in 19th-century society is discussed in Thomas Christensen, "Four-Hand Piano Transcription and Geographies of Nineteenth-Century Musical Reception." *Journal of the American Musicological Society* 52/2 (Summer 1999): 255–298.

Chapter 2

Pp. 39–42 A thorough interpretation of the "L'Homme Armé" melody and its significance is presented in Craig Wright, *The Maze and the Warrior: Symbols in Architecture, Theology and Music* (Cambridge: Cambridge University Press, 2001).

P. 51 *Monteverdi: Creator of Modern Music* is the title of a book by Leo Schrade (New York: Norton, 1969).

Chapter 3

P. 73 Wayne Senner, Robin Wallace and William Meredith, eds., *The Critical Reception of Beethoven's Compositions* by His German Contemporaries, v. 2, trans. Robin Wallace (Lincoln, NE: University of Nebraska Press, 2001), 97.

P. 83 Jonathan Bellman, *Chopin's Polish Ballade: Op. 38 as Narrative of National Martyrdom* (New York: Oxford University Press, 2010).

Chapter 4

P. 101 Virgil Thomson, *A Virgil Thomson Reader* (Boston: Houghton Mifflin, 1981), 312.

Pp. 105–106 Douglas Henry Daniels, *Lester Leaps In: The Life and Times of Lester "Pres" Young* (Boston: Beacon Press, 2002), 205.

Chapter 6

Pp. 166–167 See Gardiner's notes for his recording of Handel's *Messiah* with the same group: Philips 6769 107, LP.

P. 175 Michael Tenzer, *Gender Wayang*, <http://www.balivision.com/Article_Resources/Genderwayang.asp>, accessed February 24, 2006.

P. 180 Igor Stravinsky and Robert Craft, "A Quintet of Dialogues," *Perspectives of New Music* 1, no. 1 (August, 1962): 17.

P. 178 Vandervelde's Genesis II is discussed extensively in Susan McClary, "*Getting Down Off the Beanstalk: The Presence of a Woman's Voice in Janika Vandervelde's Genesis II,*" in Feminine Endings: Music, Gender, and Sexuality (Minneapolis: The University of Minnesota Press, 1991), 112–131.

P. 183 The shift in the perceived identity of the hero of Beethoven's "Eroica" symphony from Napoleon to the composer himself is discussed most thoroughly in Scott Burnham, *Beethoven Hero* (Princeton: Princeton University Press, 1995).

Chapter 7

P. 208 Charles Ives, *Sonata No. 4 for Violin and Piano: "Children's Day at the Camp Meeting"* (New York: Associated Music Publishers, 1942).

P. 209 Harold Courlander, liner notes to *African and Afro-American Drums*, Folkways Records Album No. FE 4502 C/D (New York, 1962), long-playing record.

Chapter 8

P. 226 Senner, Wallace and Meredith, eds., *The Critical Reception of Beethoven's Compositions*, 103.

Chapter 9

P. 259 http;//www.janikavandervelde.com

Chapter 10

Pp. 276–280 The concepts of semantic, syntactic and phonetic text setting are developed, though in reference to a different repertory, in Leo Treitler, "Music and Language in Medieval Song," in *The Medieval Lyric* (South Hadley, MA: Mount Holyoke College, 2001), CD-ROM.

Pp. 280–290 The idea of persona in the lieder repertory is introduced and explored in Edward T. Cone, *The Composer's Voice* (Berkeley: University of California Press, 1974), 20–40.

P. 289 Luigi Dallapiccola, "The Genesis of the *Canti di Prigonia* and *Il Prigoniero*: An Autobiographical Fragment," translated by Jonathan Schiller, *The Musical Quarterly* 39, no. 3 (July 1953): 359, 363.

P. 290 Herbert Lindenberger, *Opera: The Extravagant Art* (Ithaca: Cornell University Press, 1984).

Chapter 11

P. 294 For a taxonomy of the various functions of music in film scores, which presents some additional options and an overview of earlier views of the subject, see Mark W. Gallez, 'Theories of Film Music,' *Cinema Journal* 9/2 (Spring 1970): 40–47.

P. 305 Pierre-Augustin Caron de Beaumarchais, *The Barber of Seville, The Marriage of Figaro*, translated with an introduction by John Wood (London: Penguin Books, 1964), 222.

Chapter 12

P. 337 Wright, The Maze and the Warrior, 80–86. Wright makes an elaborate argument throughout the book connecting such examples of musical symbolism with the mazes that appeared in many Gothic cathedrals, whose theological significance centered on the often-neglected Christian doctrine of the Harrowing of Hell.

P. 340 Maynard Solomon, *Mozart: A Life* (New York: Harper-Collins, 1995), 187–209.

Leonard Bernstein, *The Joy of Music* (New York: Simon and Schuster, 1959), 28–29.

P. 344 Senner, Wallace and Meredith, *The Critical Reception of Beethoven's Compositions*, 97.

Pp. 354–355 See Mark Evan Bonds, *After Beethoven: Imperatives of Originality in the Symphony* (Cambridge, MA: Harvard University Press, 1996), 28–72 and Reinhold Brinkmann, *Late Idyll: The Second Symphony of Johannes Brahms*, trans. Peter Palmer (Cambridge, Mass: Harvard University Press, 1995), 223. Brinkmann sees in the last two symphonies of Brahms an anti-archetype that specifically contradicts the plot structure established by Beethoven; he finds examples of this anti-archetype in works by Berlioz, Tchaikovsky and Mahler as well.

P. 355 See McClary, Feminine Endings. The interpretation of *Vandervelde's Genesis II* presented here is based on Chapter 5 of McClary's book, titled *"Getting Down Off the Beanstalk: The Presence of a Woman's Voice in Janika Vandervelde's Genesis II."*

P. 255 Liner notes to *A La Carte*, produced by the Minnesota Composers Forum in cooperation with The McKnight Foundation, MN 104 and 105, 1986. LP.

Chapter 13

P. W7 Anthony Hicks. "Handel, George Frideric." *Grove Music Online. Oxford Music Online.* Oxford University Press, accessed October 25, 2013, http://www.oxfordmusiconline.com/subscriber/article/grove/music/40060pg22.

P. W17 John A. Lomax and Alan Lomax, compilers, Ruth Crawford Seeger, ed., *Our Singing Country: A Second Collection of American Ballads and Folk Songs* (New York: Macmillan, 1941), 249.

CREDITS

Chapter 4

Chapters 2, 4 and 6

Chapter 11

INDEX

Page numbers in bold indicate a definition. Page numbers followed by *f, t,* or *m,* indicate a figure, table, or map, respectively. Italicized page numbers indicate a photograph.